BIRNBAUM'S

Walt Disney World®

THE OFFICIAL VACATION GUIDE

2020

Expert Advice From the Inside Source

Wendy Lefkon EDITORIAL DIRECTOR

Jill Safro EDITOR

Jennie Hess CONTRIBUTING EDITOR

H. Clark Wakabayashi DESIGNER

Alexandra Mayes Birnbaum CONSULTING EDITOR

Stephen Birnbaum FOUNDING EDITOR

DISNEY
EDITIONS

LOS ANGELES • NEW YORK

CONTENTS

7 GETTING READY TO GO

Here is all the practical information you need to organize a Walt Disney World visit down to the smallest detail: when to go, how to get there, how to save money and work within a budget, and how to book Fastpass+ assignments for favorite attractions; plus sample schedules and hints for parents, international travelers, travelers with disabilities, singles, couples, and older visitors.

61 TRANSPORTATION & ACCOMMODATIONS

Two big questions about Walt Disney World are where to stay and how to get around. Accommodations range from concierge suites to modest campsites, with thousands of rooms and villas in between. Our guide describes every Disney resort, with details presented in a handy chart. And we explain the World's vast transportation system, to boot.

113 MAGIC KINGDOM

The enchantment of Walt Disney World is most apparent in the wealth of attractions and amusements that fill this, the most famous entertainment zone of all. Our land-by-land guide describes all there is to see and do, where to shop, and how to avoid the crowds, plus plenty of other insider tips and the scoop on new additions to the Kingdom.

143 EPCOT

A gleaming silver geosphere introduces Disney's wonderland of discovery— an ambitious exploration of the world of the future as well as the present. Future World and World Showcase offer every visitor the opportunity to be a global and cerebral voyager, without setting foot outside Florida. Here's how to make the most of this uniquely fascinating destination.

175 DISNEY'S HOLLYWOOD STUDIOS

Now's your chance to be part of Disney's Hollywood adventure! Everything from controlling the *Millennium Falcon* to a *Frozen* sing-along to a trip to *The Twilight Zone*™ and the excitement of daring stunts and special effects is waiting to be enjoyed. There are also opportunities to bond with Disney characters and experience a thrill ride or two. We've developed strategies for seeing this Tinseltown, ensuring the most fun possible.

195 DISNEY'S ANIMAL KINGDOM

The most sprawling member of WDW's theme park lineup celebrates the circle of life and the wonders of Earth's animal kingdom. Amid nature's majesty, guests experience a stirring safari, dodge dastardly dinosaurs, and ride raging rapids. Our coverage, which includes the park's newest land, Pandora—The World of Avatar, guarantees a fun-filled trip to a place where humans are humbly reminded of their role in the natural world.

215 EVERYTHING ELSE IN THE WORLD

Beyond the theme park boundaries lie countless acres full of just the sort of wonders for which Disney is famous: state-of-the-art water parks and the dynamic Disney Springs entertainment, shopping, and dining district among them. So if you want to ride down watery slides, dance the night away, shop at elegant boutiques, pamper yourself at a spa, or experience behind-the-scenes tours, this chapter will help you find your way.

243 SPORTS & RECREATION

Walt Disney World has more tennis courts and golf greens than most posh resorts, plus plenty of places for boating, biking, horseback riding, swimming, and fishing. Here's how to combine these options with the rest of the WDW fun.

251 GOOD MEALS, GREAT TIMES

Restaurants around Disney World property run the gamut from simple snack shops to bastions of haute cuisine. Choices are nearly endless, so we've organized them in an area-by-area directory that lets you know where each restaurant is located and what specialties it offers, plus a roundup of the dining spots we consider Birnbaum's Bests. We also tell you about dinner shows, the best family fare, where to dine with Disney characters, and where to enjoy an after-dinner drink.

325 DISNEY CRUISE LINE

Many guests choose to make a Walt Disney World visit even more magical by pairing it with a cruise to the Caribbean or the Bahamas—the ultimate Land and Sea vacation, Disney style. This "bonus" chapter tells you how to plan it.

363 COUPONS

We've stuffed the final pages of this book with valuable coupons to help you save hundreds of dollars on Walt Disney World food, merchandise, recreational experiences, and more.

WHAT'S NEW?

To spotlight attractions, shows, restaurants, and events that are making (or have recently made) their debut, listings are marked with the icon shown at left. Look for it throughout the book. Here are some of the highlights:

✳ City Works Eatery & Pour House (*page 221*)
✳ Disney Skyliner (*page 65*)
✳ Disney's Riviera Resort (*page 86*)
✳ Epcot Forever (*page 171*)
✳ Jaleo by José Andrés (*page 222*)
✳ Mickey & Minnie's Runaway Railway (*page 187*)
✳ *Millenium Falcon:* Smugglers Run (*page 188*)
✳ The NBA Experience (*page 221*)
✳ Oga's Cantina (*page 319*)
✳ Sebastian's Bistro (*page 288*)
✳ Star Wars: Galaxy's Edge (*page 188*)
✳ Star Wars: Rise of the Resistance (*page 188*)
✳ Toledo—Tapas, Steak & Seafood (*page 290*)
✳ Topolino's Terrace—Flavors of the Riviera (*page 294*)
✳ Up Close with Rhinos (*page 257*)

For Steve, who merely made all this possible.

AMC Disney Springs 24 © Copyright 2019 AMC Theatres; Arribas Brothers © Arribas Brothers; *B Resort & Spa* © *B Hotels & Resorts*®; Best Western Lake Buena Vista Resort Hotel © 2019 Best Western Lake Buena Vista Resort Hotel. All rights reserved. Each *Best Western*® branded hotel is independently owned and operated; Bibbidi Bobbidi Boutique–"Bibbidi Bobbidi Boo" © 1948 Walt Disney Music Company; Chevrolet Impala is a trademark of General Motors; DoubleTree Suites by *Hilton*®, *Hilton*® Buena Vista Palace, and *Hilton*® Lake Buena Vista © 2019 Hilton; Four Seasons Resort Orlando Copyright © 2019 Four Seasons Hotels Limited; Frontera Cocina © Frontera Cocina by Rick Bayless; The Disney movie, *The Great Mouse Detective* is based on the *Basil & of Baker Street* book series by Eve Titus and Paul Galdone; *Holiday Inn*® is a service mark owned by Six Continents Hotels, Inc., its parent, subsidiaries, or affiliates, all InterContinental Hotels Group companies. © Copyright 2019 *InterContinental*® Hotels Group; House of Blues © 2019 House of Blues Entertainment, LLC, a Live Nation© company; *Indiana Jones*™, Star Tours, and Star Wars © Disney © & TM 2019 LUCASFILM LTD; *Jenga*® Pokonobe Associates. All rights reserved; LEGO and the LEGO logo are trademarks of the LEGO Group. © 2019 The LEGO Group; Morimoto Asia © *Patina*™ and owned by Patina Restaurant Group, LLC; Pandora—The World of Avatar ©Twentieth Century Fox Film Corporation. James Cameron's *AVATAR* is a trademark of Twentieth Century Fox Film Corporation; Pixar properties © Disney/Pixar; The movie *The Princess and the Frog* Copyright © 2009 Disney, story inspired in part by the book *The Frog Princess* by E. D. Baker Copyright © 2002, published by Bloomsbury Publishing, Inc.; *Raglan Road*™ Irish Pub and Restaurant © Raglan Road; Senses, A Disney Spa at the Grand Floridian Resort: LIC#MM30134; Senses, A Disney Spa at Saratoga Springs Resort: LIC#MM31094; *Slinky*® Dog © POOF-Slinky, LLC; Splitsville Luxury Lanes © *Splitsville*™ Co, LTD.; *STK*® Orlando © The ONE Group, LLC; *Tinkertoy*® is a registered trademark of Hasbro, Inc. Used with permission. © Hasbro, Inc. All rights reserved; T-Rex Cafe: A Prehistoric Family Adventure © 2019 LANDRY'S INC.; *The Twilight Zone*™ is a registered trademark of CBS, Inc., and is used pursuant to a license from CBS, Inc.; Walt Disney World Swan and Dolphin Resort and Todd English's Bluezoo © 2019 Marriott International, Inc. All rights reserved.; Winnie the Pooh characters based on the "Winnie the Pooh" works by A. A. Milne and E. H. Shepard; *Wyndham*® © 2019 Wyndham Hotels & Resorts, Inc. All rights reserved. All hotels are independently owned and operated except certain hotels managed or owned by a subsidiary of Wyndham Hotels & Resorts, Inc.

ISBN 978-1-368-02758-8
FAC-038091-19214
Printed in the United States of America

Other 2020 Birnbaum's Official Disney Guides:

Disneyland
Walt Disney World for Kids

The Official Disney Fan Club

D23.com

SUSTAINABLE FORESTRY INITIATIVE Certified Sourcing
www.sfiprogram.org
SFI-00993

Logo Applies to Text Stock Only

A WORD FROM THE EDITOR

For some of us, our first Walt Disney World experience dates all the way back to 1971, the year this new "Disneyland in Florida" made its debut. At that time, the Magic Kingdom was the only theme park to explore. Nonetheless, for those who came, it was love at first sight, and we've returned again and again. Fast-forward nearly five decades and Walt Disney World boasts four theme parks, two water parks, dozens of hotels, hundreds of restaurants, and a whole lot more.

Editor Jill Safro consults with Mickey and Minnie, the ultimate Disney insiders.

Never before has there been so much incentive to visit (and revisit) the memory-making capital of the world. The Magic Kingdom wows guests with its mix of classic and contemporary shows and attractions, from Pirates of the Caribbean to the Seven Dwarfs Mine Train, plus a stirring fireworks spectacular: Happily Ever After. Guests control the *Millennium Falcon* and join The Resistance in a brand-new land: Star Wars—Galaxy's Edge. They are also shrunk to the size of a toy as they enter the park's beloved fun zone, Toy Story Land. And the new Mickey & Minnie's Runaway Railroad transports giddy Studios guests to a wild and wacky cartoon world. Animal Kingdom's Pandora—the World of Avatar is home to Flight of Passage, a thriller that lets guests fly on the back of a mountain banshee. The park also boasts evening safaris and a nighttime spectacular, Rivers of Light. At Epcot (which in the midst of a multi-year "re-imagining phase"), *Frozen* fans are fired up for Norway's Frozen Ever After attraction, while Soarin' Around the World continues to send guests to happy heights. And the dynamic Disney Springs is bursting with dining, shopping, and entertainment opportunities. Of course, that's just the tip of the iceberg, as so much of Walt Disney World has grown and evolved since our last edition. We are privileged and proud to provide readers with our extensively researched, insider look at some of the most cherished attractions, resorts, and eateries on Earth.

When Steve Birnbaum launched this guide in 1981, he made it clear what was expected of anyone who worked on it. The book would be meticulously revised each year, leaving no attraction untested, no snack or meal untasted, no hotel untried. First-hand experiences like these, accumulated over the years, make this book the most authoritative guide to the World. Our expertise, however, is not achieved by being escorted through back doors of attractions (although we would enjoy that). Instead, we wait in lines with everyone else, always hoping to have a Disney experience like that of any other guest. We also take advantage of WDW's ambitious (and free) Fastpass+ attraction reservation system whenever we can. We'll continue to keep a close eye on it and other additions to the Walt Disney World vacation-planning universe—homework we're happy to do for readers like you.

After more than 48 fun-filled years, the World has vastly expanded—and so has our knowledge of the most popular vacation destination on the planet. On some occasions we've encountered sweltering weather and swelling crowds—times when even the happiest of travelers can turn into Grumpy for a moment or two. Had we known then what we know now, we could have spared ourselves some trying experiences. In one case, a staffer waited more than an hour to take a tour at the Studios. Standing in line with a notebook, she was asked by another guest if there was a quiz at the end. When she explained what she was doing, he expressed surprise to learn that she was waiting with the masses. But that's always been our strategy. We believe the best way to gather useful advice for a Walt Disney World guest is to be one. Over and over again!

TAKE OUR ADVICE

We have done our best to keep you from making any tactical mistakes. We realize that even the most meticulous vacation planner needs detailed, accurate, and objective information to prepare a successful itinerary. To achieve that goal, we encourage the sharing of insight and information from Walt Disney World staffers—however, the decision of whether or not to include such information is entirely up to the discretion of this book's editor.

To that end, we have packaged handy bits of advice in the form of sample itineraries and "hot tips" throughout the book. This advice comes directly from the copious notes we've taken during our thousands of days spent in Walt Disney World. We've also used our "Birnbaum's Best" stamp of approval wherever we deemed it appropriate, highlighting favorite attractions and restaurants—the crowd-pleasers we believe stand head, shoulders, and ears above the rest.

You, the reader, benefit from the combination of our many years of experience that, together with our access to current insider information, makes this guide unique. We like to think it's indispensable, but we'll let you be the judge of that a few hundred pages from now.

CREDIT WHERE CREDIT IS DUE

Enormous thanks to the teams of dedicated, detail-conscious Walt Disney World Cast Members from Guest Communications, the Disney Reservation Center, Food & Beverage, Merchandise, Resort Operations, Sports & Recreation, Attractions Operations, Disney Cruise Line, Disney Vacation Club, Marketing, and Disney Parks Synergy.

Kudos to Michelle Olveira for her diligent fact-checking and to Jessica Ward for her meticulous proofreading. Immeasurable gratitude also to copy editor extraordinaire Diane Hodges and to Kathy Crummey, Jennifer Eastwood, Jerry Gonzalez, Monica Vasquez, Marybeth Tregarthen, Devon Munroe, and Kinden Sevorwell for their editorial support and production panache.

Hats off to those for whom doing Walt Disney World research is truly a labor of love. The "volunteer" class of 2020 includes the Safro family (Irene, Joy, Hayden Fullerton, and Delaney Irene), the Henning family (Amy, Chris, Avery, Elle, and Reid), Linda Verdon, Trace Schielzo, Mary Jeanne Anderson, Kevin Anderson, Tim Gallagher, Denise Kiernan, Joe D'Agnese, Bob Cook, Stacey Cook, and Christina Fontana.

Of course, no list of acknowledgments would be complete without mentioning our founding editor, Steve Birnbaum, whose spirit, wisdom, and humor still infuse these pages, as well as Alexandra Mayes Birnbaum, who continues to be a guiding light—to say nothing of being a careful reader of every word.

Don't Forget to Write!

No contribution is of greater value to us in preparing the next edition of this book than your comments on its usefulness and your own experiences at Walt Disney World. Drop us a postcard or send a letter to the address on the right.

Jill Safro
Birnbaum's Walt Disney World 2020
Disney Editions
125 West End Avenue, 3rd Fl.
New York, NY 10023

THE LAST WORD

Finally, it's important to remember that every worthwhile travel guide is a living enterprise; the book you hold in your hands is our best effort at explaining how to enjoy Walt Disney World at this moment, but its text is in no way etched in stone. Disney is constantly changing and growing, and in each annual edition we refine and expand our material to serve your needs even better. For this year's edition, though, this must be the final word.

Have a great visit!

— Jill Safro, Editor

GETTING READY TO GO

"To all who come to this happy place: Welcome." —Walt Disney

8	When To Go
14	How to Get There
17	Planning Ahead
21	Theme Park Tickets
28	Money-Saving Tips
32	Sample Schedules
46	Customized Travel Tips

The key to a fabulous vacation at Walt Disney World is advance planning. This remarkably varied complex is too vast and diverse to allow a spontaneous visit to be undertaken with much success—especially when you consider the rapid rate at which the World has expanded and the introduction of Fastpass+, a system that allows WDW resort guests to reserve attraction times up to 60 days in advance. It does not mean that even the most casual visitors can't have some significant fun, but they are bound to have regrets about things they missed because of time pressures or a simple lack of information. The purpose of this guide is to eliminate potential frustration while getting the biggest bang for your vacation buck.

What follows, then, is meant to provide a sensible scheme for planning a satisfying visit to Walt Disney World, one that will offer the most fun and the least amount of disappointment. But how do you know which of the countless activities will be the most enjoyable for you and your family? Do your homework. The best strategy is to make sure you have a clear idea of all that is available long before you arrive in the Orlando area. Details are subject to change.

When to Go

When talk finally turns to the best time to make a trip to Walt Disney World, Christmas and Easter are often mentioned, as well as the traditional summer vacation period—especially if there are children in the family. But there is also good reason to avoid these periods, namely the tremendous crowds they attract. And when Disney World is crowded, it can be very crowded, indeed. On the busiest days, visitors may wait in line more than two hours to experience the most popular attractions. That's at least twice as long as during less busy times of the year. Weekends, in general, are quite popular with locals. Sunday night through Wednesday tends to be a bit less densely populated.

Considering seasonal hours, weather, crowd patterns, and Disney resort rates, optimal times to visit Disney are usually mid-January through early February, late April through late May, and September through December (except for Martin Luther King Day weekend, and Thanksgiving and Christmas weeks).

Note that during some of the less crowded times of the year—particularly during the winter—some attractions are closed for renovations. In addition, water parks are often closed for refurbishment during cooler months. Check the My Disney Experience mobile app or website, visit *www.disneyworld.com*, or call 407-824-4321 for a current schedule.

Early November through December is a festive time of year the world over, and Walt Disney World is no exception. The theme parks are decorated to the nines for the holiday season. (It seems to turn from Halloween to Christmas overnight.) Epcot holds stirring Christmas concerts, and the Magic Kingdom drapes Cinderella Castle in thousands of sparkling lights. Many other special events are held during this period, including Mickey's Very Merry Christmas Party in the Magic Kingdom (a separate admission ticket is required). The party brings a dusting of "snow" to Main Street from about 7 P.M. to midnight for several days between mid-November and the first three weeks of December. It also features holiday shows around the park, including Mickey's Once Upon a Christmastime Parade, plus a unique holiday fireworks show. Select performances from Mickey's Very Merry Christmas Party are also staged in the park during regular hours on the days leading up to, including, and following Christmas. This event often sells out way ahead of time. Get tickets in advance by using the My Disney Experience website or app, or by calling 407-W-DISNEY (934-7639). Advance purchase prices start at about $90 (same-day purchases are higher). It's usually easier to snag tickets for dates earlier in the season.

Epcot celebrates with its International Festival of the Holidays, including the nightly Candlelight Processional, complete with a mass choir, 50-piece orchestra, and a reading of the story of Christmas by a celebrity narrator. Dinner packages are available for some World Showcase restaurants. (We recommend the dinner package: It guarantees a table for dinner as well as seating at the Candlelight Processional. Without a package, you should arrive at least two hours before showtime or risk being shut out of your preferred performance.) Disney's Hollywood Studios presents Jingle Bell, Jingle BAM! on select evenings throughout the season. The show comes to life on and above the Chinese Theatre with colorful projections, special effects, fireworks, and festive holiday tunes.

Disney Springs gets into the jolly spirit of the season with Christmas trees, twinkling lights, and holly-jolly entertainment—including visits by Saint Nick himself. There are happy holiday decorations at each Walt Disney World resort hotel, too, including a Victorian Christmas at the Grand Floridian, a seaside party at the Yacht & Beach Club, and a Cajun holiday at Port Orleans Riverside.

For reservations, go to *mydisneyexperience.com* or call 407-W-DISNEY (934-7639), a travel agent, or the Walt Disney Travel Company (407-828-8101). For more info, visit *mydisneyexperience.com*, or *disneyworld.com*, or call 407-939-7630. Special-event tickets are sold separately.

HOT TIP!

The period of time between the week after Thanksgiving weekend and the week before Christmas is one of the less crowded and most festive times of the year.

Crowd Patterns

DAY-TO-DAY TRENDS

Weekends tend to be among the most crowded days at Walt Disney World theme parks, followed by Mondays, Thursdays and Fridays. Morning through early afternoon is a bustling time for the theme parks and their popular "E-ticket" attractions. Days that offer Extra Magic Hours tend to be more crowded at their respective theme parks (refer to page 22). When the weather's especially steamy, the Disney water parks tend to pack them in—so be sure to get an early start if you're headed to Blizzard Beach or Typhoon Lagoon.

When the time comes to plot an itinerary for your WDW visit, it's helpful to know about crowd patterns beyond the four theme parks as well. As a rule, Disney Springs (formerly known as Downtown Disney) and Disney's water parks host their largest throngs on weekends. Of course, in these circles, a bigger crowd could possibly mean a better time. Golfers should note that weekend tee times are typically in the highest demand, while Monday and Tuesday tee times tend to be the easiest to come by.

SEASONAL SHIFTS

The chart below indicates the density of crowds in the theme parks throughout the year. Though it's tough to generalize about a property as big and ever-changing as Walt Disney World—special events (such as the Disney Marathon and Epcot's International Food & Wine Festival) and package deals can swell park attendance during a period typically marked by smaller crowds—the chart highlights historic trends.

Least Crowded means that there will be lines (there always are!); however, most shows and attractions may be experienced with a bit less waiting than during busier times of the year.

Average Attendance refers to times when there are lots of people around, but lines for shows and attractions are relatively manageable.

Most Crowded reflects times when lines at popular attractions can mean a wait of as much as two to three hours (or more). As a rule, when school is out, the crowds are most definitely in at Walt Disney World.

LEAST CROWDED

- 2nd week of January through 1st week of February (excluding WDW Marathon Week and Martin Luther King Day Weekend)

- Weeks before and after Labor Day (excluding the holiday weekend itself)

- Week after Thanksgiving until the weekend at the start of Christmas week

AVERAGE CROWDS

- 1st week of January (excluding New Year's Day, which is "most crowded")

- 2nd week of February until Presidents' week

- End of February through 2nd week of March

- Last week of April through May

- Period after Epcot's International Food & Wine Festival ends until the weekend before Thanksgiving

MOST CROWDED

- All major holidays

- Presidents' week

- WDW Marathon Week

- 3rd week of March through 3rd week of April

- Easter week

- June through the 3rd week of August

- Epcot Food & Wine Festival

- Thanksgiving week

- Christmas through New Year's Day

- Any time school's out

Holidays & Special Events

Special events are staged at Walt Disney World all year, not only to mark holidays but also to celebrate other interests. The dates and details below are subject to change without notice; call 407-824-4321 to confirm, or pay a visit to *www.disneyworld.com* for up-to-the-minute information about specific events in 2020.

JANUARY

Walt Disney World Marathon Weekend (January 8–12, 2020): Some 26,000 entrants run through parks and other areas of the World during this 26.2-mile race (January 12). Characters and Cast Members are on hand for inspiration. Similar hoopla surrounds the half marathon (January 11). The 2-day Goofy Race and a Half Challenge (January 11 and 12) covers 4 theme parks and 39.3 miles. There is a 10K run (January 10) and a 5K family run on January 9. (It's okay to walk the 5K, but you must maintain a 16-minute mile.) Runners may take the "Dopey Challenge"—all of the aforementioned events within the pacing requirements—and earn a Dopey Challenge finisher medal. Packages are available. Call 407-939-4786 for package details or to book. For marathon weekend event information and schedules, go to *www.rundisney.com*, or call 407-938-3398. Registration for this event generally opens in the April prior to the January races—and fills up within hours. Rooms are in high demand for this event. For details on other Walt Disney World running events, visit *www.rundisney.com*.

Epcot International Festival of the Arts (January–February): Epcot itself is a celebration of culture, cuisine, art, and entertainment. This festival takes those elements to the next level in a special salute to the creative arts. Expect curated art exhibits, live performances—including the crowd-pleasing Disney on Broadway concert series at the America Gardens Theatre, kiosks featuring fanciful, artistic nibbles, workshops, lectures, and more. For details about the Epcot's Festival of the Arts, visit *Disneyworld.com/ArtfulEpcot*, use the My Disney Experience mobile app or website, or call 407-939-3463.

MARCH–JUNE

Saint Patrick's Day (March 17): Everyone is Irish on Saint Patrick's Day—especially at Raglan Road's Mighty St. Patrick's Festival at Disney Springs. The family-friendly festivities include music, dancing, dining, and more. (The festivities usually run several days on either side of March 17.) Of course, every day is a celebration of the Emerald Isle at Raglan Road, the Landing's Irish pub. Epcot's United Kingdom pavilion marks the day with Irish dining, dancing, and green beer.

Easter (April 12, 2020): Most of the Disney parks stay open late during the two weeks straddling Easter Sunday. The Easter Bunny greets guests in the Magic Kingdom. Epcot hosts an "Egg-stravaganza" hunt—cost is about $6 for a map with stickers (find all the eggs and win a prize). And many of the Disney World resorts offer special Easter-themed fun. Catholic and Protestant services may be offered at the Contemporary resort. Call 407-W-DISNEY for specifics. This is an extremely busy time to visit.

Epcot International Flower & Garden Festival (Early March–Memorial Day): Epcot is blooming with elaborate gardens (including more than 30 million fragrant blossoms) and topiary displays, behind-the-scenes tours, and concerts. Pick up a Garden Passport and stamp it as you explore the Outdoor Kitchens throughout the day. Passports are free and may be found at park entrances, at Outdoor Kitchen stations, and at many Epcot shopping locations. Each Outdoor Kitchen has its own unique stamp.

Another popular element of the Flower and Garden Festival is the Garden Rocks concert series, presented at the America Gardens Theatre near the American Adventure pavilion. Past performers have included

the Village People, Rick Springfield, Smash Mouth, Lonestar, and The Spinners. All shows are included with Epcot admission. Some seats may be reserved via Fastpass+ (see page 25)—the rest are available on a first-come, first-served basis.

Mother's Day (May 10): Celebrate Mom by treating her to a special Mother's Day buffet. Several WDW restaurants, such as Animal Kingdom Lodge's Boma—Flavors of Africa, Chef Mickey's and The Wave at the Contemporary, Ale & Compass Restaurant at Yacht Club, and the Swan's Garden Grove (dinner), have been known to offer Mother's Day meals. For details on the 2020 options, call 407-WDW-DINE (939-3463). Note that Walt Disney World resorts are very busy on Mother's Day weekend—book early.

JULY

Fourth of July Celebration: Double-size fireworks presentations over the Magic Kingdom, Epcot, and Disney's Hollywood Studios make for a very colorful night. Ben Franklin, Betsy Ross, and Disney characters greet guests at Epcot's American Adventure pavilion throughout the day. That pavilion's America Gardens Theatre hosts a patriotic show featuring an expanded cast of the Voices of Liberty. The evening's nighttime spectacular (presented on World Showcase Lagoon) may feature a patriotic finale. This is an exceptionally busy time to visit Walt Disney World.

AUGUST–NOVEMBER

Epcot International Food & Wine Festival (late August–mid-November): Epcot celebrates the flavors of many different countries (even those not usually represented in World Showcase) through tastings (about $3 to $12 per tapas-style plate), demonstrations from top chefs, the Eat to the Beat concert series, and wine and cooking seminars. It's an exceptionally satisfying way in which to wander through the park. It's also insanely popular, so expect lots of company—especially in the evening. For additional details or to make a reservation for a special event (which you should do as far in advance as possible), visit *www.epcotfoodfestival.com*.

Halloween (late August–November 1, 2020): The festivities vary a bit from year to year. What follows is a sampling of what to expect:

Fort Wilderness Resort and Campground usually hosts a pumpkin-carving contest and a kids' costume contest,

followed by a screening of a spooky movie. It also offers Halloween-themed wagon rides with storytelling and various surprises along the way.

The Magic Kingdom will play host to its Halloween spectacular, **Mickey's Not-So-Scary Halloween Party**, mid-August through October. The special-ticket activities include a parade, fireworks, dancing, appearances by Disney villains (including a new Castle Forecourt show called **Hocus Pocus Villain Spelltacular**), trick-or-treating, and a special (new) fireworks presentation. This is an extremely popular—and crowded—Magic Kingdom event. Purchase tickets as far in advance as possible. And don't forget to wear a costume. (For Disney's costume

A Tisket, A Tasket . . .

. . . a "Welcome to Walt Disney World Basket." The Disney Florist can deliver this and a striking array of themed surprises to any room on Disney property (and many that aren't). There's no occasion they can't rise to—from a birthday to Earth Day, from honeymoons to golden wedding anniversaries. One call (or click) to the Disney Florist (the only one serving Walt Disney World) can yield custom-tailored bouquets, gift baskets, and even Christmas trees. (They also have a division dedicated exclusively to Walt Disney World engagements.)

Not satisfied with a simple delivery to a resort room? The Florist folks encourage creativity. Do you have a favorite Disney character? Into the basket he or she goes! One package known as "Create a Fairy Tale" (complete with slipper and tiara) can actually be delivered to guests enjoying a romantic carriage ride.

For further information or to place an order, visit *www.disneyfloralandgifts.com*, or call 407-939-4438 (daily from 8 A.M. to 6 P.M.).

three weeks of December, complete with snow flurries on Main Street and complimentary cookies and hot cocoa. Entertainment for the special-ticket party includes **Mickey's Once Upon a Christmastime Parade** and a special edition of the fireworks show. Select performances are staged during regular hours just before Christmas. Magic Kingdom may offer a holiday Jungle Cruise, aka the Jingle Cruise. Finally, Queen Elsa lights the Castle on a nightly basis (with the help of Anna and Olaf). Note that the Magic Kingdom is densely populated during Mickey's Very Merry Christmas Party. Guests with tickets to the Christmas Party may enter the Magic Kingdom as early as 4 P.M. Details are subject to change in 2020.

Epcot International Festival of the Holidays (mid-November–late December) features the Christmas Candlelight Processional, including a choral concert, plus a celebrity narrator who reads the story of Christmas. The event is included with park admission, but seating is limited and it is exceptionally popular. Arrive at least 90 minutes before showtime, or book a dinner package (which combines dinner at a World Showcase eatery with guaranteed Processional seating). For details, call 407-939-3463. Holiday kitchens serve sweet and savory treats throughout the holiday season.

Disney Springs gets into the holiday spirit with a cheery mix of twinkling lights, music, a towering tree, and visits from the North Pole's most famous resident. Past years have brought carolers, stilt-walkers, and a lively holiday dance party.

New Year's Eve Celebration (December 31): There are extra-spectacular fireworks in the skies above the Magic Kingdom, Epcot, and Disney's Hollywood Studios (though there are no fireworks at all at Animal Kingdom—imagine the stampede!). These parks stay open until approximately 1 A.M. Many of the resort restaurants, as well as the nightspots at Disney Springs, also welcome the new year Disney style.

HOT TIP!

On dates when the Magic Kingdom hosts "special-ticket" events, such as Mickey's Not-So-Scary Halloween Party and Mickey's Very Merry Christmas Party, the park closes early to day guests (usually 6 or 7 P.M.).

guidelines, visit *www.disneyworld.com*.) Note that guests with tickets to the Halloween Party may be able to enter the park as early as 4 P.M. (Ask when you buy your ticket.) As a spooky bonus, **Mickey's Boo-to-You Halloween Parade** makes its way through the Kingdom during the not-so-scary Halloween party. Advance purchase prices range from about $79–$135 for adults, $72–$130 for kids (plus tax; same-day purchases are higher). For details, call 407-827-7200.

Thanksgiving (November 26): All Disney World restaurants are open on Turkey Day, many of them offering Thanksgiving specialties. For details, call 407-WDW-DINE (939-3463).

AdvoCare Classic (Thanksgiving weekend): This early-season college basketball tournament features 8 NCAA teams and 12 games. Each team competes in one game per day and advances through a bracket-tournament format. Book your hotel early if you want to stay at a Walt Disney World resort for this extremely popular weekend. For additional information, visit *espnevents.com/advocare-international*.

NOVEMBER–DECEMBER

Disney's Magical Holidays: Decorations and festivities abound in WDW's parks and resorts. The Magic Kingdom park hosts **Mickey's Very Merry Christmas Party** on select nights from early November through the first

HOT TIP!

Special-ticket events such as Mickey's Very Merry Christmas Party are more popular than ever before. Get your tickets early— and expect to have lots of fellow revelers partying in the park. For details on this and other events, visit *www.disneyworld.com*.

Keeping WDW Hours

Since operating hours fluctuate, use the My Disney Experience app or website, visit *www.disneyworld.com*, or call 407-824-4321 for current schedules.

THEME PARKS: Disney theme park hours vary seasonally. In May, September, October, parts of November and December, and all of January, the Magic Kingdom is usually open from 9 A.M. to 8 P.M.; Epcot is typically open from 9 A.M. to 9 P.M. (some Future World attractions may close at 7 P.M.), later during peak seasons; Disney's Hollywood Studios is open from 9 A.M. until about an hour after sunset; and Animal Kingdom is usually open from 9 A.M. till about 8 P.M. (or later). The theme parks take turns offering Extra Magic Hours throughout the week. That is, on any given day, one park may allow Disney resort guests to enter an hour early or stay in the park for two hours after it closes to the public. Participating Walt Disney World resorts have schedules at the Front Desk. (Note that while Extra Magic Hours are—by far—the best time to visit for guests craving shorter lines, some attractions do not operate during E.M.H.)

The Magic Kingdom park keeps later hours through summer and other busy periods, including Christmas and Easter weeks. The parks may be open until 1 A.M. on New Year's Eve. Disney's Hollywood Studios often stays open until 10 or 11 P.M. in the summer, too.

DISNEY SPRINGS—MARKETPLACE, LANDING, AND TOWN CENTER: Shops are generally open from about 10 A.M. until 11 P.M. Sunday through Thursday; 11:30 P.M. on Friday and Saturday. Restaurant hours vary, with most venues open until 11 P.M. or midnight.

DISNEY SPRINGS, WEST SIDE: At the AMC cineplex, movies begin as early as 10 A.M. Restaurants are open from about 11:30 A.M. to midnight. Most shops are open from about 10:30 A.M. to 11 P.M. (midnight on Friday and Saturday).

WATER PARKS: Disney water parks are usually open from about 10 A.M. to 5 P.M., but extend hours during summer months. Cabanas should be reserved in advance (see Hot Tips on page 226 and 229).

WDW PARK TRANSPORTATION: Bus, boat, Disney Skyliner (gondolas), and monorail service generally begin one hour prior to park opening time and continue until about an hour after the parks close. Boats, Disney Skyliner, and monorails do not operate for Extra Magic Hours.

WALT DISNEY WORLD WEATHER

| | Temperature | | Rainfall |
| | AVERAGE | | AVERAGE |
	HIGH	LOW	(INCHES)
JANUARY	71	49	2.4
FEBRUARY	74	52	2.5
MARCH	78	56	3.8
APRIL	83	60	2.7
MAY	88	68	3.5
JUNE	91	72	7.6
JULY	92	74	7.3
AUGUST	92	74	7.1
SEPTEMBER	90	73	6.1
OCTOBER	85	66	3.3
NOVEMBER	79	59	2.2
DECEMBER	73	52	2.6

How to Get There

BY CAR

While most visitors to the Orlando area fly in, quite a few choose to drive. If you opt for a road trip, figure on logging no more than 350 to 400 miles a day—a distance that won't wear you down so much that you can't enjoy your trip.

If you plan to navigate with GPS, note Walt Disney World's address in the Hot Tip at the top of page 15. Contact state tourist boards to inquire about free maps, too (yes, they still make maps!); for a Florida map and guide, call 888-735-2872, or pick up a copy of *Rand McNally Road Atlas* or the *AAA North American Road Atlas*; both are sold in bookstores.

From Orlando International Airport

By car: During rush hour, take the airport's South Exit to the Central Florida Greeneway (Route 417) to Route 536, which leads to Walt Disney World. The tolls run about $4–$6.

For the shortest route, take the North Exit to Route 528, going west toward Tampa. Pick up I-4 west, and go to a WDW exit. Tolls are about $4–$6. The route is usually heavily trafficked, but manageable during non-rush periods of the day. It's busiest on weekday mornings and evenings and any time when a theme park is scheduled to open or close.

By Disney's Magical Express: This tailor-made, complimentary transportation program is available to guests staying at select Disney resorts. For more information, turn to page 16.

By car service: Lyft and Uber are authorized to transport guests to and from WDW. Be sure to download the app before your trip. Disney's Minnie Van service (accessed via the Lyft app) costs $150 each way (to and from Orlando International Airport) for up to 6 passengers and 6 medium-sized bags. (For Minnie Van details, see page 64.) Reliable towncar service is available from Noris Limousines. The company offers a special round-trip rate for Birnbaum readers—mention this book and expect to pay about $125 for up to three passengers for a towncar, or about $225 for up to 6 passengers in an SUV. Reservations are required and cancellations must be made at least 48 hours ahead. Call 407-240-4533, or visit *www.norislimousines.com*. Prices may increase if there is a big jump in prices at the pump.

Florida Towncar also offers direct service to all Disney Area resorts. And they offer our readers a special rate, too. Simply mention the Birnbaum Guide when you book and expect a round-trip flat rate of $100 for up to 5 passengers (to and from Orlando International Airport only). That's $15 off the regular price. Call 407-277-5466 (from Florida) or 800-525-7246 (from out of state) up to 24 hours ahead, or visit *www.floridatowncar.com*. Online reservations should be made at least 24 hours ahead of pickup time.

By shuttle: At Orlando International Airport, Mears Motor Shuttle offers vans and buses 24 hours a day. It serves the Swan and Dolphin, Hotel Plaza Boulevard properties, and other non-Disney area hotels. Shuttles make multiple stops; a trip can take an hour or more. On the return trip, Mears requires guests be picked up at least 3 to 4 hours prior to flight times. Reservations should be made 24 hours ahead. There is often a long wait at the airport (even with a reservation), and employee attitudes fluctuate wildly. This is not our preferred mode of transit.

The shuttle cost to most hotels is $24 one way, $38 round-trip per adult; $19 one way, $29 round-trip per child ages 4 through 11; free for children under 4. Fares to International Drive properties are a little lower. Service is not direct. Call 855-463-2776 for information, or visit *www.mearstransportation.com*.

By taxi: Metered cabs usually cost between $60 and $70 each way, depending on the destination—and the integrity of the driver (prices listed at the Orlando International Airport taxi stand are estimates). Some taxis can accommodate up to 9 people (for the price of one). Bell Services can call for a cab at any WDW resort. Note that many drivers do not have SunPass, so it'll cost you at least 45 cents a minute while waiting to pay each toll. What's more, many drivers do not know the area streets (or pretend not to)—resulting in bigger fares than necessary. Until cabs offer a flat rate to and from the airport, we are sticking with Magical Express or car services.

Note that gratuities are not included in transfer rates. It is customary to tip for good service.

➤

HOT TIP!

Driving to Walt Disney World and in need of an address to plug into the GPS? Look no further: 1180 Seven Seas Drive, Lake Buena Vista, FL 32830 (this takes you to the Magic Kingdom area of WDW—follow signs to your final Walt Disney World destination).

Reputable automobile clubs offer help with break-downs; towing; insurance that covers personal injury, accidents, arrest, bail bond, and lawyers' fees for defense of contested traffic cases; and travel-planning services, including free maps and route mapping. Services vary from one club to the next, and membership fees range widely, from about $50 to $120 a year.

BY AIR

When it comes to airfares, there is no real trick to unearthing the most economical ones: Simply shop around. Call a travel agent, browse the Internet, and keep these tips in mind:

➤

HOT TIP!

If you are flying home via Orlando International Airport (MCO), allow an extra 60 to 90 minutes to get through airport security. The lines there can be unimaginably long—and you will have to wait your turn, even if it means missing your flight. Plan ahead.

• Take advantage of advance-purchase fares (lower rates that apply if a ticket is bought up to several weeks prior to departure).

• Fly when most people don't: For vacation destinations, that usually means leaving the ground on Tuesday or Wednesday.

DID YOU KNOW?

It's perfectly legal to make a right turn at a red light in Florida (after coming to a complete stop and yielding to traffic and pedestrians).

Resources for Road Trippers

There are a variety of reputable national automobile associations to choose from. Among the leading clubs to consider:

• **Allstate Motor Club**
  Customer Service Center
  P.O. Box 660598
  Dallas, TX 75266
  877-810-2920
  www.allstatemotorclub.com

• **American Automobile Association (AAA)**
  1000 AAA Dr. #28
  Heathrow, FL 32746
  407-444-7000 or 800-564-6222
  www.aaa.com

• **Auto Club of America**
  P.O. Box 21443
  Oklahoma City, OK 73156
  800-411-2007
  www.autoclubofamerica.com

• **Ford Customer Relationship Center**
  P.O. Box 6248
  Dearborn, MI 48126
  800-392-3673; *www.ford.com*

• **Geico**
  800-207-7847
  www.geico.com

• **Signature's Nationwide Auto Club**
  Attention: Customer Service
  P.O. Box 968008
  Carol Stream, IL 60173
  800-323-2002
  www.autoclub.com

Travelers may also check with state tourist boards for free maps. Other map sources are the *AAA North American Road Atlas* and the *Rand McNally Road Atlas*; they are sold in many bookstores.

• Keep in mind that the lowest airfares usually carry a penalty if you have to revise or cancel your ticket, and that most discounted tickets are nonrefundable.

• When you call to make a reservation, ask about any fare restrictions, including an obligatory Saturday night stay-over.

• Visit airline websites. They may e-mail details about discounted fares. Most offer a small discount for purchasing tickets online.

BY TRAIN

Amtrak serves the Orlando, Florida, area twice daily to and from New York City, with stops made along the way. The journey usually takes about 22 hours and costs from about $240 to $660 round-trip, coach. (Book early for lower fares; discounts are often available, so be sure to ask. Passengers over the age of 18 must present valid government-issued photo ID upon request.) If you're staying at a Walt Disney World resort, plan to take a cab or shuttle to your hotels. Rental cars are also available. They are not on-site, but are easily reached by shuttle.

For reservations and additional train information, call 800-USA-RAIL (872-7245), visit the Amtrak website at *www.amtrak.com*, or contact a travel agent.

BY BUS

Greyhound provides frequent direct service to Orlando and Kissimmee (the latter is closer to Walt Disney World). From either destination, you can take a taxi to your hotel, but first check if your hotel offers shuttle service. For more information, contact Greyhound at 800-231-2222, or visit *www.greyhound.com*.

Disney's Magical Express Service

Disney's Magical Express service is for guests booked at a Walt Disney World–owned-and-operated resort and arriving at Orlando International Airport. Meant as a money-saver as well as a convenience, the service lets guests check luggage at their airport of origin, bypass baggage claim, and board a bus to their WDW resort. The luggage, which guests affix with special tags before leaving home, is usually delivered to the resort room within several hours of arrival. (Note that bags are delivered to rooms for flights landing between 5 A.M. and 10 P.M. If your flight arrives after 10 P.M., you'll need to claim your bags and take them to the Magical Express bus.) On the final day of a trip, prior to boarding the bus to the airport, guests who fly domestically with participating airlines (at press time, that included Alaska, American, Delta, jetBlue, Southwest, and United) check their luggage at their resort and receive a boarding pass for their airline. (Airline luggage fees apply.) Once at the airport, guests can skip the airline check-in counter and proceed to security. If you'd prefer to schlep your own bags, you can still hitch a free ride on the bus (provided that you are headed to a Disney resort). Here are some specifics:

• Magical Express service is booked when you book your resort and must be done at least 10 days prior to arrival. (Have flight information handy when you make the call.) Be sure to confirm.

• Reservations may be made via *www.disneyworld.com*, 407-W-DISNEY, or a travel agent.

• Tip the driver as you would had you paid for the trip: $1–$2 per bag is appropriate.

• Special luggage tags will be sent to the party that makes the reservation. These tags must be put on all bags that will be checked at the airport.

• Upon landing at Orlando International Airport (MCO), skip baggage claim (only if you tagged your bags) and go to the Disney Welcome Center, located in the Main Terminal Building on the B side, Level 1. Don't forget to have your transfer vouchers, MagicBands (see page 24), and a photo ID handy.

• On the return trip, expect to be picked up 3 to 4 hours before your scheduled flight departure time for domestic flights and 4 to 5 hours ahead for international flights.

• If a member(s) of your party uses a wheelchair or scooter, tell the reservationist when booking your trip on Disney's Magical Express. Confirm reservations before you leave home.

• Guests flying on "non-participating" airlines are entitled to the free shuttle service, too.

The good news? It is super convenient, and it is a real money-saver. In fact, a family of four can shave $120 to $300 off their total vacation cost by taking the Magical Express as opposed to other forms of transportation. And it is beyond liberating to leave the lugging of the luggage to someone else. It's also delightful to bypass check-in at the airport on the return trip. And each bus has an onboard bathroom—handy for emergencies. The downside? Well, to call any service "magical" is to elevate expectations. It's not really express, either—as most buses make multiple stops at Disney resorts. So if time is of the essence, it might not be the best choice. Same goes for the transportation of luggage. While the service truly eases the burden of many a family, it may take one to three hours to arrive at your resort room. So if you'll need anything right away—swimsuits, pajamas, medication, snacks, etc.—be sure to pack it in a day bag, carry it onto the plane, and transport it to the resort yourself. We could do without the video that's played throughout the journey, but the bus is comfy and the price is right.

Planning Ahead
Logistics

Organizing a trip properly takes time, but most travelers find the increased enjoyment well worth the effort. The fact is, planning a Disney visit can be a pleasant sort of "armchair" exercise for the whole family. Kids will enjoy their visit to Disney all the more if they, too, are involved in the process. Take it from us, the more information you can gather, the better.

To assist in that effort, we recommend *Birnbaum's Walt Disney World For Kids*, a colorful look at the World, written for readers ages 7 through 14. For parties who plan to pair a Disney cruise with a Walt Disney World visit, cruise information beginning on page 325 is a good place to start.

HOT TIP!

So you're using the Birnbaum Guide to plan your trip to Walt Disney World. What are you going to do next? Go to *www.disneyworld.com*! There you can get WDW news and park hours, purchase tickets, make dining reservations, and more.

INFORMATION SOURCES

For additional information about Walt Disney World, use the My Disney Experience app or website, visit *www.disneyworld.com*, or call 407-W-DISNEY (407-934-7639). Specifics such as park hours, ticket prices, refurbishment schedules, and directions are available through an automated system 24 hours a day. For information by mail, write to: Walt Disney World, P.O. Box 10000, Lake Buena Vista, FL 32830-1000.

Internet and smartphone users can tap into updates about happenings in the World, get information on trip planning, reserve a resort room, order tickets, book dining reservations, and get park operating hours and special-events listings by visiting *www.disneyworld.com*, *mydisneyexperience.com*, or the My Disney Experience mobile app. Disney Cruise Line vacation packages may be booked at *www.disneycruise.com*.

For details and discounts on (non-Disney) area attractions, restaurants, and hotels, contact the Official Orlando Visitor Center, 8102 International Drive, Orlando, FL 32819 (it's a satellite office of the Orlando Convention & Visitors Bureau); 407-363-5872, or 800-972-3304; *www.visitorlando.com*.

For details about other Central Florida attractions, contact Visit Florida; 888-735-2872 (to request a complimentary visitors guide and map) or 850-488-5607; *www.visitflorida.com*.

On-site Resources: Those staying at a WDW resort should consider their Lobby Concierge desk a primary resource. Resort guests also receive information via their room's TV. Fort Wilderness campers are advised to stop at the Pioneer Hall Info and Ticket Window, call extension 2788, or touch 11 on a phone near any restroom. Tablet and smartphone users can access *mydisneyexperience.com* or use the free app.

What to Pack

While there's no formal dress code at Walt Disney World, neat, casual clothing is the rule, with few exceptions. Most notably, jackets are required for men at Victoria & Albert's restaurant in the Grand Floridian resort. Generally speaking, T-shirts and shorts are fine during the day. For evening, slacks, jeans, or Bermuda-length shorts are appropriate. Bathing suits are a must, along with the appropriate attire for any sport you want to pursue.

Light sweaters are necessary even in summer—to wear indoors when air-conditioning gets chilly. From November through March, warmer clothing is a must for evening. Pack for weather extremes so you'll be comfy should it become unseasonably warm or cool. Bring sunscreen and bug spray. Adults must have government-issued photo ID. (Leave selfie sticks at home—they are not allowed in Disney theme or water parks. Also forbidden: weapons of any kind, including toys.) If possible, pack rain gear (a poncho is best). One of the most important items of all? Comfortable walking shoes.

Guests staying at the resorts on Hotel Plaza Boulevard may access a tourist-information television station of their own. Some other area hotels also show a version of the programming, usually aiming to provide an overview of all Central Florida attractions.

For Day Visitors: When purchasing one-day admission to a given theme park, guests receive a complimentary guidemap and entertainment Times Guide for that park. Ticket holders may receive all four park guides upon request. Extra park guidemaps are available at City Hall (in the Magic Kingdom) and at Guest Relations (in Epcot, Disney's Hollywood Studios, and Disney's Animal Kingdom), as well as in many shops and restaurants throughout the theme parks.

PACKAGE POINTERS

The sheer number and diversity of packages offering vacations in Central Florida are enough to bewilder even the savviest traveler. Still, such plans are worth exploring. Most offer the convenience of a vacation that's completely organized in advance, and one that will generally cost less than the sum of the same transportation, accommodations, and admission elements purchased separately. In addition, since most package providers purchase blocks of Disney resort rooms, they are an excellent source for securing a room on Walt Disney World property when the hotel of your choice is booked solid.

Southwest Vacations (800-243-8372), American Airlines Vacations (800-321-2121), *www.expedia.com*, *www.travelocity.com*, and the Walt Disney Travel Company (407-939-6244 or *www.disneyworld.com*) all offer packages that feature Walt Disney World on-site hotels, as well as choice off-property accommodations. Certain packages may sweeten the deal by including (relatively) low-cost air transportation.

Vacations and other travel packages may include certain perks and discounts. For possibilities, check travel websites, the travel section of your local paper, or consult a travel agent.

Walt Disney Travel Company offers four vacation plans: Magic Your Way base package, Magic Your Way Plus Dining package, Magic Your Way Plus Quick Service Dining package, and Magic Your Way Plus Deluxe Dining package. (Go to *www.disneyworld.com/dvd* to order a complimentary vacation-planning DVD.) Walt Disney Travel Company packages may include extras such as miniature golf vouchers and savings on participating recreation, dining, and shopping locations throughout Walt Disney World.

Travel agents may design packages around a specific type of vacation: say, a golf getaway, honeymoon, or family reunion. They may include extra elements such as unlimited tee times or a carriage ride. Still others are tied to an annual event, such as the Walt Disney World Marathon (see Holidays & Special Events on page 10). Air transportation, rental car, travel insurance, or airport transfers can be added to most packages.

The value of a package depends on your party's needs. Before considering options, use this book to help determine which of the accommodations, activities, and attractions most appeal to you. There's genuine value in certain package elements, such as airport transfers. Several packages also include meals with the Disney characters, tennis lessons, golf greens fees, spa treatments, boat rentals, and the like.

Never choose a package that includes elements you don't want or won't have time to enjoy. While extras such as welcoming snacks may sound appealing, their cash value is negligible. Also beware of any packages that tout certain services as selling points that are actually available to every Disney guest.

Finally, we highly recommend insuring your trip when purchasing a package, as cancellation fees can be steep and emergencies do happen. Insurance ensures peace of mind (and wallet).

HOT TIP!

When purchasing a Walt Disney World package, pay attention to the type of WDW ticket that's included—and make sure you are able to customize the ticket to meet your needs. See page 21.

"Magic Your Way" Packages

"Magic Your Way" is the name of the game when it comes to Disney World vacation packages. The phrase, meant to reflect each individual's freedom to customize a vacation, covers quite the gamut of options. Most of all, it covers four vacation packages: Magic Your Way, Magic Your Way Plus Dining, Magic Your Way Plus Quick Service Dining, and Magic Your Way Plus Deluxe Dining. They can be booked through the Walt Disney Travel Company (407-939-7675), travel agents, and *www.disneyworld.com*.

The packages have some elements in common. They're all intended to be flexible and include a Disney resort stay and a theme park ticket of some kind. They come with "magical extras" such as discounts at select Walt Disney World dining, recreational, and shopping locations, as well as admission to one of WDW's mini golf courses and ESPN Wide World of Sports Complex. They must be paid for in full. Packages must be canceled at least 31 days before the trip to avoid a penalty. (For cancellations made 31 days or more prior to arrival, amounts paid minus fees assessed by third-party suppliers will be refunded.) Everyone staying in a resort room must have the same package and ticket options. Finally, Magic Your Way packages come with the following perks (which are also extended to guests with room-only reservations):

• Extra Magic Hours benefit: Walt Disney World resort guests may enjoy exclusive access to theme parks on select mornings and evenings. (For details, see page 22.)

• Disney's Magical Express service: complimentary transportation to and from the Orlando International Airport, plus complimentary baggage collection and delivery to your resort room. (See page 16 for details.)

• Complimentary use of the Walt Disney World transportation system.

Magic Your Way Package: This package includes a stay at any Walt Disney World–owned-and-operated resort paired with a theme park ticket. The important decisions to be made here are (1) which Disney resort to reserve, and (2) the number of days and add-ons (if any) you want on your park ticket. (For additional information about Walt Disney World theme park ticket structures and pricing, turn to pages 21–24 of this chapter.)

"Enchanting Extras"

Disney offers an ever-changing slate of adventures, tours, and seasonal events, collectively known as the "Enchanting Extras Collection." The most widely offered experiences are detailed on the pages of this book. Seasonal offerings, aka "Limited Time Events," and new adventures join the lineup throughout the year. For details or to make reservations for Disney's Enchanting Extras Collection, call 407-WDW-PLAY (939-7529), or visit *https://disneyworld.disney.go.com/events-tours/enchanting-extras-collection/*.

Magic Your Way Plus Dining Package: Take the Magic Your Way package, throw in a Disney Dining Plan, and you've got a vacation plan with the option to pre-pay for meals and choose from more than 100 eateries. This package includes one quick-service meal, two snacks, plus one meal at a table-service restaurant per person, per night of your vacation. (For more on the Dining Plan, see the sidebar at right.) The package also includes a Magic Your Way base ticket and a Rapid Fill refillable mug for each member of your party (see page 285).

Magic Your Way Plus Quick Service Dining Package: This plan includes two quick-service meals and two snacks per day, per guest. (Note that all meals must be of the quick-service variety.) It includes a Rapid Fill refillable mug for each member of the party participating in this package (see page 285).

Magic Your Way Plus Deluxe Dining Package: This plan is similar to the two aforementioned packages, but it comes with three meals a day, all of which can be cashed in at any eatery that is a Dining Plan participant (regardless of whether it is quick service or table service).

VIP Tours

You may have noticed them in the theme parks—those cheery folks in the plaid vests. They are VIP guides, leading guests on customized WDW trips.

The point is to minimize the hassle factor, while maximizing the overall magic component. Though participating in a VIP tour won't necessarily let you cut the line, it may yield some special seating for stage shows and parades. One tour guide can host up to 10 guests at a cost of about $175–$315 per hour. There is a 6-hour minimum per trip. Parties larger than 10 will require a second guide. Make your needs known when you book the tour. Cancellations must be made at least 48 hours in advance to avoid a fee. Call 407-560-4033 for additional VIP tour information or to make a reservation.

Disney Dining Plan

The Disney Dining Plan lets guests pre-pay for meals before they arrive at Walt Disney World. While convenient for some, it's not a money-saver. For details on Disney Dining Plan options, visit *www.disneyworld.com*. Consider just how much your party can consume before selecting a plan, as some include much more sustenance than others. Here's a summary of the standard (non-deluxe) table-service plan (specifics are subject to change at any time):

Each day of the 2020 plan—which costs about $78 a day for adults and $31 for kids (ages 3 to 9) and is offered as part of the Magic Your Way Plus Dining package—includes:

• One table-service meal, including entrée, dessert (lunch or dinner), and one drink.
• One quick-service meal, including an entrée and one beverage.
• Two snacks, such as ice cream, popcorn, or a medium soft drink at select quick-service spots or snack carts.
• The option of exchanging two table-service meals for one meal at a high-end "Signature" restaurant or a WDW dinner show, such as the Hoop-Dee-Doo Musical Revue.

To sum up: Say your family of four purchases a five-night package. Together you're entitled to 20 quick-service meals, 20 table-service meals, and 40 snacks. And you are free to use them in any way you want. That is, if you want to skip a meal one day or have 5 meals in a single day, by all means go for it. (Remember there is a finite number of meals allotted.) Usage can be tracked via My Disney Experience (see page 23), at Guest Relations in the parks and Walt Disney World resorts, and by keeping your meal receipts. Present a MagicBand (see page 24) or room key card. Tax is included, gratuities are not. Be sure to tip your servers. Note that guests age 21 and older have the option of ordering an alcoholic beverage (where available).

In addition to traditional table-service meals, certain "character dining" experiences are available to Dining Plan participants, as are some Disney Springs locations. A Quick-Service Only Dining Plan is offered, as well. Children ages 3 through 9 must order from the kids' menu where available.

To find out which restaurants are participating, turn to our *Good Meals, Great Times* chapter. For updates, call 407-939-3463, or go to *www.disneyworld.com*.

Dining Plans must be purchased at the same time a WDW resort stay is booked. *If you get a Dining Plan with table-service meals, you must make reservations for restaurants.* Do so as far ahead as possible—180 days.

All About Theme Park Tickets

PHOTO BY JILL SAFRO

Buying a park ticket can be very simple. Do you plan on visiting one park on one day? Just pick up a One-Day Base Ticket. Perhaps you are a frequent visitor and expect to pass through theme park gates dozens of times over the next year. In that case, an Annual Pass is what you're looking for. Now, if your park-going plans lie somewhere in between (and most do), you will have to be a little more strategic.

When it comes to selecting the perfect type of admission ticket, it pays to do some homework. Study all the options, evaluate your priorities, and make no hasty decisions. For starters, there are several major factors to consider: (1) total number of days you would like to visit theme parks, (2) the actual dates you want to visit the parks, (3) to park-hop or not to park-hop, and (4) whether you want to pre-pay (and save some time) for "extras" such as admission to the WDW water parks, mini golf courses, the Memory Maker photo package, etc. The following information was correct at press time and is meant to help you make wise choices. Keep in mind that most WDW ticket prices are likely to increase in 2020—they always do. For pricing updates, use the My Disney Experience mobile app or website, visit *www.disneyworld.com*, or call 407-824-4321.

DISNEY THEME PARK TICKETS

Date-based Tickets: Available for 1 to 10 days. Valid for admission to one theme park per day—the Magic Kingdom, Epcot, Disney's Hollywood Studios, or Disney's Animal Kingdom. The ticket does not allow for park-hopping, but that option may be added. (Guests may customize tickets to fit their vacation needs.) Prices

vary, depending on the day of the week and time of year. To get a sense of "peak" pricing, see page 26. To see ticket prices during each day of your planned visit to Walt Disney World, go to *www.disneyworld.com* and study the interactive calendar.

> ## HOT TIP!
>
> You cannot use a second day's admission to enter a second theme park on the same day you visited another theme park—even if you have days remaining on a multi-day ticket. To do that you must add the Park Hopper option to the ticket or buy a one-day ticket to enter the second park.

Expiration: Date-based tickets must be used within a certain time period. A 1-day ticket must be used on the specific date for which it was purchased; 2-day tickets must be used within 4 days after the start date; 3-day tickets must be used within 5 days of start date; 4-day tickets must be used within 7 days after start date; 5-day tickets must be used within 8 days of start date; 6-day tickets must be used within 9 days of start date; 7-day tickets must be used within 10 days of start date, 8-day tickets must be used within 12 days of the start date; 9-day tickets must be used within 13 days of the start date; and 10-day tickets must be used within 14 days of start date. Guests who purchase the Park Hopper Plus option get an extra day to use the 2- through 10-day tickets.

The No Expire option was discontinued in February 2015; tickets that were purchased prior to then should be honored at the parks, provided they have the No Expire option. Tickets bought before 2005 are valid, too—they pre-date the No Expire option. For information on how to use older tickets, visit a Walt Disney World ticket booth or call 4017-824-4321.

Flexible-Date Tickets: Flexible-date tickets live up to their name in that they may be used at any time before the end of the year. Like the old "Magic Your Way" tickets, they expire within 14 days of first use. With flexibility comes sticker shock: Flexible-Date tickets cost significantly more than Date-Based tickets.

Park Hopper Option: This add-on lets guests visit more than one theme park on a single day. The privilege extends through the length of the ticket. It costs about $60 to add it to a one-day theme park ticket; about $70 for two- and three-day tickets to all parks; and about $80 for all other base tickets (regardless of the number of days on the ticket). We recommend checking operating hours for your planned visit. In our opinion, hopping is a worthwhile option *only* if the parks are open very late.

Park Hopper Plus Option: This add-on covers entry to Blizzard Beach and Typhoon Lagoon water parks, Disney's ESPN Wide World of Sports Complex, miniature golf, or a round of golf at Disney's Oak Trail golf course. For about $80 to $100 extra (depending on the number of days on the ticket), you will get two to ten visits to these spots. The total number of visits depends on the number of days on your base ticket—the more days, the more visits.

Theme Park Platinum Annual Pass: This pass offers admission to the four Walt Disney World theme parks for a full year with no block-out dates. It can be used in more than one park on the same day (also known as park-hopping), and includes use of the Disney transportation system, as well as free standard parking at the theme parks, and a full year's worth of PhotoPass downloads. Annual passes can be purchased at the entrance to any of the theme parks (they can be renewed there or by mail). A valid, government-issued photo ID must be presented for purchase by adults and may be required for future use of the pass. All passes are non-transferable. At press time, the cost was about $1,119 for adults and kids age 3 and up.

Annual Pass-bearers qualify for many Walt Disney World discounts and benefits, such as reduced rates at select Disney resorts at certain times of year. A newsletter called the *Mickey Monitor* and *DisneyPassholder.com* provide updates regarding discount offers. The pass expires one year after it's first used. A discounted renewal rate may apply if a pass is renewed before expiration. (The old pass must be presented in order to receive the discounted renewal rate.) A pass may be renewed by mail, online, or at any Disney theme park.

Platinum Plus Annual Pass: This pass has everything the Platinum Pass has to offer and more—namely, admission to both water parks, ESPN Wide World of Sports Complex (non-premium events only), a year's worth of PhotoPass downloads, plus a round of golf at the Oak Trail golf course. Platinum Plus Annual Passholders are eligible for the same discounts and

Extra Magic Hours

How'd you like to visit a Disney theme park before it opens to the public? Or stick around after it's officially closed for the day—at no extra cost? Well, if you're a guest staying at a Walt Disney World–owned-and-operated resort, the Swan, Dolphin, Shades of Green (see page 110), Four Seasons Orlando (see page 111), or a Hotel Plaza Boulevard resort near Disney Springs (see page 104), you can! It is one of the major perks that comes with staying on Disney property.

Here's how it works: One park opens its doors an hour early or stays open two hours late on a particular day. Basically, the park becomes something of a members-only private playground for Walt Disney World resort guests. So, provided that you have a WDW resort ID and valid admission media, you're in! No secret password necessary. Keep in mind that you will need park-hopping privileges if you plan to visit a park other than the one offering extra hours on any given day. If you don't plan to park-hop, you must visit the theme park offering Extra Magic Hours on that particular day. When a park opens early in the morning, guests are admitted starting one hour prior to the official opening time. Transportation to the park usually starts about 30 minutes before that. Be sure to have your MagicBand or Walt Disney World resort ID handy. Flash (or scan) it and you will be allowed to visit some (but not all) attractions and mingle with favorite Disney characters.

In our opinion, Extra Magic Hours is the single-most valuable perk available to Walt Disney World Resort hotel guests.

Details about Extra Magic Hours are subject to change. Visit *www.disneyworld.com* for updates and the schedule for your visit.

benefits as Platinum Annual Passholders. Platinum Plus Annual Passes can be purchased at the entrance to any of the four theme parks (they can be renewed there or by mail). Adults must present a government-issued photo ID and may be required to show one for future use. Passes are non-transferable and they expire one year after first use. The cost is about $1,219 for adults and kids (over the age of 3).

Premier Annual Pass: This pass provides admission to all Disney theme parks and water parks within the United States (including Disneyland Park and Disney California Adventure) for one year. It also includes one year's worth of unlimited PhotoPass downloads, admission to the ESPN Wide World of Sports Complex (non-premium events only), and the Oak Trail golf course. Unlimited park-hopping and standard theme park parking are included, as are the same discounts offered with Disney's other annual passes (select merchandise, food, and resort discounts).

The Premier Pass costs about $2,099, plus tax. It must be purchased in person at a U.S. Disney theme park. Guests already bearing a WDW or Disneyland Resort Annual Pass may upgrade to the Premier Pass. For details, call 407-824-4321 or visit *disneyworld.com*.

> # HOT TIP!
> If your child "outgrows" his or her park ticket (by turning 10), you can upgrade the ticket at any of the theme parks.

DECIDING FACTORS

Choosing the Right Ticket: Before you make a decision, it helps to map out your vacation. Remember, all tickets start as Base Tickets. They are a bare-bones, admission-to-one-theme-park-at-a-time deal. That's perfect for many folks—especially those planning a relatively short stay. Still, the first step for every potential guest is to decide just how many days they plan to spend in the theme parks. Keep in mind that as days are added, the average price per day goes down. Unused days expire after the ticket's start date whether activated or not. For expiration details, see page 21. Once the length of stay and the start date are determined, it's time to customize the ticket. If the total number of days is undetermined, err on the side of caution—unused days cannot be refunded. You can, however, add days to a ticket at a park Guest Relations window on the final date of an activated ticket. After that, you'll have to purchase a new ticket. Do you want to park-hop? Add about $60–$80. Want to add the Park Hopper Plus Option? That's about $80–$100.

If you are planning a long visit, or two trips in one year, consider an Annual Pass. In addition to unlimited admission to the parks, an Annual Pass entitles bearers to discounts on everything from dinner shows to resort room rates.

Note: Only one person per party needs to have an Annual Pass to net a discount on a WDW resort (when available). This option is great for travelers with flexible schedules, as the discounts do vary, and they are often announced shortly before going into effect.

Tickets with Unused Days: Prior to 2005, WDW tickets never expired. That is no longer the case. Days remaining on a multi-day admission ticket now expire 2 to 14 days after the ticket's start date (with the exception of Flex-Date tickets and Annual Passes). Unused one-day tickets have expiration dates, too.

Attractions Outside the Theme Parks: Typhoon Lagoon and Blizzard Beach water park prices start at about $69 for a day and about $139 for an annual pass for adults; $63 for one day and about $139 for an annual pass for kids (ages 3 to 9). ESPN Wide World of Sports Complex runs about $19 for adults, about $14 for kids (general admission). Prices are apt to rise in 2020.

MY DISNEY EXPERIENCE

"My Disney Experience" is the all-encompassing moniker attached to the vacation-planning tools managed via the My Disney Experience website or mobile app. It also links ticket cards and MagicBands (wristbands that are connected to various Disney vacation features) and includes the complimentary Fastpass+ attraction reservation system (see page 25).

My Disney Experience: An app that can be downloaded for free and is compatible with most Android and Apple iOS smartphones and tablets, My Disney Experience is a tool for reserving tables at WDW eateries and dinner shows; booking, revising, and keeping track of Fastpass+ assignments at theme park attractions; viewing wait times, room charges; track Dining Plan entitlements, and more. The app can even be used to open your WDW-owned-and-operated resort room via "digital key." For guests traveling without smartphones or tablets, *MyDisneyExperience.com* can be accessed by personal computer. It allows for the same advance

> # HOT TIP!
> Value remaining on an expired, unactivated, Date-Based park ticket may be put toward a new ticket (for use within a year). Details are subject to change. For specifics, call the WDW Ticket Services Department: 407-566-4985 (press Option 4).

HOT TIP!

Adults should always carry a government-issued photo ID. You'll need it should you have any issues with your MagicBand and to purchase alcohol while at WDW.

planning. The service is free and requires guests to create an account (to which all members of the traveling party should be linked). Note that kids under age 13 are not permitted to have live, individual accounts. Instead, parents create and manage a profile for each child (kids' profiles are attached to their parents'). There is a bit of a learning curve, so get started as soon as you can.

After linking a WDW resort reservation or vacation package and tickets to an account, guests may link MagicBands, make and monitor dining reservations, book and track Fastpass+ times, and load the Memory Maker Photo Package (see page 27). It is important to link all accounts in your traveling party (parties larger than 10 should call 407-939-5277).

All guests may use this service, whether they stay on Disney property or not, provided they can access the website or utilize the app.

MagicBands: This accessory is something of a technological wonder—it can serve as a resort room key and be linked to theme park and water park tickets. Guests can also use it to make purchases throughout Walt Disney World (provided the MagicBand is backed up with a credit card and a personal PIN code has been selected); use it for Disney's PhotoPass (see page 135), Fastpass+ (in conjunction with *MyDisneyExperience.com* or the associated app); and more. To use it to make a purchase in a shop or restaurant, just tap the not-so-

hidden Mickey on the band to the Mickey head on the console. MagicBands are complimentary for guests at Disney–owned-and-operated resorts. The standard version comes in gray but may be customized in one of 8 different colors. (We recommend using different colors for each member of a party.) Bands customized 11 or more days ahead of arrival can be sent to your home. Bands customized within 6 to 10 days of your visit will be sent to your Disney–owned-and-operated resort. MagicBands ordered within 5 days cannot be customized and may be collected at your resort's Front Desk. MagicBands cannot be shipped to all countries.

MagicBands are included with your Disney hotel reservation, but specialty versions may be purchased in the parks, via the My Disney Experience app or website, or at *shopdisney.com*. Non-WDW resort guests may buy MagicBands at WDW theme parks and *shopdisney.com*.

The MagicBand is waterproof (but does not float), hypoallergenic, and can be adjusted to fit most wrists. If a Band is lost, it can be disabled via the My Disney Experience app (and the website) or with the help of a Cast Member. MagicBands are non-transferable. No personal information is stored on the band— it only links to entitlements that were pre-purchased. Remember, you will need to use a PIN code to pay for

HOT TIP!

We recommend wearing the MagicBand on your dominant hand. That should make it easier to align it with Mickey heads when endeavoring to make a purchase or open a resort room door.

How Do You Book a Room? Let Us Count the Ways

You're ready to reserve a room at a resort on Walt Disney World property. How nice for you! But before you dial 407-W-DISNEY (934-7639) or a travel agent, know this: There are three different ways to book your WDW stay. It's best to know what you prefer in advance. It will save you time and spare confusion while on the phone or while using the My Disney Experience website or mobile app. Here's the scoop:

• Room-Only Reservation—What you hear is what you get: a hotel room only. It requires an advance deposit and allows you to cancel up to 5 days prior to the start of the reservation (penalty-free). It comes with a 12-digit confirmation number.

• Walt Disney Travel Company Basic Plan—A package that includes room, luggage tags, and a round of mini-golf for the entire party. Must be paid in full 30 days before check-in and must be canceled at least 31 days prior to check-in to avoid a paying a penalty. (The confirmation number has 8 digits.) We recommend adding trip insurance to the package (at an additional cost), just in case.

• Magic Your Way Base Package—Includes room and theme park tickets. It may be customized in many ways, such as adding the Disney Dining Plan, Water Park admission, and more (see page 21). Must be paid in full 30 days before check-in and must be canceled at least 31 days prior to check-in (any later and there will be hefty penalties). Once reserved, expect to get an 8-digit confirmation number.

Save Time in Line with FASTPASS+

Walt Disney World's Fastpass+ is a service that was designed to allow guests to bypass the traditional standby line and enjoy a number of theme park shows and attractions with less of a wait. It's a virtual queue—one you join by visiting "My Disney Experience" via the Internet (with a computer, tablet, or smartphone). Once you've established an account, you can link your ticket (and those in your party) and access Fastpass+ to book times to visit attractions during a pending visit to a Walt Disney World theme park.

To WDW veterans, the term Fastpass conjures happy memories of bypassing lines after securing assignments while visiting the parks. That concept is still the same, but the procedure has changed quite a bit. In fact, we wish they had called the new system something other than Fastpass+, because it really is a bold departure from the original. Think of Fastpass+ as an *advance reservation system*—one that is free to all guests bearing a valid park ticket. (Guests staying in Club Level rooms in select WDW resorts may purchase additional Fastpass+ assignments. For details, see page 105.)

Popular WDW attractions and shows (aka E-Ticket experiences) are often very crowded, with long waits and no guarantee you'll get in. By using Fastpass+, you can reserve a time to enjoy at least one popular ride (and several other attractions) during each day of your WDW visit. In most cases, you won't walk right in, but you will have an expedited wait time and guaranteed admission to some crowd-pleasers such as Toy Story Mania!, Soarin' Around the World, Avatar Flight of Passage, and Peter Pan's Flight. Ideally, Fastpass+ aims to spread guests throughout the parks, making traditionally congested areas less so. For folks who prefer to do things on the fly or who find the new system a bit daunting or difficult to navigate, traditional standby lines will always be available. That said, tech-savvy, detail-minded guests may relax a bit, knowing each day of their vacation is pre-planned.

Begin by paying a visit to My Disney Experience via the Internet or mobile app. Set up an account and link it with your park ticket. Then, if it's within 30 days of your visit (60 if you are staying in a WDW–owned-and-operated resort, Swan, Dolphin, Four Seasons Orlando, or select Disney Springs area resorts on Hotel Plaza Boulevard), you can start booking Fastpass+ assignments starting at 7 A.M. Eastern Standard Time. When the one-hour Fastpass+ window kicks in, go to the attraction and touch your MagicBand or ticket card to the Fastpass+ console, wait for the light, and head inside.

We highly recommend using Fastpass+ assignments for your must-sees. We've placed our Fastpass+ symbol (**FP+**) beside the listing for all shows and attractions that were included at press time. However, since experiences may be added or dropped, visit *www.mydisneyexperience.com* for updates. And remember, all WDW attractions continue to offer the option of standing in a traditional queue. But Fastpass+ is a true bonus option for folks who like to plan ahead. By using it, we have gleaned the following:

• To make advance Fastpass+ reservations, you must have access to the Internet.

• It's possible to reserve a same-day Fastpass+ assignment via the mobile app and at a park kiosk—but getting convenient, same-day access to popular attractions is tough. Start early!

• Fastpass+ lets you experience at least 3 attractions or shows per day without waiting in the (usually) longer standby line. You may be able to get more same-day assignments via the app and at in-park kiosks once your first three have been used or the time has expired (pending availability).

• Although you are able to book up to 3 Fastpass+ assignments in one park in advance, you can make changes after you use your first Fastpass+ assignment of the day. Changes to original selections must apply to shows and attractions within the same park. To revise your selections, visit *mydisneyexperience.com*, use the My Disney Experience app, or go to an in-park kiosk.

• Fastpass+ allows for park-hopping after the first 3 Fastpass+ assignments have been used or the times have expired. After that you can make a selection for another park via the mobile app or at an in-park kiosk. Additional Fastpass+ assignments are available one at a time.

• Fastpass+ times are linked to your MagicBand (see page 24) or park ticket card and can be viewed, modified, or canceled via smartphone, tablet, computer, or in-park Fastpass+ kiosk. To use a Fastpass+ assignment, you'll need to touch a MagicBand or ticket card to a Fastpass+ reader device at the attraction.

• Fastpass+ assignments are non-transferable.

• Need to coordinate Fastpass+ assignments for a group? Start by inviting all members of your party to connect to your "My Friends and Family" list in your My Disney Experience account. Then, when your Fastpass+ window opens up, you can reserve Fastpasses for everyone in your group. (All guests must have valid theme park tickets linked to their respective My Disney Experience accounts.)

• Write the assignment times on paper if you don't have a smartphone or in case your smartphone battery dies. You can check times at a park kiosk, too.

• All shows and attractions continue to offer traditional standby lines.

• Disney's Fastpass+ is an ever-evolving system. Details are subject to change.

	1-Day	2-Day	3-Day	4-Day	5-Day	6-Day	7-Day	8-Day	9-Day	10-Day
Base Ticket* AGES 10 & UP	$159	$311 ($155.50/day)	$449 $149.67/day)	$562 ($140.50/day)	$570 ($114/day)	$576 ($96/day)	$582 ($83.14/day)	$593 ($74.13/day)	$597 ($66.33/day)	$606 ($60.60/day)
Base Ticket* AGES 3–9	$154	$301 ($150.50/day)	$434 $144.67/day)	$545 ($136.25/day)	$552 ($110.40/day)	$558 ($93/day)	$563 ($80.43/day)	$573 ($71.63/day)	$576 ($64/day)	$586 ($58.60/day)
ADD: Park Hopper**	$60	$70	$70	$80	$80	$80	$80	$80	$80	$80
ADD: Park-Hopper Plus Option***	$80 2 visits	$90 2 visits	$90 3 visits	$100 4 visits	$100 5 visits	$100 6 visits	$100 7 visits	$100 8 visits	$100 9 visits	$100 10 visits
ADD: Memory Maker****	$169/ $199	$169/ $199	$169/ $199	$169/ $199	$169/ $199	$169/ $199	$169/ $199	$169/ $199	$169/ $199	$169/ $199

† These are advance-purchase, Date-Based prices and do not include tax. Prices are lower during non-peak times of year. All prices are subject to change.

* Base Ticket admits guest to one theme park each day of use. Park choices are Magic Kingdom, Epcot, Disney's Hollywood Studios, and Disney's Animal Kingdom.

** Park Hopper Option entitles guest to visit more than one theme park on each day of use. Park choices are any combination of theme parks on each day of use.

*** Park-Hopper Plus option entitles guest to a specified number of visits to a choice of entertainment and recreation venues. Choices include Disney's Blizzard Beach water park, Disney's Typhoon Lagoon water park, and ESPN Wide World of Sports Complex.

**** Guests who pre-pay for Disney's Memory Maker photo package pay the first price, those who make the purchase within 3 days of their WDW visit pay the second price. If you purchased Memory Maker at the advance purchase price, photos taken within 3 days of the date of purchase will not be included in Memory Maker and must be purchased separately. The Memory Maker Photo package is available to all guests. For details, see page 27.

things with your MagicBand. If you lose your Magic-Band while at Walt Disney World, go to the nearest Guest Relations location or your Disney Resort hotel Lobby Concierge and they'll deactivate it for you. A replacement band may be provided (for a fee).

Fastpass+: WDW's reservation system for most attractions, shows, and character meet and greets at its four theme parks is a free service, available to guests with valid theme park tickets. It may be accessed up to 30 days in advance via the My Disney Experience app or website. Guests with a reservation at a Disney–owned-and-operated resort and other select resorts may book Fastpass+ assignments up to 60 days prior to checking in. It's possible to make same-day Fastpass+ reservations, too—by using the aforementioned ways and by visiting a Fastpass+ kiosk in any of the WDW theme parks. Note that it is not possible to get Fastpass+ assignments at the attractions themselves. For details on Fastpass+, turn to page 25.

Memory Maker Photo Package: Memory Maker includes all photographs and videos taken in the parks, including those snapped on select attractions and character meal locations for your length of stay. You can view and download the photos via the My Disney Experience app, or via the PhotoPass website: *https://mydisneyphotopass.disney.go.com/*. It's possible to customize your photos with banners and Disney art, too. At press time, the same-day price was about $199; about $169 if pre-ordered. (We think Memory Maker is a worthwhile investment—especially for large parties and those who expect to purchase more than 10 Photo-Pass photos. For more information about Disney's PhotoPass package, see page 131.)

PURCHASING TICKETS

Admission tickets are sold at all Walt Disney World park entrances and resorts, the Four Seasons Orlando resort, the resorts on Hotel Plaza Boulevard, WDW's Transportation and Ticket Center (TTC), and at the Ticket Center at Disney Springs (located in Town Center). Cash, traveler's checks, American Express, Visa, MasterCard, Diner's Club, Discover, JCB Card, and Disney gift cards are accepted. (Disney Dollars are still accepted as payment for most Walt Disney World purchases, but they are no longer sold.) Not all tickets are available at each of the aforementioned locations, so call 407-934-7639 to confirm.

We recommend buying tickets in advance (it can save time when you arrive at the parks) from a travel agent, or in one of these ways:

Tickets by Phone: All tickets can be purchased by phone; call 407-W-DISNEY (934-7639). Allow 15 days for standard delivery; $15 for express delivery (allow 7 days); and $25 for international delivery (allow 12 days). There is no handling fee for pickup at a Walt Disney World Will Call window.

Tickets Online: Tickets can be bought online via the My Disney Experience mobile app or website or *www.disneyworld.com*. The fees for delivery are the same as those listed above.

Tickets by Mail (select tickets only): Allow at least three to five weeks for processing, and include a return address. Send a money order (for total amount due, plus a $4 handling fee), payable to The Walt Disney World Company, to: Walt Disney World, Box 10140, Lake Buena Vista, FL 32830-0030. Attention: Ticket Mail Order.

Ticket Tag System

As a means of enforcing the non-transferability aspect of all Walt Disney World tickets, Disney has devised a system to trace each ticket to its rightful owner. The procedure is as follows: Touch your MagicBand or ticket to the shiny orb at any park entrance. While the machine is crunching the data encrypted on your MagicBand or ticket, gently press the tip of your forefinger onto the glowing gizmo perched beside the orb. Remove your finger and presto! Your MagicBand or ticket will link to your forefinger, giving you the green light to enter. All guests over age 3 have to do this every time they use the ticket. Remember to use the same finger every time you enter a park. (It's a good idea to wash your hands after this process.)

Money-Saving Tips

A Walt Disney World vacation can be an exceptionally expensive undertaking, but it is possible to keep costs down a bit. When budgeting for your trip, keep in mind that WDW prices are comparable to those in a big city. Here are a few tips to help you conserve cash.

LODGING

• When it comes to saving money on hotel accommodations, timing is truly key. While off-season dates tend to vary depending on the hotel, value season for most Walt Disney World resort hotels generally means January through mid-February, late August through late September, early November, and early December. Weeknights are generally less expensive than weekend nights year-round.

• The Walt Disney World Swan and Dolphin resorts often have rate specials when other WDW resorts have peak rates. Check *www.swandolphin.com*.

• Consider how much time you will actually spend at your hotel, and don't pay for a place with perks you won't have time to enjoy. Off-property hotels often allow kids to stay free in parents' rooms, but the cutoff age varies. Be sure to inquire in advance.

• When weighing the cost-effectiveness of off-property lodging, remember to factor in the time, money, and inconvenience of the commute to and from Walt Disney World and nearby attractions.

• Realize, too, that the advantages of staying on Walt Disney World property (tops among them the Extra Magic Hours perk, free airport transfers courtesy of Disney's Magical Express, a 30-day jump on making Fastpass assignments [refer to page 25], and access to WDW's extensive transportation system) also apply to those staying in the least expensive rooms in Disney's hotels. The most important addresses for budget-watching Disney fans, the All-Star and Pop Century

HOT TIP!
To save money on Walt Disney World dining, merchandise, golf, behind-the-scenes tours, and much more, use the coupons at the back of this book!

resorts, offer the lowest rates on Disney property. Rooms at Caribbean Beach and Port Orleans French Quarter & Riverside are slightly higher-priced. Also, note that the only difference between the least and most expensive rooms in a hotel is often the view.

• The resorts on Hotel Plaza Boulevard, located near Disney Springs, offer lovely rooms starting at about $130 per night. (See page 106.)

FOOD

• Club Level accommodations can absorb the cost of some meals, snacks, and cocktails—the more folks in the room, the better the value.

• Carry snacks and sandwich fixings and enjoy them picnic style wherever possible.

• Consider lodgings with kitchen facilities. The savings on food may be more than the extra accommodations expense. Note that there is a small fridge in all rooms at WDW–owned-and-operated resorts (no charge).

• Staying at a Walt Disney World-owned-and-operated resort? We recommend the purchase of a Rapid Fill refillable mug. Each mug costs about $19 (plus tax) and is good for unlimited soft-drink refills (coffee, tea, soda pop, and more) for the length of your stay. (See page 285.) Note that Rapid Fill Mugs are included with most Disney Dining Plans. Be sure to ask.

• Snack stands are plentiful, but not always handy or cost-efficient. Be sure to pack snacks and refillable water bottles before you arrive.

• Don't plan on three big table-service meals a day. It gets expensive (and time-consuming).

• Save money by having supplies delivered to your resort. Items such as bottled water, snacks, fruit, and breakfast bars can be enjoyed in the room or out of a backpack throughout the day. Our go-to for groceries is *gardengrocer.com*. (This company is authorized to deliver to all Walt Disney World resorts, but is not affiliated with the Walt Disney Company.)

• The Disney Dining Plan is appealing for the convenience of pre-paying for your vacation meals—but it is no more cost-efficient than paying as you go.

Satisfying Substitutes

Fewer frills rarely mean less fun at Walt Disney World. Here are money-saving alternatives to two of Disney's higher-priced treats:

If you would rather not spring for admission to Disney Springs West Side venues, consider taking a trip to the BoardWalk resort. Among other diversions, you will find Jellyrolls (a sing-along piano bar with a cover of about $15), Atlantic Dance Hall (a nightclub with no cover charge), and ESPN Club (a cover-free sports bar). Magicians and jugglers entertain guests on the boardwalk on a nightly basis. A short walk will take you to the Swan hotel, home to the karaoke-friendly Kimonos Lounge and Il Mulino New York Trattoria, where live music is presented in the lounge on Friday and Saturday evenings.

If the Grand Floridian doesn't quite fit into your budget, consider staying in a Mansion room at Port Orleans Riverside. Southern hospitality replaces Victorian splendor, and though the guestrooms aren't quite as spacious, the air of sophistication makes for a most satisfying stay. And for a sweet deal on a suite, consider the family suites at the vibrant resort known as Disney's Art of Animation.

DISCOUNTS

• Theme Park Annual Passholders receive so many discounts on meals, dinner shows, tours, room rates, and more that it may be worth purchasing an Annual Pass for longer visits or if you plan to take more than one trip within a calendar year.

• WDW resorts that offer Annual Passholder discounts vary from month to month, and discounted rooms aren't always available for booking very far in advance. It's best to be flexible with travel dates. Annual Passholders may net deals on recreational opportunities, too. For details, call 407-W-DISNEY (939-7639). Passholders can save 20 percent at many WDW eateries by joining the Tables in Wonderland program (for a fee). For details, call 407-WDW-DINE (939-3463).

• Discounts on Walt Disney World resort rates and theme park tickets are available to Florida residents, and seasonal promotions occur. Call 407-W-DISNEY (939-7639) for specifics.

• The Swan and Dolphin, as well as some off-property hotels, offer discounts to seniors and the Automobile Association of America (AAA) or AARP members, nurses, and teachers. Some AAA branches provide discounts on park passes, as well as discounts on rooms, and more. Touch base with your local AAA branch for additional information.

> ### HOT TIP!
> It may be cheaper to get a family suite or spread out over two rooms in a "value" or "moderate" resort than to have everyone stay in one room at "deluxe" Disney digs.

> ### HOT TIP!
> Bring inexpensive, lightweight rain gear from home. It's likely you'll need it—especially in the stormy months of summer.

• *Travelocity.com* offers a variety of Walt Disney World vacation packages. Vacation Outlet sometimes offers packages at a reduced rate; call 800-825-3633, or visit *www.vacationoutlet.com* for details.

• Visit Orlando is an organization that offers information and discounted tickets to several area parks, shows, restaurants, hotels, and more. To learn about Visit Orlando discount offers and to purchase tickets, go to *www.visitorlando.com/discounts-and-tickets/*.

• Disney Visa® Cardmembers who pay with their Disney Visa Card enjoy savings on merchandise, dining, and guided tours. Cardmembers may use the Disney Visa card wherever Visa is accepted. Details are subject to change. For additional information, visit *DisneyRewards.com* or *DisneyDebit.com*.

• Okay, so it's not exactly a discount, but we think that multi-day Date-Based WDW park tickets are worth their weight in gold. The more days you purchase, the lower the cost is per day. (Just don't over-purchase days—unused days expire. Extra days can be added as needed, provided the ticket has not yet expired.)

• Visit *disneyworld.disney.go.com/special-offers/* to see if any discounts apply for your WDW visit.

• For discounts on dozens of WDW restaurants, tours, recreational experiences, and more, see the coupons starting on page 363 of this book.

MAKING A BUDGET

A stay at Disney's kingdom need not cost a king's ransom (though it certainly can). A well-planned budget can help ensure that money spent at Walt Disney World is money well spent.

Vacation expenses fall into five major categories: (1) transportation (which may include any combination of costs for airfare, airport transfers, train tickets, car rental, gas, parking, tolls, and taxi service); (2) lodging; (3) theme park tickets; (4) meals; and (5) miscellaneous (recreational activities, cover charges, tips, souvenirs, forgotten items, and home expenses such as house-sitting, pet boarding, etc.).

When planning your budget, first consider what level of service suits your needs. Some people prefer to spend fewer days at Disney but stay at a deluxe hotel or dine at pricier restaurants, while others would rather make their money cover a longer vacation that includes a value-priced resort and less-expensive meals. The choice is up to you. Once you've established your spending priorities, determine your price limit. Then make sure you don't exceed it when approximating your expenses—without a ballpark figure to work around, it's easy to get carried away.

SAMPLE BUDGET

The following is an example of a low- to moderately priced budget designed for a family of four during "peak" season (two adults and two kids planning to stay at Walt Disney World for five nights and six days). Totals do not include transportation expenses or sales tax. Plan your budget accordingly.

SAMPLE BUDGET*

Our 6-night Walt Disney World Vacation

Lodging:
Disney's Art of Animation: about $187–$555 per night (x 6 nights)
Lodging total (before tax) = $1,122–$3,330

Theme Park Tickets:
Adult 5-day (peak) Date-Based Ticket: $570 (x 2 people)
Child 5-day (peak) Date-Based Ticket: $552 (x 2 people)
Tickets total (before tax) = $2,244

Meals:
(2 inexpensive and one moderate meal per day, plus 1 snack)
Average adult: $140 (x 6 days) (x 2 people)
Average child: $75 (x 6 days) (x 2 people)
Meals total = $2,580

Miscellaneous:
Average adult: $40 (x 6 days) (x 2 people)
Average child: $25 (x 6 days) (x 2 people)
Miscellaneous total = $780

VACATION TOTAL = $6,726–$8,934

Disney may offer discounts on select resort accommodations throughout the year. For details, visit *https://disneyworld.disney.go.com/special-offers/*.

The resort prices listed here represent average nightly rates for a 5-night stay. Prices don't include tax.

Unsure of how many days you will ultimately spend in the parks? Know that extra days may be added to any Date-Based ticket on or before the ticket's last day. (Upgrade tickets at a Guest Relations window before leaving the theme park on the last day of your ticket.)

Even if you stick to fast food, expect to spend at least $60 per adult and $30 per child, per day.

Careful packing should cut down on miscellaneous expenses, which often include forgotten toiletries like toothpaste, insect repellent, or the all-important sunscreen.

* Prices exclude tax and are subject to change. Resort rates fluctuate based on date, season, view, etc. Flexible Date park ticket prices are higher. For resort prices during your visit, use the My Disney Experience website or app, or go to *disneyworld.com*.

PLANNING YOUR ITINERARY

FIRST THINGS FIRST

- Make hotel and transportation arrangements as far ahead as possible. Note that many Walt Disney World hotels fill up more than six months ahead. Book via the My Disney Experience app or website or call 407-W-DISNEY (934-7639); your confirmation should arrive within two weeks. Log it and other pertinent info in a notebook for future reference.
- Check park hours for your planned visit. (Hours are available up to 7 months ahead; use the My Disney Experience app or website, visit *www.disneyworld.com*, or call 407-824-4321.) Closing times will be particularly helpful when making evening plans. Create a day-by-day schedule, deciding which area of WDW to visit on each day of your trip.

6 MONTHS

- Choose dining spots from those listed in the *Good Meals, Great Times* chapter. To make reservations, use the My Disney Experience app or website, visit *www.disneyworld.com/dine*, or call 407-WDW-DINE (939-3463). Guests with a confirmed reservation at a Walt Disney World–owned-and-operated resort may call 180 days before scheduled check-in date and book dining reservations for up to 10 days of their planned stay.
- Popular dining experiences such as those at Cinderella's Royal Table, Be Our Guest Restaurant (lunch and dinner), and Le Cellier should be booked 180 days ahead. Call 407-WDW-DINE (939-3463) and have a credit card handy.
- Dinner-show reservations may be secured up to 180 days in advance. Use the My Disney Experience app or website, visit *www.disneyworld.com*, or call 407-WDW-DINE (939-3463) for reservations.
- Unless you have a package that includes park admission, it's time to order tickets. Refer to pages 21–24 for details, and call 407-824-4321. You can save money by purchasing select tickets in advance.
- Specialty cruises (see page 242) may be booked by calling 407-WDW-PLAY (939-7529).

6 MONTHS (continued)

- If you will be staying at a Walt Disney World resort or a resort on Hotel Plaza Blvd., you may book a tee time on one of WDW's golf courses now (see pages 244–245 for details). Golf lessons may also be reserved now. Call 407-WDW-GOLF (939-4653) for reservations. Those not staying on WDW property may make reservations 60 days ahead.
- Fishing excursions (see page 247) may be booked by calling 407-939-2277 or 407-WDW-PLAY (939-7529).
- Tennis lessons (offered at select Walt Disney World resorts) may be reserved by calling 321-228-1146. Turn to page 245 for additional tennis information.
- Trail-ride reservations may be made up to 180 days in advance. Call 407-WDW-PLAY (939-7529).
- If you'd like to add a behind-the-scenes tour to your vacation, now is the time to make a reservation.

3 MONTHS

- Double-check park hours for your stay, as they may have changed. Take note of Extra Magic Hours (extended park hours for guests registered at a Walt Disney World–owned-and-operated resort and other select resorts at WDW).

60 DAYS

- If you have valid park tickets linked to a reservation at a participating WDW resort, you may book Fastpass+ selections for your entire stay starting 60 days ahead of the day you intend to check in (at a WDW–owned-and-operated resort and other select resorts), via the My Disney Experience website or app. For Fastpass+ details, see page 25.

30 DAYS

- If you have valid WDW theme park tickets but aren't staying in a Disney resort, you may book Fastpass+ up to 30 days ahead.

11 DAYS

- If you haven't already customized your MagicBand color(s), today is the last day to do it and have the package shipped to your home. If customized between 10 and 6 days before arrival, MagicBands will be sent to your Walt Disney World resort. (All others may be picked up at your WDW–owned-and-operated resort. Non-customized bands are usually gray.)

1 WEEK

- Reconfirm all reservations. Finalize your schedule, including confirmation numbers and Fastpass+ times. (We like to print this information, just in case.)

The following sample schedules assume that you eat breakfast at your resort (unless otherwise stated) and arrive up to 20 minutes before the official opening time. These schedules, though tirelessly tested and proven successful by Birnbaum's editors, are not carved in stone. Use them as a guide, tailoring the itineraries to suit your family's individual tastes. And use them in conjunction with complimentary theme park Times Guides (available at park entrances).

Note that we have not included specific instructions with regard to Fastpass+ in our sample itineraries. It's not because we don't use the service. In fact, we highly recommend using Fastpass+, even if working it into a daily schedule is an inexact science. Without it, there is always the risk of a long line or missing out on a "must-see." By all means, take advantage of the free Fastpass+ opportunity every chance you get—especially for the ultra-popular attractions. Not only might it make you feel like a VIP, but it will free up time in your schedule for things you otherwise might not have gotten to. (If you didn't pre-book Fastpass+ assignments, head to an in-park kiosk to see what, if anything, is still available.)

Many visitors have a deep desire to cover each and every inch of Walt Disney World in the span of a few short days. While we hesitate to discourage these most ambitious of travelers, we feel the need to enlighten them: Walt Disney World is a staggeringly large place. In fact, it's nearly as big as San Francisco and jam-packed with about as many diversions as you might expect from a city that size. You could spend two full weeks on Walt Disney World property and still not have time to do it all. The theme parks alone require every bit of four days just to see the major attractions.

What's the best strategy for organizing a Walt Disney World visit? Make a list of the parks, attractions, and activities you most want to see and use it to create an itinerary. Don't forget to allow time for swimming, boating, or relaxing on a lakeside swing.

Assuming you've narrowed your "must-do" list to the barely manageable, we recommend a stay of at least four to five days. This allows for a visit to each of the theme parks and some time to enjoy many of the recreational activities at your resort, not to mention relaxing a bit. You are on vacation, after all. Longer stays can include water parks, Disney Springs, a dinner show, and more. When planning your days (which you should do before leaving home), be sure to take into account theme park hours and seasonal temperatures in Central Florida.

ONE-DAY SCHEDULE

- 💮 Begin the day with a brisk stroll down Main Street, U.S.A.—it opens earlier than the rest of the park. You can use the extra time to shop, relax, or have a light breakfast before watching Let the Magic Begin—the Magic Kingdom's "welcome to the park" show presented at Cinderella Castle. If you haven't pre-booked Fastpass+ assignments, do so via your smartphone or tablet or stop at an in-park kiosk. Check a park map for kiosk locations. Then head to Splash Mountain and Big Thunder Mountain Railroad. Move to Adventureland for Pirates of the Caribbean, Jungle Cruise, The Magic Carpets of Aladdin, or Walt Disney's Enchanted Tiki Room.

- 💮 Make your way over to Liberty Square to see The Muppets Present . . . Great Moments in American History.

- 💮 Consider lunching at Columbia Harbour House or Pecos Bill's.

- 💮 If time allows, squeeze in The Haunted Mansion before the Festival of Fantasy parade. Watch the parade and move on to Fantasyland.

- 💮 See as much of Fantasyland as possible, including Dumbo the Flying Elephant, It's a Small World, Peter Pan's Flight, Seven Dwarfs Mine Train, and Under the Sea—Journey of The Little Mermaid.

- 💮 If the timing's right, head to the front of Cinderella Castle for a live stage show (with oodles of Disney characters), or take a relaxing ride on Tomorrowland's PeopleMover.

- 💮 Haven't seen Tom Sawyer Island, the Haunted Mansion, Hall of Presidents, or the Country Bear Jamboree? Go for it!

- 💮 Visit Space Mountain, Buzz Lightyear's Space Ranger Spin, Monsters, Inc. Laugh Floor, and the Tomorrowland Speedway.

- 💮 Find a spot near the Castle or in the middle of Main Street to view the nightly presentation of Happily Ever After fireworks show. (Check a Times Guide for the schedule.)

- 💮 If there's time, revisit a favorite attraction (guests are usually admitted right up until closing time).

(Continued on page 34)

MAGIC KINGDOM

(Continued from page 33)

MAGIC KINGDOM MUSTS:

Here's a list of the attractions that put the magic in the Magic Kingdom. Note that everything on the list is a Fastpass+ attraction:

Splash Mountain

Big Thunder Mountain Railroad

The Haunted Mansion

Pirates of the Caribbean

Peter Pan's Flight

It's a Small World

Space Mountain

Buzz Lightyear's Space Ranger Spin

The Many Adventures of Winnie the Pooh

Seven Dwarfs Mine Train

Under the Sea—Journey of The Little Mermaid

LINE BUSTERS:

Even when the park is packed, there are some attractions with shorter or faster-moving lines. Among them are Tomorrowland Transit Authority People-Mover, Hall of Presidents, The Enchanted Tiki Room, Carousel of Progress, Mickey's PhilharMagic, Country Bear Jamboree, and Tom Sawyer Island.

IF YOU HAVE YOUNG CHILDREN:

- Head directly to Fantasyland (walk right through the Castle if you can) and visit It's a Small World, Peter Pan, The Many Adventures of Winnie the Pooh, Under the Sea—Journey of The Little Mermaid, and Dumbo the Flying Elephant. Cool off at Casey Jr. Splash 'N' Soak Station.

- Stop for a spin in a teacup or a ride on Prince Charming Carrousel on the way to Frontierland. Sing along with Big Al and the gang at the Country Bear Jamboree.

- Check the schedule for Mickey's Royal Friendship Faire, the Castle stage show.

- Line up for the afternoon parade about 30 minutes early. Or skip the parade, finish up Fantasyland, and take a magic carpet ride in Adventureland. If it's hot (and your tot has swim diapers), visit the camel near the magic carpets. It spits cool water!

- Most little ones enjoy Tom Sawyer Island and Monsters Inc. Laugh Floor.

MORE FASTPASS+ ATTRACTIONS:

Ariel's Grotto

The Barnstormer

Dumbo the Flying Elephant

Enchanted Tales with Belle

Jungle Cruise

Mad Tea Party

The Magic Carpets of Aladdin

Mickey's PhilharMagic

Monsters, Inc. Laugh Floor

Princess Fairytale Hall

Tomorrowland Speedway

Town Square Theater

ONE-DAY SCHEDULE

- If you haven't booked Fastpass+ assignments, you can do so via your smartphone or tablet and/or a park kiosk. Check a guidemap for locations. Then make a beeline for Future World's Soarin' Around the World and Test Track. Guests with no health issues and no susceptibility to motion sickness whatsoever should experience the out-of-this-world adventure known as the "highly intense" Mission: SPACE Orange Mission. (Otherwise, ride Mission: SPACE Green Mission—the gentler, non-spinning version.) Follow it up with The Seas with Nemo & Friends.

- World Showcase generally opens at 11 A.M., but Norway's Frozen Ever After usually welcomes guests a bit earlier. (Check a park Times Guide.) It is an extremely popular attraction—arrive early. We recommend booking Fastpass+ as far in advance as possible.

- Stop for lunch at The Land's Sunshine Seasons, Coral Reef Restaurant in The Seas with Nemo & Friends, or La Cantina de San Angel in Mexico.

- After exploring The Land, take time to screen the Disney & Pixar Short Film Festival in the Imagination pavilion. Afterward, visit ImageWorks, a small, high-tech playground. Kids love it—almost as much as they do the enthralling "leapfrog" fountains just outside the pavilion.

- If you're up for some pin trading (or shopping), stop by the collector pin shop near Spaceship Earth. Cast Members displaying pins are always willing to swap a Disney pin for another Disney pin.

- The line for Spaceship Earth should have dwindled by now. Head to the giant geosphere to experience an intriguing journey through time.

- Make your way back to World Showcase by early evening and start your world tour at Canada. Proceed counterclockwise around the lagoon. Don't miss the *Impressions de France* movie in the France pavilion. And take in as much live entertainment as you can—World Showcase has a lot to offer!

- After dinner, scope out a spot to watch the park's nighttime spectacular. (There are excellent viewing locations all around World Showcase Lagoon.) Return to your viewing spot about 30 to 40 minutes before the show.

TIMING TIP: If you have a World Showcase restaurant reservation, allow 30 to 45 minutes to get there from the front gate. Taking a FriendShip water taxi can save some time, but it isn't much faster than brisk walking.

(Continued on page 36)

EPCOT

(Continued from page 35)

EPCOT ESSENTIALS:

There is a lot to see and do at Disney's discovery park. Don't leave Epcot without investigating these outstanding attractions:

Soarin' Around the World

Frozen Ever After

Test Track

Spaceship Earth

Turtle Talk with Crush

Disney & Pixar Short Film Festival

Living with the Land

Epcot Forever (nighttime spectacular)

The Seas with Nemo & Friends

The American Adventure show

Mission: SPACE

IF YOU HAVE YOUNG CHILDREN:

- Begin the day by visiting with Disney characters (check a park Times Guide for details) and exploring The Seas with Nemo & Friends. Then head over to Imagination! to experience Journey Into Imagination with Figment and the ImageWorks play zone.

- At World Showcase, head to Norway's Frozen Ever After attraction. Afterward, hit Mexico's boat ride: Gran Fiesta Tour Starring the Three Caballeros.

- Visit the Kidcot Fun Stop in each country. Don't miss the koi pond in Japan and Germany's tiny village.

- If the weather is warm, let little ones splash in the interactive fountain on the pathway joining Future World with World Showcase or the spray zone in front of Test Track.

LINE BUSTERS:

Tired of long lines? Go to Disney & Pixar Short Film Festival in Imagination!, the movies in China, Canada, and France (*Impressions de France* only; the new *Beauty and the Beast* sing-along has a much bigger following). The Spaceship Earth line thins out in the afternoon, as do the lines for the attraction inside The Seas with Nemo & Friends and Gran Fiesta Tour starring the Three Caballeros in the Mexico pavilion.

FASTPASS+ ATTRACTIONS*:

Group A:

Test Track

Soarin' Around the World

Frozen Ever After (in Norway)

Epcot Forever (nighttime spectacular)

Group B:

Mission: SPACE

Spaceship Earth

Living with the Land

Turtle Talk with Crush

Journey Into Imagination with Figment

The Seas with Nemo & Friends

Disney & Pixar Short Film Festival

* At press time, guests could reserve a Fastpass+ time for one attraction from Group A and two from Group B. That may change in 2020. Visit *www.MyDisneyExperience.com* for updates.

ONE-DAY SCHEDULE

- Some attractions open later in the morning; consult a park Times Guide for exact times. Also, many shows here run on a schedule (e.g., For the First Time in Forever: A Frozen Sing-Along Celebration, and Beauty and the Beast—Live on Stage). Use a tablet or smartphone or stop at a park kiosk to get Fastpass+ assignments if you haven't booked them in advance.

- This park has a brand-new land known as Star Wars: Galaxy's Edge. Get there early to ride the wildly popular *Millenium Falcon:* Smugglers Run and Star Wars: Rise of the Resistance.

- Toy Story Land attractions are quite popular. Arrive as early as possible and pre-book Fastpass+ assignments if you can.

- Daredevils should make Rock 'n' Roller Coaster a priority, followed by some eye-opening drops at *The Twilight Zone*™ Tower of Terror.

- Peruse a park Times Guide. Select a time to take in For the First Time in Forever—A Frozen Sing-Along Celebration. Arrive early, just in case.

- If Beauty and the Beast is playing soon, grab a seat. Otherwise, plan to come back later and go to Voyage of The Little Mermaid.

- Pause for lunch at 50's Prime Time Cafe or Sci-Fi Dine-In Theater (with a reservation), Woody's Lunch Box, Sunset Ranch Market, or the Backlot Express.

- See Muppet*Vision 3-D, followed by Star Tours—The Adventures Continue, and the Indiana Jones Epic Stunt Spectacular. Take tots to see Disney Junior Dance Party!

- If you missed Beauty and the Beast—Live on Stage, go now, and if you haven't hit it yet, be sure to experience Tower of Terror.

- If Fantasmic! is being presented, you want to get a spot in line at least 50 minutes before showtime. Note that if you choose to skip Fantasmic!, plan to exit the park before the last performance breaks. If you do stay for the show, know that you can meander through select shops while the throngs exit.

- Is Star Wars: A Galactic Spectacular happening tonight? Make a point of catching the stellar fireworks display.

(Continued on page 38)

(Continued from page 37)

STUDIOS STANDOUTS*:

If you're short on time, be sure to catch as many of the following four-star attractions at Disney's Hollywood Studios as possible. At press time, Star Wars: Galaxy's Edge attractions did not offer Fastpass+. That may change in 2020.

Group A:

Alien Swirling Saucers

Toy Story Mania!

Slinky Dog Dash

Rock 'n' Roller Coaster—Starring Aerosmith

The Twilight Zone™ Tower of Terror

Group B:

Beauty and the Beast—Live on Stage

Fantasmic!

Muppet*Vision 3-D

Star Tours—The Adventures Continue

* At press time, guests could reserve a Fastpass+ time for one attraction from Group A and two from Group B. That may change. Visit *www.MyDisneyExperience.com* for updates.

MORE FASTPASS+ ATTRACTIONS:

In addition to those listed above, these attractions are classified by Disney as Group B:

Disney Junior Dance Party!

Indiana Jones Epic Stunt Spectacular

Voyage of The Little Mermaid

For the First Time in Forever: A Frozen Sing-Along Celebration

LINE BUSTERS:

When lines abound at Disney's Hollywood Studios, we suggest the following: Indiana Jones Epic Stunt Spectacular (the theater fits about 2,000 guests at a time); Muppet*Vision 3-D; For the First Time in Forever: A Frozen Sing-Along Celebration (this indoor theater also has a high capacity); Lightning McQueen's Racing Academy, and Star Wars Launch Bay.

IF YOU HAVE YOUNG CHILDREN:

- Begin with Toy Story Mania! if your child is old enough to wear 3-D glasses. Follow that up with a spin on Alien Swirling Saucers. Next, head to Muppet*Vision 3-D. (If your tot won't wear 3-D glasses, bypass the Muppets and go directly to Disney Junior Dance Party!)

- Have lunch at Sunset Ranch Market on Sunset Boulevard, then check out Beauty and the Beast—Live on Stage and Voyage of The Little Mermaid (but warn kids about moments of darkness and a thunderstorm). Zoom over to Lightning McQueen's Racing Academy, but Skip Fantasmic!—parts of the show tend to spook wee ones.

- Catch up with Disney characters at Animation Courtyard and Commissary Lane.

ONE-DAY SCHEDULE

❤ Guests who arrive prior to park opening may wait for the "rope drop" after passing through The Oasis. Many shows here run on a schedule, so check for times throughout the day. If you want to experience Kilimanjaro Safaris or Expedition Everest without a big wait, book Fastpass+ or arrive as early as you can. Check the schedules for Festival of the Lion King, UP! A Great Bird Adventure, and Finding Nemo—The Musical. Note that if you haven't booked Fastpass+ assignments, you can make same-day arrangements with your smartphone or tablet and/or at a Fastpass+ kiosk in the park (pending availability).

❤ As you enter the park, pass through the Oasis and go to Pandora—World of Avatar. (Daredevils should make a beeline for Flight of Passage. This ride may begin operating prior to the officially posted park opening time.) If the line for Na'vi River Journey is on the short side, go for it. If not, move on to Asia.

❤ In Asia, tackle Expedition Everest, ride Kali River Rapids, then visit the tigers and gibbons at the Maharajah Jungle Trek and see UP! A Great Bird Adventure at the Caravan Stage.

❤ Plan to arrive at The Festival of the Lion King theater at least 45 minutes prior to your preferred showtime. If possible, mingle with Mickey and Minnie (at the Adventurers Outpost) before seeing Festival of the Lion King.

❤ Stop at Yak & Yeti, Harambe Market, Flame Tree Barbecue, or Nomad lounge (inside Tiffins Restaurant) for lunch. Then board the Wildlife Express train to Rafiki's Planet Watch and visit the Affection Section petting farm. Be sure to collect Wilderness Explorer badges along the way.

❤ After experiencing Africa's Kilimanjaro Safaris, take a relaxing hike on the animal-laden Gorilla Falls Exploration Trail.

❤ Make your way to DinoLand, stopping to take in It's Tough to be a Bug! along the way. After riding Dinosaur, catch Donald Duck and friends at Donald's Dino–Bash! Then head to Finding Nemo—The Musical. Take young kids to the play in Boneyard—and possibly meet Pluto—before leaving the area.

❤ Revisit favorite attractions. Keep in mind that Kilimanjaro Safaris operates day and night—it's definitely worth checking out after the sun sets.

❤ When the sun sets, watch the Tree of Life "awaken" and cap off the day with the park's waterborne nighttime show: Rivers of Light. If you haven't booked Fastpass+ for Rivers of Light, get in line at least an hour before it is scheduled to begin. (It is presented on most nights.)

(Continued on page 40)

(Continued from page 39)

ANIMAL KINGDOM ACES:

An abbreviated visit to Disney's Animal Kingdom is enough to make anybody growl. The following shows and attractions are sure to soothe the savage beast, er, guest:

Avatar Flight of Passage

Dinosaur

Kali River Rapids

Kilimanjaro Safaris

Gorilla Falls Exploration Trail

Donald's Dino-Bash!

Expedition Everest

Finding Nemo—The Musical

Maharajah Jungle Trek

Festival of the Lion King

UP! A Great Bird Adventure

It's Tough to be a Bug!

Winged Encounters—The Kingdom Takes Flight

FASTPASS+ ATTRACTIONS:

Dinosaur

Expedition Everest

Festival of the Lion King

Finding Nemo—The Musical

It's Tough to be a Bug!

Kali River Rapids

Primeval Whirl

Kilimanjaro Safaris

Rivers of Light

Avatar Flight of Passage

UP! A Great Bird Adventure

Na'vi River Journey

LINE BUSTERS:

When herds of guests mob Disney's Animal Kingdom shows and attractions, there are a few places to escape the stampede: The Oasis, Gorilla Falls Exploration Trail, Maharajah Jungle Trek, Discovery Island Trails, The Boneyard playground, and Rafiki's Planet Watch. (You'll need to take the Wildlife Express train to reach Rafiki's Planet Watch.)

IF YOU HAVE YOUNG CHILDREN:

- Explore the Oasis on your way into the park. As you cross the bridge to Discovery Island, stop at the Wilderness Explorer Headquarters and get started collecting badges. Then go to the Adventurers Outpost to meet Mickey and Minnie.

- Stop by the Tree of Life to discover all of the animal carvings in its trunk. (Note that the show inside the tree, It's Tough to be a Bug!, is very intense and may frighten young children.)

- Make a point of experiencing Donald's Dino-Bash! (Check a park Times Guide to see when Disney characters will be present.) In the evening hours, guests may join a dance party with a couple of "chipmunkosauruses!" The interactive party is fun for guests of all ages. It's a great opportunity to meet Disney characters, too.

- Eat lunch at Pizzafari or head to Restaurantosaurus. Be sure to explore The Boneyard playground, see UP! A Great Bird Adventure, and ride Triceratop Spin.

- In Asia, go to the Maharajah Jungle Trek. Ride Africa's bumpy Kilimanjaro Safaris. See the Gorilla Falls Exploration Trail. Then take the Wildlife Express train to Rafiki's Planet Watch.

MAGIC KINGDOM
HALF-DAY SCHEDULE

MORNING/AFTERNOON*

○ Arrive early—Main Street, U.S.A., opens before the rest of the park. Use extra park time to shop, nosh, and catch the park's welcoming show: Let the Magic Begin. Where to go next? It's a big decision. Know that the area you postpone may have long lines by the time you get there. We like to start in Adventureland.

○ Visit Pirates of the Caribbean, then head over to Splash Mountain (if you don't mind getting a little soggy) and Big Thunder Mountain Railroad.

○ Visit The Haunted Mansion, and then (if you plan on staying through the afternoon) grab a spot for the afternoon parade, Festival of Fantasy.

○ Watch the Festival of Fantasy parade (and wave hello to Anna and Elsa!) in Frontierland. Or skip the processional and head to Peter Pan's Flight, Winnie the Pooh, It's a Small World, Under the Sea—Journey of The Little Mermaid, and (if the line's not too long) Seven Dwarfs Mine Train.

○ Head over to Tomorrowland to experience Space Mountain. Follow it up with Buzz Lightyear's Space Ranger Spin. Take youngsters for a relaxing trip on the PeopleMover (but warn them that there will be moments of total darkness).

HALF DAY WITH YOUNG KIDS

Start at Town Square Theater. Meet Mickey inside. If it's close to parade time, grab a spot on the curb. After exploring Fantasyland (do not miss It's a Small World), consider the Country Bear Jamboree. Watch Mickey's Royal Friendship Faire at Cinderella Castle. Soar on a magic carpet in Adventureland, then head to Tomorrowland for Tomorrowland Speedway and Buzz Lightyear's Space Ranger Spin. Cap off the day with the Once Upon a Time castle projection show (best viewed from the Castle forecourt).

AFTERNOON/EVENING*

○ Check a Times Guide and choose a time to take in Mickey's Royal Friendship Faire stage show (at Cinderella Castle). And don't miss the Festival of Fantasy parade. (Warn little ones about a possible appearance by a fire-breathing dragon.)

○ Explore Town Square Theater. If the wait to meet Mickey Mouse is more than 45 minutes, consider coming back in the evening—or get a Fastpass+ assignment.

○ Start in Adventureland. Ride the Jungle Cruise and Pirates of the Caribbean.

○ Head to Frontierland. Do Splash Mountain and Big Thunder Mountain Railroad. Then see the Country Bears or Tom Sawyer Island (the latter closes at dusk).

○ Hit the best of Fantasyland, including It's a Small World, Seven Dwarfs Mine Train, Peter Pan, Journey of The Little Mermaid, The Many Adventures of Winnie the Pooh, and the Mad Tea Party.

○ Join the afternoon street party known as Move It, Shake It, Dance & Play It! if it is offered (on Main Street, near Cinderella Castle).

○ Pop in at The Haunted Mansion and be sure to see The Muppets Present . . . Great Moments in American History before dinner.

○ Now it's time for Tomorrowland. Go to Space Mountain or Buzz Lightyear's Space Ranger Spin.

○ Catch Once Upon a Time—a festive light show that is projected onto Cinderella Castle. And don't miss the Happily Ever After fireworks spectacular.

* For details on where to meet Disney characters, see page 139.

EPCOT
HALF-DAY SCHEDULE

MORNING/AFTERNOON

○ Head directly to Norway's popular Frozen Ever After attraction, followed by Test Track and Soarin' Around the World (this requires a bit of legwork, but it is worth hitting the park's biggies as early as you can). If you're up for the "intense" Mission: SPACE voyage to Mars, go for it. (We prefer the "less intense," non-spinning version of the attraction, aka The Green Mission.)

○ Visit The Seas with Nemo & Friends and Imagination! pavilions before moving on to World Showcase—most of it opens at 11 A.M. Save Spaceship Earth for later, when the line dies down a bit. When hunger calls, stop for lunch. See the countries that interest you most, making sure to see Norway's Frozen Ever After (if you haven't already!), the show inside The American Adventure, and Mexico's boat ride: Gran Fiesta Tour Starring the Three Caballeros.

AFTERNOON/EVENING

○ If you don't have restaurant reservations and would like to try for dinner at a table-service restaurant, use the My Disney Experience mobile app or stop by Guest Relations to make them. If not, consider dining at the nearby BoardWalk resort (it's a short stroll or FriendShip ride away). Note that reservations are necessary for most locations.

○ See as much of Future World as possible before heading to World Showcase. (Both sections of the park generally stay open until about 9 P.M., but some Future World attractions close at 7 P.M.)

○ Spend the evening touring World Showcase. Keep an eye on the clock so you can secure a good spot around the lagoon to watch the park's nightly pyrotechnic spectacular.

○ Avoid the crush of exiting crowds by browsing the wares in the MouseGear shop in Future World.

MEET THE CHARACTERS*

American Adventure (Daisy Duck)

China (Mulan)

France (Belle and Aurora)

Future World (Mickey and Goofy)

Germany (Snow White)

Mexico (Donald Duck)

Morocco (Jasmine)

Norway (Anna and Elsa, in the Royal Sommerhus)

United Kingdom (Mary Poppins, Alice in Wonderland; Winnie the Pooh)

World Showcase Gazebo (Pluto and Minnie)

*Characters and locations are subject to change. Check a park Times Guide for specifics during your visit.

HALF DAY WITH YOUNG KIDS

Begin with a visit to Norway's Frozen Ever After, followed by The Seas with Nemo & Friends pavilion (take a ride in a clam-mobile, see Turtle Talk with Crush, and romp in Bruce's Shark World). Follow it up with a visit to Spaceship Earth. If your child is old enough to wear 3-D glasses, take in at least the first film in Imagination's Disney & Pixar Short Film Festival. It's a blast! Visit the Kidcot Fun Stops throughout the park and stop by the mini village in Germany. If time allows, take in Journey Into Imagination with Figment and Image-Works in the Imagination pavilion (if they are operating during your visit to the park).

DISNEY'S HOLLYWOOD STUDIOS
HALF-DAY SCHEDULE

MORNING/AFTERNOON

○ Kick-start the day with a visit to the park's new land—Star Wars: Galaxy's Edge.

○ Make a beeline for Slinky Dog Dash, followed by Toy Story Mania!, Alien Swirling Saucers, and trips to Rock 'n' Roller Coaster and Tower of Terror (just don't ride them on a full stomach). From there, wander over to Muppet*Vision 3-D, and Star Tours—The Adventures Continue.

○ See Beauty and the Beast—Live on Stage and For the First Time in Forever: A Frozen Sing-Along Celebration.

○ For a quick bite, stop at The Backlot Express, Woody's Lunch Box, or Sunset Ranch Market.

○ If time permits, go to Voyage of The Little Mermaid and/or revisit a favorite attraction.

MEET THE CHARACTERS*

Hollywood Boulevard at park opening time (characters vary)

Animation Courtyard (Pluto and Disney Junior friends such as Fancy Nancy, Doc McStuffins, and Vampirina)

Grand Avenue (Goofy, Chip, and Dale)

Commissary Lane (Minnie, Mickey)

Toy Story Land (Woody, Buzz, Jessie, and the Green Army Corps)

Hollywood Boulevard (Donald and Daisy)

Star Wars Launch Bay (Chewbacca, BB-8, Kylo Ren, and Rey)

Celebrity Spotlight near Commissary Lane (Olaf)

*Characters are subject to change.

AFTERNOON/EVENING

○ Explore planet Batuu in Star Wars: Galaxy's Edge.

○ Begin with Tower of Terror, Rock 'n' Roller Coaster, and Beauty and the Beast—Live on Stage.

○ Visit Toy Story Land attractions: Toy Story Mania!, Slinky Dog Dash, and Alien Swirling Saucers.

○ Take in Star Tours; Muppet*Vision 3-D; For the First Time in Forever—A Frozen Sing-Along Celebration; and Voyage of The Little Mermaid.

○ Take in the Indiana Jones Epic Stunt Spectacular (if it is operating today), then jump in line for Fantasmic! Or skip Fantasmic! and revisit favorite attractions. Try to catch the Wonderful World of Animation show on Hollywood Boulevard. And don't miss Star Wars: A Galactic Spectacular—it's a truly impressive fireworks show.

HALF DAY WITH YOUNG KIDS

Start with Toy Story Land attractions: Alien Swirling Saucers and Toy Story Mania! (if your child is old enough to wear 3-D glasses), followed by For the First Time in Forever—A Frozen Sing-Along Celebration, Disney Junior Dance Party!, Voyage of The Little Mermaid, and Beauty & the Beast—Live on Stage, and Lightning McQueen's Racing Academy. Youngsters ages 4 to 12 can harness the Force at the Jedi Training Academy. Skip Fantasmic!—it's just too intense (and a bit long) for most tykes.

DISNEY'S ANIMAL KINGDOM
HALF-DAY SCHEDULE

MORNING/AFTERNOON

○ Go directly to Pandora—World of Avatar to ride Flight of Passage. Then head to Asia to ride the thrilling Expedition Everest and the soaking Kali River Rapids, and hike the Maharajah Jungle Trek.

○ Experience UP! A Great Bird Adventure on the way to Kilimanjaro Safaris and the Gorilla Falls Exploration Trail.

○ Check a Times Guide to see when the Festival of the Lion King show is playing today. Plan to arrive up to 45 minutes before showtime.

○ Finish up with a performance of Finding Nemo—The Musical; Dinosaur; and It's Tough to be a Bug!—though the last two are intense for tots. Take little ones to The Boneyard playground instead.

MEET THE CHARACTERS*

Park Entrance at park opening (characters vary)

Discovery Island (Timon and Flik)

Discovery Island Character Landing (Pocahontas)

Adventurers Outpost on Discovery Island (Mickey and Minnie)

Rafiki's Planet Watch (Rafiki and Doc McStuffins)

DinoLand Service Station (Pluto and Goofy)

It's Tough to be a Bug! entrance (Russell and Dug)

Donald's Dino—Bash! in DinoLand, U.S.A. (Donald, Daisy, Goofy, Pluto Chip, Dale, and Launchpad McQuack)

*Characters are subject to change.

AFTER LUNCH

○ Check a Times Guide for Festival of the Lion King schedule. Arrive up to 45 minutes before showtime. Then visit Mickey and Minnie at the Adventurers Outpost on Discovery Island. Be sure to soar on a mountain banshee at Flight of Passage in Pandora—The World of Avatar.

○ Head to the Kilimanjaro Safaris ride. Then do the Gorilla Falls Exploration Trail and Wildlife Express train to Rafiki's Planet Watch.

○ Ride Expedition Everest and Kali River Rapids, and experience the Maharajah Jungle Trek. Try to catch UP! A Great Bird Adventure, too (the first performance takes place in the late morning).

○ Wander the Discovery Island Trails before pausing to see It's Tough to be a Bug!

○ Before dinner, dodge dastardly dinos on Dinosaur.

○ Watch the Tree of Life awaken and line up for the evening's presentation of The Rivers of Light (plan to arrive at least an hour early). Or use the time to revisit favorite attractions.

HALF DAY WITH YOUNG KIDS

Scope out animal life in The Oasis before stopping at the Wilderness Explorer Headquarters on the bridge to Discovery Island. Then head to the Adventurers Outpost to meet Mickey and Minnie, followed by a visit to DinoLand U.S.A. Explore The Boneyard and ride TriceraTop Spin. If time allows, take the train to Rafiki's Planet Watch, where kids can bond with live animals (mostly goats). A bird show known as UP! A Great Bird Adventure captivates guests of all ages. And Donald's Dino-Bash! (in DinoLand, U.S.A.) is fun for everyone.

Making the Most of Longer Visits

Longer stays allow the chance to sample some of the World's myriad offerings. Spend another day in the one park you most enjoyed. Lounge by the pool, go biking, or play tennis or golf. Go shopping at Disney Springs. Cool off at one of Disney's innovative water parks. Have lunch at a WDW resort, and try a special dinner at Victoria & Albert's in the Grand Floridian or at Flying Fish at the BoardWalk resort. Sample the restaurants at Disney Springs or spend the evening at the BoardWalk. Take golf, tennis, or surf lessons. Go fishing or horseback riding. Visit a relaxing day spa. See a movie. Participate in a behind-the-scenes program. Play a round or two of miniature golf. Catch a game at the ESPN Wide World of Sports Complex. Enjoy the many activities offered by your WDW resort. Or just sit back and chill. For even more ideas, see our *Sports & Recreation*; *Everything Else in the World*; and *Good Meals, Great Times* chapters.

How to Save a Rainy Day

Florida rain showers come and go with such regularity that you could almost set your watch by them, especially during summer months. They're usually brief, though torrential. Of course, there are times when gray clouds linger longer. Here are some ways to make the most of a soggy day:

- See a movie (or two!) on one of AMC Theatres' many screens at Disney Springs.
- Head for an arcade—many Walt Disney World resorts have one. Games are appropriate for guests of all ages. (The arcades at Art of Animation and Contemporary are larger than most.)
- Don your rain gear and go to Epcot. The pavilions in Future World house a bounty of sheltered diversions. Ponchos are sold throughout WDW for about $10 each. (Keep in mind that crowds at all of the parks tend to dwindle a bit during inclement weather—as do the lines for popular attractions.)
- On soggy days, the Magic Kingdom may offer a splashy character parade in lieu of its usual afternoon processional. If the Rainy Day Cavalcade is offered during your visit, be sure to catch it. Feel free to sing and splash along.
- Swap your shoes for alley-friendly footwear and pound some pins at Splitsville—a bodacious bowling zone located at Disney Springs West Side. They serve food and drinks, too. (See page 223 for details.)
- Consider taking in an indoor event at the ESPN Wide World of Sports Complex. For schedules and pricing information, visit *www.espnwwos.com*, or call 407-939-1500.

Customized Travel Tips
Traveling with Children

Tell kids that a Walt Disney World vacation is in the works and the response is apt to be overwhelming! Our guide *Birnbaum's Walt Disney World For Kids 2020*, written for children age 7 and up, can be a useful resource for getting them involved in the planning from the outset. Filled with information about the World from a kid's perspective, it can be used as a reference before and during the trip, a place to collect character autographs, and a post-trip souvenir keepsake.

Walt Disney World ranks among the most appealing spots on Earth for families with kids. Keep in mind, however, that a child under age 14 must be accompanied by a guest age 14 or older to enter the theme parks and kids under age 7 must be accompanied by a person over age 14 to board theme park attractions; kids under 10 must be accompanied by an adult at the water parks.

Child Care: In-room child-care service can be summoned to all Disney-owned resorts. The service is available 24/7, though it is not run by Disney. Kid's Nite Out offers one-to-one babysitting in your Walt Disney World Resort hotel room. Arts and crafts, reading and playing games are among the activities for children 6 months to 12 years of age. For pricing and to make a reservation with Kid's Nite Out, visit *www.kidsniteout.com*, call 800-696-8105 (from 8 A.M. until 9 P.M. daily), or inquire at your resort's Lobby Concierge. You can also arrange for a childcare expert to accompany your family during visits to Disney theme parks, providing assistance when needed. Another company, Super Sitters, offers similar services. To reach them, visit *www.supersitters.com*, or call 407-382-2558. While authorized to operate at WDW, neither Kid's Nite Out nor Super Sitters is run by the Walt Disney Company.

Children's Activity Centers: Camp Dolphin operates daily from 5 P.M. to midnight and accepts kids ages 4 to 12. Camp Dolphin costs $12 per hour, per child and includes supervised arts, crafts, movies, board games, themed activities, and more. A meal can be included for an extra $10. For details, call 407-934-4000. Four Seasons Orlando offers a complimentary Kids Camp for youngsters ages 4 through 12. For details and operating hours, call (407) 313-7777, or visit *www.fourseasons.com/orlando/*.

Note that Children's Activity Centers previously operated by Polynesian Village, Animal Kingdom Lodge, Yacht & Beach Club, and Wilderness Lodge closed their doors in 2018.

Baby Care Centers: Located in all theme parks, these centers are for parents with young children. They are not meant as day care. All kids must be accompanied by a parent or guardian. There are rocking chairs and comfy couches in feeding rooms for nursing mothers and screenings of Disney films for kids. Centers have facilities for changing diapers, preparing formula, warming bottles, and washing bottles. Diapers, bottles, formula, pacifiers, and baby food are among the supplies for sale. Baby Care Center locations are listed on theme park guidemaps. There are changing tables in most women's, many men's, and all family restrooms.

Lost Children: Disney employees (also known as Cast Members) will know what to do if a child starts to call for his or her parents. If your child wanders off, tell the nearest Cast Member and stop at the Baby Care Center or City Hall in the Magic Kingdom (on Main Street, U.S.A.); at Guest Relations or the Baby Care Center in Epcot; at Guest Relations in Disney's Hollywood Studios; or at Guest Relations in Animal Kingdom. A computerized system allows for a detailed description of the child and his or her status, helping to reunite families quickly. It helps if your child has your mobile phone number, too. In emergencies, an all-points bulletin can be put out among Cast Members. The Guest Relations staff at each Disney park can help, too.

Parental Perk

Families with babies or small children should know about the "rider switch" policy (aka "baby swap") at the theme parks. At attractions with age or height restrictions, a parent who waits nearby with a young child while the other parent rides the attraction can go right on soon after the first parent comes off. Be sure to ask the attendant at the attraction's entrance. They'll tell you how to proceed.

Prepare youngsters for the possibility of an accidental separation. Direct him or her to contact the nearest park worker (someone wearing a costume and a name tag) and ask for help.

Refrigerators: For parents of young children, an in-room fridge is not a mere luxury, it's a necessity. Accommodations at all WDW–owned-and-operated resorts come equipped with a small fridge, free of charge. Many Disney Vacation Club Villas accommodations are equipped with full-size refrigerators.

Baby Food: Many parents choose to ship a box of food and baby supplies to their resort before they leave home. (Note that there is a $6 fee for any package or mail that goes through a WDW resort Front Desk.) It is possible to purchase baby food at most Disney resorts, but the selection is small. For a wider variety of foodstuffs to choose from, make a trip to the Winn-Dixie at 11957 South Apopka-Vineland Road. (To get resort addresses for a GPS, inquire at your resort's Front Desk.)

Publix and Walmart, as well as several nearby convenience stores, are also within a reasonable driving distance. Be sure to hire an authorized cab for the trip. Your resort staff can make the arrangements and give you an estimate of the cost. Another option is to order groceries from *gardengrocer.com*. They are authorized to deliver to most Disney-area hotels and stock a wide variety of items, including many organic, gluten-free, and kosher selections.

If you have a milk (or other food) need after hours, know that the following Disney resorts have 24-hour snack bars: Grand Floridian Resort & Spa, Polynesian Village, Dolphin, and Hilton Lake Buena Vista.

Bed rails: If you'd like bed rails for a child, it's best to request them in advance (and confirm). Call 407-934-7639 and ask that they be added to your Walt Disney World resort reservation. Bed rails may be used on standard-size beds, but not smaller pull-down beds. Inquire about bed rails when you book your room.

Cribs: Some Walt Disney World resort rooms come with a small, portable playpen-like crib. Look for it in the closet. If it's not there, call to have one sent to your room. They're free, but somewhat flimsy. If you'd like something bigger or sturdier, consider renting a crib from A Baby's Best Friend. To do so, call 407-891-2241, or visit *www.abbf.com*. This company is authorized to operate at WDW, though not run nor endorsed by The Walt Disney Company.

Diapers: Each Disney resort has at least one shop in which to pick up diapers. If you're brand loyal, pack your own. (Consider shipping diapers to your resort so you don't have to pack them.) Be sure to throw extra swim diapers into your bag each morning. You never know when you'll run into an interactive fountain on Disney property. They're necessary for pool use, too.

Resort Fun: Many WDW resorts have little playgrounds as well as kid-friendly pools (complete with supervised pool parties and life jackets to borrow), plus nightly campfires and screenings of Disney films—all

---

HOT TIP!

Walt Disney World is stroller central. Make yours easier to spot in sprawling stroller parking zones by adorning it with a colorful sign, scarf, balloon, or flag—or all of the above. You'll be happy you did.

Tips for Tots

Walt Disney World is as toddler-friendly as it gets. Here are a few pointers to make it even more so:

• Familiarize your child with Disney characters before your trip. That way they'll be more likely to enjoy meeting them and less likely to be frightened by them.

PHOTO BY MIKE CARROLL

• Disney resort rooms are designed with little ones in mind, but we recommend packing baby-proofing items such as outlet plugs and doorknob covers or locks.

• Fireworks (and thunder) can scare little ones silly—and the booms can hurt sensitive ears. Pack noise-cancelling headphones. If your tot is spooked by loud noises, be prepared to make a hasty exit once the booms begin. The Studios' Fantasmic! show also tends to terrify tots.

• Be sure to bring snacks when you head out for the day. It's tough to find toddler-friendly nibbles once you leave your resort.

• You will be asked to collapse your stroller before boarding a WDW resort bus or boat—but not on the monorail or Disney Skyliner.

• Don't forget sunscreen that's sensitive to toddler skin. Pack a hat for an infant.

• Pack a small, familiar toy from home and keep it with you at all times.

• Don't underestimate the play value of a good splash. Take time to relax and enjoy the invaluable amenity that is the Walt Disney World resort pool. Of course, swim diapers are a must.

• Remember that your child may enter the parks for free until his or her third birthday.

• Pack a thermometer and your baby-friendly analgesic of choice—just in case.

HOT TIP!

If you have a baby, you'll need a stroller during your Walt Disney World visit. Although they may be rented at the theme parks, consider bringing one from home. It will save you money and the hassle of getting one each time you visit a park. Plus, there's the convenience of using it all over WDW property. (Disney rents strollers at the parks and Disney Springs, but they are made of uncomfortable hard plastic and can't leave the place from which they are rented.)

When we choose to rent a stroller, our go-to company is Magic Strollers (866-866-6177; *www.magicstrollers.com*). For more information, turn to page 68.

included with the resort reservation. Additional resort activities are offered for a fee. For details, see page 232.

Strollers: Available for $15 for one day and $13 per day of a multi-day, Length of Stay rentals are offered at stroller rental areas at each of the theme parks. (If you will need a stroller for several days, the Length of Stay rental ticket is the way to go.) Disney Springs rents

single strollers for about $15 a day, plus a $100 refundable deposit (with a valid USD credit card). Guests may rent strollers from Sundries, near the Disney Springs bus depot. Strollers are not available for rent at either of the Walt Disney World water parks. Double strollers cost $31 for one day and $27 per day of a multi-day rental. Walt Disney World strollers are made of hard plastic and are not ideal for babies. They are designed to accommodate children weighing up to 50 pounds. A limited number of infant-friendly single strollers may be offered. Length of Stay rentals must be paid for in full at the time of rental. Put your receipt in a safe place— that's what you'll need to show to get a stroller on the remaining days of your stay. That receipt will also come in handy should your stroller go missing. Simply present it at the nearest stroller rental location and you will receive a replacement stroller.

Strollers are not permitted inside attractions (they should be parked in designated stroller parking zones) and cannot be removed from the park in which they are rented. It's very important to park in a stroller zone. Otherwise, your stroller will likely be re-parked by a Cast Member in the nearest designated stroller spot.

If you rent a stroller in the morning and plan to hop to another park, just present your receipt for a replacement at the second park. Strollers should be returned to a rental location before leaving a theme park.

Notes: You will be asked to remove the child and fold your stroller before boarding Disney World buses and boats. There's no folding necessary when boarding the monorail or the skyliner. (For details about the new Disney Skyliner, turn to page 65.)

You may bring your own stroller to Walt Disney World, but wagons and strollers with front-protruding wheels are not permitted. Strollers can be no larger than 31 inches wide and 52 inches long. No exceptions.

Tips for Teens

When it comes to teenagers at Disney World, *The Little Mermaid*'s Ariel has plenty of company. Of course, be they of the fish or human variety, teenage guests have special needs all their own. Here are some tips from our WDW teen experts:

• Have some of your own money on hand. If it's your hard-earned cash, you probably won't spend it as quickly as you would Mom and Dad's!

• Pack a hat. Why? It's much easier to throw a hat on than waste time doing your hair.

• Try to get along with your brothers and sisters— even if it isn't always easy. Don't bug them to do the things you want to do all the time. Try to do things they want to do, too.

• One of the coolest things for teens to do is an Extra Magic Hours evening at a theme park. Another good thing to do at night is to explore Disney Springs.

• Attention, parents! Try to include your teens in planning the trip. If they get a say during planning, they'll be much happier when they arrive at Disney World. Also, don't make them get up every morning at 6 A.M. Try to give them a day or two to wake up late and lounge around the pool or a water park.

Traveling without Children

Walt Disney World has become an extremely popular destination for adults travelling without children, appealing to singles, couples, and empty nesters alike. And Disney has responded to the growing demand with an ever-growing entertainment and dining selection for big kids without youngsters in tow. Just add mouse ears.

COUPLES

There is a place for lovebirds at Walt Disney World. Actually, there are many spots in Walt's World that are perfectly suited to those with romantic intentions (provided, of course, that privacy is not a prerequisite!).

• Grown-ups love to roam the parks unencumbered by little ones and strollers. The Magic Kingdom's carousel-and-castle combo invokes the enchantment in true fairy-tale tradition. Epcot's World Showcase has the aura of a whirlwind tour (and the inspiration for a future trip?), with countries as exotic and far-reaching as Japan and Morocco. Disney's Hollywood Studios recaptures an era of starry-eyed elegance. And what could be more enjoyable than sharing a safari through Disney's Animal Kingdom park?

By day, there is romance in the theme parks for couples who are already inclined to hold hands; by night, the parks sparkle with an intensity that inspires sudden mushiness in those who never considered themselves the type, and that's before the fireworks.

The Most Romantic Places in the World

WDW RESORTS

• Animal Kingdom Lodge
• BoardWalk Resort
• Contemporary
• Grand Floridian
• Polynesian Village
• Port Orleans Riverside
• Wilderness Lodge

WDW RESTAURANTS

• Cinderella's Royal Table
• Cítricos
• Enzo's Hideaway
• Flying Fish
• Jiko—The Cooking Place
• Le Cellier Steakhouse
• Monsieur Paul
• Narcoossee's
• Paddlefish
• Sanaa
• Victoria & Albert's

WDW LOUNGES

• Belle Vue Lounge at BoardWalk
• The Boathouse (dock seating) at Disney Springs
• Cítricos Lounge at Grand Floridian
• Il Mulino New York Trattoria Lounge at the Swan
• The Edison in Disney Springs
• Nomad Lounge at Disney's Animal Kingdom
• Rooftop lounge at Disney Springs' Paddlefish

WDW THEME PARK SPOTS

• All of Epcot's World Showcase
• Happily Ever After fireworks presentation at the Magic Kingdom
• Star Wars: A Galactic Spectacular fireworks show at Disney's Hollywood Studios

• As Disney's themed resorts go about transporting guests to various times and places, they make quite a few passes through settings straight out of everyone's favorite fantasy escape textbook—from the Victorian charms of the Grand Floridian to the exotic island getaway that is the Polynesian Village resort. You won't find a more inspirational backdrop than that at the rustic Wilderness Lodge, marked by geysers and steamy hot springs, and a grand stone fireplace. At the nostalgic BoardWalk resort, surrey bikes are available for romantic rides along the waterfront. And a peaceful stroll around Crescent Lake is a lovely way to cap off the day.

• The myriad of recreational activities that couples may enjoy at Walt Disney World includes tennis, golf, ballooning, carriage rides, couples treatments at one of four on-property spas, and more.

OLDER TRAVELERS

Disney World can sometimes be challenging for older travelers. And the heat, particularly in summer, can be hard to take. But with the proper planning and precautions, it's just as delightful for older visitors as for kids.

• Make special requests when you reserve your room. For example, if you need a wheelchair-accessible room or grab bars in the bath—ask for them, and confirm requests before arrival.

• For slower times, visit the parks Monday through Wednesday. (Thursdays through Sundays tend to attract lots of locals.)

Vacation Insurance

No one books a vacation expecting to cancel it at the last minute—yet sometimes life intervenes and it's simply unavoidable. So it may be worth working travel insurance into your vacation budget (we do). It may include coverage for trip cancellation and interruption, travel delay, loss of baggage, medical expenses, and more. Be sure to ask about travel insurance when you reserve your trip.

• The Florida sun tends to be brutal year-round. Always wear sunscreen (don't forget hands and feet) and a hat.

• Try to eat early or late to avoid the big mealtime crowds. In the Magic Kingdom, select restaurants such as Tony's Town Square Restaurant and Columbia Harbour House. Or take the monorail to the peaceful Polynesian Village, Contemporary, or Grand Floridian resorts, where pleasant dining options abound (check ahead to find out which restaurants serve lunch). In Epcot, the Coral Reef restaurant and La Hacienda are pleasant spots. At Disney's Hollywood Studios, the Hollywood Brown Derby offers a relaxing meal, as does Mama Melrose's Ristorante Italiano.

• If you need to refrigerate medicine, know that small refrigerators are included with the room rate at all Walt Disney World–owned-and-operated resort hotels. Refrigerators can be provided at most other area resorts for a small fee. All park First Aid Stations will store medicine, too. (No charge.)

• Don't underestimate distances at Epcot or Animal Kingdom; you may need to walk more than three miles in a day in each of these parks. Wear comfortable shoes and remember to take breaks.

HOT TIP!

Even the fittest of seniors may want to avoid some of Walt Disney World's more physically challenging attractions. Do heed all warning signs at attraction entrances to thrill rides and consider steering clear of high-activity-level experiences such as the Magic Kingdom's Swiss Family Treehouse (seemingly endless stairs!), the Maharajah Jungle Trek, and Gorilla Falls Exploration Trail at Disney's Animal Kingdom (lots of walking and few places to rest).

fishing excursion (407-939-2277 or 407-939-7529) or surfing lessons (407-939-7873), and watching a game (at ESPN Wide World of Sports). Call 407-939-7529.

• Disney Springs' lounges and restaurants can prove to be fertile meeting places. The BoardWalk is another lively destination. Sports fans find its ESPN Club most inviting. And suds fans appreciate the home-brewed libations at Big River Grille & Brewing Works. Sushi lovers fit right in at the California Grill sushi bar (in the lounge section of the eatery).

• The lounges at most Walt Disney World resort hotels are relaxed and welcoming. The same convivial atmosphere prevails at the Tune-In Lounge in the 50's Prime Time Cafe at Disney's Hollywood Studios and at the Rose & Crown Pub (in the United Kingdom pavilion at Epcot's World Showcase).

• Pace yourself. It's smart to head back to your hotel for a swim or a nap in the afternoon and then return to the parks later on. The hotels connected by monorail are particularly convenient for this.

• Many Orlando-area hotels and attractions offer discounts to seniors and AARP members. Contact the Official Visitor Information Center (407-363-5872) for additional information.

• Be sure to pack extra doses of any medication—in case of travel delays or other reasons for an extended visit. Pack contact info for your doctors and copies of all prescriptions, too. It pays to be prepared.

SOLO TRAVELERS

Those who travel alone (be it for business or just for fun) can have as memorable a time here as they would anywhere else.

• Solo travelers with extra time should consider taking a behind-the-scenes tour.

• Many of the finer restaurants now have counters at which to eat—perfect for chatting with other diners.

• Sometimes, being a solo traveler can mean shorter wait times at attractions. Test Track is among those with "single rider" lines.

• Other opportunities for unencumbered travelers include ballooning (at Disney Springs), horseback riding (at Fort Wilderness), taking a spin in a motor boat at a Disney resort, enjoying an early morning bass

Important Telephone Numbers

AdventHealth Celebration Hospital:
407-303-4000

Behind-the-Scenes Tours:
407-WDW-TOUR (939-8687)

Central Reservations:
407-W-DISNEY (934-7639)

Dining Reservations:
407-WDW-DINE (939-3463)

Disney's Magical Express:
866-599-0951

Dr. P. Phillips Hospital:
407-351-8500

Disney Floral & Gifts:
407-WDW-GIFT (407-939-4438)

Emergency: 911

ESPN Wide World of Sports Complex:
407-939-1500

Golf Reservations:
407-WDW-GOLF (939-4653)

Recreation:
407-WDW-PLAY (939-7529)

Walt Disney Travel Company:
407-828-8101

Walt Disney World Information:
407-824-4321

Weather: 407-824-4104

Tips for International Travelers

Visitors from outside the U.S. need not feel like strangers in a strange land when they arrive at Walt Disney World—even if they speak a language other than English. Information is readily available in many different languages. These tips may also be helpful:

• International guests with reservations on Disney's Magical Express (D.M.E.) should proceed directly to the D.M.E. check-in area when they arrive at Orlando International Airport (MCO).

• A valid passport or government-issued photo ID is required to check in at a Walt Disney World resort hotel.

• Free park guidemaps can be found in Spanish, French, German, Portuguese, and Japanese at the entrance to all Walt Disney World Disney parks, as well as at Guest Relations locations.

• Free translation services are available at all four theme parks and include a specially designed translation device called Ears to the World, Disney's Show Translator. The units are lightweight headsets that use wireless technology to provide synchronized narration at several theme park attractions. They are available in French, German, Japanese, Portuguese, and Spanish. There is no charge to use the service, but a $25 (refundable) deposit is required to borrow one.

• Several Disney resorts offer services for their international guests. Ask about them when making reservations.

• When making your reservations through 407-WDW-DINE (939-3463) or WDW-PLAY (939-7529), ask to speak with a foreign-language host or hostess.

• Most Disney restaurants offer menus in various languages. Some have picture menus.

• Guests must be at least 21 years old to consume alcoholic beverages in the state of Florida.

• Foreign currency exchange is offered at Guest Relations in the Disney theme parks. Traveler's checks may be purchased at the SunTrust bank in Celebration, Florida.

• Disney's MagicBands can act as a charge card (as well as a room key). Most purchases made at Walt Disney World can be billed to a credit card that is linked to an active MagicBand.

• Many Disney employees are fluent in more than one language. Languages spoken (in addition to English) are noted on employee name tags.

• Guests traveling long distances and through time zones should conserve their energy. It might be wise to relax by the pool on the day of arrival, instead of trying to fit in a full day at a theme park—it's never beneficial to start a vacation exhausted!

• Phone cards good for international calls can be purchased at several Disney World shops and in many resorts. Inquire at Guest Relations. Resist the urge to direct dial calls from resort rooms (see below).

Telephone Dos and Don'ts*

It's a common practice for hotels to assess a massive surcharge for phone calls, and Disney is no exception. To avoid whopping bills, use your mobile phone, and keep these tips in mind for the hotel phone:

• A direct-dialed, long-distance call will set you back the cost of the call at the AT&T operator-assisted day rate, plus a 65 percent surcharge! The rate applies to both domestic and international long-distance. Applicable taxes are included.

• Prepaid phone cards are available for purchase in most WDW resort lobbies.

• There is no extra fee for guests making credit card, prepaid phone card, or any type of operator-assisted calls from a resort-room telephone.

• There is no charge to call an 800 number from a Walt Disney World resort room.

• Landline directory assistance 411 phone calls cost $1.99 each; a 555-1212 call costs $1.40.

• There's no charge to call from room to room within a resort—but there may be a charge to call one Disney resort from another.

• Check with your cell-phone carrier to avoid tallying up "roaming" charges. And switch your phone from roaming to Wi-Fi when possible.

• All Walt Disney World—owned-and-operated resorts support mobile computing via laptop and tablet. Wi-Fi service is free.

*Details are subject to change.

Travelers with Disabilities

Disney tends to get high marks from travelers with disabilities because of attention paid to special needs. For details, go to *https://disneyworld.disney.go.com/guest-services/guests-with-disabilities/* or call 407-824-4321. Here is an overview of services:

GETTING AROUND: Special parking is available for guests at the theme parks. From the Transportation and Ticket Center (TTC), the Magic Kingdom is accessible by ferry or by monorail. All monorail stations are accessible to wheelchairs. The ramps are lengthy and a bit steep, but manageable.

Wheelchairs: Guests may bring their own wheelchairs. They also have the option of renting them at a theme park, BoardWalk resort, or from a local vendor. Wheelchairs may be rented in theme parks for $12 per day ($10 per day with a Length of Stay rental). In the Magic Kingdom, they are available at the Stroller and Wheelchair Rental. Epcot's rental areas are at the main entrance and at the International Gateway entrance. Oscar's Super Service rents wheelchairs at the Studios. At Animal Kingdom, wheelchairs may be rented at Garden Gate Gifts Stroller Rental area.

If you plan to visit the parks for several days, consider getting a multi-day wheelchair rental. Called a Length of Stay rental, it comes at a $2-per-day discount. Pay for the entire stay when you first visit a theme park. Simply show your receipt to the attendant the next time you visit a rental location.

The water parks have a small number of wheelchairs and ECVs on hand. Wheelchairs cost $12 per day, while ECVs rent for $50 a day. Both require a $100 refundable deposit. Disney Springs rents wheelchairs for $12 a day, plus a $100 refundable deposit from Sundries (located near the bus depot). Electric Conveyance Vehicles (ECVs) are available there for $50 per day with a $100 deposit. Wheelchairs at ESPN Wide World of Sports run $12 per day with a $100 refundable deposit. WDW Resorts with zero-depth-entry pools may have a small

number of wheelchairs available to assist guests entering the swimming pools.

Electric Conveyance Vehicles (ECVs) are available for rent in every theme park. They cost $50 for a day, plus a $20 refundable deposit. They usually sell out early. A word of advice: Practice makes perfect. So before you head into a thicket of park guests, take it for a test drive—and please don't exceed the speed of an average pedestrian.

Equipment rented at a park cannot leave that park. If you will need to use it for the whole trip, consider calling a company that rents standard and electric wheelchairs, as well as scooters. Keep in mind that you will have to transport the wheelchair or scooter from your resort to your daily destinations. (Monorails and buses are equipped to accommodate, but some boats are not.) Companies from which to rent include Scoot-Around (888-441-7575) and Walker Mobility (407-518-6000). Pickup and delivery (often for free or with a small surcharge) are available at all hotels in the WDW area (not just those on Disney property). In our opinion, guests are often better off renting from a local vendor or bringing their own equipment. The quality is generally better, and you don't have to worry about availability. The Walt Disney Company is not affiliated with, nor does it endorse, these companies.

Buena Vista Scooters has a presence at Disney's Board-Walk resort. They have a few first-come, first-served ECVs. The cost is about $31 per day. It's possible to reserve in advance; visit *www.buenavistascooters.com*, or call 866-484-4797. These scooters have a two-day-minimum rental period. The company provides free pickup and delivery to all Disney-area resorts.

▶▶

Attraction Access

Most park attractions are accessible to guests who are able to get out of their wheelchairs (with or without assistance). And a growing number have queues that can be navigated in a wheelchair. When that's the case, guests are urged to do so. If a wheelchair cannot be accommodated in the queue area, ask an attendant to direct you to an auxiliary entrance. Such entrances are intended for guests using wheelchairs or with service animals. For specifics on this policy, guests should visit a Guest Relations location.

There are designated areas for guests using wheelchairs to view the fireworks at Epcot and to view the parades in each of the theme parks. Check a park guidemap for locations.

Accessibility: It's relatively easy to get around the parks by wheelchair and scooter. Most attractions are accessible to guests who can be lifted from chairs with assistance from a member of their party, and some can accommodate guests who must remain in wheelchairs. Consult each park's *Guide for Guests with Disabilities* (for a free set, write to Walt Disney World Guest Correspondence, P.O. Box 10000, Lake Buena Vista, FL 32830) for details about access, or check with the ride host or hostess. At the water parks, life jackets are available for travelers with disabilities.

Most WDW hotels have accommodations suitable for guests with disabilities, including roll-in showers. Other features—which vary, depending on the resort—include wheelchair-accessible bathrooms, bed accessories, strobe-light smoke detectors, in-room Text Typewriters (TTYs), and more. The following WDW resorts have zero-depth-entry pools: Art of Animation, Animal Kingdom Lodge, Caribbean Beach, the Contemporary's Bay Lake Tower, Grand Floridian, Polynesian Village, and Saratoga Springs. For help finding a hotel that fits your requirements, ask for the Special Reservations Department when you call Central Reservations (Voice: 407-939-7807; TTY: 407-939-7670).

RESOURCES: Visual Disabilities: Guests can get a handheld device that verbally describes each park as well as many attractions. Each requires a $25 refundable deposit. Portable tactile maps may be borrowed from Guest Relations in each theme park (with a refundable deposit). Braille guides, Braille menus at most restaurants, and Braille maps are also available.

Hearing Disabilities: Sign Language interpretation for some live theme park shows is offered on a rotating basis. For the schedule, go to *MyDisneyExperience.com* or visit a Walt Disney World Guest Relations location. Sign language is offered for select dinner shows and special events. For information and to make arrangements, call 407-824-4321 at least two weeks ahead.

Assistive-listening devices that amplify attraction audio are available at City Hall in the Magic Kingdom and at Guest Relations in Epcot, Animal Kingdom, and Disney's Hollywood Studios. A $25 refundable deposit is required. Sites with assistive-listening systems are listed on park guidemaps.

Captioning systems, including reflective and handheld devices, are available at theme park Guest Relations locations. The former project show dialogue onto panels; the latter provide captioning on personal devices at certain attractions. A $25 deposit is required.

Booking the Trip: These organizations specialize in assisting disabled travelers:

• The Society for Accessible Travel & Hospitality (2175 Hudson Street, Fort Lee, NJ 07024; 212-447-7284; *www.sath.org*)

• Accessible Journeys (35 W. Sellers Avenue, Ridley Park, PA 19078; 610-521-0339 or 800-846-4537; *www.accessiblejourneys.com*)

• Ventures Travel (*www.venturetrvels.com*; 866-692-7400) offers customized trip planning services.

Vehicles: Mobility Works (1-877-275-4915; *www.mobilityworks.com*) rents wheelchair-accessible vans and offers pickup and delivery for Orlando International Airport and most Walt Disney World–area hotels. Side- and rear-entry ramps are available, as are hand-controlled vans.

WDW Weddings & Honeymoons

Honeymoon Registry

Launched, appropriately, on Valentine's Day, the honeymoon registry is a service for happy couples planning a Disney honeymoon. Gifts include theme park tickets, resort accommodations, carriage rides, spa treatments, and more. For additional information or to sign up for the free Disney Honeymoon Registry, visit *www.disneyhoneymoonregistry.com,* or call 877-699-5884 during regular business hours.

Believe it or not, Walt Disney World is one of the most popular honeymoon destinations in the United States. Why the appeal? The resorts offer romantic stretches of white-sand beaches for evening strolls, fine restaurants, and a host of recreational activities to rival almost any other destination. Add to that the fantasy of the Magic Kingdom, the wonder of Epcot, the glamour of Disney's Hollywood Studios, and the majesty of Animal Kingdom—plus Disney Springs and BoardWalk nightlife, water parks, and the nearby Disney Cruise Line—and it's not hard to see why Walt Disney World is tops with newlyweds.

After years of fending for themselves, folks looking to honeymoon here now have help at hand. A variety of options caters to newly married couples, as well as blended families joining together for the first time. For additional information, visit *www.disneyweddings.com/honeymoons/,* or call toll-free: 877-566-0969.

Over the years, the folks at Walt Disney World have received oodles of requests from couples wanting to get married at one of the theme parks. They responded by creating Disney's Fairy Tale Weddings and have been making wedding dreams come true for more than 25 years. Happy couples can tie the knot in fairy-tale ceremonies at some theme parks, as well as many other spots around Walt Disney World.

The Yacht & Beach Club, BoardWalk, Polynesian Village, and Port Orleans Riverside resorts host their share of weddings each year. The elegant Wedding Pavilion, on the grounds of the Grand Floridian Resort and Spa, offers a Victorian-style indoor setting with a prime view of Cinderella Castle and the Seven Seas Lagoon. The pavilion, which overflows with romantic ambiance, has seating for approximately 250 guests. Couples can fill their wedding albums with photos taken at Picture Point, under a trellis of climbing white roses, with the faraway castle in the background.

Weddings range from elegant affairs, with no hint of Disneyana, to ceremonies in which the bride arrives in Cinderella's horse-drawn Crystal Coach and Mickey and Minnie Mouse are among the guests at the reception.

At Franck's Bridal Studio, Disney experts work with couples to customize each wedding. Among the services offered are cakes, photography, flowers, and entertainment. They can help secure accommodations, rehearsal dinners, bachelor and bachelorette parties, and more. Feel free to stop by during your next WDW visit. F.Y.I.: Franck's was named for the character portrayed by Martin Short in the Disney film *Father of the Bride.*

For more information about planning a Walt Disney World wedding or honeymoon packages, call 321-939-4610, or visit *www.disneyweddings.com.*

PHOTO BY JILL SAFRO

My Disney Experience

My Disney Experience is "a whole new way to plan and share your Walt Disney World vacation." All guests are invited to visit *MyDisneyExperience.com* or download the free app. After setting up a profile, guests can use the site to book most elements of a Disney vacation, including hotel, restaurant reservations, Fastpass+ assignments for select theme park attractions—and even track the arrival times for buses at Walt Disney World. For details, see pages 23–27.

Fingertip Reference Guide

Flash photography is not permitted inside any Disney attraction. Note that when capturing moments with Disney characters as video, refrain from using camera lights. (The lights are much too bright for the characters' sensitive eyes.)

Camera Supplies: If you plan to use a digital camera while visiting Walt Disney World, be sure to pack an extra memory card or two—they are not stocked by many WDW shops (if at all). One-time-use cameras may be available at several retail locations scattered throughout the World. Note that film is not available.

BARBERS AND SALONS

One of the most amusing places to get a haircut is the Magic Kingdom's old-fashioned Harmony Barber Shop. It's located beside the Car Barn in the Town Square section of Main Street, U.S.A. Cost is about $19 for adults and $18 for kids. Colored hair gel is $5 (kids love it). Treat tots to a special "my first haircut" experience for $25. Hours are 9 A.M. to 5 P.M. daily. Walt Disney World resort guests may make reservations by calling 407-939-7529. Walk-ins are accommodated on a first-come, first-served basis.

Haircuts, coloring, manicures, and other services are offered at Ship Shape at the Yacht & Beach Club (407-939-7727), Ivy Trellis at the Grand Floridian Resort & Spa (407-824-3000, ext. 2581), Mandara Spa at the Dolphin (407-934-4772), the salon at Four Seasons Orlando (407-313-6970), and the Casa de Belleza at Coronado Springs (407-939-7727).

BUSINESS SERVICES

Disney provides a range of services for those who simply must mix business with pleasure. Copiers, fax machines (also found at Guest Relations in the theme parks), and FedEx materials may be available at the Lobby Concierge or Business Center at many Disney resorts.

The Contemporary, Grand Floridian, Animal Kingdom Lodge, Yacht & Beach Club, Swan, Dolphin, and Coronado Springs resorts can also provide computers and printers. There's a video-conferencing center near Disney Springs. For additional information about WDW business services, call 407-827-2000.

CAMERA NEEDS

Disney's PhotoPass photographers will happily snap shots of you with their camera (for details about Photo-Pass, see page 135) or with your camera or mobile phone. Note that selfie sticks are not allowed in WDW theme parks or water parks.

CAR CARE

There are three Speedway gas stations (complete with convenience stores) at Walt Disney World, all open 24/7. One is at 1475 Buena Vista Drive across from Disney Springs; another is near the Magic Kingdom Auto Plaza at 1000 Car Care Drive. The 300 Buena Vista Drive location, across the street from Disney's BoardWalk resort, also has a car wash.

Breakdowns happen, but they don't spell disaster. All Disney roads are patrolled by police and security officers who can call for help. If you need a tow or other services, call the WDW Car Care Center (407-824-0976). The service is available to all Walt Disney World resort guests. Located in the Magic Kingdom Auto Plaza, the Car Care Center offers full mechanical services and free towing on-property, Monday through Friday, 7 A.M. to 7 P.M.; Saturdays 7 A.M. to 4 P.M.; Sundays 8 A.M. to 3 P.M. After hours, call 407-230-5598. For off-property car care, guests can rely on Riker's Roadside Services (407-855-7776) for vehicle towing, Riker's Automotive & Tire (407-238-9800) for repairs, or AAA (provided you're an active AAA member).

DRINKING LAWS

In Florida, the legal drinking age is 21. Minors may accompany their parents to Walt Disney World lounges and bars, but might not be allowed to sit at the bar. Magic Kingdom table-service eateries serve liquor at lunch and dinner (dinner only at Be Our Guest Restaurant). Alcohol is available throughout the other theme parks and Disney Springs.

Spirits are sold in at least one retail location at most Disney resorts. A limited selection of liquor products may be purchased from room service at the Animal Kingdom Lodge, Contemporary, Grand Floridian, Polynesian Village, Yacht & Beach Club, BoardWalk, Swan, and Dolphin resorts; beer and wine are usually available for delivery at other Walt Disney World resorts.

LOCKERS

Lockers can be found in the following theme park locations: to the right, just inside the Magic Kingdom entrance; beside Spaceship Earth (to the right, as you enter) in Epcot; near Oscar's Super Service at the Studios; and inside the entrance (to the left) at Animal Kingdom. Lockers are also available at the Transportation and Ticket Center (TTC).

All parks have small (12.5 by 10 by 17-inch) and large lockers (15.5 by 13 by 17-inch). The cost is about $10 per day for small lockers and $12 for large ones. Epcot and Magic Kingdom also offer jumbo lockers. The super-size storage compartments measure 17 by 22 by 26 inches and cost $15 per day. Items may not be stored overnight. Lockers are cleaned out after the park closes.

Note: Locker rentals are not transferable from theme park to theme park. Plan accordingly.

LOST & FOUND

The extensive indexing system maintained by Walt Disney World's Lost and Found department is impressive, especially when a prized possession goes missing, whether it's false teeth or a camera. (Both have been lost in the past; the dentures were never claimed.)

If you lose something, immediately report it to one of these Lost & Found locations: City Hall in the Magic Kingdom, the Guest Relations lobby near Spaceship Earth at Epcot, at Guest Relations in Disney's Hollywood Studios, Guest Relations near the Animal Kingdom park entrance, or the Lobby Concierge at any Walt Disney World resort. At Fort Wilderness, dial 7-2726 from a comfort station telephone; from outside the campground, phone 407-824-2726 between 8:30 A.M. and 5 P.M. EST.

Items lost in a theme park may be claimed on the day of the loss at the park's Lost & Found. After your visit to WDW, you may realize that you left an item behind. If so, you should fill out an online form at *https://www.chargerback.com/disneyworld*. Once you've submitted the form, you'll receive an email with your lost item claim number. The Lost & Found team will continue to look for your item and provide an email update within 48 hours. For additional Lost & Found information, visit *https://disneyworld.disney.go.com/guest-services/lost-and-found/*.

We highly recommend attaching your contact information to electronic equipment (including mobile phones) and other valuables.

MAIL

Postage stamps are sold at all WDW resorts; World of Disney at Disney Springs; at the Newsstand shop in the Magic Kingdom; at shops near the lockers in Epcot, Disney's Hollywood Studios, and Animal Kingdom.

The old-fashioned mailboxes in Disney parks are not official United States Post Office mailboxes, but postcards and letters (with postage) can be sent from them. Postmarks read "Lake Buena Vista," not "Walt Disney World."

Don't mail anything that is time-sensitive—it takes much longer for mail to reach its destination when sent from here.

Mail may be addressed to guests in care of their hotel. It should clearly feature the word "Guest" on the front and the intended recipient's arrival date. Note that a $6 per package handling fee will apply to all packages received through the Front Desk or delivered to a Walt Disney World resort hotel room.

MEDICAL MATTERS

Travelers with chronic health issues should carry copies of all prescriptions and get names of local doctors from hometown physicians. Disney is equipped to deal with minor medical issues. In the Magic Kingdom, next to the Crystal Palace restaurant, there is a First Aid Center staffed by a registered nurse; there is another such facility at Epcot in the Odyssey Center complex. At Disney's Hollywood Studios, the First Aid Center is inside the Guest Relations building at the main entrance. Animal Kingdom's First Aid Center is located on Discovery Island near the back side of Creature Comforts (aka Starbucks). **In the case of a medical emergency, call 911 and alert a Cast Member.** Paramedics will arrive as promptly as possible.

HOT TIP!

Nobody starts the day expecting to lose something. But trust us, it pays to plan ahead. Put your name and contact number on your valuables, especially cameras. Disney does a good job of tracking lost items, but it's a whole lot easier to pick a labeled camera out of the heap of look-alikes than it is to find your "little silver" one. (Yes, it happened to us!)

Walt Disney World resort guests and theme park day guests staying at other area hotels have access to nearby services providing medical care. AdventHealthCentra Care Walk-In Urgent Care (*www.centracare.org*), owned and operated by Florida Hospital, has 20 area locations, most near pharmacies and with X-ray facilities. Guests in need of additional care will be transported to the hospital when necessary.

The main Centra Care facility is located at 12500 South Apopka Vineland Road (407-934-2273; close to Disney Springs and Hotel Plaza Boulevard) and is open 8 A.M. to midnight weekdays and 8 A.M. to 8 P.M. weekends. The Centra Care Walk-In facility at 8014 Conroy-Windermere Road (407-291-8975; near the resorts at Universal Studios Orlando) is open 8 A.M. to 8 P.M. weekdays and 8 A.M. to 5 P.M. on weekends. One location in Kissimmee is at 8201 W. Irlo Bronson Highway (407-465-0846). It's open 8 A.M. to 8 P.M. weekdays and 8 A.M. to 5 P.M. weekends. There is also a 24-hour in-room physician service (407-238-2000).

Round-trip courtesy transportation is provided from most area hotels to AdventHealth Centra Care clinics, and there is a no-tipping policy. Waits in clinics can be lengthy, but drivers can call ahead to learn which has the shortest wait. The most common maladies reported by Walt Disney World guests? Sunburn, blisters, fevers, earaches, and injuries from falls.

For Diabetics: All Disney parks and resorts can provide refrigeration services for insulin. WDW–owned-and-operated resort accommodations have refrigerators, and small refrigerators may be rented at most other resorts for a small fee. The fee may be waived for folks who need the fridge to store medicine, but a doctor's note may be required.

Prescriptions: Turner Drugs (407-828-8125) delivers medications to many Orlando-area resorts, including those on Disney property.

MONEY

Cash, traveler's checks, American Express, MasterCard, Visa, Discover Card, Diner's Club, JCB Card, Disney Dollars, and Disney gift cards are accepted as payment for most WDW charges.

Guests staying at a WDW–owned-and-operated resort enjoy a purchasing perk: Provide a major credit card at check-in and a MagicBand or hotel ID may be used to cover most expenses incurred at Walt Disney World. (They may be used to make purchases until midnight after you check out.)

ATMs: Automated teller machines are scattered throughout WDW. Theme park locations include Magic Kingdom (near the locker rental, in City Hall on Main Street, U.S.A., in Frontierland near the Shootin' Arcade, and by Pinocchio Village Haus in Fantasyland); Epcot (near the front entrance, on the path between Future World and World Showcase, at the American Adventure, and at International Gateway); Disney's Hollywood Studios (at the entrance and near Keystone Clothiers); and Animal Kingdom (near the entrance and by Chester & Hester's in DinoLand U.S.A.); plus the Transportation & Ticket Center (TTC) near the Magic Kingdom. Most resorts have ATMs; the Fort Wilderness ATM is at Pioneer Hall. There are five at Disney Springs: in the Welcome Center and by Marketplace Snacks in Town Center, next to Tren-D in the Marketplace, and near the West Side's House of Blues and Starbucks. Most bank and credit cards are accepted; fees range from about $2 to $3 (free for customers of Chase Bank).

Note: It's always a good idea to notify your bank that you'll be using your debit (or credit) card while on vacation. That should keep fraud protection software from freezing your account when you use it outside your home banking zone.

Banking: SunTrust, in Celebration, Florida (about 4 miles from Disney Springs), offers a variety of services. Guests can get cash advances up to $5,000 on MasterCard, Discover, and Visa credit cards; receive incoming wire transfers up to $3,000 (for a $50 fee); and cash, replace, or purchase American Express traveler's checks. Fees may apply. This branch is open from 9 A.M. to 4 P.M. Monday through Thursday; 9 A.M. until 6 P.M. Fridays; and 9 A.M. to 12 P.M. on Saturdays; drive-through is open Monday through Friday from 8 A.M. to 6 P.M. It is located on Celebration Water Tower Place, 74 Blake Blvd., Celebration, FL; 407-964-3333.

Disney Dollars: While Disney stopped selling Disney Dollars in May 2016, Mickey's money may still be used for purchases at most Walt Disney World shops, eateries, and WDW-owned-and-operated resorts.

Traveler's Checks: Even the most careful vacationer occasionally loses a wallet. Traveler's checks can take the sting out of that loss. Stash the receipt bearing the check numbers in a place separate from the checks themselves, along with a piece of identification such as a duplicate driver's license or a spare credit card to speed the refund process should your checks get lost.

To purchase, cash, or replace American Express traveler's checks, guests may go to the SunTrust bank in Celebration, Florida (74 Blake Blvd.; 407-964-3333). Call for hours. (If you do not have a record of the check numbers, first contact the place where you purchased the traveler's checks. Then, an American Express referral number is required; call 800-221-7282.)

Foreign Currency Exchange: Up to $50 per person in foreign currency may be exchanged daily at Guest Relations in the theme parks, and up to $500 at the Concierge desk at Disney resorts.

PETS

No pets (other than trained service animals) are allowed in the theme parks, Disney Springs, or the water parks. Of course, that's no reason to leave Fifi or Fido at home—especially when you can treat them to a pampered getaway at the Best Friends Pet Resort, a sprawling luxury facility (please don't call it a kennel!) complete with cat condos, doggy suites, and special accommodations for "pocket pets," including birds and hamsters. Cats or dogs from shared households may share quarters, but cats and dogs are not permitted to cohabitate (for obvious reasons).

The facility, which is now the only dedicated place to board animals at Walt Disney World, provides a full range of hospitality services, including day care (boarding in suites), grooming services, and doggy day camp (group sessions where the pups play games and frolic with other dogs under the supervision of a trained animal counselor).

Best Friends Pet Resort is located at 2510 Bonnet Creek Parkway, across from Disney's Port Orleans resort. Its services are available to everyone, but guests staying at WDW resorts net discounts. Indoor boarding (which includes two walks) costs $41 per day for Walt Disney World resort guests; indoor/outdoor boarding (with one walk) runs $45 a day; vacation villas (one walk, play group, flat-screen TV, and a turndown biscuit) cost $86, and VIP luxury suites (two walks, two play groups, flat-screen TV, webcam, and bedtime story) cost $101 a day (and, with a 3-day minimum, they throw in a "Go Home Fresh" grooming service).

To prevent separation anxiety, guests are encouraged to visit pets during regular operating hours. Though hours vary, Best Friends is generally open from approximately one hour before the earliest theme park opening to about one hour or so after the latest park closing. The center is not open to the public 24 hours, but it is staffed around the clock (a convenient service for guests who

experience travel delays or other emergencies). There are several certified veterinary technicians on staff, and all associates are trained in animal first aid. For directions, details on services, or to make reservations, visit *www.bestfriendspetcare.com/waltdisneyworldresort/*, or call 407-209-3126.

Be sure to bring your pet's certificate of vaccinations, since Florida law requires proof of immunization for animals involved in biting incidents. Elderly pets must be in good health with bladder and bowel control, and be mobile. Pack your pet's favorite blanket or toy, too. And never leave your pet in the car—it is extremely dangerous, and it's against the law.

Note: Pets are permitted at some campsites at Walt Disney World's Fort Wilderness Resort & Campground.

Outside Walt Disney World: A few hotels in the Orlando area, including the Rosen Inn at Pointe Orlando, let pets stay with guests (there is a $15 pet fee, plus tax, per night; 407-996-8585). Call Visit Orlando (407-363-5872) for a list of more pet-friendly hotels.

RELIGIOUS SERVICES

Though religious services are occasionally offered on Disney property, regular services are available at local houses of worship.

Protestant: Services are offered Sundays at 8 A.M., 9:30 A.M., and 11 A.M. at the Community Presbyterian Church, 511 Celebration Ave., Celebration, FL; 407-566-1633; *www.commpres.org*.

Muslim: Prayer takes place five times a day at the Islamic Center of Orlando, 11543 Ruby Lake Rd.; 407-238-2700; *www.icorlando.org*.

Catholic: The closest Catholic church is Mary, Queen of the Universe Shrine, 2½ miles southeast of Lake Buena Vista, at 8300 Vineland Ave. This church seats 2,000 people. For current mass times, visit *www.maryqueenoftheuniverse.org*, or call 407-239-6600.

Jewish: Reform services are held at the Congregation of Reform Judaism (928 Malone Dr., Orlando; 407-645-0444; *www.crjorlando.org*), near Winter Park, about 20 miles from WDW. Conservative services are held at Temple Ohalei Rivka, aka the Southwest Orlando Jewish Congregation (11200 South Apopka Vineland Road; 407-239-5444; *www.sojc.org*), approximately two miles from Disney Springs.

SHOPPING FOR NECESSITIES

At least one retail location in every Walt Disney World resort stocks a small selection of toiletries. In addition, over-the-counter health aids, plus many other useful items, may be available at the Emporium in the Magic Kingdom; they're kept behind the counter, so ask for what you want.

Aspirin, sunscreen, and sundries are also available at the Mickey's Star Traders shop in Tomorrowland.

In Epcot, a selection of sundries is sold in at least one shop in World Showcase and in Future World. At Disney's Hollywood Studios, stop by the Crossroads of the World souvenir stand. At Animal Kingdom, pick up the bare necessities at Island Mercantile.

Local supermarkets include Winn-Dixie (7840 W. Irlo Bronson Memorial Hwy., Kissimmee) and Publix (29 Blake Blvd., Celebration). WDW Speedway stations have convenience stores offering some grocery items, snacks, drinks, and sundries. It's also convenient (and cost-efficient) to have groceries delivered to the hotel (all WDW resort rooms have a mini fridge in which to store perishables). Our go-to source for groceries is *www.gardengrocer.com*. A $14 delivery fee will be added per grocery delivery when order is placed at least 2 days in advance. Same-day deliveries incur higher fees. Note that the aforementioned companies are not affiliated with or endorsed by the Walt Disney Company.

SMOKING

Smoking (including e-cigarettes/vaping) is prohibited in all indoor and outdoor spaces at Walt Disney World, unless specifically designated as "smoking areas." All eateries are smoke-free, as are clubs and lounges. Walt Disney World resort guestrooms (and balconies) are also smoke-free zones. A $250–$500 cleaning fee will be added to the resort bill for guests who smoke in their room or on the balcony. Tobacco products are not sold in the theme parks. Guests older than age 18 may buy tobacco products at some Disney resorts and Disney Springs venues (with government-issued photo ID). This is a statewide tobacco smoking policy, so if you venture off Disney property, the same rules apply. If you have questions about the smoking policy at WDW, ask a Cast Member or visit *https://disneyworld.disney.go.com/guest-services/designated-smoking-areas/*. Smoking marijuana is not permitted at any time.

TELEPHONE CALLS

Every time a local call is placed from a Central Florida landline, callers must dial the area code and seven-digit number. The rule applies to calls made within the same area code as well as for those that connect with other area codes.

Lost Adults

Occasionally, traveling companions get separated in the crush of the crowds, or someone may fail to show up at a meeting spot. When this happens, it's good to know that messages can be left for phone-free or battery-drained fellow travelers at Guest Relations in any of the Walt Disney World parks.

HOT TIP!

The point is to escape the real world, so turn off that mobile phone whenever possible—or at least stick to texting. If you have to make a call, kindly do so by the nearest public phone station. And *PLEASE* do not use a mobile phone while experiencing any Walt Disney World shows or attractions. Otherwise, the noise and the light will disrupt the magic for you and those around you.

Local calls made from pay phones cost about 50 cents each. Rates charged by non-Disney resorts can vary quite a bit (for all calls). Ask about rates and fees before making calls beyond your resort. See page 52 for more phone tips.

TIPPING

Tips are no less valued at Walt Disney World resorts than at any other hotel—$1 to $2 per bag is appropriate for lugging luggage; $2 to $3 per person, per night for housekeeping services (include a note to avoid confusion). Gratuities of 15 to 20 percent (excluding tax) are customary at full-service restaurants. (If the service is exceptional or otherwise, adjust accordingly.) Gratuity is included in the room-service bill at all WDW resorts and some off-property hotels. Meals that are prepaid with the Disney Dining Plan (except for dinner shows and Cinderella's Royal Table) *do not include gratuity*—please tip your servers.

Give cab drivers at least a 15 percent tip for good service. Baggage handlers at the train station and airport expect about $1 to $2 per bag. The same goes for Magical Express drivers. The ride is free, but it's customary to tip when bags are handled. (See page 16 for details about Disney's Magical Express service to and from Orlando International Airport.)

WEATHER

Call Walt Disney World Weather Information (407-824-4104), or check The Weather Channel website (*www.weather.com*).

WILDLIFE

Florida is home to a vast array of fauna, including alligators, snakes, owls, armadillos, manatees, and more. Never feed wild animals. Doing so alters their natural behavior and is often against the law.

TRANSPORTATION & ACCOMMODATIONS

"My business is making people, especially children, happy." —Walt Disney

62   Getting Oriented

63   WDW Transportation

66   WDW Accommodations

106   Resorts Near Disney Springs

The popularity of Walt Disney World has made the region around Orlando one of the world's major tourism and commercial centers, and transportation sources—from a state-of-the-art airport to an efficient network of highways—bring visitors to the area by the millions.

There's no doubt that getting to and around the Walt Disney World region can be confusing. The only more perplexing dilemma may be choosing the best accommodations for your group from the huge assortment of resort hotels and motels.

The accommodations owned and operated by Disney itself range from futuristic towers to cabins buried deep in piney woods. In between are resorts that evoke striking images of Africa, the South Pacific, historic Florida, the Pacific Northwest, the Caribbean, New England, early Atlantic City, New Orleans, Spain, and the sports, movie, and music worlds, plus a sprawling, well-maintained campground. And that list doesn't include the many villas or the studios and one-, two-, and three-bedroom "homes" that can be rented or "purchased" through a special vacation-ownership system (aka Disney Vacation Club). What follows should help travelers sort out the broad range of lodging options within the borders of Walt Disney World. Regardless of where you plan to stay, we offer this important piece of advice: Book your room as far in advance as possible. You'll be glad you did.

Getting Oriented

The Central Florida city of Orlando is the municipality with which Walt Disney World is most closely associated. Disney World, however, is located in a far smaller community called Lake Buena Vista, 15 miles from Orlando's business center. All Walt Disney World hotels and restaurants are located in Lake Buena Vista.

ORLANDO-AREA HIGHWAYS: The most important traffic artery in Orlando is I-4, which runs diagonally through the area from southwest to northeast, cutting through the southern half of Walt Disney World. It then angles on toward Orlando and Winter Park, ending near Daytona Beach at I-95, which runs north and south along the Atlantic coast.

> ## HOT TIP!
> Parking lots are cleverly labeled throughout Walt Disney World. Yet many drivers still misplace their vehicles. Avoid being dopey: Always snap a photo or jot down your parking location!

All the city's other important highways intersect I-4, and each has a name as well as a number. From south to north, they include U.S. 192 (aka Irlo Bronson Memorial Highway), which takes an east-west course that crosses the Walt Disney World entrance road and leads into downtown Kissimmee on the east; S.R. 528, aka the Beachline Expressway (formerly the Beeline), which shoots eastward from I-4; S.R. 435 (aka Kirkman Road), which runs north and south and intersects International Drive, where many motels catering to Walt Disney World visitors are located; U.S. 17-92-441 (aka Orange Blossom Trail), which runs north and south, paralleling Kirkman Road on the east; and S.R. 50 (aka Colonial Drive), which runs east and west. S.R. 429 (aka the Western Expressway), leads to a WDW entrance near Coronado Springs resort (exit 8).

WALT DISNEY WORLD EXITS: The nearly 40-square-mile tract that is Walt Disney World is roughly rectangular. I-4 runs through its southern half from southwest to northeast. Major Walt Disney World destinations can be reached by taking the I-4 exits suggested in the paragraphs that follow; off the highway, clear signage makes it easy for visitors to get anywhere in the World.

> ## DID YOU KNOW?
> When it comes to fashion, Walt Disney World is the biggest clotheshorse of them all. There are more than 2.5 million garments in its corporate costume closet, making it the largest working wardrobe in the world.

This road is congested more often than not. Keep in mind that construction work and special events will often require rerouting of traffic patterns on I-4:

• **Exit 64A**, marked "192/Magic Kingdom," leads to the Magic Kingdom, Fort Wilderness, and Palm and Magnolia golf courses, as well as the Grand Floridian, Polynesian Village, Contemporary, and Wilderness Lodge resorts.

• **Exit 65** leads to Disney's Hollywood Studios, ESPN Wide World of Sports Complex; Disney's Animal Kingdom; Blizzard Beach; Art of Animation; Coronado Springs; All-Star Music, Sports, and Movies; Pop Century; and Disney's Animal Kingdom Lodge. It is also a good alternate route to Disney's Hollywood Studios park.

• **Exit 67**, marked "Epcot/Disney Springs," leads to Epcot, Typhoon Lagoon, Disney Springs, Lake Buena Vista golf course, Disney's Saratoga Springs Resort & Spa, the BoardWalk, Caribbean Beach, Riviera, Swan, Dolphin, Yacht & Beach Club, Port Orleans Riverside and French Quarter, and Old Key West resorts.

• **Exit 68**, marked "S.R. 535/Lake Buena Vista," is the best route to the resorts on Hotel Plaza Boulevard and the Crossroads of Lake Buena Vista shopping center. It can serve as an alternate route to Epcot.

> ## HOT TIP!
> The cost to valet park a vehicle at any WDW—owned-and-operated resort is $33 per day (not including gratuity). Self-parking is $15, $20, and $25 per night at Value, Moderate, and Deluxe resorts.

WDW Transportation

Walt Disney World transportation is extensive, with boats, buses, the monorail, and the new Disney Skyliner (airborne gondolas that debuted in 2019) all doing their part to shuttle guests around.

One of the system's hubs is called the Transportation and Ticket Center (TTC), and is located near the Magic Kingdom. Monorail, bus, and ferry service connect the TTC to points throughout the World. Day visitors must park (or be dropped off) here before taking a monorail or ferry to the Magic Kingdom. (Most Walt Disney World resort guests can bypass the TTC via direct buses to and from their respective resorts.)

The monorail runs along a circular route near the Magic Kingdom, making stops at the TTC, Polynesian Village, Grand Floridian, Magic Kingdom, and Contemporary. A separate monorail route connects the TTC to Epcot. Bus service is the cornerstone of the WDW transportation system. Buses usually operate starting one hour before park opening time until about an hour after closing; bus stops are clearly marked. Travel times vary, depending on the route.

Although Walt Disney World resort guests are provided with complimentary transportation to all sites on-property, that transportation is not always direct.

Should You Rent a Car?

If you plan to spend all of your time on Walt Disney World turf, you can probably spare yourself the car-rental expense (and parking expenses). Ride-sharing, towncar, taxi, and shuttle service from the airport to all area hotels is available around the clock. Within WDW, an exhaustive network of transportation brings guests from point to point (if not always immediately or directly). Most area hotels offer their own bus service to and from Disney theme parks (inquire in advance about schedules and costs, if any). Note that strollers must be collapsed before boarding Disney bus and water taxi transportation.

For those planning to resort-hop within Walt Disney World or any attractions outside Walt's world, taxis and services such as Lyft, Minnie Van, and Uber can often do the trick. A rental car is an option, too. It is easy (but pricey) to rent a car at the airport: National (800-227-7368), Alamo (800-327-9633), Avis (800-331-1212), Budget (800-527-0700), or Dollar (800-800-4000)—but note that the rates are much higher than at other locations due to hefty airport fees. For day (or multi-day) trips, consider Alamo or National at the Disney Car Care Center (407-824-3470; free shuttle service is available from select Disney resorts) or one of the rental agencies that have desks at the resorts on Hotel Plaza Boulevard, or simply inquire about car rental at the Front Desk of your resort. It is also possible (and convenient) to rent a car from National or Alamo at the Walt Disney World Dolphin resort. There is a daily fee to park a vehicle at a Walt Disney World resort hotel. Be sure to factor that into your travel budget. Keep in mind that area traffic can be brutal—always allow extra time to reach your destination, especially if you have a restaurant reservation.

Build in extra time for travel, especially if you have restaurant reservations or Fastpass+ assignments. Also, know that traveling between resorts usually requires at least one transfer. From several WDW locales, water taxis usher guests to the Magic Kingdom, Epcot, Disney's Hollywood Studios, Disney Springs, or between resorts. Boats depart every 20 to 25 minutes. Walt Disney World buses generally run in intervals of 20 to 50 minutes (or more)—plan accordingly. The new Disney Skyliner connects Pop Century, Art of Animation, Caribbean Beach, and Riviera (see page 86) resorts with Epcot and Disney's Hollywood Studios. What follows is a rundown of the components that make up the Walt Disney World Transportation System.

MINNIE VAN SERVICE: Polka-dotted, 6-passenger "Minnie" vans whisk guests around Walt Disney World—provided they have activated the Lyft app on a smart device. Simply open the app from anywhere within Walt Disney World Resort to access the service, request a ride, and pay for the trip. Cars are usually minutes away. All rides have a base rate of $15 per ride, regardless of the number of passengers (up to 6). (Prices are subject to change.) The total cost of the trip varies based on distance traveled. Note that Minnie Van rates are generally a bit higher than trips of equal distance provided by Lyft, Uber, or taxi.

Each Disney Cast Member-driven car is equipped with 2 car seats, and specially outfitted vehicles may be requested for folks who use wheelchairs or Electric Convenience Vehicles (ECVs). Once the Minnie Van service is selected, the Lyft app will offer the estimated arrival time for the vehicle.

Minnie Van service is offered between 6:30 A.M. and 12:30 A.M. Guests at WDW resort hotels may arrange for Minnie Van service to and from Orlando International Airport (MCO) for about $150 per trip. To book, call 407-939-7529. Details are subject to change.

DISNEY'S MAGICAL EXPRESS: Free round-trip motor coach transportation (aka bus) to and from Orlando International Airport (aka MCO) is available to all guests with a confirmed reservation at a Walt Disney World-owned-and-operated resort hotel. The service includes complimentary luggage delivery to and from the airport. For more information, refer to page 16, or call 866-599-0951.

THE MONORAIL: The Walt Disney World monorail system has two main loops, which converge at the Transportation and Ticket Center (TTC). One loop connects the TTC with the Magic Kingdom, plus the Polynesian Village, Grand Floridian, and Contemporary resorts. (The Magic Kingdom is the third stop on the resort track

Transportation Tips

- Most WDW buses are equipped with wheelchair lifts. Such buses have a blue emblem on the windshield and rear door.
- When using the WDW transportation system to get from a resort to a theme park, or from one park to another, allow an extra 45 minutes (or more) to get to your destination.
- The interval between the arrivals of Disney buses is about 20 to 50 minutes (possibly more, possibly less).
- Be forewarned: It takes a long time to travel by bus from resort to resort. Plan on a trip of up to 100 minutes and at least one transfer (at a theme park or at Disney Springs).
- Monorails usually run until one hour after the Magic Kingdom closing time (and they don't always run during Extra Magic Hours).
- There is no direct transportation between Disney's BoardWalk and most WDW resorts. You must travel to Disney Springs or a park and transfer to the appropriate bus (or take the Disney Skyliner [to Epcot's International Gateway], a car-sharing service, or a taxi).
- Try to avoid vacating a theme park or water park just as it closes. Instead, plan to linger a bit in a shop, or grab a seat and watch the crowds crawl toward their respective buses, boats, airborne gondolas, cars, and monorails.
- If all seats are filled, guests will be asked to stand during transport on a bus or monorail (often at park opening and closing times).
- Keep in mind that the most obvious method of transportation may not turn out to be the quickest. For example, it is often much faster to walk to the Magic Kingdom from the Contemporary resort than it is to take the monorail.
- It's possible to rent a car from any Walt Disney World-owned-and-operated resort (plus many others). For details, inquire at the Lobby Concierge desk, or contact the Front Desk.
- Guests staying at a WDW-owned-and-operated resort receive complimentary, standard self-parking at all theme parks. Details are subject to change.

and the first stop on the express track.) Another loop links Epcot with the TTC. Monorails run from about 7 A.M. until about one hour after park closing. Strollers don't have to be collapsed to board the monorail.

Timing Tips: It can take 5 to 10 minutes to travel between stops on the Magic Kingdom resort loop, making for a grand circle total of 25 to 50 minutes. However, there are times during the day when the trains are taxed with greater volume than usual, causing delays at the station and on the beam. If there's an alternate form of transportation available at busy times of day (bus, boat, your feet, etc.), consider taking it. Otherwise, plan ahead and anticipate delays. Monorails may not run during Extra Magic Hours. For the current schedule, pick up a Times Guide at any WDW resort Front Desk or theme park Guest Relations location.

CAR SERVICE: Ride-sharing services Lyft and Uber may transport guests throughout Walt Disney World—as does Disney's Minnie Van service (see page 64 for details). For assistance with taxis, go to a Bell Services desk. To reserve a Minnie Van, download the Lyft mobile app. (Disney's Minnie Van works with the Lyft app, but is operated by Disney Cast Members.)

DISNEY WATER TRANSPORTATION: FriendShip water taxis connect the Disney's Hollywood Studios theme park with the Swan, Dolphin, Yacht, Beach, and BoardWalk resorts, and Epcot's International Gateway entrance. FriendShips also traverse Epcot's World Showcase Lagoon.

Water taxis also connect the Magic Kingdom with the Contemporary, Grand Floridian, Polynesian, Wilderness Lodge, and Fort Wilderness resorts. Ferry boats transport guests between the Transportation and Ticket Center and the Magic Kingdom. The Sassagoula Express ferries guests to Disney Springs from Port Orleans (French Quarter and Riverside) and Saratoga Springs resorts. Most routes run on 10- to 25-minute intervals. Hours of operation vary based on weather conditions. No luggage or alcohol is permitted. All strollers must be folded and stowed out of the aisle.

TAXI SERVICE: Authorized taxis (run by Mears Transportation) are available for about $4 for the first mile, $2.50 per extra mile (407-422-2222). Payment may be made with a credit card or cash. Stick with authorized taxis. Unauthorized services may charge outrageous, unregulated rates. Inquire at the Bell Services desk at your resort's front entrance. They'll direct you to an authorized taxi or order one on your behalf. (Pay attention to the route the driver takes—we've been taken on "the scenic route" on several occasions.)

DISNEY SKYLINER: This grand airborne gondola system connects Disney's Hollywood Studios and Epcot's International Gateway entrance with four WDW resort hotels: Disney's Art of Animation, Pop Century, Caribbean Beach, and the new Riviera (see page 86). Many of the colorful cars are adorned with Disney character illustrations and all provide a scenic, free-of-charge way to travel among the aforementioned properties. Many gondolas can accommodate guests using wheelchairs. The units use cross ventilation to maintain air flow (not traditional A.C.). For details about the high-flying Disney Skyliner, use the My Disney Experience mobile app or website, or visit *www.disneyworld.com*.

DISNEY BUS TRANSPORTATION: Motor coaches can get you just about anywhere you need to go on Disney property. Bus service from WDW resort hotels begins 45 minutes prior to park opening and ends an hour prior to park closing. Return service to the hotels ends two hours after park closing. Bus service to Disney Springs from Disney resorts begins 45 minutes before opening until 1 A.M. Return service to WDW hotels ends at 2 A.M. One-way bus service from the Disney theme parks to Disney Springs runs daily from 4 P.M. until 11 P.M. or 2 hours after theme parks close, whichever is earlier. Some routes require you to transfer buses. Wonder when the next bus will arrive at your resort? Open the My Disney Experience app to view your account screen and tap "See Bus Times."

Note: No alcohol or luggage of any type is permitted on Disney buses. All strollers must be folded (prior to boarding the bus) and kept out of the aisle.

WDW Accommodations

With a myriad of resorts in the Orlando area to choose from, it's definitely a challenge to select a hotel. Here's a bit of advice.

Weigh the Options: First decide whether to stay on or off Walt Disney World property. Many opt for a Disney resort because the conveniences and perks offered to resort guests are appealing (see page 67). Given that, there are still two major factors that tend to lure guests off Walt Disney World property: vacation budget and itinerary.

Travelers on a tight budget may find off-property options that are quite reasonable. However, Disney offers rooms as low as about $130–$250 per night (depending on hotel and season), so choose off-property digs only if the price difference is substantial. WDW room rates are based on double occupancy. Additional adult guests will result in an increase in the rate. There is no charge for kids age 17 or younger.

Guests who will spend only part of their trip exploring Walt Disney World may also prefer an off-property hotel—one that's closer to the other area attractions on their itinerary.

There's also the issue of what one considers deluxe. Disney–owned-and-operated "deluxe" resorts do tend to provide more amenities and services than their "moderate" and "value" counterparts, but they do not always rival comparably priced accommodations in the real world.

Deciding Factors: Once the on- or off-property decision has been made, it's time to look at hotels. The big differences among on-property WDW accommodations are in the proximity to theme parks, size of the rooms and bathrooms, level of service, dining and transportation options, recreational facilities, views, landscaping, and, of course, the all-important *cost*.

Consider how much time you'll spend in the room, whether you'd like to return to the hotel during the day, and if you'll have time to use all the amenities that are included. Parties with five or more members have an additional concern: how best to accommodate their group. It may be less expensive to reserve two value-priced rooms or a family suite (at All-Star Music or Art of Animation) instead of one luxe room or villa.

Ask the Right Questions: Once a hotel that meets all basic criteria is selected, it's best to do some further research to avoid surprises at check-in.

For example, ask about any possible hidden costs, like fees for shuttle service to and from Walt Disney World destinations or taxes that may not be included in the quoted price. Though most off-property hotels offer transportation to Disney, price, trip frequency and the number of buses vary. Find out the exact schedule and the number of stops made. Ask where the bus picks up and drops off, too. Try to avoid those that stop in the middle of busy parking lots.

Some hotels advertise a misleading proximity to Disney. While a hotel may be a short distance from the border, the commute to the parks may be considerable. Get specifics. (Distance from your favorite park is also a factor to consider when staying on-property.)

Last but not least, do not underestimate the value of Extra Magic Hours—a free perk offered to guests staying at all Walt Disney World–owned-and-operated resorts, plus the Swan and Dolphin, Shades of Green, Four Seasons Orlando, and the resorts on Hotel Plaza Boulevard (see page 22 for details).

Reserve a Room: Found the perfect hotel for your vacation needs? Book it before someone else does, and don't forget to ask about any special discounts, seasonal promotions, and cancellation policies.

A Room with a View

There's a lot to be said for throwing back the curtains and gazing at a breathtaking view, provided you have the time to appreciate it and your view is within your price range. The following is a breakdown of "views" you may select from at WDW resorts. It will help you choose the best category for your budget.

Although the categories vary, depending on the resort type, the "standard" view room is always the lowest rate available:

Value Resorts
Standard or Preferred = Location specific.
   The view can be parking lot, pool, garden, or anything else

Moderate Resorts
Standard View = Parking lot or landscaping
Water View = Pool, marina, lake, river

Deluxe Resorts
Standard View = Parking lot
Garden View = Landscaping
Water View/Lagoon View = Pool, lake, lagoon, or other water
Savanna View = Animal pastures
   (at Disney's Animal Kingdom Lodge only)
Theme Park View = Magic Kingdom

Walt Disney World Resorts

Walt Disney World hotels fall into two categories: Disney–owned-and-operated and non-Disney–owned resorts. Of all the WDW properties, the Swan and Dolphin, Four Seasons Orlando, and the resorts on Hotel Plaza Boulevard don't belong to Disney. Services and benefits in these resorts are slightly modified (see pages 89, 106, and 111).

On-Property Perks: Walt Disney World resorts offer guaranteed admission (with ticket) to the parks in most instances (though there are times when a park hits capacity and no further admissions are allowed); use of the WDW transportation system; the convenience of charging most purchases to the hotel bill; free package delivery to resorts from most WDW shops; nightly campfires, Movies Under the Stars; and the invaluable Extra Magic Hours benefit, which allows extra time in a select park on select days. Guests who stay at a Disney–owned-and-operated resort and arrive via air at Orlando International Airport are entitled to Disney's Magical Express service (see page 16). They also have a 60-day advance window for booking Fastpass+ assignments (non-WDW-resort-guests have a 30-day window).

Room Amenities: Disney resort hotel rooms all come with a small safe, shampoo, phone with voice mail, a flat-screen TV, and free Wi-Fi. There is a hair dryer, iron (with board), small (unstocked) refrigerator (in all WDW–owned-and-operated resorts regardless of their category), and a coffeemaker (with coffee, sugar, and powdered creamer) in most rooms. Guest laundry facilities, dry cleaning, and room service are offered in most resorts (for a fee).

RESORT PRIMER

Payment Methods: Hotel bills and deposits may be paid by credit card, gift cards, traveler's checks, money order, cash, Disney Dollars, or personal check. Checks must bear the guest's name and address, be drawn on a United States bank, and be accompanied by proper ID (a valid driver's license or government-issued passport will do the trick).

Room Deposit Requirements: When booked through Disney's Central Reservations, a deposit equal to one night's lodging (or campsite rental) is required within

Online Check-in

Are you planning a stay at a Disney–owned-and-operated resort? If so, you can take advantage of Disney's online check-in service. Meant to streamline the check-in experience, the virtual service is available in advance of and up through arrival day.

How does one check in via the Internet? Simply visit *www.disneyworld.com*, or the My Disney Experience app or website. Checking in online does not mean you can check in early—unless, of course, there is a room available (a happy surprise that has been known to happen). When your room is ready, you'll receive the number via text.

Online check-in expedites the arrival experience by getting the pesky paperwork out of the way prior to arrival. Before you log on, know that you'll be asked to provide the following: the credit card that will be used for room charges, mobile number, address, arrival time, and room-location requests (but know that special requests are subject to availability).

With all that info already in the system, guests just need to get to the resort, wait for a text with the room number, and open the door with a MagicBand or a mobile phone by tapping Unlock Door via the My Disney Experience app. Of course, friendly Front Desk folks are on hand to answer all questions and offer guidance should you need it.

14 days of the time that a reservation is made. Reservations are automatically canceled if deposits are not received by the 14-day deadline. (Reservations booked less than 30 days prior to arrival will receive special instructions for deposits.) Reservations booked through the Walt Disney World Travel Company are subject to a substantial cancellation fee. Ask about the cancellation policy when you book your room.

When booking by telephone, guests may pay the deposit with a major credit card. Those who wish to use another payment method may do so by mailing it with the payment stub that comes with the reservation confirmation. Call to confirm that your payment was received.

Cancellation Policy: With the exception of Magic Your Way packages, deposits for resort stays will be fully refunded if the reservation is canceled at least five days before the scheduled arrival. Vacation packages must be canceled at least 31 days ahead.

Parking Fees: The nightly fee to park a standard-size car at a WDW–owned-and-operated hotel is $15 (value resorts), $20 (moderate resorts), and $25 (deluxe resorts). Prices include tax and are subject to change.

Check-in and Checkout: The relatively early check-out time (11 A.M. at all Walt Disney World-owned-and-operated lodgings) and the late check-in times (3 P.M. in most hotels and campsites, 4 P.M. at Disney Vacation Club [DVC] accommodations) often come as bit of a surprise. Guests who arrive before check-in time can pre-register, store luggage at Bell Services (without a fee), and head to the parks or relax by the resort pool.

Magic Strollers

Brought to you by the folks behind Owner's Locker (above, right), this stroller-rental program is truly magical to the parenting populace. For starters, the strollers are all from the popular Baby Jogger City Mini and Summit series; they're delivered directly to any Walt Disney World resort (and many other area hotels) by 6 A.M. on the day guests check in (when the reservation is made at least 24 hours in advance—otherwise delivery is later in the day) and picked up before 5 P.M. on the day guests head home; and the convenience of using the strollers anywhere and everywhere is a major plus.

Magic Strollers pricing is based on reservation length. To receive a price quote, simply go to www.magicstrollers.com and plug in your rental dates. We recommend getting the insurance, too. For a flat fee of $25, you're covered for any damage or theft that may occur during the time you have the stroller. For details or to make a reservation, visit www.magicstrollers.com, or call 866-866-6177. To save $5 off a stroller rental, use the coupon at the back of this book!

PHOTO BY AMY HENNING

Stash Your Stuff

If you count yourself among the merry multitudes who travel to Walt Disney World at least once a year, a system called "Owner's Locker" was devised with you in mind. Simply put, it lets you stash your vacation gear in a private purple locker in the WDW area and have it delivered to you each time you visit the Mouse. That means you'll have less to check at the airport (the locker is great for storing liquids and "must-check" items) and lighten your load overall. Say good-bye to lugging items such as sunscreen, baby supplies, rain gear, cooking items, non-perishable snacks, first aid supplies, toys, DVDs, rainy-day activities, and more.

It's called Owner's Locker because customers are given an industrial-strength, secure storage bin when they join the program (extra lockers may be purchased at any time). After a one-time $75 membership fee—*waived for Birnbaum readers with a valid coupon**—expect to pay about $105 a year (or $10.50 per month) for the Moderate Plan (including one round-trip visit a year; $27.50 for each additional visit), or about $190 a year (or $19 per month) for the Deluxe Plan, which allows for unlimited visits at no additional charge.

How does it work? As soon as you plan your Walt Disney World trip, schedule a round-trip delivery via www.ownerslocker.com. Your locker will make its way from a climate-controlled storage facility to your resort before check-in time. Call the Bell Services desk and expect the purple chest to arrive in minutes (don't forget to tip accordingly). Owner's Locker service is available at all Disney resorts and many other area hotels (though the business is not owned or operated by the Walt Disney Company). For details or to join, call 800-431-6588, or visit www.ownerslocker.com.

* The coupon at the end of this book will net you a $75 savings on the initial Owner's Locker membership fee. You're welcome!

Walt Disney World MagicBands: Issued to guests upon check-in at Disney resorts (if not pre-ordered; see page 24 for details), the bands (which double as room keys) entitle guests to use of all Disney transportation (through the last day of your stay) and charging privileges (if linked to a major credit card) to cover most purchases at Walt Disney World. You will be asked to program a personal pin code at check-in. Should you use your MagicBand to make a purchase at WDW, you'll use that pin code to complete the transaction.

Note: Charges that are incurred on a MagicBand or hotel ID after checkout will be reflected in a revised bill, which may be requested at the resort's Front Desk or sent via email. Swan and Dolphin guests may use their resort IDs to charge meals inside the two hotels only.

Walt Disney World Resort Rates: One key factor in determining WDW hotel pricing is *resort category*. Disney has three main categories for its resort hotels: Deluxe, Moderate, and Value (refer to the Category Conundrum sidebar below right for details). Deluxe digs cost the most, value resort rooms the least, and moderates fall somewhere in between. When it comes to Walt Disney World accommodations rates, the calendar is another key factor. Traditionally, prices are higher during peak times of year (weekends, holidays, summer, school vacations, etc.) and lower during times surrounding holidays and when school is in session. Many Walt Disney World resorts offer lower rates on some weeknights year-round.

Rates within a Disney resort vary based on the room's view and the type of accommodation—studio, villa, suites, campsite, etc. Want to enjoy a deluxe resort's Club Level service? It will add to the nightly rate of your accommodations (but could take a bite out of your daily dining budget). Resorts such as Caribbean Beach and Port Orleans Riverside offer rooms with an extra layer of Disney magic. Rates for specially themed "pirate" or "princess" rooms run a bit higher than for the traditionally appointed rooms.

HOT TIP!

For Walt Disney World resort rates, use the My Disney Experience website, visit *www.disneyworld.com*, or call 407-939-1936. For rates at the Four Seasons resort at Walt Disney World, call 800-267-3046, or visit *www.fourseasons.com/orlando/*. For the Swan and Dolphin, visit *www.swandolphin.com*, or call 888-828-8850. For the properties on Hotel Plaza Boulevard (near Disney Springs), visit *disneyspringshotels.com*.

HOT TIP!

On weekends and when peak rates are in effect at Walt Disney World—owned-and-operated resort hotels, rates at Swan and Dolphin are often much lower. Conversely, Swan and Dolphin tend to have their highest rates on business days and during traditional convention times of year.

For additional information and pricing details or to make a Disney resort reservation, call 407-934-7639, use the My Disney Experience mobile app or website, or visit *www.disneyworld.com*.

Category Conundrum

Value vs. Moderate vs. Deluxe—which resort category is best for you? Categories reflect the price of a room, the style of the accommodation, and the level of service.

• Deluxe properties (the most expensive) are defined by their larger, practically appointed rooms, several restaurants, and such amenities as extended room service hours. This category generally includes Disney Vacation Club properties.

• Moderate properties (which are in WDW's middle range, price-wise) feature comfortably sized rooms, full-service restaurants and food courts, and bellhop luggage service.

• The Fort Wilderness Camping category covers campsites, but not Wilderness Cabins (which fall into the Moderate resort category).

• Value properties (the least expensive category) offer fewer frills and smaller quarters. Meals are offered at food courts. Recreation and transportation options are limited at these resorts.

WALT DISNEY WORLD

NAME & LOCATION	Setting/ Theme	Favored By	Romantic Hideaways
Animal Kingdom Lodge* Animal Kingdom Resort Area (page 100)	African wildlife preserve	Animal lovers—nearly every room affords a view of wandering wildlife Art aficionados—authentic African artwork abounds Disney Vacation Club members	Private balconies by moonlight Sunset lounge overlooking the savanna
BoardWalk Inn* Epcot Resort Area (page 92)	Turn-of-the 20th-century Atlantic City	Night owls—the entertainment options are numerous and right in the backyard Epcot lovers, who will appreciate the short commute Disney Vacation Club members	Moonlight strolls along the boardwalk A special fireworks cruise
Contemporary* Magic Kingdom Resort Area (page 80)	Retro-futuristic exterior, thoroughly modern interior	Families—the monorail whisks through it, and the Magic Kingdom is a short walk away Professionals, who can take advantage of the hotel's many business services Disney Vacation Club members	The rooftop lookout (available exclusively to patrons of the California Grill), which helps make up for the resort's otherwise less-than-romantic atmosphere
Disney's Riviera* **Resort** Epcot Resort Area (page 86)	A celebration of the grandeur of Europe	Fireworks fans—a rooftop restaurant offers prime views of theme park pyrotechnics Admirers of the Disney Skyliner. (The airborne gondola system stops nearby.) Disney Vacation Club members	Topolino's Terrace late in the day. Peaceful strolls around the nearby Barefoot Bay.
Grand Floridian Resort & Spa* Magic Kingdom Resort Area (page 80)	Victorian seaside resort	Honeymooners—who will love spending much of their vacation basking in the resort's unebbing romantic atmosphere Magic Kingdom and monorail fans Disney Vacation Club members	Manicured rose gardens The Grand Lobby for a cocktail while an orchestra performs on the balcony
Polynesian Village* Magic Kingdom Resort Area (page 78)	South Pacific	Romantics—fireworks views and lush, tropical setting may make you swoon Vacationers looking for a hotel with a real resort feel Magic Kingdom and monorail fans Disney Vacation Club members	Beach swings for two Tropical, torch-lit evening strolls
Swan & Dolphin Epcot Resort Area (page 89)	Beachfront whimsy	Guests who want many of the Disney perks but not necessarily the Disney hotel Bargain hunters—when WDW resorts are "peak," these resorts may offer discounts	A peaceful area beside the grotto pool waterfall

* Animal Kingdom Lodge, Beach Club, BoardWalk, Contemporary, Grand Floridian, Polynesian, Riviera, and Wilderness Lodge have Disney Vacation Club accommodations.

RESORT FINDER

Kids Adore	Dining Tip	Resort Category & Amenities	
The kopje, a rocky outcropping from which to spy on critters Story time beside the lobby fireplace Rustic bunk beds (on request) Animal-watching Lobby activities	Sample the exotic eats and atmosphere of Boma while savoring the sights of the savanna.		
The Keister Coaster, a 200-foot waterslide at the main pool The live entertainment on the boardwalk at night Board games in Belle Vue Lounge (available for use throughout the day)	Snack on Ample Hills Creamery's fabulous, freshly made ice cream while strolling the boardwalk. ♥ Club Level resort guests are treated to delightful dinner delicacies prepared by an "in-lounge" chef.	Full-service restaurants, fast-food spots, room service Luggage service Valet parking ($33 a night) Swimming pools	
The "party" held every 45 minutes at Chef Mickey's fabulously fun character meals Watching the monorail whoosh through the resort Boat rides from the marina	Reserve California Grill for a time that's likely to coincide with the Magic Kingdom's fireworks show—or eat early and come back for the show with your receipt in hand. The view is amazing. ♥	Beaches on which to stroll and build sand castles. ‡	
The S'il Vous Play interactive water play area. Inspired by the grand public fountains of Europe, the splash zone features a ballet of friendly Fantasia characters. Having breakfast with Disney pals at Topolino's Terrace—Flavors of the Riviera	Topolino's Terrace offers bird's-eye views of fireworks at Disney's Hollywood Studios. Check the schedule for the day you plan to dine here and book a table accordingly. Le Petit Café morphs from a coffee bar into a wine bar every afternoon. ♥	On-site recreation, such as boat rentals ‡ On-site kids' activities Most rooms sleep five guests	DELUXE
Nightly marshmallow roasts and alfresco Disney films Having dinner with Cinderella and her friends at 1900 Park Fare Zero-depth-entry pool and a Mad Hatter–themed splash zone	Have a spot of traditional afternoon tea, accompanied by a scone, at the Garden View Lounge. ♥	Monorail, bus, or boat transport to all parks Movies Under the Stars (outdoor screenings of classic Disney films)	
The hula lessons offered in the Great Ceremonial House (on select days) The slide- and waterfall-endowed lava pool, plus a cool splash zone	The sushi served at Kona Cafe is second to none. Order it (and other menu items) to go and have a poolside picnic. (Place your order with a waiter near the counter seats at Kona Island.) ♥	‡ Except Disney's Animal Kingdom Lodge	
The swan-shaped pedal boats The giant swan and dolphin statues perched atop their respective resorts A grotto pool complete with waterfall and winding waterslide	The Swan's Kimonos Lounge serves sushi with a side of karaoke. ♥		

♥ These resorts host character meals.

WALT DISNEY WORLD

NAME & LOCATION	Setting/Theme	Favored By	Romantic Hideaways
Wilderness Lodge* Magic Kingdom Resort Area (page 82)	America's grandest national parks	Sweethearts—love is always in the air at this resort Winter visitors—the warm, cozy atmosphere is even more inviting when the many fireplaces are roaring Disney Vacation Club members	Steamy, bubbling "hot springs" whirlpools The cozy alcoves hidden on each floor of the main building
Yacht & Beach Club* Epcot Resort Area (page 100)	Martha's Vineyard and Nantucket Island	Ambitious guests—those who plan to see and do everything Disney has to offer will like the central location Epcot fans, who enjoy the proximity of Disney's discovery park Disney Vacation Club members	The Yacht Club's peaceful gazebo Secluded whirlpools The beach—perfect for strolling hand in hand
Old Key West Disney Springs Resort Area (page 98)	Key West	Guests looking for a homey, village atmosphere Disney Vacation Club members Those who appreciate roomy rooms	Private whirlpool tubs—they come with all accommodations but the studios
Saratoga Springs Resort & Spa Disney Springs Resort Area (page 97)	Historic Saratoga Springs, New York	Peace seekers—the atmosphere is meant to soothe Disney Vacation Club members Space seekers. The accommodations are a bit more spacious than at other resorts.	Pretty gardens and meandering pathways Private whirlpool tubs—they come with all accommodations but the studios
Caribbean Beach Epcot Resort Area (page 85)	Tropical islands	Families—the colorful design, themed pool, and beach setting make this hotel ideal for families Pirate fans! The main pool and 384 rooms have a buccaneer theme.	Aruba beach—the hotel's longest, most secluded stretch of sand
Coronado Springs Animal Kingdom Resort Area (page 102)	A celebration of Mexican, Spanish, and South American cultures	Conventioneers—which means more business services (and a health club), higher food prices, and slightly less family entertainment than at the other moderate resorts at WDW	The waterfront in the peaceful Casitas area Secluded corners of Rix Cafe The delightful Dahlia Lounge
Port Orleans French Quarter & Riverside Disney Springs Resort Area (pages 95–96)	New Orleans French Quarter and Antebellum South, respectively	Lovebirds on a budget—the Riverside decor is like many of Disney's deluxe hotels, as is the romance factor, but the price is considerably less Big Easy fans. The French Quarter provides a peaceful, urban environment	Any room in Magnolia Bend's stately mansions The peaceful gardens scattered about the Riverside quarters

* Animal Kingdom Lodge, Beach Club, BoardWalk, Contemporary, Grand Floridian, Polynesian, Riviera, and Wilderness Lodge have Disney Vacation Club accommodations.

RESORT FINDER

Kids Adore	Dining Tip	Resort Category & Amenities
Totem poles, an erupting geyser, and countless Hidden Mickeys—there's even a free tour to help guests find them	Storybook Dining at Artist Point offers guests an exclusive chance to meet the Queen from *Snow White and the Seven Dwarfs*. (Snow White, Dopey, and Grumpy are there, too!) Savor morning coffee from a fireside rocking chair. ♥	**DELUXE** See details on page 71.
Stormalong Bay—the sprawling sand-bottomed, three-acre pool, with a waterslide and a neat shipwreck on which to play	Cape May Cafe's bountiful nighttime clambake has many a surf-and-turf fan lining up for more. ♥	
Crafts and games offered at Community Hall One super pool slide and poolside activities The pool's sand castle slide	Olivia's pleases all palates with a nice mix of pastas and fresh fish. The conch chowder is a yummy way to start a meal.	**DELUXE VILLA RESORTS (DVC) †** Kitchens or kitchenettes, restaurants, pizza delivery Luggage service Swimming pools and on-site recreation such as bike rentals Front-door parking Villas sleep 4–12 Bus transport to all parks Washers and dryers Boat to Disney Springs Movies under the Stars (outdoor screenings of Disney films)
The kids-only water-spray area near the pool Kid-oriented activities offered at Community Hall	Turf Club is a low-key, local dining room. Disney Springs and its tempting array of eateries is just across the lake—and easily accessed by a walking path or water taxi.	
The fortress pool and Caribbean Cay Island The coconut postcards sold at the Calypso Trading Post (real coconuts!) Pirate-themed rooms. *Arrrr!*	Spyglass Grill and Banana Cabana raise the bar for poolside quick-service eateries. At quick-service Centertown Market, guests pick up their breakfast from walk-up windows when their buzzer goes off; at dinner, orders are delivered to the table.	**MODERATE** Restaurant, food court, limited room service Luggage service Swimming pools with slides On-site recreation, such as bike or boat rentals Movies under the Stars (outdoor screenings of Disney films) Rooms sleep four to five guests Bus transport to all parks
The Dig Site—which encompasses the resort's playground, whirlpool, and main pool with its Mayan temple waterslide	To start the day in a pleasant way, consider breakfast at Rix Sports Bar & Grill. For a quicker start to the day, head over to El Mercado de Coronado or the grab-and-go area of Rix Cafe.	
The pool, fishing hole, and play area at the Riverside's Ol' Man Island. And the "Royal Guest Rooms" rock! The French Quarter's Doubloon Lagoon—a sea-serpent-themed family pool	Sample the fresh beignets from the food court. You'll think you're in the Big Easy.	

♥ These resorts host character meals.

† Known as "Disney Deluxe Villa Resorts" on *www.disneyworld.com*

WALT DISNEY WORLD

NAME & LOCATION	Setting/Theme	Favored By	Romantic Hideaways
All-Star Movies, Music, & Sports Animal Kingdom Resort Area (page 99)	Larger-than-life fun	Penny savers of all ages—these resorts offer fun, colorful theming, plus all the WDW perks, at a much lower price than at most other Disney resorts Space cravers—who adore the family suites at All-Star Music	All-Star Music's Jazz and Broadway areas
Art of Animation ESPN Wide World of Sports Area (page 104)	Classic and colorful Disney animation	Extended families and families with babies—it's great to have the extra sleeping area that comes with the family suites	The Drop Off pool bar is a sweet spot for a (quasi) quiet evening interlude
Pop Century ESPN Wide World of Sports Area (page 103)	American pop culture	Budget watchers and nostalgia buffs—this sprawling resort celebrates pop history with bright colors and big icons Young athletes and their families—ESPN Wide World of Sports is located nearby	Sipping specialty cocktails poolside
Fort Wilderness Cabins and **Campground** Magic Kingdom Resort Area (page 83)	Rustic woods	Seasoned RV enthusiasts—Disney's hookups are considered top-notch Families—who appreciate the modern amenities of the cabins, which fit six and fall into Disney's "moderate" category	Horse-drawn carriage rides The Fort Wilderness beach— perfect for viewing the Electrical Water Pageant on Bay Lake

** Wilderness Cabins fall under WDW's Moderate resort category.

RESORT FINDER

Kids Adore	Dining Tip	Resort Category & Amenities
Awe-inspiring, super-size icons—the movie and sports themes score the highest points Extra-large arcades Organized pool games and on-site activities for kids and families	Pick up a pizza at the pickup window in the food court and have a pizza party by the pool.	
The Righteous Reef soft-surface squirt zone Super-size icons from *Finding Nemo*, *Cars*, *The Lion King*, and *The Little Mermaid*	Dine in one of the loveliest food courts Disney has to offer: Landscape of Flavors. Indulge in made-to-order smoothies, hand-scooped gelato, and Mongolian barbecue.	Food court, pizza delivery Luggage service Swimming pools Movies under the Stars (outdoor screenings of Disney films) Bus transport to all parks
The state-of-the-art arcade Wildly oversize cell phones, yo-yos, bowling pins, and more The interactive water fountain near the playground	There are daily dance parties in the food court! At 8 A.M. each morning, the whole place does "The Twist," and at 6 P.M. guests may join Cast Members as everyone does "The Hustle."	
Pony rides, wagon rides, a blacksmith's shop, and campfire marshmallow roasts with Chip and Dale	Join the nightly campfire circle and roast marshmallows with Disney's famous chipmunk duo. Trail's End Restaurant offers hearty fare at a relatively reasonable price.	Recipient of perfect ratings from *Trailer Life* and *Woodall's* magazines Bus transport to all parks Water transportation to Magic Kingdom

VALUE

FT. WILDERNESS

Magic Kingdom Area

CONTEMPORARY & BAY LAKE TOWER

PHOTO BY JILL SAFRO

Watching the monorail trains disappear into the Contemporary's 15-story A-frame tower never fails to impress. The sleek trains look like long spaceships docking as they glide inside the resort.

Passengers, for their part, are impressed by the cavernous lobby, with its tiers of balconies and, at its center, the soaring 90-foot-high, floor-to-ceiling tile mural depicting scenes from the Southwest. (Look carefully and you may spot the five-legged goat.)

This imposing structure has 656 rooms in its main tower and garden building, plus those in Bay Lake Tower—available to all guests when not booked by members of the Disney Vacation Club. There are shops, a snack bar, restaurants, lounges, a marina, health club, and more. The pool area incorporates two whirlpools and a waterslide. The convention center offers business services. One of the resort's most notable features is its 15th-floor observation deck. From here, guests dining at the resort's California Grill can enjoy a bird's-eye view of the Magic Kingdom. Another huge bonus: a walking path to the Magic Kingdom (it's a 6- to 10-minute stroll away).

A club-level package is available for guests who stay in the hotel's 14th-floor suites. Amenities include express check-in and checkout, complimentary (light) continental breakfast, evening refreshments, and nightly turndown service. The 12th floor also provides guests with special club-level privileges. The phone number for the Contemporary resort is 407-824-1000.

ROOMS: Boasting a sleek and contemporary design, the standard rooms here are evenly apportioned among the main tower and garden building. All rooms located in the tower have private balconies and (magnificent) views of Bay Lake or the Magic Kingdom. Want to wake up with a view of Cinderella Castle? Request an odd-numbered, park-facing room in the Tower. Most Contemporary rooms can accommodate five guests (plus a child under 3). Typical units have a daybed and two queen-size beds; some rooms have a king-size bed and a daybed. And every room has a flat-screen TV.

Business-minded folks appreciate the desk space and Wi-Fi(free of charge). While the ceiling fans have gone away, room temperature may be set as low as 68 degrees. A heads-up: The bathrooms here, though elegant in design, could be more user-friendly. There's not much shelf or counter space, the flat sinks tend to stay wet throughout the day, the floor can be slippery, and the sliding doors don't lock.

Connecting rooms may be requested, though not guaranteed. Suites, consisting of a living room and one or two bedrooms, can sleep 4 to 12 people. Amenities include iron (with board), hair dryer, shampoo and conditioner, and coffeemaker (complete with coffee and sweetened, powdered creamer).

The monorail may be heard from lower rooms in the main tower. For maximum quiet, request a park view on a higher floor or stay in the garden wing. Of course, all rooms get serenaded by the nightly fireworks at the nearby Magic Kingdom park.

The 15-story Bay Lake Tower, a Disney Vacation Club (DVC) property that sits next to the Contemporary and is connected by a covered walkway, mimics the color scheme and strong horizontal lines of its neighbor. The tower's crescent shape hugs a lakeside pool.

Studios sleep up to four and offer a kitchenette, queen-size bed, and double sleeper sofa. Sleeping up to five, the one-bedroom villas have full kitchens, two bathrooms, a king-size bed in the master bedroom and queen sleeper sofa, and a sleeper chair in the living room. Two-bedroom villas sleep up to nine, and the two-story grand villas sleep up to 12. All configurations feature a flat-screen TV and free Wi-Fi.

WHERE TO EAT: In addition to the many restaurants and snack spots, 24-hour room service provides a wide range of offerings.

California Grill: On the 15th floor. The specialty is California fare—flatbreads, grilled meats, seafood, and market vegetables. An extra-special treat: the dramatic, panoramic view of the Magic Kingdom fireworks for dining guests. Check-in is on the resort's second floor.

Chef Mickey's: Mickey and his pals host daily buffets at this fourth-floor institution. Breakfast and brunch feature Mickey-shaped waffles, as well as traditional items. Dinner offers carved meats, daily specials, and a variety of entrées, plus a sundae and dessert bar.

Contempo Cafe: A quick-service spot with high-quality, freshly prepared fare (there's a grab-and-go selection, too), this snack bar is on the fourth floor.

The Wave . . . of American Flavors: A first-floor eatery, The Wave offers three meals a day.

WHERE TO DRINK: The Contemporary is home to some of the World's most inviting lounges.

California Grill Lounge: On the resort's 15th floor, adjoining the California Grill. Enormous picture windows provide a dramatic backdrop for sipping California wines and other drinks and nibbling on appetizers. Seating is limited.

Contemporary Grounds: This lobby coffee bar serves cappuccino, espresso, latte, and other coffee drinks, plus smoothies, pastries and snacks.

Outer Rim: On the fourth-floor concourse, overlooking Bay Lake, the Outer Rim serves beer, wine, cocktails, and specialty drinks.

Sand Bar and Cove Bar: These poolside spots offer drinks and light snacks.

The Wave . . . of American Flavors Lounge: Inside The Wave restaurant, this bar features wine flights, locally crafted beer, specialty drinks, cocktails, and The Wave's full menu. It's a good destination if you find yourself caught without a dinner reservation.

WHAT TO DO: Volleyball nets may be set up on the beach. Fishing excursions may be arranged (see *Sports & Recreation* for details). A resort entertainment schedule is available at the Front Desk.

Arcade: The Game Station, a spacious arcade, can be found on the resort's fourth floor.

Bass Fishing: See page 247.

Boating: Sea Raycer motorboats, Boston Whaler Montauks, and other boats may be rented at the Boat Nook by the resort's marina.

Campfire: Complimentary campfires and marshmallow roasts take place nightly, weather permitting. Afterward, everyone is treated to an alfresco screening of a Disney film—aka "Movies Under the Stars."

Health Club: The third-floor Olympiad Fitness Center has strength machines, bikes, sauna, treadmills, lockers, and massage (by appointment). Equipment use is free to Contemporary guests.

Jogging: A nearly one-mile jogging path loops around Bay Lake Tower and the resort's Garden Wing.

Shopping: The fourth-floor concourse is home to three shops. Fantasia sells plush toys, games, accessories, clothing for kids, and more. Fantasia Market proffers magazines, books, snacks, soft drinks, and liquor. Bay View Gifts (BVG) carries Disney character merchandise and apparel for all ages, items with the Contemporary resort logo, jewelry, and kitchenware. Baked goods and candy are also available.

Swimming: In addition to a round, lakeside pool, the free-form pool features a 17-foot-high slide, a squirt zone for little ones, and a whirlpool or two. Life jackets may be borrowed at no cost. Organized pool games are offered on most days. Cabanas can be rented at Bay Lake pool. Call 407-W-DISNEY for pricing and reservations.

Tennis: Two tennis courts are available to guests of the Contemporary resort. There is no charge to play. Racquets and tennis balls may be borrowed from Community Hall at Bay Lake Tower.

Yoga: A 30-minute gentle yoga class is offered on Tuesdays and Thursdays at 7:30 A.M. Space is limited to 15 Contemporary resort guests. Kids must be accompanied by an adult. Mats and towels are provided on-site.

TRANSPORTATION: The Contemporary resort is connected to the Transportation and Ticket Center (TTC) and Magic Kingdom by monorail. From the TTC, Epcot can be reached by transferring to another monorail. Buses take guests to Disney's Hollywood Studios, Animal Kingdom, Blizzard Beach, Typhoon Lagoon, and Disney Springs. (A transfer may be required for the water parks.) Watercraft travel from the marina to Fort Wilderness and Disney's Wilderness Lodge. Guests may walk to the nearby Magic Kingdom theme park (it takes about 7 to 12 minutes).

HOT TIP!

Guests staying in rooms with a park view may gaze upon the Magic Kingdom and its fireworks presentations. The nighttime viewing experience may be enhanced by tuning the in-room TV to channel 105—it plays the soundtrack to Happily After After.

POLYNESIAN VILLAGE

The Polynesian Village resort is as close an approximation of the real thing as Walt Disney World's designers could create. The vegetation is lush, and the architecture summons the tropics. The mood is set by a cavernous lobby that features open areas and sweeping vistas of the Seven Seas Lagoon. The structure in which it is housed, the Great Ceremonial House, is the central building in the Polynesian Village. The Front Desk, shops, and most of the restaurants are located here. Flanking the Ceremonial House on either side are 11 two- and three-story village longhouses named for various Pacific islands. The Bora Bora Bungalows on the Seven Seas Lagoon are part of the Disney Vacation Club accommodations at the resort. The monorail stops at this hotel, making it a convenient place to stay; in fact, it's just a short ride to the Magic Kingdom theme park.

Club-level service offers such amenities as express check-in; continental breakfast; snacks and drinks every afternoon; cocktails, hors d'oeuvres, and desserts in the evening; and a lounge with a prime view of the Seven Seas Lagoon and Cinderella Castle (and the nightly fireworks display). Club-level rooms and suites are located in the Tonga and Hawaii buildings. The phone number for the Polynesian Village is 407-824-2000.

DID YOU KNOW?

The white sand on the beaches near the Polynesian and Grand Floridian resorts and along the Seven Seas Lagoon actually came from the bottom of Bay Lake, located behind the Contemporary resort.

ROOMS: Many of the tropically appointed rooms have balconies, and most have a view of the gardens, Seven Seas Lagoon, or one of the resort's swimming pools. Many rooms have two queen-size beds and a daybed, and can accommodate five guests (plus a child under the age of 3). Adjoining rooms may be requested (but are not guaranteed). The Polynesian's suites—located in the Tonga building—can accommodate four to nine guests. Some have a king-size bed in the bedroom and one queen-size bed in the parlor. Amenities include a flat-screen TV, free Wi-Fi, coffeemaker (with coffee), hair dryer, and a small refrigerator. This is one of a few Walt Disney World resorts to offer snacks and soft drinks via vending machines.

WHERE TO EAT: Room service is available between 7 A.M. and midnight. There's also a selection of eateries at which to dine:

Capt. Cook's: On the lobby level of the Great Ceremonial House, this 24/7 quick-service spot is good for light fare throughout the day. In addition to packaged salads and sandwiches, there are items such as pastries and fresh fruit, plus a made-to-order section, too. This is the place to head when you wish to fill your refillable resort mug. (For a one-time purchase fee, you're entitled to unlimited soft-drink refills at all Rapid Fill locations for the length of your stay.)

Kona Cafe: A family eatery on the second floor of the Great Ceremonial House, Kona Cafe serves lunch and dinner with an Asian flair (including sumptuous sushi), while the breakfast menu is filled with traditional American selections.

Kona Island: This spot serves as a coffee bar by day, featuring fresh-brewed Kona coffee (including many specialty drinks), plus pastries, fruit, and bagels. In the evening, this casual corner morphs into an extension of the Kona Cafe (featuring sushi and other items). Grab a seat and place your order with a member of the Kona Cafe waitstaff. Details are subject to change.

Oasis Grill: Set beside the Oasis pool and available exclusively to Polynesian resort guests, the Grill serves up items such as cheeseburgers, fish tacos, chicken avocado wraps, and more. Note that guests must use a MagicBand or room key to access this area.

'Ohana: On the second floor of the Great Ceremonial House, 'Ohana serves family-style dinners roasted over a fire pit. Disney characters (including Lilo and Stitch) host a breakfast each morning.

Pineapple Lanai: The Polynesian Village is a happy place for fans of that chilly, tropical treat known as the Dole Whip (frozen, non-dairy pineapple dessert). It is served (plain, with vanilla soft-serve, or as a float) at this kiosk near the Lava pool.

Spirit of Aloha dinner show: For details on this nightly luau, turn to page 315.

WHERE TO DRINK: As might be expected, both the drink offerings and the settings in which they are served are as tropical as they come. Guests may sip at the following:

Barefoot Bar: Adjacent to the Lava Pool, this watering hole is open seasonally.

Oasis Bar: An alfresco lounge, Oasis offers beer, wine, sangria, specialty cocktails (we dig the Frosty Pineapple), and drinks sans alcohol. The Oasis Bar is available exclusively to Polynesian resort guests.

Tambu Lounge: There's a tropical air about this lounge near 'Ohana. There's a full bar, but we go straight for the creamy, frozen piña coladas (available with or without alcohol).

Trader Sam's Grog Grotto: The spirited first-floor lounge is next to Captain Cook's snack bar. Sam's is a delightful Disney lounge offering tropical drinks and small plates in a richly themed locale. There is indoor and outdoor seating, with the outdoor patio tables much easier to snag than the bar stools inside.

F.Y.I.: Trader Sam is the "head salesman" in the Magic Kingdom's Jungle Cruise attraction.

WHAT TO DO: A wide range of activities is available at the Polynesian, including a jogging path. Fishing excursions can also be arranged. A resort entertainment schedule is available at the Front Desk.

Bass Fishing: Refer to page 247 or call 407-WDW-BASS (939-2277).

Boating: Sea Raycer boats, Boston Whaler Montauks, and pontoon boats may be rented at the resort's marina. Specialty cruises are available.

Health Club: Polynesian guests are invited to use the Grand Floridian Health Club. (Get there via lakeside walking path or monorail.)

Shopping: BouTiki is the go-to place for resort-wear, souvenirs, sweet treats and more. Moana Mercantile sells Disney souvenirs, toys, magazines, and fashions. It's also stocked with food, spirits, soft drinks, snacks, and other fixings for an impromptu party.

Swimming: There are two pools here: the Oasis, an unguarded, zero-depth-entry pool near the Samoa, Niue, Hawaii, Tokelau, and Rarotonga buildings; and the larger free-form Lava pool, near the marina. The latter is complete with slide and zero-depth-entry. There is also the Kiki Tiki Splash area (an aquatic playground for little ones, located near the Lava pool), a hot tub with views of Cinderella Castle, and an expanded poolside deck. A limited number of wheelchairs are available to borrow for use in the pool. The beaches are strictly for sunbathing, sand-castle-building, afternoon snoozing, and fireworks viewing (no swimming allowed).

PHOTO BY JILL SAFRO

HOT TIP!

Swimming and wading are not permitted in any of Walt Disney World's lakes. The rule is meant to protect guests from unguarded water and from exposure to naturally occurring bacteria and dangerous wildlife, such as alligators and snakes, common to Florida lakes.

TRANSPORTATION: The Polynesian Village is on the monorail line to the Magic Kingdom and the Transportation and Ticket Center (TTC). It's also possible to get to the TTC via walkway (it takes 5 to 10 minutes). From the TTC, Epcot may be reached by transferring to another monorail. Buses take guests to Disney's Hollywood Studios, Animal Kingdom, Epcot, Blizzard Beach, Typhoon Lagoon, and Disney Springs. (A bus transfer may be required for the water parks, depending on the time of year.) Water taxis ferry guests from the marina to Magic Kingdom. Guests may reach the Grand Floridian by monorail or via lakeside walking path.

GRAND FLORIDIAN RESORT & SPA

At the turn of the 20th century, Standard Oil magnate Henry M. Flagler saw the realization of his dream: The railroad he had built to "civilize" Florida had spawned along its right-of-way an empire of grand hotels, lavish estates, prominent families, and opulent lifestyles. High society blossomed in winter, as the likes of John D. Rockefeller and Teddy Roosevelt checked into the Royal Poinciana in Palm Beach, enjoying the sea breezes from the oceanside suites.

Unfortunately, the hotel was lost to a fire, and Florida's golden era faded with the Depression. But nearly a century after Flagler first made Florida a fashionable resort destination, Walt Disney World opened a grand hotel—an 867-room Victorian structure with gabled roofs and carved moldings—on 40 acres of Seven Seas Lagoon shorefront, between the Magic Kingdom and the Polynesian Village.

Like its late-19th-century predecessors, the Grand Floridian resort boasts abundant verandahs, intricate latticework, turrets, towers, and red-shingle roofs. And yet it offers all the advantages of modern living, including monorail service. With five restaurants, multiple lounges, four shops, a convention center, two pools, a kids' splash zone, a marina, and full-service health club and spa, the Grand Floridian is not only a grand hotel but also a complete resort.

The main building houses the Grand Lobby, a palatial space soaring five stories to a ceiling of stained-glass domes and glittering chandeliers. Palms and an aviary decorate the sitting area; an open-cage elevator carries guests to the shops and restaurants on the second floor. The turn-of-the-20th-century theme is everywhere, from the employees' costumes to the shop displays, restaurants, room decor, and music played by the lobby band. The phone number for the Grand Floridian resort is 407-824-3000.

ROOMS: The rooms are filled with charm, decorated as they might have been a century ago—with elegant light fixtures and marble-topped sinks. Amenities include hair dryer, bathrobes, mini fridge, TV, nightly turndown service (by request), coffeemaker (with coffee), and free Wi-Fi service.

The main building houses club-level rooms and suites; lodge buildings, each four and five stories high, contain standard rooms, slightly smaller "attic" chambers, and suites. Villas, located in a building near the Beach pool, are available to rent when not occupied by Disney Vacation Club members.

Most rooms measure more than 400 square feet and include two queen-size beds, plus a daybed, to accommodate up to five people. Many rooms have a terrace. Suites include a parlor, plus one, two, or three bedrooms; there are queen-size beds in the bedrooms. Most of the 15 Deluxe King Rooms, located on the second, third, fourth, and fifth floors, enjoy wonderful views.

On the third floor, the club-level desks offer such services as reservations and information. The fourth floor features a quiet seating area where continental breakfast and evening refreshments are served. Club-level service is also available in the Sugarloaf building.

WHERE TO EAT: Most restaurants and lounges are located on the first two floors of the main building. In-room dining is offered, too.

Cítricos: The largest of the hotel's restaurants serves market-fresh cuisine from southern Europe. It's open for dinner only. All menu items are available in the lounge, too. (Order from the bartender.)

Gasparilla Island Grill: This 24-hour snack bar offers sandwiches, salads, flatbreads, and more.

Grand Floridian Cafe: Its verandah-like feel makes this a relaxing place for a simple sit-down meal. All meals are served. There is limited outdoor seating.

Narcoossee's: This sophisticated spot has a romantic shoreline location. The seasonal menu includes items such as sustainable seafood paired with award-winning wines. Guests may sip cocktails on the verandah.

1900 Park Fare: A buffet restaurant decorated with carousel horses, plants, and Big Bertha, the carnival organ. Characters host meals daily. This character experience is a nice alternative to Cinderella's Royal Table in the Magic Kingdom and easier to reserve.

Victoria & Albert's: The upscale eatery is named after the former queen and prince consort of England. It serves a (pricey) prix-fixe menu of 7 to 10 courses (to guests ages 10 and up). Jackets are required for men, and reservations are a must.

WHERE TO DRINK: The refined lounges here can be lovely escapes. Cítricos and Narcoossee's both have bars, complete with a full menu for dining. Drinks (bought from any Grand Floridian bar) may also be enjoyed in the Grand's majestic lobby.

Cítricos: Proof that good things do indeed come in small packages (8 bar stools and 4 tables), this lounge has an extensive wine list, specialty coffees, and full menu.

Garden View Tea Room: This pretty spot offers a view of the hotel's lush, landscaped garden and pool area. Afternoon tea is served (as are finger sandwiches and small desserts).

Second Floor Lounge: There's a new, *Beauty and the Beast*–inspired watering hole in the space formerly occupied by Mizner's Lounge and Commander Porter's shop. If you time your visit right, you may be serenaded by a band known as the Grand Floridian Society Orchestra. Bonus! (Note that the band's last set ends at 9 P.M., but the lounge is usually open until about midnight.) There's indoor and outdoor seating.

Narcoossee's: Located in the heart of the restaurant, this lounge offers an extensive wine list and craft beer selection, plus a full bar and menu.

Pool Bars: These bars (known as Courtyard and Beaches) both feature a variety of beverages, while Beaches also serves lunch and dinner.

WHAT TO DO: The Grand Floridian Resort & Spa offers many of the recreational facilities of a beach resort. Fishing excursions can be arranged (refer to the *Sports & Recreation* for details). The Grand Floridian resort entertainment schedule is available at the Front Desk.

Arcade: The pocket-sized Arcadia Games is adjacent to the Gasparilla Island Grill (near the marina).

Basketball: Hoops may be shot on a half-court near the health club. Registered Grand Floridian guests may borrow basketballs on a first-come, first-served basis.

Bass Fishing: See page 247.

Boating: Boston Whaler Montauks, pontoon boats, and Sea Raycer speedboats are available for rent (by the hour or half hour) at Captain's Shipyard Marina. The *Grand 1* yacht (including a captain and first mate) can be rented. Prices start at about $399, plus tax, per hour. Larger boats accommodate up to 18 guests. Rates may vary depending on the time of day.

Campfire: Grand Floridian guests are invited to gather around the fire and roast marshmallows (the marshmallows are free and s'mores kits start at about $5). Afterward, everyone is treated to an alfresco screening of a Disney film—aka "Movies Under the Stars." Both events may be cancelled due to inclement weather.

Golf: This resort is close to Disney's Magnolia, Palm, and Oak Trail golf courses. Call 407-WDW-GOLF (939-4653), or visit *www.disneyworldgolf.com* for information or to reserve tee times.

Health Club: The full-service exercise facility, adjacent to the Senses spa, is outfitted with modern fitness equipment. (Oddly enough, there is no restroom. Health Club patrons may use the facilities at the nearby restroom by the pool.)

Salons: The Ivy Trellis salon offers a full line of hair-care services. Bibbidi Bobbidi Boutique offers royal makeovers for young guests.

Shopping: On the first floor of the main building is Summer Lace, specializing in women's and men's resort-wear and swimwear, and Sandy Cove, for gifts, sundries, and home decor. One level up is the cheerful M. Mouse Mercantile character shop, and Basin for soaps and bath supplies.

Spa: The spa at Disney's Grand Floridian resort is a pampering palace called Senses—A Disney Spa. In addition to treatments offered at its sister spa at the Saratoga Springs resort (see page 241), this spot also offers many soothing packages.

Treatment hours are usually 8 A.M. to 8 P.M. daily. Prices start at about $135 for a 50-minute massage and about $150 for a facial. To book an appointment, call 407-WDW-SPAS (939-7727). For information, visit *http://disneyworld.com/spas/*.

Swimming: There are two large pools for guests to cool off in. Both have zero-depth-entry, and the Beach Pool also has waterfalls and a 181-foot slide. There's an *Alice in Wonderland* splash zone for kids up to 48 inches tall (and their guardians). Kids get absolutely giddy when the Mad Hatter's gigantic hat tips over, dumping massive amounts of water onto bathers below.

TRANSPORTATION: The Grand Floridian Resort & Spa is connected to the Transportation and Ticket Center (aka TTC) and Magic Kingdom by monorail. (All guests pass through a security check before boarding.) From the TTC, Epcot may be reached by transferring to another monorail. Buses transport guests to Disney's Hollywood Studios, Animal Kingdom, Blizzard Beach, Typhoon Lagoon, and Disney Springs. (A transfer may be required for the water parks.) Watercraft travel from the marina to the Magic Kingdom park.

DID YOU KNOW?

Movie buffs may find the Grand Floridian resort strangely familiar. Its design is based, in part, on that of the Hotel Del Coronado in California. Scenes from the classic film *Some Like It Hot* were shot there.

WILDERNESS LODGE, VILLAS, & CABINS

This resort artfully recalls the spirit of the early American West and the feeling of the National Park Service lodges built during the early 1900s. These grand structures architecturally unified the elements of the unspoiled wilderness parks, kept harmony with nature, and incorporated the culture of Native Americans. The Wilderness Lodge artfully recaptures this rustic charm.

The resort is located between the Contemporary and Fort Wilderness on Bay Lake. The majestic lobby is an eight-story, log-structured building. Massive bundled log columns support a series of trusses, while two Pacific Northwest totem poles soar 55 feet into the air. Four levels of corridors surround the lobby, providing access to guestrooms, sitting nooks, and terraces. The monorail does not stop here. Club-level service is available on the top floor of the Lodge. There are villas, here, too: Boulder Ridge Villas and Copper Creek Villas & Cabins (Copper Creek joined the Disney Vacation Club family in 2017). The telephone number for the Wilderness Lodge is 407-824-3200.

ROOMS: Most of the Lodge's 725 guestrooms have two queen-size beds and a balcony. Some have a queen-size bed and bunk beds. Bathrooms have separate vanity areas with double sinks. The wallpaper has a Native American–motif border and the curtains add to the decor. Images of wildlife complete the theme. Rooms include an iron (with board), hair dryer, coffeemaker (with coffee, sweetener, and non-dairy creamer), mini refrigerator, free Wi-Fi, and flat-screen TV.

The 126 Boulder Ridge villas are housed in a five-story building adjoining the Lodge. This tribute to turn-of-the-20th-century design is also one of the two Disney Vacation Club (DVC) properties at this resort. The style of the villas building was inspired by the grandeur of Rocky Mountain geyser country. At Copper Creek (the other DVC property), guests may choose from studios, 1-, 2-, and 3-bedroom villas, and lakeside cabins.

Each studio has a queen-size bed, a double sleeper sofa, and a pull-down twin-size bunk bed, plus a kitchenette with microwave, coffeemaker, and mini refrigerator. Villas sleep 4 to 12 guests and have dining areas, kitchens, laundry facilities, master baths with bubble-jet tubs, and DVD players. They include a king-size bed in the master bedroom, a living room with a queen sleeper sofa, and either two queen-size beds or a queen-size bed and a double sleeper sofa in the extra bedrooms.

Each of the 26 waterfront Cascade Cabins features two bedrooms (and sleep up to 8 guests), two bathrooms, large dining and living room spaces, floor-to-ceiling windows, exposed wooden beams, and an interior-exterior stone-hearth fireplace.

Villas and cabins are available to all guests when not occupied by Disney Vacation Club members.

WHERE TO EAT: The Northwest theme is carried out with flair in the hotel's eateries. Room service generally runs from 6:30 A.M. to 11 A.M. and 4 P.M. to midnight.

Artist Point: Decorated with art representing painters who first chronicled the Northwest landscape, this spot features a prix-fixe dinner hosted by Snow White, Dopey, Grumpy, and the evil Queen.

Geyser Point Bar & Grill: With its cedar beams and natural stone, this rustic, open-air waterside spot invites guests to pair small plates with beverages from the Pacific Northwest. It's a delightful spot.

Roaring Fork: Quick service food and light snacks are available at this snack bar. This is also the site of the resort's "refillable mug" station. (For details, refer to page 285.) Roaring Fork hours are usually about 6 A.M. until midnight.

Whispering Canyon Cafe: A boisterous, family-style restaurant with top-notch all-day dining.

WHERE TO DRINK: Two pleasant spots are available for a relaxing break.

Geyser Point Bar & Grill: Geyser Point is a waterside retreat with a full bar featuring an array of beer, wine, cocktails, and soft drinks—and a great fireworks vantage point is just steps away.

Territory Lounge: This low-key, lobby-adjacent lounge honors the survey parties who led the move westward. In addition to specialty drinks, wine, micro-brewed beer, and snacks (popcorn, fries, olives, and mac & cheese) are served.

WHAT TO DO: The resort offers many recreational activities. Teton Boat & Bike Rental is in the Colonel's Cabin by the lake. Fishing excursions may be arranged (refer to the *Sports & Recreation* chapter for details). Pick up a resort entertainment schedule from the Front Desk.

Arcade: The Buttons and Bells Arcade has about 30 different games to enjoy.

Bass Fishing: See page 247.

Biking: Due to ongoing construction in the surrounding area, bike rentals have been suspended indefinitely. Wilderness Lodge guests may rent bikes any other WDW resort that offers the service.

Boating: A variety of watercraft may be rented for trips around Bay Lake and the Seven Seas Lagoon.

Carolwood Pacific Room: A fireplace and railroad memorabilia add atmosphere to this relaxing room, equipped with comfy seating, tables, and games. It is located in the Wilderness Lodge Villas building.

Campfire: Resort guests are invited to gather round the campfire (on select nights) and roast marshmallows. (Marshmallows are complimentary for Wilderness Lodge guests; s'mores kits start at about $5.) Afterward, everyone is treated to a screening of a Disney film—aka "Movies Under the Stars." The movie lawn is located between the marina and Geyser Point Bar & Grill. For the screening schedule, check with the resort's Front Desk.

Health Club: The only thing rustic about the Sturdy Branches health club is the structure it's housed in. Open 24 hours, it features modern equipment, a sauna, and more. Massage and facial services are available. To make an appointment, call 407-939-7727.

Salon by the Springs: In the market for a manicure, pedicure, hair styling, or other spa services? Spring to this salon! It's open daily from 9 A.M. to 5 P.M., and reservations can be made by calling 407-WDW-SPAS.

Shopping: Wilderness Lodge Mercantile stocks necessities and sundries, as well as a line of clothing with the Wilderness Lodge logo and Disney character merchandise. There is a small selection of grocery items, too. The mercantile is usually open until about 11 P.M. There's a pin-trading cart in the lobby.

Swimming: The zero-depth-entry Boulder Ridge Cove pool looks as if it were carved from a natural rockscape. A beach, a kiddie pool, two whirlpools, and a geyser complete the design. Fire Rock Geyser erupts on the hour from early morning until 10 P.M. Most kids enjoy the splash zone.

TRANSPORTATION: Boats (aka water taxis) ferry guests to the Magic Kingdom, Contemporary, and Fort Wilderness. Buses transport folks to the Magic Kingdom, Epcot, Disney's Hollywood Studios, Disney's Animal Kingdom, Blizzard Beach, Typhoon Lagoon, and Disney Springs. (A transfer may be required for the water parks, depending on the time of year.)

FORT WILDERNESS RESORT & CAMPGROUND

The very existence of this canal-crossed expanse—with more than 750 acres of cypress and pine—always surprises visitors who come to Walt Disney World expecting to find nothing more than theme parks.

Tucked among the campsites are hundreds of Wilderness Cabins for rent, complete with housekeeping service. The cost is comparable to that of some of the more expensive rooms at Disney resorts, but each sleeps up to 6 guests and offers about 500 square feet of space. The phone number for the Fort Wilderness resort and campground is 407-824-2900.

PHOTO BY JILL SAFRO

The Chuck Wagon: Dinner vittles such as brisket sandwiches, burgers, hot dogs, salads, marshmallows, s'mores kits, ice cream, and cotton candy are served from a retro camper near the Meadow Trading Post.

P&J's Southern Takeout: Aka Trail's End To Go, this venue serves hearty fare throughout the day. Place your order at the counter on the far left of the Trail's End eatery. You can chow down at nearby tables or take the grub to go.

Trail's End: This log-walled spot in Pioneer Hall serves home-style fare for breakfast and dinner. Spirits are available. The Trail's End breakfast buffet delivers a nice bang for the buck—provided you come hungry!

WHERE TO DRINK: Cocktails, soft drinks, and pub grub are served at Crockett's Tavern in Pioneer Hall.

FAMILY ENTERTAINMENT AFTER DARK: The Hoop-Dee-Doo Musical Revue is quite popular and offered year-round. (Another beloved dinner show, Mickey's Backyard BBQ, is on hiatus while Imagineers build a new Fort Wilderness resort: Reflections—A Disney Lakeside Lodge.) There's a free nightly campfire/sing-along with Chip and Dale, followed by a screening of a Disney movie near the Meadow Trading Post. Fees apply for marshmallows and s'mores kits.

WHAT TO DO: There's plenty of free activities to choose from, including two pools (the Meadow Swimmin' pool has an aquatic play zone for tots and a slide), tennis, and campfire sing-alongs with Chip and Dale. For a fee, guests can enjoy wagon, pony, and carriage rides, fishing, archery, boats, and more. For details, see *Everything Else in the World* and *Sports & Recreation* and pick up an entertainment schedule at the Fort Wilderness check-in desk.

TRANSPORTATION: Buses circulating at 15- to 40-minute intervals provide transportation within the campground, while buses and boats connect Fort Wilderness to the rest of the World. Magic Kingdom, Contemporary, and Wilderness Lodge are best reached via watercraft that depart from the marina. Buses to Wilderness Lodge depart from the Settlement stop only. Buses to Epcot, Animal Kingdom, Disney's Hollywood Studios, Blizzard Beach, Typhoon Lagoon, and Disney Springs leave from the Outpost stop. (A transfer may be required for the water parks.)

Electric golf carts and bikes may be rented outside the Reception Outpost as an alternative means of getting around within the campground. Call 407-824-2742 for golf cart reservations. Available to Fort Wilderness guests only, golf carts cost about $67 per night (plus tax). To drive a golf cart, guests must have a valid license and be at least 18 years old.

CAMPSITES: Fort Wilderness has 843 traditional sites. They feature electricity hookups (30/50-amp), water, sanitary disposal, complimentary Wi-Fi, and cable TV. Partial-hookup campsites supply electricity and water hookups only. All campsites feature a paved driveway pad, picnic table, and charcoal grill. Most loops have at least one air-conditioned comfort station complete with restrooms, private showers, ice machine, phones, free Wi-Fi, and a laundry room. A site allows for occupancy by up to ten. Each site has room for one car, plus the camping vehicle. Other cars may be parked in the main lot at Fort Wilderness.

The various campground areas are designated by numbers. The 100–500 loops are closest to the beach, the Settlement Trading Post, and Pioneer Hall. The 1500–2000 loops are farthest away from the beach and many other Fort Wilderness activities, but they are quieter and more private. Premium campsites are big-rig friendly and are wider and deeper to accommodate large vehicles. Pets are welcome at certain campsites for a nightly charge of $5. They can frolic at Waggin' Tails Dog Park, the "off leash" pet play area.

WILDERNESS CABINS: These woodland dwellings offer a rustic escape (with all the comforts of home, plus housekeeping). Falling into WDW's "moderate" resort category, the interiors of the six-person, log cabin-like buildings are decorated with wilderness accents. Each one is shaded by a pine canopy. Cabins include air-conditioning, full kitchen, free Wi-Fi, two TVs, full bath, hair dryer, iron, a deck, picnic table, and charcoal grill. DVD players are available upon request.

Note: No extra camping equipment allowed; all guests must be accommodated in a cabin.

WHERE TO EAT: There is a bona fide restaurant here, but many folks opt to cook their own meals. A small selection of supplies is sold at the Meadow Trading Post and the Settlement Trading Post. Ask about nearby grocery stores when you check in to the resort, or use *www.gardengrocer.com.*

Epcot Area

PHOTO BY JILL SAFRO

CARIBBEAN BEACH

This vibrant, tropical hotel—which is southeast of Epcot and near Disney's Hollywood Studios—offers an idyllic island-style getaway. Introduced to the World in 1988, Caribbean Beach has been thoroughly revamped and revitalized. The resort is composed of brightly colored "villages" surrounding the 45-acre Barefoot Bay. Villages are identified with Caribbean islands: Barbados, Jamaica, Martinique, Trinidad, and Aruba.

A village consists of a cluster of two-story buildings, a guest laundry, and a lakefront stretch of white-sand beach. Old Port Royale acts as a "port of entry," providing a tropical atmosphere for guests to check in, access lobby concierge services, shop, dine, and relax. Decor, and staff costumes all reflect the Caribbean theme. Stone walls, pirates' cannons, and lush landscapes add to the immersive atmosphere.

The lakeside recreation area includes a pool with waterfalls and a slide; the Barefoot Bay Bike Works, where bicycles may be rented; and a 1.2-mile promenade around the lake that's perfect for biking, walking, or jogging. Kids love it here. The telephone number for the Caribbean Beach resort is 407-934-3400.

ROOMS: Rooms are located in two-story buildings in the island villages. A typical 340-square-foot room has two queen beds, and most sleep up to four. Some rooms can sleep up to five (with a fold-down bunk-size bed). The rooms here are a bit larger than standard rooms at Disney's other moderate resorts. Rooms are decorated in tones softer than the colors found on the exterior. Many have a super-kid-friendly pirate motif.

(Rates for pirate rooms run higher than for standard rooms.) Each room has a small fridge, coffeemaker (with coffee), and free Wi-Fi. A note for the budget-conscious: Rooms are identical in terms of size and comfort, but rates differ depending on location, the view, and the aforementioned pirate theming.

WHERE TO EAT: Guests may dine at Sebastian's Bistro, Centertown Market, and Spyglass Grill. The Banana Cabana poolside lounge offers first-rate fare, too.

Centertown Market: The indoor market sells freshly prepared quick-service meals with Caribbean influences. There is a grab-and-go section, too.

In-room Dining: Guests may have pizza, sandwiches, and pasta delivered to their room from 4 P.M. until midnight. To order, press Pizza Delivery on the in-room phone. Note that an 18 percent gratuity and a $3 delivery charge applies to in-room orders.

Sebastian's Bistro: A casual, waterside locale, Sebastian's serves creative fare with Latin and Caribbean flair. Dinner only.

Spyglass Grill: A walk-up counter near the Trinidad pool area, Spyglass serves three meals a day. Meals may be enjoyed on a patio overlooking Barefoot Bay.

HOT TIP!

Avast, ye hearties! About 400 rooms at Caribbean Beach resort were designed to appeal to the swashbuckler in all of us. The pirate-pleasing parlors are perfect for swapping sea stories. Kids love them.

WHERE TO DRINK: Soft drinks and cocktails may be purchased at all resort dining spots, but the best bet for bending elbows is Banana Cabana—an open-air oasis offering luscious libations, satisfying small bites, and menu items from the nearby Sebastian's Bistro.

WHAT TO DO: Barefoot Bay provides many a recreational opportunity. Fishing excursions and pirate cruises take place on the lake, while biking, walking, and jogging happen around it. A resort entertainment schedule is available at the Front Desk.

Biking: Bicycles may be rented at Barefoot Bay Bike Works. Rides may take guests around the resort's scenic 45-acre lake known as Barefoot Bay.

Fishing: Guided fishing excursions are offered on Barefoot Bay. Call 407-WDW-BASS (939-2277) for additional info and to make a reservation.

Playground: There is a small playground to explore.

Pirate Adventure Cruise: Young buccaneers (ages 4 to 12) can don bandannas and set sail on a 2-hour pirate adventure! Each excursion is kids-only and takes place daily (weather permitting) from 9:30 A.M. to 11:30 A.M. Cruises depart from Caribbean Cay, a tropical island located in the middle of Barefoot Bay. To make reservations, call 407-939-7529.

The Unsolved Mysteries of Barefoot Bay: Scallywag sleuths ages 10 through 16 band together to solve the mystery of Captain Calico's disappearance. Nightly cruises cost about $39 per pirate and include a snack. For reservations, call 407-939-7529; walk-ins are accepted based on availability.

Shopping: Calypso Trading Post carries Disney merchandise, swimwear, sundries, snacks.

Swimming: Each village has its own pool, and the main pool, dubbed Fuentes del Morrow, has a Caribbean-themed setting, conjuring up images of high-seas pirate adventures—has 2 slides, 2 whirlpool spas, and a splash zone for kids under 48 inches tall. Youngsters simply adore it.

TRANSPORTATION: Buses go to the Magic Kingdom, Epcot, Disney's Hollywood Studios, Animal Kingdom, Blizzard Beach, Typhoon Lagoon, and Disney Springs. (A bus transfer may be required for the water parks.)

HOT TIP!

Portable playpen-like cribs that accommodate one child under age 3 are available at all Disney resorts. Ask about them when you call to reserve your room. They're free. (If you'd like a more substantial sleeping apparatus for your toddler, refer to page 47 of the *Getting Ready to Go* chapter.)

The Disney Skyliner gondola transportation system stops at this resort. It whisks guests to Epcot and Disney's Hollywood Studios. (See page 65 for details.) Getting around within the resort is done via buses bearing an "Internal Resort Shuttle" sign.

DISNEY'S RIVIERA RESORT

Walt and Lillian Disney marveled at the majesty of Europe and the Mediterranean coastline— and this resort pays tribute to their travels and the region that inspired them. It's a compelling blend of Disney artistry and the sights, sounds, tastes, and heritage of the sun-drenched Riviera.

Disney's Riviera Resort is the 15th Disney Vacation Club (DVC) property, and its rooms are available to all guests when not reserved by DVC members. (At press time, the resort was expected to open in fall 2019.) For additional information about the new hotel, use the My Disney Experience website or mobile app, visit *www.disneyworld.com*, or call 407-824-4321.

VILLAS: Many of the 300 units have balconies or a patio and most have a view of lush landscapes or pools. Amenities include a flat-screen TV, free Wi-Fi, coffeemaker (with coffee), hair dryer, and a small refrigerator. Deluxe studios sleep up to 5 guests and feature a kitchenette; one- and two-bedroom villas have fully equipped kitchens with a dining space that opens to a living area; an en-suite luxury bath; and a laundry area with a washer and dryer. Details are subject to change.

WHERE TO EAT AND DRINK: Room service is available. There's also a selection of eateries at which to dine:

Bar Riva: Visit this open-air pool bar with seaside decor for snacks, drinks, and views of the pool.

Le Petit Café: Coffee bar by day, wine bar by night, this elegant French patisserie specializes in beverages and casual bites throughout the day.

Primo Piatto: With a modern design and a traditional feel, this quick-service spot offers family-friendy fare.

Topolino's Terrace: A rooftop retreat with French and Italian influences, Topolino's serves breakfast with Disney characters and (character-free) dinner daily.

F.Y.I.: Topolino is what Mickey answers to in Italy.

WHAT TO DO: In addition to on-site diversions, Riviera guests may partake in many recreational activities at the nearby Caribbean Beach and all other WDW resorts.

Health Club: Guests may work out in a modern facility known as The Athlétique Fitness Center.

Shopping: The resort's resident retail outlet sells Disney souvenirs, toys, magazines, and fashions. It's also stocked with assorted spirits, soft drinks, snacks, and other grocery items.

Swimming: There are two pools here: the tranquil Beau Soleil leisure pool; and the Riviera pool, which features a winding stone turret water slide. The S'il Vous Play splash zone is ideal for little ones.

TRANSPORTATION: Buses go to Magic Kingdom, Epcot, Disney's Hollywood Studios, Animal Kingdom, Blizzard Beach, Typhoon Lagoon, and Disney Springs. The Disney Skyliner stops near this resort. It whisks guests to Epcot and Disney's Hollywood Studios.

YACHT & BEACH CLUB, AND BEACH CLUB VILLAS

The New England seaside exists at Walt Disney World in the form of the Yacht & Beach Club, and the Beach Club Villas. Situated near Epcot's International Gateway entrance, the resorts are set around a 25-acre lake. The adjacent properties, designed by noted architect Robert A. M. Stern, share most facilities—including a convention center offering business services—and transportation options.

The Yacht Club's design evokes images of the New England seashore hotels of the 1880s. Guests enter the five-story beige clapboard building along a wooden-planked bridge. Spartan guestrooms feature blue curtains; walls, furniture and accents in shades of brown and beige; and faux wood floors throughout (no carpet). A lighthouse on the pier serves as a beacon to welcome guests back to the hotel from WDW attractions. To contact the Yacht Club, call 407-934-7000.

Distance from the ocean is irrelevant over at the sand-and-surf-focused Beach Club resort. There's a sandy volleyball court and beachside swings on the white-sand shore of Crescent Lake. Guests are met by hosts and hostesses dressed in colorful beach resort costumes of the 1870s. The phone number for the Beach Club resort is 407-934-8000.

ROOMS: The Beach Club's rooms are amply sized and a bit more modern than the resort's overall motif. Yacht Club rooms are also roomy, if a bit more austere. Most rooms feature two queen beds or one king bed (higher than the beds in most WDW resort rooms), and many have a daybed (a couch that converts to a single bed). Most of the suites have a king-size bed, as well as two sleeper sofas and a fold-down, single bunk. In the bathrooms, there is a separate vanity with double sinks. Each room has an iron (with board), hair dryer, free Wi-Fi, mini fridge, coffeemaker (with coffee, sugar, and powdered creamer), and a digital safe. Club-level rooms (with exclusive access to a room with a concierge, snacks, and drinks) are available.

A five-story building beside the Beach Club is home to 177 two-bedroom equivalents. The villas are available to Disney Vacation Club members. (They are open to all guests when not occupied by Vacation Club members.) Each studio has a queen-size bed, a double sleeper sofa, and a fold-down bunk-size bed, plus a kitchenette with a microwave, coffeemaker, and mini fridge, as well as a flat-screen TV and DVD player. Larger villas sleep four to eight guests, and all have a dining area, kitchen, laundry room, and a master bath with whirlpool tub. They include a king-size bed in the master bedroom, living room with queen sleeper sofa, and either two queen-size beds or a queen-size bed and a double sleeper sofa. Yacht Club guests may have up to two dogs stay in their room for an additional $75 per night.

WHERE TO EAT: The themes of yachting and the sea play a role in the eateries found at their respective resorts. Room service is available.

Beach Club Marketplace: Stop here for hot and cold breakfast items such as scrambled eggs, croissants, and pastries, as well as soup, salads, sandwiches, and snacks. Rapid Fill mugs may be purchased and filled here, too.

Beaches and Cream Soda Shop: An old-fashioned spot with massive appeal, this classic soda fountain doles out frosty shakes, malts, and varied ice cream sundaes. Burgers and sandwiches are served as well. The newly refurbished and expanded happy place is located near the Stormalong Bay pool.

Cape May Cafe: An indoor clambake is held here at the Beach Club each night. The varied and bountiful buffet features several types of clams and mussels, plus beef ribs and chicken. A character breakfast (hosted by Minnie and friends) is presented daily.

Ale & Compass Restaurant: The lighthouse-themed eatery serves three meals a day. It's at Yacht Club, just off the lobby (next to Ale & Compass Lounge).

Hurricane Hanna's Waterside Bar & Grill: Sandwiches, seafood rolls, salads, burgers, and snacks are served here. A full bar is offered and poolside beverage service is available. If you buy a refillable resort mug, this is one spot to top it off during your stay.

Market at Ale & Compass: A sleek snack bar, the Market offers freshly prepared selections for breakfast, lunch, and dinner. Breakfast items include spinach and feta pastries; ham, egg, and cheese rolls; oatmeal; and sticky buns. Lunch and dinner feature paninis (grilled chicken, veggie, or Italian), soup, and more. There is a grab-and-go area with snack items to choose from. Rapid Fill mugs may be purchased and filled here.

Yachtsman Steakhouse: Select cuts of aged beef are the specialty of the house. Fresh seafood, pasta, and poultry are also offered. A special wine-tasting event takes place here beginning at 3 P.M. on the second Wednesday of each month.

WHERE TO DRINK: The lounges in the Yacht and Beach Club resorts offer a variety of specialty drinks in relaxing seaside settings.

Ale & Compass Lounge: This Yacht Club lounge features a full bar, plus a small bites menu. Revelers may imbibe from about 11:30 A.M. until about 1 A.M. The popular watering hole can be quite cacophonous.

Crew's Cup: A cozy lounge, Crew's Cup is the place to try local beer and brews shipped from the world's seaports—as well as spirits, soft drinks, and appetizers. It's next door to Yachtsman Steakhouse.

Martha's Vineyard: This relatively quiet lounge at the Beach Club offers selections from American and international vineyards, served by the glass or bottle, as well as a full bar and appetizers.

WHAT TO DO: There is enough to do here to fill a vacation. A sand volleyball court may be found near the Beach Club. Equipment is available at no cost at the Ship Shape health club. Bikes and boats may be rented. Kids may train to be a pirate or a mermaid in special kid-only programs (fees apply). Pick up a resort entertainment schedule at the Front Desk.

Fantasia Gardens Mini Golf complex is close by, and guided fishing excursions may be arranged (see *Sports & Recreation*). And last but not least, the BoardWalk entertainment district is a short walk around the lake.

Boating: Pontoons, Boston Whaler Montauks, Sea Raycers, and other boats are available for rent at Bayside Marina (shared by the Yacht and Beach Club resorts).

Campfire: Resort guests are invited to gather round the campfire (on select nights) and roast marshmallows. (Marshmallows are free for Yacht or Beach Club guests; s'mores kits start at about $5.) Afterward, everyone is treated to a screening of a Disney film. The campfire may be cancelled due to inclement weather.

Health Club: The Ship Shape health club has strength and cardio machines and is open around the clock to resort guests age 14 and older. (Use your MagicBand or request an "after hours" key card during operating hours.) Massage and facial services are available. For an appointment, call 407-939-7727.

Salon: The Ship Shape salon sits between Yacht & Beach Club, poolside. It offers a full line of hair care services; call 407-939-7727.

Shopping: At the Yacht Club, Market at Ale & Compass is an all-purpose shop stocked with character merchandise, and sundries. At the Beach Club, the Beach Club Marketplace has a similar selection.

Swimming: Between the marina and the beach is the centerpiece of the dual resort—Stormalong Bay, a three-acre pool that's like a mini water park. There is a lagoon expressly for relaxed bathing, and another with currents, jets, and sand-bottomed areas. Several whirlpools are scattered throughout the area. Adjacent to the main pool is a shipwreck, where guests can enjoy a waterslide. There is one unguarded pool and whirlpool at the far end of each hotel. There is also an unguarded pool by the Beach Club Villas. Guests may sunbathe on the beach, though swimming is not permitted.

Tennis: There is one lighted tennis court on the Yacht Club side of the property. Rental equipment is available at the Bayside Marina.

TRANSPORTATION: Guests travel to Epcot and Disney's Hollywood Studios via FriendShip water taxis or walkways. (It takes about 3 to 5 minutes to walk to Epcot's International Gateway entrance and about 20 to hoof it to the Studios.) Buses go to Magic Kingdom, Animal Kingdom, Disney Springs, Typhoon Lagoon, and Blizzard Beach (a bus transfer may be required for the water parks).

PHOTO BY JILL SAFRO

WDW resort benefits, most notably access to Extra Magic Hours and a 60-day advance window for Fastpass+ selections. (To do so, you must create a My Disney Experience account via the mobile app or website and link your hotel confirmation number and the last name on the reservation.) One notable difference: Guests cannot use their room keys to charge purchases on Walt Disney World property, with the exception of within the Swan and Dolphin resorts themselves. The direct line for the Swan and Dolphin is 407-934-3000. Reservations for either resort may be made visiting *www.swandolphin.com*, through Facebook at *www.facebook.com/swananddolphin*, or by calling 888-227-1500.

HOT TIP!

The Swan and Dolphin resorts run seasonal promotions throughout the year. For information, call 888-828-8850, or visit *www.swandolphin.com.*

SWAN & DOLPHIN

These sister resorts, situated near the shores of Crescent Lake, can easily be distinguished by the 47-foot swan and 56-foot dolphin statues that top them. The waterfalls, rows of palm trees, and beachfront location all reflect the tropical Florida landscape that was their inspiration. Both hotels were designed by noted architect Michael Graves as examples of "entertainment architecture." The turquoise waves on the colored facade of the Swan's 12-story main building and two 7-story wings are clearly evidence of this design, as is the Dolphin's exterior mural, which features a banana-leaf pattern. The soaring 27-story triangular tower at the center of the Dolphin is flanked by four 9-story guestroom wings.

The resorts—which recently underwent a $150 million renovation—share extensive convention facilities, many recreational options, and a host of restaurants. The Swan and Dolphin are operated by Westin and Sheraton, respectively, but are treated as Walt Disney World resorts; guests here enjoy most

ROOMS: All rooms have a fresh look, with soothing hues of white, blue, and gray, plus sleek, modern furniture. Amenities include weekday newspaper delivery, digital safes, mini fridge, coffeemaker (with tea and Starbucks coffee), irons and boards, two dual-line telephones (with complimentary, unlimited local and long-distance service), two bottles of water per day, and enhanced high-speed, wireless Internet access. Rooms equipped for guests with disabilities are available. Valet parking is $33 per day (plus tax); self-parking costs about $24 a day.

There are 756 rooms and 55 suites at the Swan, each with one king-size or two queen-size "Westin Heavenly Beds." At the Dolphin, the 1,514 rooms and 112 suites feature two double beds or one king-size heavenly bed. Swan rooms also include a vanity and dressing area.

Meetings and Conventions

Convention centers at Walt Disney World range in size from about 20,000 to 300,000 square feet. The Dolphin's center is the largest. The Contemporary has three ballrooms and a spacious pre-function area with lots of natural light. The convention center at the Yacht & Beach Club is reminiscent of a grand turn-of-the-century New England town-meeting hall. The Grand Floridian Resort and Spa has a lavish center with silk brocade walls. The BoardWalk offers a smaller conference area with a lakeside gazebo for outdoor events. And Coronado Springs, the first moderately priced Disney resort to offer convention facilities, boasts one of the largest hotel ballrooms in the U.S.

Among the unique services available to Disney conventioneers is the use of Disney characters and performers for events. Special events can even be held in the parks. Resort business centers have clerical staffs and computers, in addition to faxing and photocopying equipment. (These services are available to all resort guests.)

Those interested in scheduling a convention should call 321-939-7221. Organizers are advised to book their events six months in advance, especially for large groups.

WHERE TO EAT: In addition to many restaurant choices, 24-hour room service provides an extensive all-day dining menu. (The room service here is among the best at Walt Disney World.)

Cabana Bar & Beach Club: This poolside spot near the Dolphin serves burgers, grilled chicken sandwiches, flatbreads, and more. The bar serves specialty drinks.

The Fountain: Homemade ice cream is the specialty at this Dolphin eatery. Huge sundaes, shakes, malts, and burgers are also offered.

Fresh: Designed to resemble a cheerful marketplace, this Dolphin spot serves breakfast and lunch only. The menu features "healthy, sustainable, and organic" fare.

Fuel: The chic Dolphin snack bar invites guests to fuel up with specialty coffees, baked goods (including bagels, muffins, and croissants), ready-made sandwiches, salads, beverages, and snacks, plus a make-your-own frozen yogurt sundae bar.

Garden Grove Cafe: This Swan eatery, which features a park-like atmosphere, serves three meals daily. A buffet breakfast with Disney characters is held on Saturdays and Sundays, while a character dinner takes place nightly.

Il Mulino New York Trattoria: The highly acclaimed Italian restaurant is located on the first floor of the Swan. The setting, which is somewhat reminiscent of an old-world trattoria, is relaxed yet vibrant. Features such as *Piatti per il Tavolo* (family-style dining) and wood-fired pizzas complement Il Mulino New York's family-friendly Walt Disney World locale.

Picabu: A cafeteria with a bit of flair. The 24-hour convenience store here sells snacks and sundries. It has Starbucks coffee, too.

Shula's: An upscale celebration of two American favorites: steak and professional football. It's a bit pricey, but the steaks are superb and the side orders are big enough to share. There is a kids' menu (chicken, cheeseburgers, etc.). The (enforced) dress code at Shula's is business casual.

Splash Terrace: A poolside cafe near the Swan serving specialty sandwiches, pizza, and snacks. A full-service bar is also located here.

Todd English's bluezoo: This eatery features coastal cuisine, beef, and chicken dishes with international and domestic influences.

WHERE TO DRINK: It's easy to find a nice cocktail spot in this neck of the woods.

Java Bar: This lobby spot at the Swan offers a quick bite for early birds on the go. Enjoy specialty coffees, light breakfast items, soft drinks, and fresh pastries until 6:30 P.M. most days.

Kimonos: The Asian decor makes this Swan lounge an inviting place for sake, sushi, and other Japanese selections. Karaoke is a house specialty. This place is generally hopping a bit later than most other Walt Disney World resort lounges.

Phins: A snazzy Dolphin lobby lounge featuring beer, wine, specialty drinks, and appetizers. Hours are generally 12 P.M. to 2 A.M.

Shula's Steak House Lounge: Settle into a comfy chair and sip a drink in this swanky lounge adjacent to Shula's dining room.

WHAT TO DO: The Swan and Dolphin share many recreation options. Volleyball nets and hammocks are set up on the beach. The Fantasia Gardens Miniature Golf complex and BoardWalk are nearby (the proximity to BoardWalk and Epcot is a big plus). Disney's Hollywood Studios is a FriendShip water taxi ride (or about a 20-minute walk) away.

Arcade: A game room with video games, air hockey, and more is located near Picabu on the first floor of the Dolphin. Fees apply.

Boating: Watercraft are available for rent on the beach between the Swan and Dolphin. Swan-shaped paddle boats may be borrowed for free by guests staying at the Swan or Dolphin (weather permitting). Simply present a valid resort ID and an attendant will escort you to your fine feathered float. Life jackets should be worn by all passengers.

HOT TIP!

As part of a "green initiative," the Swan and Dolphin resorts reward guests for passing up housekeeping services. For each eligible night that service is declined guests receive one $5 Food and Beverage voucher for participating outlets. (Note that rooms are automatically serviced every four days.)

Campfire: Nightly campfires—complete with complimentary s'mores fixin's for registered Swan and Dolphin guests—take place on the resorts' shared White Sand Beach. The campfire may be cancelled due to inclement weather.

Children's Program: Camp Dolphin welcomes kids (potty-trained) ages 4 through 12 and has supervised activities throughout the day. There's no charge from 11 A.M. to 4 P.M. (a parent must be present). From 4 P.M. to midnight, cost is about $12 per child, per hour (no parent presence required). Guests get two hours for free when they dine at Shula's, Todd English's bluezoo, or Il Mulino or get a 75-minute treatment at Mandara spa. A same-day receipt is required. Camp Dolphin space is limited, so book ahead.

Health Clubs: There is a fitness center near the pool area at the Dolphin and a smaller health club near Splash Terrace at the Swan.

Playground: A sandy play area with swings and jungle gyms is near the grotto pool.

Shopping: Disney Cabanas, located in the Swan lobby, sells character merchandise and sundries. There are three shops at the Dolphin: Accents offers resort-wear for men and women; Disney Gifts & Sundries is the place to find essentials and character goods; the Cabana Beach Hut, near the Dolphin pool area, offers "pool-fun" essentials. And the 24-hour convenience store within Picabu sells grocery items and sundries.

New Resort Report

Disney's Riviera resort may be the newest hotel on WDW property for now, but it's soon to be joined by several newcomer neighbors. Over the course of the next several years, Walt Disney World's resort landscape will expand to include The Cove, Reflections—A Disney Lakeside Lodge, and a highly anticipated Star Wars-themed resort.

The Cove is brought to you by the folks behind the Walt Disney World Swan and Dolphin. The 14-story tower, which takes over the area once occupied by Swan and Dolphin tennis courts, is expected to have about 350 rooms and an elegant rooftop eatery (perfect for fireworks viewing). It should be open for business in 2020. To learn more, call 407-934-4290.

Reflections—A Disney Lakeside Lodge is slated to be the 16th Disney's Vacation Club property. On track to open by 2022, the 900-room "celebration of nature" is currently under construction near Disney's Fort Wilderness Resort & Campground (on the site of the long-defunct water park known as River Country).

Last, but certainly not least, is the much ballyhooed Star Wars-themed hotel. Billed as an immersive luxury resort, guests "leave Earth" when they check in and enter a Star Wars-riddled realm. How thorough is the theming? Every window offers a view of space! As of press time, an opening date for this Disney's Hollywood Studios-area resort had not yet been revealed. For details on this and the aforementioned resorts-in-progress, use the My Disney Experience app or website, or visit *www.disneyworld.com*.

Spa and Salon: The Mandara Spa (at the Dolphin) offers full-service body treatments, plus hairstyling, manicures, pedicures, and more.

Swimming: There are two lap pools, a themed grotto pool with slides, and a kiddie pool between the Swan and Dolphin. Several whirlpools are scattered about the area. All pools are unguarded. Life jackets may be borrowed (no charge). Be sure to keep an eye on your little splashers at all times.

TRANSPORTATION: Guests may travel to Epcot and Disney's Hollywood Studios via FriendShip water taxis or walkway. (It takes about 10 minutes to walk to Epcot's back entrance and about 20 minutes to reach Disney's Hollywood Studios on foot. Water taxis don't move much faster—and they make multiple stops—so allow plenty of time to reach either destination.) Buses go directly to the Magic Kingdom, Animal Kingdom, and Disney Springs. A transfer may be required for Typhoon Lagoon and Blizzard Beach.

PHOTO BY JILL SAFRO

BOARDWALK INN & VILLAS

The enchantment of a bygone era is recaptured at the BoardWalk. The resort combines a waterside entertainment complex with deluxe hotel accommodations and vacation villas. Dining, recreation, shopping, and entertainment venues line the boardwalk, and twinkling lights trim the buildings. The ambience continues throughout, with detailed architecture featuring colorful facades, flagged turrets, and striped awnings, all reminiscent of the turn of the 20th century. Board-Walk resort guests may walk or take a water taxi to Epcot's International Gateway entrance and Disney's Hollywood Studios. The phone number for BoardWalk Inn & Villas is 407-939-5100.

ROOMS: Accommodations here evoke the charm of early Eastern-seaboard inns. Most have private balconies or patios. The BoardWalk Inn has 372 deluxe hotel rooms decorated with cherrywood furniture, boardwalk postcard-print curtains, and light green accents. Guestrooms at the inn sleep up to five, and feature two queen-size beds (or one king-size bed) and a single, sleeper couch. Romantic two-story garden suites each have a private garden enclosed by a white picket fence. They sleep four, and have a living room on the first floor and a king-size bed in the unenclosed, bedroom loft. The inn also has club-level rooms and suites.

The 282 two-bedroom equivalents are collectively called BoardWalk Villas. These are Disney Vacation Club villas, available to everyone when not occupied by members. Each studio has a queen-size bed and double sleeper sofa, plus a kitchenette with microwave, coffee-maker, and small refrigerator. Larger (one-, two-, and three-bedroom) villas sleep 4 to 12 people, and feature dining areas, fully equipped kitchens, laundry facilities, master baths with whirlpool tubs, and flat-screen TV with DVD player. They also include a king-size bed in the master bedroom, a living room with a queen sleeper sofa, and a queen-size bed, plus a double sleeper sofa in any additional bedrooms. All rooms have an iron and board, hair dryer, and free Wi-Fi.

WHERE TO EAT: This resort has a wealth of dining and snacking options. A variety of vendors along the boardwalk tempt with hot dogs, pizza, crêpes on a stick, gourmet coffee, and more. For those looking to eat in, room service is available.

Ample Hills Creamery: Enjoy handcrafted ice cream made with hormone-free milk from grass-fed cows and organic cane sugar at this shop next to the ESPN Club. If you can't commit to one (or two) of the day's flavors, fear not: a small sample will help a heap. Ice cream is served in cups, cones, and in sundaes. Every flavor can be made into a creamy milk shake.

Big River Grille & Brewing Works: This working brewpub features a full menu, complemented by fresh specialty ales. Guests may observe the brewmaster through floor-to-ceiling glass walls.

BoardWalk Bakery: A popular stop that offers baked goods, sandwiches, soups, and salads. This is also the place to purchase and refill a Rapid Fill resort mug.

BoardWalk Pizza Window: This handy walk-up window sells pizza by the slice and the pie. It's open for lunch and dinner.

BoardWalk Carts: Stands along the boards offer snacks such as hot dogs, funnel cakes, pretzels, nachos, wings, and chili fries.

ESPN Club: A serious sports bar for serious sports fans, ESPN provides sports video entertainment and all-day dining. Get there early if a big game (or game day) is scheduled.

Flying Fish: The Fish features a show kitchen, and its upscale menu emphasizes expertly prepared seafood, steak, and fresh seasonal items.

Trattoria al Forno: An Italian eatery, Trattoria features old-world favorites for the whole family. The morning meal is a character affair.

WHERE TO DRINK: Guests have a multitude of options right in their backyard.

AbracadaBAR: This enchanting enclave proffers potent potables and alcohol-free elixirs in an escapist environment.

Atlantic Dance Hall: This waterfront nightclub is an elegantly designed dance spot. You must be at least 21 to enter. There's usually no charge, but there are exceptions for special events.

Belle Vue Lounge: Listen to old-time tunes on antique radios and play board games in this cocktail lounge near the lobby. The room is open all day, but the bartender doesn't arrive until about 5 P.M.

Jellyrolls: Dueling pianos provide entertainment in a casual warehouse atmosphere. The cover charge is about $15 nightly. You must be at least 21 to enter Jellyrolls and able to prove it. Note that this place cranks the A.C. year-round.

Leaping Horse Libations: The carousel-themed pool bar at Luna Park serves a variety of cocktails, as well as sandwiches and snacks.

Resort Roundup

What's the best place to stay at Walt Disney World? It's a tough question—and one that Birnbaum editors are asked all the time. The answer? Well, it depends. Do you have a favorite park? What's your price range? Will a clown's tongue that doubles as a pool slide make your day? All factors to consider. Here are our favorites in each of WDW's price categories:

BIRNBAUM'S ★BEST★ **DELUXE**

BoardWalk: In addition to a picturesque setting, this resort is all about location. For starters, you can walk to Epcot (and the Studios if you're feeling ambitious). Of course, you can always take a water taxi. You're a stone's throw from the more serene Yacht & Beach Club resorts, but get to enjoy the bustling excitement of the Board-Walk entertainment district. Strolls around Crescent Lake are soothing for the soul. Excellent dining options abound. And the circus-themed pool area is fun for all ages. In our opinion, BoardWalk is as Disney as it gets.
Honorable mentions: Contemporary, Grand Floridian, and Polynesian Village

BIRNBAUM'S ★BEST★ **MODERATE**

Port Orleans Riverside: One need not be a Southern aristocrat to live like one. Many of the guest buildings at this resort, formerly known as Dixie Landings, were designed to look like historic mansions. Even the food court has a certain Southern ambience. There's a table-service restaurant and a cozy lounge (which may offer entertainment). Kids enjoy dropping their hooks in the fishing hole (strictly catch-and-release) and splashing in the free-form pool on Ol' Man Island. Pretty gardens and a relatively reasonable price add to the appeal.
Honorable mention: Caribbean Beach Resort

BIRNBAUM'S ★BEST★ **VALUE**

Art of Animation: This colorful WDW Value property has some of the boldest theming around and a top-notch food court—but what sets it apart is the splashy Big Blue Pool. The family suites, which fall under Disney's Moderate resort category, are a good value (during most times of year). We're particularly fond of the *Cars*–themed accommodations, but all areas get a happy thumbs-up. And having two bathrooms (in the suites) is a valuable bonus for most traveling parties. The resort is part of the Disney Skyliner transportation system, too.
Honorable mention: Pop Century

WHAT TO DO: The three-quarter-mile pathway encircling Crescent Lake provides a ready venue for walkers and joggers. Guests may rent boats from Yacht & Beach Club's Bayside Marina. The Fantasia Gardens Miniature Golf complex is nearby. At the resort itself, Ferris W. Eahlers Community Hall lends and rents equipment for many recreational pursuits and hosts rainy day activities. Fishing excursions can be arranged. A resort entertainment schedule is available at the resorts Front Desk.

Arcade: Side Show Games Arcade has a small selection of interactive games.

Surrey Biking: A (strenuous) trip around Crescent Lake on a pedal-powered surrey bike (a canopied quadracycle) is also offered on the boardwalk. Bikes, which accommodate 2 or 4 people, rent for about $25.

Health Club: Muscles & Bustles health club has steam rooms, modern exercise machines and circuit-training equipment. The health club is open 24 hours a day for BoardWalk resort guests.

Midway Games: This area on the BoardWalk's WildWood Landing features games of luck and skill similar to those found along traditional boardwalks. There is a charge to play.

Shopping: Dundy's Sundries in the lobby is the source for basic necessities. Character Carnival on the boardwalk has children's apparel as well as character merchandise. Screen Door General Store stocks some groceries, dry goods, snacks, and beverages. Thimbles & Threads, also on the boardwalk, carries apparel for men and women. Wyland Galleries features marine and environmental art.

Swimming: The BoardWalk's swimming area, Luna Park, has a pool with a 200-foot slide, "Keister Coaster," patterned after a wooden roller coaster. The resort has two unguarded pools. There are three whirlpools, one in each pool area.

Tennis: There are two tennis courts (with lights). Rent equipment at Community Hall.

TRANSPORTATION: Guests travel to Epcot and Disney's Hollywood Studios via boats or walkways. (It takes about 10 minutes to walk to International Gateway, aka Epcot's back door. The stroll to Disney's Hollywood Studios takes about 20 minutes.) Buses transport guests to the Magic Kingdom, Animal Kingdom, Typhoon Lagoon, Blizzard Beach (a bus transfer may be required for the water parks), and Disney Springs.

Disney Vacation Club

Disney Vacation Club (DVC) grants members the convenience of flexible vacations from year to year, with the ability to choose when and where to visit, how long to stay, and the type of accommodations. It starts with the purchase of a real estate interest in a DVC property. For a one-time purchase price and annual dues, members can enjoy vacation stays at Aulani Resort & Spa (in Oahu, Hawaii); Bay Lake Tower at Contemporary resort, Animal Kingdom Villas, The Villas at Disney's Grand Floridian Resort & Spa, Old Key West Resort, Beach Club Villas, BoardWalk Villas, the Boulder Ridge Villas and Copper Creek Villas & Cascade Cabins at Disney's Wilderness Lodge (note that the "Boulder Ridge Villas" and the "Copper Creek Villas & Cascade Cabins" are separate DVC properties), Saratoga Springs Resort & Spa, the Polynesian Villas & Bungalows, and the new Riviera resort at WDW; Disney's Vero Beach Resort in Florida; Disney's Hilton Head Island Resort in South Carolina; and the Villas at Disney's Grand Californian Resort & Spa in Anaheim, California; plus access to additional destinations around the globe. Through Member Getaways, DVC members may also elect to stay at their choice of more than 500 resorts around the globe, including most Disney owned-and-operated resorts and the Disney Cruise Line.

Disney's Vero Beach Resort is a two-hour drive from Walt Disney World. It has villa-type accommodations comparable to those at Disney's Old Key West Resort—with lush surroundings, the beach, and local sights. The proximity makes it easy to tack a beach vacation onto a WDW visit.

Disney Vacation Club information centers may be found at each of the Walt Disney World hotels and theme parks. For more information, call 800-800-9100, or visit *www.disneyvacationclub.com*.

Disney Springs Area

PORT ORLEANS FRENCH QUARTER

This 1,008-room resort invites comparisons to the historic French Quarter of New Orleans.

Starting at the entrance gate, with its wrought-iron portal and overgrown landscape, the appeal of the Delta City surrounds arriving guests. The entry drive leads to the heart of the "city," which is Port Orleans Square. The central building was based on a turn-of-the-20th-century mint. The Mint houses check-in facilities, a shop, food court, and an arcade. It has a vaulted ceiling, and the check-in desks are designed as bank-teller windows. The musical notes in the mural are the notes to "When the Saints Go Marching In." To reach Port Orleans French Quarter, call 407-934-5000.

ROOMS: The guestrooms are located in seven 3-story buildings (with elevators). Each room has two queen beds; some king-size beds are available. The rooms are a bit smaller than the standard rooms at the more expensive Disney hotels, but they are comfortable for a family of four. (Rooms with a small bunk can fit 5, provided that the fifth person is kid-sized.) Buildings are brightly colored and have wrought-iron railings of varying designs. Connecting rooms may be requested but can't be guaranteed. The least expensive rooms overlook gardens or parking areas, and the most expensive rooms offer water views. All guestrooms have a coffeemaker (with coffee), mini fridge, and Wi-Fi.

PHOTO BY JILL SAFRO

WHERE TO EAT: A counter-service food court has several dining options. Disney Springs, and its plethora of eateries, is accessible by boat or bus.

Sassagoula Floatworks & Food Factory: A variety of specialty foods is available in this food court, including gumbo, chicken with red beans and rice, freshly made beignets, and other traditional Creole dishes. Cheeseburgers, veggie burgers, pizza, ice cream, and baked goods are also on the menu.

WHERE TO DRINK: A pool bar operates seasonally, and guests on a quest for a cocktail may head to Port Orleans Riverside—it's a short bus ride away. Of course, there's always Disney Springs or any theme park. (Epcot has quite a few sipping spots.)

WHAT TO DO: A themed pool is the highlight of the recreational opportunities here.

Arcade: South Quarter Games is located at Port Orleans Square. The arcade has a selection of state-of-the art, interactive games.

Biking: Bicycles and surrey bikes are available for rent at Port Orleans Riverside.

Carriage Rides: Refer to page 233 for details on horse-drawn carriage rides.

Fishing: Two-hour guided fishing excursions are available (see *Sports & Recreation*).

Shopping: Jackson Square Gifts & Desires, located at Port Orleans Square, features Disney character merchandise, clothing bearing the Port Orleans resort logo, and sundries.

Swimming: A pool dubbed Doubloon Lagoon was built around a bright blue sea serpent. The waterslide is the mythical creature's tongue—kids love it. There is a whirlpool, too. Port Orleans French Quarter guests are also invited to swim in the pool at Ol' Man Island at Port Orleans Riverside.

TRANSPORTATION: Buses transport guests to the Magic Kingdom, Epcot, Disney's Hollywood Studios, Animal Kingdom, Typhoon Lagoon, Blizzard Beach (a transfer may be required for the water parks), and Disney Springs. Small water taxis transport guests along the Sassagoula River to Disney Springs, too.

PHOTO BY JILL SAFRO

PORT ORLEANS RIVERSIDE

Here, the city feel of the French Quarter gives way to the rural South. The resort is divided into "parishes." Closest to the "city," guestrooms are found in Mansion homes; farther upriver are the Bayou guestrooms, with a more rustic feel. The phone number for the Port Orleans Riverside resort is 407-934-6000.

ROOMS: The 2,047 Mansion and Bayou rooms are of the same size, and each has two queen beds (some king-size beds are available); nearly 400 of the Bayou rooms have a bunk-size bed (recommended for kids under age 9) as well. The Magnolia Bend Mansion rooms are situated in elegant manor homes with stately columns and grand staircases. The Bayou rooms are in rustic, weathered-wood buildings that are tucked among flora native to the area. Although all of the buildings have two to three floors, only the Magnolia Bend Mansions have elevators.

The Bayou guestrooms surround Ol' Man Island, a 3½-acre recreational area with a pool, playground, and fishing hole. Decorative touches include wood and tin armoires and pedestal sinks with brass fittings. The closet space is not enclosed. The rooms are a bit small, but they can accommodate four guests. Rooms have a coffee-maker (with coffee), fridge, and Wi-Fi (free).

More than 500 Riverside rooms invite guests to live like royalty. These "Royal Guest Rooms" have special touches inspired by Disney's animated classics (all featuring royalty of some sort), ornately decorated beds with fiber-optic special effects, custom bed coverings and drapes, artwork featuring Princess Tiana and other Disney royals, and more. If you want the royal treatment while residing at Port Orleans Riverside, make your wishes known when you book the room. Note that the rates for these rooms run higher than for standard rooms.

WHERE TO EAT: In addition to a restaurant and food court, the hotel offers limited pizza delivery from 4 P.M. until midnight.

Boatwright's Dining Hall: This 200-seat table-service eatery, located next to Riverside Mill, serves Cajun specialties and American fare for dinner. Reservations are recommended.

Riverside Mill: This food court resembles an old-fashioned cotton mill with a working waterwheel that powers the cotton press inside. The five counter-service stands offer all sorts of choices. The basic selections are available for breakfast. **Pizza 'n' Pasta** has pasta dishes, pizza, and bread sticks; **Grill Shop** offers fried shrimp, chicken nuggets, and burgers; Carving Station serves freshly sliced turkey; **Specialty Shop** offers soup and sandwiches; and the **Bakery** serves pastries, ice cream, seasonal cobbler, and more. If you buy a resort refillable mug, the Riverside Mill is where you'll do the refilling.

WHERE TO DRINK: Two lounges possess an enticing degree of charm.

Muddy Rivers: The poolside bar serves beer, wine, cocktails, and soft drinks. Seasonal.

River Roost: Situated in a room designed as a cotton exchange, this lounge features specialty drinks, pub grub, and cabaret-style entertainment (on select evenings).

WHAT TO DO: A wealth of activities are offered at Ol' Man Island, a recreation center featuring a pool, whirlpool, wading pool, interactive fountains, and a playground. Swing by the Front Desk to pick up a resort entertainment schedule.

Arcade: The Medicine Show Arcade features a small selection of games.

Biking: Bicycles may be rented by the hour or the day.

Carriage Rides: Horse-drawn carriages take guests for 25-minute rides throughout the resort grounds. Carriages hold up to 4 adults or 2 adults and 3 small kids. Each trip departs from the marina. Call 407-939-7529 for reservations.

Fishing: Two-hour guided fishing excursions are available (turn to the *Sports & Recreation* chapter for details). It's also possible to drop a line at the Fishin' Hole on Ol' Man Island. Catch-and-release only.

Playground: An elaborate play area is located on Ol' Man Island next to the pool.

Shopping: Fulton's General Store in the Riverside building stocks Disney character merchandise, clothing, and sundries.

Swimming: In addition to the main pool and kiddie pool at Ol' Man Island, there are five unguarded pools (aka "quiet pools") at the resort. Guests may also swim in the Port Orleans French Quarter pool.

TRANSPORTATION: Buses go from Port Orleans Riverside to Magic Kingdom, Epcot, Disney's Hollywood Studios, Animal Kingdom, Typhoon Lagoon, Blizzard Beach, and Disney Springs. (A transfer may be required for the water parks.) Small water taxis ferry guests to and from Disney Springs. A walking path connects this resort with Port Orleans French Quarter.

SARATOGA SPRINGS RESORT & SPA

Just across the lake from the happy hustle and bustle of Disney Springs (reachable by bus, boat, or convenient walkway), this Disney Vacation Club resort is a calm complement to its nearest neighbor. Disney's Saratoga Springs Resort & Spa aspires to recapture the heyday of upstate New York country retreats of the late 1800s. The resort covers 65 acres. Some accommodations are nearly a mile from the main building. To contact Saratoga Springs, call 407-827-1100.

ROOMS: There are studios and villas with one, two, and three bedrooms. A studio is a room with a queen bed and a double sleeper sofa, bathroom, kitchenette, microwave, and coffeemaker. All units have a porch or a balcony, access to guest laundry facilities, and free high-speed Wi-Fi.

One-bedroom villas have a king-size bed in the master suite and a queen-size sleeper sofa in the living room. The one bathroom has a whirlpool tub. The full kitchen has a fridge, stove, microwave, toaster, coffeemaker, dinnerware, and dishwasher. Each unit has a washer and dryer.

Two-bedroom villas at Saratoga Springs have an additional bath and bedroom, with either one queen-size bed and a double sleeper sofa or two queen-size beds. The three-bedroom Grand Villa has similar features as the two-bedroom models, but is about twice the size and has four bathrooms.

The resort's Treehouse Villas, elevated on pedestals and designed to blend into the woodsy environment, offer serene views of the surrounding treetops. Each "cabin-casual" villa features a full kitchen, flat-panel TVs, three bedrooms, and two bathrooms, and sleeps up to nine guests.

WHERE TO EAT: There are two eateries here and dozens across the lake. Several barbecue areas are available to resort guests. Note that the only room service is pizza delivery.

The Artist's Palette: Supposedly set in a converted artist's loft, this spot offers all meals. Among the simple selections are salads, sandwiches, thin-crust pizzas, and baked goods.

Turf Club Bar & Grill: Dinner is served in this spot with a horse-racing motif.

Groceries: In-room grocery delivery is available from Artist's Palette. If you've got a car, ask for directions to a grocery store.

WHERE TO DRINK: In addition to local bars, guests imbibe at nearby Disney Springs.

Backstretch Bar: A poolside watering hole.

On the Rocks: A pool bar serving the usual battery of cocktails.

Turf Club Bar & Grill: This spot serves a variety of drinks, plus it has a pool table.

WHAT TO DO: Besides spa treatments, guests may rent bikes, play basketball, swim, walk, swat tennis balls, and more. Be sure to pick up a resort entertainment schedule at the Front Desk.

Arcade: Expect to find the usual bells and whistles at "Win, Place, or Show."

Biking: Bicycles may be rented from Horsin' Around Rentals. (Kids age 16 and under must wear bike helmets.)

Golf: The resort is adjacent to the Lake Buena Vista course. (Non-metal spikes are required.)

Health Club: This spot features strength and cardio machines and weight lifting equipment.

Playground: The small play area near an unguarded pool is open to kids ages 2 through 12. Be sure to supervise youngsters at all times.

Shopping: The Artist's Palette stocks a variety of souvenirs and sundries.

Spa: Senses, the award-winning spa, offers massage therapy, manicures, facials, aromatherapy, and more. Call 407-939-7727 for an appointment.

Swimming: High Rock Spring cascades down rugged rock work and feeds into a free-form, heated zero-depth-entry pool. The splash zone has a waterslide, two whirlpools, and a play area for kids. There are four unguarded pools, too.

Tennis: Two clay courts are available on a first-come, first-served basis from 9 A.M. to 10 P.M. Equipment may be borrowed from Horse Around Rentals.

TRANSPORTATION: Buses go from the resort to all theme and water parks. Boats ferry guests to Disney Springs (it's about 10 to 25 minutes on foot). The internal bus makes 7 stops throughout the resort. Buses arrive every 20 to 60+ minutes.

PHOTO BY JILL SAFRO

DISNEY'S OLD KEY WEST RESORT

Escape to the spirit of the Florida Keys. Disney's Old Key West Resort is the original Disney Vacation Club property, but villas not occupied by members are available for nightly rental. It has the laid-back feel of a resort community and all the amenities that go with resort life. The homey, modern accommodations have lots of space and the convenience of kitchen facilities, making the resort nice for longer stays. The telephone number for Old Key West is 407-827-7700.

VILLAS: A studio consists of a large room with two queen-size beds, a table and chairs, a small fridge, free Wi-Fi, microwave, and sink. Bathrooms are spacious. Each of the one-bedroom villas has a king-size bed in the master bedroom and a queen-size sleeper sofa and a sleeper chair in the living room; the master bath has a whirlpool tub, sink, and shower.

The two-bedroom villa features a king-size bed in the master bedroom, two queen-size beds in the second bedroom, living room with queen-size sleeper sofa and TV with DVD player, free Wi-Fi, dining room, and a kitchen with a fridge, dishwasher, toaster, and coffee-maker (with coffee), plus plates, flatware, cooking utensils, and more.

The master bathroom is divided into two rooms with an extra-large whirlpool tub and a sink in one and an oversize shower, sink and vanity, and toilet in the other. There's a porch or balcony off the living room and bedroom, and ceiling fans in each room. The configuration of the two-story, three-bedroom Grand Villas is similar to that of the two-bedroom models, but adds a third bedroom with two double beds. As for capacity, studios sleep 4 and one-bedroom villas sleep 5 people; two-bedroom villas sleep 9 guests, and the two-story, three-bedroom villas accommodate 12.

WHERE TO EAT: In addition to the restaurant, there are grills and picnic tables. Select food and pizza delivery is available from 4 P.M. to midnight.

Good's Food to Go: The perfect place to pick up ham and cheese on Texas toast, bread pudding, and breakfast platters in the morning. Burgers, chicken nuggets, salads, sandwiches, ice cream, pastries, and other snacks are offered later in the day. Soft drinks, cocktails, and (more than a dozen) beers are served.

Olivia's Cafe: This full-service restaurant serves Key West favorites, plus more traditional American fare, for breakfast, lunch, and dinner. Menus change seasonally. Reservations are recommended.

WHERE TO DRINK: The watering holes at Old Key West are as laid-back as they come.

Gurgling Suitcase: This tiny bar serves specialty drinks, wine, beer, soft drinks, and small bites. It's possible to order "to-go" items from Olivia's Cafe, too.

Turtle Shack: This seasonal, poolside spot serves drinks, pizza, sandwiches, and light snacks.

WHAT TO DO: At Conch Flats Community Hall, table tennis, board games, a large-screen TV, DVD rentals, and planned activities are offered. There are basketball, shuffleboard, and volleyball courts, and equipment is available at Hank's Rent 'N Return. Pick up a resort entertainment schedule at the Front Desk.

Arcades: O.K.W. boasts two arcades: Electric Eel Game Room and Flying Fish Game Room.

Biking: Bikes and surrey bikes may be rented from Hank's Rent 'N Return.

Health Club: The Fitness Center offers a nice variety of exercise equipment.

Playground: There are three kids' play areas located throughout the resort.

Shopping: Conch Flats General Store has groceries, books, sundries, and more.

Swimming: The main, guarded pool is located behind the Hospitality House. It features a 125-foot waterslide inside what appears to be a giant sand castle. There is a whirlpool, a kiddie pool, and a sandy play area nearby. The resort has three unguarded pools.

Tennis: There are two lighted tennis courts by the main pool, plus a third on Old Turtle Pond Road.

TRANSPORTATION: Buses go to the theme parks, water parks, and Disney Springs. (A transfer may be required for the water parks, depending on the season.) Build in a bit of extra time for bus travel. Water taxis also make the trip between the resort and Disney Springs.

Animal Kingdom Area

ALL-STAR MOVIES, MUSIC, & SPORTS

The All-Star resorts are among the most vividly themed at Walt Disney World. Each resort has 1,500 to 1,920 rooms housed in ten buildings devoted to five Disney movies, types of music, and sports.

The All-Star Movies resort celebrates five different Disney films: *Toy Story*, *The Mighty Ducks*, *Fantasia*, *101 Dalmatians*, and *The Love Bug*. Resort buildings are adorned with such icons as 40-foot Dalmatians and wildly oversize versions of Buzz Lightyear and Woody.

At the All-Star Music resort, Broadway, country, jazz, rock, and calypso are the themes. A walk-through, neon-lit jukebox; a three-story pair of cowboy boots; and a Broadway theater marquee are among the oversize icons.

Sports fans will find themselves in a world of baseball, football, tennis, surfing, or basketball at the All-Star Sports resort. Brightly colored, larger-than-life football helmets, surfboards, tennis balls, basketball hoops, and baseball bats adorn the buildings.

As value resorts, the All-Star properties offer relatively few frills, but the service and whimsical atmosphere are pure Disney.

Guests check in at Cinema Hall for All-Star Movies, Melody Hall for All-Star Music, or Stadium Hall for All-Star Sports. To reach All-Star Movies, call 407-939-7000; to phone All-Star Music, call 407-939-6000; to contact All-Star Sports, call 407-939-5000.

ROOMS: The guestrooms, measuring 260 square feet, are rather small compared with those at Port Orleans, which are 314 square feet. Each guestroom has two double beds, a vanity area with a sink, a bathroom, free Wi-Fi, a small dresser, and a small table with chairs.

All-Star Music has 215 Family Suites. Each one sleeps up to six and has two bathrooms, a "master" bedroom with its own TV, Wi-Fi (free of charge), and a kitchenette with counter space, mini fridge, sink, microwave, and coffeemaker (with coffee).

WHERE TO EAT: There are three food courts—World Premiere in Cinema Hall, Intermission in Melody Hall, and End Zone in Stadium Hall. Each features a bakery, grab-and-go items, and stations geared to pizza, pasta, salads, and burgers. Each food court has a seating area with a beverage bar. The All-Star resorts deliver pizza and salads to rooms from about 5 P.M. to 1 A.M.

WHERE TO DRINK: There are no traditional lounges at the All-Star resorts; however, the convivial Silver Screen Spirits, Singing Spirits, and Grandstand Spirits pool bars serve drinks throughout the day and evening.

WHAT TO DO: Guests may swim in any of the All-Star resort pools. They may rent boating equipment at any Walt Disney World resort marina. Pick up a resort entertainment schedule at the Front Desk.

Arcades: Each of the All-Star resorts has its own arcade filled with classic and modern games.

Playground: A small playground is located in each hotel's courtyard area.

Shopping: Maestro Mickey's in Melody Hall, Sport Goofy's Gifts and Sundries in Stadium Hall, and Donald's Double Feature in Cinema Hall all have hats, shirts, pins, books, character items, snacks, and sundries.

Swimming: Each hotel has two pools and a kiddie pool. The main pool at All-Star Movies has a *Fantasia* theme (look for Sorcerer Mickey). The smaller Duck Pond Pool is based on *The Mighty Ducks*. At the All-Star Music resort, the Calypso Pool is in the form of a giant guitar, while the Piano Pool bears a striking resemblance to a grand piano. At All-Star Sports, Surfboard Bay has an ocean motif. The smaller Grand Slam Pool pays tribute to our national pastime.

TRANSPORTATION: Buses make pickups at the All-Star Resorts' Cinema Hall, Melody Hall, and Stadium Hall for trips to each of the theme parks, water parks, and Disney Springs. A bus transfer may be required for the water parks.

A word about All-Star resort transportation: The bus service at these "value" resorts tends to be slightly more efficient than at other locations. The combination of fewer stops and connections is a bonus for guests staying here.

PHOTO BY MIKE CARROLL

savanna that practically surround the resort. Birds and all manner of hoofed animals, including giraffes, zebras, and Thomson's gazelles, call the wildlife reserve home. With the freedom to wander within a dozen or so yards of the lodge itself, these enthralling critters allow guests to go on safari without leaving their balconies.

The resort is located about one mile from Disney's Animal Kingdom park (which is accessible by bus). The lobby is a huge, high-ceilinged room, richly appointed with colorful African artwork and artifacts. The biggest draw here is the four-story observation window overlooking the savanna. It's one of many portals through which to gaze upon wildlife.

Like the African game lodges on which it is based, Disney's Animal Kingdom Lodge was constructed using a semicircular design. From overhead, it looks a bit like a horseshoe. This allows for maximum animal-viewing potential. Indeed, a large number of the resort's guestrooms have direct views of the savanna areas. Be sure to specify your viewing preference when you book a room. The telephone number for Disney's Animal Kingdom Lodge is 407-938-3000.

DISNEY'S ANIMAL KINGDOM LODGE & VILLAS

At first glance, Disney's Animal Kingdom Lodge evokes images of a sleepy, little thatched-roof game lodge in the wilds of southern Africa. Upon closer examination, however, it's clear that the only things sleepy or little about this place are the small creatures that live in its shadow. Those animals, along with their more sizable cousins, inhabit acres of meticulously re-created African

ROOMS: The 970 rooms, which are notably smaller than those at other deluxe Disney resorts, feature dark-wood furniture, sand-colored walls, and earth-tone carpets. Deluxe rooms are a tad more spacious than their standard counterparts. Most rooms have two queen beds (some king beds are available) and sleep up to four people; bunk beds are available in some rooms. All rooms have balconies. Suites include a parlor, plus one or two bedrooms; there are king-size or queen-size beds in the bedrooms. Bathrooms have a separate vanity area with double sink. Rooms have

an iron (with board), hair dryer, free Wi-Fi, and small fridge. Club-level service is available.

The Villas are located in Jambo House and in the Kidani Village, an area that features thatched-roof, hewn-timber homes. Also included in this village are a pool, modern fitness center, shop, table-service restaurant, and more. As with all Disney Vacation Club resorts, the homes are available to guests when not being used by members. For information on this member of the Disney Vacation Club family, call 800-800-9100, or visit *www.disneyvacationclub.com.*

HOT TIP!

Balloons are not permitted at Disney's Animal Kingdom Lodge—it's a safety issue for the animals. You can check yours at the Bell Services desk, free of charge.

WHERE TO EAT: In addition to its restaurants, the hotel offers round-the-clock room service.

Boma—Flavors of Africa: Boma is modeled after a bustling African marketplace. The restaurant boasts many types of cuisine in what chefs describe as a "global fusion" style. Served buffet style, the cuisine is a marvelous mix of French, Malaysian, Indian, Chinese, and English.

Jiko—The Cooking Place: The colors of sunset are the backdrop for this reliable restaurant. Wines are from South Africa.

The Mara: A high-quality quick-service eatery, The Mara offers made-to-order flatbreads, African stew, chicken pita, and salads, plus kid-pleasers such as burgers and chicken nuggets.

Sanaa: This Kidani Village star features African- and Indian-inspired cuisine.

WHERE TO DRINK: The lounges here are rustic and inviting. Some even offer the opportunity to sip beverages while observing wildlife.

Cape Town Lounge and Wine Bar: Located inside Jiko—The Cooking Place, this spot features a selection of fine wines from South Africa.

Maji and Uzima Springs: These poolside bars serve specialty and traditional drinks.

Sanaa: A 24-seat lounge, inspired by African spice markets, is within the restaurant of the same name.

Victoria Falls: Set alongside a soothing waterfall, this mezzanine-level lounge offers appetizers, South African wines, beer, and assorted cocktails.

WHAT TO DO: Spying on African wildlife is the main event in these parts. However, if you can manage to

pry yourself away from those hoofed exhibitionists for a bit, there are plenty of other diversions available— including tennis, basketball, shuffleboard, and a barbecue pavilion. Note that guests are welcome to partake in recreational activities offered at other Disney resort hotels, too. An Animal Kingdom Lodge entertainment schedule is available at the Front Desk (at Jambo House and Kidani Village).

Arcades: Pumbaa's Fun & Games and Safari So Good are both stocked with the latest games.

Health Club: The Zahanati Massage and (24-hour) Fitness Center has exercise equipment, sauna, and spa services, including massage, facial, and nail services. To make an appointment, call 407-939-7727. Kidani Village's Survival of the Fittest also offers state-of-the-art exercise equipment.

Playground: The Hakuna Matata playground is located near the Uzima pool.

Shopping: The Zawadi Marketplace stocks Africa-themed gifts, Disney-character merchandise, clothing with the Animal Kingdom Lodge logo, and sundries. Johari Treasures tempts shoppers at Kidani Village.

Swimming: The resort's main pool, Uzima, is meant to resemble a watering hole. More impressive than the size of the zero-depth-entry pool, however, is the view from the pool deck. There is a kids' pool and two whirlpools nearby. Kidani Village is home to another swimming pool (Samawati Springs) and to Uwanja Camp, a watery playground.

Tennis: There are two clay courts available to all Animal Kingdom Lodge guests.

TRANSPORTATION: Buses go to the Magic Kingdom (a 25- to 35-minute ride), Epcot, Disney's Hollywood Studios, Animal Kingdom, Typhoon Lagoon, Blizzard Beach (a transfer may be required for the water parks), and Disney Springs. Buses arrive every 5 to 60 minutes.

CORONADO SPRINGS

An oasis set on the shore of Lago Dorado, the re-imagined resort celebrates the spirit of Spanish, Mexican, and South American explorers, artists, writers, and architects. There is a blend of classic influences, imaginative Disney touches, and modern comforts inside and out. The 2,400 rooms are found in four guest areas that stretch around Lago Dorado, a 22-acre lake. The new 15-story Gran Destino Tower features a two-story lobby and a scenic, rooftop eatery.

It can take 5 minutes or more to walk to the farthest rooms. (Many guests opt to use the bus that makes a loop around the resort.) There is an upscale food court, elaborately themed table service eateries, and a lovely bar and grill atop a new island in Lago Dorado. A convention center offers access to business services. The phone number for Coronado Springs is 407-939-1000.

ROOMS: Standard rooms are a bit smaller than those at Disney's deluxe hotels, but adequate for up to four; each has two queen beds (some king-size beds are available). The sleek rooms are awash in shades of brown with the occasional splash of color and feature faux wood floors (no carpet). Amenities include a coffeemaker, tiny fridge, mini safe, hair dryer, and free Wi-Fi. In the Casitas area, where most suites are located, terra-cotta guest buildings occupy a city-like landscape. In the pueblo-style Ranchos, scattered along a dry streambed, rooms have a rustic feel. Cabanas, located along the rocky palm-lined beach, reflect the casual feel of their namesake. There are Club Level rooms in Gran Destino Tower.

WHERE TO EAT: In addition to four full-service restaurants and food court, limited room service is available for breakfast and dinner.

Cafe Rix: A quick-service eatery, Rix has offerings for breakfast, lunch, and dinner.

Maya Grill: Open for dinner, Maya offers seafood, steak, and authentic Mexican dishes.

El Mercado de Coronado: This nontraditional food court feels like an open-air market. The fare includes tacos, pizza, pasta, and made-to-order omelets.

Rix Sports Bar & Grill: This table-service spot serves three meals a day, and is in the main building.

Three Bridges Bar & Grill: Choose one of three bridges to reach this happy place built in the middle of Lago Dorado. Beer, wine, sangria, Spanish specialty coffees, and cocktails are served here, as is full menu of solid sustenance with a Spanish flair.

Toledo—Tapas, Steak, & Seafood: Perched on the top of Gran Destino Tower, Toledo serves Latin-inspired cuisine and bird's-eye views of Walt Disney World.

WHERE TO DRINK: There are currently five places at which to wet your whistle at Coronado Springs.

Barcelona Lounge: This Gran Destino Tower lobby locale is a coffee house by day and an artisanal cocktail bar by night.

Dahlia Lounge: Perched on the top of Gran Destino Tower, this vibrant lounge (near Toledo—Tapas, Steak, & Seafood) serves beer, wine, cocktails, and small plates.

Laguna Bar: A lagoonside lounge outside the lobby, this spot serves drinks daily.

Rix Sports Bar & Grill: This spot offers a full bar, plus substantial grub.

Siestas Cantina: In the Dig Site area, this pool bar lets swimmers and archaeologists enjoy drinks and light fare (three meals a day).

WHAT TO DO: The resort has volleyball, a short nature trail, and other recreational diversions.

Arcade: Iguana Arcade is in the Dig Site area.

Biking: Rent bikes and surrey bikes at La Marina. Details are subject to change. (Coronado Springs guests are also welcome to rent bikes at any WDW resort.)

La Vida Health Club—Massage, Salon & Fitness: The fitness center offers strength and cardio equipment 24/7. Spa services such as massage and custom facials are offered. And the salon provides hair care services (including a "Perfectly Prepared Princess" package), beard and mustache trim, plus manicures, and pedicures. Hours are usually 9 A.M. until 7 P.M. To make an appointment, call 407-939-7727.

Playground: The Explorer's Playground, part of the Dig Site area, includes a sandbox, complete with Mayan carvings waiting to be excavated.

Shopping: Panchito's Gifts & Sundries is where to find souvenir items with a Southwestern flavor, Disney merchandise, and necessities.

Swimming: The main pool is in the Dig Site recreation area. It surrounds a 50-foot Mayan pyramid and has a 123-foot waterslide. There's a 22-person hot tub (the largest one at WDW) and toddler pool in the Dig Site, too. The resort offers 3 unguarded pools.

TRANSPORTATION: Buses go to the Magic Kingdom, Epcot, Disney's Hollywood Studios, Animal Kingdom, Typhoon Lagoon, Blizzard Beach (a transfer may be required for the water parks), and Disney Springs.

ESPN Wide World of Sports Area

POP CENTURY

What do you get when you mix decades of American pop culture with a Disney resort? Pop Century! Like the All-Star resorts, Pop Century is a vivid celebration of Americana. The 2,880-room resort represents the second half of the twentieth century. The resort's larger-than-life "time capsules" commemorate the toys, fads, dance crazes, and catchphrases that swept the nation from the 1950s through the 1990s. It's groovy . . . you dig?

As a Walt Disney World value resort, the Pop Century property offers few frills, but the service is good, the atmosphere's colorful, and the transportation is efficient. There's even a peaceful lake to stroll around on temperate days. (It's shared by Pop's next-door neighbor, Disney's Art of Animation resort.) Guests check in at Classic Hall, which also features a food and merchandise location, arcade, and guest services desk. To contact Disney's Pop Century resort, call 407-938-4000.

ROOMS: Guestrooms measure 260 square feet (a bit smaller than Port Orleans' rooms, which are 314 square feet). Each room has a queen bed and a pull-down double bed, a vanity area with a sink, a bathroom, a small dresser, a table with chairs, a fridge, and free Wi-Fi.

WHERE TO EAT: The food court features a bakery and a convenience market, plus several stands geared to pizza, pasta, and burgers. The Pop Century resort delivers pizza to guestrooms from about 4 P.M. to midnight. For

security reasons, it is best to ignore flyers placed under your door by unauthorized companies.

WHERE TO DRINK: Liquid refreshments are served at Petals, a bar located near the Hippy Dippy pool.

WHAT TO DO: Guests may swim in any of the Pop Century resort pools and enjoy a 1.4-mile walk or run around Hourglass Lake. Pick up a resort entertainment schedule at the Front Desk.

   Arcade: Revisit classic video games or discover some new ones at Fast Forward arcade.

   Playground: There is one soft-surface playground.

   Shopping: The Everything Pop shop has a selection of books, character merchandise, sundries, and snacks.

   Swimming: The hotel has three pools (shaped like a bowling pin, computer, and a flower), plus a kiddie pool.

TRANSPORTATION: Buses stop at Classic Hall for trips to all theme parks, plus Blizzard Beach, Typhoon Lagoon, and Disney Springs. (A transfer may be required for the water parks.) The new Disney Skyliner stops here, too. (For Skyliner details, see page 65 and visit *www.mydisneyexperience.com*.)

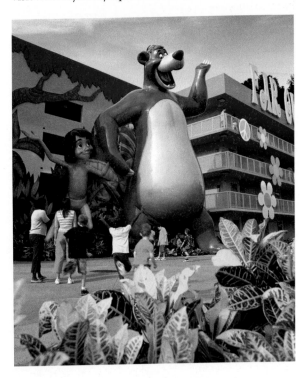

ART OF ANIMATION

The Walt Disney World resort landscape has gotten a serious burst of color thanks to this exceptionally vivid celebration of Disney animation. A Value resort, Disney's Art of Animation made its debut in 2012.

Pop Century's next-door neighbor (the resorts share access to Hourglass Lake and the nearly 1.4-mile jogging path that surrounds it), Art of Animation boasts

WDW Resort Fun

Walt Disney World resort hotels are famous for their immersive theming and enviable proximity to the theme parks, but they can also be playgrounds in and of themselves. Recreation and relaxation opportunities abound, and many of them are complimentary for registered WDW resort guests. Here is a sampling of the possibilities:

• Sunrise yoga
• Games and dance parties at the pool
• Resort tours (i.e., "Jambo House Art Tour" at Animal Kingdom Lodge and "Wonders of the Lodge Art & Architecture Tour" at Wilderness Lodge)
• Trivia challenges
• Nightly campfires (marshmallow roasting optional)
• Disney movies under the stars
• Arts & crafts (fees may apply)

Activities vary from resort to resort (and month to month) and may be cancelled due to inclement weather. For the lineup during your stay, request a Recreation Calendar when you check in.

colossal figures from classic animated films. It also has three themed pools, playgrounds, festive courtyards, a sizable arcade (one of the best at WDW), and a splash zone featuring everyone's favorite clownfish, Nemo. The resort also offers free Wi-Fi, laundry, and dry cleaning (fees apply for the last two services).

ROOMS: The 864 standard rooms, which are housed in *The Little Mermaid*–themed buildings, sleep up to 4 and come with the usual amenities afforded to Walt Disney World's Value resorts (see pages 73–74 for details). Each measures 277 square feet and has two double beds, a vanity area with a sink, a bathroom, a small dresser, a table with chairs, and free Wi-Fi. The 1,120 festive family suites (considered Moderate by Disney), which are themed to *Cars*, *Finding Nemo*, and *The Lion King*, feature 3 separate sleeping areas, accommodate up to 6 guests, and come with 2 flat-screen TVs, a queen-size bed, double-size pull-down bed, and sleeper sofa. Each 565-square-foot suite has a living room, 2 bathrooms, and a kitchenette (with a small refrigerator, microwave, and coffeemaker with coffee and non-dairy creamer).

WHERE TO EAT: The brilliantly hued Landscape of Flavors food court features four unique cooking stations serving international favorites, Mongolian barbecue, burgers, sandwiches, pizza, pasta, fresh smoothies, and hand-scooped gelato. It's open for breakfast, lunch, and dinner. There is a grab-and-go selection, too. In-room pizza delivery is also an option. Guests are welcome to pop over to the nearby Pop Century resort for a bite or a drink, too.

WHERE TO DRINK: The Drop Off is a full-service bar located near the Big Blue Pool.

WHAT TO DO: Guests may swim in any of the Art of Animation resort pools, walk or jog around Hourglass Lake, hit the arcade, and enjoy poolside activities such

Swimming: The hotel has three pools: Flippin' Fins, Cozy Cone, and the recently refurbished Big Blue Pool, plus a *Finding Nemo*–themed splash zone known as The Schoolyard Sprayground.

TRANSPORTATION: Buses stop at Animation Hall for trips to Walt Disney World theme parks, water parks, and the Disney Springs shopping, dining, and entertainment district. (A transfer may be required for the water parks.) The new Disney Skyliner stops here, too. It connects guests with Epcot, Disney's Hollywood Studios, Caribbean Beach resort, and the new Riviera resort. For Skyliner details, see page 65.

as bingo, trivia, dance parties, and more. A resort entertainment schedule is available at the Front Desk. Hair wraps and temporary tattoos are offered (for a fee) from 10 A.M. to 7 P.M. near the Drop Off Pool Bar.

Arcade: Pixel Play Arcade is in Animation Hall, across from Landscape of Flavors. You'll need to purchase a game card to play. Available to all WDW resort guests, the arcade is open round the clock. Boasting a wide variety of gaming diversions, Pixel Play is one of the best arcades at Walt Disney World.

Jogging and Walking: The resort is encircled by a scenic trail that's 1.38 miles long.

Playground: The Righteous Reef playground can be found in the middle of the Finding Nemo courtyard.

Shopping: The cheery Ink and Paint Shop stocks books, pins, character merchandise, Art of Animation resort–themed souvenirs, sundries, snacks, and more.

PHOTO BY JILL SAFRO

Club Level Digs

When selecting a WDW resort you'll find there is a lot to consider: proximity to the parks, recreational opportunities, restaurants, budget, and more. While there's a plethora of possibilities under that "more" umbrella, one of most enticing temptations is known as Club Level. It's a special room category offered at Coronado Springs (in Gran Destino Tower) and most of Disney's Deluxe resort hotels, including Beach Club, BoardWalk, Contemporary, Grand Floridian, Polynesian Village, Saratoga Springs, Wilderness Lodge, and Yacht Club. Prices vary, but for an extra $150 to $300+ per night, Club Level provides a bevy of benefits. Among them: extra Fastpass+ opportunities (for an extra $50 per person, per day, you can get three extra Fastpass+ assignments in addition to the three you get for free) per day on stays of three nights or longer; personalized check-in; evening turn-down service; itinerary planning assistance; printed daily itineraries placed in your room each night; newspapers; access to the Club Level lounge, and more.

While specifics vary a bit from resort to resort, all Club Level lounges serve early-morning coffee and tea, continental breakfast, afternoon snacks, dinnertime appetizers, and evening desserts and cordials. Soft drinks and alcoholic beverages are included. The offerings are more ample at some resorts (BoardWalk, Grand Floridian, and Contemporary spring to mind), but all usually have something for everyone in the party to enjoy. BoardWalk, Contemporary, and Polynesian Village offer fireworks views, too—with the Contemporary and Poly providing the most dramatic fireworks-viewing vistas.

With the exception of Grand Floridian and Contemporary (which have two lounges each), there is one Club Level lounge at every participating resort. These pleasant rooms have a homey feel and are yours to enjoy until midnight of the day you check out of the resort.

Bottom line? Club Level digs definitely fall into the "super splurge" category of vacation indulgences—certainly worth considering if budget allows. And depending on the size of your party and the amount of time you spend bonding with your resort, you may even save a few bucks. Note that details are subject to change.

Resorts near Disney Springs

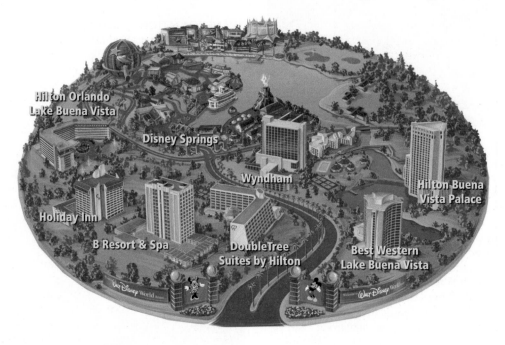

These hotels—Best Western Lake Buena Vista, Double-Tree Suites by Hilton, Wyndham, B Resort & Spa, Hilton Buena Vista Palace, Hilton Orlando Lake Buena Vista, and Holiday Inn—though inside WDW boundaries, are neither owned nor operated by Disney. However, a few have been here since the park opened in 1971 or soon thereafter (under different names), accommodating Mickey enthusiasts from the very beginning. The hotels are not Disney-themed, though several have meals hosted by Disney characters and all have Disney shops. For details, visit *disneyspringshotels.com*.

Often referred to as Disney Springs Resort Area Hotels, they line the mile-long Hotel Plaza Boulevard. The Hilton, Buena Vista Palace, and Wyndham are across from the Disney Springs Marketplace, with its shops, restaurants, and nightlife. The other four properties are a 10- to 25-minute stroll away. The privileges of staying in one of these hotels include:

• Guests who link their reservation to a valid park ticket via the My Disney Experience mobile app or website may enjoy WDW's "Extra Magic Hours" benefit. For additional information, refer to page 22. All details are subject to change.

• Guests at Hotel Plaza Boulevard properties may be able to book Fastpass+ selections as far as 60 days before arrival. (Refer to page 25 for details on this system that allows guests to book advance reservation times for theme park shows and attractions.) Details are subject to change.

• Free bus service to the four theme parks, with limited service to Disney Springs, Typhoon Lagoon, and Blizzard Beach. The buses, which are not part of the Disney transportation network, make stops every 30 minutes, beginning one hour prior to park opening; be sure to allow extra time for bus travel. One bus serves the Hilton, DoubleTree, Holiday Inn, and B Resort & Spa; another serves the other hotels (it takes at least ten minutes to stop at all resorts on the loop). Note that buses load and unload in the middle of the parking lot at some of the parks.

• Easily accessed pedestrian bridges connect Hotel Plaza Boulevard with Disney Springs Marketplace at Disney Springs.

• Flexibility to book tickets for both on- and, in most cases, off-Walt Disney World-property attractions.

• Preferred access to Disney golf courses.

• A "Passport to Savings" coupon book with discounts on dining, shopping, and entertainment.

• Advanced reservations for Disney restaurants.

Guests staying in the resorts on Hotel Plaza Boulevard have to pay to park at Disney theme parks ($25–$50) and they can't charge purchases made at WDW shops and restaurants with a resort ID—though they can buy MagicBands to link with park tickets and

Fastpass+ assignments via the My Disney Experience mobile app or website.

To reserve a Disney Springs Area/Hotel Plaza Boulevard resort, go to *disneyspringshotels.com*, call the resort directly, or contact Walt Disney World Central Reservations (407-934-7639). These resorts are included in several Walt Disney Travel Company packages.

All of the following hotels offer accommodations for travelers with disabilities. To get to Hotel Plaza Boulevard from I-4, take Exit 68. For more information, visit *disneyspringshotels.com*.

BEST WESTERN LAKE BUENA VISTA RESORT:
This 18-story hotel recently underwent an extensive refurbishment. Each of the 308 spacious, smoke-free rooms and suites features either one king-size bed and a queen sofa bed or two queen-size beds, plus floor-to-ceiling windows and furnished balcony. Rooms also come with free high-speed Wi-Fi, flat-screen TV, coffeemaker, refrigerator, electronic safe, hair dryer, and full-size iron with board. Baths have one sink and plenty of counter space. Rooms on the seventh floor and higher offer views of Disney Springs or the other resorts on Hotel Plaza Boulevard.

The hotel also has a fitness center, 24/7 business center, heated swimming pool, small kiddie pool, sundry store, Disney gift shop, and coin-operated guest laundry facilities.

Trader's Island Grill is open for breakfast and dinner. For each paying adult, one child (age 10 or younger) eats at the breakfast buffet for free. The Flamingo Cove offers poolside or inside seating and serves dinner, drinks, and snacks. For guests on the go, there's Marketplace Café.

It offers a variety of grab-and-go items, as well as Pizza Hut Express selections.

Room rates for this hotel range from about $99 to $299. Parking fees apply for both self- and valet parking ($7 and $12 per day, respectively). There is an additional daily resort fee. Best Western Lake Buena Vista Resort, 2000 Hotel Plaza Boulevard, Lake Buena Vista, FL 32830; 407-828-2424 or 800-528-1234; *www.lakebuenavistaresorthotel.com*.

DOUBLETREE SUITES BY HILTON:
The only all-suite hotel in the Disney Springs area, the DoubleTree Suites by Hilton has a stellar staff, homey atmosphere, and low-slung façade reminiscent of WDW's Contemporary hotel. Upon check-in, guests receive the hotel chain's signature warm chocolate chip cookies. Each of the 229 roomy suites (625 square feet) has a separate living and sleeping room. Every living room features a sofa sleeper, a wet bar area with a small refrigerator, coffeemaker and microwave, safe, and a small dining/work area. The one-bedroom suites sleep up to six people with either two queen beds or one king bed. Two bedroom suites are available.

Recreational facilities include a heated pool and whirlpool as well as a splash pad and playground for the kids. For fitness buffs, there is a newly updated fitness center, two lighted tennis courts, and a jogging trail. Evergreen Cafe offers breakfast buffet, lunch, dinner, and room service. The Reef serves up poolside drinks and snacks starting at noon each day. A lobby market provides snacks, drinks, and groceries. There is a Disney store, too.

Rates range from $99 to $399. Parking fees apply for self and valet parking. A daily resort charge includes additional amenities (inquire with the hotel). DoubleTree Suites by Hilton Disney Springs, 2305 Hotel Plaza Blvd., Lake Buena Vista, FL 32830; 407-934-1000 or 800-222-8733; *www.doubletreeguestsuites.com*.

PHOTO BY JILL SAFRO

WYNDHAM: The Wyndham offers two distinct lodging opportunities: A 19-story tower with 232 rooms is known as Wyndham Lake Buena Vista, while the Wyndham Garden section features 394 rooms spread over two 5-story buildings. (Be sure to make your preference known when you make your reservation.) The resort sports a spiffy look, obvious upon stepping into the cheerful Bermuda-themed lobby. Most rooms have two double beds, though 77 king-bed rooms are available. There are 7 spacious suites. All accommodations include a refrigerator, coffeemaker, complimentary Wi-Fi, TV, plush bedding, a safe, hair dryer, iron, and daily newspaper (available upon request). Guests receive a discount at many shops and restaurants at nearby Disney Springs—safely and easily accessible via pedestrian bridge.

Extensive recreational facilities include an exercise room, two lighted tennis courts, a sand volleyball court, and a basketball court. The impressive Oasis Aquatic Playground features a heated pool with zero-depth-entry, interactive features such as water cannons, and a hot tub. Kids-only activities are offered. There's a health club, arcade, and business center, too.

Lakeview Restaurant (on the mezzanine level) serves breakfast and dinner. Breakfast is hosted by Disney characters on Tuesday, Thursday, and Saturday. Sundial is open 24 hours and offers light fare. For beer, wine, cocktails, snacks, and soft drinks, head to the Eclipse lobby bar and Oasis pool bar.

A lobby merchandise shop sells assorted sundries and a selection of Disney-themed souvenirs. Room rates range from about $119 to $209 year-round; suites range from $150 to $350. There is an additional (daily) resort fee for other amenities, as well as a $20-per-day parking fee. Wyndham, 1850 Hotel Plaza Boulevard, Lake Buena Vista, FL 32830; 800-624-4109 (Wyndham Lake Buena Vista); 844-482-8444 for Wyndham Garden; *www.wyndhamlakebuenavista.com*.

HILTON LAKE BUENA VISTA: Aka Hilton Orlando Lake Buena Vista, this hotel gets high marks for its 23 well-groomed acres, laid-back ambience, pool area, and upscale shops. The 814 non-smoking rooms, all of which have been extensively refurbished, are outfitted with two queen or one king bed (suites are available for larger parties) and have minibars, voice mail, safes, and high-speed Internet access.

In addition to its two heated pools, whirlpool, and kiddie pool, the resort has a 24-hour video arcade. There is a 24/7 business center, too.

Among the resort's restaurants and lounges, Andiamo Italian Bistro, open daily from 5:30 P.M. until 11:30 P.M., offers American and Italian cuisine, while Benihana Steakhouse and Sushi serves Japanese favorites, plus entertainment (both eateries serve dinner exclusively); Covington Mill serves breakfast and lunch (with Disney characters attending Sunday breakfast); Rum Largo Poolside Bar and Cafe serves burgers, sandwiches, salads, and tropical drinks alfresco; Mainstreet Market, open 24 hours, is part deli, part country store (serving Starbucks coffee). For light meals, snacks, or drinks, drop

PHOTO BY JILL SAFRO

by John Ts lounge. There is an Avis car rental on the premises. And Disney Springs is a 5- to 10-minute walk away, across a pedestrian footbridge.

Recreational facilities include a fitness room and large game room. Rates range from $99 to $299; suites are $149 to $1,500. Parking charges apply for self-parking and valet parking. Hilton, 1751 Hotel Plaza Blvd., Lake Buena Vista, FL 32830; 407-827-4000 or 800-782-4414; *www.hiltonorlandoresort.com*.

HOLIDAY INN: This family-friendly hotel features 323 nonsmoking rooms that have either one king or two queen beds. Some are available with views of nearby Disney Springs. Guestrooms are decorated with modern touches and include a flat-screen TV with DirecTV, coffeemaker (with coffee), microwave, mini refrigerator, safe, and hair dryer. Bathrooms have granite countertops and feature Bath & Body Works products. Free high-speed Wi-Fi is available in all guestrooms and restaurants, as well as in the lobby.

The Palm Breezes Restaurant, located in the atrium, serves three meals a day (kids under age 11 and under eat free). Palm Breezes has a grab-and-go section, a bar, and provides room service. There is a zero-depth-entry heated pool, a whirlpool, poolside sundeck, Disney store, 24-hour fitness center, and a 24-hour game room. Laundry and dry-cleaning services are offered (fees apply). Parking charges apply for self- and valet parking. There is an additional daily resort fee.

Rates range from approximately $109–$272. Holiday Inn; 1805 Hotel Plaza Blvd., Lake Buena Vista, FL 32830; 407-828-8888 or 888-465-4329; *www.hiorlando.com*.

B RESORT & SPA: A glitzy resident of Hotel Plaza Boulevard, B pulls out all the modern stops in its 394 guestrooms and suites. Amenities include l47-inch HD flat-screen TVs, bunk beds (in select rooms), in-room safe, beverage cooler, and iPad/iPod docking stations. Select rooms have sleeper sofas. Kitchenettes are available in the suites. Free wireless Internet service is a perk offered to all guests. Complimentary loaner gaming consoles are available upon request.

Resort guests may enjoy the outdoor, heated infinity-edge saltwater pool with interactive water features, the 5,000-square-foot B Indulged full-service spa and wellness center, and the B Active fitness center. American Kitchen Bar & Grill, the resort's signature restaurant, features "farm to table dining" and presents a salad bar on the back of a 1950s cherry-red Ford pickup truck that sits proudly in the middle of the restaurant. The Bar at American Kitchen, which offers happy hour from 5 P.M. to 7 P.M. daily, is open until midnight. Stop by the Pick-Up—a casual one-stop shop and ice cream parlor just off the lobby—which serves quick breakfasts, snacks, beverages, sundries, and, of course, ice cream.

B Resort, 1905 Hotel Plaza Boulevard, Lake Buena Vista, FL 32830. For reservations or additional information, visit *www.bresortlbv.com*, or call 407-828-2828 or 888-662-4683.

HILTON BUENA VISTA PALACE: The tallest hotel in the Disney Springs area and the largest of the resorts based at Hotel Plaza Boulevard (it's actually near the intersection of Hotel Plaza Boulevard and Buena Vista Drive) is a cluster of towers set on 27 acres. The resort, which is also known as Hilton Orlando Buena Vista Palace, is quickly (and safely) connected to Disney Springs via pedestrian bridge.

Each of the 1,011 rooms has two queen beds or one king, a coffeemaker, 32-inch flat-screen TV, Wi-Fi, ceiling fan, and weekday newspaper in the lobby. Most rooms have a balcony or patio. In addition, there are 103 one- and two-bedroom suites and two-story penthouses with microwaves. Twin/queen sofa beds are in suites and rooms with king beds. Guestrooms have a small safe and mini fridge. Children's videos may be rented for in-room viewing.

The hotel also provides daily room service (breakfast is served from 6 A.M. to 11 A.M. and dinner is offered from 4 P.M. to 11 P.M.), a Disney shop, and a guest laundry room. Dining spots include the lakeside Letterpress restaurant, which serves breakfast, lunch, and dinner. Disney characters are in attendance on Sunday mornings from 8:30 A.M. till 11:30 A.M. Citrus 28 Grab N Go, open from 6 A.M. to 11 A.M., features freshly prepared light meals and snack items, plus drinks (including Starbucks coffee); Sunnies Lobby Lounge offers appetizers, snacks, and cocktails until 1 A.M., and Shades Pool Bar & Restaurant serves burgers, fries, wraps, beverages, and more.

PHOTO BY JILL SAFRO

Shades of Green

Shades of Green is a recreational retreat for active and retired military personnel and their families, members of the reserves and the National Guard, and U.S. Department of Defense employees. This 586-room resort is near the Grand Floridian but is not linked with the monorail system.

The resort features two tennis courts, two pools, a small health club, restaurant, bar and lounge, gift shop, arcade, laundry facilities, and free transportation around WDW.

Room rates are based on military or civilian grade. Select multi-day tickets are offered at a discount. The property's three golf courses—the Palm, the Magnolia, and Oak Trail—are open to all Walt Disney World guests (see *Sports & Recreation* for details). All other activities are for hotel guests and their families only.

Disney's Magical Express motor coach service is not available to guests staying at this resort. The phone number for Shades of Green is 407-824-3400; *www.shadesofgreen.org*.

The resort's impressive recreation zone features a zero-depth-entry pool with lazy river Float Lagoon, a pool designated for grown-ups, and poolside food and beverage service. Pool cabanas may be rented. There's a fitness center with Life Fitness Equipment and accessible equipment for guests with disabilities.

Rates for most rooms are generally about $125 and up per night (no charge for kids under 18); suites, which sleep four to eight, are $149 and up. Rollaway beds cost $35 per night; cribs are free. There is an Alamo/National car rental desk here, too. Hilton Buena Vista Palace, 1900 Buena Vista Dr., Lake Buena Vista, FL 32830; 407-827-2727 or 866-397-6516; *www.buenavistapalace.com*.

> ## HOT TIP!
>
> **The Hilton Buena Vista Palace is just a 5-minute walk from the Marketplace at Disney Springs. It is directly across the street, safely and easily accessed by an elevated pedestrian walkway.**

Resort on Dream Tree Blvd.

FOUR SEASONS ORLANDO

Walt Disney World welcomed a Four Seasons resort into its happy hotel fold in 2014. The 443-room luxury property boasts more than 26 lakeside acres of elegant design, as well as a multitude of recreational diversions and high convenience for Disney guests. Spanish Revival architecture reflects Florida's Golden Age mansions and is surrounded by a vibrant array of foliage. Check-in begins at 4 P.M. daily. Checkout time is 12 P.M. There is a 24-hour business center, plus ample meeting space suitable for conferences and social functions. Four Seasons Orlando resort is an AAA Five-Diamond award winner. For additional information or to make reservations for the hotel, call 800-267-3046, or visit *www.fourseasons.com/orlando*.

ROOMS: All rooms have furnished balconies, one king or two double beds, twice-daily housekeeping service, newspaper delivery, 24-hour room service, and high-speed Internet and Wi-Fi. Rooms also come with a safe, coffeemaker (with coffee), DVD player, iPod docking station, flat-screen TV, and minibar. There are terry-cloth bathrobes to use throughout your stay (kids' robes are available upon request). Accommodations feature marble bathrooms with double sinks and soaking tub, hair dryer, lighted makeup mirrors, and a TV in the mirror (yes, in the mirror!). Hypoallergenic bedding is available upon request. Cribs may be requested (no charge), as can high chairs, bottles, and toddler toys. Babysitting services may be arranged for an hourly fee (reservations must be made at least 2 weeks in advance).

The resort has many rooms that are accessible for guests with disabilities. Make your needs known when you book the room. Four Seasons is a nonsmoking resort.

Room categories include (distant) Park View, Lake View, Golden Oak View, and Four Seasons Rooms. Park View rooms offer a distant view of the Magic Kingdom and Happily Ever After, the park's nightly fireworks presentation. Lake View rooms have views of a lake, golf course, or pool area. Golden Oak rooms offer "residential views" of privately owned homes, while Four Seasons rooms have limited views.

Suites have king beds, two bathrooms, and a living area with a queen sleeper sofa. To book a room, call 800-267-3046. For suites (including Royal Suite, which can connect up to 9 bedrooms, and the Presidential Suite, which can connect up to 4), call 407-313-6734.

The lobby's convenient Disney Planning Center assists with the purchase of park tickets, making Disney dining reservations, reserving special events, and more. When it comes to Walt Disney World privileges, the resort is similar to the Swan and Dolphin and the resorts on Hotel Plaza Boulevard. Among the perks:

• Complimentary transportation to the four Walt Disney World theme parks may be provided by a Four Seasons luxury motor coach. (There are on-site vehicles available for rent, too.)

• Guests may use the theme parks Package Express delivery service. Merchandise can be delivered directly to the resort from any WDW theme park and many shops (no charge).

• Four Seasons guests may be able to book Fastpass+ selections as far as 60 days before arrival. (Refer to page 25 for details on this system that allows guests to book advance reservation times for theme park shows and attractions.) Details are subject to change.

• Guests who link their reservation to a valid park ticket via the My Disney Experience mobile app or website may enjoy WDW's "Extra Magic Hours" benefit. For additional information, refer to page 22. All details are subject to change.

• Disney characters visit Ravello for the "Good Morning Breakfast" on Thursdays and Saturdays year-round (and on Tuesdays during school breaks and major holidays). Expect Goofy and his pals.

WHERE TO EAT: There are four full-service eateries and a coffee bar, plus 24-hour in-room dining. Reservations are recommended for Capa and Ravello (call 407-313-6161). Note that Four Seasons resort guests are welcome to dine at any WDW resort restaurants, too. To book, use the My Disney Experience app or website, or call 407-WDW-DINE (939-3463).

Capa: This contemporary, Spanish-style steakhouse specializes in prime cuts, tapas (appetizer portions), and local seafood such as freshly shucked oysters. There is indoor and outdoor seating at this rooftop hot spot. Capa is open for dinner only, 6 P.M. to 10 P.M.

Lickety-Split: Located in the lobby, this is the perfect place for gourmet coffees and quick bites. Selections include breakfast pastries, grab-and-go items, gelato, and more. There is indoor and outdoor seating.

PB&G: Think rotisserie chicken, gyro style lamb, grilled fish tacos, burgers, and salads at this Southern-style open-air eatery, located poolside (all seating is alfresco). Open 11 A.M. to 6 P.M.

Plancha: Located at the Tranquilo golf course, this lakeside restaurant serves a mix of American clubhouse favorites and Cuban-inspired dishes. The cocktail menu includes mojitos and Hemingway daiquiris. The hours are 10 A.M. till 6 P.M.

Ravello: Guests are invited to watch the action in this Italian eatery's open kitchen. In addition to regionally influenced specialties, Ravello serves fresh bread and pizza, and housemade pasta. Two private dining rooms are also available. Ravello is open for breakfast (6:30 A.M. to 11 A.M.) and dinner (5:30 P.M. to 10 P.M.). The dress code here is "smart casual."

WHERE TO DRINK: Guests may quench their thirst and enjoy creatively prepared nibbles at a duo of lovely (and lively) lounges.

Lobby Bar: Drinks mix well with the appetizers, entrées, and desserts at this lounge.

Capa Bar: As you sip a beverage on the patio, you may also enjoy the Magic Kingdom's fireworks. Capa Bar is open from 5 P.M. to 11 P.M.

WHAT TO DO: There's no getting bored in these parts. The Explorer Island play province could be enjoyed for days on end. In addition to a swimmer's paradise, the amusing island boasts a rock-climbing wall, volleyball and basketball courts, Ping-Pong, and more. Outdoor movies are presented on select nights.

Children's Program: The resort's complimentary "Kids for All Seasons" program is open daily to youngsters ages 4 to 12. Check with the hotel for hours. Trained staffers supervise and entertain kids throughout the day. Little ones under the age of 4 are welcome to participate if accompanied by a guardian.

Fun and Games: The Mansion on the resort's Explorer Island is a family-focused hangout with outdoor activities such as table tennis, bocce ball, and pool (the kind you play with a cue stick). The Hideout has video games, basketball hoops, and beach volleyball.

Golf: Golfers may argue that the resort's crowning glory is the secluded Tranquilo course at Four Seasons Golf and Sports Club Orlando. The Tom Fazio–designed, 18-hole, 6,968-yard, par 71 course is a certified Audubon sanctuary with abundant opportunities to view local wildlife between swings. Amenities include a pro shop, instruction, driving range, putting green, club rental, and a restaurant (Plancha). The course is exclusively available to guests of the hotel and members (fees apply). To reserve tee times, call 407-313-7777. For information on Walt Disney World's other golfing opportunities, turn to page 244 of the *Sports & Recreation* chapter.

Health Club: The 24-hour Fitness Centre has cardiovascular equipment, weights, and yoga, plus a steam room and whirlpool spa. Certified trainers are on hand, too (for a fee).

Movies: The resort presents alfresco films on select nights at the Star Struck "dive-in" movie screen (near the pool on Explorer Island).

Spa: The Spa at Four Seasons evokes the peace and natural beauty of Florida's Everglades. The Zen zone features 18 treatment rooms, which include 6 couples suites (2 of which are bungalows for ultra-private retreats). There are also outdoor lounges and a whirlpool. The Salon offers hair-styling, manicures, pedicures, and other services. There is a Magical Moments for Kids package, too. In it, little ones are transformed into princesses and knights. To book an appointment, visit *https://www.fourseasons.com/orlando/spa/*.

Swimming: The resort's swimming areas are part of an enormous playground known as Explorer Island: the Oasis, a lakeside adults-only pool; the Explorer Pool, a zero-depth-entry family pool; Splash Zone, a soft-surface interactive fountain area that sprays water up to 30 feet in the air; a 1,203-foot-long lazy river, complete with a waterfall and bubbling rapids; and two 242-foot waterslides.

Tennis: The resort sports three Har-Tru tennis courts for play and instruction (fees apply to both activities).

Weddings: From the rehearsal dinner to the ceremony, reception, and even the honeymoon, Four Seasons can accommodate the wishes for most fairy-tale occasions, from intimate to grand. Wedding specialists may be reached by calling 407-313-6745, or visiting *www.fourseasons.com/orlando/weddings*.

TRANSPORTATION: A complimentary bus goes to the Transportation and Ticket Center (TTC) every 30 minutes or longer (from there, guests take a ferry or monorail to the Magic Kingdom); buses go to Epcot, Disney's Hollywood Studios, and Animal Kingdom once every hour. The resort staff recommends using a car service as the most efficient means of getting around Walt Disney World property and for travelling to and from the airport.

MAGIC KINGDOM

"Here you leave today—and visit the worlds of yesterday, tomorrow, and fantasy." —Walt Disney

115 Getting Oriented

116 Park Primer

118 Attractions

133 Shopping

137 Entertainment

140 Hot Tips

The Magic Kingdom is the most enchanting part of the World. Few who visit it are disappointed, and even the most blasé travelers manage a smile. The sight of the soaring spires of Cinderella Castle, the gleaming woodwork of the Main Street shops, and the crescendo of music that follows the parades never fail to have an effect. Even when the crowds are large and the weather is hot, a visitor who has toured this wonderland dozens of times can still look around and think how satisfying this place is for the spirit.

What makes the Magic Kingdom timeless is its combination of the classic and the futuristic. Both childhood favorites and space-age concepts have a home here. Every "land" has a theme, carried through from the costumes worn by the hosts and hostesses and the food served in the restaurants to the merchandise sold in the shops, and even the design of the trash cans. Thousands of details contribute to the overall effect, and recognizing these touches makes any visit more enjoyable.

But the delight most guests experience upon first glimpse of the Magic Kingdom can disappear when disorientation sets in. There are so many bends to every pathway, so many sights and sounds clamoring for attention, it's too easy to wander aimlessly and miss the best the Magic Kingdom has to offer. So we earnestly suggest that you study this chapter before your visit.

MAGIC KINGDOM

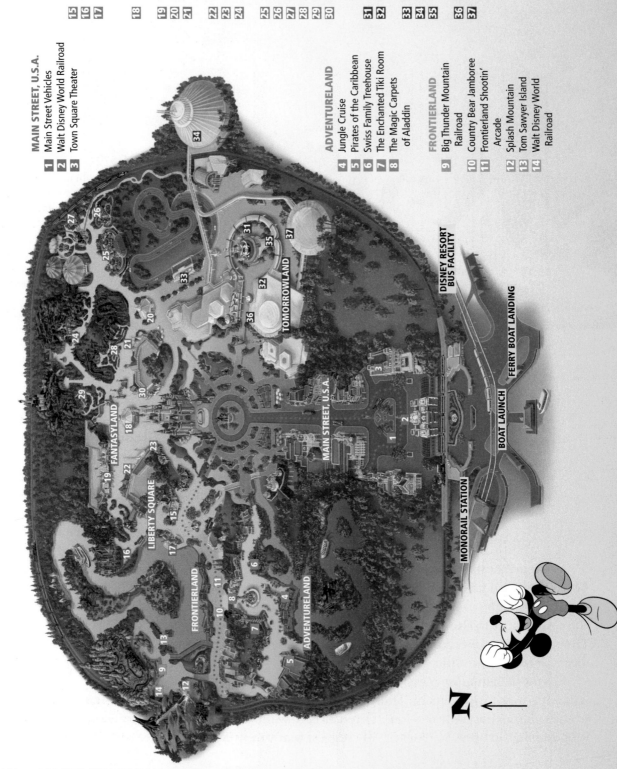

MAIN STREET, U.S.A.
1 Main Street Vehicles
2 Walt Disney World Railroad
3 Town Square Theater

LIBERTY SQUARE
15 The Hall of Presidents
16 The Haunted Mansion
17 Liberty Square Riverboat

FANTASYLAND
18 Prince Charming Regal Carrousel
19 It's a Small World
20 Mad Tea Party
21 The Many Adventures of Winnie the Pooh
22 Peter Pan's Flight
23 Mickey's PhilharMagic
24 Under the Sea—Journey of The Little Mermaid
25 Dumbo the Flying Elephant
26 The Barnstormer
27 Walt Disney World Railroad
28 Seven Dwarfs Mine Train
29 Enchanted Tales with Belle
30 Princess Fairytale Hall

TOMORROWLAND
31 Astro Orbiter
32 Buzz Lightyear's Space Ranger Spin
33 Tomorrowland Speedway
34 Space Mountain
35 Tomorrowland Transit Authority PeopleMover
36 Monsters, Inc. Laugh Floor
37 Walt Disney's Carousel of Progress

ADVENTURELAND
4 Jungle Cruise
5 Pirates of the Caribbean
6 Swiss Family Treehouse
7 The Enchanted Tiki Room
8 The Magic Carpets of Aladdin

FRONTIERLAND
9 Big Thunder Mountain Railroad
10 Country Bear Jamboree
11 Frontierland Shootin' Arcade
12 Splash Mountain
13 Tom Sawyer Island
14 Walt Disney World Railroad

.... Parade Route

Getting Oriented

When you visit Walt Disney World's original theme park, it's vital to know the lay of the "lands." The Magic Kingdom has six themed lands—Main Street, U.S.A.; Adventureland; Frontierland; Liberty Square; Fantasyland (including the Storybook Circus area); and Tomorrowland. Main Street, U.S.A., begins at Town Square, located just inside the park gates, and runs directly to Cinderella Castle. The area in front of the castle is known as the Central Plaza or the Hub. Bridges over the waterways here serve as passages to each of the park's themed lands.

As you enter the Hub, the first bridge on your left goes to Adventureland; the next, to Liberty Square and Frontierland. On your right, the first bridge heads to Tomorrowland; the second, to Fantasyland. The end points of the pathways leading to the lands are linked by a street that is roughly circular, so that the layout of the Magic Kingdom resembles a wheel.

Guidemaps and Times Guides are available at the park entrance, at City Hall in Town Square, and at many shops. You will find them to be valuable navigational and scheduling resources.

HOW TO GET THERE

Take Exit 64B off I-4. Continue about four miles to the Auto Plaza and park; walk or take a tram to the main entrance complex, known as the Transportation and Ticket Center (TTC). Choose a seven-minute ferry ride or a slightly shorter trip by monorail for the last leg of an anticipation-filled journey.

By WDW Transportation: From the Grand Floridian and Polynesian Village: monorail or boat. From the Contemporary: monorail or walkway. (It's roughly a 7- to 15-minute stroll, depending on the pace.) From Epcot: monorail to the Transportation and Ticket Center (TTC), then transfer to the Magic Kingdom monorail or ferry. From Disney's Hollywood Studios and Animal Kingdom: bus. From the resorts on Hotel Plaza Boulevard: bus to the TTC, then transfer to a monorail or ferry. From Fort Wilderness: boat or bus. From Wilderness Lodge: boat or bus. From Disney Springs: bus to any Walt Disney World resort and transfer to the Magic Kingdom bus (or monorail). From all other Walt Disney World resorts: buses.

PARKING

All-day car parking at the Magic Kingdom starts at $25 for day visitors (free to WDW resort guests with a valid resort ID, MagicBand, or an annual pass; trucks, trailers, and RVs cost more; preferred parking costs $45–$50). Bear left after passing through the Auto Plaza; attendants will direct you into a lot. Several preferred lots are within walking distance of the Transportation and Ticket Center; all others are served by trams.

Note the section and aisle in which you park. (Even better, take a photo with your mobile phone.) The parking ticket allows for re-entry to the parking area throughout the day.

HOURS

The Magic Kingdom park is generally open from 9 A.M. to about 8 P.M. However, during busy seasons, it's open later. It's best to arrive up to an hour before opening time. Guests are allowed to wander about Main Street, U.S.A., before the rest of the park opens for the day. It's possible to shop and grab breakfast before Let the Magic Begin—the Castle stage show that kicks off each day. If you prefer to avoid the morning crush, consider postponing your visit until 1 P.M. or later.

Note that on select days, the Magic Kingdom opens early or stays open late for select Walt Disney World resort guests only (this happy perk is known as Extra Magic Hours). For details, visit *www.disneyworld.com*, or call 407-824-4321. The park tends to be more crowded on such days, so plan accordingly. We recommend booking Fastpass+ assignments in advance.

GETTING AROUND

Horseless carriages, horse-drawn trolleys, and a fire engine take turns offering one-way trips up and down Main Street (during non-peak hours). Walt Disney World Railroad steam trains—which usually make a 20-minute loop of the park, stopping to pick up and drop off passengers at stations on Main Street, U.S.A., Frontierland, and Fantasyland—will not be running in 2020 (while Imagineers continue to build a new *TRON*-themed thrill ride in Tomorrowland). You can expect to do a lot of walking during your visit to the Magic Kingdom—wear comfortable shoes.

Park Primer

BABY FACILITIES

The best place in the Magic Kingdom to take care of little ones' needs is the Baby Care Center. This cheery site, equipped with changing tables and facilities for nursing mothers, is next to the Crystal Palace restaurant. Disposable diapers are for sale at the Baby Care Center (if possible, bring your own—the packages are small and a tad pricey). All Magic Kingdom restrooms are equipped with changing facilities.

DISABILITY INFORMATION

Most Magic Kingdom shops and restaurants, and many attractions, are accessible to guests using wheelchairs. Additional services are available for guests with visual or hearing disabilities. The (free) *Guide for Guests with Disabilities* provides an overview of all services, including transportation, parking, and attraction access. You can pick one up at the park entrance or at City Hall on Main Street. For more information, see the "Travelers with Disabilities" section of the *Getting Ready to Go* chapter.

FERRY VERSUS MONORAIL

For guests arriving by car or bus, it's necessary to decide whether to travel to the Magic Kingdom by ferry or monorail. The monorail usually makes the trip from the Transportation and Ticket Center (aka TTC) in about 7 to 10 minutes, while the ferry takes about 10. During busy seasons, the ferry will often get you there faster (long lines can form at the monorail, and most people don't make the short walk to the ferry landing). Guests who use wheelchairs should note that while the monorail platforms are accessible, the ramp leading to the boarding area is a bit on the steep side, prompting many guests to opt for the ferry.

FIRST AID

A registered nurse tends to minor medical problems at the First Aid Center during regular park hours. If you have medicine that requires refrigeration, The Center

will store it for you. (All medication must be in its original container and be clearly labeled.) Special containers can be provided for safe disposal of hypodermic needles. If you have other special needs, contact Disability Services by emailing *disability.services@disneyparks.com*, or calling 407-560-2547.

You'll find the First Aid Center between the Crystal Palace and Casey's Corner restaurants, just off Main Street. **For medical emergencies, call 911 from any phone and alert a Cast Member.**

INFORMATION

City Hall, just inside the park entrance, serves as the Magic Kingdom's information headquarters. Guest Relations reps can answer questions and help with MagicBands. Guidemaps and Times Guides, updated weekly (including details about entertainment and character greeting times and locations), are also available here. Should you have problems with your ticket or a question about the number of unused days remaining on a ticket, City Hall is a good place to go.

LOCKERS

Unattended lockers are located just inside the park entrance, all the way to the right. Standard lockers cost $10 per day; large lockers run $12 per day; and jumbo lockers cost $15 per day. Park-hoppers take note: Locker rental is not transferable from park to park—if you hop from M.K. to another Disney park, you'll need to rent another locker at your new destination.

LOST & FOUND

On the day of your visit, report lost articles at City Hall on Main Street, U.S.A., or fill out a lost item report at *www.chargerback.com/disneyworld*. After your visit, go to the aforementioned website.

LOST CHILDREN

Report lost children at City Hall or the Baby Care Center and alert the nearest Disney employee to the problem. To expedite reunions, supply kids with a copy of your mobile number before you visit the park.

HOT TIP!

Certain shows and attractions keep shorter hours than the Magic Kingdom itself (e.g., The Enchanted Tiki Room, The Country Bear Jamboree, and Tom Sawyer Island). To make sure you catch your favorites, check a Times Guide as you enter the park.

MONEY MATTERS

The Magic Kingdom has several automated teller machines (ATMs): near the locker rental site; in City Hall on Main Street, U.S.A.; near the Frontier Shootin' Arcade; and near Pinocchio Village Haus. Most foreign currency can be exchanged (in limited amounts) at City Hall on Main Street, U.S.A.

Credit cards (American Express, Visa, MasterCard, JCB, Discover Card, and Diner's Club) are accepted as payment for admission, merchandise, and at most dining locations. Traveler's checks and Disney gift cards are accepted at most places, as are MagicBands and WDW resort ID cards (backed up with a major credit card). Some food and souvenir carts may accept cash only.

While no longer sold, Disney Dollars are accepted for dining and purchases at most Walt Disney World locations and may be exchanged for U.S. currency. (Production of Disney Dollars was discontinued in 2016.)

PACKAGE PICKUP

Individual shops can arrange for purchases to be transported to the Package Pickup at the Main Street Chamber of Commerce, next to City Hall, for pickup between noon and park closing time (at least three hours after purchase). Packages may be sent to most Disney resorts, too. The delivery service is free.

PARK RULES

To ensure a comfortable, safe, and enjoyable experience for all guests, visitors are asked to comply with all Park rules, signs, and instructions including:

- All bags are subject to inspection.
- Guests are subject to screening via wand and/or metal detector.
- Proper attire is required.
- Smoking (including e-cigarettes and vaping) is not permitted in any Disney park. Marijuana smoking is prohibited throughout Walt Disney World.
- Selfie sticks are not permitted in Disney parks.
- Weapons (including toys) are prohibited.

For additional information and a complete listing of Disney park rules, visit Guest Relations or go to *www.disneyworld.com/ParkRules*.

SAME-DAY RE-ENTRY

Wear your MagicBand if you used it for admission or retain your ticket if you leave the park and plan to return to it later the same day.

SECURITY CHECK

All guests entering the Magic Kingdom are subject to a thorough security check, including a metal detector screening. Backpacks, parcels, handbags, etc., will be searched by security personnel before guests may pass through the entrance.

HOT TIP!

Will you need a stroller during your visit? Consider bringing one from home. It will save you money, and it can be used all over WDW. (Disney rentals may not be removed from the parks.) Chances are your baby buggy is more comfortable than the ones in the parks, too—they are made of hard plastic. If yours is too cumbersome for travel, consider buying an "umbrella" stroller or renting a user-friendly carriage from a company such as Magic Strollers (see page 68).

STROLLERS & WHEELCHAIRS

Wheelchair Rental, located just inside the entrance, all the way to the right, offers wheelchairs (some oversized) and Electric Conveyance Vehicles (ECVs). Strollers are available under the Main Street Train Station. The cost for strollers is $15 per day ($13 per day with a multi-day rental); double strollers cost $31 per day ($27 a day with a multi-day rental); wheelchairs are $12 per day, $10 with multi-day rental; $50 per day for ECVs, with a $20 refundable deposit. Quantities are limited. Hold on to your receipt; it can be used on the same day to get a replacement stroller or wheelchair at any of the theme parks. Multi-day rentals, called Length of Stay tickets, save you two dollars off the daily price. Remember to keep your receipt in a safe place.

To prevent your stroller from getting lost in a sea of stroller clones, consider personalizing it with an item such as a ribbon or a sign. Do not leave valuables in an unattended stroller.

Admission Prices

ONE-DAY BASE TICKET*
(Restricted to use only in the Magic Kingdom. Prices are for Date-Based tickets. Rates for Flexible Date tickets are higher. **Prices exclude tax and are likely to rise in 2020.**)

Adult .... $109–$159
Child** .... $104–$154

* 1-Day tickets are valid only on the selected date. Flexible Date tickets purchased in 2020 must be used by December 31, 2021. This is the cost of a 1-day/1-park-only ticket. Terms are subject to change. For updates, visit *https://disneyworld.disney.go.com/admission/tickets/*.

** 3 through 9 years of age; children under age 3 free (no ticket required)

Main Street, U.S.A.

PHOTO BY JILL SAFRO

Stepping onto Main Street, U.S.A., feels like jumping through a time portal. Welcome to turn-of-the-twentieth-century America! Double-decker buses and horse-drawn trolleys are the transportation of choice, peppy patriotic music underscores the bustle of merry, moving masses, and the tantalizing aroma of fresh-baked goodies perfumes the air.

A rose-colored retrospective? Maybe. But this is Disney's version of a small-town Main Street—and the charm of this nostalgic land is lost on no one. Anchored by an old-fashioned train station at one end and a fairy-tale castle at the other, Main Street, U.S.A., whisks you from reality to fantasy in a few short blocks.

All of the addresses here feature fresh coats of paint, curlicued gingerbread moldings, and pretty details. Add to that the baskets of hanging plants and gaslights, and Main Street, U.S.A., becomes a true showplace—both in the bright light of high noon and after nightfall, when the tiny lights edging all of the rooflines are flicked on.

The street represents an ideal American town. Although such a town never really existed, many claim to have served as the inspiration for it. Chances are Walt Disney got the idea from Marceline, Missouri, the tiny rural town that was his boyhood home.

Most of the structures along the thoroughfare are given over to shops, and each one is different. Some emporiums are big and bustling, others are relatively quiet and orderly; some are spacious and airy, others are cozy and dark. Inside and out, maintenance and housekeeping are superb.

White-suited sanitation workers patrol the street to pick up litter and quickly shovel up any evidence of the horses that pull the trolley cars from Town Square to the Hub. As in the rest of the Magic Kingdom, the pavement here is washed down every night with hoses. There's one crew of maintenance workers whose sole job is to change the little white lights around the roofs; another crew devotes itself to keeping the woodwork painted. As soon as these people have worked their way as far as the Hub, they start all over again at Town Square. The greenish, horse-shaped, cast-iron hitching posts are repainted 20 times a year on average—and totally scraped down each time.

The "attractions" along Main Street, U.S.A., are relatively minor compared to the really big deals such as Tomorrowland's Space Mountain, Frontierland's Splash Mountain, or The Haunted Mansion in Liberty Square. But each and every shop has its own quota of merchandise that is meant as much for show as for sale. It's almost as entertaining to watch the cooks stir up gooey batches of fudge or peanut brittle at the Main Street Confectionery as it is to actually savor a sample. The shop windows, particularly at the Emporium, are also worth a look.

Once you start to meander along Main Street, be sure to notice all of the names embossed on the second-story windows. Above the Uptown Jewelers store (near the Confectionery) is that of Walt Disney's nephew, Roy E. Disney. And you will see Walt's name above the ice-cream parlor. Other names are those of people closely connected with The Walt Disney Company.

HOT TIP!

Attention, early birds: Guests (with tickets) are welcome to visit Main Street, U.S.A., before the posted Magic Kingdom opening time. You can spend 30 to 45 minutes moseying along the nostalgic thoroughfare, grabbing some breakfast (for dining details, refer to *Good Meals, Great Times*), and shopping for souvenirs (packages can be held at the park's Package Pickup location free of charge). As park opening time approaches, head to the Castle forecourt stage for a lively, character-laden show known as Let the Magic Begin.

HOT TIP!

Kids under age 14 must be accompanied by someone age 14 or older when visiting any WDW theme park or water park.

WALT DISNEY WORLD RAILROAD: A beloved staple of a Magic Kingdom visit, the Walt Disney World Railroad has temporarily run out of steam. Fear not, fans. For this steam-powered classic *will* chug again—but not until Disney Imagineers finish building a brand-new *TRON*-themed attraction in the park's Tomorrowland (possibly by the end of 2020, but more likely in 2021).

Until then, those loco for locomotives can bond with Disney trains at the Main Street station. Bring a camera or have your smartphone ready: guests may strike a pose with one of the Magic Kingdom's four meticulously restored, narrow-gauge trains—originally built between 1916 and 1928.

Walt Disney himself was a railroad aficionado. During the early years of television, viewers watched films of him circling his own backyard in a one-eighth-scale train, the Lilly Belle (named for his wife). The 1928 steam engine is the same age as Mickey Mouse.

The Walt Disney World Railroad also has a Lilly Belle among its quartet of locomotives. The others are named Roy O. Disney, Walter E. Disney, and Roger E. Broggie (a Disney Imagineer who shared Walt Disney's enthusiasm for antique trains). All of them were built in the U.S. around the turn of the century and later taken to Mexico to haul freight and passengers in the Yucatán, where Disney scouts found them in 1969. The United Railways of Yucatán was using them to carry sugarcane. Brought north once again, they were completely overhauled, and even the smallest of parts were reworked or replaced.

Another way for guests (over the age of 10) to enjoy the Walt Disney World Railroad during its prolonged

service interruption is the "Magic Behind our Steam Trains" guided tour. For details on this 3-hour behind-the-scenes experience, turn to page 236 of the *Everything Else In the World* chapter. Fees apply.

HOT TIP!

Guests staying at the Contemporary resort can walk to and from the Magic Kingdom's front gate. The trip takes about 7 to 15 minutes. It's handy when there's a long line for the resort monorail.

MAIN STREET VEHICLES: A number of vehicles can be seen traveling up and down Main Street—horseless carriages and jitneys patterned after turn-of-the-century vehicles; a spiffy scarlet fire engine; and a troop of trolleys drawn by Belgians and Percherons, two strong breeds of horse that once pulled plows in Europe. These animals—weighing in at about a ton each and shod with plastic (easier on their hooves)—pull the trolley the length of Main Street about two dozen times during each of their working days. Between shifts, they can be seen resting inside Main Street's Car Barn. Feel free to stop by the entrance to wave hello. At day's end, they go home to their barn at Fort Wilderness.

Note: Main Street Vehicles generally operate during daytime hours on off-peak days.

TOWN SQUARE THEATER: + Elaborately themed as a Victorian-era theater, this is an ideal spot to meet and mingle with Mickey Mouse. Of course, this being a magic kingdom, Mickey has a few tricks up his sleeve. Yep, in addition to all his other skills, the Mouse is a master magician. Who knew? Note that this is strictly a "backstage" experience, as Mickey's magic show is still in the rehearsal stage. The wait here can be quite long—get a Fastpass+ if you can.

HOT TIP!

Tuesday and Wednesday tend to be the least crowded days at the Magic Kingdom.

PHOTO BY JILL SAFRO

Adventureland

Adventureland seems to have even more atmosphere than the park's other lands. That may be due to its neat separation from the rest of the Magic Kingdom by the bridge over Main Street on one end and by a gallery-like structure (where it merges with Frontierland) on the other, or, possibly, it's because of the abundance of lush landscaping.

A centrally located attraction, The Magic Carpets of Aladdin, sets the tone for this corner of the Kingdom. Surrounded by tropical splendor, the area has the look and feel of a bustling marketplace—the likes of which one might stumble upon in Agrabah. Shops here offer imports from around the globe.

As guests stroll away from Main Street, U.S.A., they just may hear the sound of beating drums, the squawks of parrots, and the regular boom of a cannon. Paces quicken. And the wonders that are soon to be encountered do not disappoint.

SWISS FAMILY TREEHOUSE: This is everybody's idea of a dream treehouse, with its multiple levels and comforts—patchwork quilts, mahogany furniture, candles stuck in abalone shells, even running water in every room. Based on the wondrous banyan-tree home in Disney's 1960 rendition of the classic story *Swiss Family Robinson*, it rarely fails to intrigue. It's easy to understand why, when given the chance to leave the island (several adventures later), all but one member of the Robinson family chose to stay on. The only modern convenience the Robinsons could use? An elevator! Expect to burn off a few calories climbing up and down the stairs. Be sure to enjoy the view of the park from the tree-top.

The Spanish moss draping the branches is real; the tree—unofficially dubbed *Disneyodendron eximus*, a genus that is translated roughly as "out-of-the-ordinary Disney tree"—was constructed by the props department. Some stats: Its concrete roots poke 42 feet into the ground, about 300,000 lifelike polyethylene leaves "grow" on the tree's 1,400 branches, and there are 116 stairs to climb from beginning to end. Keep that in mind before you commit to this breezy tour.

JUNGLE CRUISE: FP+ Inspired in part by the 1955 documentary *The African Lion* and the classic film *The African Queen*, this ten-minute adventure is one of the crowning achievements of Magic Kingdom landscape artists for the way it takes guests through surroundings as diverse as a Southeast Asian jungle, the Nile Valley, and an Amazon rainforest. Along the way, passengers encounter zebras, giraffes, lions, headhunters, and more (all of the Audio-Animatronics variety); they also see elephants bathing and tour a temple—while listening to an amusing, though corny, spiel delivered by the skipper. (Bet you didn't know that Schweitzer Falls was named after the famous doctor Albert . . . Falls.)

This classic adventure, which is best enjoyed by daylight, is one of the park's slower-moving attractions. It's popular with guests of all ages.

Calling All Pirates!

Captain Jack Sparrow needs your help. He knows there's treasure to be found and enemies to fight in Adventureland (yeah, that means you, Captain Barbossa!), but Captain Jack can't do it alone. So he's recruiting Magic Kingdom guests to join his pirate posse. That's where you come in!

The interactive quest, "A Pirate's Adventure—Treasure of the Seven Seas," begins at The Crow's Nest, near the Pirates of the Caribbean attraction. That's where potential pirates use a MagicBand or talisman (which activates magical effects throughout the land) and a mission map. There are five missions in all, some of which involve dodging blow darts and cannon fire. It's free to play (how's that for a little hidden treasure?!), and the maps and talisman are yours to keep. Arrrrr!

FP+ = Fastpass+ attraction (see page 25)

>

HOT TIP!

The Jungle Cruise has a dedicated entrance for guests who use wheelchairs. When the accessible boat arrives, Cast Members will put a ramp in place. Folks who can transfer may park their wheelchair in an area near the attraction's exit.

WALT DISNEY'S ENCHANTED TIKI ROOM: Welcome to a tropical (and blissfully air-conditioned) paradise. After a pre-show greeting courtesy of talented toucans known as Clyde and Claude, guests stroll into the legendary Tiki Room. Here, fine-feathered legends José, Michael, Pierre, and Fritz take center stage—as they did when the attraction first opened at Disneyland in 1963. Cherished for its historical significance (the Tiki Birds starred in the original Audio-Animatronics attraction), the show has evolved a bit over time.

The performance features the aforementioned friends, plus some 200 additional birds, flowers, and tiki statues singing up a tropical storm. Let's all sing like the birdies sing!

THE MAGIC CARPETS OF ALADDIN: FP+ Adventure-land's high-flying attraction is conveniently located in the Agrabah-themed center of the action. It features not one, but 16 carpets that soar through the air in a fashion similar to those airborne elephants over in Fantasyland. Each flying carpet accommodates four guests at a time. Depending on where you sit, you'll have control of the carpet's movement (vertical controls are in the front row; side to side are in the back row). Be prepared to dodge the occasional stream of liquid, courtesy of an expectorating camel.

BIRNBAUM'S **★BEST★** **PIRATES OF THE CARIBBEAN:** FP+ Quite simply, this is one of the very best of the Magic Kingdom's classic adventures. The beloved ten-minute cruise originated in Disneyland and was added to Walt Disney World's Magic Kingdom park (in slightly revised form) due to popular demand. Here, guests board a small boat and set sail for a series of scenes showing a pirate raid on a Caribbean island town, dodging cannon fire and weathering one small, though legitimate, watery dip along the way. There are singing donkeys, plastered pigs, and marauding miscreants; the observant may note a few familiar rapscallion residents. Beloved scallywag Captain Jack Sparrow has dropped anchor here, as has his nefarious nemesis, Captain Barbossa. And there's a new pirate in town! Following an extensive ride refurbishment in 2018, the famous redhead (and longtime resident of the attraction) has joined forces with the local marauders and hopes to help the townspeople "unload" their valuables at the Mercado Auction.

While it may not be the World's most politically correct attraction, the rendition of "Yo Ho, Yo Ho, a Pirate's Life for Me"— the catchy theme song—makes the somewhat unsavory scenario into something that comes across as good fun.

And, yes, this is the attraction that inspired the *Pirates of the Caribbean* movies—which, in turn, inspired the attraction.

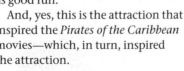

FP+ = Fastpass+ attraction (see page 25)

Frontierland

With the Rivers of America lapping at its borders and Big Thunder Mountain rising in the distance, this re-creation of the American Frontier encompasses the area from the Mississippi River to the Southwest, from the 1770s to the 1880s. In these parts, the shops, restaurants, and attractions have unpainted barn siding or stone or clapboard walls, and there are several wooden sidewalks of the sort Marshal Matt Dillon used to stride along. The Walt Disney World Railroad has a station here.

FRONTIERLAND SHOOTIN' ARCADE: This modest arcade is set in an 1850s town in the Southwest Territory. Positions overlook Boothill, a town complete with bank, jail, hotel, and cemetery.

Genuine Hawkins .54-caliber buffalo rifles have been refitted, and when the infrared beam strikes any of the targets, an interesting result is triggered. Struck tombstones rise, sink, spin, or change their epitaphs; hit a cloud and a ghost rider gallops across the sky; a bull's-eye on a grave digger's shovel causes a skull to pop out of the grave.

There is an additional charge to play here (usually about a buck—bring quarters).

COUNTRY BEAR JAMBOREE: The Country Bears may never make it to the Grand Ole Opry, but they don't seem to mind. Disney's brood of banjo-strummin' bruins has been playing to packed houses in Grizzly Hall for nearly half a century. Judging by all the toe tappin' and hand clappin' that accompany each performance, the show remains a countrified crowd-pleaser. As for the few folks who aren't charmed by the backwoods ballads and down-home humor, well, they just have to grin and bear it.

As guests are settling into their seats (all of which provide a decent view of the show), Buff, Max, and Melvin are beginning to grumble. Despite their status as permanent fixtures in the theater, the mounted animal heads would rather not "hang around all day" waiting for the show to get going. The 11-minute revue opens with a rousing ditty by the Five Bear Rugs. The wheels set in motion, the remaining songs come fast and furious. Together, they capture the spirit of a music genre that has a tendency to celebrate and lampoon itself simultaneously.

For example, Bunny, Bubbles, and Beulah bemoan "All the Guys That Turn Me On Turn Me Down"; Henry, the easygoing emcee who sports a coonskin cap (still attached to the 'coon), belts out "The Ballad of Davy Crockett"; and Big Al, the oversize tone-deaf fan favorite, woefully croons "Blood on the Saddle," much to the delight of the giggle-prone audience.

Timing Tip: This attraction typically opens at 11 A.M. each day, even when the rest of the park opens earlier in the morning.

TOM SAWYER ISLAND: This tranquil patch of land in the middle of the Rivers of America has hills to scramble up; a working windmill, Harper's Mill, with an owl in the rafters and a perpetually creaky waterwheel; and a few pitch-black caves. To reach the island, guests take a raft across the river. (It's the only way to get there and back.)

Pleasant paths wind this way and that, and it's easy to get disoriented. Keep an eye out for mounted maps scattered about the island.

There are two bridges here—a suspension bridge and a barrel bridge, which floats atop some lashed-together wooden barrels. When one person bounces, everybody lurches—and all but the most chickenhearted laugh. Both of the bridges are easy to miss, so be sure to keep your eyes peeled.

Across the suspension bridge is Fort Langhorn. Poke around and you should discover a twisting and slightly scary escape tunnel. Walk along the pathway on the banks of the Rivers of America and you'll find your way back to the bridges.

The whole island seems as rugged as backwoods Missouri and, probably as a result, it actually feels a lot more remote than it is—enough to be able to provide some welcome respite from the bustle.

One particularly enjoyable way to relax here is at a waterside table. It's sometimes possible to buy a snack—and you are always welcome to bring your own. Restrooms are beside the main raft landing and inside Fort Langhorn.

Timing Tip: This attraction closes at dusk.

BIRNBAUM'S **★BEST★** **SPLASH MOUNTAIN:** FP+ On the day this attraction made its official 1992 Walt Disney World debut, everyone got soaked—thanks in part to a particularly potent Florida rain cloud. But the rain wasn't entirely responsible for the sea of soggy Magic Kingdom guests. The five-story drop into an aqueous briar patch was. And a steady stream of thrill-seekers has been taking the drenching plunge ever since.

In this guaranteed smile inducer, guests enjoy a waterborne journey through brightly colored swamps and bayous, and down waterfalls, and are finally hurtled from the peak of the mountain to a briar-laced pond five stories below.

Splash Mountain is based on the animated sequences in Walt Disney's 1946 film *Song of the South*. The scenery entertains as the story line follows Br'er Rabbit as he tries to reach his "laughin' place." It's tough for a first-time rider to take in all the details, since the tension of waiting for the big drop is all-consuming.

It is a bit terrifying at the top, but once back on the ground, it seems most riders just can't wait for another trip—even though they may get drenched. (Water-wary guests are sometimes seen wearing rain ponchos on this attraction. On the other hand, if you want to get soaked, try to sit up front or on the right; seats in the back receive a smaller splash.)

By the second or third time around, it's possible to relax a bit, enjoy the interior scenes, and take in the spectacular views of the Magic Kingdom from the top of the mountain. At this point, you may even manage to keep your eyes open for the duration of the final fall—or at least part of it.

Splash Mountain's designers not only borrowed characters and color-saturated settings from *Song of the South*, but also used quite a bit of the film's Academy Award–winning music in this attraction. As a matter of fact, the song in Splash Mountain's final scene, "Zip-a-Dee-Doo-Dah," has become something of a Disney anthem over the years.

Note: You must be at least 40 inches tall to ride Splash Mountain. The final drop may be too scary for some kids (and grown-ups!). There's a small play area for parents to tend to tykes while older kids ride. If you'd like to absorb as little precipitation as possible, sit on the left side of the log—though no seat is splash free.

HOT TIP!

If you'd like to get soaked on Splash Mountain, sit on the right side of the log.

BIRNBAUM'S ★BEST★ **BIG THUNDER MOUNTAIN RAILROAD:** FP+ It's certainly not hard to spot Big Thunder, the lone red rock formation this side of the Mississippi. Even newcomers to the Magic Kingdom will be able to distinguish the landmark from its famed counterparts—Splash and Space mountains—because it's the only one that looks like an actual mountain range. The attraction's designers took Utah's Monument Valley as inspiration, and the resemblance is quite remarkable.

According to Disney legend, the 2.5-acre mountain is chock-full of gold. Unfortunately for the residents of Tumbleweed, the local mining town, a flood has ruined any chance of uncovering the remaining gold. Before the prospectors find drier land, they are having one last party at the saloon to celebrate their riches. Even though in danger of washing away, they don't seem too worried—and guests who decide to take a trip on the Big Thunder Mountain Railroad have nothing to worry about, either.

After passing through the new interactive queue area, guests are advised to "hang on to your hats and glasses 'cause this here's the wildest ride in the wilderness." Do heed the warning, but don't despair. The ride, though thrilling, is relatively tame, so relax and enjoy the sights. (Passengers seated nearest the caboose

Sorcerers of the Magic Kingdom

Uh-oh! Disney villains are trying to take over the Magic Kingdom, and you can help defeat them. How? First, Merlin the magician will make you (and everyone with you) an apprentice sorcerer. Then you'll use magic spell cards to beat the bad guys and save the park.

The interactive game starts at the Firehouse on Main Street, U.S.A., or in Liberty Square, behind Ye Olde Christmas Shoppe (the Liberty Square location operates during "peak" seasons). Simply present your valid park ticket or MagicBand and you'll receive a special key card, five magic spell cards, and a map. (The folks behind the counter can answer questions, too.) As you follow the clues, you will try to prevent villains from stealing Merlin's crystal ball and keep the Magic Kingdom safe.

There is no extra charge to play, and the magic spell cards are yours to keep. You may get a new set of cards each day you visit the park. Having trouble getting a complete set? Know that other guests are often eager to trade. Many guests—of all ages—enjoy collecting the cards as much as they do playing the game.

PHOTO BY MIKE CARROLL

experience more turbulence than those seated closer to the front of the train.)

A bleating billy goat atop a peak, a family of possums hanging overhead, and a dark cavern full of bats, not to mention chickens, donkeys, and washed-up miners, can be spotted along the way. Be sure to keep an eye out for the not-yet-sunken saloon—it's easy to miss the first time around.

A continuous string of curves and dips around Big Thunder's pinnacles and caverns is sure to please thrill-seekers of all ages, but the adrenaline surge is caused by more than just the speed of the trip. The added sound of a rickety track, a steam whistle that blows right before the train accelerates into a curve, and an unexpected earthquake all compound the passengers' anticipation, making this attraction one of the Magic Kingdom's most popular.

Notes: You must be at least 40 inches tall and free of motion sickness, back and neck problems, and other health issues to ride Big Thunder Mountain Railroad. Seats in the front of the train provide a less wild ride than those toward the caboose. Expectant mothers should not ride.

Timing Tip: Plan to visit early in the morning, during a parade, or just before closing time. Of course, you can always plan ahead and reserve a Fastpass+ assignment.

Liberty Square

The transition between Frontierland on one side and Fantasyland on the other is so smooth that it's hard to say just when you arrive at Liberty Square, yet ultimately, there's no mistaking the location. The small buildings are clapboard or brick and topped with weather vanes; the decorative moldings are Federal or Georgian in style; the glass is sometimes wavy; and there are flower boxes in shop windows. The square is home to two of the park's most famous attractions—The Haunted Mansion and The Hall of Presidents. There's also a convincing replica of the Liberty Bell, a living, century-old "Liberty Tree," and a Christmas shop.

THE HALL OF PRESIDENTS: The attraction has evolved since making its debut way back in 1971. The current version is an epic theatrical production that brings the story of the American presidency to life. The show, which takes place in a 700-seat theater, pays tribute to the ordinary people who have risen to the nation's highest office and led Americans through extraordinary circumstances. It begins with an original film—developed by a Pulitzer Prize–winning historian— which relays the dramatic story of the United States of America. At the film's conclusion, a curtain rises to reveal (an Audio-Animatronics version of) each and every person who has served as president of the United States.

The patriotic production explores America's enduring origins, the framing of the United States Constitution, and the hard-fought struggles along the way—such as the American Revolution and the Civil War.

All 45 U.S. presidents are represented in the show. Observant guests may note that there are only 44 Audio-Animatronics figures on the stage. No, Disney Imagineers did not misplace a president. Grover Cleveland served two non-consecutive terms, so he is actually the 22nd and 24th U.S. president.

Shows run throughout the day. A large clock beneath the marquee indicates the next available showtime.

Displays in the pre-show area give guests a chance to gaze upon bits of Americana, such as painted eggs from a White House Easter egg hunt and dresses from former first ladies (exhibit items will change from time to time).

Prior to popping in on the presidents, catch a performance of The Muppets Present . . . Great Moments in American History. (Check a park Times Guide for the schedule.) It's Muppet-ational!

THE MUPPETS PRESENT . . . GREAT MOMENTS IN AMERICAN HISTORY: Hear ye, hear ye! Great moments in history (all American) are being reenacted in Liberty Square—courtesy of the most American of entertainers: The Muppets! Town crier James "J.J." Jefferson alerts the masses as each show is about to begin (check a Times Guide if you'd like to plan ahead) and he's joined by the likes of the super patriotic Sam Eagle, Kermit the Frog, Miss Piggy, The Great Gonzo, and other fuzzy patriots. Gather below the windows at and beside The Hall of Presidents attraction as Kermit and Company act out such historical moments as Paul Revere's famous ride, the ratification of the U.S. Declaration of Independence, and much more. This Muppet-y celebration of American life, liberty, and the pursuit of happiness is fun for all ages.

PHOTO BY JILL SAFRO

LIBERTY SQUARE RIVERBOAT: Based in Liberty Square and built in dry dock at Walt Disney World, the *Liberty Belle* is a genuine steamboat. Its boiler turns water into steam, which is then piped to the engine, which drives the paddle wheel that propels the boat. It's not the real deal in one key respect, however: It moves through the nine-foot-deep Rivers of America on an underwater rail.

The pleasant ride, with narration by an actor playing Mark Twain, is a good way to beat the heat on steamy afternoons. En route, a variety of props creates a sort of Wild West effect: moose, deer, a burning cabin, and the like. The tour is completed within 17 minutes. Note that this aquatic attraction usually opens an hour or so after the park itself and shuts down earlier than most other Magic Kingdom attractions.

BIRNBAUM'S **THE HAUNTED MANSION:** FP+
★BEST★ This eerie, eight-minute experience is among the Magic Kingdom's most enjoyable. However, guests who expect to be scared silly when they enter the big old house, modeled after those built in New York's Hudson River Valley in the eighteenth century, will be just a tad unfulfilled. This haunted house steers clear of anything too terrifying, and a good-spirited voice-over keeps the mood light. Still, some of the scenes, as well as the darkness, may be too much for some tykes.

Once you're inside the portrait hall, entered after passing through the front doors, you'll be asked to step to the *dead* center of the room. It is also where you will meet your "Ghost Host" and learn how he met his demise. As the space begins to stretch it's fun to speculate: Is the ceiling moving up, or is the floor dropping?

The spooky journey through the mansion takes place in a Doom Buggy. The attraction is full of tricks and treats for the eyes; just when you think you've seen it all, there's something new: staircases to nowhere, bats' eyes on the wallpaper, a terrified cemetery watchman and his mangy mutt, and the image of a creepy lady in a floating crystal ball (aka Madame Leota).

One of the biggest jobs of the maintenance crews here is not cleaning up, but keeping things dirty. The manse is littered with some 200 trunks, chairs, dress forms, harps, rugs, and knickknacks and requires a lot of dust. Cobwebs are bought in liquid form and strung up by a secret process.

When waiting to enter, take time to enjoy the interactive queue area. And on the way out, take a moment to pay your respects at the pet cemetery. Mr. Toad, we hardly knew you. *Sniff, sniff.*

Fantasyland

Walt Disney called this a "timeless land of enchantment," and his successors termed it "the happiest land of all"—and it is, for many. It is also the home of a number of rides that are particularly well liked by children of all ages. Head here for a quintessential Disney theme park experience.

CINDERELLA CASTLE: Just as Mickey stands for all the merriment in Walt Disney World, this storybook castle represents the hopes and dreams of childhood—a time in life when anything is possible and dreams really do come true.

Rising to a height of 189 feet (and sporting 27 turrets), Walt Disney World's Cinderella Castle is nearly twice the height of Disneyland's Sleeping Beauty Castle. For inspiration, Disney Imagineers looked to the palaces of author Charles Perrault's France, still showplaces of Europe. The design took the form of a romanticized composite of such courts as Fontainebleau, Versailles, and famed chateaux of the Loire Valley. Of course, they also turned to the original designs for the fairy-tale castle in Disney's 1950 classic, *Cinderella*.

Unlike real European castles, this one is made of steel and fiberglass; in lieu of dungeons, it has service tunnels. However, like many fabled castles, it is protected by a moat. And from any vantage point, Cinderella Castle looks as if it came straight from the land of make-believe.

Mosaic Murals: The elaborate murals beneath the castle's archway rank among the true wonders of the World. They tell the story of the little cinder girl and one of childhood's happiest happily-ever-afters, using a million bits of glass in some 500 different colors, plus real silver and 14-karat gold.

Cinderella Wishing Well: This pleasant alcove, nestled along a path to Tomorrowland, is a nice spot from which to gaze at the castle. Any coins tossed into the water are donated to children's charities. Don't forget to make a wish as you part with your penny.

PRINCE CHARMING REGAL CARROUSEL: Not everything in the Magic Kingdom is a Disney version of the real article. This carrousel, discovered at the now-defunct Olympic Park in Maplewood, New Jersey, was built back in 1917 (technically making it the oldest attraction in the park). That was the end of the golden century of carrousel building, which began around 1825. During the Disney refurbishment, many of the original horses were replaced with horses made of fiberglass. No two of the 90 horses are exactly alike. Can you spot Cinderella's horse? Hint: It's the only one with a golden ribbon on its tail.

ARIEL'S GROTTO: FP+ The Little Mermaid spends most of each day greeting guests in her Fantasyland grotto. Ariel loves to pose for photos and sign autographs. PhotoPass photographers will happily snap your photo with her, too.

FAIRYTALE GARDEN: This special spot is tucked beside Cinderella Castle. Several times a day, Merida (the heroine from *Brave*) stops by to visit with guests. Check a park Times Guide for appearance schedule. Character subject to change.

MICKEY'S PHILHARMAGIC: FP+ Mickey Mouse and a panoply of his pals (including Donald, Simba, and Ariel) strut their musical stuff in this 3-D production.

The 12-minute show is a lively amalgam of music, effects, and animation. Of course, this being Fantasyland, the film is by no means ordinary. It's colorful, crisp, and to the delight of many a goggle-wearing guest, three-dimensional. The spirited presentation unfolds on a 150-foot wide canvas. Special effects and surprises take place off-screen, too.

As with many attractions, there are moments of darkness. If you're unsure as to whether your child might find this (or any attraction) unsettling, express your concern to an attendant. They will help you make the right decision. Note that all guests must wear 3-D glasses to enjoy the show.

PHOTO BY JILL SAFRO

BIRNBAUM'S ★BEST★ **PETER PAN'S FLIGHT:** FP+ "Come on, everybody, here we go!" So says Peter Pan at the start of this nonstop flight to Never Land. The 3-minute adventure, which takes you soaring in a pirate ship, fancifully retells the story of Peter Pan—a boy with a knack for flying and an immunity to maturity. The effects in this classic Fantasyland attraction are simple, but enchanting.

The journey starts in the Darling family nursery—which siblings Wendy, Michael, and John quickly abandon to follow Peter Pan on a trip to his homeland. As in Disney's animated feature, one of the most beautiful scenes—and one that makes this attraction a treat for grown-ups as well as smaller folk—is the sight of nighttime London, dark blue and speckled with twinkling lights. Keep your eyes peeled for Big Ben and Tower Bridge. It's quite lovely.

By the time you spot your first mermaid, you're deep in the heart of Never Land. Alas, something is terribly wrong—Captain Hook and his buccaneer buddies have taken the Darling kids captive. It's all really a trap for Peter (Hook is still peeved at Pan for serving his hand to Tick Tock the crocodile). Does everyone live happily ever after? We'll never tell.

HOT TIP!

Many Fantasyland attractions are dark, and, in some cases, special effects may be too intense for tots and small children. However, they all tend to love It's a Small World. Nothing scary about that!

PRINCESS FAIRYTALE HALL: FP+ Practice your curtsy as you approach this hall—once inside expect to meet regal folks such as Cinderella, Elena of Avalor, Rapunzel, and Tiana. Characters vary. This royal residence occupies the space formerly occupied by the Snow White's Scary Adventures attraction. And the line here can be scary—get a Fastpass+ if you can.

IT'S A SMALL WORLD: FP+ *Hola! Guten Tag! Hello!* No matter what language you speak, what you look like, or where you live, you still have a lot in common with folks the world over (including an especially high tolerance for a singsong melody that repeatedly reminds us that it's a small world after all). That's the message driving this pleasant 10-minute boat trip around the world.

Originally created for New York's 1964–65 World's Fair, the attraction is an oldie but goodie (and it is exceptionally popular with young children). The ride moves at slightly swifter than snail's pace, drifting past hundreds of colorfully costumed dolls from around the world—all of whom know all the words to the ride's famously infectious theme song (written by Disney Legends, the Sherman Brothers).

A showcase of diversity, the attraction is a simple celebration of human similarities. It's also a relaxing alternative to many of the Magic Kingdom's higher-tech, longer-line attractions.

DUMBO THE FLYING ELEPHANT: FP+ This is purely and simply a kiddie ride, though children of all ages have admitted to loving it.

A beloved symbol of Fantasyland, the ride relocated to the Storybook Circus neighborhood and doubled in size—but rest assured, the Dumbo experience remains the same. Consider stopping here first thing in the morning, or during a parade, when the line—which is often prohibitively long—thins a bit. Inspired by the 1941 Disney film classic *Dumbo*, the ride lasts a memorable two minutes.

Note: Guests in Dumbo's standby line receive a pager and are free to frolic in a covered play zone while they wait to ride. The lines for Dumbo tend to dwindle late in the day, especially when the park is open late.

FP+ = Fastpass+ attraction (see page 25)

THE BARNSTORMER: [FP]+ At this mini roller coaster attraction, guests of most sizes follow the same fluky flight path taken by the daredevil pilot known as the Great Goofini. Don't let the size fool you: This one-minute ride proves that big thrills do indeed come in small packages. Although guests as young as 3 may ride, they must be at least 35 inches tall. It may be too turbulent for some. Don't snack before riding!

CASEY JR. SPLASH 'N' SOAK STATION: The famous locomotive Casey Jr. invites Magic Kingdom guests to cool off in this colorful splash zone, conveniently located beside Fantasyland's train station. Be sure to dress tykes in swim diapers.

MAD TEA PARTY: [FP]+ The theme of this two-minute ride—in a group of oversize teacups that whirl and spin wildly—was inspired by a scene in the Disney Studios' 1951 movie production of *Alice in Wonderland*. During the sequence in question, the Mad Hatter hosts a tea party for his un-birthday.

Unlike many rides in Fantasyland, this is not just for younger kids; the 5-to-20-something crowd seems to like it best. Keep in mind that when the cups stop spinning, your head may continue to do so. Skip this ride if you suffer from motion sickness or if you have recently enjoyed a meal or a snack. And don't miss the woozy mouse that pops out of the teapot at the center of the platform—he ignored our advice.

BIRNBAUM'S ★BEST★ **THE MANY ADVENTURES OF WINNIE THE POOH:** [FP]+ Everyone's favorite honey-lovin' cub treats Magic Kingdom guests to wild and whimsical 3½-minute tours of his home turf—the Hundred Acre Wood.

The attraction features a most unlikely method of transportation: honey pots! They whisk (and bounce) guests through the pages of a giant storybook and into the Hundred Acre Wood, where the weather's most blustery. The wind is really ruffling the feathers of one

of the locals. Sight gags abound, from a bubble-blowing Heffalump (hey, this is Fantasyland) to a treacherous flood that threatens to sweep Tigger, Piglet, and the rest of the gang away. When Pooh saves the day, it's time to celebrate—and everyone is invited to the party.

Like other Fantasyland attractions, parts of this one take place in the dark. Some young children may find it a bit unsettling. That said, most little ones dig Pooh's interactive queue area. While waiting to ride or for others to do so, youngsters can bang on big vegetable "drums," play tug-of-war with a gopher, and scrawl their names in a flowing wall of honey.

UNDER THE SEA—JOURNEY OF THE LITTLE MERMAID: [FP]+ In the Magic Kingdom's first attraction to feature everyone's favorite Disney mermaid, guests are invited to board continuously moving clam-mobiles and embark on a jolly journey above and below sea level. Along the way, they join Ariel, Flounder, and all of their aquatic acquaintances, and enjoy major musical movements and pivotal plot points from the classic animated feature. It's fun for the whole family.

BIRNBAUM'S ★BEST★ **SEVEN DWARFS MINE TRAIN:** [FP]+ Heigh-ho, heigh-ho! A roller coaster is whimsically transporting guests on a musical journey through the workplace of the Seven Dwarfs—the mine where a million diamonds shine. The ride vehicles swing back and forth a bit as they zoom along the track, so folks with motion sickness or other health issues should sit this one out. Intensity-wise, the family-friendly attraction fits between the Barnstormer coaster and Big Thunder Mountain Railroad. The queue has a few interactive surprises, too. This 2½-minute attraction is extremely popular—get a Fastpass+ assignment if you can. Guests must be at least 38 inches tall to ride.

ENCHANTED TALES WITH BELLE: [FP]+ This clever mix of show and character meet and greet is one of those "you have to see it to believe it" experiences. Located in Maurice's exquisitely detailed cottage, the 30-minute experience includes lifelike Audio-Animatronics versions of Lumiere and Madame Wardrobe, plus an audience-participation performance by Belle in Beast's library. There are lots of parts to play—be sure to volunteer!

Tomorrowland

The original Tomorrowland attempted a serious look at the future. But as Disney planners discovered, it isn't easy to portray a future that persists in becoming the present. So the old Tomorrowland has given way to a friendlier, space-age town whose neighborhood atmosphere is more in keeping with the other lands in the Magic Kingdom. This is the future that never was, the fantasy world imagined by the science-fiction writers and movie-makers of the 1920s and '30s. It's a land of sky-piercing beacons and glistening metal, where shiny robots do the work, whisper-quiet cars glide along an elevated highway, and even time travel is possible.

BIRNBAUM'S
★BEST★ **BUZZ LIGHTYEAR'S SPACE RANGER SPIN:** FP+ The Evil Emperor Zurg is up to no good. As soon as he rounds up enough batteries to power his ultimate weapon of destruction—KERPLOOEY!—it's curtains for the toy universe as we know it. It's up to that Space Ranger extraordinaire Buzz Lightyear and his trusty Junior Space Rangers (that means you) to save the day.

So goes the story line of Tomorrowland's video-game-inspired spin through toyland. The adventure is experienced from a toy's point of view. Guests begin their 4½-minute tour of duty as Space Rangers at Star Command Action Center. This is where Buzz gives his team a briefing on the mission that lies ahead. Then it's off to the Launch Bay to board the ride vehicles. The ships feature dual laser cannons, glowing lights, and a piloting joystick.

Once Junior Space Rangers blast off, they find themselves surrounded by Zurg's robots, who are mercilessly ripping batteries from toys. As Rangers fire at targets,

beams of light fill the air. For every target hit, you will be rewarded with sound effects and points. The points are accumulated throughout the journey and tallied automatically. Although the vehicles follow a rigid "flight" path (they're on a track), the joystick allows

---

HOT TIP!

To up your score at Buzz Lightyear's Space Ranger Spin, keep the trigger depressed at all times. Also, be sure to aim for moving or distant targets— they provide some of the biggest point payoffs. The target on top of the volcano is quite valuable, and the one beneath Emperor Zurg will net you a whopping 100,000 points every time you zap it!

---

riders to maneuver the spaceships, arcing from side to side or spinning in circles while taking aim at their intended targets.

When the star cruiser arrives at Zurg's spaceship, it's showdown time. Will good prevail over evil? Or has time run out for the toy universe? And will you score enough points to be a Galactic Hero (999,999)? Most people improve their scores with a little practice. Note that the seat on the left side of the ride vehicle tends to have better access to the high-point-yielding targets in the first room.

MONSTERS, INC. LAUGH FLOOR: FP+ That Mike Wazowski is one enterprising eyeball. It seems the fuzzy fellow from *Monsters, Inc.* has opened a comedy club. Why? Well, it turns out his hometown is experiencing a bit of an energy crisis. Mike's clever plan is to tap into a decidedly alternative (not to mention free) fuel source to provide power for Monstropolis . . . laughter. But where can he gather enough giggles to fuel an entire city?

In a 400-seat theater in Tomorrowland, that's where. To accomplish his goal, monster of ceremonies Mike has recruited a couple of cornball comedians. Their job is to make you laugh yourself silly. And they are not too proud to resort to slapstick while doing so. Guests are encouraged to text a joke while waiting in the queue. (Standard text messaging rates apply.)

PHOTO BY JILL SAFRO

Coming Attraction

E-ticket alert! Walt Disney World is soon to reveal a brand-new thrill ride known as TRON Lightcycle Power Run (T.L.P.R.). The roller-coaster-like experience will occupy a piece of Tomorrowland real estate beside the park's Space Mountain attraction. T.L.P.R. will send intrepid park guests on a dramatic race through the digital frontier. Guests will experience the out-of-this-world adventure while aboard a zippy neon train of 2-wheeled lightcycles.

The new Magic Kingdom attraction—which was originally launched in Shanghai Disneyland—is on track to open in time for Walt Disney World's 50th anniversary celebration in 2021. For additional details and updates about the new attraction (including height requirements), visit *www.disneyworld.com* or use the My Disney Experience mobile app or website.

TOMORROWLAND TRANSIT AUTHORITY PEOPLE-MOVER: Boarded near Astro Orbiter, these open-air trains (known to Disney purists as the WEDway) move at a speed of about seven miles per hour along almost a mile of track, beside or through most of the attractions in Tomorrowland. They are operated by a linear induction motor that has no moving parts, uses little power, and emits no pollution.

The breezy excursion through Tomorrowland takes about ten minutes. There is usually less than a 15-minute wait to board (though lines can build up on busy days). It's one of our favorites. However, moments of darkness (as the train passes through Space Mountain) may be a bit unsettling for some little ones. Warn them before you climb aboard.

ASTRO ORBITER: Here, passengers fly for two minutes in machine-age rockets designed to look more like oversize Buck Rogers toys than twenty-first-century space shuttles. Riders are surrounded by vibrantly colored, whirling planets as they are treated to an astronaut's-eye view of Tomorrowland.

TOMORROWLAND SPEEDWAY: FP+ Little cars that burn up the tracks at this attraction provide quite a bit of the background noise in Tomorrowland. Young kids especially enjoy the not-especially-speedy, herky-jerky driving experience.

The vehicles have rack-and-pinion steering and disc brakes, but unlike most cars, they run along a track. Yet even expert drivers have trouble keeping them going in a straight line. (Resist the urge to panic when you notice the lack of a brake pedal—when you take your foot off the gas, the car comes to a quick, if not screeching, halt.) The one-lap tour of Tomorrowland takes about four minutes.

Notes: You must be at least 52 inches tall to drive the car by yourself. Guests must be at least 32 inches tall to ride as a passenger. Babies younger than 12 months may not participate.

BIRNBAUM'S ★BEST★ SPACE MOUNTAIN: FP+ This E-Ticket attraction, which blasted onto the Magic Kingdom scene in 1975 (and was completely refurbished in 2009), is a can't-miss crowd-pleaser for throngs of thrill-seekers. Rising to a height of more than 180 feet, this gleaming steel-and-concrete cone houses an attraction that most people call a roller coaster. The ride takes place in an outer-space-like darkness that gets inkier and scarier as the journey progresses. The rockets that roar through this blackness attain a maximum speed of just over 28 miles per hour—but somehow it feels a whole lot faster.

The Space Mountain experience is wild enough to send glasses, purses, wallets, and even an occasional set

of false teeth plummeting to the bottom of the track, so be sure to find a safe place for your possessions before the ride starts. It's also turbulent enough to upset the stomachs of those so unwise as to ride it immediately after eating. (Those who change their minds at the last minute have access to a "chicken" exit. Ask a ride attendant for directions to the door.)

Note: Guests who are under 44 inches are not permitted to ride, and must be in good health and free from heart conditions, motion sickness, back or neck problems, or any other physical limitations to ride. Expectant mothers must skip the trip. Children under age 7 must be accompanied by a guest age 14 or older.

WALT DISNEY'S CAROUSEL OF PROGRESS: First seen at New York's 1964–65 World's Fair and moved here in 1975, this 20-minute experience showcases the evolution of the American family and how life changed—and ostensibly progressed—with the advent of electricity. The hook here is that as a scene ends, the audience moves to the next one—not unlike being on a carousel (hence the name of the attraction). This is a great place to escape the crowds and heat, not to mention take a much-needed load off weary feet.

FP+ = Fastpass+ attraction (see page 25)

Magic Kingdom Shopping

No one travels to the Magic Kingdom exclusively to shop. But as many a visitor has learned, shopping is one of the most enjoyable pastimes here.

The Magic Kingdom's boutiques and stores may stock much more than just Disneyana. Along with the more predictable items in Main Street shops, it's possible to find cookbooks, glassware, and dishes, pirate hats, designer handbags, 14-karat gold charms, and filigreed costume jewelry. In Adventureland, shops may boast items imported from the exotic regions the area represents. Throughout the park, stores generally have merchandise that complements the themes of the various lands and the attractions that occupy them.

In some shops, you can watch people at work: a candy maker hand-dipping caramel apples in the Main Street Confectionery, a glassblower crafting wares in Main Street's Crystal Arts, etc.

THE CHAPEAU: This Town Square shop is the place to buy mouse ears and have them monogrammed, and to shop for straw hats, baseball caps, pins, and assorted other headgear. Feel free to pick up the receiver on the old-fashioned phone and eavesdrop away.

CURTAIN CALL COLLECTIBLES: After visiting Mickey Mouse at the Town Square Theater, guests may shop for souvenir items featuring assorted Disney characters, including the Big Cheese himself.

CRYSTAL ARTS: Cut-glass bowls, vases, glasses, and plates glitter in the cases of this crystal-chandeliered emporium. They have a lovely selection of miniature Disney characters meticulously crafted from glass. An engraver or a glassblower is often at work. There's a

---

HOT TIP!

Your Walt Disney World shopping spree does not have to end when your vacation does. Simply download the free Shop Disney Parks mobile app and you may continue to shop away. To download, visit *www.DisneyWorld.com/shop*.

We recommend shopping in the early afternoon, rather than at the end of the day, when the shops are more crowded. However, keep in mind that Main Street shops do stay open about a half hour after park closing, in case you need any last-minute gifts on the way out.

MAIN STREET

THE ART OF DISNEY: Tucked inside the Main Street Cinema, the shop showcases Disney-inspired fine art and collectibles, books, puzzles, and more. There may even be a Disney artist on hand to personalize a sketch just for you. This spot also sells collector pins. You can watch classic Mickey Mouse cartoons here, too.

BOX OFFICE GIFTS: Housed within the Town Square Theater, this shop may offer camera supplies such as batteries, camera straps, and disposable cameras. It's also the place to view and pick up PhotoPass photos and purchase MagicBand paraphernalia.

Where to Eat in the Magic Kingdom

A complete listing of all Magic Kingdom eateries—full-service restaurants, fast-food eateries, and snack shops—can be found in the *Good Meals, Great Times* chapter. See the Magic Kingdom section, beginning on page 252.

fireplace, too. Stop here to watch craftspeople mold shields and carve metal—impressive!

DISNEY CLOTHIERS: This shop offers clothing for young girls, including shirts and sleepwear, all of which incorporate Disney characters. Look for bags, accessories, and trendy trinkets.

EMPORIUM: Framed by a two-story-high portico, the Magic Kingdom's largest gift shop stocks stuffed animals and toys, T-shirts, kitchen items, home decor, hats, mugs, and much more.

The cash registers always seem to be busy, especially in the late afternoon hours and just before park closing time. Nearby lockers make for convenient storage of purchases. (Fees apply.)

You may choose to begin your Magic Kingdom day by shopping here, as Main Street opens about an hour before the rest of the park does. If you do, remember to take advantage of the aforementioned lockers, (free) package pickup, or delivery to your Walt Disney World resort. And make a point of peering into the Emporium's windows, which usually feature elaborate displays ranging from seasonal themes to character tableaux.

HARMONY BARBER SHOP: Situated next door to the Main Street Car Barn, the quaint, old-fashioned setting for this working shop (with occasional appearances by a harmonizing quartet) merits a peek even if

Let It Rain

The show doesn't stop just because of a little storm. Instead, shops throughout the Magic Kingdom sell plastic Disney Parks—branded ponchos and umbrellas to outfit guests who find themselves in need. (If there is lightning in the area, some attractions will temporarily cease operation. Safety first.)

you have no need for a trim. It's open from 9 A.M. to about 5 P.M. daily. This is a popular spot for a child's first haircut, but they serve grown-ups, too (haircuts and beard/mustache trims). Colored gel hair treatments are offered, too. For an appointment, call 407-WDW-PLAY (939-7529). Walk-ins are accepted, too (though there may be a wait).

MAIN STREET CHAMBER OF COMMERCE: This is the place to go if you have any Magic Kingdom purchases "sent to the front of the park" (aka Package Pickup). Allow at least three hours for the package to get here. It's located near City Hall.

MAIN STREET FASHION AND APPAREL: Character-related gifts and apparel are the hallmarks of this spot. The shop also stocks golf shirts, bags, hats, sweatshirts, and accessories. You'll find it next to Casey's Corner.

MAIN STREET CONFECTIONERY: Tasty treats are sold in this old-fashioned pink-and-white paradise. A delight at any time of day, but more so when the cooks in the shop's glass-walled kitchen dip apples in gooey caramel or roll out freshly made crispie treats. Then the candy sends up clouds of aroma that you could swear were being fanned out onto the street. There is a selection of fresh-made fudge, chocolate-dipped strawberries, and candy-coated marshmallows, along with jelly beans, and dozens of other confections that will satisfy any sweet tooth.

NEWSSTAND: No newspapers are sold in the Magic Kingdom—even at its newsstand, which is near the park entrance. (It's to the left, just inside the entrance.) The stand sells character items, stamps, and souvenirs.

THE SHADOW BOX: Watching Rubio Artist Co. silhouette cutters snip black paper into the likenesses of children is one of Main Street's more fascinating diversions. The Shadow Box is at the corner of Main and Center streets.

UPTOWN JEWELERS: Designed to resemble a turn-of-the-twentieth-century collectibles shop, this spiffy store specializes in jewelry, watches, handbags, scarves, purses, wallets, shoes, phone cases, and other gifts. Uptown Jewelers is also home to the Disney Parks/PANDORA Jewelry Collection. A notable addition to the shelves: garments and accessories from The Disney Dress Shop. Other wares may include cosmetics, tote bags, backpacks, and more.

WHEELCHAIR AND ECV RENTAL: Guests may rent strollers at a spot under the Main Street Train Station. Wheelchairs and Electric Conveyance Vehicles (ECVs)

Disney's PhotoPass

As you wander the theme parks, Disney Cast Members will be happy to snap your picture—just ask! After mugging for the camera, you'll be asked to scan your MagicBand (see page 24) or a PhotoPass card. It will link all such photographs together for viewing on the Internet. You can ogle and e-mail the low-res images for free for up to 45 days after they are taken. High-quality prints of various sizes are for sale. To buy or peruse photos, visit *mydisneyphotopass.com* or use your My Disney Experience account. Each park has a spot for photo viewing. Check a park guidemap for locations. Individual photo downloads start at about $16.95, while the unlimited Memory Maker Package runs about $169 if purchased in advance. (This is a bit of splurge, but a very convenient way to get quality shots of your whole party.) Note that Disney World photographers will gladly capture a moment using your camera, too. Say cheese!

are offered at a separate location, directly across from the Newsstand, just inside the park entrance. (The supply of ECVs is limited—get there early.) All rentals are offered on a first-come, first-served basis. Hold on to the receipt—it will get you a replacement stroller or wheelchair should yours disappear during the day or if you "hop" to another park. Note that anything rented here cannot be taken out of the Magic Kingdom.

ADVENTURELAND

AGRABAH BAZAAR: Stop here and find clothing and accessories covered with animal prints and images, toys and costumes with a safari theme, and items featuring Jasmine and Aladdin. The bazaar also stocks musical instruments, tumbled stones, snacks, and souvenirs themed to Moana, Simba, and other Disney pals.

BWANA BOB'S: Stop here for tropically themed jewelry, bags, pins, and hats, plus sunglasses, bottled soft drinks, and more.

ISLAND SUPPLY: This small tropical shop features a large selection of sunglasses and sunglass accessories.

THE PIRATES LEAGUE: More than just a crew of plank-walkers, this group of savvy pirates transforms guests into one of their own—in exchange for loot, of course. Once you're swashbuckled up, they'll snap your photo

in the "secret" treasure room. Call 407-WDW-CREW (939-2739) for pricing or to make a reservation. The Pirates League is in the Plaza del Sol Caribe Bazaar, by the Pirates of the Caribbean.

PLAZA DEL SOL CARIBE BAZAAR: Ahoy there, mateys! A swashbuckler's delight, the joint adjoining the Pirates of the Caribbean sells stuff celebrating both the attraction and the feature films of the same name. It also stocks other pirate booty, including Jolly Roger flags, rings, dolls, pirate costumes, themed hats, and eye patches. If that's not enough treasure for you, check out the candy and snacks. The pièce de résistance for pirate fans? Pirate makeovers! (See the previous entry, The Pirates League.) This is one of our favorite shops.

FRONTIERLAND

BIG AL'S: Named for one of the most popular (and least talented) member of the Country Bears, this riverfront locale is known for its selection of headwear, including Davy Crockett-style caps.

BRIAR PATCH: Toys and cuddly character items, plus kids' apparel and hats for the whole family, are featured wares at this shop, located near the Splash Mountain exit. There's also a pair of rocking chairs for those who need to take a load off.

FRONTIER TRADING POST: This is the place to shop for collector pins and the associated accoutrements. Since it's got the largest selection of pins in the park, they might want to rename this the Pin Trading Post. The Trading Post also boasts a selection of Western-themed shirts, plus hats, decorative rocks, MagicBands, and Sorcerers of the Magic Kingdom spell card binders. (For details about Sorcerers of the Magic Kingdom, turn to page 124.) There is a station at which guests may customize MagicBands and mobile phone cases (Disney style), too.

PRAIRIE OUTPOST & SUPPLY: Stop by this turn-of-the-twentieth-century general store for candy (including a wall of jelly beans), coffee, cookies, pastries, jellies, and kitchen accessories.

LIBERTY SQUARE

LIBERTY SQUARE PORTRAIT GALLERY: In the midst of Liberty Square, guests may have their portraits or caricatures drawn in this open-air studio.

MEMENTO MORI: Welcome, foolish mortals—to a spooky and spectacular shop dedicated to all things Haunted Mansion. Here you'll find everything from gargoyle candle holders and hourglasses to "Ghost Host" gear and hitch-hiking ghost figurines. It's also possible to have your portrait taken, Haunted Mansion style. Yep, for about twenty bucks, you can be transformed into a spirited version of your future, ghoulish self. So creepy, but so cool.

YE OLDE CHRISTMAS SHOPPE: A wide variety of festive Yuletide items, including decorative Disney-themed gifts and ornaments (many of which can be personalized), is available year-round. Look for items such as stockings, tree toppers, and Christmas cards.

FANTASYLAND

BIBBIDI BOBBIDI BOUTIQUE: Housed within Cinderella Castle, this shop offers young guests the opportunity to be transformed into princesses and knights. Magical makeovers are available from 8 A.M. to 7 P.M. Prices vary. Magic Kingdom admission is required to enter this location. (There is an additional Bibbidi Bobbidi Boutique shop at Disney Springs. While there is no admission fee, there is a charge for services at both locations.) For pricing information or to book a reservation, call 407-WDW-STYLE (939-7895). Photo packages are available, too. Reservations are strongly recommended.

BIG TOP SOUVENIRS: A not-so-hidden gem, Big Top is joyfully themed and full of energy. Step inside the tent and discover Disney merchandise galore. At the center of the tent is Big Top Treats—a circus-themed confectionery dispensing caramel corn, chocolate-dipped strawberries, cupcakes, crispie treats, candy-coated marshmallows, and other sweet treats. Yum.

BONJOUR VILLAGE GIFTS: Visit this charming boutique in Fantasyland for items inspired by Disney's *Beauty and the Beast*. Expect to find apparel, T-shirts, toys, royal dinnerware, Cogsworth clocks, glowing goblets, tapestries, castle artwork, and more. Also sold: jigsaw puzzles, Mrs. Potts tea sets for kids, and books. (Belle would appreciate that.)

CASTLE COUTURE: Stop here for royal playthings, costumes, dolls, and kids' princess and knight apparel, plus jewelry and accessories.

FANTASY FAIRE: Set beside the Mickey's Philhar-Magic attraction, this faire focuses on Disney-themed headwear, plus shirts, bags, and toys. Many items may be personalized (for a fee).

HUNDRED ACRE GOODS: Located at the exit of The Many Adventures of Winnie the Pooh attraction, this small shop is stuffed with wares featuring friends from the Hundred Acre Wood (among other places). Among the items Pooh bear proffers are toys, hats, shirts, baby clothing, snacks, and bottled soft drinks.

SIR MICKEY'S: Expect to find Disney princess-themed clothing and souvenir items in this shop with a design based on *The Brave Little Tailor*, the cartoon in which Mickey defeats a fearsome giant to win the heart of Princess Minnie. (It was one of the most elaborate and expensive Mickey Mouse cartoons ever made.) Mouse ears may be purchased and monogrammed here.

TOMORROWLAND

MERCHANT OF VENUS: The place to go for anything and everything Stitch, plush toys, games, and sunglasses. There is a station at which to have your picture placed in a decidedly Disney scene, too. (Fees apply.) Details are subject to change.

MICKEY'S STAR TRADERS: This is one of the better places to go in the Magic Kingdom for Disney-themed items: plush toys, hats, shirts, candy, etc. Sunglasses and sun-care products are also sold. The Tomorrowland Transit Authority passes through here, too. (To catch a glimpse of the T.T.A., look up!)

Magic Kingdom Entertainment

In this most magical corner of the World, a slate of live performances ranks among the more serendipitous discoveries. The Magic Kingdom's entertainment mix includes dazzling high-tech shows and old-fashioned numbers alike.

While details may change in 2020, what follows is a good indication of the park's entertainment repertoire. Check the park Times Guide or the My Disney Experience app or website for the schedule and showtimes during your visit to the Magic Kingdom.

CASEY'S CORNER PIANIST: A peppy pianist tickles the ivories of a snow-white upright, just outside Casey's Corner on Main Street, U.S.A. Twenty-minute performances take place throughout the day.

ONCE UPON A TIME: A 14-minute animated, musical celebration of Disney storytelling, this takes place on Cinderella Castle. Yes, *on* the castle. (The beloved WDW icon has evolved into a high-tech canvas for Disney artists without losing any of its charm.) The action starts with Chip (from *Beauty and the Beast*) asking his mom to tell him a story. Mrs. Potts doesn't need to be asked twice—and starts to tell stories that begin with "Once upon a time..." And then a montage of memorable movie moments lights up the night. Chip and Magic Kingdom guests hear stories and songs from Disney classics, including *Alice in Wonderland, Tangled, Peter Pan, Cinderella, Winnie the Pooh,* and more. How do all the stories end? Happily, of course! The front and sides of the Cinderella Castle offer slightly different viewing experiences—so if you've already enjoyed it from one vantage point, you might want to try another. In addition to the regular show, Once Upon a Time may include seasonal updates. Check a Times Guide for this nighttime show's performance schedule.

CITIZENS OF MAIN STREET: Performers clad in 19th-century costumes interact with Magic Kingdom guests throughout the day. They've even been known to burst into song from time to time. Keep an eye out for the Socialite, the Fire Chief, and the Suffragette crusading for women's right to vote. Don't forget your high-tech, picture-taking contraptions—the old-timey characters are pleased as punch to pose for photos.

DAPPER DANS: You just might encounter a barbershop quartet while strolling down Main Street. Conspicuously clad in straw hats and striped vests, the ever-so-jovial Dapper Dans tap-dance and let one-liners fly during their short, four-part-harmony performances. Each show runs about 20 minutes.

BIRNBAUM'S ★BEST★ **HAPPILY EVER AFTER:** A dynamite, pyrotechnic/digital projection extravaganza, Happily Ever After is presented most evenings when the Magic Kingdom stays open after dark. This jubilant nighttime spectacular takes place on and above Cinderella Castle. Showtimes vary—check a park Times Guide for specifics. Happily Ever After is ideally viewed from Main Street, U.S.A., but can be seen from many perspectives throughout the theme park. The 18-minute show is typically presented nightly, rain or shine, but it may be canceled due to inclement weather.

FAIRYTALE GARDEN: Merida from *Brave* greets guests in this nook beside Cinderella Castle each day (on the right side when facing the Castle from Main Street). Check a Times Guide for specifics. Details are subject to change.

FLAG RETREAT: At about 5 P.M. each afternoon (check a current Times Guide), patriotic music fills the air as a color guard marches to Town Square, in Main Street, U.S.A., and takes down the American flag that flies from the flagpole.

BIRNBAUM'S ★BEST★ FESTIVAL OF FANTASY PARADE: FP+ A musical celebration of Disney Animation, this parade wends its way down Main Street once a day. The festival focuses on Disney friends who frequent Fantasy-land. Kids love to wave to favorite characters—especially Anna and Elsa. The elaborate floats are quite impressive.

The Festival of Fantasy parade highlights the classic tales of *Tangled*, *The Little Mermaid*, *Sleeping Beauty*, *Pinocchio*, *Brave*, *Dumbo*, and more.

HOEDOWN HAPPENING: Every now and then a happy hoedown happens in Frontierland. Disney pals such as Bre'r Bear, Bre'r Fox, and Bre'r Rabbit pop in, as do several of those musically inclined Country Bears. An interactive display, this hoedown usually wraps up with the Hokey Pokey. Do join in! The seemingly spontaneous party isn't listed in the Times Guide—so you best ask a local Cast Member about the next possible performance.

MICKEY'S ROYAL FRIENDSHIP FAIRE: Mickey and his band of merrymakers are hosting a joyous festival in front of Cinderella Castle, and they are welcoming friends old and new—including you!

Goofy has invited folks from *The Princess and the Frog*; Donald Duck's guests include friends he met at the Snuggly Duckling in the Land of the Enchanted Woods; and Daisy Duck introduces her guests Rapunzel and Flynn Ryder. Mickey has a very special surprise for *Frozen* fans: He traveled all the way to The Land of Mystic Mountains to invite Olaf, Anna, and Elsa (who brings along a little of her trademark icy magic). Festivities include lively dancing, special effects, and memorable music—including an original song. The show is presented daily (but may be canceled due to inclement weather). We recommend viewing this show just before or just after a parade. Check a park Times Guide for the day's performance schedule.

LET THE MAGIC BEGIN: The Magic Kingdom park kicks off each morning with a whimsical welcome ceremony. The 5-minute show begins as the Royal Majesty Maker invites guests to gather 'round the Castle forecourt. Mickey Mouse soon takes the stage to greet eager parkgoers. He's joined by Minnie, Pluto, Chip, Dale, princes, princesses, and one very special Fairy Godmother. With a wave of her wand and a "Bibbidi bobbidi boo!"—the Magic Kingdom's day has officially begun. Have fun! (Main Street opens before the rest of the park, so get there as early as you can.)

MAIN STREET PHILHARMONIC: Clad in bright red and white, Disney World's merry marching band serenades guests with old-school marches, big-band standards, and classic Disney ditties. Each perky performance lasts about 20 minutes.

MAIN STREET TROLLEY SHOW: A dozen colorfully costumed performers arrive via horse-drawn trolley and put on a cheery song and dance show "right down the middle of Main Street, U.S.A."

MOVE IT, SHAKE IT, DANCE & PLAY IT!: Whether you are celebrating a special occasion or just the fact that you are in the Magic Kingdom, this dance party is a treat. A spectacle of music and dance, the 35-minute jubilee invites guests to join in the fun as dancers and Disney characters take over the street by Cinderella Castle. Check a Times Guide for the schedule.

THE MUPPETS PRESENT . . . GREAT MOMENTS IN AMERICAN HISTORY: The Muppets are coming, the Muppets are coming! In fact, they come to Liberty Square several times a day to reenact the drafting of the Declaration of Independence and Paul Revere's Ride. The fuzzy cast is as follows: Kermit the Frog, Miss Piggy, Gonzo, Fozzie Bear, and that super patriotic bird: Sam Eagle. The show takes place in the windows above and next door to Hall of Presidents. Standing room only. (The action is easily viewed from most vantage points in the square—just look up.) Check a park Times Guide for showtimes.

HOLIDAY HAPPENINGS

It's a rare holiday that passes quietly in Disney's Magic Kingdom. During certain holidays, such as Christmas, New Year's Eve, and the Fourth of July, the park breaks curfew, staying open extra late and stepping up its nighttime entertainment. On these occasions, special performances of parades and the fireworks are often in store. Entertainment plans are subject to change, so it's wise to visit *www.disneyworld.com* or call 407-934-7639 for information and schedules.

EASTER: Easter is a delightful, though quite busy, time to visit the Magic Kingdom. Mr. and Mrs. Easter Bunny have been known to appear in the park to help guests celebrate the occasion.

FOURTH OF JULY: The busiest day of the summer—and with good reason: There's a double-size fireworks extravaganza that lights up the skies above Cinderella Castle and the Seven Seas Lagoon. It is a thrilling spectacle. Arrive at the park as early as possible for this packed, patriotic occasion.

HALLOWEEN: This most spooky of holidays is celebrated on (many) select nights from August through October with a special-ticket event: Mickey's Not-So-Scary Halloween Party. The park closes a bit early on nights when the party takes place. (Guests bearing tickets to the party can stay in the park.) Expect characters in costume, creepy music and fog effects, and trick-or-treating throughout the park. It's a real hoot! Mickey's Boo-to-You Halloween Parade takes place, as does a special edition of the fireworks show. Visit *www.disneyworld.com/halloween*, or call 407-824-4321 to order tickets to the party.

CHRISTMAS: A towering Christmas tree goes up in Main Street's Town Square, and the entire Magic Kingdom is decked out as only Disney can do it. (Cinderella Castle is draped in 250,000 sparkling lights!)

On select nights in November and December, Walt Disney World's original park hosts a special-admission celebration known as Mickey's Very Merry Christmas Party. The festivities, complete with hot cocoa, holiday cookies, and snow flurries on Main Street, U.S.A.,

include a running (or two) of Mickey's Once Upon a Christmastime Parade, festive shows, and a special fireworks show. Disney characters are on hand, too.

Mickey's Very Merry Christmas party is a popular (and enjoyable) event. Purchase tickets way ahead of time. And don't forget to don your holiday apparel; *www.disneyworld.com/christmasparty*. On dates when the Christmas party is offered, the park closes early to day guests. Plan accordingly.

NEW YEAR'S EVE: It has always been true that on December 31 the throngs here are body to body. Expect a dazzling, supersize fireworks display (which is also offered on December 30) and oodles of happy holiday decorations. There's often plenty of nip in the air as the evening goes on, so we recommend dressing in layers.

Where to Find the Characters at Magic Kingdom

Mickey and his pals make appearances throughout the day—but you can often find him at Town Square Exposition Hall. Tinker Bell greets guests there, too. Alice and her Wonderland friends may appear near the Mad Tea Party. Pooh and Tigger frequent Fantasyland. Disney royals such as Rapunzel, Tiana, and Elena visit Princess Fairytale Hall. You'll find Goofy, Donald, Daisy, and (possibly) Pluto or Minnie at Pete's Silly Sideshow in Fantasyland. Peter Pan has been known to hang out by his attraction. Ariel greets folks in her Fantasyland grotto. Gaston has been known to flex his muscles near his tavern in Fantasyland. And Anna and Elsa lead the Festival of Fantasy parade. Feel free to wave hello!

Check a Times Guide for updated information. Park eateries such as Cinderella's Royal Table and the Crystal Palace offer opportunities to mingle with various Disney characters, too. (See page 298.)

Hot Tips

- Start at a Fastpass+ kiosk or use a smartphone to book Fastpasses for as many attractions as possible (if you haven't reserved in advance).

- Get to the Magic Kingdom entrance about an hour before opening time—guests may visit Main Street before the rest of the park starts up for the day.

- If you're driving to the Magic Kingdom, start very early. Most visitors arrive between 9:30 A.M. and 11:30 A.M., and the adjoining roads and parking lots are jammed.

- No matter what your mode of travel, allow extra time to reach the park entrance. Area traffic and security checks can cause delays—especially during peak times.

- For the best fireworks view, stand on Main Street between Town Square and Casey's Corner. (If you stand too close to the castle, some of the show may be obstructed.)

- All Disney parks provide free Wi-Fi, but charging stations are hard to come by. We recommend you bring a battery pack from home or buy a portable phone charging system from a park kiosk for about $30.

- The Main Street plaza gardens are a lovely place for a picnic (on the lawn).

- On super soggy afternoons, the park's usual parade may not be presented. Instead, guests may be treated to the short-but-very-sweet Rainy Day Cavalcade. Catch it if you can!

- Eager to meet Mickey Mouse? Head for the Town Square Theater on Main Street (near the train station). He likes to greet guests there. Get a Fastpass+ assignment if you can.

- Travel light. The fewer bags you have, the faster you'll pass through security.

- Avoid the mealtime rush hours by eating early or late: before 11:30 A.M. or after 2 P.M., and before 5 P.M. or after 8 P.M.

- Table-service restaurants are in high demand in this park. Book yours as early as possible. And don't forget to confirm your reservations.

- At busy times, take in these (usually) less-packed attractions: The Country Bear Jamboree, The Enchanted Tiki Room, Walt Disney's Carousel of Progress, and the Hall of Presidents.

- Use a smartphone to check all attraction wait times via the My Disney Experience app (which may be downloaded for free).

- If your party decides to split up, set a meeting place and time. Avoid regrouping in front of Cinderella Castle, since this area can become quite congested.

- Jazz up the time spent waiting in line with Play Disney Parks—a free mobile app that entertains with attraction-themed fun, interactive in-park adventures, trivia and more.

- Park guests have the right to chicken out at any time while waiting in line. In other words, should you or a member of your party have second thoughts about soaring on Space Mountain, visiting with the grinning ghosts of the Haunted Mansion, or braving another attraction, simply inform an attendant and you'll be discreetly whisked out a special exit.

- If you have rented a stroller, plan to return it just before the nightly fireworks presentation. That way, after the show, you can make a bee-line for your pillow rather than stand in a line to return the stroller.

- Some of the merchandise found in the shops at Walt Disney World may be purchased with the Shop Disney Parks app and at *shopdisney.com*.

- You can usually get in line for an attraction right up until the minute the park closes.

- If the park closes early on the day you plan to visit, consider booking dinner at a Magic Kingdom area resort (Contemporary, Grand Floridian, Polynesian Village, or Wildernesss Lodge). But keep in mind that transportation to and from the Magic Kingdom and its parking lot only runs for about an hour after the park closes. Plan accordingly.

HIDDEN MICKEYS

Disney Imagineers have hidden Mickey's image all over Walt Disney World. Some are easier to track down than others. Here are some of the most popular "Hidden Mickeys" at the Magic Kingdom. How many can you find? Check the circle when you spot each one!

Pirates of the Caribbean: As you enter the ride's main building and jump on the standby line (the queue on the left), keep your eyes peeled for four large gun cabinets hanging on both sides of the wall (you will pass a set of smaller ones on the right before reaching these). The locks on the cabinets form Hidden Mickeys. ○

Splash Mountain: About halfway through the ride and in the room with jumping water, look quickly to your right and find a turtle floating on its back on a small geyser. Now look just above and behind the turtle for one of the most creative Hidden Mickeys in the park: It's a plastic bobber attached to a fishing line. There's a more obvious one in the cloud formation by the riverboat in the "Zip-a-dee-doo-dah" room, after the big splash. ○

Big Thunder Mountain Railroad: At the very end of the ride and after the train slows down, look to your right to find two sets of gear shifts laying on the ground. The second set forms a Hidden Mickey, although you may notice that the dimensions are not quite proportional (Mickey's "ears" are significantly smaller than his "head"). ○

The Haunted Mansion: In the ghostly party scene, look at the bottom left corner of the banquet table for a Hidden Mickey made of two saucers and a plate. (An H.M. that is easily replicated at home!) ○

Carousel of Progress: In the Christmas scene, look to the far left for nutcrackers lined up on top of the fireplace. The nutcracker farthest to the left is a Mickey nutcracker. Also in this scene, look for a Mickey plush toy in a box under the Christmas tree and a special pepper grinder on the kitchen counter (it's best seen from seats on the right side of the revolving theater). ○

Buzz Lightyear's Space Ranger Spin: Once you enter the interior queue, look for a poster on the right called "Planets of the Galactic Alliance" and find the planet "Pollost Prime." One of the continents forms a Mickey profile. Keep your eyes open during the attraction's last room and you'll see this same planet on the left side. ○

Under the Sea—Journey of The Little Mermaid: When entering the scene where everyone's favorite crab sings "Under the Sea," you may spot several purple corals that form Mr. Mouse's head. (Hint: Two are on the floor and one is on a wall.) ○

It's a Small World: Don't rush into the queue, because the wait time sign forms a Hidden Mickey if you tilt your head to the left. Once on the ride, pay close attention to the Africa room and search for purple leaves hanging from the ceiling that form several Hidden Mickeys. (Hint: You'll find them by the giraffes.) ○

The Magic Carpets of Aladdin: You'll feel like a pro once you find this small but very cool Hidden Mickey. First find the Agrabah Bazaar shop (across from the Magic Carpets of Aladdin exit) and find the pole with a thick blue stripe at the bottom. Take about three steps toward the attraction and look down to find a charm in the cement with a Hidden Mickey in the center. ○

Tomorrowland Transit Authority PeopleMover: Toward the end of the ride, you will glide past a futuristic woman getting her hair done. That fashionable future-dweller has a Hidden Mickey on her belt buckle. (Hint: She's on the right side of the ride vehicle's forward motion.) ○

Swiss Family Tree House: As you make the trek up (and down) the treehouse stairs, take a good look at the giant tree trunk. Cleverly camouflaged by moss and bark? A subtle-but-familiar silhouette. ○

Peter Pan's Flight: The sign above the attraction's stand-by entrance includes a Hidden Mickey that's best described as *cumulus*. ○

Specifics may change during 2020.

WHERE IN THE WORLD?

All of the photos on this page were taken at the Magic Kingdom. Do you know where? We challenge you to find all the spots where these images were shot and snap a (non-flash) photo for yourself as you discover each one. Happy hunting! (For locations, turn to page 362.)

PHOTOS #3 AND #4 BY JILL SA

EPCOT

"It's kind of fun to do the impossible." —Walt Disney

145 Getting Oriented

146 Park Primer

147 Future World

157 World Showcase

171 Entertainment

172 Hot Tips

Imagine a place with an entertainment inventory that includes both a rich sampling of world cultures and a fun, enlightening journey to the technological frontier. You now have an inkling of the eye-opening and mind-broadening potential of Epcot—a place that has evolved most imaginatively since the day it opened.

Walt Disney suggested the idea back in 1966: "Epcot will be an experimental prototype community of tomorrow that will take its cue from the new ideas and technologies that are emerging from the creative center of American industry." It would never be completed, he said, but would "always be introducing and testing and demonstrating new materials and systems." On October 1, 1982, Walt Disney's dream became a reality. Test Track puts guests on the thrilling inside track of the fast-paced world of automobile design. A re-imagined Soarin'—known as Soarin' Around the World—delivers the breathtaking sensation of flight. And old favorites like Turtle Talk with Crush and Spaceship Earth continue to ignite the creative forces within us all. In keeping with the ever-evolving tradition, Epcot guests will be treated to major enhancements for years to come.

The park consists of two areas of exploration: Future World and World Showcase. The former examines ideas in science, technology, and other topics in ways that make them downright irresistible. The latter celebrates the diversity of the world's peoples, portraying a stunning array of nations, with extraordinary devotion to detail.

Think of Epcot as Disney's playground for curious, thoughtful, and adventurous guests of all ages. The experiences it delivers—all of them wonders of the real world—continue to amaze, educate, inspire, and (of course) entertain.

EPCOT

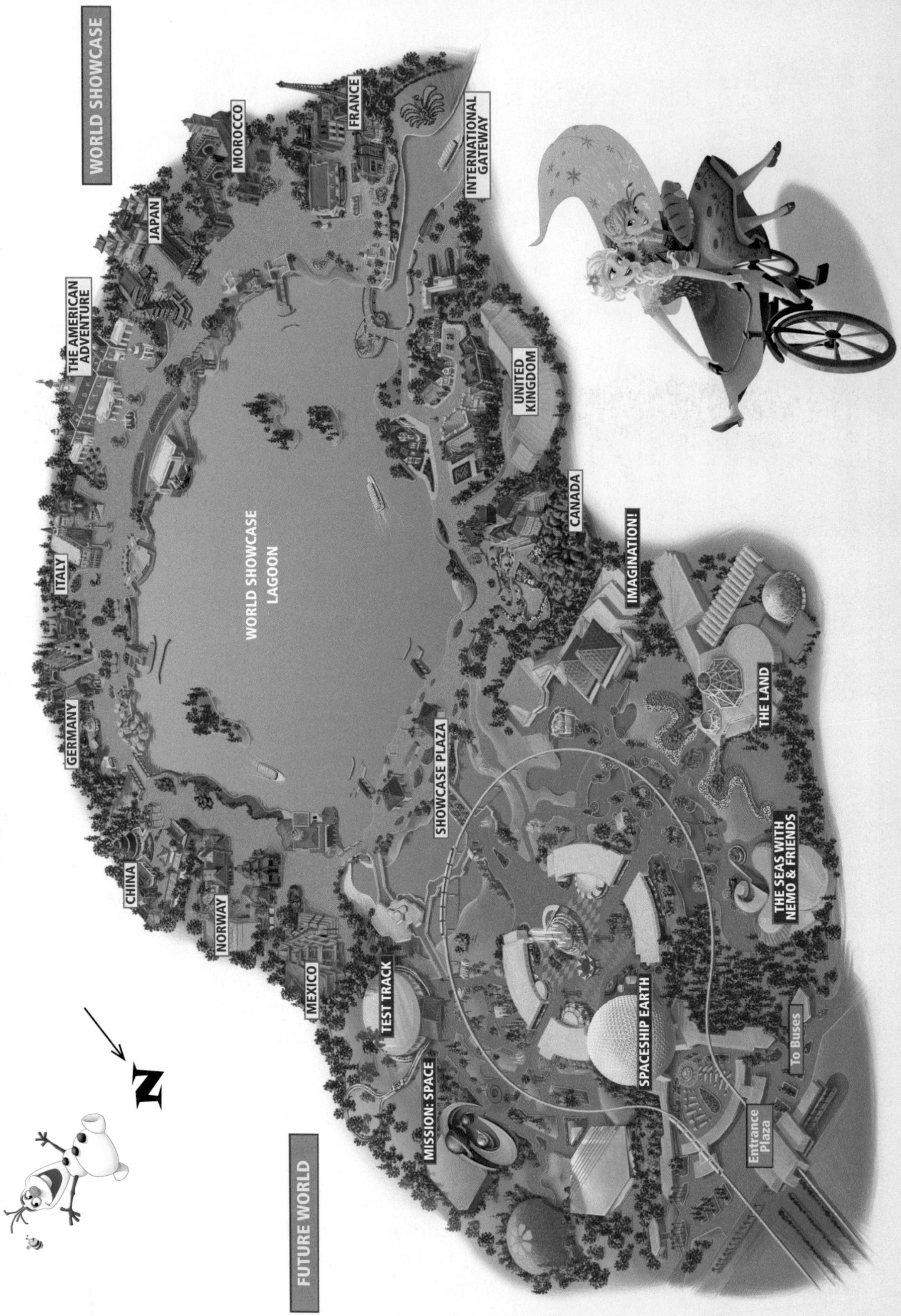

MOROCCO

FRANCE

JAPAN

INTERNATIONAL GATEWAY

THE AMERICAN ADVENTURE

ITALY

UNITED KINGDOM

WORLD SHOWCASE LAGOON

GERMANY

CANADA

IMAGINATION!

THE LAND

CHINA

SHOWCASE PLAZA

THE SEAS WITH NEMO & FRIENDS

NORWAY

MEXICO

TEST TRACK

MISSION: SPACE

SPACESHIP EARTH

To Buses

Entrance Plaza

N

FUTURE WORLD

Getting Oriented

Triple the Magic Kingdom park and you have an idea of the size of Epcot. As for layout, the park is shaped something like a giant hourglass. The pavilions of Future World fill the northern bulb, while the international potpourri called World Showcase occupies the southern bulb. Future World is anchored on the north by the imposing silver "geosphere," dubbed Spaceship Earth.

As you pass through Epcot's main Entrance Plaza (which is being re-imagined in 2020), Spaceship Earth looms ahead. Pathways curve around the 180-foot-tall geosphere, depositing guests in the Future World area of the park. There are two roughly symmetrical north-south avenues; these are dotted with the pavilions that form the outer perimeter of Future World. Mission: SPACE and Test Track flank Spaceship Earth on the east side, while Imagination!, The Land, and The Seas with Nemo & Friends lie to the west.

In World Showcase, the international pavilions are arranged around World Showcase Lagoon, with The American Adventure on the lake's southernmost shore. Several paths from Future World lead to World Showcase Promenade, a 1.2-mile thoroughfare that wraps around the lagoon, winding past each pavilion in the process.

HOW TO GET THERE

Take Exit 67 off I-4. Continue along to the Epcot Auto Plaza; if you park in a distant parking lot, take a tram to Epcot's main entrance.

By WDW Transportation: From the Grand Floridian, Contemporary, and Polynesian Village: hotel monorail to the Transportation and Ticket Center (TTC), then switch to the TTC-Epcot monorail. From Magic Kingdom: express monorail or resort monorail to the TTC, then switch to the TTC-Epcot monorail. From Disney Springs: bus to any resort, then transfer to an Epcot bus or boat From Disney's Hollywood Studios: water taxi, bus, or Disney Skyliner. From Disney's Animal Kingdom, all other Walt Disney World resorts, Four Seasons resort, and the resorts on Hotel Plaza Boulevard: buses.

The back entrance to the park, known as International Gateway, provides access via the World Showcase section of Epcot. Located between the France and U.K. pavilions, it may be reached via walkways and FriendShip water taxis from BoardWalk, Yacht & Beach Club, Swan and Dolphin resorts, and Disney's Hollywood Studios. The Disney Skyliner connects International Gateway with Disney's Hollywood Studios, plus Caribbean Beach, Pop Century, Riviera, and Art of Animation resorts. It is possible to purchase park admission here, at Epcot's "back door."

PARKING

All-day car parking at Epcot starts at $25 for day visitors (standard parking is free to WDW resort guests and most annual passholders; trucks, trailers, and RVs cost more; preferred parking costs $45–$50). Attendants will direct you to a lot. Trams circulate regularly, providing transportation between the distant lots and Epcot's main entrance. Be sure to note the section and aisle in which you park. Parking receipts allow for re-entry here (and other Disney theme parks) throughout the day.

HOURS

Future World is usually open from about 9 A.M. to 9 P.M. (though some attractions may close at 7 P.M.). World Showcase hours are about 11 A.M. to 9 P.M. (though some attractions may open earlier). During certain holiday periods and summer months, Epcot hours are extended. It's best to arrive a bit before the park's posted opening time. Guests staying at Disney owned-and-operated resorts may take advantage of Extra Magic Hours (see page 22). For schedules, use the My Disney Experience app or website, or visit *www.disneyworld.com.*

GETTING AROUND

Water taxis, called FriendShips, ferry guests across the World Showcase Lagoon. It's not much quicker than brisk walking, but it's a nice way to rest weary feet. FriendShip docks are located near Mexico, Canada, Germany, and Morocco. (The only other way to traverse the vast section of this park is on foot.) Boats do not operate during the Epcot's nightly fireworks spectacular.

Admission Prices

ONE-DAY BASE TICKET*
(Restricted to use only in Epcot. Prices are for date-based tickets. Rates for Flexible Date tickets are higher. **Prices exclude tax and are likely to rise in 2020.**)

Adult	$109–$159
Child**	$104–$154

* 1-Day tickets are valid only on the selected date. Flexible Date tickets purchased in 2020 must be used by December 31, 2021. This is the cost of a 1-day/1-park-only ticket. Terms are subject to change. For updates, visit *https://disneyworld.disney.go.com/admission/tickets/.*

** 3 through 9 years of age; children under age 3 free (no ticket required)

Park Primer

BABY FACILITIES

There are changing tables, a feeding area with high chairs, a kitchen with a microwave oven and sink, and comfy facilities for nursing mothers at the Baby Care Center, located between Test Track and the Mexico pavilion. Disposable diapers may be kept behind the counter at some Epcot shops; just ask.

CAMERA NEEDS

The World Traveler shop at International Gateway may stock batteries and disposable cameras. Memory cards are no longer sold. It's best to bring camera necessities from home. Note that selfie sticks are not permitted in any Disney theme park or water park.

DISABILITY INFORMATION

Nearly all of Epcot's attractions, shops, and restaurants are accessible to guests using wheelchairs. Parking for guests with disabilities is available. Additional services are available for guests with visual and hearing disabilities. The complimentary *Guide for Guests with Disabilities* is available at the park entrances and at Guest Relations. It provides a detailed overview of all services. For more information, turn to the *Getting Ready to Go* chapter of this book and visit *www.disneyworld.com*.

FIRST AID

Minor medical problems can be handled at the First Aid Center, between Test Track and the Mexico pavilion. Keep in mind that many guests could avoid a trip to First Aid simply by staying well hydrated. **If you have an emergency, notify an employee and call 911.**

INFORMATION

Guest Relations, which has one location to the right of the main entrance plaza (near the bus depot) and another near Spaceship Earth, is equipped with guidemaps, Times Guides, and a helpful staff.

LOCKERS

Lockers are found next to Spaceship Earth and at the International Gateway entrance. Cost is $10–$15 for unlimited use throughout the day (in Epcot only).

LOST & FOUND

Report lost items to Guest Relations or fill out a lost item report at *www.chargerback.com/disneyworld*. After your visit, go to the aforementioned website. If you find an item, kindly give it to a park employee.

LOST CHILDREN

Alert an employee and report lost children at Guest Relations or the Baby Care Center. Kids who become separated from their parents will be looked after at the Baby Care Center until picked up by a parent.

MONEY MATTERS

There are automated teller machines (ATMs) at the main entrance, on the path between Future World and World Showcase, at International Gateway (near United Kingdom), and at The American Adventure. Some foreign currency may be exchanged at Guest Relations. Major credit cards (American Express, JCB, Discover, Diner's Club, Visa, and MasterCard), traveler's checks, Disney Dollars, and Disney gift cards are accepted throughout WDW. MagicBands and Walt Disney World resort IDs are accepted at most park locations (if backed up with a major credit card).

PACKAGE PICKUP

Epcot shops can arrange for most purchases to be transported (no charge) to the Gift Stop in Entrance Plaza or the World Traveler shop at International Gateway (in World Showcase) for later pickup.

SAME-DAY RE-ENTRY

Be sure to wear your MagicBand (if you used it for admission to the park) or retain your ticket if you plan to return to Epcot later the same day.

SECURITY CHECK

Guests entering Disney theme parks are subject to a thorough security check. All bags will be searched by security personnel before guests may enter the park. A metal detector screens park guests. Weapons (including toys) are prohibited. For details and a complete listing of Walt Disney World Park Rules, visit Guest Relations or go to *www.disneyworld.com/ParkRules*.

STROLLERS & WHEELCHAIRS

Strollers, wheelchairs, and Electric Conveyance Vehicles (ECVs) may be rented from venues at both park entrances. Wheelchairs are also available at the Gift Stop. The cost is $15 for single strollers, $31 for double strollers, and $12 for wheelchairs. A Length of Stay rental yields a $2-per-day discount. It's $50 a day for an ECV, plus a $20 refundable deposit. Quantities are limited. Hold on to your rental receipt; it can be used that same day to get a replacement at Epcot or another Disney theme park.

Future World

A mere listing of the basic themes covered by the pavilions at Future World—agriculture, the ocean, the land, car design, communication, imagination, technology, and space—tends to sound a tad academic. But when these intriguing topics are presented with a special flair, they become part of an experience that ranks among Disney's most entertaining.

Some of these subjects are explored in the course of lively and unusual "adventures," involving a whole arsenal of motion pictures, special effects, and Audio-Animatronics figures so lifelike that it is hard to remain unmoved. The basic elements are also appealing in their own right, from the palm-tree-dotted Entrance Plaza (which is undergoing refurbishment) to the path under Spaceship Earth, the many-faceted "geosphere" that has become the universal symbol of Epcot.

The park is so vast that it's hard to know what to do first. Many guests stop at Spaceship Earth on their way into Future World. As a result, they end up spending more time waiting in line than they need to. A wise alternative is to save Spaceship Earth for later in the day (when the lines inevitably thin out), and head for Soarin' Around the World, the "less intense, non-spinning" Green Team version of Mission: SPACE, The Seas with Nemo & Friends, and Test Track (if jarring motion isn't an issue for you) as soon as the park opens (the lines tend to stay long throughout the day). Take in Frozen Ever After (the World Showcase attraction usually opens at 9 A.M.) and as many Future World attractions as time allows. Refer to page 35 for a more detailed version of this Epcot touring plan.

Another strategy—one that requires quite a bit of extra walking, but can help skirt a long line or two—is to explore World Showcase early in the day, while many guests interact with Future World attractions. Then, in the late afternoon—when many folks have migrated to World Showcase—return to Future World. Although long lines can be found during peak seasons at Soarin' Around the World, Mission: SPACE (both versions), Spaceship Earth, The Seas with Nemo & Friends, Living with the Land, and Test Track throughout most of the late morning and afternoon, it's usually a bit less hectic from late afternoon until park closing time. But don't forget to make it back to World Showcase Lagoon in time to see the park's new nighttime spectacular, Epcot Forever (which replaced IllumiNations: Reflections of Earth in 2019). There are excellent viewing locations throughout World Showcase promenade.

HOT TIP!

Epcot is in the midst of an exciting, multi-year "re-imagining" phase. Imagineers are hard at work, creating new restaurants and attractions throughout the theme park. Most of the pixie dust should be settled by 2021, the year WDW celebrates its 50th birthday. For updates, visit *disneyworld.com*.

Left a Legacy?

Epcot has invited guests to "Leave a Legacy" near its front gate since its big Millennium Celebration. And more than 550,000 have done so. They left their mark, in the form of a one-inch-square tile affixed on massive stone walls. The sales period has come to a close, but the tiled cluster of monoliths are still on display. While Epcot's entrance is redesigned in 2020, Leave a Legacy tiles will move to an area just outside the park entrance (where they may be visited for the foreseeable future.) Details are subject to change.

SPACESHIP EARTH

FP+ As it looms impressively just above the Earth, this great, faceted silver structure looks a little bit like a spaceship ready to blast off. It appears large from a distance, and it seems even more immense when viewed from directly underneath. It's no surprise that some visitors simply stop beneath it and gawk.

The show inside, which explores the continuing quest by human beings to create the future, remains one of Epcot's most compelling—if slower moving—attractions. It's an intriguing, narrated journey through time. It also has a high-tech, interactive element that's a real hoot.

A common misconception about Spaceship Earth is that it is a geodesic dome. Not so. It is a geo*sphere*. A geodesic dome is only half a sphere, while Spaceship Earth is almost completely round. Affectionately known to many simply as "the Ball," Spaceship Earth is a sight to behold.

Noted science-fiction writer Ray Bradbury, together with a team of consultants from the Smithsonian

HOT TIP!
The line for Spaceship Earth is usually quite long during the early morning hours and relatively short in the late afternoon and evening.

DID YOU KNOW?
Spaceship Earth weighs 16 million pounds! Its silver outer "skin" is made up of 11,324 aluminum and plastic-alloy triangles. And rainwater never falls off the sphere—it's channeled into the ball and surreptitiously funneled away.

Institution, the Los Angeles area's prestigious Huntington Library, the University of Southern California, and (among others) the University of Chicago, collaborated with Disney in developing this memorable 14-minute journey. It begins in an inky-black time tunnel, complete with a musty smell that suggests the dust of ages, and continues through history from the days of Cro-Magnon man (30,000 or 40,000 years ago) to the future.

Every scene is executed in exquisite detail. The symbols on the wall of the Egyptian temple really are hieroglyphics, and the content of the letter being dictated by the pharaoh was excerpted from a missive actually received by an agent of a ruler of the period. Later on you'll catch a glimpse of a 1970s mainframe computer room and a garage scene depicting the creation of the personal computer.

All of these sights are enough to keep heads turning as the "time machines" wend their way upward. The most dazzling scene is saved for the ride's finale, when the audience is placed in outer space—with a prime view of our beautiful, blue planet, aka Spaceship Earth.

> HOT TIP!

Many of Walt Disney World's moving attractions—such as Spaceship Earth—can be slowed down to make the boarding process safer for guests with physical limitations and guests who can transfer from a wheelchair (with assistance from someone in their party). Ask a Cast Member as you and your party enter the attraction.

The journey winds down with a custom look at your own future, courtesy of a nifty touch screen in the ride vehicle. Specifics are subject to change.

The post-show area—Project Tomorrow—features several interactive areas all emphasizing technology and its influence on daily life. Themes include medicine, power, and accident avoidance. Plan to spend up to an hour in this high-tech playground. Kids love it.

MOUSEGEAR: This (temporarily relocated) shop offers a superb selection of Disney merchandise. MouseGear stocks character memorabilia, key chains, T-shirts, hats, candy (including jelly beans and various gummy treats), MagicBands and associated paraphernalia, mugs, photo albums, jewelry, towels, footwear, toys, and much more—making this the best source for character merchandise in Epcot. There are also items related to Epcot itself, along with Disney-themed apparel and kids' clothing. MouseGear stays open about a half hour later than the park does. For many, MouseGear is considered one of the best places to shop at WDW.

THE SEAS WITH NEMO & FRIENDS

Welcome to one of the largest facilities ever dedicated to humanity's relationship with the ocean. It was designed by Disney Imagineers, in cooperation with oceanographic experts and scientists. Note that details are subject to change in 2020.

Though it enjoys the distinction of being one of Future World's original pavilions, what used to be known as The Living Seas is as fresh as ever—thanks to a familiar little clownfish called Nemo and some of his aquatic acquaintances.

Once inside, guests can find the animated critters' real-life counterparts, including clownfish, blue tangs, sharks, and puffer fish.

The pavilion also features a Nemo-themed ride, a nifty interactive encounter with an animated turtle, and an engaging post-show area. Little ones enjoy Bruce's Shark World—a hands-on play area that celebrates the ocean's toothiest residents. From there, take a look at a simulated Caribbean coral reef environment. For many, the crowning jewel of this pavilion is the simple-but-spectacular Turtle Talk with Crush. This pavilion is an excellent destination for big and little kids alike.

Under the Sea

Three behind-the-scenes Epcot tours offer guests a closer look at life in The Seas with Nemo & Friends underwater environs: DiveQuest gives certified scuba divers the opportunity to explore one of the world's largest aquariums. Epcot Seas Aqua Tour lets folks snorkel The Seas. And Dolphins in Depth offers guests the opportunity to learn about dolphin behavior as they closely observe researchers and trainers interacting with dolphins. Reservations for any tour can be made by calling 407-WDW-TOUR (939-8687). Save money by using the coupons at the end of this book. For details on all of these programs, turn to pages 235–238 of the *Everything Else in the World* chapter.

SEA BASE ALPHA SHOP: All visitors to this pavilion filter though this shop on their way back to Future World—and many stop to peruse the wares. In addition to many a *Finding Nemo*–themed souvenir, this area celebrates other creatures of the sea—in the form of shirts, hats, and plush toys.

THE SEAS WITH NEMO & FRIENDS ATTRACTION: FP+ Imagineered in the style of classic Disney family attractions, this undersea adventure is fun for everyone. In it, guests climb aboard a clam-mobile and enter a colorful coral reef. It seems Nemo has wandered off yet again, and his teacher, Mr. Ray, needs help finding him. So keep your eyes peeled!

This ride feels like a little bit of the Magic Kingdom's Fantasyland swam off to Epcot. The colorful mixture of animated and authentic sea life makes for a nicely layered experience. There's a bit of suspense involved—including several moments of darkness, an appearance by Bruce the shark, and a stressful jellyfish encounter—but rest assured, it all ends happily.

BRUCE'S SUB HOUSE: Explore this small adventure zone within Sea Base Alpha and you just may learn a thing or two about Bruce (from *Finding Nemo*) and his toothy pals. There are several hands-on activities (including a chance to learn what shark skin feels like), exhibits such as Bruce's scrapbook, and fishy photo ops.

BIRNBAUM'S ★BEST★ TURTLE TALK WITH CRUSH: FP+ If ever there was an attraction that left guests smiling and asking, "How do they do that?!"—this is it. The concept is simple enough—a 10-minute, animated show featuring the surfer-dude sea turtle from *Finding Nemo*. The amazing part? The cartoon critter interacts with the audience. In doing so, he imparts turtle-y wisdom, answers questions, and cracks more than a few jokes. You have to see it to believe it. To do that, you'll have to wait your turn—it's popular with guests of all ages. Oh, and Dory, Hank, Bailey, Destiny, Marlin, and Squirt have been known to pop in for a visit, too. Note that kids are encouraged to sit on the floor in front of the big screen. There are benches to accommodate the rest of Crush's guests. The typical guest reaction to this show? It's totally awesome, dude!

CARIBBEAN CORAL REEF: The man-made reef exists in an enormous tank that holds about six million gallons of salt water and more than 60 species of sea life. Among the 4,000 or so inhabitants are turtles, angelfish, sharks, dolphins, and diamond rays. It's worth it to stop by as when breakfast or lunch is served. The feeding frenzy is fun to watch.

Guests sometimes get to see scuba divers testing and demonstrating diving gear and monitoring equipment as they carry on training programs with dolphins.

The Caribbean Coral Reef aquarium is also home to two rescued manatees named Lou and Li'l Joe. Each of these wondrous creatures gobbles up nearly 100 heads of lettuce per day. They're a sight to behold.

HOT TIP!

Try to position yourself near the Caribbean Coral Reef at 10 A.M. or 3 P.M. That's feeding time for the fish!

FP+ = Fastpass+ attraction (see page 25)

THE LAND

Occupying six acres, this enormous skylighted pavilion examines the nature of one of everybody's favorite topics—food. It also gives guests a chance to soar above the clouds in a celebration of flight. A boat ride explores farming in the past and future. Narration gives visitors the chance to learn about the experimental agricultural techniques practiced in the pavilion.

Timing Tip: The Land pavilion's Soarin' Around the World is an exceptionally popular attraction. So much so that Fastpass+ assignments may all be gone early. It's best to visit first thing in the morning or get a Fastpass+ as far in advance as possible!

LIVING WITH THE LAND: FP+ This pavilion's 13½-minute boat ride through meticulously re-created natural locales opens with a dramatic storm scene. Guests sail through tropical rainforests, prairie grain fields, and a family farm. As the boat passes through each realistic setting, recorded narration offers commentary on humanity's ongoing struggle to cultivate

HOT TIP!

A new cinematic experience has landed at The Land's Harvest Theater. *Awesome Planet* is a visual exploration of the beauty, diversity, and dynamic story of the astonishing orb that we all call home. For updates on this Epcot addition, brought to you by Industrial Light & Magic, use the My Disney Experience app or website, or visit *disneyworld.com*.

and live in harmony with the land. Note the details that make each setting so convincing, such as sand blowing over the desert and light flickering from the television in the farmhouse window.

In the next segment, guests enter a plant research laboratory and solarium. Here, our planet's major food crops are being grown in research projects, along with rare new crops that may someday help meet Earth's ever-growing dietary needs.

Also of interest are the experiments being conducted to explore the practice of farming fish, and a desert farm area, where plants get nutrients through a drip

HOT TIP!

Got a rumbly in your tumbly? Head for Sunshine Seasons in The Land pavilion. There's a variety of counter-service choices— apt to please even the pickiest of eaters.

irrigation system that delivers just the right amount of water—important in a dry climate.

As unreal as they appear, all the plants on view in the experimental greenhouses are living. In contrast, those in the biomes (the ecological communities viewed from the boat ride) were made in Disney studios out of lightweight plastic that simulates the cellulose found in real trees. The trunks and branches were molded from live specimens; the sycamore in the farmhouse's front yard, for example, duplicates one that stands outside a Burbank, California, car wash. Thousands of polyethylene leaves were snapped on.

Note that all of the greenhouse flora is quite real—please resist the urge to touch plants or the sand in which they live. Details may change in 2020.

BIRNBAUM'S ★BEST★ SOARIN' AROUND THE WORLD:

FP+ Up, up, and away! On this high-flying Epcot ride (it's one of the most popular attractions in all of Walt Disney World), you will be suspended in a hang-glider-type vehicle up to 45 feet in the air, above a giant IMAX projection dome, and treated to an aerial tour of awe-inspiring landscapes and treasured landmarks. Soarin' has been delighting park guests with its wraparound glory since 2005—but these days, instead of hovering over just one state (California), park visitors are treated to a much broader aerial tour of the planet.

Soarin' Around the World showcases some of the world's most glorious sights: The Great Wall of China, the plains of Africa, the oceans of Fiji, the Grand Canyon, Egyptian pyramids, and much more. With

PHOTO BY JILL SAFRO

Mad About the Mouse?

Can't get enough of all things Disney? Then D23 is the place to be. It's the official community for Disney superfans. To join, you'll need nothing more than a computer or smartphone and an unebbing enthusiasm for the House that Walt built. Upgrade to Gold Membership ($80 annual dues) to net access to special events, an official membership card and certificate, a subscription to the D23 magazine, a collectible gift (plus the opportunity to purchase exclusive merchandise), and more. For details or to join the club, visit *www.d23.com*. F.Y.I.: Walt Disney founded what would become the Disney Studios in 1923. Hence, the name D23.

the wind in your hair and your legs dangling in the breeze, the hang glider feels so real that you may even be tempted to pull up your feet for fear of tapping the rooftops and landscapes below.

The flight takes about 6 minutes and employs synchronized wind currents, scent machines, and a rousing musical score set to a film that wraps 180 degrees around you. The re-imagined version of this attraction touched down in 2017. It features a high-tech digital screen and projection system and is a hit with all ages—reserve a Fastpass+ assignment if you can.

Note: You must be at least 40 inches tall and free of back problems, heart conditions, motion sickness, and other physical limitations to ride. It's calmer than traditional "thrill" rides, but the sensation of flight is quite

>

HOT TIP!

Epcot is much bigger than it seems, so allow lots of time to get from place to place. (It can take more than a half hour to walk from Spaceship Earth to The American Adventure.) Keep this in mind if you have a restaurant reservation or hope to snag a nice viewing location on the World Showcase promenade for the park's new nighttime spectacular: Epcot Forever.

realistic. If you're afraid of heights, sit this one out. Place loose items (including flip-flops) in the pouch under your seat or on the floor in front of you—and be sure to collect them at the end of the flight.

IMAGINATION!

The oddly shaped glass pyramids that house the Imagination! pavilion are quite a striking sight to behold. They certainly set the stage for the atypical experiences inside. One of the attractions is Journey Into Imagination with Figment, a slow-moving tour of the Imagination Institute. Also located here is the Disney & Pixar Short Film Festival.

Another pavilion highlight is the set of classic, quirky fountains outside—the Jellyfish Fountains, which spurt streams of water that spread out at the top, looking for an instant like their namesake sea creature, and the Leap Frog Fountains, which send out smooth streams of water that arc from one garden plot to another in the most astonishing fashion. Kids just can't seem to get enough of them.

BIRNBAUM'S ★BEST★ **DISNEY AND PIXAR SHORT FILM FESTIVAL:** FP+ Head to the Magic Eye Theater to enter the imaginative worlds of three animated shorts. Though films are subject to change, the one that is expected to play throughout 2020 is *Get a Horse*. It stars everyone's favorite mouse as he, Minnie, and their pals Horace Horsecollar and Clarabelle Cow delight in a manic, musical wagon ride. It combines with two other films to make for a most merry movie experience. The animated shorts are presented in 3-D (pick up your glasses on the way into the theater) and feature entertaining "4-D" effects.

This unexpectedly delightful attraction has appeal for guests of all ages, provided they are old enough to wear 3-D glasses. (It's also a nice way to enjoy some restorative air-conditioning!) For updates on the films set to be screened during your stay, visit *disneyworld.com* or use the My Disney Experience website or mobile app.

FP+ = Fastpass+ attraction (see page 25)

JOURNEY INTO IMAGINATION WITH FIGMENT:
FP+ Figment, the beloved purple dragon with the orange wings and yellow eyes, is on hand to guide guests on an imaginative quest. The intended goal? To figure out, once and for all, the best way to capture your imagination.

The journey takes place inside the Imagination Institute, where guests are invited to tour the institute's various labs, such as the Sight Lab, the Sound Lab, and

Smell Lab. All in all, it's a very tame experience, save for the occasional blast of air or flashing lights. The disappearing butterfly is a highlight.

Nostalgia buffs, take note: The classic song "One Little Spark," which made its debut with the original incarnation of this ride, underscores the show once more. Attraction details are subject to change in 2020.

IMAGEWORKS LABS: It's a rare tot-aged ImageWorks visitor who doesn't experience at least some of the emotion felt by the little one who cried when her parents tried to tear her away. There used to be more to explore, but it's still worth a look-see.

TEST TRACK

BIRNBAUM'S ★BEST★ FP+ Fasten your safety belt! This high-octane pavilion puts guests through the creative and frenetic motions of automobile design and testing. The experience starts with guests designing a vehicle in the attraction's high-tech pre-show area. What is important to you in a car: efficiency, power, responsiveness, or capability? Use a touch screen to design your car with your priorities

PHOTO BY MIKE CARROLL

in mind, then take your virtual "Sim Car" over to the Sim Track and give her a test drive. (They easily could have dubbed this attraction Sim Track—a Test Track by any other name would be just as cool.)

HOT TIP!

If you don't mind splitting up your party, head for the "single rider" line at Test Track. It's generally shorter than the standby line.

The 4-minute ride is similar to the original version of Test Track—there's lots of zigging and zagging on the front end, followed by a dramatic near-miss with a big noisy truck. Along the way, you'll learn how well your car did in each of the categories featured in the design stage. Finally, a long straightaway feeds into a series of banked turns and another straight shot that sends vehicles rocketing around the pavilion at top speed (up to 65 mph!). The computer-controlled, six-seater vehicles are equipped with video and audio, but no steering wheels or brake pedals. After all is said and done, guests may create a 15-second commercial for their new car and send the video to a friend via e-mail.

Note: Kids who are less than 7 years old must be accompanied by a guest over the age of 14; guests under 40 inches cannot ride; passengers must be free of back problems, heart conditions, motion sickness, and other physical limitations. Pregnant women are advised to sit this one out.

HOT TIP!

Is someone in your party too young or small to ride Test Track? If so, make a beeline for the Post Show area. It's a high-tech, hands-on car showcase—providing big thrills for pint-sized park-goers.

MISSION: SPACE

FP+ Think you've got "the right stuff"? Well, this is your chance to prove it. Epcot's out-of-this-world attraction has a bold mission—to give you a chance to feel the excitement and extreme intensity of space travel without ever leaving the planet.

There are two ways to experience this attraction: the "highly intense" Orange Mission to Mars, and the "less intense" Green Mission around Earth. The original Mission: SPACE attraction provides a galaxy of thrills for many brave and sturdy theme park guests. The adventure begins with a white-knuckle blast-off of a spacecraft (which has snug seating for four) on an important mission to Mars. The sustained G-force during the launch is intended to be most realistic. Once en route, expect a rather strange, spectacular sensation. It's not quite weightlessness, but according to astronauts who've felt the real thing, it's pretty darn close. (So much so that it also tends to duplicate the not-so-spectacular sensation of space sickness. In fact, Mission: SPACE has the dubious distinction of being the first attraction in theme park history to be equipped with motion-sickness bags.)

Throughout the journey, you're expected to work with your fellow crew members (assuming the roles of navigator, captain, engineer, and pilot) to accomplish the mission. For the "highly intense" version, we recommend ignoring this call to duty and keeping your eyes glued directly to the screen. This will allow you to sit back and enjoy the ride and decidedly down-size the dizziness factor.

The intense version of this attraction can wreak havoc on the equilibrium. To cut the chances of losing your lunch, keep your eyes open at all times and fixed on the screen in front of you. You may be tempted to tilt your head or shut your eyes. Don't. (We promise you will arrive safely on Mars whether you fulfill your astronaut duty or not.)

Bottom line? Most guests who don't get queasy on the "highly intense" Orange Mission tend to rave about it. For us, well, we admit we prefer the ride's gentler version—aka the Green Mission. It's intended for those who would rather not spin. The experience is a bit different on "Mission: SPACE-lite," but it gives everyone a chance to travel through space without getting queasy. The effects may be toned down, but they are still quite extraordinary. We completely enjoy the "less intense" mission around our home planet.

Note: Guests must be at least 40 inches tall for the (less intense) Mission: SPACE Green mission. For the Orange Mission, guests must be at least 44 inches tall and free of back and heart problems, motion sickness, and any other physical limitations. Pregnant women must skip the trip, as should anyone with claustrophobic tendencies. And don't eat just before riding!

Epcot's Backstage Adventures

Epcot offers an intriguing and inspiring lineup of "backstage" opportunities. Experiences range from a walking "world tour" to an up-close encounter with majestic creatures of the sea. Tours, dates, and prices are subject to change in 2020; for information or to make reservations, call 407-WDW-TOUR (939-8687).

BEHIND THE SEEDS (Daily; between 10:30 A.M. and 4:30 P.M.): An opportunity for guests of all ages to get a closer look at the greenhouses and fish farm that are part of The Land pavilion at Epcot. During the tour, guests will have close encounters with insects and plants. A skilled guide shares knowledge of hydroponics growing systems and crops from around the planet. Expect to be on your feet for the full hour of this experience. Cost is $25 per adult, $20 per child (ages 3–9). This tour is best enjoyed by sturdy adults and older kids. Reservations may be made in advance or at the tour desk on the lower level of The Land (near the entrance to the Soarin' Around the World attraction). Theme park admission is required, but not included.

DIVEQUEST (Tuesday–Saturday; 4:30 and 5:30 P.M.): The highlight of the 3-hour program is a 40-minute underwater adventure—complete with sharks, turtles, rays, and other fish—in The Seas with Nemo & Friends aquarium. Participants must show proof of current scuba certification. Cost is about $180 per person. Guests ages 10 through 12 must dive with a parent or guardian. Gear is provided. Epcot admission is neither required nor included in the price of the tour.

DOLPHINS IN DEPTH (Tuesday–Saturday; 9:45 A.M.): This 3-hour Epcot program (about 30 minutes takes place in the water) teaches guests about dolphin behavior as they interact with the social sea creatures and observe researchers and trainers working with them. Cost is about $199 per person. The minimum age is 13. Guests ages 13 to 17 must be accompanied by a paying adult. Park admission is not required or included. Wet suits are provided; wear your own swimsuit.

EPCOT SEAS AQUA TOUR (Tuesday–Saturday; 12:30 P.M.): A 2½-hour program (about 30 minutes of which is in the water) that lets guests learn about and interact with ocean life in The Seas with Nemo & Friends pavilion. First, guests watch a video about sea creatures, then they join them in their habitat using a Supplied-Air Snorkel system. Cost is about $145. Gear is included, as are light refreshments, a souvenir gift, and a group photo. Guests must wear swimsuits. The tour is open to guests age 8 and up. Park admission is not required or included.

THE UNDISCOVERED FUTURE WORLD (Offered seasonally on Monday, Tuesday, Friday, and Saturday; 8:30 A.M.): Walt Disney dreamed about making the world a better place. In this 4-hour tour, guests are taken back to the creation of Epcot and learn about Walt's lofty ambitions and his legacy.

Guests walk to Future World pavilions and learn how each area celebrates humanity's accomplishments and challenges. The goal is to share the vision behind the park.

Cost is about $69 per person. Guests must be at least 16 years old to take this walking program. Park admission is required but is not included.

WORLD SHOWCASE: DESTINATIONS DISCOVERED (Monday, Tuesday, Friday, and Saturday; 8:15 A.M.): A 4½- to 5-hour walking tour of World Showcase, the experience covers the culture, architecture, and design details of several of the park's international pavilions. Lunch is included at the Rose & Crown dining room in the U.K. pavilion. Cost is about $109 per person. Theme park admission is required, but not included. For pricing, schedules, and additional details, call 407-939-8687, visit *www.disneyworld.com*, or use the My Disney Experience website or mobile app.

HOT TIP!

The power was turned off at Epcot's Universe of Energy in 2017, and Disney Imagineers are currently building a brand-new "E-ticket" ride to take its place. The new, high-energy attraction will be based on the rockin' and action-packed world of Guardians of the Galaxy. It is expected to be open by 2021—in time for Walt Disney World's 50th anniversary celebration. For details, visit *www.disneyworld.com*.

World Showcase

Noble sentiments about humanity and the fellowship of nations, which have motivated so many World's Fairs in the past, also inhabit World Showcase. But make no mistake about it: This area of Epcot is unlike any previous international exposition.

The group of pavilions that encircles World Showcase Lagoon (a body of water that is the size of several football fields, with a perimeter of about 1.2 miles) demonstrates Disney conceptions about participating countries in remarkably realistic, consistently entertaining styles. You won't find the real Germany here—rather, the country's essence, much as a traveler returning from a visit might remember what he or she saw in the actual Deutschland.

Shops, restaurants, and attractions are housed in a group of structures that is an artful pastiche of all the elements that give that nation's countryside and towns their distinctive flavor. Although occasional liberties have been taken when scale and proportion required them, careful research governed the design of every nook and cranny.

Equally impressive is the cuisine. With no fewer than 14 upscale eateries to choose from, it's no wonder some guests here do nothing but nosh. (That is especially true during Epcot's popular International Food & Wine Festival, a time when dozens more nations contribute to an already fortified international menu. See page 11 for additional information.)

In the shops, many of the wares represent the country in whose pavilion they are sold. Skilled craftspeople are occasionally on hand to demonstrate their arts. Thanks to special cultural-exchange programs and recruiting efforts, many World Showcase staffers hail from the countries the pavilions represent.

A diverse lineup of entertainment ensures that all visitors experience more than a little culture, foreign or otherwise. The entertainment is as authentic as the Disney casting directors can make it, with native performers commonly featured and new festivities always in the works.

Pavilions are described in the order in which they are encountered while moving counterclockwise around the World Showcase Lagoon after crossing the bridge from Future World. All entertainment offerings are subject to change.

HOT TIP!

Most World Showcase pavilions open at about 11 A.M. However, guests may use the International Gateway entrance as much as a half hour prior to Future World's official opening time—allowing plenty of time to reach favorite attractions.

Phineas and Ferb: Agent P's World Showcase Adventure

Calling all secret agent wannabes! How would you like to help Perry the Platypus save the world from the evil Dr. Heinz Doofenshmirtz? Well, here's your chance. The interactive game is based on the Disney Channel show *Phineas and Ferb*. Of course, one need not be familiar with the show to get a kick out of the Epcot version. Just grab your trusty mobile device (or a parent's) and go to *www.agentpwsa.com* to start an adventure.

If you and your team follow instructions and find the clues, you will complete your bold mission: to save the world!

There are five pavilions in which to play this World Showcase–based game: Mexico, United Kingdom, France, Germany, and Japan. There's no extra charge to participate. Details are subject to change in 2020.

CANADA

Celebrating the many beauties of the U.S.A.'s neighbor to the north, the area devoted to the Western Hemisphere's largest nation is complete with its own mountain, waterfall, rushing stream, rocky canyon, mine,

PHOTO BY JILL SAFRO

and splendid garden massed with flowers. There's even a totem pole, a trading post, and an elaborate, mansard-roofed hotel similar to ones built by Canadian railroad companies as they pushed west around the turn of the twentieth century. All this is imaginatively arranged somewhat like a split-level house, with the section representing French Canada on top, and another devoted to the mountains alongside it and below. From a distance, the Hôtel du Canada, the main building here, looks like little more than a bump on the landscape—as does Epcot's single Canadian Rocky Mountain. But viewed up close, they both seem to tower as high as the genuine article.

The gardens were inspired by the Butchart Gardens, on Vancouver Island, British Columbia, a famous park created on the site of a limestone quarry. The hotel is modeled, in part, after Ottawa's Victorian-style Château Laurier. Musical entertainment takes place at the Mill Stage, a theater on the World Showcase Promenade (on the United Kingdom side of the pavilion).

O CANADA!: Step into the Circle-Vision 360 film, *O Canada!*, and find yourself surrounded by the breath-taking sights and sounds of this northern nation. Of course, you won't be alone—Canadian actor Martin Short stars as your guide, taking guests through prairies, plains, snowfields, rivers, rocky mountainsides, and beyond. Humor and hockey are included. The motion picture provides a you-are-there feeling that makes all of this spectacular scenery still more memorable. Know that you'll have to stand for the show, as there are no seats in this theater. At press time, updates were in store for the film. For details, use the My Disney Experience app or website, or visit *disneyworld.com*.

NORTHWEST MERCANTILE: Found to the left upon entering the pavilion's plaza, this spot features Canada-themed shirts, attire celebrating sports (hockey, lacrosse, and curling), plush toys (moose, owls, otters, etc.), maple-flavored snacks, tiny totem poles, pajamas, plus other Canada-themed collectibles. Quirky item of note: "Moose Spit" soap. Skeins of rope, tin scoops, lanterns, and antique ice skates hanging from the long beams overhead set the mood, together with the structure itself.

UNITED KINGDOM

In the space of only a few hundred feet, visitors to this pavilion stroll from an elegant London square to the edge of a canal in the rural countryside—via a bustling urban English street framed by buildings that constitute a veritable rhapsody of historic architectural styles. But one scene leads to the next so smoothly that nothing ever seems amiss. Do note the meticulous attention to detail: the half-timbered High Street structure that leans a bit, and the hand-painted "smoke" stains that make the chimneys look as if they have been there for centuries. When a thatched roof is required, it's right where it should be—though the roof may be made of plastic broom bristles because fire regulations prohibit the real thing. Off to the side is a pair of scarlet phone booths identical to those that used to be found around the U.K. And there are eight architectural styles characteristic of the streetscapes, from English Tudor to Georgian and Victorian.

There is no major attraction in this pavilion; instead, it features half a dozen shops and a pub that serves a selection of beers and ales that would be the toast of any "local" in London itself. The Rose & Crown serves snacks, too. There's lots of entertainment in Epcot's United Kingdom, including visits from Mary Poppins and Alice from *Alice in Wonderland*. In the Rose & Crown pub, a lively pianist has been known to play throughout the afternoon. A crowd-pleasing band known as British Revolution plays classic rock favorites in the garden courtyard. They're a true crowd-pleaser. Note that the entertainment at this pavilion is subject to change in 2020.

THE CROWN & CREST: This shop looks like a backdrop for a child's fantasy of the days of King Arthur, with its high rafters decked out with bright banners, fireplace (and crossed swords above), and wrought-iron chandelier. Souvenirs featuring the Union Jack are the stock-in-trade at this emporium adjoining the Sportsman's Shoppe. Name histories and family crests are also sold, as are chess sets, swords, shields, and knights in shining armor. There's also a line of Guinness Stout merchandise (think glasses, shirts, coasters, bottle openers, etc.) and items that pay tribute to British bands.

HOT TIP!

A pleasant place from which to view the park's nighttime spectacular is the patio area at the Rose & Crown Pub in the United Kingdom pavilion. Try to snag one of the few lagoonside tables—whether within the pub's boundaries or in the self-serve sitting area nearby—at least 45 minutes before showtime. If you miss out on a seat, grab a Guinness and enjoy the standing-room view.

SPORTSMAN'S SHOPPE: Head here for clothing and accessories centered on uniquely British locales and sports. You can expect to find a large selection of golf and football (soccer) team gear. Don't miss the tartan map on the wall opposite The Crown & Crest; it identifies plaids from Glen Burn and Gordon to Langtree and St. Lawrence. There's a sizable selection of shirts and souvenirs featuring the Rose & Crown Pub (the U.K. pavilion's local watering hole), too. Outside, the shop resembles a stone manor built during the last half of the sixteenth century.

PHOTO BY JILL SAFRO

THE TEA CADDY: Fitted out with heavy wooden beams and a broad fireplace to resemble the Stratford-upon-Avon cottage of William Shakespeare's wife, Anne Hathaway, this shop stocks English teas, both loose and in bags, in a variety of flavors. Other items include teapots, china, jewelry, biscuits, and candy.

THE TOY SOLDIER: There's a selection of items here, celebrating beloved British shows, plus merchandise featuring Peter Pan, Alice in Wonderland, and the gang from the Hundred Acre Wood: Pooh, Piglet, Eeyore, and Tigger, too. Paddington Bear is also represented.

THE QUEEN'S TABLE: This shop is one of the loveliest in all of Epcot. That is particularly true of the store's elegant Adams Room, embellished with elaborate moldings and a crystal chandelier. The refined setting is a fitting background for the handbags, jewelry, and other fragrant items that are available.

Don't neglect to inspect small, serene Britannia Square outside the shop farthest from the promenade. But for its diminutive size and the Florida climate, it feels a bit like London itself.

INTERNATIONAL GATEWAY

Known to many as Epcot's back door, the International Gateway is between the United Kingdom and France pavilions. There's a ticket window just outside the gate. (Yes, it's possible to enter and exit the park here.) Note that guests are subject to a thorough security screening. All bags are searched here and guests must pass through a metal detector before they may enter the theme park. International Gateway is also home to:

DISNEY SKYLINER STATION: Walt Disney World's new airborne gondola system connects Epcot with Disney's Hollywood Studios theme park, and Caribbean Beach, Pop Century, Art of Animation, and Riviera resorts. The Disney Skyliner (see page 65) is the newest addition to WDW's vast transportation network.

FRIENDSHIP LANDING: Disney's water taxis, known as FriendShip boats, ferry guests to the Yacht & Beach Club, BoardWalk, and the Swan and Dolphin resorts, and to Disney's Hollywood Studios (the last stop before the boat returns to the resorts and back to Epcot). The dock is just outside the International Gateway entrance. It's possible to walk to all of the aforementioned destinations, too. (It takes about 25 to 35 minutes to stroll to the Studios, depending on your pace.)

STROLLER AND WHEELCHAIR RENTAL: Strollers and wheelchairs may be rented here. Hold on to your rental receipt; it can be used on the same day in all WDW theme parks should you leave and return later on. It's possible to get a replacement stroller here. Note that ECVs are only available at the park's front entrance.

Where to Eat in Epcot

A complete listing of all Epcot eateries— full-service restaurants, fast-food eateries, and snack shops—can be found in the *Good Meals, Great Times* chapter. See the Epcot section, beginning on page 260.

WORLD TRAVELER: Snacks, Epcot souvenirs, Disney fashions, books, kitchen items, disposable cameras, backpacks, and a package pickup depot are located at this spot near "Epcot's back door."

FRANCE

The buildings here have mansard roofs and casement windows so Gallic in appearance that you may expect to see a Bohemian poet looking down from above. A canal-like offshoot of the lagoon seems like the Seine itself; the footbridge that spans it recalls the old Pont des Arts. There's a kiosk like those that punctuate the streets of Paris and a bakery whose heavenly rich aromas announce its presence long before it's visible.

Shops sell perfumes, wine, and other items. Their roofs are of real copper or slate, and the cabinetry is finely crafted. Galerie des Halles—the iron-and-glass-ceilinged market that Paris once counted as one of its most beloved institutions—lives again. But perhaps most special of all are the people. Hosts and hostesses who hail from Paris and the French provinces answer questions in French-accented English. Keep an eye out for Serveur Amusant, the comedic waiter who does one heck of a balancing act.

An interesting background note: The main entrance to the pavilion recalls the architecture of Paris, most of which was built during the Belle Epoque ("beautiful age"), the last decades of the nineteenth century.

Don't miss the garden area on the right side of this pavilion. It is one of the most pleasant places in World Showcase—and Aurora occasionally mingles with park guests at a nearby gazebo.

BEAUTY & THE BEAST SING-ALONG: There's something here that wasn't here before: a new sing-along experience in the France pavilion's Palais du Cinéma. The new, interactive experience was created by Disney legend, Don Hahn, who produced both the animated and live-action versions of the *Beauty & the Beast*. The show is enjoyed by guests of all ages.

BIRNBAUM'S ★BEST★ **IMPRESSIONS DE FRANCE:** Shown in the Palais du Cinéma, a quaint little theater that's not unlike the one at Fontainebleau, this enchanting 18-minute film takes viewers on a trip through France.

The film shows off a tree-dotted estate, fields and vineyards at harvest time, a flower market and a pastry shop, a glacier, and a harbor full of squawking gulls. Viewers visit the Eiffel Tower; Versailles and its gilt Hall of Mirrors (just outside Paris); Mont Saint Michel; the French Alps; and Cannes, the star-studded resort city on the Mediterranean coast. All this is even more appealing

thanks to a superb soundtrack, consisting almost entirely of the music of French classical composers.

Though not a Circle-Vision 360 film like the movies shown at China and Canada, the wide screen adds yet another dimension to the viewing experience. The France film used only five cameras, and it is shown on five large projection surfaces—200 degrees around.

F.Y.I.: *Impressions de France* is recognized by the *Guinness World Records* as the longest-running daily screened film in the world.

PLUME ET PALETTE: One of the loveliest shops in World Showcase, this Art Nouveau–inspired location is home to the Givenchy Shop—the only location in the world that carries the complete line of Givenchy fragrances, skin care products, and cosmetics.

LA SIGNATURE: Aka Guerlain Paris, this boutique features Guerlain cosmetics and fragrances.

LES HALLES BOUTIQUE DE CADEUX: Everything from Eiffel Tower statuettes to Impressionist-style prints is offered at this location near the exit of the cinema. Mugs, bags, T-shirts, berets, flags, and picture frames are among the offerings available. The area is based on Paris's now-demolished Les Halles, the city's old fruit and vegetable market. This space is also the location of the ever-popular bakeshop known as Les Halles Boulangerie & Patisserie.

Coming Attraction

Epcot's France pavilion is ready to welcome a new tenant . . . Remy the rat! Yep, there's a new rodent coming to town. The star of Disney's animated film *Ratatouille* is set to star in a brand-new, family-friendly attraction called Remy's Ratatouille Adventure. For updates, visit *www.disneyworld.com*, or use the My Disney Experience website or mobile app.

>>

LES VINS DE FRANCE: Selections in this rustic wine shop range from the inexpensive to the pricey, from *vin ordinaire* going for several dollars to upward of $99 for a rare vintage. Wine tastings are held here to sample the offerings (for a fee). Other wares include wine glasses with a World Showcase theme, books about wine, bottle openers and toppers, aprons, candy, and kitchenware. Toward the back of the shop you will find perfumes, soaps, sachets, and more.

MOROCCO

Nine tons of tile were handmade, hand cut, and shipped from Morocco to Epcot to create this World Showcase pavilion. To capture the unique quality of this North African nation's architecture, Moroccan artisans came to Epcot to practice the mosaic art that has been a part of their homeland for thousands of years. Koutoubia Minaret, a meticulously detailed replica of the famous prayer tower in Marrakesh, stands guard at the entrance. A courtyard with a fountain at the center leads to the medina (Old City). Between the traditional alleyways and the more modern sections are the pointed arches and swirling patterns of the Bab Boujeloud gate, a replica of the one that stands in the city of Fez. An ancient working waterwheel irrigates the gardens, and the motifs repeated throughout the buildings include carved plaster and wood, tile, and brass. Live entertainment is presented on World Showcase Promenade, while Jasmine greets guests at Lamps of Wonder. Check a Times Guide for specifics.

THE BRASS BAZAAR: Interspersed among the decorative brass plates in this enchanting emporium are pitchers, pots, bottles of rosewater, serving sets, wooden collectibles, shoes, books, mirrors, baskets, tiles, tabbouleh mixes, lamps, spices, and various other Moroccan selections.

THE ART OF HENNA: In the market for a temporary henna body decoration? Look no farther than this cozy corner of the Morocco pavilion. Henna "tattoos" are available—for a fee—in various sizes and designs between 1 P.M. and 9 P.M. daily (hours may vary).

CASABLANCA CARPETS: In addition to handmade carpets, this store features an intriguing and eclectic selection of merchandise. Look for lamps, fez hats, jewelry, books, and more.

MARKETPLACE IN THE MEDINA: Hand-woven baskets, sheepskin wallets and bags, assorted straw hats, drums, sandals, postcards, scarves, jewelry, clothing, and small carpets are among the available wares.

SOUK AL MAGREB: This waterside enclave located on the World Showcase promenade spills over with handcrafted keepsakes. Look for Moroccan lamps, baskets, jewelry, rosewater, and spices.

TANGIER TRADERS: Ensconced within the Brass Bazaar, T.T. is the go-to place for Moroccan lamps, leather wallets, sandals and purses, and other traditional Moroccan clothing and accessories. As shops go, it's quite the gem.

JAPAN

Serenity rules in Japan. Except, of course, when the pavilion resounds with traditional music performed by a drum-playing duo or group.

The landscaping, designed in accordance with traditional symbolic and aesthetic values, contributes to the pavilion's peaceful mood. Rocks, which in Japan represent the enduring nature of the Earth, were brought from North Carolina and Georgia (since boulders are scarce in the Sunshine State). Water, symbolizing the sea (which the people of Japan consider a life source), is abundant; the Japan pavilion garden has a stream and pools inhabited by koi (fish). Evergreen trees, which in Japan are symbols of eternal life, are here in force.

Disney horticulturists created this very Japanese landscape using few plants native to that country because the climate there is so different from that of Florida. Among the few trees here native to Japan are

the sago, near the courtyard entrance to the Katsura Grill; the two Japanese maple trees, identifiable by their small leaves, not far away (near the first stairway from the promenade on the left side of the courtyard as you face it); and the prickly monkey-puzzle trees, near the walkway to the promenade, on The American Adventure side of the pagoda. Needle-sharp thorns make the latter the only species of tree that monkeys are unable to climb.

The pagoda was modeled after an eighth-century structure located in the Horyuji Temple, in Nara, Japan. The striking torii gate on the shore of World Showcase Lagoon derives from the design of the one at the Itsukushima shrine in Hiroshima Bay.

BIJUTSU-KAN GALLERY: Housing an ever-changing cultural display, this small museum has offered, among other exhibitions, the Kitahara Collection of Tin Toys, featuring toys produced between 1880 and 1970. Most recently, the exhibit "Kawaii—Japan's Cute Culture" was featured here.

MITSUKOSHI MERCHANDISE STORE: There are kimonos, T-shirts bearing Japanese characters, fine jewelry, and a selection of bowls and vases meant for flower arranging for sale at this spacious store set up by Mitsukoshi—a four-centuries-old retail firm.

The shop features a wall of sake selections (and a small sake bar), plus chopsticks, bonsai, jewelry, china, paper fans, and origami products. There is also a bounty

DID YOU KNOW?

The five stories of the Japanese pagoda symbolize earth, water, fire, wind, and sky.

of toys, bags, snacks, and teas. You can even buy an oyster and discover a pearl! The pleasant atmosphere and variety of merchandise make this destination a rewarding experience for both the casual browser and the serious shopper. The building's design was inspired by the Gosho Imperial Palace, which was constructed in Kyoto in 794 A.D.

THE AMERICAN ADVENTURE

BIRNBAUM'S ★BEST★ When it came to creating The American Adventure pavilion, the centerpiece of World Showcase, Disney Imagineers were given relatively free rein. So the 110,000 bricks of the imposing Colonial-style structure that houses a stirring show, quick-service restaurant, and shop are the real thing—patiently crafted by hand from soft Georgia clay.

The show inside stands out because of its wonderfully evocative settings, its detailed sets, and the 35 superb Audio-Animatronics players, some of the most lifelike ever created by the Disney organization.

A stirring a cappella vocal group called Voices of Liberty periodically serenades guests in the building's foyer. By all means, catch a performance.

THE AMERICAN ADVENTURE SHOW: One of the most ambitious Epcot attractions, this 26-minute presentation celebrates the American spirit from the nation's birth. Beginning with the arrival of the pilgrims at Plymouth Rock and their harsh first winter on the western shore of the Atlantic, the Audio-Animatronics narrators—a lifelike Ben Franklin and a thoroughly convincing Mark Twain—recall key people and events in American history: the Boston Tea Party, George Washington and the grueling winter at Valley Forge, the influential abolitionist Frederick Douglass, the celebrated nineteenth-century Nez Perce chief Joseph, and many more. The Philadelphia Centennial Exposition is remembered, along with women's rights campaigner Susan B. Anthony, telephone inventor Alexander Graham Bell, and the steel giant and philanthropist Andrew Carnegie. Naturalist John Muir converses onstage with Teddy Roosevelt. Charles Lindbergh, Rosie the Riveter,

Jackie Robinson, and Walt Disney are represented. So are John Wayne, Lucille Ball, Margaret Mead, John F. Kennedy, Martin Luther King Jr., and Billie Jean King.

The idea is to recall episodes in history, positive and negative, that contributed to the growth of the spirit of America, by engendering "a new burst of creativity" (in the designers' words) "or a better understanding of ourselves as partners in the American experience."

To learn how each of the many featured historical figures spoke during his or her lifetime, researchers contacted historians and cultural institutions—the Philadelphia Historical Commission, the State Historical Society of Missouri, the Department of the Navy's Ships Historical Branch, and others. When recordings were not available, educated guesses were made: Alexander Graham Bell's voice was created on the basis of contemporary comments about his voice's clarity, expressiveness, and crisp articulation, combined with the fact that his father taught elocution. A highlight of the show is the majestic music played by the Philadelphia Symphony Orchestra. The inspirational "Golden Dreams" finale was updated in 2018, as was the sound system. (There's a new digital-projection screen, too.)

If you have some extra time before the show begins, be sure to read the inspirational quotes that line the walls of Disney's Independence Hall— Jane Addams, Charles Lindbergh, Ayn Rand, Herman Melville, Althea Gibson, and Walter Elias Disney are among the notable Americans who are quoted.

AMERICAN HERITAGE GALLERY: Inside the pavilion (on the right side of the grand lobby), this is one of six art galleries at Epcot. Its new exhibit, "Creating Tradition: Innovation and Change in American Indian Art," celebrates historical and contemporary American Indian art and cultures. It showcases 89 objects, representing 40 tribal nations from seven North American regions. Exhibit visitors hear native languages and blended contemporary music styles, experiencing first-hand how American Indian art is both ancient and timeless.

HOT TIP!

The Voices of Liberty, a stellar 8-member a cappella vocal group, serenade guests in the American Adventure's main rotunda several times a day. For the best experience, sit or stand as close to the rotunda circle as possible to get the full benefit of the acoustics. Their last performance is usually around 4 P.M. Each show runs about 15 minutes.

HERITAGE MANOR GIFTS: Visit this shop to a special assortment of Disney collectibles. The store showcases a variety of art inspired by Disney Animation and theme parks. There is a collection of unique pieces by acclaimed artists, including prints, sculptures, and figurines.

THE AMERICA GARDENS THEATRE: An ever-changing slate of entertainment is presented in this lakeside amphitheater in front of The American Adventure. Concert series such as Eat to the Beat, Disney on Broadway, and Garden Rocks take place on this stage, too (during Epcot's International Food & Wine Festival and Flower & Garden Festival)—as does the Candlelight Processional, which is offered during the holiday season. Showtimes are posted at the theatre and in the park Times Guide. For details, use the My Disney Experience mobile app or website, or visit *www.disneyworld.com*.

ITALY

The arches and cutout motifs that adorn the World Showcase reproduction of the Doge's Palace in Venice are just the more obvious examples of the attention to detail lavished on the structures in this relatively small pavilion. The angel perched atop the scaled-down campanile was sculpted on the model of the original, right down to the curls on the back of its head. It was then covered with real gold leaf, despite the fact that it was destined to perch almost 100 feet in the air.

The other statues in the complex, including the sea god Neptune presiding over a fountain, are similarly exact. And the pavilion even has an island like Venice's own, its seawall appropriately stained with age, plus moorings that look like barber poles, with several Venetian gondolas tied to them. St. Mark the Evangelist is also remembered, together with the lion that is the saint's companion and Venice's guardian. These can be seen atop the two massive columns that flank the small arched footbridge that connects the island to the mainland. The only deviation from Venetian reality is the alteration of the site of the Doge's Palace in reference to the real St. Mark's Square.

The quaint pavilion is equally interesting from a horticultural point of view. The island boasts kumquat

trees and citrus plants typical of the Mediterranean. The tall, narrow trees that stand like dark columns are Italian cypresses, which are common in their native country. And the plant climbing a trellis beside the fountain is an honest-to-goodness grape vine.

ENOTECA CASTELLO: This shop on the edge of the piazza features a selection of red and white Italian wines. (If it's early in the day, take advantage of Epcot's Package Express service and have bottles sent to the park exit— so you don't have to carry them all day.) Wine tasting is offered, too (for about $8–$15). It's also possible to purchase an ice cold Italian beer. *Salute!*

IL BEL CRISTALLO: This shop boasts a large assortment of exquisite, handcrafted Venetian masks (which range in price from about $30 to $500).

LA BOTTEGA ITALIANA: Stop here for items such as cappuccino makers, wine glasses, olive oil, spices, cookies, chocolate, espresso, truffle sauce, balsamic vinegar, aprons, cookbooks, bags, kitchen items, mugs, glassware, and coffeemakers.

LA GEMMA ELEGANTE: There is an abundance of Italian fragrances, shirts, and accessories, plus purses, wallets, bags, and accessories inside this shop (just off the promenade on the Germany side of the piazza).

GERMANY

There are no villages in Germany quite like this one. Inspired by various towns in the Rhine region, Bavaria, and the German north, it boasts structures reminiscent of those found in urban enclaves as diverse as Frankfurt, Freiburg, and Rothenburg. There are stair-stepped rooflines and towers, balconies and arcaded walkways, and so much overall charm that the scene seems to come straight out of a fairy tale. The beer hall to the rear is almost as lively as those at Munich's famed Oktoberfest. The shops, which offer a range of merchandise from wine and sweets to ceramics and cuckoo clocks, teddy bears, steins, and freshly prepared caramel treats are so tempting that it's nearly impossible to leave the area empty-handed.

The elements that constitute the Germany pavilion are described here as they would be encountered while walking clockwise around the cobblestone-paved plaza. (The plaza is known as St. Georgsplatz, after the statue at its center.) St. George, the patron saint of soldiers, is depicted with a dragon that legend says he slew during a pilgrimage to the Middle East.

Try to time your World Showcase peregrinations to take you to the Germany pavilion on the hour, when the handsome, specially designed glockenspiel at the plaza's rear can be heard chiming in a melody composed specifically for the pavilion.

DAS KAUFHAUS: This two-story structure, with an exterior that is patterned after a merchants' hall known as the Kaufhaus (located in the German town of Freiburg im Breisgau), stocks athletic apparel and footwear. Looking to add some lederhosen to your wardrobe? Head here!

DER TEDDYBAR: Located adjacent to the Volkskunst clock shop, this is a toy store with a bit of flair. It's home to one of WDW's best selections of playthings, including an assortment of stuffed keepsakes. The selection of plush toys extends beyond teddy bears: look for lions, penguins, pigs, pandas, ducks, and unicorns. They also stock bears of the gummy kind.

KARAMELL-KÜCHE: This caramel display kitchen tempts with housemade sweet treats made from buttery caramel. Many items are made fresh in the on-stage kitchen. Favorites include fresh strawberries hand-dipped in chocolate and drizzled with gooey caramel, caramel-filled chocolate chip cookies, crunchy apples enveloped in caramel, chocolate or vanilla cupcakes topped with rich vanilla icing with a dab of caramel on top, caramel corn, packaged Werther's candies, and much more. Don't come here on an empty stomach— you could go bankrupt!

KUNSTARBEIT IN KRISTALL: This shop to the left of the Biergarten features Austrian and crystal jewelry (including tiaras), beer mugs, wine glasses in traditional German tints of green and amber, and crystal decanters. Glassware may be etched on the spot.

STEIN HAUS: The "house" is really a tiny shop that celebrates *bier*, featuring steins, mugs, shirts, and collectibles. *Prost!*

VOLKSKUNST: Small and appealing, this establishment is filled with a burgher's bounty of German timepieces, plus a smattering of other items made by hand in the rural corners of the nation. As for cuckoo clocks, some are small and unobtrusive, while others are so immense that they'd look appropriate only in some cathedral-ceilinged hunting lodge. This is also one place to find a traditional German beer mug, wine accessories, bells, books, crafts, and music.

WEINKELLER: Germany's local wine shop, situated toward the rear of St. Georgsplatz, offers about 50 varieties of German wine. Wine tastings are held here daily (for a fee). The selection includes vintages meant for everyday consumption, plus some fine estate wines. These are white (with a few exceptions), because white wine constitutes the bulk of Germany's vinicultural output. (Only 20 percent of German wine bottlings are red.) Bottles of wine and liqueur, wine glasses, artisanal cheese plates, and candy are sold, too. The setting itself is rather charming—low-ceilinged and quite cozy.

DIE WEIHNACHTS ECKE: A shop like this can set a visitor's mind to thoughts of Christmas—even on the steamiest dog days of summer. Ornaments, decorations, and gifts manufactured by various German companies line the merry shelves.

One item of note is the pickle ornament. Pickle ornaments are considered a special Christmas tree decoration by many families in Germany. Historically, it is always the last ornament hung on the tree, with a parent hiding it among the other ornaments. Kids gleefully search for it—and the one who finds it gets a special little present from St. Nicholas, left for the most observant child. Can you find the pickle ornament on each tree in the shop? It's not easy!

CHINA

Dominated by the Disney equivalent of Beijing's Temple of Heaven and announced by a pair of banners that proclaim good wishes to passersby (the Chinese characters translate to: "May good fortune follow you on your path through life" and "May virtue be your neighbor"), this pavilion conveys a level of serenity that offers an appealing contrast to the hearty merriment of the bordering Germany and the gaiety of nearby Mexico. Part of this quiet environment is the by-product of the soothing, traditional Chinese music. The gardens also make a major contribution. They are full of rosebushes native to China, and there is a century-old mulberry tree (to the left of the main walkway into the pavilion), with a pomegranate tree and a wiggly-looking Florida native known as a water oak nearby.

The number of stones in the floor of this pavilion's main structure is not random; the center stone is surrounded by nine stones because nine is considered a lucky number in China. Around the edge of the outer room rise 12 columns—because 12 is the number of months in the year and the number of years in a full cycle of the Chinese calendar. Be sure to stand on the round stone in the center: Every whisper is amplified.

A spacious emporium is devoted to wares from China, and two eateries add to the overall atmosphere. However, all this

is secondary to the motion picture shown inside the Temple of Heaven—a Circle-Vision 360 film that is one of the most diverting World Showcase attractions. Keep in mind that this movie is a standing-room-only viewing experience.

CIRCLE-VISION FILM: A new cinematic presentation shows the beauties of a land that few Epcot visitors have seen firsthand—and does it so vividly that it's possible to see the film twice and still not fully absorb all the wonderful sights.

This new film experience is set to replace *Reflections of China*, the Circle-Vision 360 movie that's concluding a successful run at Epcot's China pavilion. Just as with its predecessor, filmmakers used a total of nine cameras to capture cultural and scenic images that wrap completely around the audience. The majestic tour includes some rural stops, plus visits to cities such as Hong Kong, Macau, Beijing, and Shanghai.

The previous version of the movie featured footage of many landmarks, such as the 2,400-year-old Great Wall and Tiananmen Square, as well as some newer cultural developments. Overall, it showcased the majesty of this ancient country and highlighted some of the more dramatic changes that have taken place over time. Film details will differ in 2020—but China remains the star of the show. Note that the theater has no seats.

HOUSE OF GOOD FORTUNE: This vast emporium, located off the narrow, charming Street of Good Fortune, offers a huge assortment of merchandise—lanterns, hats, wine, beer, fine jewelry, silk robes, shoes (including a variety of sandals and flip-flops), prints, porcelain

Village Traders

Located between the Germany and China pavilions, this open-air shop sports a selection of handcrafted gift items from Africa, India, Spain, and Australia. Browse through such souvenirs as wind chimes, handbags, hats, and, of course, T-shirts.

items, tea sets, candles, neckties, Buddah statues, chess sets, (non-prescription) reading glasses, and much more. Kids adore the huge variety of panda-themed plush toys. Handheld fans may be personalized on the spot.

HOUSE OF WHISPERING WILLOWS: When exiting the movie, pass by the House of Whispering Willows, an exhibit of ancient Chinese art and artifacts. Changed periodically, it invariably includes fine pieces from well-known collections.

NORWAY

Set between Mexico and China is Norway, a pavilion added to the World Showcase mix in 1988. Built in conjunction with Norwegian companies, the pavilion celebrates the rich history, folklore, and culture of one of the Western world's oldest countries.

The cobblestone town square is an architectural showcase of the styles of such Norwegian towns as Bergen, Alesund, and Oslo. There's also a Norwegian castle fashioned after Akershus, a 14th-century fortress still standing in Oslo's harbor; the castle here houses the Akershus restaurant. Few can resist walking into the bakery for a taste of its treats. In a show of modernity, a statue of Norway's legendary marathoner Grete Waitz stands behind the bakery. Shops stock handicrafts and folk items: hand-knit woolens, wood carvings, and glass and metal artwork.

Frozen fans can also visit Arendelle, in the popular attraction Frozen Ever After. And for those guests who would like to meet Anna and Elsa of *Frozen* fame—great news: They're here!

ROYAL SOMMERHUS—MEET ANNA & ELSA: Attention, *Frozen* fans! Princess Anna and Queen Elsa greet guests throughout the day in this pavilion's Royal Sommerhus. Fastpass+ is not offered for this regal meet and greet, but the posted wait time is usually accurate. F.Y.I.: Arendelle, the fictional kingdom in which the ladies live, is said to be in Norway.

FROZEN EVER AFTER: **FP**+ Be prepared to let it go as you're swept off to the queendom of Arendelle in this enchanting boat ride. The snowy adventure celebrates the story from the film *Frozen* and the characters that have become near and dear to just about everybody's heart: Anna, Elsa, Olaf, Kristoff, and Sven—plus the Snowgies from the *Frozen Fever* animated short. The attraction, which replaced Maelstrom, immerses guests in favorite moments and music from the film. This attraction can have exceptionally daunting waits—we highly recommend reserving a Fastpass+ assignment well in advance. Otherwise, head here as soon as Epcot opens for the day.

THE FJORDING: Here you should find a nice variety of Norwegian gifts. Sweaters, active wear, high-quality winter wear, Viking helmets, trolls, toys, fragrances, fine jewelry, and candy are among the wares for sale at The Fjording. The back room offers all things *Frozen*. Want to pose for a photo with a giant troll? You've come to the right place! You may also pick up a bottle of Glogg—a traditional, non-alcoholic beverage popular in Scandinavia.

STAVE CHURCH GALLERY: Inside the wooden stave church, there is an exhibit that explores Norwegian culture. It's interesting (and sad) to note that only about 30 stave churches remain in Norway today.

PHOTO BY JILL SAFRO

MEXICO

The lush tangle of tropical vegetation surrounding the great pyramid that encloses this pavilion and the Mexican restaurant on the edge of World Showcase Lagoon provides only the barest suggestion of the immersive and charming area inside.

Dominated by a re-creation of a quaint plaza at dusk, the pyramid's interior is rimmed by balconied, tile-roofed, colonial-style structures. Crowding a fountain area is a quartet of stands selling Mexican handicrafts, and to the left is a shop stocked with other handsome wares. A visit by a Mariachi Cobre band keeps things lively—as does the tequila bar. To the rear, the San Angel Inn serves authentic fare. Behind it, a waterborne attraction features a whirlwind Mexican tour.

Take a look at the cultural exhibit inside the pyramid entrance on the way in. Note that the building was inspired by Meso-American structures dating from the third century A.D. Afterward, take a duck break—Donald greets guests next to the Mexico pavilion throughout the day.

GRAN FIESTA TOUR STARRING THE THREE CABALLEROS:
Big news: The Three Caballeros (that would be Donald Duck, Panchito, and José Carioca) are reuniting for a big show in Mexico City! Unfortunately, the ever mischievous Donald Duck has gone missing in Mexico—and guests join Panchito and José in the quest to find him. In doing so, you will be treated to a whirlwind (slow-moving) boat tour of the country. The cheery montage of film, props, and Audio-Animatronics figures is reminiscent of It's a Small World, though on a much smaller scale.

Trivia buffs should note that the Audio-Animatronics versions of the Three Caballeros that appear in the finale made their original Disney World debut in 1971. They were a part of the Magic Kingdom's original Mickey Mouse Revue in the Fantasyland Theatre—and remained there until 1980 (when the show left WDW for Tokyo

Disneyland). This attraction generally opens at 11 A.M. Details are subject to change.

EL RANCHITO DEL NORTE: Located on the lagoon side of World Showcase Promenade, this spot features gifts and souvenirs.

LA PRINCESSA DE CRISTAL: Presented by Arribas Brothers and located next to the entrance to the Gran Fiesta Tour Starring the Three Caballeros attraction, this alcove offers crystal tiaras, character figurines, rings, bracelets, necklaces, and glass slippers. If you're timing's right, you may get to watch glass blown by an in-house artisan.

LA TIENDA ENCANTATA: Visit this cheery store inside the pyramid and you'll discover mini piñatas, jewelry, bags, scarves, accessories, and assorted fashions.

PLAZA DE LOS AMIGOS: Brightly colored artwork, sombreros, baskets, decorative parrots, mariachi music (available on CD), musical instruments, and pottery make this mercado (market) at the plaza's center as bright and almost as lively as one in Mexico itself. Brilliantly hued papier-mâché piñatas figure strongly in the scenery here. Authentic pre-Columbian figures are on display. Also available for purchase are spices, hot sauce, salsa, liquors, cocktail accessories, and candy. The plaza is also a fitting space in which to peruse items themed to the film *Coco* and the Mexican holiday known as *Dia de los Muertos* (Day of the Dead).

SHOWCASE PLAZA

DISNEY TRADERS: Merchandise combining the charm of classic Disney characters and Epcot themes is the primary stock-in-trade. Sundries are also sold.

PORT OF ENTRY: A shop carrying fashions for the whole family, accessories, plush dolls, and toys. It has food and wine-related items, too.

Epcot Entertainment

Epcot presents a dynamic array of live performances each day, making it very important to consult a park Times Guide when you arrive. For details and scheduling information, go to *www.disneyworld.com*, use the My Disney Experience website or app, call 407-824-4321, or refer to a complimentary park Times Guide.

AMERICA GARDENS THEATRE: The lagoon-side venue at The American Adventure pavilion hosts an ever-changing program of live entertainment, such as the popular Garden Rocks, Disney on Broadway, and Eat to the Beat concert series. The beloved Epcot Candlelight Processional is traditionally presented here during the holiday season.

EPCOT FESTIVALS: When it comes to parties, Epcot is celebration central. Throughout the year, the theme park plays host to the International Festival of the Arts (January–February), International Flower & Garden Festival in which the park undergoes a fragrant bloom boom (March–May); International Food & Wine Festival (mid-August through mid-November); and International Festival of the Holidays (mid-November–late December). Epcot fests feature food, drink, entertainment, and special-ticket events with an international flair.

JAMMITORS: When they're not tidying up Future World, these jolly janitors drum up fun with the most unlikely of musical instruments: trash cans! Each rhythmic jam lasts about 10 minutes. Check a park Times Guide for showtimes.

KIDCOT FUN STOPS: There is an activity area in each of the countries of World Showcase. These spots invite kids to play games, draw, color, and collect activity cards at Epcot's international pavilions.

EPCOT FOREVER: FP+ When the curtain closed on IllumiNations—Reflections of Earth in 2019, a new show was introduced: Epcot Forever. This rousing, temporary, nighttime spectacular—which mixes lasers, fireworks, special effects, kites, and classic Epcot music—is expected to yield the lagoon to another new show at some point before WDW marks its 50th anniversary (in 2021). That vibrant new, high-tech production will celebrate how Disney music inspires people around the world and will feature massive floating set pieces, custom-built LED panels, choreographed fountains, lights, pyrotechnics, lasers, and music (of course!).

Epcot's nighttime extravaganza is visible from anywhere on the World Showcase promenade and takes place nightly at closing time.

WORLD SHOWCASE PERFORMERS: It's all but impossible to complete a circuit of World Showcase without catching performances while en route. Keep an eye on the schedule and be sure to take in entertainment at each pavilion, often performed by natives of the country represented. Among the possibilities: worldly acrobats, a Mexican mariachi band, an American a cappella group, Moroccan belly dancers, and Japanese drummers.

HOLIDAY HAPPENINGS

During certain holidays, such as Easter week, the Fourth of July, Thanksgiving, Christmas week, and New Year's Eve, Epcot usually offers extended hours and presents extra entertainment to celebrate the respective occasion.

CHRISTMAS: The park is exceptionally festive throughout the holiday season. Epcot's International Festival of the Holidays is an international yuletide extravaganza. It features the joyous holiday traditions of all 11 World Showcase nations, complete with musical performances, seasonal food and drink, and decorations galore. Of course, the 2020 holiday celebration will include the park's popular candlelight choral processional.

The Candlelight Processional, a stirring presentation of traditional holiday songs, includes a reading of the Christmas story by a celebrity narrator. This is an exceptionally popular event. (See page 12 for details.)

HOT TIPS

- Use a smartphone or stop at a Fastpass+ kiosk to book Fastpasses for as many attractions as possible (if you haven't reserved in advance).

- On your way into the park, pick up a free guide-map and a Times Guide. Consult the entertainment schedule first thing.

- Lines throughout Epcot are longest at midday and shortest in the early evening.

- During peak seasons, preferred reservation times at Epcot's table-service restaurants book quickly—make reservations as far in advance as possible. However, some tables may be available on a first-come, first-served basis (with a bit of a wait). Plan to arrive at least a few minutes ahead of your reservation time.

- Most World Showcase restaurants seat guests until park closing. To make advance plans, call 407-WDW-DINE (939-3463).

- Kids can have autograph books or World Showcase passports (sold for about $10 inside the park) stamped in each of the 11 countries represented in the park. It's a nice added layer to an Epcot "world tour."

- Interactive fountain areas at Epcot provide guests of all ages with an opportunity to cool off. Be sure to pack swimsuits (and waterproof diapers) for little ones who will undoubtedly spend time splashing in the water.

- If you plan to stay until park closing and are traveling by WDW bus, take your time getting to the depot—the wait time will be longer than usual as Epcot's day comes to an end. Wait out the exodus at the MouseGear shop or relax on a bench as the masses stroll by.

- Allow plenty of time to explore the post-shows at Spaceship Earth and Mission: SPACE.

- Epcot is a good park to "hop" to from another park (provided your ticket has the hopper option). It's usually open until at least 9 P.M.

- FriendShip water taxis are unlikely to transport you across World Showcase Lagoon any faster than a brisk walk, but they are a foot-friendly way to make the half-mile-plus journey.

- For a dynamite view of Epcot's nighttime extravaganza, book dinner at Mexico's La Hacienda de San Angel up to an hour before showtime.

- At press time, Starbucks (aka Fountain View) and Epcot's beloved Club Cool (Coca-Cola tasting station) were on temporary hiatus. They do, however, factor into the park's future. Check *disneyworld.com* for updates on their status.

Where to Find the Characters at Epcot

PHOTO BY JILL SAFRO

The original Epcot Character Spot has closed, but rest assured Epcot is still character central. The Gazebo near Showcase Plaza is a good place to meet Disney friends (possibly Minnie or Pluto), while Mickey and Goofy have been known to visit Future World. Daisy socializes with visitors near the American Adventure pavilion. Princesses host meals at Norway's Akershus Royal Banquet Hall. Characters such as Mickey, Pluto, Chip, and Dale host meals at Garden Grill in The Land. Anna and Elsa meet folks in Norway's Sommerhus. Snow White visits with guests in Germany. Mary Poppins, Alice in Wonderland, and Winnie the Pooh mingle at the U.K. pavilion. Donald Duck greets guests in Mexico. Aurora and Belle visit France, while Mulan appears in China. Disney pals such as Winnie the Pooh, Joy, and Baymax may greet guests, too. Note that character appearance specifics may change without notice. Check a Times Guide for greeting locations and appearance schedules during your visit.

HIDDEN MICKEYS

These are some of the most popular "Hidden Mickeys" at Epcot. How many can you find? Check the circle when you spot each one!

Mission: SPACE: When your ship lands on Mars, you may spy a Mickey on a rooftop to the right of the landing strip. (It's made of satellite dishes.) ○

After you exit the ride and enter the gift shop, look up in the center of the room to find a side profile of Mickey painted on the ceiling. ○

Mexico: Toward the end of the Gran Fiesta Tour boat ride, you'll see a barge on your left. On that barge is a Hidden Mickey made of strategically arranged bongo drums. ○

Living with the Land: As you walk through the queue, try to find the three bubbles on the large mural that come together to form a Hidden Mickey. (Hint: It's near the middle of the mural.) ○

About halfway through the attraction, you may notice a water hose coiled into the shape of Mickey Mouse's noggin'. ○

Soarin' Around the World: As you soar over Utah's Monument Valley, keep an eye out for a trio of hot air balloons that briefly converge to form an H.M. ○

As the ride comes to a finish, note pyrotechnic bursts that strategically line up with Spaceship Earth. ○

The American Adventure pavilion: Look for a painting of early American settlers crossing a river with covered wagons. One of the wagon-pulling oxen has a Mickey near its left front leg. ○

Another painting features workers constructing a building. Check out the tops of the beams behind the construction team. They form a classic Hidden Mickey! (The painting is on the first floor, on the right, and toward the back of the rotunda.) ○

France: Head to Monsieur Paul to find swirly-shaped Mickey heads on the marquee at the entrance, as well as on the top of the menu display. ○

Be sure to eyeball the grates surrounding the trees near the entrance to Les Chefs de France. There are several H.M.s in the intricate grillwork. ○

While visiting Epcot's France pavilion, pay very close attention to the wedding party scene in the *Impressions de France* film—there is a Hidden Mickey on a second-floor window! ○

Canada: It's easy to find the totem poles in this pavilion—but it's a bit more challenging to find the Hidden Mickey on the left one. ○

The Seas with Nemo & Friends: In Bruce's Shark World, look for two large posters—one titled "Did You Know?" and the other titled "Bruce's Shark World" (they are on opposite sides of the room). Each has an oyster in the lower right-hand corner that contains Mickey-shaped pearls. If you pay attention at the shark tank, you'll be rewarded with a Hidden Mickey sighting (or two). The Mouse's head appears on the bottom of the tank, shaped by strategically placed rocks. ○

Journey Into Imagination with Figment: About halfway through the ride and as you move through Figment's house, look up in the bathroom. Figment's commode forms a Hidden Mickey with two red circles on the ground next to it. ○

Spaceship Earth: In the Renaissance scene, look quickly to your left to find the first painter standing in front of a table (his back is to you). On the top left of the table, three white-paint circles form a Hidden Mickey. ○

Later on, keep your eyes open for a Hidden "W.D.I." (the abbreviation for Walt Disney Imagineering) on the microphone of the radio broadcaster (on the left side of the ride vehicle's forward motion). ○

Germany: Look up to spot three armor-wearing fellows festooning a facade to the right of the clock in St. Georgsplatz. The suit closest to the glockenspiel sports an H.M. ○

Japan: Finding the koi pond here is easy—but can you find the Hidden Mickey in the pond? And no, it's not a Mickey fish! ○

Specifics may change during 2020.

WHERE IN THE WORLD?

All of the photos on this page were taken at Epcot. Do you know where? We challenge you to find all the spots where these images were shot and snap a (non-flash) photo for yourself as you discover each one. Happy hunting! (For locations, turn to page 362.)

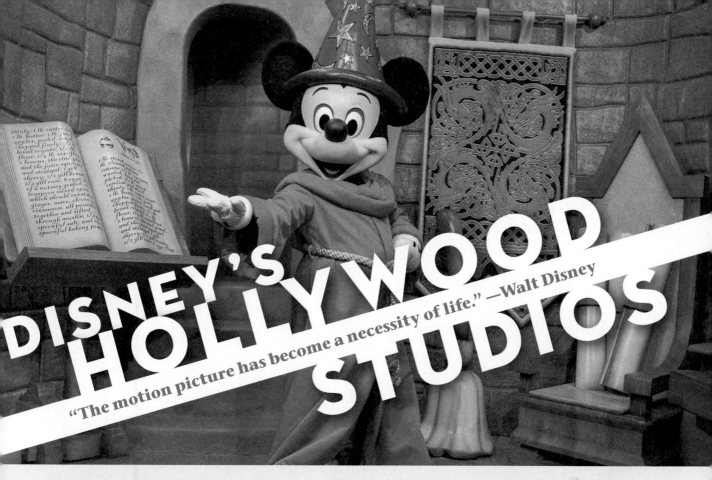

DISNEY'S HOLLYWOOD STUDIOS

"The motion picture has become a necessity of life." —Walt Disney

177 Getting Oriented

178 Park Primer

179 Attractions

189 Shopping

191 Entertainment

192 Hot Tips

Disney's Hollywood Studios has been described as "the Hollywood that never was and always will be." A bit hokey, perhaps— but also true. Enter the gates and the mosaic of flashy neon, chromed Art Deco, streamlined architecture, and star-gazing street characters immediately plunges you into the Hollywood of the 1940s. A nostalgic view of the movie-making capital has been combined with a variety of current TV- and movie-themed attractions and a delightful selection of eateries to create this Walt Disney World enclave. The combined result is an entertainment lineup worthy of a rave review.

Since opening in 1989, the park has continued to grow and evolve. The bright and cheery Toy Story Land made its debut in 2018 and an immersive new adventure zone called Star Wars: Galaxy's Edge blasted onto the scene last year. While visiting the distant planet of Batuu, intrepid park visitors can take the controls of the *Millennium Falcon* starship and join an epic battle between the First Order and the Resistance.

The park's collection of attractions boasts such classic crowd-pleasers as *The Twilight Zone*™ Tower of Terror, the rollicking Rock 'n' Roller Coaster, the zany Toy Story Mania!, an explosive struggle between good and evil in Fantasmic!, and a rousing fireworks extravaganza: Star Wars: A Galactic Spectacular. Each adds a new dimension to the Hollywood term "action."

DISNEY'S HOLLYWOOD STUDIOS

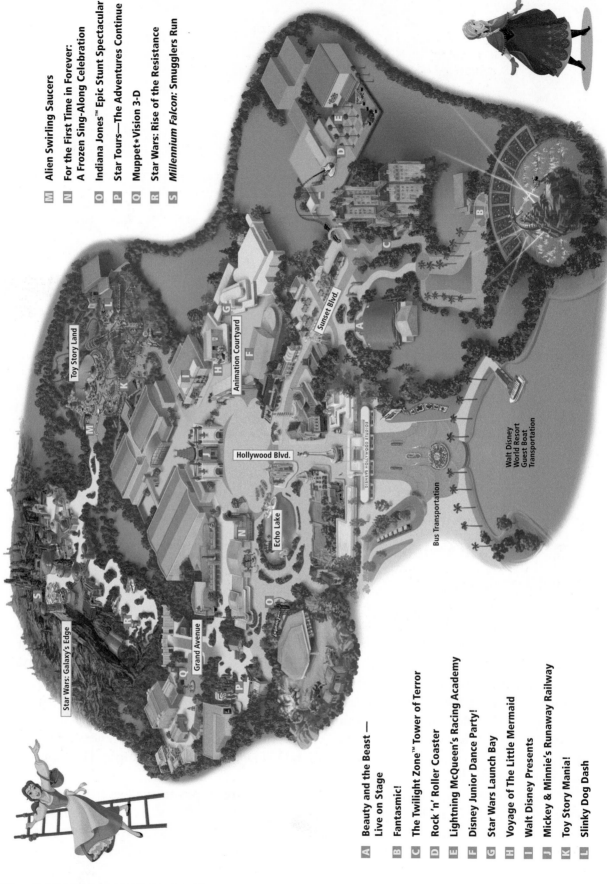

M Alien Swirling Saucers

N For the First Time in Forever:
A Frozen Sing-Along Celebration

O Indiana Jones™ Epic Stunt Spectacular

P Star Tours—The Adventures Continue

Q Muppet✶Vision 3-D

R Star Wars: Rise of the Resistance

S Millennium Falcon: Smugglers Run

Toy Story Land

Animation Courtyard

Sunset Blvd.

Hollywood Blvd.

Echo Lake

Grand Avenue

Star Wars: Galaxy's Edge

Bus Transportation

Walt Disney
World Resort
Guest Boat
Transportation

A Beauty and the Beast —
Live on Stage

B Fantasmic!

C The Twilight Zone™ Tower of Terror

D Rock 'n' Roller Coaster

E Lightning McQueen's Racing Academy

F Disney Junior Dance Party!

G Star Wars Launch Bay

H Voyage of The Little Mermaid

I Walt Disney Presents

J Mickey & Minnie's Runaway Railway

K Toy Story Mania!

L Slinky Dog Dash

Getting Oriented

Disney's Hollywood Studios theme park has a layout with no distinctive shape or main thoroughfare. As such, the park can be a bit of a challenge to navigate. Study a guidemap as you enter.

The park entrance deposits guests on the shop-lined Hollywood Boulevard. This avenue leads to an ornate replica of the Hollywood landmark Grauman's Chinese Theatre. Walking along the Boulevard, you will come to Hollywood Junction. Here, a palm-tree-dotted street known as Sunset Boulevard branches off to the right.

Stroll to the end of Sunset Boulevard and you will come across the Hollywood Hills Amphitheater, home of Fantasmic! and Rock 'n' Roller Coaster. At the street's far end is *The Twilight Zone*™ Tower of Terror. The strip is also graced with shops, the Sunset Ranch Market, and the Theater of the Stars Amphitheater, where Beauty and the Beast—Live on Stage is performed daily.

Stand in Hollywood Plaza, facing the Chinese Theatre, and you'll notice an archway just off to your right. This leads to Animation Courtyard, home to Disney Junior Dance Party! and Star Wars Launch Bay. Nearby Toy Story Land is home to Toy Story Mania!, Slinky Dog Dash, and Alien Swirling Saucers. If you turn left off Hollywood Boulevard, you're on course for Echo Lake attractions such as Indiana Jones Epic Stunt Spectacular and Star Tours—The Adventures Continue. Beyond Star Tours there are two entertainment zones: Grand Avenue, home to Muppet*Vision 3-D and the brand-new land known as Star Wars: Galaxy's Edge.

HOW TO GET THERE

By car, take Exit 64B off I-4. Continue about half a mile to the parking area. Take a tram to the park entrance.

By WDW Transportation: From the Swan, Dolphin, Yacht & Beach Club, and BoardWalk resorts: boat or walkway. From Fort Wilderness: bus from the Outpost stop. From Epcot: boat, bus, or the new Disney Skyliner gondola system. From Caribbean Beach, Pop Century, Art of Animation, and Riviera (see page 86) resorts: bus or Disney Skyliner. From the Magic Kingdom, Animal Kingdom, all other WDW resorts, and the resorts on Hotel Plaza Boulevard: bus only. From Disney Springs: bus to any Walt Disney World resort and transfer to a bus, or boat, or the Disney Skyliner.

PARKING

All-day parking starts at $25 for day visitors (standard parking is free to WDW resort guests and annual pass-holders; $45–$50 for premium lots). Trams circulate regularly, providing transportation to and from the parking area to the park entrance. Please note the section and the aisle in which you park. The ticket allows for re-entry to the parking area throughout the day.

HOURS

Disney's Hollywood Studios is usually open from about 9 A.M. until about one hour after sunset. During certain holiday periods and summer months, hours may be extended. It's best to arrive about 20 minutes before the posted opening time—guests are often let in early. Depending on the season, some stage shows do not open until late in the morning.

Admission Prices

ONE-DAY BASE TICKET*
(Restricted to use only in Disney's Hollywood Studios. Prices are for Date-Based tickets. Rates for Flexible Date tickets are higher. **Prices exclude tax and are likely to rise in 2020.**)

Adult	$109–$159
Child**	$104–$154

* One-Day tickets are valid only on the selected date. Flexible Date tickets purchased in 2020 must be used by December 31, 2021. This is the cost of a 1-day/1-park-only ticket. Terms are subject to change. For updates, visit *https://disneyworld.disney.go.com/admission/tickets/*.

** 3 through 9 years of age; children under age 3 free (no ticket required)

HOT TIP!

The information on these pages was accurate at press time, but some details are apt to change. For updates on the shows and attractions at Disney's Hollywood Studios, use the My Disney Experience mobile app or website, or visit *www.disneyworld.com*.

Park Primer

BABY FACILITIES

Changing tables and facilities for nursing mothers can be found at the Baby Care Center at Guest Relations near the park entrance.

DISABILITY INFORMATION

Most Walt Disney World attractions, restaurants, shops, and shows are accessible to guests using wheelchairs. Additional services are available for guests with visual or hearing disabilities. Stop by the park's Guest Relations location when you arrive. For a detailed overview of the services offered, including transportation, parking, attraction access, and more, pick up a free copy of the *Guide for Guests with Disabilities*. For more information, refer to the *Getting Ready to Go*.

FIRST AID

Minor medical problems can be handled at the First Aid Center, located next to Guest Relations at the park entrance. **For medical emergencies, alert a Cast Member and call 911.**

INFORMATION

Guest Relations, located just inside the park entrance (on the left), has free guidemaps, Times Guides, and an ever-resourceful staff. To make dining arrangements for certain Studios eateries, visit *www.disneyworld.com*, use the My Disney Experience website or mobile app, or call 407-939-3463.

LOCKERS

Lockers, found by Oscar's Super Service, just inside the park's entrance, cost $15 per day for jumbo lockers, $12 a day for large lockers, $10 a day for small ones for use all day (at Disney's Hollywood Studios only). Payments are made at a self-service kiosk (via cash or major credit card; guests paying with MagicBands should seek out a Cast Member at the nearest merchandise location).

LOST CHILDREN

If you become separated from a child, alert the nearest Cast Member to the problem.

LOST & FOUND

Report a lost item to Guest Relations, just inside the park's entrance or fill out a lost item report online at *www.chargerback.com/disneyworld*. To report lost items after your visit, go to the aforementioned website.

MONEY MATTERS

There is an automated teller machine (ATM) just outside the park entrance and by the Sunset Club Couture shop. In addition to U.S. currency, credit cards (Visa, American Express, JCB, MasterCard, and Diner's Club), traveler's checks, Disney gift cards, Disney Dollars, MagicBands, and WDW resort key cards are accepted at most park locations. (MagicBands and resort key cards must be backed up with a major credit card.)

PACKAGE PICKUP

Shops can arrange for purchases to be transported to Package Pickup, next to Oscar's Super Service (by the park entrance), where they can be picked up later in the day. Packages may take several hours to get to Package Pickup—plan accordingly. The service is free to all guests at Disney's Hollywood Studios.

SAME-DAY RE-ENTRY

Be sure to wear your MagicBand (if you used it for admission) or retain your ticket if you plan to return later the same day.

SECURITY CHECK

Guests entering Disney theme parks are subject to a thorough security check. All bags will be searched by security personnel before guests may enter the park. A metal detector screens guests. Weapons (including toys) are prohibited. For details and a complete listing of Walt Disney World Park Rules, visit Guest Relations or go to *www.disneyworld.com/ParkRules*.

STROLLERS & WHEELCHAIRS

Strollers, wheelchairs, and Electric Conveyance Vehicles (ECVs) may be rented from Oscar's Super Service, inside the park entrance on the right. Cost for strollers is about $15; about $12 for wheelchairs. A double stroller costs $31. A Length of Stay rental ticket saves wheelchair and stroller renters $2 a day. Cost for ECVs is $50, plus a $20 refundable deposit. Keep the receipt—it can be used on the same day for a replacement at any WDW theme park. Quantities are limited (especially for ECVs).

Sunset Boulevard

Disney's Hollywood Studios has a brand of attractions altogether unique. Some offer guests behind-the-scenes looks at the creative and technical processes that generate television shows and movies. Others go so far as to allow guests to gain a bit of showbiz experience along with the insight. Still others present popular characters and stories in new forms—from stage shows to thrill rides.

Unlike the twisty version of the real street, Disney's version of Sunset Boulevard is a straightaway that lets guests make a beeline for some of the park's biggest thrills. Said thrills include Rock 'n' Roller Coaster, Fantasmic!, and Tower or Terror.

THE TWILIGHT ZONE™ TOWER OF TERROR

BIRNBAUM'S ★BEST★ **FP+** The Hollywood Tower Hotel is the creepy home of a spectacular thrill ride. On the facade of the 199-foot-tall building hangs a sparking electric sign. As the legend goes, lightning struck the building on Halloween night in 1939. An entire guest wing disappeared, along with an elevator carrying five people.

The line for the ride runs through the lobby, where dusty furniture, cobwebs, and old newspapers add to the eerie atmosphere. As guests enter the library, they see a TV brought to life by a bolt of lightning. Rod Serling invites them to enter The Twilight Zone.

Guests are led toward the boiler room to enter the ride elevator. (This is your last chance to change your mind about riding—ask an attendant to point you toward the "chicken exit.") Once you take a seat in the elevator, the doors close and the room begins its ascent. At the first stop, the doors open and guests peek down a corridor. Among the effects is a ghostly visit by the hotel guests who vanished. The doors close and you continue the trip skyward.

At the next stop, you enter another dimension, a combination of sights and sounds reminiscent of the classic television series *The Twilight Zone*. In fact, Disney Imagineers watched each of the 156 original *Twilight*

Zone episodes at least twice for inspiration. This part of the ride is a somewhat disorienting experience, in part because the elevator moves horizontally.

What happens next depends entirely upon the whim of Disney Imagineers, who have programmed the ride so that the drop sequence is chillingly random. At the top (approximately 157 feet up), passengers can look out at the Studios below. Once the doors shut, you plummet 13 stories. The drop lasts about two seconds, but it seems a whole lot longer.

Just when you think it's over, the elevator launches skyward, barely stopping before it plunges again. And again. As you exit, Rod Serling claims this is the kind of thing "they don't tell you about in any guidebook." It's been our privilege to prove him wrong.

From the time you are seated, the trip takes about five minutes. Note that you must be at least 40 inches tall to ride Tower of Terror. It is not recommended for pregnant women, people with heart conditions, or with back or neck problems. Though thrilling (and scary), the drops are surprisingly smooth. Still, if you'd rather not experience the sensation of being a human yo-yo, sit this one out.

PHOTO BY JILL SAFRO

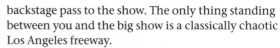

backstage pass to the show. The only thing standing between you and the big show is a classically chaotic Los Angeles freeway.

In an effort to get to the show on time, you will zip through the nighttime Los Angeles streets in a stretch limo. The ride vehicles (designed to resemble limousines) are equipped with a high-tech sound system (five speakers per seat make for a mega-decibel ride), and the remainder of the journey features rockin' synchronized sound— adding a dramatic dimension to the roller coaster experience most daredevils have come to expect. Each limo-train is equipped with 120 speakers and features a different Aerosmith song—all of which were custom-recorded for the attraction.

You must be free of back, neck, and heart problems to experience this topsy-turvy tour. Expectant mothers should sit this one out. Guests must be at least 48 inches tall to ride Rock 'n' Roller Coaster.

BEAUTY AND THE BEAST— LIVE ON STAGE

BIRNBAUM'S ★BEST★ FP+ Several times each day, Belle, Beast, Gaston, Lumiere, Mrs. Potts, and the rest of the cast of the classic Disney film *Beauty and the Beast* come to life at the 1,500-seat Theater of the Stars, near the Tower of Terror, on Sunset Boulevard.

The 30-minute show is as entertaining as they come. The staging is just right, and the music's simply addictive as it traces the classic tale—from Belle's dissatisfaction with her life in a small French town to the climactic battle between the staff of the Beast's castle and Gaston and the townspeople. Lumiere and friends perform the song "Be Our Guest" with a delightful display of dancing flatware. Check a park Times Guide for the schedule. Latecomers can often find

ROCK 'N' ROLLER COASTER STARRING AEROSMITH

BIRNBAUM'S ★BEST★ FP+ The fastest roller coaster in Walt Disney World history is guaranteed to rock your world. Rock 'n' Roller Coaster is ideally suited for those who consider the Tower of Terror just a little on the tame side.

The indoor attraction reaches a speed of nearly 60 miles per hour—in 2.8 seconds flat. The feeling is not unlike that of sitting in a supersonic jet as it blasts off the deck of an aircraft carrier. Other twists include two rollover loops and a corkscrew—marking the first time Disney has turned guests upside down on American soil. Each ride covers a half mile of track and lasts a memorable (if harrowing) 1 minute, 22 seconds.

The ride's premise is this: The rock band Aerosmith has cut their recording session short because they are late for a concert. As they rush out, they offer you a

---

HOT TIP!

You'll need to stop at a locker (near the park entrance) before riding Rock 'n' Roller Coaster—there's no place to store loose articles in the ride vehicles.

PHOTO BY JILL SAFRO

FP+ = Fastpass+ attraction (see page 25)

seats in the bleachers (in the back of the theater). Note that some scenes (especially when Gaston leads a brigade to hunt down the Beast) can be intense for some young children.

LIGHTNING MCQUEEN'S RACING ACADEMY

FP+ Get ready to start your engines and learn what it takes to be a racing champ from Lightning McQueen himself. The Piston Cup legend doles out dramatic Driver's Ed wisdom at his Racing Academy throughout the day. He kicks off each session by sharing tricks of the trade via state-of-the-art simulator and a wraparound screen. Things don't always go smoothly, but his pals from Radiator Springs are on hand to help him navigate bumps in the road and get back on course. Will he emerge victorious? Zoom on over to find out. After

the show, everyone gets to meet and pose for photos with Cruz Ramirez (pictured above).

The approximately 10-minute show—which made its debut in 2019—is most popular with young *Cars* fans. It takes place inside Sunset Showcase, a theater that neighbors the Rock 'n' Roller Coaster attraction.

Trip the Light Fantasmic!

BIRNBAUM'S ★BEST★ FP+ Fantasmic!, a lavish musical production, plays on select nights at the Hollywood Hills Amphitheater on Sunset Boulevard. A dramatic mix of fireworks, fountains, lasers, and Disney characters, it invites guests to take a peek into the dream (and nightmare) world of Mickey Mouse.

Though similar to its Disneyland counterpart, half of this 26-minute production is original. The action follows Mickey through a series of dreams. In the first dream, he appears at the base of a mountain, shoots fireworks from his fingertips, and conducts an orchestra of colorful fountains. (Guests seated up front may get spritzed.) Soon, Mickey is plagued by nightmares as Disney villains take over his dreams. (This aspect has been known to scare small children.) In the end, the Mouse and his pals prevail (of course!).

Seating begins about 90 minutes before showtime—though some guests line up even earlier. Get there early, even if you have a Fastpass+ assignment. Check a Times Guide for the schedule.

We recommend sitting toward the back—the view is good and it's easier to get out after the show. There is standing room, too. After the finale, sit for a bit. It can take 20 minutes for the crowd to exit the theater.

Timing Tip: The show is presented on most nights. Check a Times Guide for the schedule during your visit. On nights when Fantasmic! is presented twice, see the later show. Afterward, as the masses exit the park, take some time to browse the shops that keep their doors open after hours.

Animation Courtyard

PHOTO BY JILL SAFRO

Disney's Hollywood Studios park pays tribute to the art of animation with Disney Junior Dance Party!, The Voyage of The Little Mermaid, and a celebration of revered animation pioneer Walt Disney in an exhibit known as Walt Disney Presents.

VOYAGE OF THE LITTLE MERMAID

FP+ One of Disney's Hollywood Studios' most popular attractions for little ones, this is a 17-minute live musical production, adapted from the Disney animated classic *The Little Mermaid*. The show is presented in a theater with an underwater feel. In it, many of the film's beloved animated characters, such as Flounder, Scuttle, and Sebastian, are brought to life by puppeteers. The show opens with a lively rendition of "Under the Sea," then animated clips from the movie are shown as human performers join the puppets on stage.

Ariel is the star and performs songs from the film. Prince Eric makes an appearance, and an enormous Ursula glides across the stage to steal Ariel's voice. Of course, as in the movie, the happy ending prevails. The story line is a little bit disjointed, hopping from scene to scene, and some of the signature songs are missing. However, most viewers are familiar with the film, so this choppiness doesn't detract much from the show.

There are a number of special effects, including cascading water, lasers, and a lightning storm that may be a bit frightening for some very young children. Note that many of the effects are best enjoyed from the middle to the rear of the theater. All audience members get spritzed with water—don't wear silk.

Keep in mind that, although this is a Fastpass+ attraction, performances are still presented at scheduled times throughout the day. Current showtimes are listed in the Times Guide. Plan to arrive at least 15 to 30 minutes before the scheduled start time. This attraction may not operate in 2020.

DISNEY JUNIOR DANCE PARTY!

FP+ A jolly celebration of Disney Junior, this show is most popular with very young guests—who are the most enthusiastic members of the audience. The performance space holds large crowds of (mostly tiny) people at a time. Seating is minimal, but there's plenty of room to sprawl out on the carpeted floor. All guests are invited to sing, dance, catch bubbles, and laugh themselves silly. Disney Junior favorites such as

Sofia the First, Doc McStuffins, Timon—and, of course, Mickey Mouse and Minnie Mouse—join the party, too. The show is presented daily. The park's Times Guide lists the schedule.

PHOTO BY JILL SAFRO

STAR WARS LAUNCH BAY

Guests who don't get their fill of the Force in Star Wars: Galaxy's Edge can get their fix here—Star Wars Launch Bay offers an immersive atmosphere in which to experience both the Light and Dark sides. Housed in the space formerly occupied by Art of Animation, Launch Bay features props and movie memorabilia (some genuine, some convincing replicas) celebrating Star Wars and the re-awakened Force. In addition to Light and Dark galleries, guests may encounter characters such as Chewbacca, BB-8, and Kylo Ren. Details may change in 2020—for updates, check *www.disneyworld.com*, or the My Disney Experience app or website.

WALT DISNEY PRESENTS

Follow Walt Disney from "Mickey Mouse to the Magic Kingdoms" in this multi-media exhibit next to the Voyage of The Little Mermaid attraction. Among the treasures included in this tribute to the man behind the mouse are Walt's second-grade school desk, the original Audio-Animatronics Abraham Lincoln from the 1964 New York World's Fair, *Mickey Mouse Club* props, Jungle Cruise and Spaceship Earth models, costumes from *Mary Poppins*, and more. A small movie theater screens sneak peeks of upcoming Disney films. Character meet and greets are occasionally offered here, too. Details are subject to change in 2020. This attraction was previously known as Walt Disney: One Man's Dream.

HOT TIP!

The Star Wars Guided Tour is a 5.5-hour adventure including nearly all the Star Wars action this park has to offer. It currently includes reserved seating for stage shows, guaranteed enrollment in the Jedi Training Academy (for kids ages 4 to 12), a trip to hyperspace on Star Tours—the Adventures Continue, a character meet and greet opportunity, a Star Wars–inspired meal at Backlot Express, reserved viewing spot for the fireworks (Star Wars: A Galactic Spectacular), a personalized souvenir, and more. Cost is about $93 (plus tax) per person (park admission is necessary). For details or to make reservations, visit *www.disneyworld.com*, use the My Disney Experience website or mobile app, or call 407-939-7529—and experience the "Power of the Park Side." All details subject to change.

Toy Story Land

PHOTO BY JILL SAFRO

Toy Story Land, a happy new play zone located just beyond Animation Courtyard, lets guests experience the world from a toy's point of view. The joyfully elaborate re-creation of Andy's backyard features three attractions for honorary toys to enjoy: Slinky Dog Dash, Alien Swirling Saucers, and Toy Story Mania. To Toy Story Land—and beyond!

PHOTO BY JILL SAFRO

SLINKY DOG DASH

BIRNBAUM'S ★BEST★ FP+ Welcome to Andy's backyard— the site of a very special roller coaster. Yep, Andy has successfully assembled his Mega Coaster Play Kit, complete with Slinky Dog ride vehicles. The only thing missing are some action figures to ride 'em. That's where *you* come in!

Channel your inner toy and climb aboard Slinky's back to enjoy a zippy trip through Toy Story Land. The family-friendly ride is tamer (and smoother) than the park's Rock 'n' Roller Coaster, but it offers big thrills, including dramatic drops and bouncy hops.

Guests must be at least 38 inches tall to ride. Skip this ride if you are pregnant, or suffer from motion sickness or other health issues.

ALIEN SWIRLING SAUCERS

PHOTO BY JILL SAFRO

FP+ The Little Green Men were beyond delighted when Andy opened the playset he won at the Pizza Planet—it came with a set of flying saucers! Our alien friends have powered up said saucers and are ready to take you for a ride. So jump inside a rocket-shaped toy and hang on. The aliens may not be very good pilots, but don't worry—the ride vehicles never leave the ground. However, they do swirl beneath "The Claw" while a peppy, intergalactic soundtrack plays in the background.

Guests must be at least 32 inches tall and free of motion sickness to take this spinning saucer trip. Don't ride on a full stomach.

FP+ = Fastpass+ attraction (see page 25)

TOY STORY MANIA!

BIRNBAUM'S ★BEST★ FP+ This engaging experience is an energetic, interactive toy box tour with a twist: Guests wear 3-D glasses as they take aim at animated targets with toy cannons. The adventure is about as high-tech as they come, yet rooted in classic midway games of skill. As points are scored, expect effusive encouragement from a cast of cheerleaders—*Toy Story*'s Woody, Buzz Lightyear, Hamm, Rex, Trixie, and, of course, the Green Army Men.

Fans of the Magic Kingdom's Buzz Lightyear's Space Ranger Spin will no doubt delight in this adventure, which takes the experience of the interactive attraction into a whole new dimension. As far as skill level goes, there's something for everyone at Toy Story Mania—from beginners to seasoned gamers alike.

Note: This is a wildly popular attraction with guests of all ages. Get there as early in the morning as you can, and try to snag a Fastpass+ assignment as far ahead as possible. The herky-jerky motion of this ride (as the vehicles move from scene to scene) may be too much for folks with sensitive backs or other health issues.

HOT TIP!

Don't sweat the accuracy number in Toy Story Mania!—it's meaningless. Fire as fast and furiously as possible. That way, you'll hit more targets in less time!

Grand Avenue

A brief stroll down Grand Avenue deposits guests at Grand Park—the site of the Muppet-ational attraction, Muppet•Vision 3-D—complete with its glorious finale called A Salute to All Nations, but Mostly America.

MUPPET•VISION 3-D

BIRNBAUM'S ★BEST★ FP+ One of the most entertaining attractions at the Studios, this 3-D (though some describe it as 4-D) movie is quite remarkable. A funny 12-minute pre-show gives clues about what's to come. Once inside the theater, many will notice that it looks just like the one from Jim Henson's classic TV series *The Muppet Show*. Even the two curmudgeonly fellows, Statler and Waldorf, are sitting in the balcony, bantering and offering their typically critical commentary on the show.

The production comes directly from Muppet Labs, presided over by Dr. Bunsen Honeydew—and his long-suffering assistant, Beaker—and introduces Waldo, the "Spirit of 3-D." Among the highlights is Miss Piggy's solo, which Bean Bunny turns into quite a fiasco. Sam Eagle's grand finale leads to trouble as a veritable war breaks out, culminating with a cannon blast to the screen, courtesy of everyone's favorite Swedish Chef.

Including the pre-show, expect to spend about 29 minutes with Kermit and company. Shows run continuously throughout the day. Note that guests must wear 3-D glasses to enjoy this show. If your child is too young to keep the glasses on, skip this Muppet encounter.

FP+ = Fastpass+ attraction (see page 25)

Echo Lake

Once you spot a dinosaur noshing on some seaweed, you know you've entered the Echo Lake region of Disney's Hollywood Studios. In addition to Dinosaur Gertie's Ice Cream of Extinction, this zone offers guests the chance to learn about movie-making effects, to fly with C-3PO, and to sing along with Anna and Elsa.

FOR THE FIRST TIME IN FOREVER: A FROZEN SING-ALONG CELEBRATION

FP+ Have you ever heard of a song called "Let It Go"? Yes, we thought so. But have you ever had the privilege of singing it with Queen Elsa herself? Now's your chance! In fact, most of the *Frozen* gang is on hand for a spirited audience-participation sing-along.

Presented in the Hyperion Theater, the 30-minute show features a retelling of the *Frozen* story, courtesy of a duo of Arendelle storytellers. It includes clips from the beloved film (presented on a ginormous screen) and live appearances by Anna, Kristoff, and (eventually) Elsa. Guests of all ages are encouraged to sing along with a few *Frozen* ditties. Don't know all the words? Just follow the bouncing snowflake.

This celebration is very popular with *Frozen* fans of all ages—book a Fastpass+ selection if you can. You won't regret it. Oh and don't wear your finest attire—you *will* get snowed on!

INDIANA JONES™ EPIC STUNT SPECTACULAR

FP+ Earthquakes, fiery explosions, and other dramatic events give guests insight into the science of movie stunts and effects at this 2,000-seat amphitheater. Stunt people re-create scenes from Indiana Jones films and demonstrate the skills required to keep audiences on the edge of their seats. But the 30-minute show isn't all flying leaps. Guests also see how the elaborate stunts are pulled off—safely—while the crew and an assistant director explain what goes on both in front of and behind the camera.

In one segment, a dramatic scene from *Raiders of the Lost Ark* is staged. A 12-foot-tall rolling boulder chases a Harrison Ford look-alike out of the temple. The flames are so intense that the audience can feel the heat. The crew then dismantles the set, revealing the remarkable lightness of movie props, as assistants roll the ball uphill for the next show.

In a scene at a busy "Cairo" street market, "extras" chosen from the audience participate in a battle scene. The explosive action continues and leads to a desert finale in which the hero and his sweetheart make a death-defying escape.

There are moments during this show when audience members might wonder if something has actually gone wrong. But by revealing tricks of the trade, the directors and stars show that what appears to be dangerous is actually a safe, controlled bit of movie magic.

Indiana Jones Epic Stunt Spectacular may not operate in all of 2020. For updates and additional info, visit *www.disneyworld.com*, or use the My Disney Experience mobile app or website.

STAR TOURS— THE ADVENTURES CONTINUE

BIRNBAUM'S ★BEST★ FP+ Inspired by George Lucas's blockbuster series of Star Wars films, this beloved attraction—which originally opened in 1989—is better than ever. A new Star Tours experience touched down in 2011, complete with a new story line. The 3-D experience offers guests the opportunity to ride on (modified) StarSpeeders, the exact same type of flight simulator used by military and commercial airlines to train pilots.

A galaxy of trouble awaits Jedi wannabes, but fear not—the Force will be with you. The best part? There are nearly 70 different adventures, so multiple visits yield multiple surprises—some of which involve scenes from *Star Wars: The Force Awakens* and *Star Wars: The Last Jedi*, and more.

This is a turbulent trip—seat belts are a definite requirement. Passengers must be free of back problems, heart conditions, motion sickness, and other physical limitations to ride. Guests under 40 inches tall and kids younger than 3 may not ride. Pregnant women must skip this one. To all who ride: Fasten your seat belt and may the Force be with you.

HOT TIP!

Outside of the Indiana Jones show, there's a sign that says do not pull the rope. Ignore it and pull that rope! You'll be glad you did.

JEDI TRAINING—
TRIALS OF THE TEMPLE

Jedi Padawans can learn to harness the Force and properly wield a lightsaber right here in Disney's Hollywood Studios. The 20-minute training program is offered several times each day. To participate, all potential participants (ages 4 to 12) should sign up at the Indiana Jones Adventurers Outpost (between Indiana Jones Epic Stunt Spectacular and the 50's Prime Time Cafe) as early as possible (during regular park hours). Kids who make the cut (strictly determined on a first-come,

first-served basis) receive a receipt complete with an exact time to return.

Arrive about 30 minutes before showtime to receive a loaner cloak. When the Jedi master arrives, kids receive lightsabers (strictly for the show) and start the training session. Instruct kids to pay close attention to the lesson—they'll need their new skill set to search for a hidden temple and face their fears, not to mention simulate a lightsaber battle against Darth Vader and other dark side representatives. Check a Times Guide for the schedule.

Hollywood Boulevard

One of the park's (and Hollywood's) main drags, this boulevard is dotted with Art Deco–style shops bursting with Disney treasures. The thoroughfare is bookended by the park entrance and an elaborate replica of Grauman's Chinese Theatre—home to the rollicking new attraction, Mickey and Minnie's Runaway Railway.

WONDERFUL WORLD
OF ANIMATION

A celebration of Disney's legendary storytelling history, this nightly show is a stirring tribute to 90 years of Disney and Pixar animation.

The festivities are appropriately bookended by the mouse who started it all, Mickey himself. In between on-screen appearances by the Big Cheese, guests are taken on a colorful journey through a myriad of memorable moments—and themes such as magic, family, adventure, romance, and friendship—from *Sleeping Beauty, Aladdin, Frozen, Cinderella, The Lion King, The Incredibles, Beauty and the Beast, Wreck-It Ralph, Coco, Toy Story 4*, and more.

The state-of-the-art projection display fittingly uses the facade of the park's Chinese Theatre as its silver screen. (The structure is a full-scale replica of Grauman's Chinese Theatre, a landmark Hollywood movie palace.)

The 12-minute spectacle is presented rain or shine and is best viewed from Hollywood Boulevard, close to and facing the Chinese Theatre. With nods to the vast library from Disney and Pixar Animation Studios' long legacy, Wonderful World of Animation is an apt way to wrap up a day at Disney's Hollywood Studios.

Mickey & Minnie's
Runaway Railway

Enter the wild and wacky cartoon realm via Mickey and Minnie's Runaway Railway—a fanciful, family-friendly attraction that's chugging into Disney's Hollywood Studios. Housed inside the replica of Grauman's Chinese Theatre, the "2.5-D" (no glasses required) adventure begins with the premiere of a new cartoon that guests watch in the pre-show area. In it, Mickey and Minnie are preparing for a picnic. When a train driven by Goofy pulls up beside them, it's all aboard for everyone! Thanks to a bit of movie magic, guests are invited to step into the action and enter the zany, unpredictable world of a Mickey Mouse Cartoon Short. The train zigs and zags through nine scenes in all. The track follows a similar pattern to this attraction's predecessor: The Great Movie Ride (which faded to black in 2017).

Mickey & Minnie's Runaway Railway is suitable for guests of all ages. We recommend getting a Fastpass if it is offered. At press time, this attraction was on track to open by summer 2020 (possibly sooner). For updates about the opening date, use the My Disney Experience app or website, or visit *www.disneyworld.com*.

Star Wars: Galaxy's Edge

There's a wondrous new adventure zone in the heart of Disney's Hollywood Studios—Star Wars: Galaxy's Edge! The brand-new land is set on the planet Batuu, a remote outpost on the far reaches of the galaxy. As the story goes, Batuu was once a busy crossroads along the old sub-light-speed trade routes. Now, thanks to the rise of hyperspace travel, Batuu has pretty much fallen off the radar. It's far from deserted, however. In fact, the largest settlement on the planet, Black Spire Outpost, has become quite the haven for folks who prefer to fly under the radar: smugglers, rogue traders, and space-traveling adventurers. It's also an excellent destination for anyone trying to avoid the ruthless First Order.

In addition to exotic shops and otherworldly snack spots, there are two bona fide E-Ticket attractions here—*Millennium Falcon:* Smugglers Run and Star Wars: Rise of the Resistance. Each invites guests to live out their own Star Wars adventures.

MILLENNIUM FALCON: SMUGGLERS RUN

BIRNBAUM'S ★BEST FP+ Are you eager to jump into hyperspace on the "fastest hunk of junk in the galaxy"? Here's your chance to take the controls of Han Solo's beloved bucket of bolts, the one and only *Millennium Falcon!*

It seems Hondo (from the animated shows *Star Wars: The Clone Wars* and *Star Wars Rebels*) is running a "legitimate business" out of a spaceport and he needs extra flight crews to make some runs for him—provided they don't ask too many questions. That's where you come in.

Before entering the cockpit of the legendary starship, you and five fellow crew members are assigned a role. There are three different roles (pilot, gunner, and

engineer) and one common goal: complete the mission without banging up the ship. At the end of the thrilling (and bumpy) flight, your crew will receive a point total—and a few choice words from Hondo.

Guests must be at least 38 inches tall to experience this attraction and be free of motion sickness and other health issues. Expectant mothers should skip the jarring *Millennium Falcon:* Smugglers Run.

HOT TIP!

When Star Wars: Galaxy's Edge opened in 2019, Fastpass was not offered for its attractions. However, Fastpass may be added at any time. Use the My Disney Experience app or website or check *disneyworld.com* for updates.

STAR WARS: RISE OF THE RESISTANCE

BIRNBAUM'S ★BEST What happens when Star Wars heroes and villains end up on the same planet? A *massive* battle breaks out!

In one of the most ambitious adventures ever produced by Disney Imagineering, this immersive attraction places you in the middle of an epic battle between the First Order and the Resistance—including a face-off with the infamous Kylo Ren.

The journey takes guests aboard a full-size transport shuttle and a Star Destroyer. It's a thrilling and harrowing adventure—and not for the faint of heart. To ride, guests should be free of health issues (including pregnancy and motion sickness), and at least 40 inches tall. For additional information, visit *disneyworld.com*.

Shopping at Disney's Hollywood Studios

PHOTO BY JILL SAFRO

HOLLYWOOD BOULEVARD

CELEBRITY 5 & 10: Modeled after a 1940s Woolworth's, this shop carries housewares such as pillows, blankets, towels, teapots, pitchers, aprons, mugs, magnets, glassware, and Mickey ice-cube trays.

COVER STORY: A small area located just through The Darkroom, this is the place to pick up Disney souvenirs such as hats, pins, and autograph books.

CROSSROADS OF THE WORLD: In the middle of the entrance plaza, Mickey Mouse keeps watch from atop this Hollywood Boulevard landmark. The kiosk deals mostly in pins, but has souvenirs, sunscreen, bug spray, hand sanitizer, hats, batteries, and disposable cameras, plus park guidemaps and Times Guides. This is also the place to stop if you'd like to rent a locker using a gift card or MagicBand.

THE DARKROOM: The Art Deco facade of this shop sports a giant camera, so it's easy to spot. One would expect it to specialize in camera stuff, but it's focused on MagicBands, collector pins, and phone accessories.

KEYSTONE CLOTHIERS: Disney-themed women's and men's fashions and accessories are Keystone Clothiers' specialties of the house.

MICKEY'S OF HOLLYWOOD: The place to find character shirts, hats, plush toys, watches, magnets, socks, bags, books, snack items, slippers, beach towels, sunglasses, plus items emblazoned with the Disney's Hollywood Studios logo.

MOVIELAND MEMORABILIA: This kiosk, located just to the left of the Studios' main entrance, stocks shoes, bags, stuffed toys, hats, sunglasses, key chains, and other souvenirs. Movieland Memorabilia is accessible from both inside and outside the park entrance.

OSCAR'S SUPER SERVICE: In addition to renting strollers and wheelchairs, Oscar stocks diapers, strollers (to buy), snacks, sundries, soft drinks, bags, hats, and other souvenir items.

SUNSET BOULEVARD

BEVERLY SUNSET: This cheery locale is Toy Story Central. Pop in to peruse items such as plush toys, action figures, shirts, headbands (with aliens or Slinky Dog), pins, playing cards, and cowboy hats. Yee-ha!

LEGENDS OF HOLLYWOOD: Modeled after the Academy Theater, which was built in Inglewood, California, in 1939, this store offers items featuring Disney characters and films—with a recent emphasis on the gang from Star Wars.

MOUSE ABOUT TOWN: An excellent source for clothing featuring Mickey Mouse. Expect hats, ties, shirts, jackets, pajamas, socks, accessories, and more. There's a line of clothing with a golf theme, and another featuring ESPN.

ONCE UPON A TIME: This little shop's exterior replicates the Carthay Circle Theatre in Hollywood, where *Snow White and the Seven Dwarfs* premiered in 1937. The cheery store specializes in children's apparel, plush toys, and souvenirs with Disney touches.

REEL VOGUE: Spin your big-screen dreams from reel to real in this elegant emporium of Tinseltown treasures: toys, gifts, games, snacks.

ROCK AROUND THE SHOP: Conquer Rock 'n' Roller Coaster and earn the right to shop here. (You can also enter via the exit, should you opt out of the ride.) Look for music-related items, plus shirts, hats, and other rockin' memorabilia.

SUNSET CLUB COUTURE: A sophisticated selection of fashion accessories (watches, hats, earrings, bracelets, purses, etc.), plus family apparel with a Mickey or Minnie theme is sold here.

SUNSET RANCH PINS AND SOUVENIRS: This shop carries Disney collector pins, plus plush character toys, souvenirs, memory cards, and assorted sundries.

TOWER GIFTS: Inside the Hollywood Tower Hotel, near the Tower of Terror exit, this spot specializes in Hollywood Tower Hotel merchandise—shirts, towels, robes, Front Desk bells, glasses, bellhop hats, handbags, and Tower of Terror Jenga. They stock collector pins, too. The shop is a good place to wait for the rest of your party should you decide to skip the trip to *The Twilight Zone*™ via the Tower of Terror.

BEYOND THE BOULEVARDS

LAUNCH BAY CARGO: Located inside Star Wars Launch Bay, Cargo offers Star Wars–themed collectibles for fans of all ages. It offers a variety of autographed memorabilia, replica costumes and props, plus books and toys, and more. Guests may customize mobile phone cases, too.

THE DISNEY STUDIO STORE: Expect to find T-shirts, hats, and accessories inspired by Disney films at this Animation Courtyard shop.

IN CHARACTER: In front of the Voyage of The Little Mermaid attraction, this costume shop has everything a child needs to dress like a Disney princess—plus dolls and plush toys.

INDIANA JONES ADVENTURE OUTPOST: Next to the Indiana Jones Epic Stunt Spectacular, you will discover adventure clothing, as well as memorabilia emblazoned with the Indy insignia.

IT'S A WONDERFUL SHOP: Spot the snowman out front and you've found this perpetual Yuletide celebration. Tree ornaments, stockings, and nutcrackers line the shelves all year long. Ho ho ho!

Where to Eat in Disney's Hollywood Studios

A complete listing of eateries at the Studios park—full-service restaurants, fast-food eateries, and snack shops—can be found in the *Good Meals, Great Times* chapter. See the Disney's Hollywood Studios section, beginning on page 270.

STAGE 1 COMPANY STORE: Situated near the exit of Muppet*Vision 3-D, guests can find toys, shirts, and other merchandise with the likenesses of Kermit the Frog, Miss Piggy, Fozzie Bear, and other Muppet characters, as well as items featuring Mickey and his pals.

TATOOINE TRADERS: A shop near the Star Tours exit, Tatooine Traders has souvenirs themed to Star Wars, as well as the Star Tours attraction. This is also the place to "build your own lightsaber." Wanna brag about being selected as the Star Tours Rebel Spy? Pick up a T-shirt here!

STAR WARS: GALAXY'S EDGE

BINA'S CREATURE STALL: Stop here to adopt an otherworldly pet. Lifelike creatures from which to choose include tentacle-beast rathtars, cooing baby tauntauns, tongue-lashing worrt frogs, and growling pufferpigs.

BLACK SPIRE OUTFITTERS: Guests who wish to blend in on Batuu can suit up at this boutique. Costumes representing the light and dark side of the Force are available for guests of all ages.

DON-ONDAR'S DEN OF ANTIQUITIES: The mysterious Don-Ondar has stuffed this shop with everything from jewelry and ancient tools to rare kyber crystals, statues, and high-end lightsabers.

SAVI'S LIGHTSABERS: The First Order would not allow the manufacture of lightsabers—so Savi took that task underground. Head here to build your own, high-end lightsaber. Colors include Sith red, Jedi blue and green, and Mace Windu purple. Choose wisely.

MUBO'S DROID DEPOT: If you've ever dreamed of owning your own astromech droid, dream no more: Mubo has mini droids waiting for you to customize. There are two basic models: an R (like R2-D2 or R5-D4) or a BB unit (the ball-droid style similar to BB-8 and the evil BB-9E). Once you choose your droid pieces (as they roll by on a nifty conveyor belt), you can piece them together in the assembly area. Then head to the chip station to select a personality circuit. Last but not least, bring your droid to life at the activation center. Extra customization is available (for an additional fee).

TOYDARIAN WARES: An enterprising Toydarian (a species introduced in *Star Wars: The Phantom Menace*) has opened a street market in Star Wars: Galaxy's Edge. Stop here to peruse a preponderance of Toydarian wares, including handcrafted-style toys made by local artisans.

Entertainment at the Studios

In these parts, it's almost always showtime. The following list is a good indication of the Studios' stage presence. Check a park Times Guide for schedules.

CITIZENS OF HOLLYWOOD: This talented troupe of enthusiastic performers infuses Hollywood Boulevard with old-time, Tinseltown ambiance. Would-be starlets searching for their big break, a mobile radio station, fans seeking guests' autographs, and gossip columnists chasing leads entertain daily.

PHOTO BY JILL SAFRO

THE GREEN ARMY DRUM CORPS: Andy's army marches through the backyard several times a day, playing dramatic drum sequences as they do so.

JEDI TRAINING: TRIALS OF THE TEMPLE: Star Wars fans and Jedi-wannabes can learn the ways of the Force right here in Walt Disney World. A Jedi Master is on hand to teach young Padawans how to harness the power of the Force and wield a lightsaber (see page 187).

WONDERFUL WORLD OF ANIMATION: An action-packed projection show takes guests on a journey through 90 years of Disney and Pixar animation. The show uses the Chinese Theatre facade as its screen—line up early to get a good view. Wonderful World of Animation is presented nightly. Details are subject to change.

BIRNBAUM'S ★BEST★ STAR WARS: A GALACTIC SPECTACULAR: An aptly named extravaganza, this fireworks show is indeed spectacular. The Star Wars saga plays out in vibrant pyrotechnic bursts, colorful projections, and synchronized sound. It is presented during select times of year—be sure to catch it if you can. The best vantage point is from Hollywood Boulevard, facing The Chinese Theatre (home of the new Mickey & Minnie's Runaway Railway attraction)—but the show can be enjoyed from practically anywhere in the park: just look up. Details are subject to change.

STAR WARS: A GALAXY FAR, FAR AWAY: A live stage show presented in front of the Chinese Theatre, this intergalactic celebration features iconic moments from the Star Wars saga. Vignettes shine the spotlight on favorites such as Chewbacca, Rey, BB-8, Darth Vader, and others. There's not much to it, but audiences don't seem to mind. It seems Star Wars really is a *force* to be reckoned with! Check a park Times Guide for the performance schedule.

Where to Find the Characters at Disney's Hollywood Studios

You'll find Disney Junior characters—such as Vampirina, Doc McStuffins, and Fancy Nancy—in Animation Courtyard. Jessie, Woody, Buzz Lightyear, and other familiar playthings may be found in Toy Story Land. Mickey Mouse mingles with park-goers in a spot dubbed "Mickey and Minnie starring in Red Carpet Dreams." Of course, Minnie appears at that location, too. Goofy, Chip, and Dale greet guests on Grand Avenue. Donald Duck and Daisy Duck visit Sid Cahuenga's front porch. Olaf may be found at the Celebrity Spotlight meet and greet location. Disney characters interact with diners at the Hollywood & Vine restaurant, too. (Disney Junior characters are on hand for breakfast; Minnie, Mickey, Goofy, Donald, and Daisy host lunch and dinner.) Star Wars friends (and foes) hang out at Star Wars Launch Bay. And zoom over to Lightning McQueen's Racing Academy to meet Cruz Ramirez (from *Cars 3*).

Hot Tips

- Fantasmic! is presented on most nights. Check a Times Guide to see when it will be offered during your visit. Know that the show may be canceled due to inclement weather.

- Unless you actually enjoy waiting in line, get Fastpass+ assignments whenever you can.

- Resist the urge to eat just before riding Tower of Terror, Rock 'n' Roller Coaster, *Millenium Falcon: Smugglers Run, Star Wars: Rise of the Resistance, Slinky Dog Dash,* or *Toy Story Mania!*

- Some attractions keep shorter hours than the park itself. Check a Times Guide when you arrive. It lists current hours and schedules.

- Wanna meet a snowman? Disney's Hollywood Studios is the only Walt Disney World park in which Olaf meets and greets guests. Visit with him at Celebrity Spotlight.

- For a table-service meal, make an advance reservation for these eateries: 50's Prime Time Cafe, Mama Melrose's Ristorante Italiano, Hollywood Brown Derby, Sci-Fi Dine-In Theater, or Hollywood & Vine. For details, refer to the *Good Meals, Great Times* chapter of this book.

- Some shops on Hollywood Boulevard are open about 30 minutes past park closing time.

- Walt Disney Presents is an exhibit dedicated to the man who started it all. If it's open during your visit, be sure to see it.

- Your little one may love The Muppets, but if she or he won't wear the glasses necessary to enjoy Muppet*Vision 3-D, skip the attraction.

- There is a FriendShip water taxi link between Disney's Hollywood Studios and Epcot. The boat docks to the left as you exit the Studios. You may also reach Epcot via the new Disney Skyliner gondola system. Ambitious athletes may choose to walk. (It'll take you about 20 to 30 minutes to make the trip on foot, depending on your pace.) All other parks may be reached by bus.

- Every so often, the wait time for Twilight Zone Tower of Terror is listed as 13 minutes. If that should happen while you're in the park, make a beeline for the ride—"13 minutes" is code for virtually no wait.

- Go to Rock 'n' Roller Coaster, Tower of Terror, Toy Story Land, and Star Wars: Galaxy's Edge attractions very early in the day, before crowds build up. And book Fastpass+ assignments as far in advance as possible. You won't regret it.

- Use a park Times Guide, check the My Disney Experience mobile app or website, or visit *www.disneyworld.com* for showtimes, wait times, and park updates.

- Many attractions and shows stop admitting guests prior to the park's closing time (and some don't open until a few hours after the park does). Check a Times Guide for schedules. Attractions that you may enter up until the last minute include *The Twilight Zone™* Tower of Terror, Rock 'n' Roller Coaster Starring Aerosmith, Muppet*Vision 3-D, and Star Tours—The Adventures Continue.

- Fantasmic! is perpetually popular. Even if you have a Fastpass, get there at least 20 minutes before showtime—or risk arriving to a full house.

- If you choose to skip Fantasmic!, plan to exit the park before the show ends. This way, you'll avoid the inevitable bottleneck at the exit. If you are watching the show, consider making your exit before the big finale.

- If you lose your nerve just prior to boarding Tower of Terror or Rock 'n' Roller Coaster, fear not: both attractions have a last-minute egress opportunity (aka the "chicken exit"). Ironically, the chicken exit at Tower of Terror comes in the form of an elevator. Rest assured that the escape elevator is fully functional.

- Rock 'n' Roller Coaster has three different ways to enter the attraction: Fastpass+, Standby (the traditional way to stand in line), and Single Rider. Groups of more than one are welcome to jump on the single rider line at any time. Doing so may result in significantly less wait time than standby, but members of the party will be split up. Note that the Rock 'n' Roller Coaster Single Rider line is not always offered.

HIDDEN MICKEYS

These are some of the most popular "Hidden Mickeys" at Disney's Hollywood Studios. How many Mickeys can you find? Check the circle when you spot each one.

Front Entrance Gates: This is an easy one. Simply look for Mr. Mouse in the grillwork of the gates at the park entrance. ○

Rock 'n' Roller Coaster: In the pre-show room, look on the floor on the right side of the room just in front of the guitar stand to see some wire coiled into a Hidden Mickey. ○

Star Tours—the Adventures Continue: Keep an eye on the folks walking past the "window" in the second room you enter while waiting for the attraction. One of the droids sports mouse ears. ○

There's a Hidden Mickey in the shop at the ride's exit, too—on the front panel of a counter. ○

Twilight Zone™ Tower of Terror: Take a peek at the balcony in the lobby, and you may spot a row of Mickeys. ○

Then, as you watch the pre-show, pay very close attention to the "disappearing guests." The little girl is clutching a plush Mickey Mouse. ○

Toy Story Mania!: Keep your eyes peeled for a sign that says "Circus Fun!"—the dot in the exclamation point is a pink Hidden Mickey. (The sign is on a wall as the ride vehicle rotates into position for the last game of the ride.) ○

The Hollywood Brown Derby Restaurant: Look for two Hidden Mickeys in the cloud mural outside the restaurant. One is on the left side, above the red Stage 5 sign. ○

The other H.M. can be found on the far upper right-hand side. ○

Cover Story: There is a sign in the window of this Hollywood Boulevard shop that says "Melrose." Find it, then look below it for a pattern that creates many Hidden Mickeys in the store's structure. ○

Alien Swirling Saucers: Once you've located the Space Ranger mural on the wall, you should have no trouble spotting three buttons that form a multi-colored Hidden Mickey. ○

Sci-Fi Dine-In Theater: As you enter the restaurant's indoor waiting area, check out the bulletin board inside a glass case—it's home to two Hidden Mickeys! One is on a recycling sticker and the other is on a brochure for Disney University. ○

Tune-In Lounge: There are several tables in the lounge area of 50's Prime Time Cafe. Take a look at the tabletops to see some Hidden Mickeys! ○

The Trolley Car Cafe: Look for a number on the building's facade (near the top, facing Sunset Boulevard). It's not a traditional Hidden Mickey, but it is a significant date for the Mouse. ○

Muppet*Vision 3-D: Mickey first appears in a test pattern in the lobby. ○

Next you'll notice him in balloon form during the show's finale. ○

As you exit, you will see a poster detailing Five Reasons to Return Your 3-D Glasses. Take a close look at the artwork beside number 2. It sports a Hidden Mickey! ○

Sid Cahuenga's One-of-a-Kind Antiques and Curios Shop: On the front porch of this PhotoPass viewing location you just may spot a very special Dalmatian statue—it has a Hidden Mickey spot on its left hind leg. ○

Slinky Dog Dash: Mickey Mouse has a tendency to have his head in the clouds. Need proof? Check out the cloud formations on Andy's hand-drawn plans for Slinky Dog Dash! ○

The Voyage of The Little Mermaid: While waiting in the pre-show area, locate a framed world map on the wall. Then locate the Hidden Mickey. ○

Specifics may change during 2020.

WHERE IN THE WORLD?

All of the photos on this page were taken at Disney's Hollywood Studios. Do you know where? We challenge you to find all the spots where these images were shot and snap a (non-flash) photo for yourself as you discover each one. Happy hunting! (For locations, see page 362.)

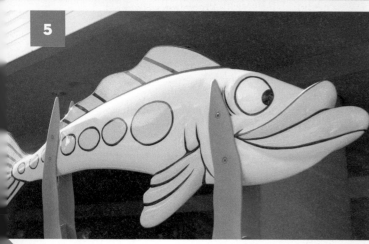

PHOTOS #1, #5, AND #6 BY JILL SAF

DISNEY'S ANIMAL KINGDOM

"The wonders of nature are endless." —Walt Disney

197 Getting Oriented

198 Park Primer

199 Attractions

211 Shopping

212 Entertainment

212 Hot Tips

With a mix of lush landscapes, thrilling attractions, and close encounters with exotic animals, this is clearly a theme park raised to a different level of excitement. Here, guests do more than just watch the action—they live it. They become paleontologists, explorers, and students of nature. And if, by doing so, they leave with nothing more than a big smile, Disney will have accomplished one of its major goals. But many guests come away with a little bit more: a renewed sense of respect for our planet and for the life-forms we share it with (not to mention a few boffo souvenirs).

The shows and attractions at Disney's Animal Kingdom are meant to engage, entertain, and inspire. They immerse guests in a tropical landscape and introduce them to creatures from the past and present—as well as a few that exist only in our collective imagination. Animal Kingdom opened on Earth Day in 1998 and now offers more opportunities for adventure than ever before. To that end, a fan favorite known as Avatar Flight of Passage has been transporting guests to other-worldly heights since it opened in 2017.

The park, which is accredited by the Association of Zoos and Aquariums, is home to more than 2,000 animals representing 300 different species. Most of the creatures are of the animate variety, as opposed to the Audio-Animatronics kind. Despite that, you won't see many beasts behind bars here. Instead, you'll go on safari and see a menagerie of wild critters living in spacious habitats, with remarkably few separations visible to the naked eye.

The following pages will help you get the most out of your visit to Disney's Animal Kingdom. It is, after all, a jungle out there.

DISNEY'S ANIMAL KINGDOM

AFRICA

A Kilimanjaro Safaris

B Gorilla Falls
Exploration Trail

C Wildlife Express
to Rafiki's Planet Watch

D Rafiki's Planet Watch

E Festival of the Lion King

DISCOVERY ISLAND

F The Tree of Life

G Discovery Island Trail

H It's Tough to be a Bug!

ASIA

I UP! A Great Bird Adventure

J Maharajah Jungle Trek

K Kali River Rapids

L Expedition Everest

DINOLAND U.S.A.

M Dinosaur

N The Boneyard playground

O Finding Nemo—
The Musical

P Chester & Hester's
Dino-Rama!

**PANDORA—THE WORLD
OF AVATAR**

Q Avatar Flight of Passage

R Na'vi River Journey

Getting Oriented

Though Disney's Animal Kingdom encompasses about five times the area of its Magic Kingdom counterpart, one need not be in training for the Olympics to tackle it. Most of the land is reserved for non-homo-sapien critters. By all estimates, pedestrians rack up about the same amount of mileage in one day here as they do in a day at Epcot.

The park's layout is relatively simple: a series of sections, or "lands," connected to a central hub. In this case, the hub is Discovery Island, an island surrounded by a river and home to the Tree of Life, the park's icon. Discovery Island is connected by bridges and paths with all other lands: the Oasis, DinoLand U.S.A., Asia, Africa, and Pandora—The World of Avatar.

As you pass through D.A.K.'s entrance plaza, you approach the Oasis. Feel free to meander at a leisurely pace, absorbing the soothing ambience of a thick, elaborate jungle, or you can proceed more quickly and plan to revisit this relaxing region later on. Each of several pathways deposits you at the foot of a bridge leading to Discovery Island. As you emerge from the Oasis, you will see the awe-inspiring Tree of Life, a 14-story Disney-made tree, looming ahead. The massive tree, which stands near the middle of the island, is surrounded by the Discovery Island Trail.

To the southeast lies DinoLand U.S.A., home of prehistoric animals, a fossil dig, a high-spirited stage show called Finding Nemo—The Musical, and an attraction that's sure to induce a mammoth adrenaline surge: Dinosaur. Behind Discovery Island and to the northwest is Africa, where guests may go on an African safari, explore a nature trail, and hop aboard the Wildlife Express train to Rafiki's Planet Watch, the park's research and education center. To the southwest is the park's newest land: Pandora—The World of Avatar. Its major draws are the thrilling Flight of Passage and the tame Na'vi River Journey. Asia lies northeast of Discovery Island. Here, guests come face-to-face with an angry Yeti (aka the Abominable Snowman) on the Expedition Everest coaster-style ride, encounter real tigers on the exotic Maharajah Jungle Trek, and take a daring journey through the rainforest on a raft at the splashy Kali River Rapids attraction.

HOW TO GET THERE

If you're driving, take Exit 65 off I-4. Then follow signs to Disney's Animal Kingdom. Trams run between the parking lot and the main entrance.

By WDW Transportation: From all Walt Disney World resorts: buses. From Disney Springs: bus to any resort or the TTC, then transfer to an Animal Kingdom bus. From Magic Kingdom: bus to Disney Springs, then transfer to an Animal Kingdom bus or take a bus to Animal Kingdom from any Magic Kingdom area resort. From Epcot, Disney's Hollywood Studios, and the resorts on Hotel Plaza Boulevard: buses.

PARKING

All-day parking at Animal Kingdom starts at $25 for day visitors (premium parking costs $45–$50); it's free to guests staying in Walt Disney World–owned-and-operated resorts. Trams circulate lots regularly, providing transportation from the parking area to the park entrance. Be sure to note the section and aisle in which you park. The parking ticket allows for re-entry to the parking area throughout the day.

HOURS

Hours may vary, but the gates are generally open daily from about 9 A.M. until 9 or 10 P.M. During summer months and other periods, hours may change. It's best to arrive up to a half hour before the official opening time. For park schedules, use the My Disney Experience mobile app or website, visit *www.disneyworld.com*, or call 407-824-4321.

Admission Prices

ONE-DAY BASE TICKET*
(Restricted to use only in Disney's Animal Kingdom. Prices are for Date-Based tickets. Rates for Flexible Date tickets are higher. **Prices exclude tax and are likely to rise in 2020.**)

Adult	$109–$159
Child**	$104–$154

* 1-Day tickets are valid only on the selected date. Flexible Date tickets purchased in 2020 must be used by December 31, 2021. This is the cost of a 1-day/1-park-only ticket. Terms are subject to change. For updates, visit *https://disneyworld.disney.go.com/admission/tickets/*.

** 3 through 9 years of age; children under age 3 free (no ticket required)

Park Primer

BABY FACILITIES

At Disney's Animal Kingdom, changing tables and facilities for nursing mothers can be found at the Baby Care Center on Discovery Island, near Creature Comforts. It's also possible to buy certain baby-centric necessities, such as formula and diapers, at this facility.

CAMERA NEEDS

Basic supplies such as batteries and disposable cameras are sold at shops such as Garden Gate Gifts, Disney Outfitters, Duka La Filimu, Mombasa Marketplace, and Chester and Hester's Dinosaur Treasures. Memory cards are no longer sold at the park. Note that selfie sticks are not permitted in any Disney park.

DISABILITY INFORMATION

Nearly all Animal Kingdom attractions, shops, and restaurants are accessible to guests using wheelchairs. (Note that the park terrain is a bit bumpy.) Additional services are available for guests with visual or hearing disabilities. The *Guide for Guests with Disabilities*, available at the park entrance, provides an overview of the various services offered, including transportation, parking, and attraction access. (For more information, refer to the *Getting Ready to Go* chapter of this book.)

FIRST AID

Minor medical problems can be handled at the First Aid Center, located on Discovery Island on the northwest side of the Tree of Life, near Creature Comforts. **In case of emergency call 911 and alert a Cast Member.**

INFORMATION

Guest Relations, located just inside the park entrance, is equipped with (free) guidemaps, Times Guides, and a helpful staff. Guidemaps and Times Guides are also available in many shops.

LOCKERS

Lockers are located just inside the main entrance area, near Guest Relations. Cost is $12 for large lockers, $10 for small ones, for unlimited use all day (at Disney's Animal Kingdom only).

LOST & FOUND

Report lost items to Guest Relations, just inside the park entrance, or fill out a lost item report online at *www.chargerback.com/disneyworld*. After your visit to Animal Kingdom, go to the aforementioned website. If you find an item, give it to a Cast Member (aka park employee). We recommend affixing contact information to valuables. That'll make them easier to track.

LOST CHILDREN

Alert the nearest Disney employee to the matter and report lost children at the Baby Care Center, on Discovery Island (by Creature Comforts).

MONEY MATTERS

There is an ATM at the park entrance and another in DinoLand U.S.A. Currency exchange is done at Guest Relations. In addition to U.S. cash, credit cards (Visa, American Express, Diner's Club, Discover Card, JCB, and MasterCard), Disney gift cards, traveler's checks, and Disney resort IDs and MagicBands (backed up with a credit card) are accepted for admission and merchandise, and meals at most restaurants. Note that Disney Dollars, while no longer sold, are still accepted as cash at most WDW venues.

PACKAGE PICKUP

Shops can arrange for purchases to be sent to Garden Gate Gifts for later pickup or directly to a Walt Disney World resort (packages should be ready for pickup about three hours after purchase). The service is free.

SAME-DAY RE-ENTRY

Be sure to wear your MagicBand or retain your ticket if you plan to return later the same day.

SECURITY CHECK

Guests entering all Disney parks are subject to a thorough security check. All bags will be searched by security personnel before guests may enter the park. A metal detector screens guests. Weapons (including those of the toy variety) and selfie sticks are among the items that are prohibited. For details and a complete listing of Disney Park Rules, visit *www.disneyworld.com/ParkRules* or any WDW Guest Relations location.

STROLLERS & WHEELCHAIRS

Strollers, wheelchairs, and Electric Conveyance Vehicles (ECVs) may be rented at Garden Gate Gifts. The cost is about $15 for strollers and $12 for wheelchairs (double strollers cost $31 a day). Length of Stay rentals yield a $2-per-day discount. It's about $50 for ECVs, plus a $20 refundable deposit. Quantities are limited (and they tend to run out early in the day). Keep your receipt; it may be used the same day to get a replacement here or at the other WDW theme parks.

The Oasis

Traditionally, one has to travel across a long, sunbaked stretch of desert in order to experience the soothing atmosphere of a tropical oasis. With that in mind, think of the Animal Kingdom parking lot as a concrete version of the Sahara. Once you've trekked across it, your journey takes you through the park's front gate and entrance plaza. What's that up ahead? Could it be a towering African tree? Here in Central Florida? It must be a mirage.

But, no. Within seconds you arrive at the Oasis, a thriving tropical garden filled with waterfalls, running streams, and lush vegetation. The transition is by no means a subtle one. Guests are immediately enveloped in a world of nature. The peaceful setting is most idyllic.

Though not a full-fledged "land" per se, this small jungle simply oozes atmosphere. It is thick and elaborate, and comes complete with critters. (Some are more difficult to spot than others. When searching for the naturally camouflaged creatures, remember to look up occasionally.) As park visitors walk along the pathways, they may catch glimpses of different kinds of animals, from babirusas and wallabies to giant anteaters and birds. As in the rest of Disney's Animal Kingdom, there is the illusion that guests are walking among the wildlife.

The Oasis is at once an exciting and calming experience. It sets the stage for what's to come. Park guests have several options once they've entered the Oasis. They can continue on a northerly path, making tracks toward the Tree of Life and across a bridge to Discovery Island. They can proceed at a more snail-friendly pace, keeping a tally of the various life-forms that they spot. Or they can simply take time to stop and smell the flowers.

Timing Tip: Making a trip through the Oasis is the only way to get in (and out of) Disney's Animal Kingdom. Some paths can become congested during the hours closest to opening and closing times. To beat the crowds, use the path to the left when you enter the park early in the day.

> "I have learned from the animal world. And what everyone will learn who studies it is a renewed sense of kinship with the Earth and all of its inhabitants."
>
> — **Walt Disney**

Discovery Island

Once you've passed through the Oasis, you will come to a bridge spanning a peaceful river. The bridge leads to Discovery Island, an area at the center of Disney's Animal Kingdom and the hub from which all other realms of the park may be reached.

Discovery Island is defined by the brilliant colors, tropical surroundings, and equatorial architecture of Africa and the South Pacific. The facades of the buildings are all carved and painted based on the art of nations from around the world. Don't fail to notice all the bright, whimsical folk-art images representing various members of the animal kingdom.

This island is the shopping and dining center of Animal Kingdom. Several of the park's restaurants can be found here, including Tiffins, Pizzafari, and Flame Tree Barbecue. (Reservations are recommended for Tiffins, which is a WDW Dining Plan Signature eatery.)

By far the most striking element standing on Discovery Island is the Tree of Life. It is on the map, but chances are you'll have no trouble finding it. Rising from the middle of the island and as tall as a 14-story building, the Tree of Life is hard to miss.

THE TREE OF LIFE

The Tree of Life is the dramatic 145-foot icon of Disney's Animal Kingdom. The imposing tree, with its swaying limbs and gnarled trunk, looks an awful lot like the real thing—from a distance. Up close, it's apparent that this is a most unusual bit of greenery. Covered with more than 325 animal images, it is a swirling tapestry of carved figures, painstakingly assembled by a team of artisans. The tree, though inorganic, stands as a symbol of the connected nature of life on Earth. We think Joyce Kilmer would have approved.

DISCOVERY ISLAND TRAIL: The walkway that wraps around the Tree of Life allows guests to get a close-up view of the trunk and even play a game of "spot the animals." (The spiraling animal images go all the way to the top of the tree. You'll need binoculars if you hope to see them all.) Scattered about the tree's massive base is a variety of animal habitats. Animals can be seen in a very open, somewhat traditional park-like setting, with lush grass, trees, and other vegetation. Others to

---

HOT TIP!

Take a minute to study a guidemap as you enter Animal Kingdom. It will give you a sense of the layout. The park Times Guide provides information about showtimes for Festival of the Lion King, Finding Nemo—The Musical, and other attractions.

HOT TIP!

Would you like to meet Mickey Mouse and Minnie Mouse before they head out on their next adventure? Make your way to the Adventurers Outpost on Discovery Island. The globe-trotting mice like to greet guests at their exploration headquarters.

which you may be introduced for the very first time as you meander through the exhibits include ring-tailed lemurs (not quite monkeys' uncles, more like cousins).

BIRNBAUM'S
★BEST★ **WINGED ENCOUNTERS— THE KINGDOM TAKES FLIGHT:** This dramatic flight features a flock of free-flying macaws. Because of their claws? No, because they're macaws! (Sorry, we couldn't resist a quote from the Enchanted Tiki Room.) Six types of this beautiful bird, some with wingspans of up to 60 inches, are included. Expect them to swoop and soar above your

Wilderness Explorers

In the movie *Up*, Russell is a very dedicated—and decorated—Wilderness Explorer. He is on a constant quest to add to his merit badge collection. Now Animal Kingdom guests can become Wilderness Explorers, too. Start by heading to the W.E. Headquarters at the Oasis bridge. After taking the official pledge, guests receive field guides describing a variety of challenges. Successfully complete a challenge and earn a badge! There are about 30 different badges to collect in all. There is no extra charge to be a Wilderness Explorer, and the badges are free. While targeted to the 7- to 10-year-old set, the challenges are fun for the whole family.

head and Discovery Island. It is quite thrilling. Check a park Times Guide for showtimes. If you think you might be spooked by a close encounter with our fine-feathered friends, stand toward the back of the crowd.

THE TREE OF LIFE AWAKENINGS: The park icon "awakens" each night with a lively projection and music show that features stirring visuals, animal spirits, and enchanted fireflies that combine to reveal stories of wonder and showcase the magic of nature.

Timing Tip: The Tree of Life Awakenings experiences begin after dark and occur approximately every ten minutes until the park closes.

BIRNBAUM'S
★BEST★ **IT'S TOUGH TO BE A BUG!:** FP+ Inside the trunk of the Tree of Life is a 430-seat auditorium featuring an eight-minute, animated 3-D film augmented by some surprising "4-D" effects. The stars of the show are the world's most abundant inhabitants—insects. They creep, crawl, and demonstrate why, someday, they just might inherit the Earth. It's a bug's-eye view of the trials and tribulations of their multi-legged world.

As guests enter The Tree of Life Repertory Theater, the orchestra can be heard warming up amid the sounds of chirping crickets. When Flik, the amiable emcee (from *A Bug's Life*), appears, he dubs audience members honorary bugs and instructs them to don their bug eyes (3-D glasses). Then the mild-mannered ant introduces some of his less-mild-mannered cronies, including a Chilean tarantula, dung beetles, and "the silent but deadly member of the bug world"—the stink bug. What follows is something of an infestation celebration.

Note: The combination of intense effects and frequent darkness tends to terrify tots and young kids. And anyone at all leery of spiders, roaches, and their ilk is advised to skip the performance, or risk being seriously bugged.

Africa

The largest section of Disney's Animal Kingdom, Africa, is bigger than the whole Magic Kingdom park. This 110-acre, truer-than-life replica of an African savanna is packed with pachyderms, giraffes, hippos, and other wild beasts. All guests enter Africa through Harambe, a village based on a modern East African coastal town. It is the dining and shopping center of Animal Kingdom's version of Africa.

The instant you walk across the bridge to Harambe, you are transported to Africa. Everything here is authentic, from the architecture to the landscaping to the merchandise in the marketplace. The result was achieved after Disney Imagineers made countless trips to the continent. After seven years of observing, filming, and photographing the real thing, they re-created it here in North America. It even feels a bit warmer here than it does at the other theme parks!

The many animals that live here, however, are not re-creations. They are quite real, most varied, and extremely abundant. In fact, this chunk of land puts the animal in Animal Kingdom.

KILIMANJARO SAFARIS

BIRNBAUM'S ★BEST★ FP+ The Kilimanjaro Safaris have something for everyone: lovely landscapes, majestic, free-roaming animals, and a thrilling adventure. It is everything you may expect from an actual trip to the African continent, and (hopefully) more.

PHOTO BY JILL SAFRO

HOT TIP!

There's no need to stampede toward the Kilimanjaro Safaris ride first thing in the morning—the animals are out and active throughout the day. That said, if you do ride early, consider coming back later in the day. The beauty of this attraction is that you tend to see something new each time you ride.

The 18-minute safari begins with a brief introduction from a guide who does double duty as your driver. Once you climb aboard the ride vehicle, look at the plates above the seat in front of you. They will help you identify the animals you see. And have those cameras ready.

As the vehicle travels along dirt roads, you'll spot free-roaming wild animals: zebras, antelope, hippos, elephants, warthogs, rhinos, lions, and more. Some animals wander near your vehicle, and others cross its path. (Don't worry—only the harmless critters can approach. Others, such as lions and cheetahs, are unable to invade your safe, personal space.)

PHOTO BY JILL SAFRO

The majesty of the Serengeti may lull you into a state of serenity, but it's merely the calm before the storm. You will soon be jostled and jolted as the ride vehicle crosses pothole-filled terrain, (seemingly) rickety bridges, and flooded dirt roads.

Good news, safari fans—evening safaris have become a reality. While the Kilimanjaro Safaris attraction is a big draw at any time of day, it's nice to ride before *and* after the sun sets. Day or night, try to get a Fastpass+ assignment—the lines can be lengthy at this popular destination. It can be a bit challenging to spot distant animals in low light, but the overall experience is pretty cool—and some animals (e.g., lions) are more active in the evening hours.

If you're prone to motion sickness, neck or back issues, or have other physical limitations, sit this one out. The ride is a rather bumpy one.

FESTIVAL OF THE LION KING

BIRNBAUM'S ★BEST **FP+** In addition to rustling up grubs in their corner of Disney's Animal Kingdom, the talented cast of *The Lion King* performs a high-energy 30-minute stage show in the Harambe Theater.

Presented in the round, this lavish musical revue is as bright and boisterous as they come. The dramatic opening features a parade of performers in colorful costumes. What follows is an intriguing, energetic interpretation of the film, including songs, dances, and acrobatics. With the exception of Timon, who plays himself, lead characters are portrayed by humans draped in bold African costumes.

Songs include Scar's nasty version of "Be Prepared," as well as "The Circle of Life," and a rousing rendition of "The Lion Sleeps Tonight."

Timing Tip: Although this theater accommodates nearly 1,400 guests at a time, plan to arrive at least 30 minutes before a performance time.

GORILLA FALLS EXPLORATION TRAIL

This self-guided walking trail winds past communities of gorillas and other rare African animals. Access it at the exit of the Kilimanjaro Safaris attraction or by the entrance in Harambe.

> "How could this earth of ours, which is only a speck in the heavens, have so much variety of life, so many curious and exciting creatures?"
>
> —Walt Disney

Up Close with Rhinos

Park guests are invited to meet the planet's second-largest land animal—the white rhinoceros—in a 60-minute, guided adventure (fees apply).

During this unique, outdoor experience, guides introduce the park's white rhinos and offer insights into the species' behavior and biology. They also address the challenges that threaten these mighty-but-gentle giants in the wild—and what *you* can do to help.

Guests must be at least 4 years old to participate. Those under age 18 must be accompanied by a paying adult. The cost is about $40 per guest. Park admission is required, but not included. For details or to make a reservation, use the My Disney Experience app or website, visit *disneyworld.com*, or call 407-939-7529. You can learn about other behind-the-scenes tours from those sources, too—and from turning to page 235 of this book.

The first major stop on the scenic trail (previously known as Pangani, which translates to "place of enchantment" in Swahili) is the Research Station. Just outside are a free-flight aviary and an aquarium teeming with fish. Not far away is the hippo exhibit, which provides close-up views of hippopotamuses both in and out of water.

Farther along the trail there is a scenic overlook point, where you can get an unobstructed view of the African savanna. This is also known as the "Timon" exhibit, featuring a family of perky meerkats. Afterward, you may catch an up-close glimpse (through a glass wall) of a cavorting gorilla or two.

As you come to the end of the suspension bridge, you'll find yourself in a beautiful green valley. Congratulations! You've finally reached the gorilla area—an experience well worth the wait. (Note that you may have to wait a little bit longer for that first gorilla sighting. Our evolutionary cousins have been known to play hide-and-seek in the lush vegetation.)

RAFIKI'S PLANET WATCH

The Harambe Train Station can be found on the east side of the village of Harambe. That's where guests climb aboard the Wildlife Express and experience a rare behind-the-scenes look at a Disney theme park while en route to Rafiki's Planet Watch.

As part of the 5½-minute, narrated trip, you'll glide past the buildings where animals sleep. All guests disembark at the Rafiki's Planet Watch station and cover the remaining distance on foot. (It's about a 5-minute walk and you may encounter animal experts en route.)

Note that you'll have to re-board the Wildlife Express train to return to Harambe Village.

While Animal Kingdom's stories often carry a conservation theme, this part really brings the message home. This is the park's conservation headquarters and veterinary lab, as well as the research and education hub. Exhibits are geared to spark curiosity about wildlife and conservation efforts around the world. At press time, changes were changes planned for this area of the park. Here are a few highlights that have called this place home:

Habitat Habit!: An outdoor discovery trail that yields glimpses of cotton-top tamarins, and helpful hints on how to share the planet with all members of the animal kingdom.

Affection Section: An animal encounter area with critters (mostly goats) to see and touch. Be sure to stop at the hand-washing station before leaving this area.

Conservation Station: The center of Disney's effort to promote wildlife conservation awareness. Be sure to take note of the huge animal murals—they are beautiful and chock-full of Hidden Mickeys. You may also find:

Animal Encounters Stage: A rotating roster of critters take the stage in shows that highlight their natural environments.

Veterinary Treatment Room: Peer through the healing center's big window and witness hands-on care of the park's animals.

Let There Be . . . Night Light!

After the sun sets on the savannah, Animal Kingdom guests gather along the Discovery River for the park's nighttime spectacular known as Rivers of Light FP+. The illuminating musical experience celebrates the magic of animals and the natural world. It features a blend of glowing lanterns that float in the air and theatrical animal imagery.

The Discovery River lagoon is a central character itself—a tranquil canvas for the unveiling of a dramatic tale. In it, the area comes to life as thousands of flickering fireflies lead a procession across the water. Giant floating flowers move about as illuminated boats bob by. The cavalcade culminates as animal images soar up into the night sky—signifying the ancient belief that when animals passed from one world to another, they danced in the sky and became beautiful rivers of light. The glow of this peaceful show can be quite enchanting for many WDW guests. Due to the preponderance of animal residents nearby, this show does not include pyrotechnics. *Note that this show may not be presented in all of 2020.*

Timing Tip: The 15-minute show is presented on select nights—and it is rather popular. Get a Fastpass+ assignment or plan to arrive at least an hour before the show begins. Check a Times Guide or the My Disney Experience mobile app for the schedule during your visit. Afterward, as the masses exit the park, take some time to browse the shops that may keep their doors open a bit after hours.

Pandora—
The World of Avatar

According to the blockbuster film *AVATAR*, Earthlings have a distant, idyllic destination to look forward to in the 22nd century: Pandora, a magnificent moon orbiting the planet Polyphemus about 4.4 light-years from Earth. Pandora, with its lush, bioluminescent rainforest environment, is home to floating mountains and incredible life-forms, including trees that stand a thousand feet tall and a myriad of infinitely diverse creatures—such as native people known as the Na'vi. These blue humanoids travel via flying mountain banshees and have a sophisticated culture based on a deep connection to each other and all life on Pandora. That connection is rendered possible via the majestic and sacred Tree of Souls.

If Pandora sounds like a place you would like to visit, you're not alone—*AVATAR* was one of the biggest movie sensations of all time. The good news is humans don't have to wait until the 22nd century to visit the wondrous world of Pandora. Thanks to Disney Imagineering magic, it has come to Disney's Animal Kingdom. This land, aka the Valley of Mo'ara, opened in 2017. Note that one need not be familiar with (or a fan of) the film to appreciate a visit here.

AVATAR FLIGHT OF PASSAGE

BIRNBAUM'S
★BEST★ FP+ The crown jewel of Animal Kingdom's newest neighborhood, Flight of Passage invites adventurers to take an exuberant trip through Pandora on the back of a flying mountain banshee (aka ikran). The joyful 3-D journey takes place in a cutting-edge, simulator-like environment and offers much more than a thrill a minute. Guests are treated to a bird's-eye view of all the sights, sounds, and smells of the majestic moon that the Na'vi call home.

A high-flying "E-Ticket" attraction, Flight of Passage is a most realistic, immersive experience. It is not recommended for guests with motion sensitivity, heart conditions, fear of heights, claustrophobia, or any other such issues. This attraction is exceptionally popular—book a Fastpass+ assignment if you can. Guests must be at least 44 inches tall to experience this ride. Note that the 3-D glasses are one size fits all. If the restraints are too tight, alert a ride attendant ASAP.

FP+ = Fastpass+ attraction (see page 25)

HOT TIP!

The escapist land has many wonders to discover—some are best enjoyed by day, while others shine at night. If time allows, revisit the Valley of Mo'ara after the sun sets. You'll be glad you did.

NA'VI RIVER JOURNEY

FP+ A placid voyage into Pandora's bioluminescent forest, this trip is calm and family-friendly (though some wee ones may be spooked by the large and somewhat daunting Na'vi shaman). The journey begins as guests board canoes and venture down a mysterious, sacred river hidden within the rainforest. The grandeur of Pandora is revealed as canoes float past exotic glowing plants and an array of exotic creatures, including native humanoids known as Na'vi. The journey culminates in an encounter with a Na'vi shaman, who has a deep connection to the life force of Pandora and sends positive energy into the forest with her music.

The tranquil Na'vi River Journey is generally appreciated by guests of all ages (though timid tykes who are spooked by darkness may find parts of this expedition a tad unsettling). This indoor attraction provides a nice opportunity to visit the Na'vi world while resting your feet and enjoying a refreshing dose of air-conditioning. If the wait time isn't overwhelmingly long (though it usually is), by all means give it a whirl.

DID YOU KNOW?

The common spirit of Pandora—where all life-forms are constantly connected to each other, the environment, and their host planet—is based on the concept of Gaia, proposed by chemist James Lovelock in 1970 and described in Isaac Asimov's novel *Foundation's Edge* in 1982.

Asia

PHOTO BY JILL SAFRO

On the far side of a Himalayan-style bridge, beyond an ancient temple, lies the tranquil village of Anandapur (a Sanskrit word meaning "place of delight"). The buildings' design was inspired by structures in Thailand, Indonesia, and other Asian countries known for their rich architectural history.

A product of Disney Imagineering, the village epitomizes the complex, enduring relationship between the animals and ecosystems of the Asian continent. The tiny village borders an elaborate re-creation of a Southeast Asian rainforest. As such, Disney's Asia is an ideal location for trekking through the lush jungle, shooting the rapids on a raging river, and gazing upon the multi-hued inhabitants of this treasured terrain.

KALI RIVER RAPIDS

FP+ Before guests board rafts at Kali (pronounced KAH-lee) River Rapids, a wise voice admonishes that "the river is like life itself, full of mysterious twists and turns." What the voice doesn't say is that this particular river is also full of splashing water and a blazing inferno. This may be business as usual for some daring souls, but for most of us, these elements make for one dramatic, drenching adventure.

All guests begin the journey in the offices of Kali River Rapids Expeditions, a river rafting company. A slide show offers a look at the sometimes unscrupulous business of logging—how it has ravaged the rainforest and deprived many animals of habitats. But, thanks to ecotourism (among other things), there is hope. Peaceful voyages give people a new appreciation and sense of responsibility for this endangered land.

A 12-seater raft whisks "ecotourists" up a watery ramp and through an arching tunnel of bamboo. It proceeds onward, through a hazy mist and past remnants of an ancient shrine. As the raft careens along curves of the raging river, guests enjoy views of undisturbed rainforest.

The tranquility is shattered by a startling sight. A huge chunk of forest has been gutted by loggers. On both sides of the river, the forest has vanished. As guests absorb the image, they are besieged by more disturbing sights and sounds. Straight ahead, the river is choked with a tangled arch of burning logs—and the raft is headed straight for it. Suddenly, the rainforest isn't the only thing endangered.

Kali River Rapids is an especially soggy experience. It is the rare guest who leaves the ride without a thorough soaking. Should you wish to repel as much precipitation as possible, pack a plastic poncho. Stash valuables in a nearby locker while you ride (no charge).

Note: This is a very bumpy adventure. In order to experience it, you must be at least 38 inches tall. It is not recommended for pregnant women, guests with heart conditions, people with back or neck problems, or anyone who hopes to stay dry.

MAHARAJAH JUNGLE TREK

Welcome to the jungle! The Maharajah Jungle Trek is a self-guided walking tour of a tropical paradise, complete with roaming tigers and dense greenery. Throughout the expedition, trekkers encounter a deluge of flora and fauna typically found in the rainforests of Southeast Asia. Komodo dragons, fruit bats, and a conglomeration of colorful birds call this corner of Animal Kingdom home. Majestic Asian tigers can be spotted stalking ancient ruins, strategically separated from

---

HOT TIP!

Everyone and everything gets wet (to varying degrees) on Kali River Rapids. Items that simply must stay dry should be stored in a locker (across the pathway at the attraction's entrance) or with a non-riding member of your party.

FP+ = Fastpass+ attraction (see page 25)

would-be prey. Deer and antelope graze and frolic nearby, blissfully oblivious of their fearsome neighbors' proximity.

About midway through the thicket stands a tin-roofed assembly hall. Step inside to witness the breathtaking sight of giant fruit bats showing off their six-foot wingspans. As you gaze upon them through the windows, thinking that the crystal clear glass was cleaned by a super diligent window washer, think again. There is no glass in some of the windows—and, therefore, nothing separating you from the giant creatures hanging about on the other side. What keeps the big bats from getting up close and personal with guests? They're a lot less interested in humans than humans are in them. (Can't say that we blame them.) Note that some viewing areas are adorned with wire mesh or glass—for guests who are more comfortable with a bat buffer.

UP! A GREAT BIRD ADVENTURE

A 1,000-seat, open-air theater, the Caravan Stage features performances by actors wearing nothing but feathers and the occasional crown—plus everyone's favorite Senior Wilderness Explorer Russell and his canine cohort, Dug. Yep, the duo from the Disney/Pixar classic film *Up* are off on another exciting adventure. Guests are invited to join in the fun as the two discover fascinating—and talented—species of birds from around the world. The dialogue is a bit contrived, but the birds are impressive. For young fans of the movie *UP*, it's a real hoot. Each show runs about 20 minutes. Check a park Times Guide for the schedule. If the thought of up-close encounters with fine, feathered friends makes you uneasy, skip this show.

FP+ = Fastpass+ attraction (see page 25)

PHOTO BY JILL SAFRO

EXPEDITION EVEREST

BIRNBAUM'S ★BEST★ FP+ Walt Disney World's mountain range is a bit more intense these days, as the world's tallest mountain—Everest—has risen from the peaceful village of Serka Zong in Animal Kingdom's Asia. Like its sister peaks, Space, Splash, and Big Thunder, this E-ticket precipice promises to deliver "coaster thrills, spills, and chills." Does it deliver on that promise? Boy, does it ever.

The attraction features an old tea train chugging and churning as it climbs up and around snowcapped peaks. Suddenly, the track comes to an end in a gnarled mess of twisted metal. Lurching forward and backward, the train hurtles through caverns and icy canyons before depositing guests in the presence of the legendary Yeti (aka the Abominable Snowman)—who's most displeased that you've scaled the mountain he so fiercely protects.

Feeling up to the challenge of a dramatic, high-speed, out-of-control train ride? If you are free of heart, back, and neck problems, are not pregnant, have no fear of heights (or abominable snowpeople), and are at least 44 inches tall, go for it. As always, never eat right before experiencing a ride as topsy-turvy as this one.

DinoLand U.S.A.

If the look and feel of DinoLand U.S.A. seems familiar, there's a reason: It was designed to capture the flavor of roadside America. It is a mixture of culture and kitsch—the likes of which you might stumble upon during a cross-country road trip. Here, you may ride a flying Triceratop, jump into gigantic footprints, and browse through a typically tacky roadside souvenir stand, where you can pick up some dinosaur mementos for the folks back home.

This corner of Animal Kingdom comes complete with its own dramatic entrance: a 50-foot skeleton of a brachiosaurus. As guests stroll beneath the bones, they find themselves smack in the middle of a paleontological dig. Here, guests of all ages (especially little ones) have the chance to play paleontologist as they dig through a fossil-packed pocket of dino discovery.

primitive tune on a bony xylophone (it's located near the car; to make a sound, firmly press on a rib), zip down prehistoric slides, and work their way through a fossil-filled maze. While exploring, watch your step: If you happen to wander into a giant dinosaur footprint, you might be greeted with a somewhat ominous roar.

While in DinoLand, be sure to check out the Olden-Gate Bridge. It's a gateway structure fashioned from a dinosaur skeleton. The bridge links one end of The Boneyard with the other. This is a good place to take young children while other members of your party ride the Dinosaur attraction.

DID YOU KNOW?

Some of the benches in Disney's Animal Kingdom are made of recycled plastic milk jugs. It takes roughly 1,350 jugs to make a single park bench.

The dinosaurs that dwell here, though often quite animated, are all of the inanimate variety. But do keep your eyes peeled for the prehistoric life-forms that actually live in this land—that is, for actual living creatures that exist in the here and now, but whose ancestors kept company with the likes of the carnotaurus and its cousins from the Cretaceous era.

The Dinosaur attraction opens with the rest of Disney's Animal Kingdom, but usually closes one hour before park closing time.

THE BONEYARD

The Boneyard gives guests—especially the very young ones—an opportunity to dig for fossils in a discovery-oriented playground. They will excavate the ancient bones of a mammoth in this re-creation of a paleontological dig (think huge sandbox). They will also unearth clues that may help them solve the mystery of how and when the creature met its untimely demise.

For serious "boneheads" who just aren't satisfied with simple digging, there are plenty of other bone-related activities here. Youngsters can bang out a

CHESTER & HESTER'S DINO-RAMA!

A colorful land-within-a-land, Chester & Hester's is an area ideally suited for roadside carnival fans. Located just beyond The Boneyard playground, this wild-and-woolly zone features old-fashioned midway games and two rides: Primeval Whirl and TriceraTop Spin.

PRIMEVAL WHIRL: FP+ A small roller coaster (with spinning cars) that seems to have been plucked from a traveling fair, this ride may have a familiar feel to it. By all means, give it a whirl—it's a truly wild ride. You

FP+ = Fastpass+ attraction (see page 25)

must be at least 48 inches tall to spin. Skip it if you are pregnant or susceptible to motion sickness or think the jarring bumps will cause you discomfort.

TRICERATOP SPIN: The ride is sure to please fans of the Magic Kingdom's Dumbo the Flying Elephant and the Magic Carpets of Aladdin. Guests ride in one of the 16 flying dinos, each of which resembles an oversize tin toy. It's rather tame when compared to its Dinosaur attraction neighbor, but certainly worth checking out— especially for young dinosaur groupies.

FOSSIL FUN GAMES: Chester & Hester's Dino-Rama is home to several silly games of skill, including Whac-A-Packycephalosaur (smack mischievous dinos with a mallet), Mammoth Marathon (roll balls into holes to move your woolly mammoth in a race to the finish line), Bronto-Score (basketball toss), Comet Crasher (toss "comets" into moving cups), and Fossil Fueler (a gas-station-themed squirt game). Just like the midway games after which they are modeled, these games come with a fee. Game coupons may be purchased at the souvenir stand in the games area and at Chester & Hester's Dinosaur Treasures. Each game costs about $5 per person. (Bundle deals are available.) Dino-themed prizes are awarded to winners.

If you'd rather stick to included-with-the-price-of-admission diversions, we recommend checking out the fun-house mirror for some simple, silly fun.

DINOSAUR

BIRNBAUM'S ★BEST★ **FP+** This dizzying adventure begins with guests being strapped into vehicles and catapulted back in time to complete a dangerous, albeit noble, mission: to rescue the last iguanodon—a 16-foot plant-eating dinosaur—and bring him back to the present. The iguanodon, which lived more than 65 million years ago (during the Cretaceous period), just might hold the answer to the mysterious disappearance of his dino brethren.

Get Involved!

When it comes to conservation efforts, the folks at the Walt Disney Company want you to do as they say—and as they do: The Disney Conservation Fund helps nonprofit groups protect and study endangered and threatened animals and habitats. The fund has supported projects from more than 330 non-profit organizations, protecting more than 400 different animal species. And guests who contribute money while making purchases at many Animal Kingdom shops and restaurants help make a difference, too.

Of course, as a trip to Animal Kingdom makes clear, there are many ways to help our planet's wild inhabitants. Stop by Rafiki's Planet Watch during your visit. There, you can get information about conservation efforts in your neck of the woods. Don't leave your enthusiasm behind when you leave the park.

Throughout the frenetic quest to locate the elusive iguanodon, you cling to an out-of-control vehicle while dodging blazing meteors and a mix of friendly and ferocious dinosaurs. Soon you will encounter a carnotaurus—a fearsome, carnivorous dinosaur. The carnotaurus, which has horns like a bull and a face like a toad, is a remarkably unsightly specimen. In fact, all of the dinos move as though they were alive. Even their nostrils move as they "breathe."

This 3½-minute attraction offers more than a thrill a minute. You rocket through time, are practically pelted by meteors, and narrowly escape becoming a dino dinner as the carnotaurus suddenly turns the tables and chases after you!

Guests reach the attraction through the Dino Institute, a museum-like building deep in the heart of DinoLand, U.S.A. Here, you'll be treated to a pre-show by Bill Nye the Science Guy (audio only) and see a dinosaur skeleton and an assortment of fossils and other artifacts.

This is an extremely rough (and dark) attraction. Guests must be at least 40 inches tall to experience it. It should be skipped by pregnant women, or people with heart conditions, back or neck problems, or any other physical limitations. Small children will most definitely be frightened.

FINDING NEMO—THE MUSICAL

FP+ DinoLand is just about as far off Broadway as one could be. Yet this show's got the ingredients of a Broadway smash: beloved characters (e.g., Marlin, the overprotective clownfish dad; Nemo, his curious son; and Dory, the endearing royal blue tang with the short-term memory loss); original songs by a Tony-winning composer (Robert Lopez—who, along with Kristen Anderson-Lopez also brought us the songs from *Frozen* and *Frozen 2*); and dancers, acrobats, and the theatrical puppetry of Michael Curry (who designed the richly detailed puppets seen in the Broadway version of Disney's *The Lion King*).

You can catch this 40-minute performance at the enclosed and air-conditioned Theater in the Wild.

Check a Times Guide or use the My Disney Experience app for showtimes—and get there early.

This show has appeal for guests of all ages, but the 40-minute run time is a tad too long for some kids (especially the wee ones).

Where to Find the Characters at Animal Kingdom

You'll discover Mickey Mouse and Minnie Mouse at the Adventurers Outpost on Discovery Island (Fastpass+ is available). Goofy mingles with guests in DinoLand, near TriceraTop Spin. Pluto has been spotted roaming around the Boneyard. Donald Duck can be found nearby. Russell and Dug are on Discovery Island, near It's Tough to be a Bug! Kevin interacts with guests on Discovery Island. Look for Pocahontas at Character Landing on Discovery Island. You may meet Timon or Flik near Creature Comforts. Characters such as Daisy, Goofy, and Mickey join Donald for meals at Tusker House in Harambe (Festival of the Lion King theater). Reservations are required for all Tusker House meals. Guests inclined to party with Donald, Daisy, Chip, Dale, and Launchpad McQuack may do so in DinoLand U.S.A., during a dance party as part of Donald's Dino-Bash! (see page 212 and check a Times Guide for the schedule).

Shopping at Animal Kingdom

ENTRANCE AREA

GARDEN GATE GIFTS: Stop here for snacks, sundries, shirts, hats, plush toys, and more. Electric Conveyance Vehicles (ECVs) may be rented. (Wheelchair and stroller rentals are nearby.) This is also the park's package pickup and PhotoPass viewing location.

OUTPOST: A small shop located just outside the park's entrance, Outpost offers character merchandise, snacks, and assorted souvenirs.

PANDORA—THE WORLD OF AVATAR

WINDTRADERS: A nice shopper's retreat, Windtraders specializes in Na'vi cultural artifacts (the Na'vi are the native inhabitants of Pandora), plus Alpha Centauri Expeditions (ACE) clothing, toys, science kits, and more. Would you like to adopt your own mountain banshee (aka ikran)? Head here.

DISCOVERY ISLAND

DISCOVERY TRADING COMPANY: This sprawling shop is themed as a shipping company that celebrates working animals—camels, elephants, and others. Here, you'll find character merchandise, clothing, candy, and Disney paraphernalia. Discovery Trading Company stays open about a half hour after the park closes for the day. It's connected to the Riverside Depot, which also sells character-themed items.

ISLAND MERCANTILE: Nature-themed gifts and apparel are the stock-in-trade at this sizable shop. There's an abundance of clothing (for the whole family), plus various items with an animal theme and Disney souvenirs.

AFRICA

MOMBASA MARKETPLACE & ZIWANI TRADERS: An African marketplace and trading company, these connected shops feature animal toys, safari clothing, T-shirts, books, and Africa-themed gifts such as pottery, masks, and musical instruments. A wood-carver makes crafts on-site.

OUT OF THE WILD: Located just outside the exit of Rafiki's Planet Watch, this open-air shop stocks a variety of souvenirs.

ZURI'S SWEETS SHOP: Guests visiting Harambe Market will discover Zuri's, a treat lover's paradise. In addition to sweets with a *Lion King* theme, Zuri sells items such as wine, African-inspired dinnerware, African-spice popcorn, spice rubs, and barbecue sauce from Animal Kingdom's Flame Tree Barbecue.

ASIA

BHAKTAPUR MARKET: A small shop with a big Asian influence, Bhaktapur sells summer shoes, bags, robes, shirts, teapots and teas, toy dragons and plush animals, chopsticks, and items with a Yak & Yeti theme.

MANDALA GIFTS: A stone's throw from Royal Anandapur Tea Company, this cozy spot offers Asian-inspired clothing, scarves, and handbags, plus souvenirs with Disney's Animal Kingdom park logo.

SERKA ZONG BAZAAR: Located at the exit of Expedition Everest (it can be accessed from the outside for those who prefer to skip the ride), this bustling bazaar sells souvenirs with a Yeti theme, plus a slew of shirts, hats, purses, postcards, books, plush toys, pins, frames, etc., that celebrate the Expedition Everest attraction.

DINOLAND U.S.A.

CHESTER & HESTER'S DINOSAUR TREASURES: Themed as an American roadside souvenir stand, this shop pays homage to all reptiles and prehistoric animals. There is a small selection of dino-themed merch, but Chester and Hester are more focused on Disney stuff.

THE DINO INSTITUTE SHOP: It should come as no surprise that you'll find dino-themed items and other souvenirs here. It's also the spot to view (and buy) that photo of you looking terrified while riding Dinosaur.

Animal Kingdom
Entertainment

DONALD'S DINO-BASH! Donald Duck has made a major discovery: His ancestors were dinosaurs! To celebrate the happy revelation, he throws daily dance parties with his pals in DinoLand U.S.A. When they're not dancing, Donald and his Disney buddies meet, greet, and pose for photos with guests. Check a Times Guide for schedules. Details are subject to change.

DI-VINE: So convincing is Di-Vine, that many a guest fail to notice she is actually a graceful entertainer and not, well, an actual vine.

PANDORA DRUMMERS—SWOTU WAYÄ: A trio of local musicians performs a traditional Na'vi drum ceremony in Pandora—The World of Avatar. Shows may not appear daily and are subject to change.

TAM TAM DRUMMERS OF HARAMBE: Park guests may dance to the beat of the Congo as these spirited musicians dance, drum, and dazzle the crowd. Each 15-minute performance takes place in the Africa section of Disney's Animal Kingdom. Check a park Times Guide for the schedule.

Where to Eat in Animal Kingdom

A complete listing of eateries at Disney's Animal Kingdom—full-service restaurants, fast-food eateries, and snack shops—can be found in the *Good Meals, Great Times* chapter. See the Animal Kingdom section, beginning on page 274.

- Most of Animal Kingdom's attractions take place outdoors. Don't become overheated! Make a point of slipping into air-conditioned shops and restaurants from time to time to cool off.

- Narrow, winding paths, grooved pavement, and hilly terrain make this the most challenging Disney theme park in which to navigate a wheelchair or heavy stroller.

- Check the My Disney Experience mobile app or website to get an idea of attraction wait times.

- When the weather gets steamy, keep a reusable water bottle with you at all times.

- Rainforest Cafe generally keeps longer hours than the park does. (Buses run until one hour after park closing time.)

- The line for Kilimanjaro Safaris tends to dwindle a bit by midday. See it then (the experience is enjoyable at any time of day). Or wait until the evening, when some animals are especially lively.

- Get a Fastpass+ for Avatar Flight of Passage as early as possible—they run out quickly.

- Bumpy rides aren't for everyone—or for every camera. When it comes to thrill (or wet) rides, it's smart to stash your camera in a locker or with a non-riding member of your party.

- Island Mercantile on Discovery Island stays open about a half hour after the park closes.

- If you plan to ride Avatar Flight of Passage (and you should), be prepared for a long wait *and* a long walk: The distance from the attraction's entrance and the ride itself is more than a quarter-mile. Wear comfortable shoes and be sure to hit the restroom before hitting the queue.

- Disney's Animal Kingdom includes a realistic reproduction of parts of Africa, right down to the climate. Beat the heat by arriving very early in the morning or "hop" to Animal Kingdom after the sun sets (on days when the park is open late).

HIDDEN MICKEYS

These are some of the most popular "Hidden Mickeys" at Animal Kingdom. How many can you find? Check the circle when you spot each one!

Tree of Life: A Hidden Mickey made of moss is on the front of the Tree of Life just to the right of the tiger and to the left of the buffalo. Although you may be able to spot it from several vantage points, the best place is right when you enter Discovery Island and before the path splits to Africa and DinoLand, U.S.A. ○

Kilimanjaro Safaris: Pay close attention to the flamingo pond on your left just after you enter elephant country. The center island is shaped like a Hidden Mickey (sit toward the left side of the ride vehicle for the best view). ○

Maharajah Jungle Trek: There are more than 10 Hidden Mickeys throughout this jungle trek, but we suggest hunting for these two to start: Inside the first archway near the tiger exhibit, pay attention to the mural on the left and look for three leaves that form a Hidden Mickey underneath the extended arm of a king. ○ Now walk to the second arch and look at the mural on the right to find a Hidden Mickey image in the clouds. ○

Gorilla Falls Exploration Trail: Okay, while not a Hidden Mickey, the Hidden Jafar (from the animated feature *Aladdin*) found in this trail is well worth searching for. Just past the gorilla viewing area, you'll reach a suspension bridge. Look directly to your right and you'll see a huge 3-D head of Jafar carved out of the rock that's covered in moss. ○

Rafiki's Planet Watch: Conservation Station is a Hidden Mickey paradise with more than twenty Mickeys in the entrance mural alone. Two favorites: Just inside the building on the right, find a possum with a Hidden Mickey in its eye. ○ Then look above it to find a butterfly with two Hidden Mickeys (one on each wing). ○ For good measure, here's a third:

Find a frog just to the right of an alligator on the left wall, then find Mickey's smiling face beneath the frog's right eye. ○

Expedition Everest: To find this Hidden Mickey, you'll need a Fastpass+ assignment for Expedition Everest. As you travel through the Fastpass+ queue, pay close attention to the Yeti Museum room. In the second display of expedition artifacts and supplies, look for a lantern on a shelf—three dents in the metal form a sideways Hidden Mickey. ○

It's Tough to be a Bug!: This is one of the more challenging Hidden Mickeys to locate at Disney's Animal Kingdom park, but Cast Members are always happy to offer some assistance. After you enter the "underground" room with all the silly musical posters (but before entering the main theater), find the other entrance to the far side of the room. Now look at the far left wall. This well-concealed (but very cool) Hidden Mickey is hiding in the shadows. ○

DinoLand U.S.A.: First, find the two large dinosaurs holding up a "Chester & Hester's Dino-Rama" sign near the TriceraTop Spin ride. Stand directly underneath the sign and close to the blue dinosaur. Look at the dino's wrist—there's a Hidden Mickey on it! ○ Then head to the dig site area of The Boneyard playground. Can you spot where two hard hats and a fan combine to form another H.M.? ○

Dinosaur: Before you travel back in time, your ride vehicle passes a laboratory scene on the left (the vehicle actually stops here for a second to give you an opportunity to look). Search carefully to find a blue Hidden Mickey drawn on the lower left corner of a whiteboard. ○

Cretaceous Trail: At the end of this short DinoLand trail sits a proud dino. We think he's proud of the Hidden Mickey on his back! ○

Specifics may change during 2020.

WHERE IN THE WORLD?

All of the photos on this page were taken at Disney's Animal Kingdom. Do you know where? We challenge you to find all the spots where these images were shot and snap a (non-flash) photo for yourself as you discover each one. Happy hunting! (For locations, see page 362.)

1

2

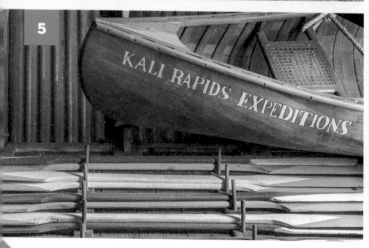

3

4

5

6

EVERYTHING ELSE IN THE WORLD

"Laughter is America's most important export." —Walt Disney

216 Disney Springs

225 Boardwalk

226 Water Parks

232 Fort Wilderness

235 Tours & Programs

239 Just for Kids

240 Spas

242 Specialty Cruises

While the total turf of the World encompasses nearly 40 square miles, the theme parks cover a mere fraction of the property. Much of the remaining Walt Disney World terrain is crammed with activities of a variety and quality seldom found anywhere else.

Within WDW's borders you'll find golf and tennis, beaches for strolling, lakes for boating and fishing, canoes to rent and winding streams to paddle along, bicycles for hire, campfire sites, horseback riding, ballooning, nature trails, and picnic grounds. The recreation options continue with Typhoon Lagoon, a lushly landscaped, state-of-the-art water park complete with surfing lagoon; and Blizzard Beach, a watery wonderland that translates the hallmarks of a ski resort to the realm of swimming.

A lineup of lavish spas and salons provides guests with ample opportunity to pamper themselves silly. Intriguing "backstage" programs invite the curious to slip behind the scenes and learn about the workings of Walt Disney World. Add to all that, Disney Springs—a dynamic dining, shopping, and entertainment district including an eclectic assortment of shops, shows, and restaurants. The expansive play zone, formerly known as Downtown Disney, has nearly 200 different venues to discover. It seems this really is a World without end.

Disney Springs

Sprinkled across 120 acres are the shops, lounges, restaurants, and entertainment sites that collectively make up Disney Springs. This timeless place, previously known as Downtown Disney, consists of four neighborhoods interconnected by a flowing spring and vibrant lakefront: the Marketplace, Town Center, The Landing, and West Side. The re-imagined enclave, which recently completed a major metamorphosis, is a definite hot spot. The spirited waterfront zone boasts close to 200 establishments—all there for your dining, shopping, and playing pleasure.

Guests staying at most Disney–owned-and-operated resorts can reach Disney Springs via bus. Water taxis ferry guests to and from Saratoga Springs, Port Orleans French Quarter, Port Orleans Riverside, and Old Key West. Safe, convenient pedestrian bridges connect the area with the resorts on Hotel Plaza Boulevard.

There is a $20 charge for valet parking. (It's available near the entrance to the Orange and Lemon parking garages from 10 A.M. till 2 A.M. and on the far end of the West Side (near the Cirque du Soleil tent), from 4 P.M. till 2 A.M.). Note that the valet fee is waived for guests with a Tables In Wonderland membership card. (See page 290 for details.) Self-parking is free. For more info, use the My Disney Experience mobile app or website, visit *www.disneysprings.com* or *www.disneyworld.com*, or call 407-934-7639.

Disney Springs Essentials

GUEST RELATIONS: Inside the Disney Springs Welcome Center in Town Center, Guest Relations is the place to go for information, to make dining reservations, for Lost and Found, to buy tickets, and more. Strollers and wheelchairs are available at Sundries Rentals, near the Orange parking garage. Details are subject to change.

HOW TO GET THERE: If you're driving, take exit 67 off I-4 to access Disney Springs.

By WDW Transportation: From Old Key West, Port Orleans French Quarter and Riverside, and Saratoga Springs: boat or bus. From all other WDW resorts: bus. There is one-way bus service from Disney theme parks to Disney Springs after 4 P.M. (There is no return bus service to the parks.) The Marketplace is within walking distance of Saratoga Springs and some resorts on Hotel Plaza Boulevard. For more details, refer to the *Transportation & Accommodations* chapter.

By Ride-Sharing Service or Taxi: Guests may use Lyft and Uber to get to and from Disney Springs. Minnie Vans (accessed via the Lyft app; see page 64), and authorized cabs serve the area, too. The cost of cabbing to most WDW resorts is usually $15 to $30 (plus tip). Minnie Vans, which transport guests anywhere on WDW property, start with a base rate of $15. Final cost depends on the destination.

The Disney Springs address is 1486 Buena Vista Drive, Orlando, FL 32830.

Marketplace

Situated along the shore of Lake Buena Vista, the Marketplace is a relaxing setting for shopping, dining, and much more. The waterside district is sprinkled with gardens featuring whimsical topiaries. Little kids are fond of the Disney Springs carousel (see Marketplace Rides, page 219). While many guests opt to eat at a table-service restaurant, others grab a bite from someplace like the Earl of Sandwich and nosh at outdoor tables. (Refer to the *Good Meals, Great Times* chapter for restaurant details.) Afterward, some gravitate toward Dockside Margaritas for live music and a nightcap.

The following pages detail many of our favorite shopping, dining, and entertainment locations. The descriptions that follow suggest the types of wares and cuisine each spot offers.

Most shops and eateries within the Disney Springs Marketplace are typically open from about 10 A.M. to 11 or 11:30 P.M. each day.

ARRIBAS BROS.: This shop sells handcrafted items  from Spanish artisans and designers. Large cut-glass bowls and vases are available, along with mugs, sculptures, and other wares, many of which can be personalized on the spot. Aspiring Cinderellas should appreciate the selection of sparkly tiaras and glass slippers. The store is located between Basin and Marketplace Co-op.

THE ART OF DISNEY: Original Disney art, porcelain figures, ceramics, posters, and other collectibles are available at this engaging gallery.

BASIN: Products designed to clean you up and calm you down are the stock-in-trade at this soothing establishment. Candles, soaps, and bath crystals are some of the wares on hand. A sampling area allows shoppers to try before they buy. The bath bombs are the best!

BIBBIDI BOBBIDI BOUTIQUE: This country parlor-inspired location gives young guests (ages 3 through 12) the royal treatment with the help of Fairy God-mothers-in-Training. Kids can get their faces painted with glitter makeup, do their nails and hair, and even don tiaras. The boutique is open daily. Youngsters are transformed into princesses and princely royal knights. Reservations are encouraged; call 407-939-7895 for reservations and pricing (cheap it is not). Note that this shop is adjacent to Once Upon a Toy.

DINO-STORE: Budding paleontologists can dig for prehistoric toys and treasures in this corner of T-Rex: A Prehistoric Family Adventure. There is an area in which to custom-build a plush dino, too.

PHOTO BY JILL SAFRO

DISNEY'S DAYS OF CHRISTMAS: Ho, ho, ho! Here is the best place to deck the halls Disney style—it's the largest Christmas shop on Walt Disney World property. In addition to character items, the shop boasts a large assortment of handcrafted ornaments. Other items to look for: Mickey Mouse nutcrackers, Santa hats with mouse ears, stockings, holiday cards, and books. Some of the ornaments can be personalized.

DISNEY'S PIN TRADERS: This shop boasts an assortment of collector pins and pin-collecting accessories, plus hats, MagicBands, and other collectibles.

DISNEY'S WONDERFUL WORLD OF MEMORIES: Preserve the memories of your Walt Disney World adventure with the frames, photo albums, and other merchandise from this shop across from Disney's Days of Christmas. There's a make-your-own Disney charm bracelet station and a wall of mouse ear hats just waiting to be personalized.

GOOFY'S CANDY COMPANY: One-stop shopping to satisfy sugary cravings, this shop has a sumptuous selection of chocolates, a dipping kitchen, and more.

On warm days, we gravitate to the corner of this shop known as Goofy's Glaciers for a frozen slushy treat, available in flavors with goofy names such as Razzle Dazzle Pink, Orange You Happy, and Pucker Purple. They also serve coffee, cookies, pastries, and ice cream. Another temptation here: the create-your-own specialty apple station.

THE HAPPY HOUND: Fetch items for Fido at this pup-centric locale. The shop specializes in toys, treats, and accessories meant to make your hound happy.

LEFTY'S: Step up to southpaw central for scissors, can openers, writing implements, notebooks, mugs, magnets, T-shirts, and more—all made especially for the differently handed. The open-air stand also sells shirts and hats lauding left-handedness.

THE LEGO STORE: World of Disney's neighbor, this playful emporium is a showcase for larger-than-life LEGO models. It also invites guests to flaunt their

HOT TIP!

Stretch your vacation dollar during your visit to Disney Springs by using the coupons at the back of this book. They'll help you save on several shopping, dining, and recreation experiences. You're welcome!

creativity in an interactive outdoor play area. A computer hub lets guests design LEGO structures and play games. The store sells a vast selection of LEGO products.

STAR WARS TRADING POST: Here's the place to find a bounty of treasures with a Star Wars theme: shirts, hats, jammies, action figures, toys, mugs, pins, books, and more. There is a special area in which guests may build lightsabers and another that allows them to create their own droids.

MICKEY'S PANTRY: Stop in for Disney-themed glasses, cookbooks, cooking utensils, wine and the associated accouterments, plus spices, teas, coffees, magnets, and mugs. Many designs are quite subtle, others not so much: Mickey-shaped pasta, anyone? Note that the Spice & Tea Exchange is located inside Mickey's Pantry (inside the main entrance, to the left).

MARKETPLACE CO-OP: A cavernous retail zone, the Co-op is home to specialty shops: **WonderGround Gallery** is a contemporary art space showcasing unusual collections and emerging artists; **Cherry Tree Lane** appeals to "the sophisticated woman with a passion for scarves, shoes, bags, and jewelry"; **D-Tech on Demand** is the place to personalize and customize electronic accessories; **Centerpiece** showcases home products for folks who dig a dash of Disney in their furnishings, textiles, and everyday ware; **Twenty Eight & Main** specializes in apparel and accessories for distinguished gentlemen who happen to love Disney parks; and

PHOTO BY JILL SAFRO

Disney Tails features whimsically designed products for pets. The variety of merchandise at the Marketplace Co-op puts this area on top of many a Disney treasure-hunter's must-do list. It's one of our favorite places to shop at Walt Disney World.

ONCE UPON A TOY: An oversize toy box, this site has plush toys, action figures, and many other playthings from which to choose.

THE PEARL FACTORY: Pick an oyster, any oyster. Then pry it open (with assistance), and *voila*—a pearl! The cost is about $16 per oyster, and you are guaranteed a genuine pearl. The open-air shop proffers pearl earrings and necklaces, too. You'll find it near Lefty's.

SILHOUETTE PORTRAITS: A stand manned by a talented artist, this spot offers single ($10), double ($20), triple ($30), and quadruple silhouettes. There are frames, too (oval and Mickey-shaped).

THE SPICE & TEA EXCHANGE: Neatly nestled into a corner of Mickey's Pantry, this fragrant destination offers the opportunity to purchase gourmet spices, salts, peppers, sugars, teas, and more. It's a unique shopping experience thanks in part to a selection of sample jars in which you are encouraged to stick your nose.

> ## HOT TIP!
> Live entertainment is presented on the Marketplace Stage throughout most days. The open-air venue is on the shore of Lake Buena Vista, across from The World of Disney shop. Expect visiting bands, dancers, kids' dance parties, and more.

SPUNKY STORK: In the neighborhood of Rainforest Café, this stand sells handmade baby clothes that are made using 100 percent organic cotton with the designs printed on a manual screen printing press.

TREN-D: The Mouse is quite a trendsetter. Need proof? Swing by this nifty boutique. It is bursting with quirky Disney merchandise, from loungewear to jeweled sunglasses and other trendy accessories.

WORLD OF DISNEY: A huge, industrial warehouse-like space stuffed with a ginormous selection of Disney merchandise, this is a popular destination for souvenir shopping. Brick walls and dark wood beams provide the backdrop for the vast array of goods. Characters are available on everything from tennis shoes to luggage. (Like at many other WDW merchandise locations, if you're an Annual Passholder, you may receive a discount when you present it at the register. It depends on the type of pass, and the discount is subject to change.) Reusable bags are available for a small fee.

Marketplace Rides

Disney Springs Marketplace has two genuine kiddie rides for adventurous tykes to enjoy: a carousel and a choo-choo train. The cost for each is $3 per child ($5 to ride twice). Be sure to purchase a token before boarding (payment can be made with Visa, MasterCard, or cash). Parents can accompany children on the train (no charge for parents, provided they ride in the same car; kids under 36 inches tall must be accompanied by a guest over age 14). The train can only accommodate two adults per trip, and grown-ups may not ride in the engine car. For the carousel, kids under 42 inches tall must be accompanied by a guest age 18 or older (who rides for free). The Marketplace rides are located between The Earl of Sandwich and the Star Wars Trading Post.

The Landing

THE ART OF SHAVING: A premium shave shop, Art of Shaving offers high-end men's grooming supplies—razors, brushes, creams, and shaving sets, and aromatherapy-based products—plus the Barber Spa: a place for guests to relax and get a shave and/or a haircut from a master barber.

THE BOATHOUSE BOATIQUE: Adjacent to The Boathouse restaurant, this shop features a bounty of nautically themed treasures. Among the wares here: clothing, jewelry, home accents, and games—plus engravable paddles and life rings.

CHAPEL HATS: Fashion-forward headwear for men and women is the stock-in-trade at this hat shop. With shelving made of reclaimed wood, decorative tables made from old shipping container hatch doors, and Arts and Crafts–style mirrors, Chapel Hats has classic appeal. They've got everything from fedoras to fascinators. Fascinating.

ERIN MCKENNA'S BAKERY NYC: Folks with dietary restrictions (and those just looking for a freshly made sweet treat) will be in the pink when they visit this bakeshop. In the words of founder Erin McKenna, the place "focuses on the underserved people with gluten, dairy, egg, and soy sensitivities, the health-minded, and allergic kids who are often unable to indulge. The goal is to make eating vegan and gluten-free fun and delicious." Mission accomplished.

ERWIN PEARL: Acclaimed jewelry designer Erwin Pearl proffers high-end fashion designs—including bracelets, earrings, necklaces, rings, pins, and charms—from a boutique across from Paradiso 37 in The Landing. The pieces here are made of enamel, and precious and semi-precious stones—and are renowned for being "distinctive, colorful, and vibrant with originality." You can save 10 percent off a $150 purchase with the coupon at the back of this book.

THE GANACHERY: A fresh take on an old apothecary, the star of this show is housemade ganache—Disney's own recipe for a luxurious mixture of melted chocolate and cream. The decadent treats aren't cheap, but many a chocolate fanatic finds them worthy of a splurge.

HAVAIANAS: Head here for vibrant flip-flops with a Brazilian flair. With more than 300 styles to choose from, Havaianas just may have a flip-flop for every possible occasion. Colorful apparel and accessories are also available. It's located across from Chapel Hats.

SANUK: Retire those pinchy old shoes and replace them with cool and comfy footwear for the whole family at Sanuk. (If we could wear our Sanuks every day, we would.) F.Y.I.: *Sanuk* is the Thai word for fun.

SAVANNAH BEE COMPANY: Do luxurious body-care goods made with locally sourced, all-natural honey sound tempting to you? How about a selection of specialty honeys, honeycombs, cookies, candies, and other sweet souvenirs? If so, make a beeline for this honey of a shop. It has it all.

Note: Savannah Bee Company is passionate about bees and advocates for education about the world's vital-but-imperiled pollinators. If you'd like to support your local honeybee, visit *www.thebeecause.com*.

SHOP FOR IRELAND: Nestled within Raglan Road (across from Morimoto Asia), this quaint boutique lines its shelves with items imported from the Emerald Isle. Among them: Irish clothing, jewelry, family crests, cookbooks, bookmarks, magnets, hats, scarves, and fragrances. You may even harness the luck of the Irish with the purchase of a four-leaf clover. *Slainte!*

HOT TIP!

Fancy a cruise in a floating car? Head to the Amphicar dock near The Boathouse restaurant (The Landing). The rare auto/boats drive into the lake and guests are treated to a 20-minute guided tour of Disney Springs (for about $125). Save $25 with the coupon at the back of this book!

Where to Eat at Disney Springs

A complete listing of restaurants, bars, and snack spots can be found in the *Good Meals, Great Times* chapter. See the Disney Springs restaurant listings, beginning on page 278. Most of the restaurants here are open from about 11 A.M. until about 11 P.M. or later.

West Side

AMC DISNEY SPRINGS 24: The most popular multi-screen movie theater complex in Florida is also one of the largest. The many screens show a wide selection of current movie releases. The seats are all roomy and comfortable—and some of the theaters offer seat-side food and beverage service (see page 278 for details). For current movie schedules, visit *amctheatres.com*.

PHOTO BY JILL SAFRO

SUNSHINE HIGHLINE: A mini version of Manhattan's High Line (an abandoned elevated roadway converted into a city park), Disney's high line provides much needed shade by day and lively international music by night. Live performances, which last about an hour, feature classic and exotic musical selections.

MUSIC ON THE LAWN: Mosey on over to the West Side Lawn (near the West Side Starbucks) for live music in a lakeside setting.

CITY WORKS EATERY AND POUR HOUSE: A sports fan's delight, City Works sits (fittingly) beside The NBA Experience. With its 165 screens, 80 tap beers (including dozens of local and global craft selections), and extensive menu including small bites (buffalo shrimp, smoked wings, flatbreads, kung pao cauliflower), salads, burgers, tacos, and entrées such as pan-seared salmon, fish and chips, pork chops, short ribs, etc., this new gathering spot aims to please. In addition to the substantial supply of suds, the bar serves specialty drinks, wine, soft drinks, and more. There is a kids' menu, too. You'll find City Works across from the House of Blues. Reservations are accepted. City Works is a Disney Dining plan participant. Details are subject to change.

HOUSE OF BLUES: A combination restaurant-music hall with standing room for 2,000, House of Blues was inspired by one of America's most celebrated musical traditions. There is a lively dose of jazz and country, plus a little bit of R&B and some rock 'n' roll thrown into the music mix. The Southern-inspired cooking lures diners here—especially on Sunday mornings, when the chefs prepare an all-you-care-to-eat buffet feast, complemented by live gospel music (and H.O.B's famous chicken and waffles). Tickets may be purchased through Ticketmaster (call 407-839-3900, or visit *www.ticketmaster.com*) or the House of Blues box office (407-934-2583).

The House of Blues restaurant features a mélange of hearty cuisine, including jambalaya, slow-smoked pulled pork, shrimp with grits, and bread pudding.

GEAR SHOP: Gear up with House of Blues hats, shirts, and other apparel at this H.O.B. shop. Art, glassware, musical instruments, and other paraphernalia are sold.

The NBA Experience

Basketball fans are drooling (or is that dribbling?) at the thought of this new interactive play zone masterminded by the folks at the National Basketball Association. The NBA Experience, which tipped off in 2019, features games, a shop, and hands-on activities for the whole family. Ever dreamed of walking through the players' tunnel and stepping into a modern-day NBA arena? Here's your chance! (Okay, it's a replica, but still super cool.) For additional information, including pricing, use the My Disney Experience mobile app or website, or visit *www .disneyworld.com*. It's located in the spot formerly occupied by DisneyQuest.

JALEO BY JOSÉ ANDRÉS: The flavors of Spain have made their way to Disney Springs. The menu at this expansive eatery features an extensive selection of tapas that celebrate the regional diversity of classic and contemporary Spanish cuisine. Think paella cooked over a wood fire and hand-carved Jamon Iberico de Bellota (premium ham). The multi-level eatery features a first-floor grab-and-go area with Spanish-style sandwiches. Reservations are highly recommended for the restaurant. For further details or to make a reservation, visit *www.disneyworld.com*, or use the My Disney Experience mobile app or website.

CANDY CAULDRON: Stop here for some homemade sweets in an open candy kitchen. Among the biggest crowd-pleasers here are the made-to-order specialty apples—fresh, crunchy apples slathered in the candy coating of your choice (for about $11 each). Yum. Kids love to peek through the windows and watch the candy makers at work.

FIT2RUN—THE RUNNER'S SUPERSTORE: A super stop for guests on the run, this shop sells footwear, apparel, performance sunglasses, jogger strollers, and more. Need help selecting the perfect shoe for you? Take advantage of this shop's complimentary evaluation and high-tech video gait analysis. There's even an indoor track to test shoes before you purchase them. Ready, set, run! You'll find it next to the Splitsville shop known as Memory Lanes.

HOT TIP!

Cirque du Soleil fans, take note: The popular Disney Springs show, La Nouba, took its final bow in 2017 (after nearly 9,000 performances!). At press time, a brand-new production, inspired by Disney's rich animation heritage, was nearing its debut. For updates, visit *www.cirquedusoleil.com* and *www.disneyworld.com*.

Up, Up, and Away!

You can float up to 400 feet above Disney Springs while beneath one behemoth of a balloon. Touted as the "world's largest tethered helium balloon," it carries up to 29 guests at a time in a gondola that measures 19 feet in diameter. Flights last 8 to 10 minutes. Guests board from a platform on the West Side (near Starbucks). Tickets are sold at a nearby window. The cost is about $20 (plus tax) for adults (guests age 10 and up) and $15 for kids ages 3 to 9. Babies fly free. Flights begin at 8:30 A.M. daily (weather-permitting) and operate on a first-come, first-served basis. It's run by Aerophile— "The World Leader in Balloon Flight."

MARVEL SUPER HERO HEADQUARTERS: Calling all would-be agents of S.H.I.E.L.D.: You can gear up at this shop, plus snag Super-Hero-themed (Spider-Man, Captain America, Guardians of the Galaxy, etc.) shirts, action figures, hats, books, mugs, glassware, and other items—all featuring characters from the Marvel Universe. One crossover item of note: Iron Man mouse ears.

DISNEYSTYLE: Spot the big yellow teacup in the window and you'll know you've arrived at the happy place known as DisneyStyle. Brimming with goodies inspired by Disney rides, attractions, animated features, and fun catchphrases, this boutique is paradise for Disney-heads. In the market for a Dole Whip plush toy? An "I speak Phoenician" T-shirt? Monorail socks? A cap inviting fellow fans to meet you at the Purple Wall? Disney Style has it all. We love this shop.

POP GALLERY: This gallery features artist-signed limited-edition sculptures and paintings, as well as high-end gift items.

SOSA FAMILY CIGAR COMPANY: For adults only, this shop specializes in premium cigars. Feel free to puff away here—the shop is a rare "authorized" smoking zone. In addition to hand-rolled cigars, Sosa features an authentic solid cedar humidor room to keep the wares as fresh as possible. Note that guests must be at least 18 years old with state-issued photo ID in order to smoke tobacco products in the state of Florida.

SPLITSVILLE LUXURY LANES™: Come for some casual bowling, stay for some food and live entertainment. This West Side venue features 30 bowling lanes, two high-end kitchens, a full bar, live music—and billiards to boot. This massive 'ville (50,000 square feet) is fun for all ages. However, some areas are restricted to guests over the age of 21 (with legal ID to prove it). It's generally open until about 2 A.M. daily; the restricted "ages 21 and up" area is open on Fridays and Saturdays after 10:30 P.M. Shoppers can peruse and purchase merchandise at Memory Lanes, a shop tucked into a corner on the first floor of the Splitsville building. Look for items such as shirts, pants, hats, glasses, jewelry, and more. For details, visit *www.splitsvillelanes.com* and refer to page 283.

STARBUCKS: That ubiquitous mermaid icon can be spotted on the shore of Lake Buena Vista. Expect all of the Starbucks specialties—from fresh-brewed, free-trade cups of joe to sweet and chilly Frappuccinos. Breakfast sandwiches, fruit, and oatmeal are served. Baked treats include cupcakes, muffins, scones, cookies, and cake pops. Teas, smoothies, veggies, juice, milk, soda, and water are also offered. (There are several Disney Dining Plan snack options to choose from.) F.Y.I.: The Green Roof and Living Walls at this location are nourished with compost made from coffee grounds. That's meant to help with recycling and offset greenhouse gases.

STAR WARS GALACTIC OUTPOST: The Force is strong with this store. So is its pull on folks strolling the promenade at Disney Springs, West Side. It boasts an impressive bounty of toys, clothes, and accessories inspired by the epic space saga: hats, shirts, dresses (yes, we once spotted a Darth Vader dress), costumes, pins, collectibles, photos, socks, glassware, plush toys,

mouse ears, lightsaber key chains, and many more items featuring characters from the Star Wars films. There's a build-your-own lightsaber station, too.

SUNGLASS ICON: Looking for some super-cool shades? This snazzy shop is full of high-end brands to protect your peepers.

PELÉ SOCCER: Fútbol fans, rejoice! You can gather garb to support your favorite club and load up on gear to tackle the game yourself—right here at the well-stocked shop named for one of the greatest soccer players of all time. This spot's goal is to meet all your soccer needs. Score!

TOM'S CUSTOM ART STATION: Stationed in the shadow of Curl by Sammy Duvall, this stand features customizable (and comfy) Tom's One For One shoes. Simply select a design and pick a pair of shoes and an artist will paint them on the spot. The artwork ranges from about $25 to $85 (plus the price of the shoes).

WETZEL'S PRETZELS: Whether you prefer pretzels on the salty or sweet side, this kiosk has something to satisfy. Also served: hot dogs wrapped in a soft pretzel, pretzel bits, lemonade, frozen lemonade, and frozen granita (a sweet, icy treat). Buy two pretzels, get one free with the coupon at the back of this book!

HOT TIP!

A visit to Disney Springs requires quite a bit of walking stamina. Expect to log a couple of miles per visit—especially if you plan to walk from the Marketplace to the West Side (and back again!). We recommend strollers for small children—and very comfortable shoes for all. And make use of the (free) Disney Springs water taxi service whenever possible. The small ferry boats—aka The Sassagoula Steamboat Company—make stops at docks in the Marketplace, The Landing, and West Side.

Town Center

The architectural design of Town Center's Town Square is "Spanish Revival," drawing from a rich history of explorers that landed in Florida centuries ago. It was ostensibly founded in the 1850s, on the banks of one of the Sunshine State's freshwater springs—where its original homestead still stands, having been restored and converted to a family restaurant (D-Luxe Burger). The commercial district of Town Center was designed in the Mediterranean Revival style that was popular in Florida in the 1920s, whereas the Welcome Center area features the wooden American revival architecture that was prevalent in the 1930s. Overall, this sophisticated area has a focus on shopping, but also brings inventive dining opportunities and other pleasant diversions. For more details about dining spots, refer to the *Good Meals, Great Times* chapter of this book.

DINING

AMORETTE'S PATISSERIE: Classic and contemporary cakes and pastries are the stars in this high-end pastry shop where guests can watch the chefs decorate signature cakes in the on-stage finishing kitchen. Amorette's lovingly packages sweet treats in old-fashioned hatboxes. Champagne, sparkling wine, hot chocolate ganache, and crepes are also served. F.Y.I.: Amorette means "little love" in French.

BLAZE FAST FIRE'D PIZZA: This eatery lets hungry guests "build their own artisanal pizzas." Custom-made pizzas are prepared in about three minutes—they don't call it "fast fire'd" for nothing. The 5,000-square-foot eatery also serves freshly prepared salads and desserts.

D-LUXE BURGER: Come for the burgers, stay for the shakes at this Town Center quick-service location. D-Luxe Burger is a comfy spot for a casual bite. The creatively prepared burgers (most big enough to share) are served on fresh-baked buns. Pair yours with freshly cut fries (which come with a variety of dipping sauces) and (scrumptious) artisanal gelato shakes (with rotating flavors such as vanilla, chocolate, raspberry, strawberry, salted caramel, and s'mores). There is a small kids' menu, too. Beer, wine, and soft drinks are served. D-Luxe Burger has ample indoor and outdoor seating (the latter overlooks the water, aka the springs).

CHEF ART SMITH'S HOMECOMIN': Created by Chef Art Smith, Homecomin' is a "farm to fork" restaurant, showcasing the flavorful bounty of the Sunshine State. The menu has Southern favorites such as Low Country shrimp and grits, deviled eggs, and Art's famous fried chicken. Desserts are made daily and delivered by a bakery in Florida's Hamilton County. Guests (over age 21 with proper ID) can quaff creative libations—including signature moonshine craft cocktails—from the adjacent Southern Shine bar.

SPRINKLES CUPCAKES: "The world's first cupcake bakery," as dubbed by Food Network, the Beverly Hills–based Sprinkles now serves said signature cakes, slow-churned ice cream, and cookies here at Town Center. The handy cupcake ATM dispenses treats 24/7.

FRONTERA COCINA: Six-time James Beard winner Chef Rick Bayless has brought his signature gourmet Mexican cuisine to Disney Springs' Frontera Cocina. The eatery features Mexican specialties such as handcrafted tortas, tacos, salads, and classic Mexican braised meat entrées, all lovingly prepared with locally sourced ingredients. Margaritas, specialty cocktails and craft beers, wine, and soft drinks are served. To save ten percent off your visit, use the coupon at the back of this book.

Retail Roundup

Disney Springs, Town Center may look retro-elegant, but the shopping opportunities here are markedly *au courant*. Treasure-seekers may peruse wares at these retail locations:

ALEX AND ANI • American Threads • Anthropologie • Coach • Coca-Cola Store • Columbia Sportswear • Edward Beiner • Ever After Jewelry Co. & Accessories • Everything But Water • francesca's • Free People • Harley-Davidson • JOHNNY WAS • Johnston & Murphy • kate spade new york • Kiehl's • Kipling • LACOSTE • Levis • Lilly Pulitzer • L'Occitane En Provence • Lucky Brand • Luxury of Time by Diamonds International • M·A·C Cosmetics • Melissa Shoes • Na Hoku • Oakley • ORIGINS • PANDORA • Ron Jon Surf Shop • Sephora • Shore • Sperry • Stance • Sugarboo • Superdry • Tommy Bahama • Tumi • UGG • Under Armour • UNIQLO • UNOde50 • Vera Bradley • Volcom • Zara

For details about these and other Town Center shopping destinations, visit *disneysprings.com*.

BoardWalk

A stroll along Disney's BoardWalk Resort is a journey back in time. Inspired by the Middle Atlantic seaside attractions of the early 1900s, BoardWalk recaptures the carefree atmosphere of that bygone era. The resort is surrounded by restaurants, clubs, and amusements similar to those enjoyed by beach-goers of yesteryear. It's bordered by a wood-planked walkway that hugs the shore of Crescent Lake. By day, BoardWalk is a peaceful place to soak up sun, enjoy lunch, or simply walk the boards. After dark, the place turns into a twinkling center of nighttime activity—some of it elegant, some of it downright raucous.

Classic midway games of the BoardWalk challenge onlookers to test their luck and skill, while strolling performers enchant passersby of all ages with magic shows, balloon tricks, or other antics.

BoardWalk is open to everyone. Although there is no admission price, individual venues may charge a cover. There is a $33 charge for valet parking (even for guests staying at a Walt Disney World–owned-and-operated resort). Self-parking was free at press time, but subject to change. For dining details, refer to this book's *Good Meals, Great Times* chapter.

CLUBS

ATLANTIC DANCE HALL: This is a lovely atmosphere in which to dance the night away. A deejay cranks up tunes, tempting guests to twist and shout on the spacious dance floor. Request your favorite music videos and bust a move while they play on the big screen.

In addition to traditional cocktails, the club serves specialty drinks. Sample one in the "big room" or on the waterfront balcony.

Guests must be 21 or older, with a legal photo ID, to enter. There was no cover charge at press time, but that could change. Hours are generally 9 P.M. until 2 A.M., Tuesday through Saturday.

ESPN CLUB: A casual sports bar/restaurant, ESPN aims to please sports enthusiasts of all kinds. It has a broadcast facility, table-service eatery, and a bar.

Nearly 100 TVs broadcast sports events, so guests always know the score. (Need to make a pit stop at a crucial moment of the game? Don't sweat it . . . there are even TVs in the bathrooms.)

As you enter the club, you're at The Sidelines area. You can catch a game on a TV above the "penalty box" bar or sit at a nearby table. Beer, wine, and soft drinks are served, as is the usual (and some unusual) pub fare.

Sports Central, the main dining area, has a big screen showing—what else?—the big game. The kitchen is usually open until 11:30 P.M. for meals, midnight for appetizers and desserts.

While ESPN Club does accept weekday lunch reservations, it's primarily a first-come, first-served establishment. However, it may offer premium seating for select "Big Games." Call 407-566-5656 for reservations.

JELLYROLLS: You might want to warm up your vocal cords before crossing the threshold. They don't call it a sing-along bar for nothing: Guests are expected to sing, clap, and join in the fun at this warehouse home of dueling pianos. You'll hear everything from Gershwin to *Grease*. The piano players take requests, so plan ahead. Write the request—a cocktail napkin will do— and slip it onto the piano. (Although it's not required, we recommend slipping a tip along, too. It'll increase the odds of you hearing the request and help the musicians pay their rent.)

Jellyrolls is open from 7 P.M. until 2 A.M. nightly. There is usually a $15 cover charge to enter. (Note that the cover charge may vary.) To get in, you must be at least 21 years old and willing to prove it. It's often quite chilly in this venue (year-round). Bring a sweater.

Water Parks
Typhoon Lagoon

This splashy playground was inspired by an imagined legend: A typhoon hit a resort village many years ago, and the storm left the village in ruins. The locals, however, were quite resourceful and rebuilt their town as this "wateropolis."

The centerpiece of Typhoon Lagoon is a huge watershed mountain known as Mount Mayday. Perched atop its peak is the *Miss Tilly*, a marooned shrimp boat originally from Safen Sound, Florida. *Miss Tilly*'s smokestack erupts every half hour, shooting a 50-foot flume of water into the air.

The surf lagoon is huge: Giant slides snake through caves, tamer ones offer twisting journeys, and tiny slides delight small kids. Guests under age 14 must be accompanied by someone over age 14.

SURF POOL: The main swimming area holds nearly three million gallons of water, making it one of the world's largest wave pools. The blue lagoon is surrounded by a white-sand beach, and its main attraction is the waves that come crashing to the shore every 90 seconds. Less

adventurous swimmers can loll about in two relatively calm tide pools, Whitecap Cove and Blustery Bay. Life jackets may be borrowed for free.

CASTAWAY CREEK: The "creek" is a 2,100-foot circular river that winds through the park and offers a lazy, relaxing orientation to Typhoon Lagoon. Tubes are the best way to make the trip along the three-foot-deep waterway. Guests pass through a rainforest, where they are cooled by mists and spray; through caves and

HOT TIP!

Guests entering Typhoon Lagoon are subject to a thorough security check. All bags will be checked and a metal detector will be used. All weapons—including toys—are strictly prohibited.

grottoes that provide welcome shade on hot summer days; and through an area where "broken" pipes from a water tower unleash refreshing showers. There are several exits along the way. It takes 20 to 35 minutes to ride around the whole park.

CRUSH 'N' GUSHER: This "water coaster" thrill ride is one of a kind. In it, daredevils are whisked along a series of flumes and tossed and turned as they weave through an abandoned tropical fruit factory. There are three spillways to choose from: Banana Blaster, Coconut Crusher, and Pineapple Plunger.

HOT TIP!

Early birds get the lounge chairs around these parts. If you want to snag a chair at either of Disney's water parks, arrive as close to park opening as possible.

GANGPLANK FALLS, KEELHAUL FALLS, AND MAYDAY FALLS: These white-water rides offer guests a variety of slippery trips, two of them in inner tubes. All of the slides course through caves and waterfalls and past rock work, making the scenery an attraction in itself. Gangplank Falls gives families a chance to ride together in a two- to four-passenger craft.

HUMUNGA KOWABUNGA: These three speed slides, reported to have been carved into the landscape by the historic earthquake, will send guests zooming through caverns at speeds of 30 miles per hour. The 214-foot slides each offer a 51-foot drop, and the view from the top is a little scary. But it's over before you know it, and once-

wary guests hurry back for another try. Guests must be at least 4 feet tall and free of back and neck trouble, heart conditions, and other physical limitations to take the trip. Pregnant women are not permitted to ride.

KETCHAKIDDEE CREEK: Open only to those children 48 inches tall or under (and their adult guardians), this area has small rides for pint-size visitors. All children must be accompanied by an adult. There are slides, fountains, waterfalls, squirting sea life, a mini-rapids ride, an interactive tugboat, and a grotto with an inviting veil of water.

MISS ADVENTURE FALLS: A family-friendly raft ride near Crush 'n' Gusher, this attraction takes guests on a tour of treasures and artifacts left behind by Captain Mary Oceaneer, an adventurous treasure hunter who became stranded at Typhoon Lagoon after a big storm. Each watery voyage takes about 2 minutes. Kids under 7 must be accompanied by an adult.

STORM SLIDES: The Jib Jammer, Rudder Buster, and Stern Burner body slides send guests zooming down winding slides, in and out of rock formations and caves, and through waterfalls. It's a somewhat tamer

Admission Prices

Prices do not include sales tax and are subject to change. **Note:** Admission is an option with a Magic Your Way ticket that includes a Park Hopper Plus add-on, and is also included with a Premium Annual Pass.

	ADULT	CHILDREN*
One-Day Ticket	$69	$63
Annual Pass	$139	$139

* 3 through 9 years of age; children under age 3 free. Tickets allow for park-hopping, provided both water parks are open on day of admission.

ride than Humunga Kowabunga, but still offers a speedy descent. The slides are about 300 feet long, and each offers a different view and experience.

SURFING: Surf clinics are offered on select mornings before the park opens. (It's challenging, but a hoot if you can get the hang of it.) For more information, call 407-WDW-SURF (939-7873).

ESSENTIALS

WHEN TO GO: Typhoon Lagoon gets very crowded early in the day. Hours vary seasonally, but the park is generally open from 10 A.M. to 5 P.M., with extended hours in the summer months. All of the park's pools are heated in the winter. Note that this water park is usually closed for refurbishment during certain winter months. The park may also close due to bad weather (including lightning and chilly temperatures). Selfie sticks are not permitted. Call 407-824-4321 for updates.

HOW TO GET THERE: Bus service begins from Walt Disney World resorts about one hour before the park opens for the day. The buses stop at the park and then at Disney Springs before 10 A.M. After 10 A.M., resort buses stop at Disney Springs and then Typhoon Lagoon. (A bus transfer may be required.) Buses stop running from the water park about one hour after it closes. There is no charge to park here.

DRESS CODE: Swimming attire must be appropriate for a family environment, and free of buckles, rivets, zippers, or exposed metal. Denim and wetsuits are not permitted. For safety, diaper-age children must wear plastic pants and/or swim diapers in all pool areas.

GUESTS WITH DISABILITIES: Disney is committed to providing access and accommodation for as many guests as possible. For specifics about Typhoon Lagoon, visit *www.disneyworld.com*.

FIRST AID: A first aid station capable of handling minor medical problems is located just to the left of Leaning Palms.

LOCKER ROOMS: Restrooms with showers and lockers are close to the entrance. Small lockers cost $10 to rent for the day, while large ones cost $15. Towels rent for $2 (it's okay to bring your own); life jackets and tubes are free.

SMOKING POLICY: Smoking (including e-cigarettes and vaping) is prohibited in all Disney parks. Typhoon Lagoon guests may smoke in a designated area outside the water park's entrance.

WHERE TO EAT: Typhoon Lagoon's two quick-service eateries offer similar fare and outdoor seating. Leaning Palms has burgers, pizza, salads, and snacks. Typhoon Tilly's (open seasonally) serves fish & chips, chicken wraps, BBQ pork sandwiches, and ice cream. Let's Go Slurpin' has frozen drinks and spirits. Guests may bring their own food and drink to enjoy in designated picnic areas. Alcoholic beverages and glass containers may not be brought into the park. Coolers are allowed. Ice packs are permitted, but loose ice and dry ice are not. Refillable Mugs (about $12 each) come with a day's worth of soft drink refills. Mugs may be reactivated for about $8.50 per day for the length of your Walt Disney World stay. For dining details, turn to page 277.

WHERE TO SHOP: Singapore Sal's is set in a ramshackle building left a bit battered by the typhoon. Swimsuits, sunglasses, hats, beach towels, sunscreen, souvenirs, water shoes, snacks, and Typhoon Lagoon logo products are among the available wares.

Blizzard Beach

A wintry, watery wonderland, Blizzard Beach is said to be the result of a freak storm that dropped a mountain of snow onto Walt Disney World, prompting the construction of Florida's first ski resort. When temperatures soared and the snow began to melt, designers prepared to close the resort. But when they spotted an animal sliding down the slopes, they realized that they had created an exciting water adventure park! The slalom and bobsled runs became downhill waterslides. The ski jump is one of the world's tallest (120 feet) and fastest (60 miles per hour) free-fall speed slides.

The centerpiece of Blizzard Beach is the snowcapped Mount Gushmore and its Summit Plummet. Most of the runs are on the slopes of this mountain, which tops out at 90 feet. At the summit, swimmers have a choice of speed slides, flumes, a white-water raft ride, and an inner-tube run. Most guests reach the top of Mount Gushmore via chairlift. The lift has a gondola for guests with disabilities. There are stairs, too. Kids under 14 must be accompanied by a guest over age 14. One-piece bathing suits are best.

HOT TIP!

Guests entering Blizzard Beach are subject to a thorough security check. All bags will be checked and a metal detector will be used. All weapons—including the toy variety— are strictly prohibited.

CROSS COUNTRY CREEK: This meandering 3,000-foot waterway circles the entire park. A slow current keeps visitors moving merrily along. Inner tubes, which are free, are the most pleasant way to travel. The ride includes a trip through a bone-chilling ice cave, where guests are splashed with the "melting ice" from overhead.

DOWNHILL DOUBLE DIPPER: Guests travel down these two parallel 230-foot-long racing slides at speeds of up to 25 miles per hour. The partially enclosed water runs feature ski-racing graphics, flags, and time clocks. You must be 48 inches tall to ride.

MELT-AWAY BAY: A one-acre pool at the base of Mount Gushmore, the "bay" has its own wave machine. There are no tsunamis here, however, just pleasant, bobbing waves—perfect for leisurely floating and body surfing.

RUNOFF RAPIDS: On this inner-tube run, guests careen down three twisting, turning flumes in a single or double tube.

SKI PATROL TRAINING CAMP: An area designed for preteens, Frozen Pipe Springs looks like an old pipe and drops sliders into eight feet of water. The Thin Ice Training Course tests agility as kids try to walk along broken "icebergs." At the Ski Patrol Shelter, guests under 60 inches grab on to a T-bar for an airborne trip. At any point in the ride they can drop into the water below. Ski patrol participants also experience Cool

Runners, where riders can count on hurtling and whirling over lots of moguls on twin inner-tube slides. No bunny slopes for these brave daredevils.

SLUSH GUSHER: This double-humped waterslide offers a brisk journey through a snowbanked mountain gully. Topping out at 90 feet, Slush Gusher is the tallest slide of its kind. You will find it on Mount Gushmore, next to Summit Plummet. Guests must be at least 48 inches tall to take the plunge.

SNOW STORMERS: A trio of flumes descends from the top of the mountain. Guests race down (headfirst while lying on a mat) on a switchback course that includes ski-type slalom gates.

SUMMIT PLUMMET: This thrilling ride begins 120 feet in the air on a platform 30 feet above the top of Mount Gushmore. Brave souls (who are at least 48 inches tall) hurtle down a 350-foot slide at a rate of about 60 miles per hour.

THE CHAIRLIFT: Guests may ascend to the top of Mount Gushmore via chairlift, provided they are at least 32 inches tall and acrophobia-free. The alternate way to reach the top is by using the stairs. Once at the summit, adventurers can access Slush Gusher, Teamboat Springs, and Summit Plummet. There is a

gondola available for guests with disabilities. Just ask a Cast Member (park employee) for assistance.

TEAMBOAT SPRINGS: One of the longest group white-water raft rides in the world, Teamboat Springs sends guests down 1,200 feet of splashy twists and turns. The gravity-fueled propulsion sends rafts careening down the slide, rotating randomly as it moves along. Each raft accommodates 4 to 6 passengers. If you have fewer than 4 guests in your party, you may be asked share a raft with other people.

TIKE'S PEAK: A kid-size variation of Blizzard Beach, this attraction features miniature versions of Mount Gushmore's slides and a snow-castle fountain play area. Adults must be accompanied by a child to enter this zone. Kids must be under 48 inches to enjoy most attractions in this area.

TOBOGGAN RACERS: An 8-lane waterslide sends guests racing over a number of dips. They lie on their stomachs on a mat and travel headfirst down the 250-foot route.

ESSENTIALS

WHEN TO GO: As a guest favorite, Blizzard Beach gets very crowded early in the day. Hours vary seasonally, but the park is generally open from 10 A.M. to 5 P.M., with extended hours in summer.

All pools are heated in winter. The park is often closed for refurbishment during certain winter months. Know that it may also close due to inclement weather (including lightning and chilly temperatures). For schedules, call 407-WDW-PLAY (939-7529).

HOW TO GET THERE: Blizzard Beach may be reached via motor coach from all Walt Disney World resorts. A transfer may be required. Parking is free.

DRESS CODE: Swimming attire must be appropriate for a family environment, and free of buckles, rivets, zippers, or exposed metal. Denim and wetsuits are not permitted. For safety, diaper-age children must wear plastic pants and/or swim diapers in all pool areas.

PHOTO BY JILL SAFRO

GUESTS WITH DISABILITIES: Disney is committed to providing access and accommodation for as many guests as possible. The water parks offer wheelchairs at Guest Relations. There is no charge to borrow one, but valid government-issued photo ID must be presented before doing so. Quantities are limited and subject to availability. For further information on all services provided at Blizzard Beach, visit *www.disneyworld.com*.

LOCKER ROOMS: There are restrooms with showers near the main entrance. Other restrooms and dressing rooms are located around the park. Small lockers cost $10 for the day, while large lockers cost $15. Towels rent for $2 (outside towels are permitted), and life jackets and tubes may be used for free.

FIRST AID: Minor medical problems are handled at this station near the main entrance (between Beach Haus and Lottawata Lodge).

WHERE TO EAT: Burgers, flatbreads, rice bowls (tofu or chicken), salads, and drinks are sold at Lottawatta Lodge. Kids selections include chicken strips and rice bowls with chicken. Avalunch offers hot dogs, sandwiches, and chef salads, while The Warming Hut stand has sandwiches and jumbo turkey legs. Polar Pub has soft drinks and adult beverages. Frosty the Joe Man Coffee Shack serves coffee drinks. Frostbite Freddy's sells loaded beef nachos, orange swirl cones, and more. There are picnic areas for those who pack their own food. Alcohol and glass containers may not be brought into the park. Coolers (smaller than 24 inches long, 18 inches high, and 15 inches wide) are allowed. Ice packs are permitted, but loose ice and dry ice are not. All-Day Refillable Mugs (about $12 each) come with a day's worth of soft drink refills. Mugs may be reactivated for about $8.50 a day for the length of your stay. For dining details, see page 228.

SMOKING POLICY: Smoking (including e-cigarettes and vaping) is prohibited in all Disney parks. Guests may smoke in a designated area outside the park entrance.

WHERE TO SHOP: Beach Haus stocks bathing suits, T-shirts, shorts, sunglasses, hats, sunscreen, beach towels, snacks, and more. It's also the place to inquire about same-day Polar Patio rental (refer to the Hot Tip on page 230 for details).

Admission Prices

Prices do not include sales tax and are subject to change. **Note:** Water Park admission is an option with a Magic Your Way ticket that includes a Park Hopper Plus add-on, and is also included with a Premium Annual Pass.

	ADULT	CHILDREN*
One-Day Ticket	$69	$63
Annual Pass	$139	$139

* 3 through 9 years of age; children under age 3 free. Tickets allow for park-hopping, provided both water parks are open on day of admission.

Fort Wilderness

In a part of the state where campgrounds tend to look like dried pastures—barren and drab—the Fort Wilderness Resort and Campground, located almost due east of Disney's Contemporary resort, is an anomaly—a forested, 750-acre wonder of tall slash pines, white-flowering bay trees, and ancient cypresses hung with Spanish moss. Native Americans from the Seminole tribe of Florida once hunted and fished here.

There are more than 800 campsites arranged in several campground loops (including sites that are big-rig ready). There are more than 300 Wilderness Cabins (which fall into Disney's "moderate" resort category) available for rent, completely furnished and fitted with all the comforts of home. For additional information about the cabins, refer to the *Transportation & Accommodations* chapter of this book.

HOT TIP!

While Imagineers continue to build Reflections—A Disney Lakeside Lodge, Tri-Circle D Ranch and associated activities may be relocated within Fort Wilderness. Activities mentioned on these pages may be suspended for some or all of 2020. For updates, visit *disneyworld.com* or call or 407-824-4321 or 407-939-7529.

Scattered throughout the campground loops are sporting facilities, including two tennis courts and many small playgrounds, basketball, tetherball, and volleyball courts. Fort Wilderness has riding stables (with rather mellow horses), two swimming pools, a marina full of boats, a canoe livery, bikes and golf carts for rent, and a scenic nature trail. Some facilities are available to Fort Wilderness guests only (including, but not limited to, swimming pools; some are open to everyone).

There's a pony farm (which offers rides to young guests for a fee) and a barn that's home to the horses that pull the Magic Kingdom's Main Street trolleys. The barn houses a small museum that celebrates horses and the cherished role they've played in Disney history.

Two stores—the Settlement Trading Post and the Meadow Trading Post—stock campers' necessities, a limited supply of groceries, and souvenirs. And then there's Pioneer Hall, the home of the Hoop-Dee-Doo Musical Revue dinner show (described in this book's *Good Meals, Great Times* chapter). This rustic structure (made of white pine shipped from Montana) also houses a popular (and reasonably priced) buffet restaurant and a small lounge area. Another dinner show, Mickey's Backyard BBQ, has been suspended while Imagineers construct Reflections—A Disney Lakeside Lodge.

ARCHERY: It takes a steady hand to hit the bull's-eye at the Fort Wilderness Archery Experience. After a brief training session led by a skilled guide, participants (age 7 and up) get to shoot for that coveted bull's-eye. Cost is about $45. To book the Fort Wilderness Archery Experience, call 407-WDW-PLAY (939-7529).

SWIMMING: There are two pools for campers' use. The Meadows Pool complex has a twisting slide and water play area. Note that the pools are open to Fort Wilderness guests only. Swimming and wading are not allowed at the beach (due to a naturally occurring bacteria found in many Florida lakes, and the presence of native wildlife such as alligators and snakes).

BIKE RENTALS: Bike rentals at Fort Wilderness have been temporarily suspended due to construction in the area. Guests are welcome to rent bikes at any WDW resort that offers the service. Bikes cost about $10 per hour or $20 per day. Florida law mandates that all guests age 16 and under wear helmets when biking.

BLACKSMITH SHOP: The pleasant fellow who shoes the draft horses that pull trolleys in the Magic Kingdom park is on hand most mornings to answer questions and talk about his job; occasionally, guests may even watch him at work, fitting the big, friendly animals with the special polyurethane-covered, steel-cored horseshoes that are used to protect the animals' hooves. The Blacksmith Shop is located at the Tri-Circle-D Ranch. Details may change in 2020.

BOATING: Fort Wilderness is ribboned with tranquil canals that make for peaceful canoe trips of one to three hours. Canoe rentals are available at the Bike Barn for about $13 per hour. For a trip around Bay Lake, zippy little Sea Raycer motorboats, Boston Whaler Montauks, and pontoon boats are available for rent at the marina, at the north end of the campground (not far from the Settlement Trading Post). They may be used to cruise on Bay Lake and the adjacent Seven Seas Lagoon. (Refer to the *Sports & Recreation* chapter for details.)

CAMPFIRE SING-ALONG: Held nightly (weather permitting) near the Meadow Trading Post at the center of the campground, this evening program features Disney movies, a sing-along, and a marshmallow roast. Chip and Dale often put in an appearance. It's open to WDW resort guests only. There is no charge to attend, but marshmallows and s'mores kits come with a small fee. You may roast your own marshmallows for free. (They're usually available for purchase at the Meadow and Settlement Trading Posts.)

CARRIAGE RIDES: Guests may enjoy a relaxing carriage ride through the picturesque grounds of Fort Wilderness or the Port Orleans Riverside resort. The rate for each 25-minute ride is $55.

Carriages can hold up to 4 adults, or 2 adults and up to 3 small kids. Reservations are a must. Rides are offered nightly. Call 407-WDW-PLAY (939-7529) for information or to make a reservation. Walk-up reservations are sometimes possible. (Ask the driver about buying tickets. If they're available, expect to pay with cash, MagicBand, or Disney Resort ID. Credit cards are not accepted.) Rides may be canceled due to inclement weather. Cancellations must be made at least 24 hours ahead to avoid paying full price.

Guests are picked up in front of Crockett's Tavern at Pioneer Hall or by the marina at Port Orleans Riverside. Feel free to bring your own liquid refreshments.

ELECTRIC CART RENTALS: Available at Reception Outpost (for about $67 per night) for sight-seeing or

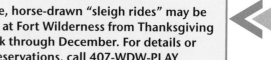

HOT TIP!

Festive, horse-drawn "sleigh rides" may be offered at Fort Wilderness from Thanksgiving week through December. For details or reservations, call 407-WDW-PLAY.

transportation. Renters must be at least 18 years old and have a valid driver's license. Reservations are recommended for electric cart rentals (and can be made up to one year in advance); call 407-824-2742.

FISHING EXCURSIONS: Disney's restrictive fishing policy means plenty of angling action—largemouth bass weighing two to eight pounds, mainly—for fishing excursion participants.

The price ranges from approximately $235 to $270 for up to five people for a two-hour trip and about $455 for a 4-hour excursion. Cost includes gear, a guide, and soft drinks (guests may not bring food on fishing excursions); no license is required. Life jackets will be provided and are required at all times for guests age 13 and under. It is recommended that adults wear life jackets, too. The price varies based on time of day, with the early-morning trips commanding the highest rate. Solo anglers may be able to book an afternoon excursion at a reduced rate.

All WDW fishing is strictly catch-and-release. Call 407-WDW-BASS (939-2277) for exact times and to make reservations. Guests may use their own equipment, but the price is the same. To stretch your Walt Disney World fishing dollar, use the coupon at the back of this book.

CANAL FISHING: Fort Wilderness is the only place on Walt Disney World property where canal fishing is allowed. In addition to bass, catfish and panfish can be caught here as well. Those without their own gear will find rods and reels for rent at the Bike Barn. No license is required. Fort Wilderness resort guests may toss their lines in right from the shore (canals only). All WDW fishing is strictly catch-and-release.

PLAYGROUNDS, VOLLEYBALL, TETHERBALL, AND BASKETBALL COURTS: These are scattered throughout the camping loops. There is no charge to use courts.

ELECTRICAL WATER PAGEANT: Originally presented for the dedication of the Polynesian Luau dinner show in 1971, this cavalcade of lights is presented nightly on the waters of Bay Lake and the Seven Seas Lagoon. The pageant consists of two strings of seven barges, each carrying a 25-foot-tall screen of lights featuring King Neptune and creatures of the sea. And it's all set to

music. The show can be seen from the beach at Fort Wilderness, as well as from the Contemporary, Grand Floridian, and Polynesian Village resorts. (We've caught it while waiting for the monorail at the Magic Kingdom, too.) Ask for the schedule at your resort's Lobby Concierge desk. Details are subject to change.

PONY RIDES: This enclave behind Pioneer Hall is home to some friendly ponies. Pony rides, offered seasonally, are available between 10 A.M. and 5 P.M. for $8 (cash only). Riders must be at least 2 years old and under 48 inches tall. The weight limit is 80 pounds. Kids must be able to hold on by themselves. A parent or guardian leads the pony. The farm is a good place to visit before experiencing Hoop-Dee-Doo Musical Revue (for details, see page 315).

TENNIS: Two tennis courts are available; play is on a first-come, first-served basis.

TRAIL RIDES: Guided horseback trips depart five times daily from the Trail Blaze Corral and take riders on a leisurely, meandering ride through the Florida wilderness, where it is not uncommon to see birds, deer, and even an occasional armadillo. Galloping is not part of the experience, so you don't need riding know-how to sign up. The cost is about $55 per person. Children under age 9 are not allowed to ride. Parents must sign consent forms for kids under age 18. The weight limit is 250 pounds. Sturdy footwear with defined heels are recommended; open-toed shoes are not permitted. Reservations are necessary; call 407-WDW-PLAY (939-7529) up to 180 days in advance.

TRI-CIRCLE-D RANCH: This corner of Fort Wilderness is the place that the world champion Percherons and draft horses that pull trolleys down Main Street in the Magic Kingdom call home. WDW guests are welcome to stop in and say hello. The Tri-Circle-D insignia above the barn door—two small circles atop a large one with a letter D inside—is the WDW brand. The barn is also the site of a museum that pays tribute to horses and their role in Disney history. The laid-back ranch is also home to the Dragon Calliope—the horse-drawn musical instrument that Walt Disney purchased for the Mickey Mouse Club Circus Parade at Disneyland Park in the 1950s. It's quite impressive.

WAGON RIDES: The wagon departs from Pioneer Hall at 6 P.M. and 8:30 P.M. and carries guests on a trip through wooded areas near Bay Lake. Each ride lasts about 25 minutes and concludes at Pioneer Hall. Purchase tickets from the wagon ride host/driver (cash only): $12 for adults, $8 for kids ages 3 through 9. Children under age 12 must be accompanied by an adult. Reservations are not accepted, so get there early.

Group wagon rides are available by calling 407-824-2832 (at least 24 hours in advance). The price is about $300 per hour. Note that wagon rides may be canceled due to inclement weather.

WILDERNESS BACK TRAIL ADVENTURE: A 2-hour "off-road" Segway tour of Fort Wilderness, this experience costs about $95 per person. Guests must be at least 16 years old, with valid photo ID. For details, refer to page 238 or call 407-WDW-TOUR (939-8687).

ESSENTIALS

HOW TO GET THERE: From outside Walt Disney World, take Magic Kingdom Exit 64B off I-4 onto U.S. 192 and follow signs for Fort Wilderness Resort & Campground. This is the most expedient way to go, even for Walt Disney World resort guests.

By WDW Transportation: Buses or boats. Buses can get you just about anywhere, but allow yourself plenty of travel time—the transportation system, while quite efficient, is time-consuming.

Water taxis are also available to and from the Magic Kingdom (it's about 30-minute ride, give or take), as well the Contemporary and Wilderness Lodge resorts (about a 25-minute ride).

WHERE TO EAT: For a description of the Trail's End restaurant and its take-out service, refer to the *Good Meals, Great Times* chapter.

The Settlement Trading Post, located near the beach at the north end of the campground, and the Meadow Trading Post, near the center of Fort Wilderness, offer a small supply of food staples. For serious grocery shopping, head to a nearby supermarket (ask the lobby concierge for driving directions), or order supplies from *www.gardengrocer.com*.

Tours and Programs

Here's your chance to experience Walt Disney World from the inside out. Adult guests may be required to carry a photo ID when attending backstage programs. Tours and prices are subject to change in 2020. For information or to make reservations, call 407-WDW-TOUR (939-8687) between 8 A.M. and 8 P.M. (daily) and have your credit card handy. Cell phone use and photography are not permitted while in "backstage" areas of Walt Disney World. Prices quoted do not include tax. For details on the Star Wars Guided Tour, a 5.5-hour adventure at Disney's Hollywood Studios, refer to the Hot Tip on page 183 and visit *disneyworld.com*, or use the My Disney Experience mobile app. Plan to arrive at least 15 minutes before each tour's scheduled start time—or risk being left behind.

BACKSTAGE MAGIC (Monday through Friday; 9 A.M.): This is one of the World's best programs. Highlighting the nearly 8-hour exploration of Disney's four theme parks may be an underground tour of the Magic Kingdom's Utilidors—Disney's tunnel system. Lunch—at Tiffins in Disney's Animal Kingdom—is included, as are a few surprises. Cost is $275, plus tax. Park admission is not required or included. Guests must be at least 12 years old. This is one of the most popular Walt Disney World experiences—book early.

BEHIND THE SEEDS (Daily; every hour between 10:30 A.M. and 4:30 P.M.): An opportunity for guests of all ages to get a closer look at the greenhouses and fish farm that are part of The Land pavilion at Epcot. During the tour, guests will have close encounters with insects and plants. A guide shares knowledge of hydroponics growing systems and crops from around the globe. Expect to be on your feet for the full hour of this experience. The cost is about $25 per adult, $20 per child (ages 3–9). This tour is best enjoyed by sturdy adults and older kids. Reservations may be made in advance or at the tour desk on the lower level of The Land (near the entrance to the Soarin' Around the World attraction). Theme park admission is required.

CARING FOR GIANTS (Daily; groups depart between 10 A.M. and 4:30 P.M.): Guests of all ages are introduced to the majestic world of African elephants in this 60-minute backstage experience. The elephant experts share strategies for day-to-day care of the gentle giants, plus a host of fascinating facts. African cultural representatives are also on hand to share stories about Disney's conservation efforts in their homeland. All the while, guests observe Animal Kingdom's elephant herd from a distance of just 80 to 100 feet. Cost is about $30 per person. Please check in at least 15 minutes prior to the scheduled start of the tour. Park admission is required, but not included with the cost of the tour.

DISNEY'S FAMILY MAGIC TOUR (Monday, Tuesday, Friday, and Saturday; 10 A.M.): Families and friends may join in this 2-hour "scavenger-hunt-style" quest to save the Magic Kingdom. Cost is $39 (it's available to all guests, but is recommended for parties with kids between the ages of 4 and 12). Magic Kingdom admission is required but is not included with the cost of the tour.

DIVEQUEST (Tuesday–Saturday; 4:30 and 5:30 P.M.): The highlight of the 3-hour program is a 40-minute underwater adventure—complete with sharks, turtles, rays, and other fish—in The Seas with Nemo & Friends aquarium. Participants must show proof of current scuba certification. Cost is about $180. Guests ages 10 to 12 must dive with a parent or guardian. Gear is provided. Epcot admission is not required or included.

DOLPHINS IN DEPTH (Tuesday–Saturday; 9:45 A.M.): This 3-hour Epcot program (about 30 minutes of it takes place in the water) teaches guests about dolphin behavior as they interact with the social sea creatures and observe researchers and trainers working with them. Cost is about $199 per person. The minimum age is 13. Guests ages 13 to 17 must be accompanied by a paying adult. Epcot admission is not required or included. Wet suits are provided; you must wear your own swimsuit underneath the wet suit.

EPCOT SEAS AQUA TOUR (Tuesday through Saturday; 12:30 P.M.): This is a 2½-hour program (about 30 minutes of which is in the water) that lets guests learn about and interact with ocean life in The Seas with Nemo & Friends pavilion. First, guests watch a video about sea creatures, then they join them in their habitat using a Supplied-Air Snorkel system. Cost is about $145. All gear is included, as are a souvenir gift and a photo of yourself in dive gear. Guests must wear swimsuits. The tour is open to guests age 8 and up. Epcot admission is not required or included.

KEYS TO THE KINGDOM (Daily; departing at 8, 8:30, 9, 9:30 and 10 A.M.): A 5-hour tour, it offers an on-site orientation to the history and workings of Walt Disney World's original theme park, the Magic Kingdom. Guests visit an attraction (waiting in the regular attraction line) and take a peek at the Utilidors (the legendary tunnels underneath the park). Cost is about $99, plus theme park admission. Lunch is included. Guests must be at least 16 years old to participate. Keys to the Kingdom Tour is an outdoor walking tour, so check the weather forecast and dress appropriately.

THE MAGIC BEHIND OUR STEAM TRAINS (Sunday–Thursday; 7:30 A.M.): Billed as a "fun- and fact-filled foray into the fascinating world of steam trains," this 3-hour tour gives guests an inside look at the Walt Disney World Railroad. In addition to an exploration of Walt Disney's passion for steam trains, guests visit the backstage "roundhouse," where the steam trains are stored, discover what it takes to keep

PHOTO BY JILL SAFRO

the antique wonders in working order, and observe Disney engineers as they go about their daily routine. Guests must be at least 10 to take the tour. Cost is about $54 per person. Theme park admission is required but not included in the tour price.

SAVOR THE SAVANNA (Daily; 4:30, 5:30, and 6:30 P.M.): A private, guided journey, this experience is limited to 12 guests per excursion. The evening safari adventure begins with a journey deep in the heart of Harambe Wildlife Preserve. It offers secluded viewing areas of the savanna, plus a sampling of African-inspired, tapas-style nibbles and regional wines, beer, and soft drinks.

Cost is approximately $169 per person, plus tax. (The price includes food, drinks, and a keepsake.) Guests must be at least 8 years old to participate in this walking program. Animal Kingdom admission is required but is not included in the tour price.

STARLIGHT SAFARI AT DISNEY'S ANIMAL KINGDOM LODGE (Nightly; 8:30 P.M. and 10 P.M.): When the sun goes away, the animals come out to play. This night-time adventure takes place on the African savannah at Disney's Animal Kingdom Lodge, but it's available to all guests over the age of 8. The adventure takes place in a rugged, open-sided safari vehicle. Hang on as the car rumbles through the savannah! Thanks to a handy night-vision device, guests can observe 30 different species of African wildlife—including zebras, giraffes, gazelles, wildebeest, and antelopes—during the approximately one-hour tour.

PHOTO BY MIKE CARROLL

Wild Africa Trek

A thrilling, 3-hour adventure, the Wild Africa Trek is not for the faint of heart or those with any trepidation about teetering high in the air on a rickety rope bridge.

The guided tour, which is offered daily at Disney's Animal Kingdom park, is a VIP safari adventure for groups of 12 or less. It includes hiking through a jungle, near the edge of a cliff, and riding over the savanna—plus many up-close encounters of the animal kind.

Available to guests age 8 and above, the rain-or-shine trek costs vary, depending on the season, and includes snacks (you can't bring your own) and an access code to view and download digital photos. Park admission is required but not included. This is a very active experience—be sure to wear comfortable shoes and attire. Note that there are no "chicken exits" here. For information, use the My Disney Experience app or website, or visit *www.disneyworld.com*. To make a reservation, call 407-939-8687.

Guests who wish to participate in a less physically taxing journey or a wheelchair-accessible trek may call 407-938-1373 to request an alternative offering.

The cost is about $75 per person, with a portion going toward Disney conservation efforts. Guests under age 18 must be accompanied by a guest age 18 or older. For your safety, you should be in good health and free from high blood pressure; heart, back or neck problems; motion sickness or other physical conditions that could be aggravated by this adventure. Expectant mothers should not participate. The safari vehicles are equipped for rain, but the Starlight Safari may be canceled due to inclement weather. The adventure takes place at the Kidani Village part of Disney's Animal Kingdom Lodge.

THE UNDISCOVERED FUTURE WORLD (Monday, Tuesday, and Saturday; 8:30 A.M.): Walt Disney dreamed about making the world a better place. In this 4-hour tour, guests are taken back to the creation of Epcot and learn about Walt's lofty ambitions and his legacy.

Guests walk to Future World pavilions and learn how each area celebrates humanity's accomplishments and challenges. The goal is to share the vision behind the park.

Cost is about $69 per person. Guests must be at least 16 years old to participate in this walking program. Park admission is required but is not included. Details are subject to change.

UP CLOSE WITH RHINOS (Daily; 11 A.M.): Guests over the age of 4 may enjoy a close-up encounter with the world's second-largest land mammal in this one-hour backstage experience at Disney's Animal Kingdom theme park. In it, guides introduce the park's white rhinos, offer fascinating insights into the species' behavior and biology, and discuss the challenges that threaten populations in the wild. The cost is about $40 per person. Park admission is required, but not included with the tour. Check in at 10:45 A.M. at the Curiosity Animal Tours kiosk, located across from the Kilimanjaro Safaris attraction entrance.

WALT DISNEY: MARCELINE TO MAGIC KINGDOM (Wednesday–Sunday; 8 A.M.): Explore how events in Walt Disney's life helped shape the Walt Disney World Resort and the attractions within it in this 3-hour walking tour. As one of Walt's final visions, the Magic Kingdom shares many similarities with the story of his life. By using the park as a walking timeline, guests discover how Walt's life inspired him to create some of the most cherished stories and attractions the parks have to offer. Guests also get an insider look at several of those aforementioned attractions. Tours cost $49 per person (plus park admission). Guests should arrive 15 minutes early and wear their most comfortable walking shoes (expect to cover a lot of ground). It's available to guests age 12 and older. (Guests under age 18 must be accompanied by a paying adult over age 18.)

WANYAMA SAFARI (daily; 3:30 P.M.): A 3-hour experience, the Wanyama Safari includes a 90-minute private tour of the animal savannas surrounding Disney's Animal Kingdom Lodge. Following the tour, guests have dinner at Jiko—The Cooking Place. (It's a family-style meal.) This tour is open to all guests age 10 and older. Cost is about $209 per person. (Price includes tax and gratuity.) The Wanyama Safari may be booked up to 180 days in advance. Use the My Disney Experience mobile app or website, visit *www.disneyworld.com*, or call 407-938-4755 for details or to make a reservation.

WILDERNESS BACK TRAIL ADVENTURE (Usually offered Tuesday–Saturday at 8:30 A.M. and 11:30 A.M.): A 2-hour experience, this adventure lets guests explore the Fort Wilderness area while aboard a Segway personal transporter. (It's a special model with off-road-type tires.) The first hour is devoted to training (it's not as easy as it looks), with the second spent exploring with a story-telling guide. Guests must be at least 16 years old and in good health. (You'll be on your feet the whole time, and operating the Segway requires more muscle than one might expect.) The cost is about $95 per person.

WORLD SHOWCASE: DESTINATIONS DISCOVERED (Monday, Tuesday, Friday, and Saturday; 8:15 A.M.): A 4½- to 5-hour walking tour of Epcot's World Showcase, DestiNations Discovered covers the culture, architecture, and design details of several of the park's international pavilions. Lunch is included at the Rose & Crown dining room in the United Kingdom pavilion. The cost is about $109 per person. Epcot admission is required, but not included. For additional tour information, visit *www.disneyworld.com*, use the My Disney Experience mobile app or website, or call 407-939-8687.

YULETIDE FANTASY (seasonal): A festive 3½-hour experience, this program showcases the way Disney weaves stories and folklore into decorations found in the theme parks and resorts. It offers a unique perspective on how colors, textures, architecture, and illusions help all of Walt Disney World deck the halls for the holidays.

The cost is about $139 per person. Theme park admission is not included or required for this experience. Guests must be at least 12 years old to participate in Yuletide Fantasy. All guests must present a photo ID.

Daredevil Disney

You've catapulted through the galaxy on Space Mountain, braved an encounter with an angry Yeti at Expedition Everest, and become something of a human yo-yo on the Tower of Terror. Now what? Believe it or not, there are plenty of thrills awaiting you outside the theme park gates. Some of them, such as the wedgie-inducing slides at the water parks, are well known. Others may be lower key, but they're definitely high octane. Here's a rundown of our favorite theme-park-alternative thrills.

Ballooning: Going up! A huge, tethered, helium balloon (run by Aerophile—"The World Leader in Balloon Flight") lifts guests 400 feet high into the sky. Moored to a landing at Disney Springs West Side, the balloon can accommodate up to 29 guests at a time—treating all to sweeping panoramic views of Walt Disney World and beyond. It operates on a first-come, first-served basis Sunday through Thursday from 8:30 A.M. until 11 P.M. and from 10:30 A.M. until midnight on Friday and Saturday. Adults pay about $20 per flight, while children (ages 3 through 9) pay about $15. Expect to be airborne for about 8 to 10 minutes. This high-flying attraction does not operate during windy or inclement weather.

Motorboating: If you've been to Disney World before, you've no doubt seen folks tooling about in zippy little motorboats. But have you ever actually given one a try? It's an experience we recommend.

For starters, the watercraft known as Sea Raycers are indeed speedy. And it's an experience everyone can enjoy—though guests need to be at least 12 years old and at least 5 feet tall to drive. Expect to pay about $32 for a half hour (for up to two passengers), $40 for 45 minutes, and $45 for one hour. (Prices do not include tax.) A signature from a parent or guardian is required for all drivers between the ages of 12 and 18. Be sure to wear a watch, as you're apt to lose track of time. For more info, turn to page 246.

Surfing: When the sun comes up, so does the surf at Disney's Typhoon Lagoon. On select days, guests can take part in a surf clinic taught by competitive surfers. Instructors control the height of the waves—and they give Mother Nature a run for her money.

If you've never hung ten before, know this: It ain't easy. But once you've managed to get up on a board, it's a blast. Lessons are offered before the water park opens for the day.

For more information, call 407-939-7873.

Just for Kids

Walt Disney World may appeal to the kid in all of us, but some activities are meant for the actual young—not just the young at heart. With the exception of the Princess Tea Party, the following programs are specifically for guests who can't remember life before smartphones. (Grown-ups can relax while their kids are entertained.) The programs are quite popular and accommodate a limited number of guests—so book early: 407-WDW-PLAY (939-7529). Note that the adventures listed are not offered every day. Reservations are required and are available up to 180 days in advance. Prices and other details are subject to change in 2020.

ALBATROSS TREASURE CRUISE: Thar be treasure at Crescent Lake! Kids are invited to follow clues and join in the hunt. The 2-hour quest takes young adventurers to several stops as they explore the aforementioned lake, as well as Epcot's World Showcase Lagoon. It includes a reading of "The Legend of the Albatross." The ship weighs anchor at the Yacht Club marina on select mornings at about 9:30 A.M. Cost per child is about $39 or $49 (depending on the time of year) and includes a drink and a light snack. It's open to potty-trained guests (no pull-ups) ages 4–12. Participants should wear socks and sneakers at all times. Epcot admission is not included nor required to participate in this treasure cruise.

PONY RIDES: Young cowpokes can ride petite ponies at the Tri-Circle-D Ranch at Disney's Fort Wilderness Resort and Campground. Guests must be at least 2 years old under 80 pounds, no taller than 48 inches, and able to hold on by themselves. Closed-toe shoes are a must. A guardian leads the pony. Rides are offered from 10 A.M. until about 4 P.M. daily. Cost is $8 per child; cash only. Reservations are not accepted.

ISLANDS OF THE CARIBBEAN PIRATE CRUISE: Ahoy there, mateys! In this adventure, young buccaneers board a battered pirate ship at the Caribbean Beach resort's Caribbean Cay—a private, tropical island in the middle of Barefoot Bay. Then they set sail with a seasoned scallywag at the helm! The captain tells tall tales and leads his crew through treacherous waters (okay, they're actually quite calm) on a hunt for treasure. The cost per child is about $39 or $49 (depending on the time of year). It is open to potty-trained guests (no pull-ups) ages 4–12. All cruise participants must wear socks and sneakers. The adventure includes a drink and a light snack. The Pirate Cruise is offered daily (weather permitting) from 9:30 A.M. till 11:30 A.M. *Arrrrrrrrrrrr!*

PERFECTLY PRINCESS TEA PARTY: Young royals (and their grown-up guardians) are encouraged to dress like their favorite princess for this festive tea party, offered on select mornings from 10:30 A.M. to noon in the Garden View Tea Room at Walt Disney World's Grand Floridian resort. The tea party is hosted by Miss Rose Petal, a magical rose from Aurora's garden that has come to life to lead storytelling, sing-alongs, and a princess parade. Guests may take a break from sipping tea and eating cake to visit with Princess Aurora, aka Sleeping Beauty.

All guests between the ages of 3 and 9 get a My Disney Girl doll, dressed as Princess Aurora, plus accessories. The cost for one adult and child (ages 3 to 9) is $334, including gratuity (tax is extra). The cost for each additional child is about $234 (plus tax), while an extra adult pays about $99 (plus tax). If you'd like a child under age 3 to receive the merchandise, they should be listed as a 3-year-old. Reservations are required and may be made up to 180 days ahead.

WONDERLAND TEA PARTY: Fans of Alice and her Wonderland friends will have a blast at this party presented at 1900 Park Fare at Disney's Grand Floridian resort. During the event, kids decorate and eat cupcakes. They are also treated to a story and have tea with the characters. The cost is about $50 per child, ages 4 to 12 (potty-trained). Cancellations must be made at least 24 hours in advance to avoid a $10 per-person fee. The tea party is offered Monday through Friday at 2 P.M.

WDW Spas

Spa Tips

• Reserve treatments far in advance and be sure to confirm all appointments.

• If you'll feel more comfortable with either a male or a female spa therapist, let your preference be known when you make your reservation. The spas will accommodate such requests whenever possible.

• Plan to arrive 30 minutes prior to your appointment. That'll give you time to change and relax. (Arriving late will reduce your treatment time.)

• Guests under age 18 must be accompanied by an adult to enjoy a spa treatment.

• If you're scheduled for a body treatment, leave clothes in a locker. Robes (and slippers) are provided.

• Leave valuables in your resort-room safe.

• Guests are required to keep cell phones and electronic devices turned off at all times.

• It's always smart to take a shower before a treatment—especially if you've been at the beach or running around theme parks.

• Drink plenty of water after your spa visit. It will counter any dehydrating effects you may experience as the result of a treatment.

• Build time into your schedule to enjoy post-treatment relaxation time at the spa. You'll want to hold on to that glow as long as possible! Bathing suits are required for whirlpools, steamrooms, and other areas.

• Like most spas in the real world, Disney spas add a 20 percent gratuity with each spa service. Additional gratuities may be added at your discretion.

• Cancellations must be made more than 4 hours in advance to avoid paying full price.

For many guests, a day at the theme parks is an exciting test of physical endurance—complete with sprinting (say, from Dumbo to Splash Mountain before that Fastpass+ time expires), weightlifting (toting tired toddlers), and long-distance hiking (covering more than a mile to reach the American Adventure from Epcot's front gate—and back again!). Fortunately, there are many ways to rest and rejuvenate weary bones, throbbing feet, and noise-addled noggins. Chief among them is a visit to a soothing spa (aah). There are four such spots on Disney property, open to all Walt Disney World visitors.

SENSES, A SPA AT DISNEY'S GRAND FLORIDIAN RESORT: You don't need a magic wand to make your stress disappear—not if you can pay a visit to the Grand Floridian pampering palace, Senses. In addition to the treatments offered at its sister spa at the Saratoga Springs resort (see page 241), this spot offers a selection of packages. Among them: the 3-hour Me Time Magic (de-stress bath, massage, organic facial, and pedicure), Gentleman's Retreat (featuring a facial, custom massage, manicure, and pedicure), and the Spa for Two package (custom firm massage for two and pedicure for two).

Services include facials for women, men, and teens, including a Berry Bliss facial and a Tropical Coconut Cream facial; revitalizing aromatherapy baths, and an herbal body-toning wrap. Massage options include: Swedish, warm stones, warm bamboo, foot and leg, and one specially designed for expectant mothers. Manicures, pedicures, and additional hand and foot treatments are also available. There are manicures for youngsters, too.

Treatment hours are usually 8 A.M. to 8 P.M. Friday through Sunday, 9 P.M. to 6 P.M. Monday through Thursday. Prices start at about $145 for a 50-minute massage and $140 for a facial, plus 20 percent gratuity. To book an appointment at the Grand Floridian spa, call 407-WDW-SPAS (939-7727). For further details, visit *https://disneyworld.disney.go.com/spas/*.

MANDARA SPA AT THE DOLPHIN:

BIRNBAUM'S ★BEST★ As exotic as it is peaceful, Mandara is on the must-do list for all guests looking to swap their stress for a big, relaxed smile.

Mandara specializes in treatments meant to reflect the "beauty, spirit, and traditions of both Eastern and Western cultures." The spa menu showcases Balinese massage, a variation of Swedish massage. It incorporates stretching, "vigorous yet relaxing" movements, and elements of acupressure. Of course, that's just one of many services offered here—all of which emphasize physical wellness and spiritual well-being. Other treatments include the Mandara customized massage, Hot Stone Therapy massage, and the Mandara Deep Tissue Muscle massage. The Elemis Superfood Pro-Radiance Facial ($145 for 50 minutes) is a nutrition boost for stressed skin. And the exotic Musclease Aroma Spa Ocean Wrap ($135 for 50 minutes) envelops the body in an aromatic seaweed mask to relieve stiff joints and muscular tension. Prices do not include (20 percent) gratuity.

In addition to Balinese-inspired architecture, two interior gardens provide retreats before guests begin the spa ritual. The goal here is to provide a place for guests to rejuvenate their minds as well as those aching "I can't believe I covered four theme parks in two days!" muscles. For more information, call 800-227-1500 or 407-934-4772, or visit *www.swandolphin.com*.

SENSES, A SPA AT DISNEY'S SARATOGA SPRINGS RESORT:

Just as Saratoga Springs in New York was developed around the healing mineral waters of the springs, this spa incorporates the healing powers of nature into its design and theming. Services include the ultimate facial to hydrate and revitalize skin (105 minutes) and a warm bamboo massage (75 minutes), the 4-hour Senses Signature package (massage, facial, and pedicure), and the "Berry Bliss Facial" (50 or 80 minutes). Also on tap: Swedish massage, warm-stone massage, and rejuvenation treatments focused on the hands and feet, plus body wraps and scrubs. Manicures, pedicures, and organic facials are options, too. Prince and princess pedicures are offered to kids ages 4 through 12 (when accompanied by an adult).

Located on the peaceful shore of Lake Buena Vista, the spa is near the Fitness Center at the Saratoga Springs resort. The hours are generally from 8 A.M. to 8 P.M. A 50-minute massage starts at about $145, with facials going for about $140 (plus gratuity). A variety of packages

is available. For more information and to make reservations, call 407-WDW-SPAS (939-7727).

THE SPA AT FOUR SEASONS RESORT ORLANDO:

The luxe, serene spa at the sprawling Four Seasons Resort Orlando evokes the natural sanctuary of Florida's Everglades. Expect to be revitalized with spa pleasures like the Citrus A'Peel facial and the exclusive Sticks and Stones therapy that massages and relaxes with sculpted basalt stones and birchwood massage sticks. This spa oasis in the midst of Disney's exclusive Golden Oak enclave features 18 tranquil treatment rooms, including couples' rooms and bungalows.

A truly special warm Healing Honey Treatment (50 minutes) uses local, raw, pure honey for a luxurious massage and immune booster; the 80-minute version adds head-to-toe exfoliation with Himalayan salt and organic tea leaves. Complimentary spa extras include an impressive fitness center and the unique-to-Florida Experience Shower with settings including "arctic mist," "island storm," "tropical rain," and even thunder and lightning effects.

Magical Moments experiences for girls and boys offer choices ranging from the Shining Knight salon grooming with "royal crown, sword of truth and shield of courage" ($40) to the Princess & Queen "Mommy & Me" salon and makeup extravaganza ($475). Yes, a princess dress and fairy dust are part of the package.

Treatment hours are 8 A.M. to 8 P.M. daily. Prices start at $175 for a 50-minute facial and $170 for a massage (plus 20 percent gratuity). For additional information and to make reservations, call 407-313-6970. Details are subject to change.

Internet Access at WDW

We are happy to report that all Walt Disney World resorts offer free in-room, wireless Internet access. (The signal isn't always strong, but the price is right.) Of course, you'll need to supply the hardware. Complimentary Wi-Fi (wireless fidelity) is also offered at all Walt Disney World theme parks, water parks, and Disney Springs. Naturally, your phone, tablet, or computer, must be Wi-Fi ready. Note that in-room, wireless Internet service is also available at the Four Seasons Orlando and the Walt Disney World Swan and Dolphin resorts.

If you'd like to access a computer but didn't pack your own, ask your Lobby Concierge to direct you to the nearest resort business center. There you can e-mail, upload, download, and print to your heart's content. Fees vary—be sure to inquire before you start using business center services.

WDW Specialty Cruises

At Walt Disney World, every evening ends with a bang—which comes in the form of pyrotechnic spectaculars. Two such presentations, the Magic Kingdom's Happily Ever After fireworks show and Epcot's extravaganza, are seen by scores of park-goers on a nightly basis. However, these displays are also enjoyed by a privileged few, far removed from the hubbub of theme park crowds yet close enough to marvel at the subtleties of each brilliant burst. These are the guests who choose a specialty cruise. This vintage vantage point is available to all, provided that rates don't break the budget and that reservations are made. Of course, there is the other extreme: a moonlit cruise on the quiet waterways of the World. This option is also available to guests who book a specialty cruise.

Reservations are accepted 24 hours to 180 days ahead. Guests are advised to make reservations as far in advance as possible. While specifics may change, the following is an indication of what was available at press time.

THE GRAND I: This striking 52-foot Sea Ray Sedan Bridge yacht escorts up to 18 guests at a time. A 3-hour tour of the Seven Seas Lagoon and Bay Lake culminates with a front-row seat for the Magic Kingdom's fireworks whenever possible. (The vessel has an audio feed that allows guests to hear the show's soundtrack.)

The *Grand I* yacht departs from the Grand Floridian, but can stop at the Polynesian Village, Contemporary, Wilderness Lodge, or Fort Wilderness on request. It starts at about $399 (plus tax) per hour to rent, with the per-boatload fee covering up to 17 guests, plus a driver and a deckhand. Butler and private dining service are available (for an additional fee). This is the most luxurious watercraft experience at Walt Disney World. Pricing depends on time of day and is subject to change. Call 407-824-2682 for additional *Grand I* yacht pricing details or to make a reservation.

PONTOON BOATS: More practical than luxurious, Disney's fleet of pontoon boats still delivers a crowd-pleasing cruise experience. The boats, which accommodate up to 10, take guests on tours of the Seven Seas Lagoon and Bay Lake, near the Magic Kingdom, as well as Crescent Lake, near Epcot's World Showcase. Those in the Magic Kingdom area are treated to VIP viewing of the fireworks show (as well as the synchronized music), while Epcot-area cruisers take in that park's new nighttime extravaganza (Epcot Forever) when available.

Pontoon cruises last about one hour. Magic Kingdom fireworks excursions depart from the Grand Floridian, Polynesian Village, Contemporary, Wilderness Lodge, and Fort Wilderness marinas. Epcot cruises leave from the Yacht Club marina. The cost for pontoon cruises (which includes a driver) starts at about $299 to $349, plus tax, per boatload (higher for fireworks cruises). Call 407-WDW-PLAY (939-7529) to make reservations.

Pirates & Pyrotechnics

Avast, ye hearties! There's a pirate–themed adventure at Walt Disney Word: The Pirates & Pals Fireworks Voyage. In it, brave buccaneers board a pirate ship—conveniently moored at the Contemporary Resort marina—and set sail on Bay Lake and Seven Seas Lagoon. Before weighing anchor, participating pirates enjoy unlimited snacks and soft drinks at the Contemporary. They can mingle with Captain Hook and Mr. Smee, who are all too eager to meet the recruits. After a pirate parade, guests board Captain Patch's ship and set sail. The captain will test your knowledge of Disney trivia, sing some sea shanties, and position your vessel in a perfect location to view the Magic Kingdom's fireworks show, Happily Ever After. The cost is about $72 per adult, $43 per child (ages 3 through 9). For more information or to make a reservation for The Pirates & Pals Fireworks Voyage, call 407-939-7529.

SPORTS & RECREATION

"Family fun is as necessary to modern living as a kitchen refrigerator." —Walt Disney

244   WDW Golf

245   Tennis

246   Waters of the World

248   ESPN Wide World of Sport Complex

249   More Sporting Fun

First-time visitors may not realize that Disney provides a plethora of sporting opportunities. Within WDW's nearly 40 square miles, there are more tennis courts than at most tennis resorts and more holes of championship-caliber golf than at most golf centers, plus so many other diversions—from fishing and golf to biking, boating, and horseback riding—that the quantity and variety are matched by few other vacation destinations.

So while the family golfers are pursuing a perfect swing on one of several first-rate, 18-hole courses, tennis buffs can be wearing themselves out on the courts, and anglers can be casting away in hopes of hooking a big bass. Those who prefer to spectate rather than participate can visit a virtual sports mecca at the ESPN Wide World of Sports Complex, an enormous, state-of-the-art facility that hosts an array of sporting events, both amateur and professional. And those who prefer the sedate can treat themselves to a soothing spa treatment.

Instruction, as well as guides, drivers, and assorted supervisors, makes every sport as much fun for beginners as for hard-core aficionados. Moreover, the ready accessibility of Walt Disney World sporting and recreational activities—via an extensive system of (free) public transportation (see *Transportation & Accommodations*)—means that no family member needs to give up playtime to chauffeur others around.

 # WDW Golf

Most people don't immediately think of Disney World for a golf outing. Yet there are superb 18-hole courses here: The Magnolia and the Palm are across from the Polynesian Village resort. Nearby is the Lake Buena Vista course. Its fairways are framed by Saratoga Springs and Old Key West resorts. And the Four Seasons resort boasts a stellar course, too. While the WDW courses won't set anyone's knees to knocking, they're demanding enough to have merited the status of a stop on the PGA Tour tournament trail.

PALM & MAGNOLIA: The wide-open, tree-dotted Magnolia measures 5,127 yards from the front tees, 6,558 from the middle, and 7,516 from the back. The Palm (which was recently redesigned by Arnold Palmer Course Design) is tighter, with more wooded fairways and nine water hazards; it measures 5,213 yards from the front, 6,339 from the middle, and 7,010 from the back. Both courses have received a four-star ("outstanding") rating from *Golf Digest* magazine. The Magnolia and Palm courses share two driving ranges and putting greens.

   Oak Trail: This nine-hole, 2,913-yard layout, is a walking course tucked into a corner within the Magnolia. It was designed for beginners and junior golfers, but it's home to some tough holes, including two par 5s. Many moderate and accomplished golfers enjoy the opportunity to tune up or play a quick 9.

FootGolf enthusiasts will be pleased to know that Disney's Oak Trail is also home to an 18-hole FootGolf course. The family-friendly game—a mix of golf and soccer—requires minimal experience to play. If you can you kick a soccer ball, you're ready for FootGolf. You may rent a ball or bring your own. For details and to reserve tee times, visit *www.golfwdw.com/footgolf*, or call 407-939-4653.

LAKE BUENA VISTA COURSE: Joe Lee's design measures 5,194 yards from the front tees, 6,264 from the middle, and 6,749 from the rearmost markers. Among the shortest of the 18-hole, par-72 courses, it has a fair amount of water, and its tree-lined fairways are WDW's narrowest. The course is well suited for beginners but challenges experienced players. A driving range and putting green are also available.

ESSENTIALS

WHEN TO GO: January through April is peak golfing season. To avoid the biggest crowds, play on a Monday or Tuesday, and tee off in the late afternoons (mornings are very busy when the mercury rises). Summer discounts may apply. From June through late September, guests pay as little as $62 after 11 A.M. After 3 P.M., the price may drop as low as $49. Florida resident, Theme Park Annual Passholder, Military, and Disney Vacation

Club member specials may be offered. Annual golf memberships are also a possibility. Call 407-939-4653 for additional information.

RESERVATIONS: Call 407-WDW-GOLF (939-4653), or visit *www.golfwdw.com*, to confirm rates and to secure tee times. From January through April, morning and early afternoon tee times should be reserved well in advance; starting times after 3 P.M. are often available at the last minute. Reservations must be made with a major credit card. Cancellations must be made at least 24 hours ahead to avoid penalties.

FEES: At the 18-hole courses, greens fees (including a required cart) vary with the course and season. Rates range from about $79 to $129 for day visitors (not staying at a Walt Disney World resort). Rates are usually discounted for guests staying at any resort on WDW property (including Swan, Dolphin, and the Disney Springs Area resorts on Hotel Plaza Boulevard).

Midafternoon rates, known as "twilight rates," may yield discounts. Available throughout the year, twilight rates run about $39 to $69.

The cost for adults to play Oak Trail is $25 to $39 for 9 holes; juniors (17 and under) pay $15 to $19 for 9 holes. Prices don't include tax and are likely to change.

INSTRUCTION: At the WDW Golf Studio at the Palm and Magnolia courses, private 45-minute lessons cost $90 for adults and $60 for juniors (up to age 17). Lessons are customized to all levels of experience. Video analysis may be used. Prices are subject to change. Walt Disney World resort guests may make reservations up to 120 days in advance; call 407-WDW-GOLF (939-4653).

> ## HOT TIP!
> Single-rider, adaptive golf carts and clubhouse accommodations are available for guests with disabilities at all Walt Disney World golf courses. For additional information, visit *www.golfwdw.com*, or call 407-WDW-GOLF (939-4653).

DRESS: Proper golf attire is required. Collared shirts or golf-style collarless shirts are necessary, and any shorts must be Bermuda length.

EQUIPMENT RENTAL: Equipment can be rented at all courses; Disney resort guests pay $40 (plus tax) for clubs, shoes, and two sleeves of golf balls, while non-Disney resort guests pay $65. Photo ID is required for rentals. Range balls are among available items. They cost approximately $7 to $11 per basket.

TRANSPORTATION: Transportation to and from the golf courses is available with complimentary taxi vouchers from Walt Disney World-owned-and-operated resort hotels. (Swan, Dolphin, Four Seasons, and resorts on Hotel Plaza Boulevard are not included in this transportation program—but taxis may be summoned from these properties, too.) Call or go to your resort's Guest Services desk at least 30 minutes prior to your desired pickup time and a Cast Member will call for your taxi. That should give you enough time to get to the course, check in at the pro shop, and spend some time at the range and practice putting green before your round. Complimentary transportation is for regular play only. Vouchers include a gratuity for the taxi driver.

Tennis

Saratoga Springs Resort & Spa has two clay tennis courts. All other Walt Disney World tennis is played on hard courts. The Yacht and the Beach Club share one court; Fort Wilderness, Saratoga Springs, Contemporary's Bay Lake Tower, Animal Kingdom Lodge's Kidani Village, and BoardWalk each have two; and Old Key West has three. Courts are free to guests staying at a WDW-owned-and-operated resort. For details or to make tennis lesson reservations, call 321-228-1146.

ESSENTIALS

WHEN TO GO: Tennis courts are often open from about 8 A.M. to 7 P.M. daily. Weather-wise, January, October, and November are prime months for playing tennis in Florida. All courts are available on a first-come, first-served basis. During very busy periods, the length of time a single group of players can occupy a court is restricted to two hours on any morning, afternoon, or evening.

Equipment rental is limited at Walt Disney World. Call 407-WDW-PLAY for details.

DRESS: Tennis whites are appropriate, but not required, for play on Walt Disney World's courts. Tennis shoes are a must.

Waters of the World

PHOTO BY AMY HENNING

BOATING

Disney World is the home of the country's largest fleet of pleasure boats. Cruising on Bay Lake and the Seven Seas Lagoon can be excellent sport, and a variety of boats are available for rent at WDW resort marinas. Bay Lake excursions originate from the Contemporary, Wilderness Lodge, and Fort Wilderness. The Polynesian Village and Grand Floridian send boaters out from their marinas on the shore of Seven Seas Lagoon. The Yacht & Beach Club, BoardWalk, Swan, and Dolphin share a boating haven in 25-acre Crescent Lake.

To rent, guests must show a valid driver's license or passport. Rental of certain craft may carry other requirements. No privately owned boats are permitted on Walt Disney World waters. All prices and times are subject to change in 2020.

AMPHICARS: It's a car! It's a boat! It's a blast from America's motoring past (the 1960s to be precise). Yep, the amphibious Amphicar is back. Disney has brought nine of these classic vehicles out of retirement and put them back to work at Disney Springs. Doing double duty as artwork/water taxi, Amphicars are next to The Boathouse eatery. Up to three guests may enjoy a 20-minute tour of Disney Springs waterways for about $125 (captain included). Tours are offered from 10 A.M. until 10 P.M. daily, weather permitting. You can save $25 with the coupon at the back of this book.

BOSTON WHALER® MONTAUK BOATS: These 17-foot motorboats are a good choice for relaxing cruises. They accommodate up to six passengers, and may be rented for about $45 per half hour at the Polynesian Village, Contemporary, Grand Floridian, Wilderness Lodge, Fort Wilderness, and Yacht & Beach Club resort marinas.

CANOEING AND KAYAKING: A long paddle down the Fort Wilderness canals is such a tranquil way to pass a misty morning that it's hard to remember that the bustle of the Magic Kingdom is not far away. Craft may be rented at the Bike Barn at Fort Wilderness (about $8 per half hour, $13 per hour). Ocean kayaks (open-top kayaks) may be rented here, too (expect to pay about $8 per half hour, $13 per hour). Note that these watercraft are for use on Fort Wilderness canals only, not for Bay Lake or the Seven Seas Lagoon.

MOTORBOATING: It seems there are always dozens of boats zipping back and forth across Bay Lake, Seven Seas Lagoon, and Crescent Lake. These are called Sea Raycers, and they're just as much fun as they look. The boats are quick enough so that a lot of watery terrain can be covered in a half hour (for about $35), though it's quite tempting to splurge on a full hour.

Sea Raycers can be rented year-round at the Grand Floridian, Polynesian Village, Wilderness Lodge, Contemporary, Yacht & Beach Club, and Fort Wilderness marinas. Guests must be at least 12 years old and 5 feet tall to rent Sea Raycer boats. Kids under the minimum age and height may ride as passengers, but they're not allowed to drive. We suggest that drivers wear a waterproof watch—it's amazing how the time flies!

PADDLE BOATS: These Swan-shaped watercraft are free for registered guests staying at the Swan or Dolphin resorts. For all other guests, the boats rent for about $7 per half hour or $11 per hour at the Dolphin marina. The majestic, pedal-powered vessels are available daily from 11 A.M. until 5 P.M. Details are subject to change.

PONTOON BOATS: Motorized, canopied platforms on pontoons are perfect for families, inexperienced boaters, and visitors more interested in serenity than in speed. Available at select resort marinas, the 21-foot craft hold up to ten passengers and cost about $45, plus tax, per half hour. Guests must be at least 18 years old (with a valid driver's license) to pilot a pontoon boat. The maximum weight per boat is 1,900 pounds.

SWIMMING: Although the beachfronts are strictly for strolling, sunbathing, and sand castle construction, swimmers may splash in one of the many elaborately themed pools that come in every shape and size imaginable. Typhoon Lagoon and Blizzard Beach water parks only add to the fun (refer to the *Everything Else in the World* chapter for water park specifics).

Walt Disney World resorts have at least one pool apiece. With the exception of sister resorts (Yacht & Beach Club; Port Orleans French Quarter and Riverside; All-Star Movies, All-Star Music, and All-Star Sports; and Swan and Dolphin), which share some of their recreational facilities, Disney hotel pools are open exclusively to guests staying at the respective resort. This policy was initiated to prevent overcrowding. All pools are heated in winter. Resort guests may borrow life jackets at no cost. Guests who cannot swim should wear life jackets at all times while in or near a pool. WDW resort guests of all ages, but especially the younger ones, may partake in a variety of engaging pool activities throughout the day. For schedules, check at your resort's front desk or at the pool itself.

Featuring one pool each are Animal Kingdom Lodge and Port Orleans French Quarter. The Grand Floridian, Contemporary, Polynesian, Fort Wilderness, the Wilderness Lodge, and All-Stars have two pools each. BoardWalk, Pop Century, and Art of Animation have three pools; Coronado Springs, Old Key West, and Saratoga Springs all feature four swimming holes; Port Orleans Riverside has six, and Caribbean Beach has seven. The Yacht & Beach Club resorts share three unguarded pools, plus a small water park known as Stormalong Bay. It features slides, a sand-bottomed wading area, and a lazy river. Saratoga Springs resort has four pools. The Swan and Dolphin share a lovely, themed grotto pool with a slide, one lap pool, and a third smaller pool. In addition, each of the resorts on Hotel Plaza Boulevard has its own pool.

HOT TIP!

Swimming and wading are not permitted in any of Walt Disney World's lakes. The rule is meant to protect guests from unguarded water and from exposure to naturally occurring bacteria and dangerous wildlife, such as snakes and alligators, common to Florida lakes.

Lifeguards are on duty during most daylight hours at each WDW resort's main pool, with the exception of the Swan and Dolphin (where all swimming is at your own risk). Keep an eye on youngsters at all times and use life jackets for little ones and weak swimmers.

FISHING

The 70,000 bass with which Bay Lake was stocked in the mid-1960s have grown and multiplied as a result of WDW's restrictive fishing policy. (It's strictly catch-and-release.) No angling is permitted on Bay Lake or the Seven Seas Lagoon, except on the guided fishing expeditions. Largemouth bass weighing two to eight pounds are the most common catch.

Excursions are presented by BASS, the world's largest fishing organization. Guests who participate in a WDW fishing excursion receive a one-year BASS membership, which includes 11 issues of *Bassmaster* magazine, a membership pack, decal, handbook, eligibility to compete in national events, discounts, and other benefits. You can save 20 percent off a 2-hour fishing excursion with the coupon at the back of this book.

Bay Lake excursions depart daily; call 407-WDW-BASS (939-2277) for details. Trips last two or four hours, accommodate up to five anglers, and include guide, gear, and refreshments (soft drinks). Guides will pick up guests at the Contemporary, Grand Floridian, Polynesian Village, Fort Wilderness, and Wilderness Lodge. Guides will pick up guests at Old Key West, Saratoga Springs, and Port Orleans Riverside and French Quarter, too. Kids under age 16 must be accompanied by an adult (over age 18).

Anglers might also consider two-hour tours that depart from the Yacht & Beach Club at 7 A.M., 10 A.M., and 1:30 P.M. All trips accommodate up to five people. A guide, gear, and soft drinks are included.

The Magic Kingdom resorts also offer two-hour excursions on pontoon boats that accommodate one or two guests. They depart from the resort marinas at 7 A.M., 10 A.M., and 1:30 P.M. daily. The $235 to $455 price includes equipment and a guide.

Reservations must be made at least 24 hours in advance and may be made up to 180 days ahead; call 407-WDW-BASS (939-2277). Note that excursions may be canceled or cut short if the weather is stormy or there is lightning in the vicinity of Walt Disney World.

Fishing on your own—remember, it is strictly catch-and-release—is permitted in the canals at Fort Wilderness. Fort Wilderness guests may toss in lines from any campground canal shore. Fishing licenses are not required. Rods and reels ($6 for 30 minutes) and cane poles ($4 for 30 minutes) are available for rent at the Fort Wilderness Bike Barn. Live bait may be purchased (worms and night crawlers cost about $6).

ESPN Wide World of Sports Complex

Variety is the name of the game at the ESPN Wide World of Sports Complex. The multimillion-dollar complex invites athletes and spectators alike to dive into more than 70 types of sporting experiences. It's a grand slam for die-hard sports fans.

The 220-acre facility—which is teamed up with ESPN—hosts events in everything from jump rope to wrestling. The home of the Pop Warner Super Bowl is also the site of the National Cheer & Dance championships.

Designed as a modern vision of old-time Floridian building styles, the architecture harks back to days when sports facilities were convenient extensions of their neighborhoods; there is even a town commons (which serves as a welcome center).

The sports complex includes a baseball stadium; a field house that accommodates basketball, wrestling, and volleyball; a track-and-field complex; tennis courts; and multipurpose fields fit for football, soccer, and more.

A general-admission ticket costs about $19 for adults and $14 for kids ages 3 through 9. Tickets may be purchased at the front gate and allow guests to watch all  "nonpremium" events. Guests are only admitted on days when events are scheduled. Tickets to premium events may be purchased through Ticketmaster (call 800-745-3000; or pay a visit to *www.ticketmaster.com*) and include general admission to the complex.

Premium-event tickets may also be purchased at the Wide World of Sports Complex box office on the day of an event, depending on availability. Prices vary from event to event.

ESSENTIALS

HOW TO GET THERE: Direct bus transportation is available at All-Star, Pop Century, and Caribbean Beach resorts (based on the events scheduled). Other Walt Disney World resort guests must take a bus (plan to transfer at a park or Disney Springs) to one of these resorts. Allow at least 90 minutes for the commute (more if you are attending a premium event). Buses run Thursday through Monday from 5 P.M. until about 11 P.M. Walt Disney World resort buses also run when events are taking place, starting about one hour prior to complex opening time, until 11 P.M. or the time the sports complex closes (whichever is later).

If you are driving, take Exit 65 off I-4 to Victory Way. The complex is between U.S. 192 and Osceola Parkway. Parking is free but limited. If you plan to attend a premium event, arrive as early as possible—or risk scrambling for a spot in an unpaved, auxiliary lot.

WHERE TO EAT: The big-ticket eatery here is ESPN Wide World of Sports Grill. (It's open on most event days.)

There are more than 30 concessions for those seeking a somewhat lighter bite. They offer hot dogs, burgers, sandwiches, snacks, soft drinks, and beer, as well as a few more substantial—yet just as portable—snacks.

Guests can pre-order boxed meals, pizza, and drinks. There is a minimum of $50 and all orders must be placed at least two days prior to the event. To place your order, go to *www.espnwwos.com*, or call 407-566-6698.

Touch Base

Get the scoop on all the scheduled action at the ESPN Wide World of Sports Complex by calling 407-541-5600 or visiting the website *www.espnwwos.com*.

More Ways to Have Fun

ARCHERY: Channel your inner Robin Hood at a Fort Wilderness program known as the Archery Experience. The 90-minute experience includes a quick but thorough lesson and lots of shooting time. It takes place every Thursday through Saturday at 2:45 P.M. Available to guests age 7 and older, the Archery Experience costs about $45 per person (plus tax). It may be booked up to 180 days in advance by calling 407-939-7529.

BASKETBALL: Guests may shoot hoops at 7 basketball courts at Walt Disney World resorts. There's no fee to play, and equipment may be borrowed by WDW resort guests (with valid ID). Courts, which range in size from quarter- to full-size, may be found at the following resorts: Animal Kingdom Lodge—Kidani Village (half-court), Contemporary, Grand Floridian Resort & Spa (half-court), Disney's Old Key West, Saratoga Springs Resort & Spa, Fort Wilderness Resort & Campground (quarter-size), and the Walt Disney World Swan (near the lap pool).

BIKING: Bikes are also available for rent year-round at Old Key West, Port Orleans, Caribbean Beach, Board-Walk, Yacht & Beach Club, and Saratoga Springs. The cost is about $10 an hour or $20 per day. Bikes with training wheels or baby seats are available. Helmets are mandatory for guests up to age 16 (but recommended for everyone) and may be borrowed for free. Note that bike rentals are temporarily suspended at Fort Wilderness Resort & Campground and Wilderness Lodge while Imagineers continue to build Reflections— A Disney Lakeside Lodge.

MINIATURE GOLF: The Fantasia Gardens Mini Golf complex, located near the Swan, Dolphin, and Board-Walk resorts, offers players two 18-hole courses themed to the Disney film *Fantasia*. The Fantasia Fairways course offers a difficult layout sure to tantalize serious golfers. It features traditional golf obstacles, such as water hazards, doglegs, and roughs. Don't be fooled by the small size of the Fantasia Fairways course—its challenges are big. (The record for the par-72 course is 47.)

Fantasia Gardens, on the other hand, is all in fun, with clever things (a dancing hippo, xylophone stairs, brooms dumping buckets of water) at every hole. The degree of difficulty varies from hole to hole, but this is an easy course to conquer. There are some serious challenges out there, however. Hole number 15, for example, is one of the trickier ones. Here, golfers aim through mini-geysers that randomly squirt water into the air. Good luck with that!

Disney's Winter Summerland miniature golf course is a mere stone's throw from the Blizzard Beach water park (they share a bus stop). Designed as a vacation retreat for Santa and his elves, the two 18-hole courses boast a festive atmosphere, complete with Christmas carol soundtracks. The sandy-surface course is a bit more challenging than its snowy-surface counterpart.

A round on any course costs about $14 for adults, $12 for kids ages 3 through 9. The second round is 25 percent off. Typical playing time is about an hour. Operating hours are generally 10 A.M. to 11 P.M. but vary seasonally. For information, call 407-WDW-PLAY (939-7529).

MOVIES UNDER THE STARS: Let's all go to the movies! Walt Disney World–owned-and-operated resort hotels offer free, nightly screenings of favorite Disney flicks. With the exception of Fort Wilderness Resort & Campground, which presents films in a mini amphitheater setting, movies are presented on a blow-up screen in an outdoor space. While snacks are typically not provided, feel free to bring your own. The show goes on rain or shine, with the fun moving indoors should the weather be rainy or otherwise inclement. Each resort has its own weekly movie lineup. The schedule may be posted near the screening location. If not, ask about at your resort's front desk. There is no cost to partake, but all guests must be registered at a WDW-owned-and-operated resort.

SPAS AND HEALTH CLUBS: Health clubs include the Contemporary's Olympiad Fitness Center, Sturdy Branches at Wilderness Lodge, Zahanati at Animal Kingdom Lodge, La Vida at Coronado Springs, Health Club at Saratoga Springs, Muscles and Bustles at Board-Walk, Health Club at the Grand Floridian, Resort Fitness Center at Old Key West, Ship Shape at the Yacht & Beach Club, Athlétique Fitness Center at Riviera, and the fitness center at the Swan. Registered guests may use their respective resort's facility for free. Guests not registered in a resort with a health club can use the facilities for a fee.

In addition to fitness centers, there are full-service spas at the Grand Floridian, Saratoga Springs, Dolphin, Four Seasons Orlando, and Buena Vista Palace resorts. There are special packages available at each location. (See pages 240–241 for details on WDW resort spas.)

PHOTO BY CHRIS HENNING

SURREY BIKES: Go four-wheelin' around Crescent Lake, along the Sassagoula River, down the promenade by Barefoot Bay, or through a rustic woodland trail on a canopied surrey bike built for 2 to 4 (possibly more). Surreys may be rented at the following WDW resorts: BoardWalk, Port Orleans French Quarter & Riverside, Old Key West, and Saratoga Springs Resort & Spa. Each half-hour rental session runs about $25.

RUNNING: Except from late fall to early spring, the weather is usually much too steamy in Central Florida for jogging. If you run very early in the morning in warm seasons, the heat is somewhat less daunting. The 1.2-mile promenade around the lake at the Caribbean Beach resort is ideal for running, as is the three-quarter-mile promenade that surrounds Crescent Lake (a waterway

that's bordered by the Swan and Dolphin, Yacht & Beach Club, and BoardWalk resorts), and the nearly mile-long path circling Coronado Springs' Lago Dorado. Old Key West also has scenic routes, averaging about a mile in length. There are also trails at All-Stars, Grand Floridian, Contemporary, Art of Animation, Port Orleans, and Pop Century resorts. Note that the 2.5-mile trail connecting Fort Wilderness and the Wilderness Lodge will remain closed as Imagineers build a new hotel: Reflections—A Disney Lakeside Lodge.

TRAIL RIDES: Guided horseback rides into pine woods and palmetto country set off from the front of Fort Wilderness four times daily. This trip is not meant for seasoned gallopers—you can't wander off on your own. All of the horses have been culled for gentleness, so trips are suitable for novices. Cost is about $55 per person for a 45-minute tour. Kids under the age of 9 are not allowed to ride, and there's a weight limit of 250 pounds. (Younger kids can saddle up on ponies at the Tri-Circle-D Pony Farm for about $8.) Reservations are necessary and may be made up to 180 days in advance by calling 407-WDW-PLAY (939-7529).

VOLLEYBALL: There are white-sand volleyball courts at the following WDW resorts: Animal Kingdom Lodge (Kidani Village), Caribbean Beach, Contemporary, Coronado Springs, Disney's Old Key West, Polynesian Village, Yacht & Beach Club, Fort Wilderness Resort & Campground, and Swan & Dolphin.

GOOD MEALS GREAT TIMES

"Fantasy and reality often overlap." —Walt Disney

252 In the Theme Parks

278 In Disney Springs

285 In the WDW Resorts

298 Character Dining

314 Reservations Explained

315 Dinner Shows

316 Bars & Lounges of WDW

Although quick-service food is in great supply, it is hardly the entire Walt Disney World dining story. Epcot adds international flavors to the WDW menu. Tempting options at the other theme parks, BoardWalk, and Disney Springs—not to mention new dining frontiers in the ever-growing brood of WDW resorts—make deciding where to eat a mouth-watering dilemma. Disney's ongoing effort to expand its culinary horizons has certainly been successful, producing prominent palate-pleasers such as Monsieur Paul, The Boathouse, Sanaa, California Grill, and Flying Fish, plus family favorites such as The Crystal Palace and 50's Prime Time Cafe.

Because there's such a large number and variety of eateries around the World, this chapter presents dining information in two formats. First, we've included an area-by-area rundown—a comprehensive section with descriptions of food purveyors, including sample menu options, that will prove most helpful when you get hungry in a particular part of the World. Second, we've compiled a collection of what we consider to be the best restaurants in a particular category. To select these standouts, we looked at the menu, theme, price, and overall enjoyability of each restaurant. And, of course, we sampled the food.

Finally, in the chapter's last section, we offer a guide to the varied lounges of the World, along with a briefing on Disney's reservations system and dinner show options—and assurance that great times are destined to follow.

The Restaurants of WDW
In the Magic Kingdom

A lot has changed since Walt Disney World's original theme park opened in 1971. Back then, when it came to quelling hunger pangs, it was pretty much burger or bust. Nowadays, the options are a lot more diverse—with everything from egg rolls to cinnamon rolls, smoked turkey legs to lamb stew, and meatloaf to Maine lobster bisque. And yes, you can still sink your teeth into a burger—beef or falafel! Regardless of tastes or budget, the six "lands" in the Magic Kingdom boast a bounty of palate-pleasers for everyone in the family. Menu specifics are subject to change.

First Things First

The red letters at the end of each entry refer to the meals served there: breakfast (B), lunch (L), dinner (D), and snacks (S).

• When you see a 🐭 at the end of an entry, it means that eatery was a Disney Dining Plan* participant at press time (see page 20).

• **SR** means the eatery is a Disney Dining Plan Signature Restaurant. As such, it requires two table-service meal credits per person, per meal. For **SR** dress code details, visit *www.disneyworld.com.*

• Eateries have been designated inexpensive (under $15 per person), moderate ($15 to $36), expensive ($36 to $60), and very expensive ($60 and up). Prices are based on an adult-sized meal consisting of a beverage, an entrée, and either one appetizer, side, or dessert (not including tax and tip). These classifications are reflected by dollar symbols at the end of each entry. Note that breakfast and lunch may cost less than dinner at some eateries.

• All Disney table-service restaurants and fast-food spots are strictly nonsmoking. Ask a server to direct you to the nearest designated smoking area.

• Reservations for Walt Disney World's table-service restaurants (and dinner shows) can (and should) be made 180 days in advance; call 407-WDW-DINE (939-3463), use the My Disney Experience app or website, or visit *www.disneyworld.com/dining/.*

Menus change often. We recommend a visit to *www.disneyworld.com* to confirm restaurant info.

*Disney Dining Plan locations are subject to change without notice at any time.

ADVENTURELAND
TABLE SERVICE

JUNGLE NAVIGATION CO. LTD. SKIPPER CANTEEN: Known to many as "The Jungle Cruise Restaurant," this jovial joint is run by off-duty Jungle Cruise skippers—and the spirit of the ride permeates the place in a most amusing manner. The menu, infused with Asian, African, and South American influences, has starters such as Ginger's "Croc" of hot and sour soup, Falls Family Falafel, and shumai. Entrées at the Skipper Canteen include sustainable fish, fried chicken, grilled steak, "A Lot at Steak" salad (get it?!), lamb chops, and Sankuru Sadie's Seafood Stew. Soft drinks, beer, wine, and specialty cocktails are served. The eatery opens daily at 11 A.M. **LD•$$–$$$•🐭**

FAST FOOD & SNACKS

ALOHA ISLE: After you sing with the birdies in the nearby Enchanted Tiki Room, stop here for all things pineapple—juice, floats, pineapple upside-down cake, and the ever-popular Dole Whip frozen pineapple soft-serve dessert. This spot has been around forever—they are definitely doing something right. **S•$•🐭**

SUNSHINE TREE TERRACE: This snack stand, across from the Swiss Family Treehouse attraction, lets you take a break with refreshing slushes (raspberry and lemonade), the classic Citrus Swirl (vanilla soft-serve swirled with orange slush), and the new Orange Cream Swirl (vanilla and orange soft-serve twist). The latter are available by the cup or as a float. It's possible to get a cup of vanilla soft-serve, plus soft drinks. The Sunshine Tree has been dishing out treats for as long as we can remember. **S•$**

TORTUGA TAVERN: The mostly covered spot across from the Pirates of the Caribbean attraction offers chipotle barbecue short ribs, jumbo turkey legs, hot dogs served with chips, chocolate chip cookies, and cookies and cream churros. Soft drinks and fruit punch "Pirate Pear" slushies are served. **LS•$–$$•🐭**

HOT TIP!

These eateries accept reservations: Be Our Guest, Cinderella's Royal Table, Crystal Palace, Tony's Town Square, Liberty Tree Tavern, and Jungle Navigation Co. Book as early as possible. Call 407-939-3463, or visit *www.mydisneyexperience.com* for details and reservations.

FANTASYLAND
TABLE SERVICE

BE OUR GUEST: Nestled beneath Beast's castle, this eatery transports guests into the realm of Disney's *Beauty and the Beast*. Guests may sit in one of three dining rooms—the cavernous Grand Ballroom, the mysterious (and dark) West Wing, or the Castle Gallery—and enjoy a quick-service breakfast or lunch or a table-service dinner. (Reservations are required for all meals.) Note that all rooms offer the same menu.

Breakfast and lunch guests enter the Beast's parlor to place their orders at touch terminals. After placing the order, grab some silverware, fill your cups, and snag a table. Servers deliver meals using MagicBand or "enchanted rose" technology. Breakfast selections include braised pork, open-faced bacon and egg sandwiches, scrambled egg whites, and more. The lunch menu includes items such as *croque monsieur* (ham and Gruyère cheese sandwich), potato leek soup, tuna niçoise salad, and vegetable quiche. The portions are a bit smaller and the prices steeper here than at other Magic Kingdom quick-service eateries. The kids' lunch menu includes whole-grain macaroni with marinara sauce, carved-turkey sandwiches, and grilled cheese.

The advance reservation allows access to the restaurant at the reserved time, but does not skip you to the front of the line. Expect a wait of up to 30 minutes to place an order. After placing the order, select a table, fetch your drinks at the beverage bar, and enjoy the ambience while waiting for your food to be delivered.

The prix-fixe dinner is a more upscale affair, with starter selections such as artisanal cheeses, French onion soup, escargot, and Maine lobster bisque. Entrées pay homage to a castle feast with spice-dusted lamb chops, herb-salted pork tenderloin, center-cut filet mignon, and pan-seared sea scallops. Beer and wine are offered with dinner. **BLD•$$–$$$•🐭 SR**

CINDERELLA'S ROYAL TABLE: You don't have to be a royal to eat like one. At least, not in the Magic Kingdom. This regal eatery, tucked inside Cinderella Castle, is a high-ceilinged, majestic mead hall. It's tiny as Disney spots go, but there's no feeling cramped—thanks to a small number of tables and towering windows. Hosts and hostesses wear Renaissance-inspired garb and address guests as "my lady," or "my lord." Cinderella welcomes "Fairytale

One Tough Ticket

Cinderella's Royal Table is consistently one of the most difficult restaurant reservations to secure at Walt Disney World. Why? For starters, Cinderella is one popular princess. And there's the allure of dining in the castle—the most famous landmark in the world's most popular theme park.

Potential guests may make a reservation by visiting *disneyworld.com/dining* or by calling 407-WDW-DINE (939-3463) at *exactly* 7 A.M. Eastern Standard Time, 180 days in advance. (It can't hurt to start dialing a few seconds early.) The meal must be paid for when the reservation is made. There's no charge for infants, but they must be included in the reservation.

Expect your credit card to be charged immediately upon making the reservation. Cancellations or changes to the reservation must be made at least 24 hours ahead to receive a full refund. The only one who can change or cancel a reservation is the one whose name is on the credit card. Reservations cannot be transferred. Guests using the Disney Dining Plan must also book the table with a credit card, but it will not be charged. However, two table-service credits are required for all meals here, as Cinderella's Table is designated a "Signature" restaurant.

Whew! That's a lot of work for one dining experience. Is it worth it? Judging by the smiles we see day in and day out, we have to say yes.

Dining" guests into her home all day and greets them in the Castle lobby, while her princess friends interact with guests in the dining room. Breakfast favorites include shrimp and grits, baked quiche, and caramel apple-stuffed French toast, along with traditional fare. Lunch and dinner showcase seasonal ingredients, with items such as beef tenderloin with shrimp, pork two ways (loin and belly), chicken, and fish. Sparkling wines and Champagne are available, but not included in the price of the meal.

The all-inclusive cost for breakfast is about $73 for adults and about $43 for kids (ages 3–9) during peak times of year; lunch and dinner cost approximately $92 for adults and $53 for kids. Prices include tax and gratuity and may differ depending on the date. Alcoholic beverages are not included. (A photo package is no longer included. Guests may pose with Cinderella and purchase a PhotoPass photo for $15 or use their own camera free of charge.) Reservations are an absolute must. **A 180-day advance booking is necessary for all meals. Full payment is required at time of booking.** Guests of Walt Disney World–owned-and-operated resorts should note our Hot Tip on page 256.

Cancellations must be made at least 24 hours in advance to avoid paying full price. Cinderella suggests that you arrive a few minutes early. This is an extremely difficult table to reserve (see page 253)—don't get little ones' hopes up until you actually book it. Good luck! BLD•$$$–$$$$•♥•SR

FAST FOOD & SNACKS

BIG TOP TREATS: Inside the Big Top Souvenirs tent, this counter offers character apples, caramel apples, cake pops, caramel corn, brownies, cookies, crispy treats, and Goofy's Glaciers (slushy treats). S•$•♥

CHESHIRE CAFE: This small stand is a good spot to cool off with raspberry or lemonade slushies (which come with a souvenir Mickey straw), orange juice, cold brew coffee, hot tea, and bottled water. The cafe also serves pastries. The cold brew coffee makes us smile like the Cheshire Cat. S•$•♥

THE FRIAR'S NOOK: This window sells hot dogs with tater tots, loaded tots, fried cream-filled sponge cakes with sweet sauce, slushies, and soft drinks. Menu items are subject to change. The Nook may operate on a seasonal basis. LS•$–$$•♥

GASTON'S TAVERN: A cozy little lodge nestled in Fantasyland's Enchanted Forest, Gaston's serves sandwiches (ham and Brie or turkey and Swiss), fruit and cheese plates, macarons, chocolate croissants, warm cinnamon rolls, and soft drinks. The specialty of this teetotaling tavern? LeFou's Brew—a not-too-sweet

concoction made from frozen apple juice with a hint of toasted marshmallow and topped with all-natural passion fruit-mango foam. It tends to please palates of all ages. And, yes, Gaston really does use antlers in all of his decorating. LDS•$$•♥

PINOCCHIO VILLAGE HAUS: One of the better spots to target with kids in tow, Pinocchio Village Haus is also a good place to take picky adult eaters. It may seem small from the outside, but there are many dining rooms through that door. One room boasts picture windows that overlook the It's a Small World loading area. It's fun to watch the boats bob by as you munch on lunch. Pinocchio offers flatbreads (aka pizza), chicken parmesan sandwiches and pasta, tomato basil soup, chicken nuggets, antipasto salad, side salad, fries, bread sticks with marinara sauce, and soft drinks. For dessert, there's Italian cream cake and no-sugar-added lemon

Healthier Options

Health-conscious folks need not abandon all restraint for want of suitable sustenance. Walt Disney World has phased out added trans fats and partially hydrogenated oils from food served in parks and resorts. Most WDW restaurants offer low-fat, low-cholesterol, low-salt, low-carb, and vegetarian entrées. Even fast-food stands feature healthier fare such as salads, grilled chicken sandwiches, fresh fruit, and veggie burgers. The WDW trend toward healthier dining extends to kids' meals, too. They come with a beverage choice of low-fat milk, 100 percent fruit juice, or water, and a side dish such as unsweetened applesauce, baby carrots, or fresh fruit. These healthy selections are easy to find on menus throughout Walt Disney World—keep an eye out for the Disney check symbol.

sorbet. Kids' picks include PB&J, chicken nuggets, pasta, and flatbreads, all served with applesauce and yogurt. **LDS•$–$$•**

PRINCE ERIC'S VILLAGE MARKET: Appropriately anchored across from The Little Mermaid attraction, this alfresco snack spot sells grapes, pickles, cookies, doughnuts, turkey legs, and soft pretzels (with or without beer cheese sauce). The prince also proffers bottled beverages and frozen soft drinks. **S•$–$$•**

STORYBOOK TREATS: Ice cream fans enjoy this window next to the Many Adventures of Winnie the Pooh attraction. It offers soft-serve cones and cups (vanilla, chocolate, swirl, and Key lime); hot fudge and strawberry sundaes; plus ice cream floats. Coffee, tea, hot cocoa, and soft drinks are also served. **S•$•**

FRONTIERLAND
FAST FOOD & SNACKS

GOLDEN OAK OUTPOST: This little wagon offers chicken breast nuggets, waffle fries (plain or with chili cheese), barbecue pork rinds, fresh-baked chocolate chip cookies, and assorted soft drinks. **LDS•$–$$•**

PECOS BILL TALL TALE INN & CAFE: Pecos Bill has been feeding hungry cowpokes for more than 40 years. The look has changed over time, as have the offerings

(the prices have gone up a bit, too). These days, Pecos Bill is serving taco burgers, beef nachos, fajita platters, Southwest salad (served plain or with chicken or spicy beef), veggie rice bowl, and "tacos three ways" (soft shell tacos with ground beef, chicken, and spicy beef). Churros and yogurt are available, too. Kids' options include burgers, beef nachos, or mac and cheese, and come with applesauce and carrot sticks and low-fat milk or bottled water. Soft drinks such as soda pop, strawberry lemonade slushies, chocolate milk, coffee, tea, cocoa, and orange juice are served. **LDS•$$•**

WESTWARD HO!: Amble on over to Westward Ho! for chips, chocolate chip cookies, frozen lemonade, and other soft drinks. Corn dogs are offered seasonally. It's across from Prairie Outpost & Supply. **S•$•**

LIBERTY SQUARE
TABLE SERVICE

THE GOLDEN HORSESHOE: An all-you-care-to-eat Saloon Feast is served for lunch and dinner ($38 per adult/$21 per child). Barbecue favorites, which arrive on family-style platters, have included beef brisket, citrus-marinated chicken, BBQ pulled pork, smoked sausage, macaroni and cheese, seasonal vegetables, baked beans, and coleslaw. A sweet ending to the meal may include buttermilk-chocolate cake, apple cobbler, or cheesecake. There is an à la carte menu for lunch. It features sandwiches, salads, and barbecue plates. This venue may operate seasonally. **LD•$$–$$$•**

LIBERTY TREE TAVERN: Step back in time at this Early American tavern where the detailed decor has a tendency to outdazzle the fare. Here, wallpaper looks as if it might have come from Colonial Williamsburg, curtains hang from cloth loops, and the rooms are filled with mementos that might have been found in the homes of Thomas Jefferson, George Washington, and Ben Franklin. The restaurant is aptly located directly across the square from the Hall of Presidents attraction.

The à la carte lunch menu (available from 11 A.M. until 3 P.M. daily) includes Tavern cheese dip, lobster fritters, pot roast, turkey pot pie, meatloaf, fish & chips, lobster rolls, and New England clam chowder. Lunch offers a family-style option, too. The all-you-care-to-eat lunch and dinner feasts feature salad, oven-roasted pork, roast turkey, pot roast, mac and cheese, stuffing, toffee cake, and more—all served family style. The menu also offers beer, wine, and hard cider. Dinner costs about $38 for adults and $21 for children ages 3 through 9. Some beverages—including those of the spirited variety—cost extra. Reservations are recommended (arrive about 20 minutes early). Disney characters do not visit here. **LD•$$–$$$•**

HOT TIP!

Perk alert! If you have a confirmed reservation at a Disney—owned-and-operated resort, you can call 180 days prior to your check-in date and book dining reservations for up to 10 days of your stay. That amounts to getting a 1- to 10-day head start on everyone else.

FAST FOOD & SNACKS

COLUMBIA HARBOUR HOUSE: This lively spot adds some interesting (and healthier) options to the quick-service lineup, including grilled salmon with vegetable rice and steamed green beans and carrots; yogurt, the Lighthouse sandwich (hummus and veggie slaw on multi-grain toast, tuna on toasted multigrain bread (formerly known as the Anchors Away sandwich), and salad (with or without chicken or shrimp). The menu also offers lobster rolls, fried shrimp, chicken nuggets, hushpuppies, mac and cheese, chicken pot pie, vegetarian chili, fries, and New England clam chowder. For dessert, choose seasonal cobbler or Boston cream pie. Kids' selections include salad with chicken, tuna sandwich, mac and cheese, chicken nuggets, and peanut butter and jelly sandwich. Fountain beverages, plus milk, coffee, tea, juice, and lemonade slushies are available.

Disney has done up this food emporium with style—complete with antiques, model ships, harpoons, nautical instruments, and lace tieback curtains. In addition to the chowder, we savor the salmon and love the Lighthouse sandwich. The upstairs dining rooms may be less crowded than those on the first floor. **LDS•$–$$•❤**

SLEEPY HOLLOW: Often missed by guests rushing toward park hot spots, this window has a lot to offer. Breakfast (egg and cheese waffle sandwich) is served until noon. After that, look for sweet and spicy chicken waffle sandwiches, foot-long corn dogs served with housemade chips, waffles with heavenly toppings (fresh fruit, chocolate hazelnut spread, strawberries and whipped cream, etc.), ice cream cookie sandwiches, and funnel cakes (dusted with powdered sugar or strawberries and cream). Drink choices include lemonade with wildberry foam, coffee, hot cocoa, milk, and orange juice. Sleepy Hollow is near the Liberty Square bridge. Eat on the patio and get a stunning view of Cinderella Castle at no extra charge. **BLDS•$–$$•❤**

MAIN STREET
TABLE SERVICE

THE CRYSTAL PALACE: What's the big draw here? Winnie the Pooh and his pals host meals all day. One of the Magic Kingdom's cherished landmarks, this spot takes its architectural cues from a similar structure that once stood in New York and from San Francisco's

Conservatory of Flowers, which still graces that city's Golden Gate Park. The place is spacious, with tables scattered amid a Victorian-style indoor garden complete with flowers and hanging greenery. Tables in the front look out on flower beds, while those at the east end have views of a courtyard. The restaurant is on a path at the end of Main Street, U.S.A.

The all-you-care-to-eat buffet features a variety of breakfast items every morning; for lunch and dinner there's spit-roasted carved meat, chicken, pastas, fish, sides, and desserts. The salad bar, with its peel-and-eat shrimp, pasta salads, greens, and grains, is most satisfying. The cost for breakfast runs about $38 for adults and $23 for kids ages 3 through 9; lunch and dinner is about $52 for adults and $31 for children. Alcoholic beverages are available for an additional fee. Reservations are a must. **BLD•$$–$$$•🐭**

PLAZA RESTAURANT: This windowed establishment next to Plaza Ice Cream Parlor is done up in mirrors with sinuous Art Nouveau frames. Breakfast brings bacon, eggs, waffles, oatmeal, biscuits and gravy, soft drinks and cocktails. Lunch and dinner selections include wedge salad, seasonal soup, burgers (and veggie burgers), meatloaf, and hot and cold sandwiches such as fried green tomato, grilled Reuben, cheese steak, Plaza club, and tuna salad—plus heavenly hand-dipped milk shakes, chocolate cake, and caramel apple pie à la mode. Soft drinks, beer, and wine are offered. Reservations are recommended. **BLD•$$–$$$•🐭**

TONY'S TOWN SQUARE: Tony's decor was inspired by Walt Disney's feature *Lady and the Tramp* (which can be viewed in the waiting area). The menu offers Italian specialties, including calamari, spaghetti, and pizza. Entrées include ravioli (plain or with chicken or shrimp), chicken Parmesan, shrimp scampi, baked rigatoni, braised short ribs, and sustainable fish of the day. If you require gluten-free pasta, just ask—Tony is happy to accommodate. Beer, wine, and sparkling fruit beverages are offered, too. Top it off with an Italian sweet (gelato, tiramisú, cannoli, cheesecake, chocolate cake, or raspberry sorbet) or foamy cappuccino. If you time it right, you can fold your napkin, pay the bill, and

Magic Kingdom Resorts

Is the Magic Kingdom open late when you plan to visit? If so, consider heading over to the Contemporary, Polynesian, Grand Floridian, or Wilderness Lodge to have an early dinner, and then return to finish the day at the park. Each of the aforementioned resorts is reachable by monorail and/or water taxi. Remember to keep sporting that MagicBand if you used it for admission or keep your ticket handy for re-entry into the Magic Kingdom. (You will have to pass through a security check to re-enter the park.) Transportation generally runs for one hour after the park's posted closing time for the day (this does not include Extra Magic Hours). Note that, as with most Walt Disney World eateries, reservations are necessary at resort restaurants. Don't forget to book that table!

mosey out to Main Street to enjoy the fireworks from one of the best vantage points in the park. Reservations are highly recommended. **LD•$$$•🐭**

FAST FOOD & SNACKS

CASEY'S CORNER: Casey's is a grand slam for baseball fans—and those who just happen to love the food associated with "America's pastime," hot dogs. This old-fashioned stop is on the west side of Main Street (near Crystal Palace restaurant). Tables line the sidewalk, where a ragtime pianist often tickles the ivories. There's a room with indoor seating. The fare retains the baseball game mood—hot dogs (plain, chili cheese, mac and cheese, plant-based, and more), corn dog nuggets, fries, brownies, and soft drinks. Hot dogs come in regular and foot-long sizes. Note that it is possible to order some items à la carte. Casey's Corner is a popular spot for a late-night snack, and a Magic Kingdom classic. **LDS•$–$$•🐭**

MAIN STREET BAKERY: This Main Street landmark resembles a turn-of-the-twentieth-century bakery and coffee shop. If the sight of this old-fashioned storefront doesn't lure you in, the aroma most certainly will. The Main Street Bakery is a nice choice for a light breakfast, salads, sandwiches, or coffee break. The vast array of juice, tea, and coffee concoctions comes courtesy of Starbucks. Assorted pastries, fresh-baked cookies, fruit and veggies, smoothies, and other snack items are also served. **BLDS•$–$$•🐭**

PLAZA ICE CREAM PARLOR: Plaza boasts the Magic Kingdom's largest variety of hand-scooped ice cream flavors (we counted 9 on our last visit, including one of the no-sugar-added variety). Tofutti and Rice Dream are available, too. This cheery spot is perfect for a before-the-parade or an on-the-way-out-of-the-park nosh. Guests of all ages enjoy the Mickey Mouse kids' cone. (To keep things moving, select your flavors and desired number of scoops before jumping in line.) They have floats and sundaes—including those served in a waffle bowl and the Mickey's Kitchen Sink for two (which is actually a sink-like version of the Mouse's red trousers). Soft drinks round out the menu. S•$•🐭

HOT TIP!

Tomorrowland Terrace's dessert party offers unlimited snacks and a viewing of Happily Ever After, the Magic Kingdom's fireworks show. Prices vary, but expect to pay up to $79 per adult and $47 per child. For details and reservations up to 180 days in advance, call 407-WDW-DINE (939-3463). The treats are served in the waterside dining area at Tomorrowland Terrace, while fireworks viewing is offered from the dessert party's reserved viewing area on Main Street, U.S.A.

TOMORROWLAND
FAST FOOD & SNACKS

AUNTIE GRAVITY'S GALACTIC GOODIES: Ice cream may not seem futuristic, but chances are it'll be around at least another billion years, give or take. Auntie G's offers strawberry smoothies, soft-serve ice cream in cones and cups (chocolate or vanilla), sundaes and floats. Soft drinks are available, too. There's virtually no atmosphere in this corner of the galaxy, but we still gravitate toward the frozen goodies. S•$• 🐭

COOL SHIP: This spaceship/snack stand is cool for two reasons. First, the water spray it provides during steamy months is beyond refreshing, and second: It serves churros with chocolate dipping sauce. Fountain drinks and assorted bottled beverages are available, too. There is no seating, but Cosmic Ray's has plenty and it's just a hop, skip, and a jump away. S•$–$$•🐭

COSMIC RAY'S STARLIGHT CAFE: Ray's seems to offer something for everyone. Head here for pulled pork sandwiches, grilled chicken club sandwiches, chicken nuggets, plant-based Sloppy Joes, bacon cheeseburgers, chicken sandwiches, Greek salads,

Magic Kingdom Mealtime Tips

• The hours from 11 A.M. to 2 P.M., and again from about 5 P.M. to 7 P.M., are the mealtime rush hours in Magic Kingdom restaurants. Try to eat earlier or later whenever possible.

• When a fast-food spot has more than one station from which to order, don't automatically jump on the nearest queue. Instead, inspect them all, because the registers farthest from an entrance may have the shortest lines.

• It is virtually impossible to snag same-day reservations for Magic Kingdom table-service restaurants (with the possible exception of Jungle Navigation Co. Ltd. Skipper Canteen). Do yourself a favor and book an advance reservation to your desired M.K. eatery.

• Reservations may be made by calling 407-WDW-DINE (939-3463), via *www.disneyworld.com*, or by using the My Disney Experience app. We recommend booking your table as far in advance as possible. That's 180 days before your scheduled visit to the Magic Kingdom! Guests with a confirmed reservation at most Walt Disney World resorts can book up to 10 days' worth of WDW restaurant reservations, starting 180 days before their check-in date.

• Consider taking the monorail or a water taxi to the Contemporary, Polynesian, or Grand Floridian to have dinner in a resort restaurant, and then return to the Magic Kingdom after you eat. Reservations are recommended. Note that it is possible to walk to and from the Contemporary. Allow 10 to 20 minutes each way. And remember to keep your ticket or MagicBand handy for re-entry to the park!

fries, fresh fruit, and s'mores. Kids may choose from PB& J sandwiches, salad with turkey, chicken nuggets, and mac and cheese. An Audio-Animatronics lounge lizard known as Sonny Eclipse entertains in the indoor dining room. There are multiple counters from which to order, but they all serve the same fare. Note that Cosmic Ray's Starlight Cafe has ample indoor and outdoor seating. **LDS•$–$$•❤**

LUNCHING PAD AT ROCKETTOWER PLAZA: If it's a snack or simple meal you're after, stop at the base of the Astro Orbiter located in the center of Tomorrowland's concrete plaza. This quick-service window dispenses barbecue pulled pork sandwiches; hot dogs; warm, cheese-stuffed pretzels; churros, Mickey pretzels; chips; soda slushies; Space Ranger Slush (grape and sour apple-layered slushy served with a candy straw), and soft drinks. **LDS•$–$$•❤**

TOMORROWLAND TERRACE: This stark spot serves simple fare such as burgers, chicken strips, and salads. Some tables on the lower terrace afford views of Cinderella Castle. It operates seasonally. This is the site of the park's popular fireworks dessert party. See the Hot Tip on page 258 for details. **LDS•$$•❤**

HOT TIP!

To help reduce your time spent waiting in line, dozens of WDW quick-service now accept mobile orders. Simply place your order via the (free) My Disney Experience app. As you arrive at the eatery, click the "I'm here" button (in the app) and the kitchen will prepare your order. When your food's ready, you'll get a notification to fetch it by the Mobile Pickup sign at the counter.

Baby Needs

Babies. They're a needy lot. Fortunately, most of the requisite supplies can be found somewhere at Walt Disney World—if you know where to look. Formula and jarred food can be purchased at the Baby Care Centers in the theme parks and all WDW resorts. Most restaurants offer kids' menus with toddler-friendly food (mac and cheese, chicken nuggets, and the like).

If your baby is partial to a specific formula or brand of food, consider shipping a box of it to your hotel before you leave home. (Note that a $6 delivery fee will be charged to your room for every parcel handled by Front Desk personnel.) Keep in mind that there are several grocery stores near Disney property. If you have a car, it is worth the trip (a Guest Relations clerk can help with directions). The selections are more varied, as are the prices. Stash any perishables in an in-room refrigerator—they are standard in all Disney—owned-and-operated resorts. Some other points of interest regarding baby diners at Walt Disney World:

• Most table-service eateries have high chairs and booster seats for little ones. Request them when you make your restaurant reservation. Quick-service spots offer high chairs on a first-come, first-served basis. Ask a Cast Member for assistance if you need help finding or transporting one to a table.

• Stroller use inside restaurants is discouraged due to fire codes. Park it outside.

• WDW restaurants are often chilly. Be sure to pack a sweater or blanket.

• Be it a fast-food or table-service restaurant, take toys to keep youngsters busy.

• The following resorts have 24-hour snack bars: Grand Floridian, Polynesian, Dolphin, Wyndham, and Hilton Buena Vista Palace (on Hotel Plaza Boulevard). The middle-of-the-night pickings may be slim, but milk and cereal are served around the clock.

• If you'd like a comfortable spot to nurse an infant, head to a Baby Care Center in any of the theme parks. They all have rooms with rocking chairs.

• If you're headed for a long day in a theme park, pack simple, healthy snacks for hungry toddlers. And look for the Disney check symbol on menus (see page 254 for details).

• To make your dining experience a little less harried, consider feeding your baby before you arrive at the restaurant.

• If you prefer organic milk (and more) for your children, consider ordering from *gardengrocer.com* or swinging by a local grocery store (for details, see Baby Food on page 47).

The eclectic, international lineup of fare offered here threatens to overshadow the attractions themselves. With no fewer than 11 different countries permanently represented in the World Showcase section of the park, Epcot provides guests with the opportunity to eat their way around the world without leaving Central Florida. Less ambitious diners will likely have all their taste needs met here, too—there's a bountiful food court in Epcot's Future World, as well as a smattering of simple yet satiating snack spots and quick-service eateries. Reservations are a very important factor in the Walt Disney World dining equation, and Epcot is no exception; be sure to book tables as far in advance as possible.

FUTURE WORLD
TABLE SERVICE

CORAL REEF (The Seas with Nemo & Friends): This peaceful, water-themed restaurant is all about nibbling on creatively prepared fish under the watchful eyes of their brethren. The place is decorated in cool greens and blues to complement its surroundings, and every table has a panoramic view of a living coral reef; some are right up against the glass. (Don't worry: You are not actually eating Epcot residents—most of Walt Disney World's catches come fresh from fishing boats each day.) Menu items run the gamut from a bounty of fresh fish and shellfish, including shrimp, mahi mahi, and salmon—prepared in a number of ways—to grilled New York strip steak and roast chicken breast for those who are satisfied by simply spying on the sea life. The menu tends to vary seasonally. Reservations are recommended. **LD•$$$•♥**

GARDEN GRILL (The Land): Garden Grill diners are often so distracted by the sights and the jovial hosts (Chip, Dale, and other Disney pals) that they don't realize the restaurant is actually *moving*. As the eatery slowly revolves, it moves past scenery featured in the Living with the Land boat ride. The view was designed with diners in mind, and provides them with a peek into a farmhouse window that's out of viewing range of the waterborne passengers.

Breakfast includes sticky buns, fruits, scrambled eggs, bacon, sausage, hash-brown-style potato barrels, and Mickey-shaped waffles. For lunch and dinner, the Grill serves salad, pot roast, turkey breast, carved pork with apple chutney, mac and cheese, buttermilk mashed potatoes, herb and leek stuffing, french fries, fresh veggies (some of which are grown inside The Land Pavilion), and shortcake. Cost for breakfast is about $41 for adults, $25 for kids; lunch and dinner run about $52 for adults, $31 for kids. (Prices are higher during peak times of year.) Soft drinks are included. Meals are served family style (communal platters for the table; there is no kids' menu). It's not an especially child-friendly presentation, as gravy is involved (at lunch and dinner) and food items touch and overlap one another. Reservations are recommended.

HOT TIP!

At press time, a new space-themed restaurant was counting down to a grand opening in Future World. The table-service eatery offers internationally-inspired cuisine in an outer-space environment. You'll find it next to the Mission: SPACE attraction. For details and to make reservations, visit *disneyworld.com* or call 407-939-3463.

To recap: This character-hosted, family-style eatery moves in a circle. It's imperceptible to most, but if you are highly sensitive to motion, it may be best to dine in a more stationary environment. **BLD•$$–$$$•**💟

FAST FOOD & SNACKS

JOFFREY'S COFFEE & TEA COMPANY (near the Epcot monorail station): Stop here for a java jolt on your way into or out of the park. This beverage stand specializes in coffee and tea, but it also offers hot cocoa, bottled water, spirited drinks, and baked treats. The coupon at the back of this book will net you a 20 percent savings on your purchase. (The coupon may be redeemed here or at any other Joffrey's Coffee & Tea Company location throughout Walt Disney World.) **S•$**

PHOTO BY JILL SAFRO

SUNSHINE SEASONS (The Land): It's the closest thing to a mall food court you'll find in a WDW park, but a bit more upscale. Located near the entrance to Soarin' Around the World on the pavilion's lower level, Sunshine Seasons is an ideal destination for parties who can't quite agree on any one type of fare—there's bound to be something for everyone. Tables are scattered in several seating areas, beneath colorful hot-air balloons. Snagging a table can be a challenge during peak mealtimes. (There can be a bit of pedestrian congestion, too, thanks to the enormous popularity of the Soarin' Around the World attraction.)

Sandwich Shop is home to the vegan flatbread with grilled vegetables, fish tacos, and more. The **Soup and Salad Shop**'s creative salads include Power Salad (with oak-fired chicken, quinoa, almonds, and honey vinaigrette) and seared tuna with sesame rice wine dressing. Soups are made fresh daily. **Grill Shop** features rotisserie

chicken and slow-roasted pork. Seasonal seafood selections are also offered. **Wok Shop** serves Mongolian beef with fried rice, sweet and sour chicken, and shrimp stir-fry. The **Bakery** offers freshly made desserts. In addition to the seasonally inspired rotating desserts—expect to find brownies, ice cream bars, and other sweet treats. There is a grab-and-go area with items such as wraps, fruit and cheese plates, fresh vegetables, salads, assorted chips, and cookies.

A word of advice: It's a good idea to split up your party and stand in several lines at the same time. That will increase your chances of actually eating together. Before you separate, select a table. That way, everyone in the group will know where to meet after they forage for their meals. It's also a nice spot to take a load off your feet while waiting for your Soarin' Fastpass+ window to kick in. **BLDS•$–$$•**💟

WORLD SHOWCASE
TABLE SERVICE

AKERSHUS ROYAL BANQUET HALL (Norway): The Norwegian castle of Akershus dominates Oslo's harbor and is considered the most impressive of all Norway's medieval fortresses. It is actually half fortress and half palace, and many of its grand halls continue to be used for elaborate state banquets. Inside Epcot's castle-like Akershus, hungry guests are treated to authentic royal Norwegian cuisine. They also get to dine with royalty—as Disney princesses interact with guests all day long.

An all-inclusive price entitles Epcot guests to enjoy dishes that don't often leave Scandinavia. Included in the family-style sampling of the Norwegian *koldbord* are smoked salmon and seafood, Norwegian cheese, and chilled salads. Norwegian-inspired entrées include

HOT TIP!

If you plan to see the park's nighttime spectacular at World Showcase, know that the show generally takes place nightly at 9 P.M. Try to time it so your evening meal winds up no later than 8:45 P.M.—and tell your server when you arrive.

seafood, beef, and poultry selections. A kids' menu is available. Dessert and soft drinks are included.

For breakfast, guests enjoy the all-you-care-to-eat fare (bacon, eggs, potatoes, and sausage are brought to your table) as Disney characters mingle with diners. Belle, Ariel, Jasmine, Snow White, Sleeping Beauty, and Mary Poppins have all popped in. The character appearance schedule varies. Reservations are necessary. Cancellations must be made at least 24 hours in advance to avoid paying the $10 per-person penalty. Breakfast costs about $52 for adults (age 10 and up) and $31 for kids (ages 3 to 9); lunch and dinner run about $63 (adults) and $37 (kids). Prices may be higher during peak times of year. **BLD•$$$•❤**

BIERGARTEN (Germany): Located in the back of the St. Georgsplatz in the Germany pavilion, this tiered eatery is a jolly stop on the Epcot world dining tour. This is partly because of the long tables that encourage togetherness among guests. But equal credit for the *gemütlich* (pleasant) atmosphere goes to the spot's spirited entertainment.

There are appearances by Bavarian musicians—each clad in lederhosen or dirndl—who play accordions, cowbells, a musical saw, and a harp-like stringed instrument known as the "wooden laughter." The entertaining shows take place on a stage in the dining hall throughout the day. Diners are usually invited to join the fun on the dance floor. Little ones love it.

The food is hearty and presented as an all-you-care-to-eat buffet, featuring bratwurst, frankfurters, chicken, spaetzle, seasonal fish, pork schnitzel, assorted cold dishes, warm potato salad, cucumber salad, pretzel rolls, and kid-friendly selections. Entertainment is intermittent and there's plenty of time to enjoy the pleasant setting. Reservations are recommended, particularly during peak seasons. **LD•$$$•❤**

CHEFS DE FRANCE (France): "Bright lights, big dining room" describes this inviting Parisian brasserie. With some of France's best chefs responsible for this kitchen, the results are usually rewarding. The menu features fresh ingredients readily available from Florida purveyors, though the restaurant imports as many key ingredients from France as possible.

The offerings are in the nouvelle French cuisine style, which involves lighter sauces using less cream and butter than in classic French cooking. Menu selections include broiled salmon, beef short ribs, and roasted chicken. Soups and appetizers such as onion soup, lobster bisque, and escargot are all-day staples. Apple tarts (with almond cream, caramel sauce, and vanilla ice cream) and vanilla crème brûlée are dessert specialties of note. Chefs de France is one of the most popular (and pricey) World Showcase eateries. Reservations are recommended (book as far in advance as possible). **LD•$$$–$$$$•❤**

LE CELLIER STEAKHOUSE (Canada): This wine-cellar-like spot is a popular dining destination. The atmospheric eatery has low ceilings, stone walls, and flickers of candlelight. Designated as a Signature restaurant for

Let 'em Eat Cake!

What could possibly make celebrating a special occasion at Walt Disney World even more special? How about a custom-made, personalized cake? You can have one delivered to just about any table-service eatery on Disney property. Simply call the Cake Hotline (407-827-2253) at least 72 hours in advance to place your order.

If you miss the ordering deadline, don't despair—no one has to go cake-less at Disney World (perish the thought!). Spontaneous cake delivery is possible, provided you request one at the podium when you check in at a restaurant. At meal's end, you'll get a small, non-personalized, Mickey–shaped cake (which serves 4 to 6 guests). It will add about $35, plus tax (and a few more calories), to the total.

both lunch and dinner, Le Cellier costs a bit more than many other Walt Disney World (and real world) eateries. The steakhouse, unsurprisingly, specializes in quality beef entrées. To start, there is a (complimentary) basket of warm bread, that includes a pretzel roll, plus sourdough and whole-grain creations. The filet mignon with mushroom risotto sauce is a perennial fan favorite. Other main course selections on the somewhat abbreviated menu include maple-brined chicken breast, châteaubriand for two, pan-seared golden tilefish, and steamed Asian-style dumplings. Many choose to start with the cheddar cheese soup made with Moosehead beer and smoked bacon, but the *poutine* (beef bourguignon or crispy soy-glazed pork belly) are appetizer options, too. Canadian beers and wines make for pairing possibilities. Reservations are a must—this is a very popular and relatively tiny Walt Disney World restaurant. **LD•$$$$•❤•SR**

LA HACIENDA DE SAN ANGEL (Mexico): Open for dinner (starting at 4 P.M.), this festive facility fits nicely on the shore of World Showcase Lagoon. The menu has starters such as *queso fundido* (melted cheese with chorizo, peppers, and onions with flour tortillas); *agua chile de camaron* (shrimp ceviche), and *crema de elote* (creamy corn soup). Entrées include a mixed grill for two, short ribs with salsa de chile, New York strip steak, grilled organic chicken breast, pork confit topped with tomatillo salad, and pan-seared snapper. We are particularly fond of the *parrillada del mar* (seafood platter for two). For dessert, there's *volcan de chocolate* (chocolate lava cake); empanadas filled with sautéed caramel apples, served with dulce de leche ice cream and *cajeta* (caramel sauce); and traditional flan. Among the handcrafted margaritas that grace the menu are Piña Loca, Orange Mango Fire, and La Cava Avocado.

If you book a table for about 8:30 P.M., you may be treated to prime seats for Epcot's nightly pyrotechnic extravaganza. While windowside tables cannot be guaranteed, there's always standing room. As an added bonus, the show's soundtrack is pumped into the eatery. It's quite impressive. **D•$$$•❤**

MONSIEUR PAUL (France): Settle in for a relaxed and memorable splurge at this ever-so-elegant bistro just one flight above Chefs de France. As your host leads you to a table, you'll pass the restaurant's stellar wine collection and framed mementos of the late, legendary Chef Paul Bocuse. His extraordinary honors include being named "Chef of the Century" in 2011 by the Culinary Institute of America.

The dinner-only menu, crafted by Chef Nicolas Lemoyne, who came from Bocuse's Michelin 3-star restaurant l'Auberge du Pont de Collonges, offers gourmet surprises like the Soupe aux Truffes featuring a delicate puff pastry that tops an oxtail broth filled with savory black winter truffles, braised beef, and vegetables. Other starters on the menu may include escargot with garlic butter or vegetarian options like endives with poached pear, Roquefort cream, and caramelized walnuts. An entrée of black sea bass encrusted in potato "scales" is sublime—the fish in this dish, as well as other menu items, may change depending on the season. And then there's the classic grilled beef tenderloin—magnifique!

Raise your glass for a toast with a specialty French martini of vodka, Chambord, pineapple juice, and lemon-lime foam, then order from the impressive, très French wine list with pairing options for every palate. The seven-course, prix-fixe dinner with an imported cheese course just before dessert is a special-occasion indulgence. You might want to stroll around the World Showcase promenade to walk off your warm chocolate almond cake with raspberry coulis and hazelnut ice cream or other sweet finish to a very special meal.

Note that this is a Disney Dining Plan Signature eatery (requiring two full-service meal redemptions). Though a bit less formal than its predecessor, Bistro de Paris, Monsieur Paul does have a "resort casual" dress code—no tank tops or tattered clothing, please. Reservations are recommended. **D•$$$$•❤•SR**

NINE DRAGONS (China): This stop on Epcot's restaurant tour transports guests to modern China when seated in the palatial dining room. À la carte selections allow

HOT TIP!

Thanks in part to the Disney Dining Plan and "Epcot After 4" (an admission pass for local Disney fans), World Showcase tends to be exceptionally busy in the evening hours year-round. Reservations for table-service eateries are an absolute must.

guests to sample provincial cuisines. The menu includes starters such as General Tso's chicken buns, steamed chicken dumplings, spring rolls, and pot stickers. Entrées range from salt and pepper shrimp to Kung Pao shrimp or chicken, veggie stir-fry, five-spiced fish, and spare ribs. (No MSG is used in any dish.) For dessert, consider sharing the banana cheesecake egg rolls, drizzled with caramel and served with ice cream or a piece of ginger cake. There is a prix fixe family style menu (including choice of one soup, one entrée, and one dessert for $26 per person). Chinese teas, beers, and wines are served. The menu features frozen daiquiris and specialty drinks, plus non-alcoholic concoctions such as the Shangri-La (strawberry-mango) smoothie and hot chai milk tea. Reservations are recommended. **LD•$$–$$$•** ❤

RESTAURANT MARRAKESH (Morocco): It's not every day that you can slip into an exquisitely tiled Moroccan palace and be entertained by belly dancers and musicians as you polish off a plate of Moroccan cuisine. Want to know how authentic this place is? The king of Morocco sent craftspeople to Epcot to make sure they were creating a real Moroccan atmosphere. The menu includes roast lamb, chicken brochette, beef shish kebab, and couscous. Sampler platters are

Special Requests

All WDW table-service eateries that accept reservations strive to accommodate food allergies and intolerances such as gluten, salt, wheat, shellfish, lactose, peanuts, etc., if requested at least 72 hours in advance. Kosher meals may be pre-ordered up to a day ahead at many table-service eateries. Note that 48 hours' notice is needed for eateries at the Swan and Dolphin, Yak & Yeti restaurant, and Rainforest Cafe. (Kosher meals are not available at Garden View Afternoon Tea [Grand Floridian resort] and Epcot's Teppan Edo and Tokyo Dining.) Make your request when booking your table by calling 407-WDW-DINE (939-3463). Note that kosher requests require a credit card guarantee and must be canceled within 24 hours of the reservation to avoid a penalty.

an option. Dessert selections include warm beignets with sweet cream; fruit salad topped with mint ice cream, toasted almonds, and orange blossom water; and an assortment of baklavas. Reservations are recommended, but it is often possible to get a table without too much of a wait. **LD•$$$•** ❤

ROSE & CROWN PUB AND DINING ROOM (United Kingdom): Don't let the word "pub" throw you. While this place serves up some excellent brews, its Dining Room is also known for such crowd-pleasing dishes as traditional fish and chips, pan-seared Scottish salmon, shepherd's pie, corned beef and cabbage, burgers, and bangers and mash (sausages with mashed potatoes). Appetizer-wise, we recommend the Rose & Crown cheese plate. One of the side dishes that makes us happy? Mushy peas! (Sort of a lumpy-but-flavorful pea porridge.) For dessert, there are lemon scones, sticky toffee pudding, and English trifle. Bass ale from England, Harp lager and Guinness stout from Ireland, and more are on tap. Wine, whisky, specialty cocktails, and soft drinks may be sipped and swigged, too.

PHOTO BY JILL SAFRO

The decor is pretty—mainly polished woods, etched glass, and brass accents. In pleasant weather, it's nice to lunch under a canopy on the terrace outside and watch the FriendShip water taxis cross the lagoon.

As for the pub's architecture, it incorporates three distinct styles. The wall facing the World Showcase promenade is reminiscent of urban establishments popular in Britain since the 1890s, while that on the south side evokes London's seventeenth-century Ye Olde Cheshire Cheese pub, with its brick-walled flagstone terrace, slate roof, and half-timbered exterior. The canal facade, with its stone wall and clay-tile roof, reminds visitors of the charming pubs so common in the English countryside.

The pub area of the Rose & Crown serves such snacks as fish and chips—along with all the brews noted earlier and traditional British mixed drinks such as shandies (Bass ale and Sprite) and black and tans (Bass Ale and Guinness stout). The pub is quite popular, so it's often necessary to queue up at the door. Note that the pub section also spills out onto the World Showcase promenade—where the first-come, first-served waterside tables make for a nice spot to sip a drink and, possibly, enjoy some fish and chips from a nearby snack stand. Reservations are not available in the pub areas, but recommended for the adjacent dining room.

If you're lucky, you'll catch a performance by the pub's artist-in-residence. Feel free to sing along as she bangs out familiar tunes on her modest upright piano. She is quite a crowd-pleaser, so expect lots of company at the bar as you sip your pint. **LDS•$$$•**🐭

PHOTO BY JILL SAFRO

SAN ANGEL INN (Mexico): The food at this moody establishment may come as a surprise to most visitors. Although the tacos and tortillas and other specialties that usually fall under the broad umbrella of Mexican food are available, the menu also offers a wide variety of more subtly flavored fish, poultry, and meat dishes.

For starters, the menu offers *tostadas de pollo* (pulled chicken on fried corn tortillas with black refried beans, green tomatillo sauce, queso fresco, and sour cream) and guacamole, plus much more. Entrées include *carne asada* (New York strip steak served with cheese enchilada), *pescado a la talla* (marinated catch of the day served with creamy poblano potatoes), and tacos (sautéed shrimp, grilled sirloin, or grilled pork). The dinner menu is a bit more elaborate than at lunch. Dessert can be flan, cheesecake, or caramel ice cream. *Bebidas* (drinks) such as Dos Equis, Sol, and Tecate beer, and margaritas make good accompaniments.

The restaurant, which is located to the rear of the plaza inside the Mexico pyramid, is a corporate cousin of the famous Mexico City restaurant of the same name. Unsurprisingly, some of the zestier dishes here have a bit of a kick—though not in an overwhelming way. In fact, some

diners may be accustomed to a bit more heat. Youngsters home in on the kid-friendly section of the menu, with (non-spicy) chicken and rice, cheese quesadillas, and tacos. Reservations are recommended. **LD•$$$•**🐭

SPICE ROAD TABLE (Morocco): Built on the shores of World Showcase Lagoon, this restaurant's style was inspired by outdoor cafés found along the scenic shores of the Mediterranean. Popular for its stunning views of the nighttime pyrotechnic spectacular and its freshly prepared, palate-pleasing fare, Spice Road Table has made its way onto Epcot diners' must-do list. The eatery's whitewashed facade is accented in icy shades of blue from the famous "Blue City of Chefchaouen" in Morocco's Rif Mountains.

The menu features Mediterranean small plates: zesty harissa chicken rolls; lamb sliders; fresh fish croquettes; Brie fondue with rosemary croutons; garlicky shrimp in a spicy chile pepper sauce; Moroccan merguez sausage with a fresh tomato salad; fried calamari, hummus fries, and more. Mediterranean specialty entrées include coriander-crusted rack of lamb, mixed grill skewers, roasted chicken, spicy yellowfin tuna, and a vegetable platter. The dessert menu tempts with a chocolate pyramid with ice cream, pistachio and saffron custard, and assorted baklava. Soft drinks, specialty cocktails, Mediterranean beer, wine, and organic sangria are served. Reservations are recommended, though walk-ups may be accommodated. **LDS•$$–$$$•**🐭

TEPPAN EDO (Japan): Tokyo Dining's lively neighbor, Teppan Edo offers a dinner-as-show experience. Guests sit around a large teppan grill and watch as a nimble chef demonstrates just how quickly enough chicken, beef, seafood, and vegetables can be chopped, seasoned, and stir-fried. Teppan Edo entrées are sizzling and satisfying. Soups, salads, sushi, desserts, and cocktails (including Japanese beer and sake) are also on the menu. Don't wear your finest attire: There's always the potential for a little splattering. Reservations are recommended. Teppan Edo's check-in desk is at the bottom of the eatery's front steps. **LD•$$$•❤**

TAKUMI–TEI (Japan): The name of this elegant World Showcase newcomer translates to "house of the artisan." Specializing in Wagyu beef selections, this upscale eatery features an à la carte menu, a multi-course tasting menu, and traditional Japanese tea service. Signature cocktails and premium sake are served, as are wine and craft beers. The dress code here is resort casual. For additional information about Takumi-Tei, use the My Disney Experience app or website, visit *disneyworld.com*, or call 407-939-3463. Reservations are recommended. **D•$$$$•SR**

TOKYO DINING (Japan): A nice escape for lunch or dinner, this restaurant features freshly prepared sushi, sashimi, edamame, tempura, grilled items, bento boxes, and prix-fixe lunch specials. Other choices: garden salad, ika salad, miso soup, grilled chicken, grilled salmon, and grilled steak/shrimp tempura combo. Finish the meal with mousse cake or soft-serve ice cream (green tea, vanilla, or green tea-vanilla swirl). Beer, wine, sake, and specialty cocktails are available. Reservations are recommended. **LD•$$–$$$•❤**

TUTTO GUSTO WINE CELLAR (Italy): A welcome retreat for grown-ups, Tutto Gusto is a wine bar that transports guests to an ancient Italian wine cellar. Tutto Italia's next-door neighbor offers more than 200 wines, including grappa; Italian beers and specialty drinks; coffee concoctions; and a marvelous small-plate menu. Nibble on imported Italian cheeses, Sicilian eggplant salad, marinated olives, seafood salad, white asparagus, cured sliced meats, paninis (pressed sandwiches on ciabatta baguette), pastas, and more. For dessert, consider the strawberries with mascarpone cream, cannoli, or mocha tiramisu. Reservations are not accepted—come in the afternoon for the smallest crowds. *Salute!* **LDS•$$–$$$**

TUTTO ITALIA RISTORANTE (Italy): There's an impressive menu at one of the most popular (and expensive) World Showcase destinations, and its indoor and outdoor tables make it one of the more appealing spots for an Epcot meal. Traditional starters such as fried calamari, fresh mozzarella with tomatoes and basil, and Caesar salad can actually make a meal in and of themselves. Entrée selections extend toward fresh pastas—spaghetti,

tortellini, fettuccine, and lasagna. The menu includes fish, steak, and chicken. Paninis are offered at lunch. For dessert, choose from gelato, sorbet, cannoli, tiramisu, and cheesecake. Wine, beer, teas, coffees, and cocktails are served. Reservations are recommended. **LD•$$$–$$$$•❤**

VIA NAPOLI RISTORANTE E PIZZARIA (Italy): Epcot's pizza-centric restaurant is tucked into the back of the Italy pavilion. Via Napoli has a casual atmosphere and seating for about 300. How serious are they about the pizza? They import the flour from Italy and select water

Frozen Ever After Sparkling Dessert Party

A sweet way to end an Epcot day, this soirée features VIP viewing of Epcot's nighttime spectacular, a steady stream of sweet and savory treats, and an after-hours boat ride at Norway's Frozen Ever After attraction. Snack selections include ice cream, cupcakes, fresh fruit, and cheese fondue. Beer, wine, cocktails, and soft drinks (melted snow!) are included. The one-hour dessert party takes place on select evenings. It costs about $79 for adults and $47 for kids (including tax and gratuity). To make a reservation, use the My Disney Experience mobile app or website, or call 407-939-3463.

so the crust tastes as authentically Neapolitan as possible. In addition to the wood-fired pizza, house specialties include pastas, salads, sandwiches, and Italian wines and signature cocktails. The Aqua Fresca is quite refreshing (signature seasonal fruit cooler). Dessert offerings include *zeppole di catarina* (ricotta cheese fritters), gelato, sorbet, cannoli, and tiramisu. Reservations are recommended. LD•$$–$$$•🐭

FAST FOOD & SNACKS

BLOCK & HANS (American Adventure): Mickey-shaped soft pretzels, anyone? You can get them here, along with cheese-y dipping sauce. Wash them down with a seasonal craft beer, hard cider, or bottled water. S•$•🐭

FUNNEL CAKE CART (American Adventure): The sweet, doughy treat known as the funnel cake wasn't born in the U.S.A., but it was Kutztown, Pennsylvania, that put it on the map. So it's fitting that funnel cakes be served at a kiosk in the American Adventure pavilion. They're available topped with powdered sugar, with chocolate sauce, and/or ice cream. In keeping with the sweet theme, the cart also dispenses cotton candy and fried ice cream. S•$

LA CANTINA DE SAN ANGEL (Mexico): Located just outside the entrance to Mexico's pyramid, this eatery serves grilled chicken with cascabel sauce over rice; beef tacos (on fresh corn tortillas); Mexican salads; nachos topped with cheese, ground beef, black beans, jalapeños, tomatoes, and sour cream; cheese empanadas; fresh,

housemade guacamole with corn tortilla chips; and *churros con cajeta* (churros with caramel). Mexican beer, sangria, margaritas (frozen and on the rocks), and soft drinks (including apple soda) are available. Kids' picks include chicken tenders and cheese empanadas (served with tortilla chips and fruit). LDS•$–$$• 🐭

LA CAVA DEL TEQUILA (Mexico): Mexico's national drink is the star of this show—there are more than 200 varieties to choose from. Also served: sangria, mezcal, beer, wine, and specialty drinks (the avocado margaritas are quite refreshing). Snack on *queso blanco* (warm, white nacho cheese with pico de gallo sauce and tortilla chips), or chips with guacamole or salsa—or go chip crazy and order them with all three. Doors open at noon. It's tiny, so expect a wait to get in. S•$–$$

REFRESHMENT OUTPOST (between Germany and China): Stop here for a snack and drink (soft drinks and adult beverages are served). Snacks include all-beef hot dogs with chips, soft-serve ice cream (chocolate, vanilla, or swirl) served in a waffle cone, and frozen cola or lemonade slushies. Fountain beverages and bottled water are served, as are beer and specialty drinks—including the Mango Starr (mango puree and African rum), Outpost Lemonade (frozen lemonade with vodka), and the Frozen Elephant (frozen cola with Amarula cream liquor). **LDS•$–$$•🐭**

FIFE & DRUM TAVERN (The American Adventure): Located on the World Showcase promenade, this small brick edifice proffers American favorites. Among the options: jumbo turkey legs, popcorn, soft-serve ice cream in a waffle cone, slushies, soft drinks, wine, beer, and frozen lemonade with cherry bourbon. Souvenir popcorn buckets cost about $10–$20 each and may be refilled for about $2 a pop for the length of your Walt Disney World visit. **LDS•$–$$•🐭**

JOFFREY'S COFFEE & TEA COMPANY (The American Adventure): One of five Joffrey's outposts at Epcot, this beverage-based stand proffers coffees, teas, hot cocoa, bottled water, spirited drinks, and baked treats.

F.Y.I.: The other Joffrey's locations at this park are between the United Kingdom and Canada pavilions, near Le Cellier Steakhouse, outside the Test Track exit, and by the monorail station. **S•$**

KABUKI CAFE (Japan): Step up to cool down at this quick-service kiosk, where the specialty of the house is Kakigori, aka shaved ice. Flavors include rainbow, tangerine, melon, strawberry, and blue raspberry. Kabuki also offers chilled edamame, sushi (California rolls, Futomaki big rolls, and sushi combo), Japanese beer (including frozen Kirin), plum wine, sake (hot and cold), Sake Mist (alcoholic shaved ice available in blood orange, coconut pineapple, or blackberry), and soft drinks. **LDS•$–$$•🐭**

KATSURA GRILL (Japan): Located on the left side of the plaza, the exterior of the restaurant was inspired by the historic sixteenth-century Katsura Imperial Villa near Kyoto, Japan.

Among the fare here is Japanese chicken cutlet curry (a peppery sauce over rice with a panko-breaded chicken breast). That, along with teriyaki chicken, shrimp, and beef (basted with soy sauce and sesame oil as it broils), sushi, spicy seafood ramen, miso soup, udon noodles

(beef or shrimp tempura), edamame, and green tea cheesecake typify the offerings. Drink choices include hot and cold sake, plum wine, green tea, beer, and soft drinks. The garden serves as a respite for those who seek a break from the hustle and bustle of a busy Epcot day. Kids dig the koi pond. **LDS•$–$$•🐭**

KRINGLA BAKERI OG KAFE (Norway): Neatly tucked between the Norway pavilion's wooden church and The Fjording shop, this newly expanded spot serves kringlas, sweet pretzels reserved for special occasions in Norway; Troll horns (flaky pastry filled with cream and tart cloudberries); *smørbrøds*, salmon and egg bagels; sandwiches such as apple and cheese; or Norwegian club; and lefse (potato flatbread rolled with sweet cinnamon butter). There are salads, frozen mini cupcakes, Norwegian school bread, fruit cups, sweet pretzels with chocolate, and rice pudding with strawberry sauce. Soft drinks, wine, beer, and coffee cocktails are served. Many of the menu items work well for breakfast—perfect for early visits to Norway's popular Frozen Ever After attraction. This spot usually opens at 9 A.M. **BLDS•$–$$•🐭**

L'ARTISAN DES GLACES (France): An artisanal ice cream and sorbet shop, this spot fills cones and cups with 16 flavors of ice cream and sorbets—all crafted in-house. The ingredients are simple and fresh: milk, sugar, cream, eggs, and fruit. There are usually more than a dozen flavors from which to choose. Specials include macaron ice cream sandwiches, iced cappuccino with ice cream, and sundaes in homemade waffle bowls. Adults over age 21 may indulge in an "ice cream martini"—two scoops with a shot of Grand Marnier, whipped cream vodka, or rum. **S•$•🐭**

LES HALLES BOULANGERIE PATISSERIE (France): The pastry shop in the France pavilion is not difficult to find: Just follow the wonderful aroma, then watch the crowds lining up to enjoy the fresh baguettes (standard and mini), croissants, quiches, cheese plates, ham and cheese or turkey sandwiches, cheese tartines, soups, salads, éclairs, fruit tarts, chocolate mousse, and more. Beer, wine, lemonade, smoothies, coffee, and other beverages are served. The patisserie is located toward the back of the France pavilion and is a favorite snack spot among Epcot veterans. There's always a line to order the treats, but it moves quickly. **LDS•$–$$•🐭**

LOTUS BLOSSOM CAFE (China): The counter-service cafe is adjacent to the House of Good Fortune shopping gallery in the China pavilion. It offers orange chicken with steamed rice, beef noodle bowls, shrimp fried rice, Sichaun spicy chicken, vegetarian stir-fry, and sesame chicken salad, plus pot stickers, pork and veggie rolls, and kid-oriented selections (sweet-and-sour chicken or

B breakfast   **L** lunch   **D** dinner   **S** snacks   /   **$** under $15   **$$** $15–$36   **$$$** $36–$60   **$$$$** $60 and up

pot stickers and spring rolls). Caramel-ginger or lychee ice cream, and smoothies (mango or strawberry) are dessert possibilities. Coffee, Chinese hot tea, soft drinks, and alcoholic beverages round out the menu. There is a small, covered seating area. **LDS•$–$$• 🐭**

REFRESHMENT PORT (Canada): A good spot for a thirst quencher or a quick snack—stop here for seasonal sweets and beverages, plus traditional poutine (fries with beef gravy and cheese curds) and signature poutine (fries with cheese curds and Canadian cheddar and bacon sauce), and Canadian cheddar cheese soup. The port also serves soft-serve ice cream floats and waffle cones. It's located on the World Showcase promenade, near Canada. Drinks include fountain beverages and light beer. **LDS•$–$$• 🐭**

REGAL EAGLE SMOKEHOUSE: CRAFT DRAFTS & BARBECUE (American Adventure): Epcot continues a proud American tradition at this classy, quick-service bastion of BBQ. The Regal Eagle is a modern barbecue smokehouse with all the accompanying sights, sounds, smells, and flavors many Americans have come to know and love. Craft beers and soft drinks pair nicely with the mouth-watering vittles. There's indoor and outdoor seating. To find this joint (which is on the left side of the American Adventure pavilion), just follow your nose. **LDS•$–$$• 🐭**

SOMMERFEST (Germany): Bratwurst or frankfurter served on a fresh-baked roll with sauerkraut and house-made paprika chips, nudel gratin (baked macaroni with cheese custard—a fan favorite), traditional cold potato salad (with eggs), jumbo pretzels, Black Forest cake, apple strudel with vanilla sauce, fountain drinks, bottled water, seasonal German beers, and Riesling wine are offered at this spot near the entrance to the Biergarten restaurant. There is limited outdoor seating in the area. **LDS•$$• 🐭**

TANGIERINE CAFE (Morocco): Named for the ancient Moroccan city of Tangier, this casual Mediterranean spot serves lentil salad, couscous salad, marinated olives, tabbouleh, Mediterranean sliders, kefta (beef), and chicken, lamb, and vegetable platters. Pastries, specialty coffees, frozen drinks, and beer are available, too. Kids can order burgers or chicken nuggets (served with applesauce, carrot sticks, and a drink). **LDS•$–$$• 🐭**

YORKSHIRE COUNTY FISH SHOP (United Kingdom): A perfect choice for a simple meal, this stand offers classic fish and chips (each portion comes with two yummy strips of fish). Don't forget the malt vinegar! Soda, iced tea, light lemonade, coffee, and hot tea are served. Bass ale and Harp lager are available on draft. For dessert, choose from Victoria sponge cake filled with jam and buttercream and whole, seasonal fruit. **LDS•$–$$• 🐭**

Epcot Mealtime Tips

- The international restaurants of World Showcase offer some of the best dining on the property. Since they're quite popular, it's smart to arrange advance reservations for all table-service restaurants. However, it's important to note that some tables may be available for same-day seating. To make arrangements, head to Guest Relations first thing in the morning, use the My Disney Experience website or app, or call 407-WDW-DINE (939-3463).
- Don't dismiss the idea of an early seating if you can get it: A 5 P.M. dinner may not only be welcome, but may provide an opportunity to spend more time enjoying the pleasant evening hours at Epcot's World Showcase.
- Lunch provides guests with another chance to enjoy the most popular Epcot restaurants. It also has an additional appeal: With reservations for 1 P.M., it's possible to spend some of the busiest hours in the park consuming a pleasant meal while other visitors wait in some of the longest lines of the day.
- If you aren't able to secure reservations for a table-service eatery, don't despair. There are several satisfying alternatives to a traditional sit-down restaurant. Tutto Gusto (Italian wine bar) and Spice Road Table (in Morocco) both offer small plates and full service (Spice Road Table accepts reservations, but can usually accommodate walk-ins). Japan has Katsura Grill, good for sushi and chicken curry. Mexican lunch specialties may be sampled at La Cantina. We also recommend the sandwiches at Kringla Bakeri og Kafe in Norway, the fish and chips in the United Kingdom (at the Yorkshire County Fish Shop), or Germany's bratwurst with house-made paprika chips (served by Sommerfest). Last, but certainly not least, do consider the heavenly offerings of France's Les Halles Boulangerie Patisserie. Bon appétit!
- The Sunshine Seasons (food court), in The Land pavilion, offers a bit of everything. However, it can get extremely congested at mealtime rush hours.
- The most timid of eaters can still find something pleasing—even in the more exotic restaurants of World Showcase. If you're undecided, ask at Guest Relations to see a booklet describing the menus. Most restaurants have menus for kids.

🐭 Disney Dining Plan participant at press time   **SR** Signature Restaurant

In Disney's Hollywood Studios

Lights, camera, lunch! This theme park, which was designed to resemble a working Hollywood backlot circa the 1940s, tackles the role of feeding guests with style and whimsy. Here you can sit in a classic car and enjoy a meal at a drive-in, rub elbows with the beautiful people at a reproduction of the Hollywood Brown Derby, and play the part of a sitcom kid as you're served by "Mom" or "Dad" at the 50's Prime Time Cafe (no elbows on the table, please!). While the attention to theming is obvious, it doesn't upstage the fare. The eateries at Disney's Hollywood Studios are a breed apart. Some feature decor that returns guests to a bygone era; others recapture memorable moments from the big or small screen. All reprise a beloved part of Hollywood's star-studded heritage. The Studios has five full-service restaurants, whose atmospheres and menus are so distinct, they satisfy altogether different moods and whims. Reservations are necessary; call 407-WDW-DINE (939-3463). Now grab a napkin, and get ready for your close-up.

TABLE SERVICE

50'S PRIME TIME CAFE: This retreat is an amusing amalgam of comfort food, kitschy 1950s-style kitchen nooks, and attentive servers of the "No talking with your mouth full" ilk. Nostalgia abounds, meant to bring guests back to the childhood of yesteryear; and TVs broadcast black-and-white clips from favorite fifties comedies (all related to food). Guests are waited on by "Mom" (and other family members) with considerable enthusiasm: They encourage everyone to keep their elbows off the table, eat their vegetables, and clean their plates (or no dessert!). Misbehave and you may have to stand in the corner for a few minutes (the 1950s version of the "time-out").

Adding to the appeal is the menu, which is packed with comfort foods. For openers, there is a choice of housemade chicken noodle soup or onion rings. Specialties of the house include meatloaf served with mashed potatoes and vegetables; fried chicken; and old-fashioned pot roast. There are wedge salads, crab cakes, and chicken pot pies, too. Ice cream sodas, root beer floats, and milk shakes are sweet accompaniments. And once you've cleaned your plate, you may order dessert! Standouts include chocolate-peanut butter layer cake (which can come à la mode), sundaes, warm apple crisp, and no-sugar-added cheesecake topped with whipped cream and strawberry sauce. A full bar is available. Guests of all ages love this place. Reservations are highly recommended. **LD•$$–$$$•**🐭

HOLLYWOOD & VINE: The distinctive Art Deco facade ushers guests into a contemporary version of a 1950s diner—all stainless steel with pink accents. An elaborate 42-by-8-foot wall mural depicts notable Hollywood landmarks, including the Disney Studios, Columbia Ranch, and Warner Bros. (back when they were the only film studios in the San Fernando Valley). At the center of the mural is the Carthay Circle Theatre, where *Snow White and the Seven Dwarfs* premiered in 1937.

The buffet breakfast, known as Disney Junior Play 'N Dine, is a character affair featuring Roadster Goofy, Doc McStuffins, Fancy Nancy, and Vampirina (attending characters are subject to change). The morning meal includes Mickey waffles, frittatas, fruit, pastries, and a create-your-own omelet station.

Minnie Mouse hosts lunch and dinner, along with Mickey, Daisy, Donald, and Goofy. Minnie's Seasonal Dine buffet may offer carved meats, pasta dishes, strip steak, chicken parmesan, and seafood offerings such as cioppino, salmon, peel-and-eat shrimp, and mussels. The dessert section includes fresh-baked treats and a kid-pleasing soft-serve sundae station. Soft drinks are included. Beer and wine are served at an extra cost.

Lunch and dinner cost about $52 for adults and $31 for kids; breakfast is about $38 for adults and $23 for kids. Prices are higher during peak times. Reservations are necessary. **BLD•$$–$$$•**🐭

HOLLYWOOD BROWN DERBY: The home of the world-famous Cobb salad is alive and well. This re-creation of the former Vine Street mainstay is quite faithful, right down to the caricatures (reproduced from the original Derby collection) that cover the walls. Old-time gossip queen rivals Louella Parsons and Hedda Hopper would fit right in here, just as they did in the heyday of the original Brown Derby. The place is decorated predominantly in teak and mahogany, and the elegant chandeliers and perimeter lamps (shaped like miniature derbies) are reminiscent of those in the original eatery.

The menu features the famed Cobb salad, created by owner Bob Cobb in the 1930s. It's a mixture of finely chopped fresh greens, tomato, bacon, turkey, egg, blue cheese, and avocado.

Desserts are tempting—particularly the cappuccino crème brûlée and the legendary grapefruit cake, a Brown Derby institution. (For those who'd like to cap off the meal with a sweet drink, the Grapefruit Cake Martini fits the bill—it's actually sweeter than the cake itself!) Some of the selections are a bit highbrow (and high-priced) for the theme park crowd, but if you're up for a splurge, this spot will likely rise to the occasion. We recommend the seafood cioppino; the filet mignon gets good marks, too.

The slightly formal atmosphere is not apt to enchant most children, but youngster-friendly fare is available. The New World wine list is excellent. Reservations are recommended. Should you find yourself caught without reservations, consider dining at the Hollywood Brown Derby Lounge (see below). **LD•$$$•❤•SR**

HOLLYWOOD BROWN DERBY LOUNGE: An alfresco oasis, the Brown Derby Lounge serves cocktails, wines by the glass, and tapas-style plates. Signature drinks of note: Grapefruit Cake Martini, sangria (red and white), Derby cocktail, and gin-gin mule. Small plates can come filled with savory treats: Derby sliders, andouille-crusted

shrimp, artisanal cheeses and charcuterie, Cobb salad, and tamarind-glazed pork belly. There's a tempting array of sweets, too—including warm blueberry cobbler, lemon cheesecake, banana toffee cake, and Brown Derby original mini grapefruit cake. Seating is limited and reservations are not accepted, so there may be a wait for a table. All drinks may be made to go. **LDS•$$**

MAMA MELROSE'S RISTORANTE ITALIANO: This pleasant Italian restaurant (with a California twist) is located in a warehouse that has been converted into a large dining room. Flatbreads are freshly prepared in a wood-burning oven. The menu also features house-made pasta, grilled fish, and vegetarian options. Favorite dishes have included seafood cioppino, charred strip steak, wood-grilled chicken and pasta, and chicken parmesan. Mama Melrose serves sustainable fish of the day, spaghetti, and penne alla vodka, too (presented plain or with shrimp or chicken). Reservations are recommended. **LD•$$–$$$•❤**

SCI-FI DINE-IN THEATER: A convincing re-creation of a drive-in theater, the atmosphere here is completely absorbing. The tables are actually flashy, 1950s-era cars, complete with fins and whitewalls. Stars twinkle overhead in the "night sky," and drive-in theater speakers are mounted beside each car. Most seats are within cars, with most featuring front- and backseat counters facing front—not terribly conducive to meaningful table talk, but ideal for viewing the large movie screen, where a 45-minute compilation of the best (and worst) science-fiction trailers and cartoons plays in a continuous loop. There are a couple of traditional tables. If this is your preference, make that known when you book the table and expect to wait a bit when you arrive.

Choose from items such as cheese steak sandwiches, pork ribs, burgers, vegan lettuce wraps, shrimp pasta, and more. Kids enjoy the mac and cheese and whole wheat

penne pasta. Desserts include sundaes and warm glazed doughnuts. Reservations are recommended. Warning: Some movie trailers feature monsters and may frighten little ones. **LD•$$–$$$•** 🐭

FAST FOOD & SNACKS

ABC COMMISSARY: Located on Commissary Lane, this spot has featured BBQ ribs, burgers, vegan burgers, chicken strips, shrimp platter, Mediterranean salads (with and without chicken), and chicken club sandwiches. The dinner sides lineup features hummus and pita, fire-roasted corn medley, and steak fries. Kids may choose BBQ quesadillas, mac and cheese, or PB&J. For dessert, consider a s'more cookie, apple almond tart, or the chocolate and banana almond crisp. Beer, wine, sangria, watermelon margaritas, and soft drinks are served. The spacious dining area resembles an actual studio commissary. Memorabilia from ABC programs is on display. Neat! Reservations are available for dinner. **LDS•$$•** 🐭

BACKLOT EXPRESS: Resembling a crafts shop on a studio backlot, this eatery is near Star Tours—The Adventures Continue. The indoor seating areas carry out the prop-shop theme, with paint-speckled floors, car engines, and various spare prop parts. Typical menu offerings include burgers, cheeseburgers, chicken and biscuits, Southwest salad (with or without chicken), tomato and mozzarella sandwiches, chicken tenders, and salads. For dessert there is Key lime custard and peanut butter brownies. Soft drinks, beer, wine, margaritas, and daiquiris are served. **LDS•$$•** 🐭

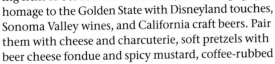

HOT TIP!

Andy's building a rootin' tootin' rodeo arena in his backyard—and when he's done, Disney Imagineers will turn it into a table-service restaurant for honorary toys. Those who visit the new eatery will find themselves enveloped by a "kaleidoscope of toys, games, and playsets" while they chow down on BBQ vittles. Yee-ha! For updates on the new Toy Story Land restaurant, use the My Disney Experience mobile app or website or visit *disneyworld.com*.

BASELINE TAP HOUSE: Housed in a red-brick building next to Sci-Fi Dine-In Theater, this lounge pays homage to the Golden State with Disneyland touches, Sonoma Valley wines, and California craft beers. Pair them with cheese and charcuterie, soft pretzels with beer cheese fondue and spicy mustard, coffee-rubbed

rib eye steak puff with olive salad and/or spiced almonds. Or wash them down with a sweet soft drink: Black cherry soda and wild strawberry lemonade are house specialties. In tribute to the building's former tenant, a silvery set of letters spells out Writer's Stop. **S•$$**

DINOSAUR GERTIE'S ICE CREAM OF EXTINCTION: Gertie serves soft-serve ice cream (vanilla, chocolate, or swirl) in a cup or cone, plus Mickey ice cream bars and cookies and cream sandwiches. **S•$•** 🐭

DOCKSIDE DINER: For the morning meal, this waterside window offers breakfast burritos, bagels, fresh fruit, and cinnamon rolls. When the lunch and dinner bell rings, stop here for foot-long hot dogs and chili cheese dogs, barbecue pulled pork sandwiches, loaded chili cheese nachos, chocolate and vanilla milk shakes, frozen lemonade (straight or spiked), soft drinks, beer, and cocktails (including a chocolate or vanilla Kahlúa and Bailey's Irish Cream milk shake). **LDS•$$•** 🐭

DOCKING BAY 7 FOOD AND CARGO: Chef Strono "Cookie" Tuggs has docked a food freighter loaded with fresh supplies and he appeases appetites with an array of exotic offerings. His flavors, while unusual, are palate-pleasing. Kids' selections are available. **BLDS•$$•** 🐭

HOLLYWOOD HILLS AMPHITHEATER: If your stomach starts growling while waiting for Fantasmic! to begin, consider this snack shack. Menu items include nachos with cheese, hot dogs, corn dogs, soft pretzels, popcorn, cookies, chips, and more. Enjoy your snack with a soft drink, beer, wine, or "wild strawberry lemonade" spiked with rum. **S•$–$$•** 🐭

ICE COLD MAIN ENTRANCE CART: Need to cool off on a hot day? Swing by this stand near the park entrance. It sells ice cream bars, cookies, chips, slushies, juices, and fizzy drinks. **S•$•** 🐭

JOFFREY'S COFFEE & TEA COMPANY: There are two Joffrey's stands at Disney's Hollywood Studios: near the entrance to Toy Story Land and by the Tower of Terror exit. These kiosks specialize in (hot and cold) tea and coffee beverages, plus drinks of the frozen and/ or spirited style. The pastry board may include fresh-baked doughnuts, cookies, and muffins. **S•$•**❤

KAT SAKA'S KETTLE: Pop over to this snack stand for a serving of Outpost Mix—a sweet and savory popcorn-based treat. **S•$•**❤

KRNR: THE ROCK STATION: In the shadow of Rock 'n' Roller Coaster's gargantuan guitar, KRNR serves hot dogs and chili dogs, chips, nachos with cheese sauce, waffle cones (chocolate, vanilla, or twist), chocolate chip cookies, floats, frozen cola, frozen lemonade, soft drinks, and specialty drinks. **LDS•$–$$•**❤

MILK STAND: This stall offer travelers a drink that's a favorite among the locals—and Luke Skywalker himself. The fruity plant-based (non-dairy) frosty beverage comes in blue or green. **S•$$**

OASIS CANTEEN: A tin shack near the theater housing the Indiana Jones Epic Stunt Spectacular, the canteen dispenses funnel cakes topped with strawberries, vanilla ice cream, powdered sugar, or cookies and cream topping with vanilla ice cream; soft-serve ice cream (chocolate, vanilla, or twist) in waffle cones; root beer floats; bottled water; fountain beverages; and draft beer. Spirited ice cream floats are available. **S•$•**❤

PIZZERIZZO: Occupying the space once filled by the Toy Story Pizza Planet, this Muppet-themed eatery continues the passable pizza tradition, plus meatball subs, antipasto salad, cannoli, and tiramisu. Also on the menu: pasta side salads and whole fruit. Assorted soft drinks, beer, wine, sangria, and margaritas are served. Pizzerizzo is located across the courtyard from the Muppet*Vision 3-D attraction. **LDS•$$•**❤

RONTO ROASTERS: To find this stand, follow your nose—the aromas of spit-roasted specialties fill the air. The menu features the Ronto Wrap (grilled sausage and roasted pork), turkey jerky (sweet or spicy), and Meiloorun Juice. The aforementioned spit, incidentally, is operated by a pit-master droid. **BLDS•$$•**❤

SUNSET RANCH MARKET: A salute to California's outdoor lifestyle, this cluster of snack stands has something for just about everyone. Rosie's All-American serves foot-long hot dogs, cheeseburgers, chicken nuggets, fried green tomato sandwiches, and desserts. Catalina Eddie's offers plain and pepperoni pizzas, chicken Caesar salads, and desserts. Vegetables, fruit,

HOT TIP!
Hollywood Brown Derby, Mama Melrose's Ristorante Italiano, and Hollywood & Vine offer a "meal and a show" combo. Seating for Fantasmic!, the park's nighttime spectacular, is included as part of the package (though tax, gratuities, and alcoholic beverages carry an extra charge). For pricing or reservations, call 407-939-3463 and request the Fantasmic! dining package (lunch or dinner). Guests should arrive at the theater 30 to 45 minutes before showtime to claim their seats.

juice, and soft drinks are sold at Anaheim Produce. Hollywood Scoops sells ice cream treats (in cones, cups, and sundaes). Head to Fairfax Fare for empanadas, pulled pork sandwiches, fajitas, rice bowls with pork or vegan chili, and baked potatoes, plus salads and desserts. Soft drinks are served, as is beer (with proper ID). **LDS•$–$$•**❤

THE TROLLEY CAR CAFE: Step into this jolly trolley station/Starbucks for coffee-based beverages, breakfast sandwiches, whole fruit, sweet treats, savory snacks, bottled soft drinks, and more. The cheery red building is on Hollywood Boulevard. Guests may purchase cups with designs unique to the park, too. **BLDS•$–$$•**❤

WOODY'S LUNCH BOX: Hunger pangs may be quelled at Woody's Lunch Box, a quick-service stand that serves three meals a day. For breakfast, try the s'more French toast sandwich, banana split yogurt parfait, or smoked turkey breakfast sandwich. Later in the day, the menu offers BBQ brisket melts, grilled three-cheese sandwiches, tomato basil soup, potato barrels, and fresh-baked tarts (strawberry or chocolate hazelnut). Beer, wine, hard lemonade, hard cider, and soft drinks are also served.

Studios Mealtime Tips

- To avoid traffic jams at fast-food spots, consider eating at a restaurant that offers advance reservations—Hollywood Brown Derby, 50's Prime Time Cafe, Sci-Fi Dine-In Theater, Hollywood & Vine, or Mama Melrose's Ristorante Italiano.
- To make reservations, use the My Disney Experience app or website, visit *www.disneyworld.com*, or call 407-WDW-DINE (939-3463). Same-day seating is next to impossible at Disney's Hollywood Studios' table-service eateries.

In Animal Kingdom

Whether you eat like a horse or more like a bird, you'll have no trouble finding something to sink your teeth into at one of D.A.K.'s eateries. Disney's nature-oriented park has four table-service spots and takes "quick service" seriously—there are plenty of places to keep stomachs from growling like the beasts over at the Kilimanjaro Safaris attraction.

TABLE SERVICE

RAINFOREST CAFE: Like the Oasis, the region it borders, this cafe is a lush, soothing jungle. Unlike the Oasis, a quiet moment here is merely a calm before the storm—as brief thunderstorms happen frequently. Waterfalls, twisting tree trunks, and colorful fish add to the ambience. The menu has a little bit of everything—sandwiches, burgers, fish tacos, salads, and pasta dishes. Dessert can come in the form of chocolate cake, root beer float, or mango sorbet. Reservations are recommended for all meals. **BLDS•$$–$$$**

TIFFINS RESTAURANT: An inviting escape, Tiffins boasts a globe-trotting menu of artfully prepared fare fit for a weary traveler. The exotic menu features cuisine from the many areas that inspired the creation of Disney's Animal Kingdom. The menu has included spiced chickpea falafel, charred octopus, artisanal cheeses, mushroom soup, Wagyu rib eye, braised short rib, pan-seared Alaskan halibut, roasted veggie platter, and whole-fried sustainable fish. Kid-friendly selections are offered. For dessert there's whipped cheesecake, chocolate ganache with caramelized banana, guava mousse, and passion fruit tapioca crème. This is a Disney Dining Plan Signature restaurant. Reservations are recommended. **LD•$$$$•❤•SR**

TUSKER HOUSE: Harambe village sets the stage for a dining adventure at this buffet restaurant. The all-you-care-to-eat selection is bountiful and satisfying to most palates. All meals are hosted by favorite Disney characters. At press time, the characters scheduled to attend were Donald, Daisy, Mickey, and Goofy (the latter three are subject to change). Reservations are highly recommended for all meals. Book as far in advance as possible. Tusker House opens at 8 A.M. **BLD•$$$•❤**

YAK & YETI: Found in the park's Asia section, Yak & Yeti opens for lunch at 11 A.M. It specializes in Asian fusion cuisine. Menu items include chicken tikka masala, coconut-crusted shrimp, kobe beef burger, Korean BBQ ribs, lo mein, and seared miso salmon. Among the dessert options are fried (sweet) wontons and mango pie. Soft drinks and cocktails are served. **LDS•$$–$$$•❤**

FAST FOOD & SNACKS

ANANDAPUR ICE CREAM TRUCK: Cool off with soft-serve (chocolate, vanilla, and swirl) from Asia's local ice cream truck. The snack is served in a waffle cone, cup, or soda float. Bottled water, soft drinks, and black cherry hard cider floats are also offered. **S•$**

CREATURE COMFORTS: A shop known as Creature Comforts has been converted into a home fit for a mermaid. Yep, the sippers' sanctum known as Starbucks is open for business on Discovery Island. It currently comforts creatures with all manner of coffee concoctions, pastries, and snacks. **BLDS•$–$$•❤**

DINO-BITE SNACKS: Restaurantosaurus's neighbor, this snack shack proffers hand-scooped ice cream, floats, ice-cream cookie sandwiches, hot fudge sundaes, fresh-baked cookies, plus Mickey pretzels, and assorted chips. **S•$–$$•❤**

DINO DINER: Found in or about Chester & Hester's Dino-Rama, the diminutive diner dispenses hot dogs and chili cheese dogs (served with chips), corn chip pie, and churros with chocolate dipping sauce. Thirsts may be quenched with fountain beverages, bottled water, frozen lemonade (with or without raspberry rum), and beer. **S•$•🐭**

DRINKWALLAH: While trekking through Asia, intrepid explorers may stop here for a refreshing pit stop. In addition to beverages, simple snacks are served (cinnamon-glazed nuts and chips). **S•$•🐭**

EIGHT SPOON CAFE: Discovery Island's mac & cheese purveyor, this quality kiosk serves it plain, with pulled pork, or with shrimp and sweet chili cheese sauce. Assorted chips, fountain drinks, and bottled water round out the offerings. **S•$•🐭**

FLAME TREE BARBECUE: To track down this eatery, just follow your nose. It serves a fragrant selection of BBQ sandwiches and platters, all wood roasted. Sample the Flame Tree's signature barbecue sauce with your chicken, pulled pork, or house-smoked St. Louis ribs. Also served: smoked pulled pork sandwiches, baked mac and cheese with pulled pork, mixed green salad

Animal Kingdom Mealtime Tips

- Satu'li Canteen, Pizzafari, Restaurantosaurus, Flame Tree Barbecue, and Harambe Market all accept advance orders via the My Disney Experience app. Payments with Mobile Order must be made with a major credit card.
- Tusker House and Rainforest Cafe are table-service places offering breakfast; a few spots, including Creature Comforts, Kusafiri Coffee Shop & Bakery, Pongu Pongu, and Yak & Yeti Local Food Cafes, have light breakfast options.
- Restaurants that accept reservations are Tusker House, Rainforest Cafe, Yak & Yeti, Pizzafari (for the "family-style" dinner only), and Tiffins. Reservations are recommended and can be made via the My Disney Experience mobile app or website, or by calling 407-WDW-DINE (939-3463). Rainforest Cafe may keep longer hours than the park itself—plan your exit transportation accordingly.
- A great place to meet Donald and pals such as Mickey, Daisy, and Goofy is at Tusker House at the daily character meals (three meals a day).

with chicken, fries (with or without pulled pork and cheese), onion rings, and housemade dessert. Most platters come with sides of beans and coleslaw. Beer, wine, and soft drinks are served. Kids may enjoy baked chicken drumsticks, turkey or PB&J sandwiches, or hot dogs. There's shaded seating along the river. Please don't feed the wildlife. It's on Discovery Island, near DinoLand, USA. **LDS•$–$$•🐭**

HARAMBE FRUIT MARKET: Sometimes a crunchy apple is just what the doctor—or hungry park guest—ordered. Apples (and other fruits) are sold at this stand by the entrance to Kilimanjaro Safaris. It has grilled corn, pickles, pretzels, chips, and drinks, too. **S•$•🐭**

HARAMBE MARKET: Enshrined in an old train station, the Harambe Market features four proprietors offering African takes on American favorites: spice-rubbed ribs, sausages, grilled chicken skewers, beef and lamb gyros, and more. You will find the Harambe-style street fare in the open-air courtyard near the Mombasa Marketplace shop. **LDS•$$•🐭**

ISLE OF JAVA: This isle is actually a Discovery Island kiosk specializing in coffees and treats for guests on the go. Among the snack items offered by Flame Tree Barbecue's next-door neighbor are Mickey pretzels with cheese sauce, elephant ear pastries, apple cider doughnut holes, cookies, and danish. Soft drinks and spirited beverages are also served. **S•$•🐭**

KUSAFIRI COFFEE SHOP & BAKERY: The bakery at Tusker House sells breakfast sandwiches, yogurt, fruit cups, croissants, and more, plus cereal, soft drinks, and specialty coffees. Sandwich options such as smoked turkey, tomato and mozzarella, and hot roast beef and cheddar (served with curry-spiced chips) may change seasonally. There are tables nearby. **BLDS•$$•🐭**

MAHINDI: Previously known as Harambe Popcorn, this snack shack still sells fresh-popped popcorn (about $5). If you purchase a refillable bucket (about $9.50), you are entitled to unlimited, discounted refills for the length of your WDW stay. (Refills cost about $2 a pop.) Other snack items include cinnamon-glazed almonds or pecans, assorted chips, fountain drinks, bottled water, and light beer. **S•$–$$**

PIZZAFARI: This colorful dining area offers freshly prepared pizzas: cheese, pepperoni, vegetable, and sausage-pepperoni. The quick-service menu also features Caesar salad (with or without chicken), garlic knots with marinara sauce, and tomato basil soup. Youngsters enjoy the Mickey pasta with turkey marinara, mac & cheese, and child-friendly plain pizza. Cannoli cake is a sweet way to finish the meal. Vibrant animal murals decorate the walls of this Discovery Island eatery. Starting at 5 P.M., this eatery also offers the option of dining "family style" (for which reservations are accepted). **BLDS•$–$$•🐭**

PONGU PONGU: Hike through the other-worldly terrain of Pandora—The World of Avatar, and you'll discover this refreshing outpost (next to the Windtraders shop). Na'vi for "Party Party," Pongu Pongu welcomes weary travelers with breakfast offerings such as sausage and egg biscuits, French toast sticks, and pineapple cream cheese spring rolls, plus milk, juice, and specialty drinks. Later in the day, this window offers colossal soft pretzels with beer cheese dipping sauce, glowing cocktails, and soft drinks. **BS•$•🐭**

RESTAURANTOSAURUS: This DinoLand spot is a fishing lodge turned commissary for student paleontologists. It offers bacon cheeseburgers, breaded shrimp, grilled chicken BLT sandwiches, chicken nuggets, black bean burgers, seasonal salad—plus chili cheese fries, soup, sides of guacamole, and warm chocolate brownies. The place is filled with fossils, dinosaur bones, and such; class notes line the walls. **LDS•$$•🐭**

ROYAL ANANDAPUR TEA COMPANY: After hiking to Asia, park guests can build up quite a thirst. That's where this tea stand comes in handy. Near the Yak & Yeti in the village of Serka Zong, the hut sells iced and hot teas, specialty coffees, and treats. **S•$•🐭**

SATU'LI CANTEEN: Look for familiar dishes with a twist at this exotic canteen, featuring bowls for diners to customize. Each bowl starts with a base of rice and black beans; red and sweet potato hash; mixed whole-grain and rice; noodles; or hearty salad. It's finished by adding chopped, wood-grilled chicken, sliced grilled beef, chili-garlic shrimp, or chili-spiced tofu, and a sauce of your choice. Kids' selections include sliced grilled beef or chicken bowls and crispy fried tofu (but not ideal for picky eaters), plus cheeseburger steamed pods,

quesadillas, and hot dogs. For dessert, choose blueberry cream cheese mousse with passion fruit curd or chocolate cake with banana cream topping. **LDS•$$•🐭**

TAMU TAMU REFRESHMENTS: Stop by this corner spot in Africa's Harambe for a sweet treat. You can choose a double chocolate chip cookie ice cream sandwich, Mickey ice cream sundae, malva cake sundae with ice cream and caramel, or the frozen pineapple treat known as a Dole Whip (with or without rum). This spot usually opens around 10:30 A.M. Coffee, soft drinks, and beer are also served. **LDS•$•🐭**

THIRSTY RIVER BAR & TREK SNACKS: Best enjoyed *after* tackling the Expedition Everest attraction, nibbles here include hummus with fresh vegetables, Mickey-shaped pretzels with cheese dip, chocolate chip cookies, frozen ice cream novelties, and assorted chips. Fountain drinks, coffee, cocoa, beer, wine, and cocktails are also on the menu. **S•$•🐭**

TRILO-BITES: Just inside the entrance to DinoLand U.S.A. (not far from the dinosaur skeleton bridge), this kiosk dispenses Buffalo chicken chips, waffle cones (soft-serve chocolate, vanilla, or twist), sundaes, and milk shakes (chocolate or vanilla), plus assorted soft drinks, margaritas, beer, and "Smokey Bones Chocolate Shakes" (made with bourbon and bacon). **LDS•$•🐭**

YAK & YETI LOCAL FOOD CAFES: Next to the Yak & Yeti, this window specializes in items with pan-Asian influences. The morning menu has breakfast sandwiches, burritos, and tacos—plus fruit and hash brown bites. Lunch and dinner entrées include teriyaki beef bowl, Asian chicken wrap, cheeseburgers, hot dogs, rib tips, and ginger chicken salad. Egg rolls and chicken fried rice are also served. For dessert, expect items such as mini mango pie, mini chocolate silk cake, and frozen lemonade. The kids' menu features cheeseburgers, chicken strips, and PB&J sandwiches. **BLDS•$$•🐭**

Water Park Dining

Disney's duo of water parks have plenty of satisfying quick-service spots at which to nosh. You may B.Y.O. (food and soft drinks only). Alcohol and glass containers may not be brought into the water park. Coolers (smaller than 24 inches long, 18 inches high, and 15 inches wide) are allowed. Ice packs are permitted, but loose ice and dry ice are not. Prefer to have someone else do the work? Read on to learn about your dining options.

TYPHOON LAGOON

HAPPY LANDINGS ICE CREAM: Tucked beside Castaway Creek, this hut serves ice cream in sand pails, soft-serve sundaes, waffle cones, root beer floats, Mickey ice cream bars, and other chilly treats. **S•$**

LEANING PALMS: Pop over to the Palms for burgers, chicken nuggets, pizza (plain and pepperoni), rice bowls, jerk chicken sandwiches, Cobb salads, hot dogs, and Italian deli sandwiches. Cake, cookies, and fruit are also available. Wash it all down with bottled water, a soft drink, beer, wine, sangria, or hard cider. Kids' meals are offered. **LDS•$–$$•🐭**

LOWTIDE LOU'S: Lou quells hunger pangs with tuna sandwiches, Italian deli sandwiches, and chicken wraps—all served with chips. Also on the menu: soft pretzels (stuffed or with cheese sauce), nachos with cheese, smoked fish dip with crackers, cake, ice cream novelties, and assorted chips. Soft drinks, beer, wine sangria, and specialty drinks are served. This spot operates on a seasonal basis. **LDS•$$•🐭**

SNACK SHACK: Relaxing in the surf pool can really work up an appetite. Fortunately, this nearby shack offers substantial snack selections. Among the choices: chicken quesadilla, shrimp cocktail, chicken wrap, "shrimp wrecked salad," Italian deli or tuna sandwich, smoked fish dip, and guacamole flight. For dessert, try

an ice cream sundae, soft-serve waffle cone, or chocolate-chip cookie. The beverage menu includes assorted fountain drinks, bottled water, light beer, piña coladas, and strawberry margaritas. **LDS•$$•🐭**

TYPHOON TILLY'S: A shipwreck-turned-snack bar, T.T.'s serves fish tacos, coconut shrimp baskets, beer-battered fish sandwiches, chicken wraps, Italian deli sandwiches, cookies, fruit cups, and an assortment of cold drinks. **LDS•$$•🐭**

BLIZZARD BEACH

AVALUNCH: Slide over to this window for quarter-pound hot dogs (plain or with various toppings), Italian sandwiches, and chef salads, plus soft drinks, beer, and sangria. **LDS•$–$$•🐭**

COOLING HUT: Strut to this hut for a tuna sandwich, chicken wrap, popcorn, hummus with veggies, chips, and frozen treats. **LDS•$–$$•🐭**

FROSTBITE FREDDY'S FROZEN FRESHMENTS: Freddy serves orange swirl cones, plus frozen drinks: blue lemonade, piña coladas, and margaritas (classic and strawberry). He also offers barbecue brisket nachos and beer cheese fondue. **LDS•$–$$**

I.C. EXPEDITIONS: Cool off with an icy sundae, waffle cone, frozen ice cream novelty, or a refreshing root beer float. **S•$–$$**

LOTTAWATTA LODGE: The lodge offers items such as burger, flatbread, tuna sandwich, chicken rice bowl, and vegetarian options. Yummy desserts include chocolate dipped Key lime pie and milk shakes (salted caramel, peppermint, chocolate, or vanilla). **LDS•$–$$•🐭**

WARMING HUT: Despite the name, most of the fare is cool. Hit the hut for sandwiches (tuna, turkey, or chicken salad), turkey legs, shrimp Louie salad, loaded potato barrels, waffle cones, brownie sundaes, cookies, crispie treats, and assorted drinks. **LDS•$–$$•🐭**

HOT TIP!

All-Day Refillable Mugs (about $12 each) come with a day's worth of soft drink refills. Mugs may be reactivated for about $8.50 a day for the length of your stay.

In Disney Springs

Disney Springs encompasses the Marketplace, the West Side, Town Center, and The Landing. Restaurants operate from about 11 A.M. to midnight; most snack spots are open from 11 A.M. to late into the night. For details, call 407-939-4636 or visit *disneyworld.com*.

AMC DINE-IN THEATRES (West Side): Popcorn and soda are upstaged by selections such as chicken Alfredo and mango margaritas in this in-theatre dining experience known as Fork and Screen. Seat-side, tabletop service (with a personal call button for the server) allows moviegoers to enjoy dinner before a screening. The menu includes appetizers, entrées, desserts, soft drinks, and cocktails—plus a variety of classic movie munchies. Seating is reserved (and is assigned when you purchase your movie ticket). Guests under the age of 18 must be accompanied by a paying adult (age 18 or older). **LDS•$–$$•**

ARISTOCRÊPES (Marketplace): Sweet and savory crêpes are the specialty of this house (okay, it's more of a hut, but you get the point). The menu tempts with ham and cheese; beef; strawberries and cream; s'mores; and banana chocolate hazelnut crêpes. Bubble waffles (ice cream cones), beer, frozen cocktails, and soft drinks are also served. **LDS•$•**

THE BASKET AT WINE BAR GEORGE (The Landing): Three words of note: *Frosé all day*. Wine Bar George's walk-up window serves this refreshingly chilly libation along with an impressive selection of wine, beer, hard cider, and soft drinks. Beverages may be paired with tasty treats such as crispy mac and cheese bites, olives and

hummus, sandwiches (prosciutto, Brie, and olive salad on a baguette; goat cheese, fig, and arugula on ficelle; and ham and Gruyère on ciabatta), and cookies. Fancy a splurge-y smorgasbord? Order the Picnic Basket (for 2 or 4 guests; $80 or $110). **LDS•$$–$$$•**

B.B. WOLF'S SAUSAGE CO. (Marketplace): Head to this stand for quick-service hot dogs (mini and foot-long), sausages, chips, and maple-bacon chocolate-chip cookie dough. Fountain beverages, frozen lemonade, and seasonal beers are served. **LDS•$–$$•**

BLAZE FAST FIRE'D PIZZA (Town Center): If you fancy a freshly custom-made pizza, make a beeline for Blaze. The 5,000-square-foot eatery fires made-to-order (aka "build your own") pizzas in just three minutes with the help of super-hot pizza ovens. Guests may customize their 11-inch pies with a vast array of toppings (included in the price), as well as pick their own cheese and sauce. Gluten-free crusts are an option. The menu features nearly a dozen signature pizzas, plus salads and desserts. S'more pie, please! **LDS•$–$$•**

THE BOATHOUSE (The Landing): An upscale and convivial waterfront destination, The Boathouse serves delightful delicacies from land and sea for lunch and dinner. Raw bar highlights include oysters on the half shell, caviar corn blinis, and crab cakes (large enough to share, though you won't want to). Entrée selections have included coriander-seared tuna, Beach and Sea Lobster Bake for Two, and baked crab-stuffed lobster. Chicken, pasta, and a large lineup of steak dishes tempt, too. A kids' menu is available. Guests may enjoy drinks and a full menu at any of the three bar settings. Doors close at 2 A.M. Reservations are highly recommended for tables at this Signature Restaurant, but bar stools are designated for walk-ins. **LDS•$$$–$$$$•🐭•SR**

CHICKEN GUY! (Town Center): This hoppin' spot boasts no fewer than 22 signature sauces in which to dip chicken tenders. Honey mustard? Check. Garlic Parmesan? Check. Sweet sriracha BBQ? Well, you get the picture. Chicken sandwiches and salads are served, as are seasoned fries, loaded fries, mac and cheese, and fried pickle chips. Save room for soft-serve ice cream. Wash it all down with bottled water, soft drinks, beer, or wine. **LDS•$–$$**

COOKES OF DUBLIN (The Landing): Raglan Road's delectable quick-service neighbor, this is the place to go for some of the best fish and chips in the World. And don't ask for the recipe—it's a Cooke family secret! Other choices include battered sausages, burgers, grilled chicken sandwiches, salads, beef and lamb pie, chicken and mushroom pie, and hog in a box (slow-roasted pork shoulder with roasted potatoes). Save room for a "lovely" dessert. **LDS•$–$$•🐭**

CITY WORKS EATERY AND POUR HOUSE: A sports fan's delight, City Works sits (fittingly) beside The NBA Experience. With its 165 screens, 80 tap beers (includ-ing dozens of local and global craft beer selections), an extensive menu including small bites (buffalo shrimp, smoked wings, flatbreads, kung pao cauliflower), salads, burgers, tacos, and entrées such as pan seared-salmon, fish and chips, pork chops, short ribs, etc., this boisterous new gathering spot aims to please. In addition to the substantial supply of suds, the bar serves specialty drinks, wine, soft drinks, and more. There's a kids' menu, too. You'll find City Works across from House of Blues. Reservations are accepted. Details are subject to change. **LDS•$$–$$$•🐭**

HOT TIP!

Is that gift card burning a hole in your pocket? Disney gift cards may be redeemed at all Disney–owned-and-operated dining, shopping, and recreation locations where credit cards are accepted. They may be used to pay for all (or part) of the bill at a Disney resort, too. If you lose track of what's left on your gift card, simply call the number on the back to find out.

THE DAILY POUTINE (Town Center): Poutine—a decadent combination of french fries and cheese curds, topped with beef gravy—comes from the Canadian province of Quebec. (Thank you, Canada!) Four different varieties of this savory snack are sold at this Disney Springs stand: Classic (beef poutine gravy and cheddar cheese curds), Latin (fried yucca and pulled pork), Italian (mozzarella and tomato sauce), and French (mushroom cream sauce and Gruyère cheese). Soft drinks, beer, and red sangria with cinnamon whisky are also served. **S•$•🐭**

D-LUXE BURGER (Town Center): D-Luxe is a sweet spot for a quick bite. The burgers (big enough to share) are served on fresh-baked buns. The freshly cut fries (which come with dipping sauces) and (scrumptious) artisanal gelato shakes are sure to please. Place your order at the counter and grab a seat while your meal is prepared—it will be delivered to your table. There's indoor and outdoor seating. **LDS•$$•🐭**

EARL OF SANDWICH (Marketplace): This counter-service spot is brimming with possibilities. Among the fare are hot and cold sandwiches (on warm bread), wraps, salads, and desserts. Other selections such as Hawaiian BBQ (ham with fresh pineapple and Swiss cheese), The Original 1762 (warm roast beef sandwich with horseradish sauce and cheddar cheese), and Caribbean jerk chicken are served, too. The veggie sandwich is an option. Breakfast includes warm sandwiches and baked goods. There are grab-and-go selections, too. Beer, wine, and Kona coffee are offered. Seating is available inside and out. The Earl welcomes hungry visitors daily from 8:30 A.M. until 11 P.M. To save some cheddar at Earl of Sandwich, use the coupon at the back of this book. **BLDS•$–$$•🐭**

FOOD TRUCKS (West Side): The Fantasy Fare food truck serves favorites from Magic Kingdoms around the world. Look for sticky chicken and waffles, corn dogs with waffle fries, shrimp & lobster mac and cheese, and chicken strips. The new Mac & Cheese Truck serves crunchy mac & cheese with six different cheeses and

---

topped with crispy cheese puffs. Other choices include chicken parm, smoked brisket, and lobster and shrimp mac & cheese. Another new addition to the food truck fleet, 4 Rivers Cantina Barbacoa, features taco cones, squash blossom quesadillas, nachos, tacos, burrito bowls, and more. Springs Street Tacos offers grilled steak, pork belly, grilled fish, adobe chicken, and rice and bean tacos. Menus and location are subject to change. The food trucks usually open between 4 P.M. and 5 P.M. **DS•$–$$•🐭**

GHIRARDELLI ICE CREAM & CHOCOLATE SHOP
(Marketplace): What is it about an old-fashioned ice cream parlor that makes just about everybody giddy? Oh, yes, the ice cream. This spot does it one better and throws in its world-famous chocolate, to boot. Stop in for a chocolaty treat, root beer float, or a malt. And there is always a possibility of a chocolaty free sample. How sweet is that?! **S•$–$$**

CHEF ART SMITH'S HOMECOMIN' (The Landing):
"Florida heritage meets New Southern cuisine" at this gustatory homage to the Sunshine State. Created by Chef Art Smith, the menu focuses on Southern favorites such as homemade pimento cheese, Church Lady deviled eggs (which, ironically, are quite heavenly), fried chicken, Low Country shrimp and grits, and pork BBQ plate. Specialty desserts such as Mockingbird Cake and fresh doughnuts make for a sweet finish.

The family-friendly destination has a design inspired by Florida architecture of the late 1800s, and it supports the "Fresh from Florida" campaign, with many of the ingredients coming from local farms, ranches, and fisheries. Reservations are recommended for all meals. **Brunch (weekend) LDS•$$$•🐭**

THE EDISON (The Landing): A lavish "Industrial Gothic"–
style venue, The Edison (modeled after the original Los Angeles version) is a 1920s-themed restaurant, bar, and nighttime destination. Designed to resemble a power plant, it recalls a robust era of invention and imagination. In addition to classic American food and drink, The Edison supplies electrifying entertainment, starting at about 9 P.M. every evening. Expect a lineup of unique acts, including contortionists, aerialists, live cabaret, deejays, and more.

The menu tempts with appetizers such as candied bacon, blackened shrimp, Mediterranean dips with pita chips, and deviled eggs. Entrée selections include jumbo lump crab cake, New York strip steak, Scottish salmon, braised pork spare ribs, fried chicken, burgers, and meatloaf. For dessert, choose a banana split, apple cobbler, or a lollipop tree (for two). Reservations are highly recommended.

Note: Guests arriving after 10 P.M. must be at least 21 years old (with government-issued photo ID to prove it) and wear venue-appropriate attire. Men may wear slacks, jeans, or dress shorts. Jackets are optional. No baseball caps, sleeveless shirts, or flip-flops allowed. For additional information, visit *theedisonfla.com*. **LDS•$$–$$$$•🐭**

ENZO'S HIDEAWAY (The Landing): A combination
tunnel bar and restaurant, Enzo's evokes a speakeasy atmosphere. Inspired by Florida's "rum-running" past, this watering hole specializing in barrel-aged cocktails has a vast selection of rums and scotches, plus beer, wine, and inventive specialty drinks (several of which are served family style).

When you're ready for some solid sustenance, choose from imported meats and cheeses, rustic pasta dishes, and a collection of Italian-inspired entrées (eggplant parm, chicken Milano, bistecca pizzaiola, etc.). Finish with a sweet treat such as cannoli, gelato, or sorbet. Late night bites are available until about midnight— among them aged cheeses, paninis, meatball sliders, and Caprese salads. Reservations are recommended. Enzo's Hideaway does not accept same-day reservations after 5 P.M. **LDS•$$–$$$$•🐭**

FRONTERA COCINA (Town Center): The brainchild
of six-time James Beard Foundation winner Chef Rick Bayless, this spot showcases his gourmet Mexican cuisine. Select from items such as handcrafted tortas, tacos, salads, freshly made guacamole, and braised meats— all prepared with locally sourced ingredients. Pair your Mexican meal with a marvelous margarita (the selection is vast). Beer, wine, cocktails, and soft drinks are also served. Reservations are recommended. There's a walk-up window from which to order take-away items such as tacos, sorbet, and sangria. **LDS•$$$•🐭**

HOUSE OF BLUES (West Side): Thanks to the mix of
its menu and rustic, folk-art-studded design, House of Blues doesn't disappoint. Menu favorites include

B breakfast   L lunch   D dinner   S snacks   / $ under $15 $$ $15–$36 $$$ $36–$60 $$$$ $60 and up

flatbreads (grilled, then finished in the pizza oven), lobster mac and cheese, tacos, cornbread, and jambalaya. House of Blues is a solid choice for a meal or a late-night bite. Live music is presented in the eatery and on the front porch on select days. There is a gospel brunch every Sunday (at 10:30 A.M. and 1 P.M.). Reservations are recommended for lunch and dinner (and necessary for brunch). To reserve a table at the House of Blues, call 407-934-2583. **LDS•$$–$$$•** 🐭

HOUSE OF BLUES SMOKEHOUSE (West Side): This walk-up window at House of Blues offers a variety of BBQ selections (pulled pork, brisket, or chicken sandwiches, smoked turkey legs, ribs, nachos, hot dogs, etc.), soft drinks, spirits, and more. **LDS•$–$$•** 🐭

JALEO BY JOSÉ ANDRÉS (West Side): The flavors of Spain have found a home in Disney Springs, thanks to world-renowned Chef José Andrés. The extensive tapas (small plates) menu features a combination of classic and contemporary España. Savory selections include hand-carved Jamon Iberico de Bellota, wood-grilled Iberico pork, and paella cooked over a wood fire. Reservations are recommended. The multi-level eatery features a quick-service area called Pepe. It offers Spanish-style sandwiches, snacks, Spanish Sangria, and other drinks. **LDS•$$–$$$**

MACGUFFINS (West Side): A little lounge in a big movie complex (AMC Disney Springs 24), MacGuffins offers a full bar and a lounge menu with wings, crab cakes, burgers, salmon, pasta, salads, and dips—plus selections from the movie theaters' Fork & Screen menu. Kids' meals are available, as are cake, ice cream, candy, and, of course, popcorn. **LDS•$$**

MARIA AND ENZO'S RISTORANTE (The Landing): Up, up, and away! Ostensibly set in a storied airline terminal from the 1930s, the edifice has morphed into an elegant eatery, thanks to a duo of enterprising immigrants named Maria and Enzo. Vintage maps and artifacts enhance the aviation theme. After checking in, passengers (aka diners) descend the grand, spiral staircase to reach an Art Deco–accented dining room. (Guests may also nosh in the cozy "First Class Lounge," on the top floor.)

The Southern Italian–inspired menu includes fried, stuffed rice balls; antipasti trio; aged prosciutto; crispy calamari; chicken or eggplant parmesan; fresh fish; seasonal vegetable soup; salads; cheese fritters; hand-crafted pasta dishes; steaks; and chops. Maria and Enzo offer desserts such as cannoli, cheesecake, gelato, and sorbet. A childrens' menu is available. Reservations are recommended. **Brunch (Sunday) LDS•$$–$$$•** 🐭

MORIMOTO ASIA (The Landing): Brought to Walt Disney World by Japanese master chef Masaharu Morimoto—TV's original Iron Chef—this modern eatery features dishes from across Asia. The two-story venue offers Pan-Asian cuisine creatively prepared in show kitchens: dim sum, sushi, shrimp wontons, and other seafood, and more. The menu features sushi and sashimi (including "towers" that serve 2 to 6 hungry guests); small plates such as edamame, shishito peppers, and portobello mushroom fries; wings; soups; salads; noodle and rice dishes; meat and poultry selections including orange chicken, angry chicken (crispy half chicken with bell peppers, bamboo, green beans, eggplant, and Thai red curry sauce), filet mignon, grilled pepper steak, and Morimoto Peking duck for two. This is a Disney Dining Plan Signature restaurant. Reservations are recommended. **LDS•$$$$•** 🐭 **•SR**

MORIMOTO ASIA—STREET FOOD (The Landing): This quick-service window, located on Morimoto Asia's patio, serves sushi, ramen (spicy kimchee or ginger chicken), pork ribs, *takoyaki* (octopus fritters), pork egg rolls, soft drinks, Japanese beers, and a specialty cocktail known as Singapore Slush. **LDS•$–$$**

PADDLEFISH (The Landing): Originally known as the Empress Lilly (after Walt Disney's wife, Lillian), and recently as Fulton's, this restaurant has been beautifully re-invented and given a new identity. Paddlefish may look as if it might set sail at any moment, but the sleek replica of a boat that houses the seafood-centric eatery is permanently docked at the edge of Lake Buena Vista. The classic WDW space features a modern interior, rooftop lounge, and two interior bars.

Paddlefish boasts an elaborate selection of appetizers and entrées featuring the day's arrivals. Look for offerings such as fried green tomatoes, charred octopus, lobster risotto, redfish, salmon, blackened catfish, Alaskan king crab, and (heavenly) lobster corn dogs. And a selection of seafood boils are sure to please. The menu offers plenty for landlubbers, too: beef skewers, filet mignon, pork osso bucco, strip steak, chicken, burgers, rib-eye, and vegetarian pasta. Youngsters appreciate the more-extensive-than-usual kids' menu.

Your meal can come to a sweet finish with spiced apple bread pudding, Key lime pie, flourless chocolate cake, New York-style cheesecake, and more. If you prefer to sip your dessert, consider a brownie milk shake or pecan chicory espresso martini. Reservations are recommended. **Brunch (Sunday) L D •$$$–$$$$•❤•SR**

PARADISO 37 (The Landing): A lively (and lovely), waterfront restaurant and bar (with indoor and outdoor seating, plus a live-performance stage), Paradiso 37 specializes in "swirl margaritas," stocks more than 100 different kinds of tequila, and offers the "coldest beer in the world." Oh, and food is served, too!

Paradiso's tapas-oriented menu focuses on "the taste" of the Americas. Starters include fire-roasted corn on the cob, salmon cakes, and P37 nachos. Entrées range from Argentinian skirt steak with chimichurri sauce to Chilean-style salmon. **LDS•$$–$$$**

PEPE BY JOSÉ ANDRÉS (West Side): Tucked within the same dynamic structure as the lively new Jaleo, Pepe features hot and cold Spanish-style sandwiches showcasing the best of José's native Spain. Highlights include *pollo frito*, *serrano* and *manchego*, and *bocatade vegetales*. The menu also includes salads, gazpacho, chips, and soft-serve treats. Beer, wine, sangria, and soft drinks are served. The counter-service eatery was designed by the acclaimed Juli Capella and features decor representing the colorful culture of Spain. **LDS•$$–$$$$•❤**

PLANET HOLLYWOOD OBSERVATORY (Town Center): Planet Hollywood is housed in a structure reminiscent of a 1900s-style observatory. The Hollywood-themed eatery has indoor and outdoor seating and a bar called Stargazers, featuring live entertainment. The menu has salads, sandwiches, pasta, burgers, and desserts. Reservations are recommended. **LDS•$$–$$$$•❤**

PIZZA PONTE (The Landing): Adjacent to Maria and Enzo's Ristorante, Pizza Ponte is a satisfying, quick-service dining experience. Step up to the counter and order pizza by the slice (tomato, spicy salami, 4-cheese, forest mushroom, etc.), sandwiches (tomato mozzarella; ham and cheese; tuna, and more), and desserts such as tiramisu, cannoli, or biscotti. Beer, wine, specialty coffee, and soft drinks are served. **LDS•$–$$•❤**

THE POLITE PIG (Town Center): Created by award-winning Orlando chefs Julie and James Petrakis, this casual quick-service destination features "modern

B breakfast   **L** lunch   **D** dinner   **S** snacks / **$** under $15   **$$** $15–$36   **$$$** $36–$60   **$$$$** $60 and up

barbecue" and Southern sides. The mouthwatering menu includes sandwich selections such as brisket melt, salmon BLT, and smoked chicken salad. Items from the smoker include pork shoulder, half chicken, brisket, wild salmon, and St. Louis ribs. There are plenty of salads and sides to mix and match, too (chopped salads, crispy Brussels sprouts, BBQ cauliflower, peel-and-eat shrimp, and much more). For dessert, choose from orange blossom honey cake or Key lime pie. Beer, wine, and cocktails are served—and there's a mighty extensive bourbon menu, too. There is indoor and outdoor seating and a full bar. **LD•$$–$$$**

RAGLAN ROAD (The Landing): As authentically Irish as you can get on this side of the Atlantic, this warm and spirited establishment blends fresh ingredients to create traditional Irish fare with a modern flair. Entrées such as fish and chips, shepherd's pie, Guinness-glazed ribs, seafood dishes, and vegetarian offerings are complemented by the welcoming atmosphere, complete with antiques and bric-a-brac, spirits, and live entertainment (starting at 4 P.M. on most days). Whistles may be wet with an extensive menu of craft beers, whiskeys, wines, and cocktails. Brunch (with live entertainment) is served on Saturday and Sunday. Reservations are recommended. **Brunch LDS•$$–$$$•❤**

RAINFOREST CAFE (Marketplace): This Amazon-emulating eatery transports diners to a makeshift rainforest, complete with banyan trees, tropical fish, waterfalls, singing birds, and trumpeting elephants.

Special effects envelop diners in tropical storms with flashes of lightning and thunder claps. American-style eats (with exotic names) have included Anaconda Pasta, Mojo Bones, and Rumble in the Jungle Turkey Wrap. Reservations may be made via the My Disney Experience app or website, or by calling 407-827-8500. Details are subject to change. **LDS•$$–$$$•❤**

SPLITSVILLE (West Side): Some go expecting just to bowl, not realizing that Splitsville's two kitchens turn out impressive casual fare such as freshly rolled sushi,

three-pepper calamari, seared ahi tuna, and sliders. They've also got pizzas, cheeseburgers, sandwiches, and salads. Many menu items are gluten free. Huge desserts include sundaes, floats, brownie à la mode, and "giant" cake. There is a bar and a mix-your-own Coca-Cola machine. Food is served lane-side or at "non-bowling" tables. Visit *www.splitsvillelanes.com* for additional information. **LDS•$$–$$$•❤**

STARBUCKS (West Side and Marketplace): The Disney Springs links of the famous coffee chain serve up all the usual Starbucks specialties all day long: fresh-brewed coffee (hot or iced), Frappuccino blended drinks, teas, smoothies, and kids' drinks, plus sweet and savory snack items—breakfast sandwiches, oatmeal, pastries, and cake pops. **BLDS•$–$$•❤**

STK ORLANDO (The Landing): Steak is the obvious star here, but this modern restaurant has a lot more to offer. Specializing in American cuisine, most palates can be pleased here. This modern-steakhouse-meets-sleek-lounge features a tempting raw bar, salads, appetizers (crispy rock shrimp, tuna tartare, mini burgers), and entrées such as burgers, fish, chicken, and all manner of steak. Enjoy your meal with sides such as jalapeño and cheddar grits, Brussels sprouts and bacon, wild mushrooms, or parmesan truffle fries. Kid-friendly selections are offered, too. Finish with a mini ice cream cone sampler, orange cheesecake, or warm berry parfait. There's a full bar and a well-rounded wine list. Guests may dine on the rooftop or in the modern main dining area. Brunch is offered on Saturday and Sunday. Reservations are recommended. **Brunch LDS•$$$–$$$$•SR**

TEA TRADERS CAFÉ BY JOFFREY'S (The Landing): The pleasant counter-service spot (with about 6 inside seats) is devoted to introducing guests to the visual beauty and taste of loose leaf teas prepared in a variety of ways: loose leaf, iced, frozen, spirited, etc. Scones, cookies, and doughnuts are at the ready. The shop also sells tea-based paraphernalia. There are outdoor tables nearby. **S•$–$$**

TERRALINA CRAFTED ITALIAN (The Landing): This waterside eatery serves as a flavorful escape inspired by Italy's famed Lake District. The menu boasts genuine Italian cuisine cooked in James Beard Award–winning Chef Tony Mantuano's signature Italian olive oil—and a selection of artisanal, hand-tossed pizzas and fresh vegetable dishes prepared in the gourmet wood-burning oven. Appetizers of note: antipasta platter, spaghetti fritters, crab crostini, and mozzarella-stuffed rice balls. The menu also features salads, sandwiches, and entrées such as citrus-herb brick chicken, slow-roasted beef short rib, housemade lasagna, and center-cut pork chop. Fans of Portobello Country Italian Trattoria, the eatery that previously occupied this spot, will be happy to note that some of their favorite menu items are still being served. With a dozen choices on the kids' menu, youngsters are sure to please their palates. For dessert, consider cappuccino crème brûlée or an ice cream sandwich. Reservations are recommended. **LDS•$$–$$$$**

PHOTO BY JILL SAFRO

T-REX CAFE: A PREHISTORIC FAMILY ADVENTURE (Marketplace): Dinosaurs throw one heck of a dinner party. See for yourself at this dino-themed feasting facility. When you enter, take note of hosts we were all led to believe were extinct. Okay, they're *mechanical* dinosaurs, but they're still pretty cool. As are the waterfalls, bubbling geysers, and fossil dig site. Appease hunger pangs with anything from Jurassic Salad to Mammoth Mushroom Ravioli. With soup, sandwiches, pasta, seafood, and steaks, this place aims to please.

Doors open at 11 A.M. and close at 11 P.M. Sunday through Thursday and at midnight on Friday and Saturday. Reservations are recommended and can be made via the My Disney Experience mobile app or website or by calling 407-828-8739. **LD•$$–$$$•**🍴

VIVOLI IL GELATO (The Landing): An 85-year-old, family-run establishment, Vivoli il Gelato comes to you from Florence, Italy. Creamy gelato is offered in 24 flavors. That could include hazelnut, salted caramel coffee, banana, peanut butter, brandied cherry, and

more. Baked treats and heavenly milk shakes are available, too. There are a few outdoor tables at this sweet spot across from The Boathouse. **LDS•$–$$**

WINE BAR GEORGE (The Landing): The masterpiece of Master Sommelier George Miliotes, this 200-seat lounge resembles a winemaker's estate. It's a cozy yet elegant environment in which to savor sips from acclaimed wineries and promising up-and-comers. There are more than 130 selections on the list, all served by the ounce, glass, or bottle. They pair beautifully with small plate offerings—crispy mac and cheese bites, grilled octopus in a lemon vinaigrette, a meat and cheese board, etc.—plus a handful of family-style entrées. Brunch is offered on Saturday and Sunday. Reservations are recommended.

F.Y.I.: George Miliotes is one of just 256 Master Sommeliers currently on the planet. Quite impressive! **Brunch LDS•$$–$$$•**🍴

WOLFGANG PUCK BAR & GRILL (Town Center): "Elegant farmhouse" is the theme behind Chef Puck's latest contribution to the Disney dining scene. Capturing the essence of laid-back California, the eatery features fresh takes on comfort classics, signature dishes with Mediterranean influences, and handcrafted specialty drinks. The menu tempts with pasta, pizza, salads, and creative entrées such as chicken weinerschnitzel, heritage farm pork chop, and seared Florida red snapper. Finish up with a sweet treat such as an apple pie sundae, Key lime pie, or cookie plate. Reservations are recommended. **LDS•$$–$$$$•**🍴

WOLFGANG PUCK GELATO BAR (Town Center): Belly up to Mr. Puck's walk-up window/bar for soft drinks (hot and cold), beer, specialty cocktails, nearly a dozen kinds of gelato, and sorbet. The frozen treats come in a cup or cone and may be topped with everything from cookie crumbs to locally grown blueberries. There is limited outdoor seating, but all items are easily taken on the go. **S•$–$$**

WOLFGANG PUCK EXPRESS (Marketplace): This high-quality, quick-service spot by Disney Days of Christmas shop serves three meals a day. Start your Disney Springs day with omelets, waffles (Belgian or chocolate chip), French toast, breakfast pizza, and oatmeal. Lunch and dinner tempt with seven different pizzas, pasta, oven-roasted salmon, rotisserie chicken, bacon-wrapped meatloaf, mac and cheese, sandwiches, wraps, soups, and salads. Kids have six entrées from which to choose, including pizza, spaghetti, and grilled chicken with mashed potatoes. For dessert, choose frozen yogurt or vanilla bean cheesecake. **BLDS•$–$$•**🍴

In WDW Resorts

Each of the dozens of resorts at Walt Disney World offers its own set of specially themed eateries. There are clambakes at the Beach Club, luaus at the Polynesian Village, wild game at the Wilderness Lodge, and beignets at Port Orleans French Quarter. Meals may be served buffet, family, or traditional table-service or fast-food style. Disney characters are often on hand, especially for breakfast, and some snack spots stay open 'round the clock. In fact, the resort dining scene has expanded and been upgraded so much of late that the (occasionally arduous) task of resort-hopping is a more worthwhile experience than ever before.

Reservations are a key part of the Walt Disney World dining circuit (call 407-WDW-DINE [939-3463]).

ALL-STAR RESORTS

There are three All-Star resorts, each with a themed food court. All-Star Sports has the End Zone food court in Stadium Hall. The Intermission food court is in Melody Hall at the All-Star Music resort. And All-Star Movies has the World Premiere food court in Cinema Hall. The food courts offer similar food stands, with Music and Sports having undergone recent refurbishments. The selections may include pasta, pizza, burgers, seafood, hot dogs, sandwiches, salads, ice cream novelties, a reliable variety of breakfast and baked goods, plus grab-and-go selections. Expect to find kid-pleasers such as fries, mac and cheese, and chicken nuggets. **BLDS•$–$$•❤**

ANIMAL KINGDOM LODGE

BOMA—FLAVORS OF AFRICA: Designed to resemble an African marketplace, Boma offers an impressively diverse selection—the fare served represents the continent of Africa. It's one big buffet with multiple stations, and the food is every bit as good as what you'd expect in a fine dining place.

The all-you-care-to-eat affair provides an excellent bang for your Disney dining buck. Breakfast features Kenyan coffee, Jungle Juice, omelets, cereals, fresh fruit, sausage, biscuits, ham, corned beef, and more. At dinner, expect to fill your plate with items such as salads (including watermelon rind salad and Tunisian couscous salad); an assortment of breads, soups, and stews; seafood; roasted meats; and a nice array of vegetarian selections. For dessert, do sample the decadent zebra domes—you'll regret it if you don't. It's tempting to overeat at a bounteous feast such as this, so consider taking tiny portions of everything. You can go back for seconds of

your favorites. Note that Boma's menu does change throughout the year. The wine list includes selections from various African vineyards. Even if you're not staying at the lodge, it's worth the trip. Reservations are required. **BD•$$–$$$•❤**

JIKO—THE COOKING PLACE: Jiko offers one of the more unusual—and enjoyable—Walt Disney World dining experiences. Its cuisine is inspired by the tastes of Africa, with influences from around the globe. Start with one of the paper-thin flatbreads (such as roasted chicken with lime chakalaka, lamb chopper cheese, and pickled sweet bell peppers), grilled wild boar tenderloin, artisanal cheeses, or seasonal salads. You may find curry-rubbed lamb loin, braised beef short ribs, maize-crusted grouper, vegetable and tofu sambusas, and oak-grilled filet mignon on the menu, too. Finish your meal with a fabulous cheese course and/or sweets such as the spiced peanut butter mousse or strawberry shortcake. The wine list is exclusively South African, one of the most extensive collections in the U.S. It's a nice spot for a grown-up splurge. Though it's not exactly a kid favorite—the sometimes exotic cuisine may not appeal to timid palates—there are child-friendly offerings. Reservations are recommended. The small lounge area offers the full menu, too. Incidentally, the word *jiko* is Swahili for "the cooking place." **D•$$$–$$$$•🐭•SR**

THE MARA: An impressive quick-service restaurant that has something for everyone—including a small grab-and-go section for those in a hurry. There are a couple of stations at which (excellent) hot entrées are freshly prepared. Among the prepackaged selections are sandwiches, salads, fruit, yogurt, and baked goods.

F.Y.I.: The eatery is named for a river that flows through Kenya and Tanzania. **BLDS•$–$$•🐭**

SANAA: Pronounced *sa-NAH*, the name of this eatery means "artwork" in Swahili. The Kidani Village spot has a family-friendly menu featuring Disney's take on African-Indian cuisine. The Indian-style bread service, perfect for sharing and served with a choice of three accompaniments, is a nice way to start the meal. Signature dishes include chicken or shrimp curry and slow-cooked beef short ribs. For lunch, try the salad sampler. Even the burgers have an Indian touch, served on soft, warm naan bread. Desserts introduce many tastes, from mango berry tapioca pudding to Tanzanian chocolate mousse. Casual breakfast options such as waffles (topped with whipped cream and berries) and scrambled-egg sandwiches are offered, too. (Some breakfast items may be ordered "to go.") Reservations are recommended. **BLD•$$–$$$•🐭**

ART OF ANIMATION

LANDSCAPE OF FLAVORS: "Better for you" options is the theme of this vividly adorned food court, where everything is made fresh once it is ordered. Breakfast offerings include egg white frittata, challah French toast, and vegetarian breakfast sandwiches on naan bread, as well as more traditional selections. Four mini shops offer soups, salads, pizza, sandwiches, burgers, create-your-own pasta, shrimp, chicken, jumbo stuffed meatballs, and grilled fish. Sweet treats include brownie bites, gelato, and cupcakes. There is a small selection of grab-and-go items, too. Made-to-order beverage options include smoothies and specialty coffees. Also available are organic teas, beers (including a gluten-free selection), wine, coffee, and juices. **BLDS•$–$$•🐭**

BOARDWALK

AMPLE HILLS CREAMERY: The handcrafted ice cream—lovingly crafted with hormone-free milk from grass-fed cows and organic cane sugar—is a bona fide crowd-pleaser. Flavor offerings may differ a bit from day to day, providing a great reason to come back. You'll find it next to ESPN Club. **S•$•🐭**

BELLE VUE LOUNGE: This cozy cocktail spot, located on the resort's second floor, offers continental breakfast each morning until 11 A.M. Expect to find items such as bagels, cereal, yogurt, fruit, muffins, and croissants, plus juice, milk, coffee, and tea (the latter two can go straight into a Rapid Fill mug). **B•$•🐭**

BIG RIVER GRILLE & BREWING WORKS: Guests may observe (and sample) as the brewmaster creates flagship ales and two seasonal brews at this working brew pub. The simple but satisfying menu generally includes burgers, steaks, and salads. Sandwiches are a cut above. Other menu favorites: flame-grilled meatloaf and blackened Creole salmon. The interior has a nice, pubby feel—but we prefer to sit at outdoor tables on the boardwalk (especially in the evening hours). Seating is available on a first-come, first-served basis. **LDS•$$–$$$•🐭**

BOARDWALK BAKERY: Trattoria al Forno's next-door neighbor offers breakfast sandwiches, baked goods, soups, salads, and beverages. Lunch and dinner sandwiches may include roast beef on focaccia and roasted vegetable on ciabatta. Sweet treats (the specialty of this house) run from éclairs and crumb cake to apple tarts

PHOTO BY MIKE CARROLL

and cupcakes. This is also the place to buy and fill refillable resort mugs. **BLDS•$–$$•🍭**

BOARDWALK JOE'S MARVELOUS MARGARITAS: Step up to Joe's window to order Mickey pretzels, cheese nachos, personal pizzas, and assorted snacks. The beverage menu boasts beer (draft, bottle, and can), piña coladas, margaritas, and soft drinks. **LDS•$**

BOARDWALK PIZZA WINDOW: Nestled into the building that houses Trattoria al Forno is an opportunity to enjoy freshly prepared pizza, served by the pie or slice (cheese; pepperoni; and combos such as kale and chicken or sausage, onions, peppers, and a balsamic glaze). Italian hoagie and meatball sandwiches, salads, cannolis, beer, sangria, and soft drinks are dispensed here, too. The top-notch quick-service window is usually open from noon until midnight. **LDS•$–$$•🍭**

PHOTO BY JILL SAFRO

ESPN CLUB: For sports fans, this joint is pure heaven. The friendly, occasionally frenzied bar/family restaurant is a hard-core sports club. If there's a game being played, chances are it's showing on one of the million (okay, hundred) TVs.

The standard, reliable fare includes wings, burgers, sandwiches, seasonal fish, and salads. Both the dining room and the bar area serve cocktails and the full menu. We make an effort to get there at least an hour ahead to get a table or a spot at the bar on days when big games are scheduled. ESPN Club usually accepts weekday lunch reservations (12 P.M. to 4 P.M.), but it's a first-come, first-served establishment at most other times. Get there early. Note that the Club may offer premium seating for select "Big Games." Call 407-939-5656 for reservations and information. On exceptionally busy sports days, ESPN Club provides bar service out on the boardwalk. **LD•$$–$$$•🍭**

FLYING FISH: The decor elevates the appeal of this upscale dining destination, which has been given a thorough and dramatic refurbishment. Look up during the meal—the flying fish chandelier is a sight to behold. As always, this restaurant gives most fine, big-city spots a run for their money. (The tab rivals said hotspots, too.)

The menu changes often, but the stars of the show are creatively prepared sustainable seafood dishes. You can always find beefy items from the grill, too—think Wagyu filet mignon, tomahawk rib eye for two, and char-crusted New York strip steak. We're routinely impressed by the service and find the menu worthy of the price tag. Reservations are highly recommended. As far as the Disney Dining Plan goes, Flying Fish is designated as a Signature restaurant. **D•$$$$–$$$$•🍭•SR**

TRATTORIA AL FORNO: Taste buds take a tour of Italy with Trattoria's tempting array of regional specialties and crowd-pleasing classics. Signature standouts include wood-fired pizzas and pastas prepared *al forno* (baked in an oven). The family-friendly eatery celebrates the diversity of Italian cuisine with housemade mozzarella atop Neapolitan-style pizzas, hand-rolled pastas, seasonal seafood, and vegetables. The exclusively Italian wine list features more than 60 offerings by the bottle and 25 by the glass. Draft and bottle beers, cocktails, grappa, and soft drinks round out the drink menu. For dessert, consider tiramisu, budino (white chocolate Italian custard), or assorted flavors of gelato. The morning meal comes with a side of Disney characters. Expect to see favorite friends from films such as *Tangled* and *The Little Mermaid* at the Bon Voyage Breakfast. The menu has selections such as omelets, pancakes with seasonal compote, calzone with scrambled eggs, and breakfast potatoes with sausage. The Bon Voyage Breakfast is most popular—book your table as far in advance as possible. **BD•$$–$$$•🍭**

CARIBBEAN BEACH

CENTERTOWN MARKET: There is quite a bit to choose from at this sleek and colorful quick-service spot. The menu is posted at the cashier station, at which guests both order and pay for meals. Once you place the order, take a pager to a table and expect delivery within a few minutes. For breakfast, choose from omelets, pancakes (plain or filled with chocolate chips or pineapple and banana), French toast, Mickey waffles, oatmeal, and seasonal fruit. The lunch menu includes salads, burgers, sandwiches, and pizza, while dinner adds pasta bowls, rotisserie chicken Alfredo, and linguine with meatballs and marinara sauce. The kids' menu includes chicken nuggets, mac and cheese, and burgers. Enjoy a sweet treat in the form of a cupcake, brownie, or tropical tart. Soft drinks, specialty coffees, beer, wine, and cocktails are served. **BLDS•$–$$• 🍭**

CENTERTOWN MARKET GRAB & GO: The perfect place to grab a cuppa joe and go about your day, this corner of the Centertown Market boasts an extensive lineup of specialty coffees, plus smoothies, beer, wine, cocktails, and soft drinks. Assorted nibbles include cereals, salads, chips, sandwiches (hot and cold), candy, pastries, and ice cream novelties. **BLDS•$–$$•❤**

IN-ROOM DINING: Resort guests may have pizza, sandwiches, and pasta delivered to their rooms from 4 P.M. until midnight. To place an order, press Pizza Delivery on the in-room phone. Beer and wine are also available. (Please have your government-issued photo ID handy to prove you are at least 21 years old.) Note that an 18 percent gratuity and a $3 delivery charge apply to all in-room delivery orders. **D•$$–$$$•❤**

SEBASTIAN'S BISTRO: The crafty crustacean who managed to evade the big silver pot in Disney's *The Little Mermaid* has loaned his name to this under-the-sea-inspired eatery. Guests of the waterside bistro indulge in surf-and-turf meals infused with Latin and Caribbean flavors. Appetizers (from which one could make a whole meal) range from crab cakes and grilled jerk-chicken wings to raw sliced tuna and Jamaican meat pies. Among the main course possibilities: sautéed shrimp and tamales, grilled skirt steak chimichurri, slow-cooked pork shoulder, citrus-stuffed

sustainable whole fish, jerk chicken or butternut squash, and Caribbean vegetable or goat curry. Youngsters have an extensive kids' menu from which to choose. Cap it all off with warm chocolate pudding, a "floating island" of fruit and meringue with guava and sorbet, or banana custard with chocolate ganache and caramel sauce. All manner of beverages are served, including pressed-pot coffee, beer, wine, and specialty drinks. Reservations are recommended. **D•$$–$$$•❤**

SPYGLASS GRILL: A walk-up counter in the Trinidad pool area, this grill sits on a patio overlooking Barefoot Bay. Head there for American fare with Caribbean flair. Start the day with pineapple-banana pancakes, breakfast yucca hash, Cuban sandwich, or more traditional selections. For lunch and dinner, consider chorizo burgers, cheeseburgers, Cuban sandwiches, tacos, salads, pastries, brownies, cupcakes, and fresh fruit. Fountain beverages, beer, wine, cocktails, and specialty coffees are also served. **BLDS•$–$$•❤**

CONTEMPORARY

CALIFORNIA GRILL: Delighting diners for decades, the World-famous California Grill still graces most guests' must-do lists. The West Coast theme shines through in dishes prepared with the freshest seasonal and local produce available. "Brunch at the Top" features vanilla bean French toast, Shashuka, poached lobster Benedict, grilled hangar steak and eggs, and other creatively prepared dishes. The fixed-price brunch costs about $80 for adults, $48 for youngsters (ages 3 to 11).

Dinner standouts include sumptuous starters such as Sonoma goat cheese ravioli, Bang Island mussels and frites, and rotisserie-smoked beef short ribs. Entrées of note include artisanal pizza; Colorado bison loin with truffle-herb potato gnocchi; pork tenderloin with goat cheese polenta; oak-fired filet of beef with tamarind BBQ sauce; and wild-caught Alaskan halibut. Sushi classics include a dragon roll with spicy tataki tuna, shrimp tempura, bell pepper, avocado, and chili-soy glaze; and a fan favorite known as the spicy kazan roll (crab, shrimp, scallops, and tuna in a spicy fireball sauce).

The encyclopedic wine list—which includes about 300 selections, 80 of which are available by the glass—is a nice mix of greatest hits and good finds. There are ten varieties of sake and a selection of (predominantly Californian) craft beers. Housemade desserts (lemon meringue cannoli, lavender doughnuts, warm Valrhona chocolate cake, etc.) provide the finishing touches, and there are sweeping views of the Magic Kingdom and the Seven Seas Lagoon (from select seats).

California Grill is always busy and the fare is first-rate. Reservations are a must. Changes or cancellations should

---

Dinner at Sea

For Disney's ultimate dinner-and-a-show splurge, consider reserving the elegant *Grand 1* yacht. You and up to 17 lucky invitees can enjoy a private tour of the lakes near the Magic Kingdom capped off with a viewing of Happily Ever After, the park's fireworks show—all the while devouring delicacies prepared by chefs at the Grand Floridian resort. The possibilities range from an intimate cruise for two, complete with dinner and champagne, to a swinging cocktail party for up to 18, with a boatload of shrimp, chips, wings, beer, wine, and soft drinks.

Cost starts at about $400 (plus tax) per hour to rent the 5-room floating fantasyland. A driver and deckhand are included; refreshments are not. Prices vary depending on the time of day. To book, call 407-WDW-PLAY at least 24 hours and up to 90 days ahead. The *Grand 1* yacht docks at the Grand Floridian Marina but can pick up passengers at the Contemporary, Polynesian Village, and Wilderness Lodge.

HOT TIP!

Would you like to watch Happily Ever After, the Magic Kingdom's fireworks display, from an exclusive perch at the Contemporary resort's California Grill? You'll need to dine at the Grill, of course—but it doesn't have to be during the show. If you finish your meal pre-fireworks, return to the second-floor check-in desk later that day, present your receipt, and you'll be escorted to the eatery via private express elevator.

be made at least 24 hours ahead to avoid the $10 per-person fee. This is a Disney Dining Plan Signature restaurant (which means it requires two table-service credits per meal, per diner).

An outdoor perch (exclusively available to California Grill patrons) affords dramatic bird's-eye views of the Magic Kingdom and its fireworks presentations (complete with the Happily Ever After show's soundtrack). Guests (including those planning to visit the lounge) check in on the hotel's second floor and are escorted to the restaurant's express elevator. Dinner starts at 5 P.M. **Brunch (Sunday) D •$$$$• ❤•SR**

PHOTO BY MIKE CARROLL

CHEF MICKEY'S: Chef Mickey and his pals host this buffet-style meal, with striking views of the monorail passing above. The eatery serves family-friendly fare for breakfast, brunch, and dinner. The ever-changing menu takes advantage of seasonal offerings; a sundae bar provides a sweet finish. At some point during the meal, Chef Mickey will stop by your table, as will Minnie and several other Disney friends. Be prepared to drop your fork and twirl your napkin at a moment's notice. This is a very popular eatery with a loyal following. Kids simply adore the experience. It's a fun place to celebrate a child's birthday, too. Reservations are an absolute must. **B Brunch D•$$$•❤**

CONTEMPO CAFE: The Contemporary snack bar can be found on the fourth floor, beside Chef Mickey's. This modest spot serves impressive made-to-order fare. (Orders are placed with a cashier.) The grab-and-go section offers drinks (including milk, juice, beer, and wine), wraps, yogurt, fruit, desserts, and more. If you buy a refillable mug, this is the place to make it happy. **BLDS•$–$$• ❤**

THE WAVE . . . OF AMERICAN FLAVORS: Serving three meals a day, this establishment offers American cuisine. For breakfast, there is a buffet and à la carte selections such as glazed doughnut French toast, eggs Benedict, omelets, and avocado toast. Lunch and dinner feature starters such as mussels, jumbo lump crab cake, salad, and rock shrimp tacos. Sandwiches and burgers are available for lunch. Evening entrées have included grilled beef tenderloin, seared gnocchi, braised beef short ribs, and noodle bowl. Desserts include the Chocolate Flight (three chocolaty treats), a trio of sorbet, and crème brûlée. The Wave is on the Contemporary's first floor.

The adjacent lounge is a perfect place for an aperitif, an after-dinner drink, a light snack, or a meal (the full menu is available to lounge guests). Reservations are recommended for the restaurant. All details are subject to change in 2020. **BLD•$$–$$$•❤**

CORONADO SPRINGS

CAFE RIX: Stop here for bagels and croissants, salads (Cobb, Greek, and house), chicken Caesar wraps, pastries, gelato, sorbet, beer, wine, soft drinks, and specialty coffee drinks. Additional snacks include fruit cups, veggies and hummus, side salads, yogurt parfait, and chocolate or Key lime mousse. **BLDS•$–$$•❤**

EL MERCADO DE CORONADO: Formerly known as Pepper Market, this busy, casual food court has a large seating area and a variety of food stations. Choose from BBQ ribs, Yucatán chicken, tacos, paninis, pizza, pasta, salads, empanadas, and other Mexican fare—all freshly prepared. For breakfast, there are eggs, Mickey-shaped waffles, breakfast bowls, Southwestern omelets, and more. Anything may be ordered to go. Given this resort's popularity with the convention set, expect a proliferation of hungry humans during traditional weekday breakfast and lunch times. **BLDS•$$–$$$•❤**

RIX BAR & GRILL: A chic but cozy environment in which to root, root, root for your home team, Rix Bar & Grill serves breakfast, lunch, and dinner in addition to pubby appetizers "with a unique spin." Breakfast runs from "ancient grain" pancakes to steak and eggs. Later in the day, items such as burgers, BBQ ribs, fish & chips, and New York Strip grace the menu. Complete the meal with sorbet, Key lime pie, or chocolate cake. There are kid-friendly menu choices, but the atmosphere is unlikely to enchant most wee ones. Reservations are suggested. **BLDS•$–$$$•**

MAYA GRILL: Guests here dine inside a Mayan pyramid, beside a volcano (dormant, of course). The menu has a bit of everything: seafood, meat, and poultry, with a touch of Latino spices added to some of the creations. Entrées range from sirloin fajitas to Veracruz-style snapper or Yucatán roasted pork. Desserts include coconut flan and panna cotta. Dinner is served from 5 P.M. to 10 P.M. Reservations are recommended. **BD•$$$•**

THREE BRIDGES BAR & GRILL: This pleasant, table-service locale is an island of sorts, sitting atop the 14-acre Lago Dorado and accessed exclusively by bridges. There's a full-service bar, plus sandwiches, salads, desserts, and more. **DS•$$–$$$•**

TOLEDO—TAPAS, STEAK & SEAFOOD: Surrealist Spanish art and 1930s avant-garde were the inspiration for this distinctive rooftop destination. The new eatery, which sits atop the resort's 15-story Gran Destino Tower, features vaulted ceilings and panoramic views of Walt Disney World. The show-kitchen serves small plates, charcutería, and cheeses, entrées such as aged, hand-cut Spanish chuletón for two (32-ounce bone-in rib eye steak), and sustainable seafood offerings—oven-roasted shrimp, scallops, tilefish, Spanish olive oil-braised octopus, and more. The expansive wine list includes Spanish and California highlights hand-selected by a Master Sommelier, as well as beer, cider, and hand-crafted cocktails. Reservations are recommended. To make reservations for parties of 11 or more, call 407-939-3890. **D•$$$–$$$•**

DISNEY'S OLD KEY WEST

GOOD'S FOOD TO GO: A walk-up window with simple yet satisfying offerings throughout the day: Hamburgers, cheeseburgers, deli sandwiches, salads, ice cream, snacks, and breakfast items are among the offerings at Good's. **BLDS•$–$$•**

GURGLING SUITCASE: This pocket-sized lounge packs a real punch. In addition to a full bar, the Suitcase features nibbles such as cheeseburgers, pulled pork nachos, conch fritters, grouper bites, and onion rings. It's possible to order from the Olivia's Cafe menu, too. Many items can be ordered to go. **LDS•$–$$$•**

OLIVIA'S CAFE: We thoroughly enjoy the Key West manner with which Olivia's approaches its theme. The laid-back setting and menu convey the spirit of the leisure-centric locale. Breakfast includes standards, but also interesting combos like poached eggs served over sweet potato hash, topped with Key West hollandaise. The lunch/dinner menu offers salads, conch chowder, crab cakes, seared scallops, burgers, and sandwiches. End with a Key lime tart, chocolate cake, or a banana bread pudding sundae. The menu changes seasonally. Wine, beer, and specialty drinks are served. Reservations are recommended for all meals. **BLD•$$–$$$•**

FORT WILDERNESS

Many folks choose to cook their own meals here. Some supplies are available at the Meadow and Settlement Trading Posts (open from 8 A.M. to 10 P.M. in winter; to 11 P.M. in summer), others may be delivered by a nearby grocery store (see page 234 for details). Trail's End is the only eat-in restaurant, but it has a corner dedicated to takeout: P & J's Southern Takeout offers breakfast, lunch, and dinner selections to bring back to a campsite or enjoy at a nearby table.

TRAIL'S END RESTAURANT: True, it's a bit out of the way for anyone but Fort Wilderness guests (and even for some of them!), but for many folks, this rustic spot is well worth the trip.

The informal log-walled restaurant offers a hearty buffet breakfast. The fare is basic but bountiful. Breakfast selections include grits, biscuits and gravy, and breakfast pizza. For dinner, expect the buffet to have smoked pork ribs, peel-and-eat shrimp, fried chicken, carved meats, a salad bar, plus a variety of side dishes

---

Tables in Wonderland

WDW Annual Passholders and Florida residents are eligible for the Tables in Wonderland (T.I.W.) discount dining program. It affords members up to 20 percent savings off food and beverages at many Walt Disney World table-service eateries. The discount is good for you and up to 9 members of your party. Present a valid photo ID and your T.I.W. card when you place an order with a server. To net the discount for the rest of the party, the check must be paid by the T.I.W. member. Membership is valid for one year and costs $150 for Annual Passholders and $175 for Florida residents (note that the price went up substantially last year). For further details, call 407-566-5858. To get a list of participating Tables in Wonderland locations, go to: *https://disneyworld.disney.go.com/faq/restaurants/tables-in-wonderland-restaurants/*.

---

and desserts. Beer and wine are served by the glass (or mason jar if you prefer). Reservations are recommended. Breakfast costs about $25 for adults, $14 for youngsters (brunch is higher); dinner is about $35 for adults, $19 for kids. After the meal, you can relax in a rocking chair on the front porch. (Allow plenty of travel time to get here, just in case.) Brunch is offered on Saturdays and Sundays. The brunch bounty includes waffles, a carving station, made-to-order eggs and omelets, shrimp, smoked salmon, pasta, fried chicken, a "dessert island," and more. **B Brunch DS•$–$$•**❤️

GRAND FLORIDIAN

CÍTRICOS: From the aromas wafting from the open kitchen, it's clear that the chef aims to wow you with cuisine from the Mediterranean, herb by fragrant herb. The fare varies seasonally but may include such items as crispy risotto with mascarpone or beef short rib. Adventurous palates are most at home here. The menu is not extensive, but the wine list sure is. Don't worry—savvy sommeliers are on hand to recommend wine pairings.

A private dining room is available for parties of up to 12. Reservations are recommended. A small lounge within Cítricos is ideal for solo diners and those caught without reservations. The dress code is business casual. **D•$$$–$$$$•**❤️**•SR**

GASPARILLA ISLAND GRILL: Gasparilla is your go-to destination for 'round the clock, casual fare. Breakfast items along the lines of egg sandwiches, Mickey waffles, quiche, oatmeal, yogurt parfaits, and cereal are served until 11 A.M. After that, made-to-order selections such as sandwiches, burgers, pizza, and freshly tossed salads are available. There's a specialty coffee station and a pastry counter. Grab-and-go options such as shrimp cocktail, pasta salad, yogurt, fresh fruit, ice cream novelties, and other snacks are on hand 24/7 in this quick-service spot near the marina. There is indoor and outdoor seating. If you purchased a refillable mug, this is a place to make it happy. (Mugs may also be filled at the resort's Beaches Pool Bar & Grill.) **BLDS•$–$$•**❤️

GRAND FLORIDIAN CAFE: A pleasant spot, the cafe is a relatively reasonably priced, low-key way to enjoy one of Disney's poshest resorts.

Breakfast extends a bit beyond the usual fare and is available until 2 P.M. Lunch and dinner menus vary seasonally but have traditional American dishes: onion soup, salad, steak, pasta, and sandwiches—including the signature Grand Floridian sandwich. The wine selection is excellent. Reservations are recommended, but it may be possible to get a table without one if you're willing to wait. **BLD•$$$•**❤️

NARCOOSSEE'S: Named for a nearby Florida town, Narcoossee's specializes in fresh sustainable seafood—with the occasional land-based entrée making surf-and-turf combinations a decadent possibility. The menu at Narcoossee's features upscale selections (and prices), but the atmosphere is rather relaxed.

The display kitchen presents sublime starters such as shrimp and crab cake, lobster bisque, and BBQ-grilled shrimp and grits. The entrée lineup may include pan-seared day boat scallops, grilled grass-fed filet mignon, wild-caught shrimp and pasta, and steamed lobster. Cap it all off with cheesecake, sorbet, or a dark chocolate-mocha bar with housemade chocolate gelato. The international wine selection is quite good—you might even enjoy a pre-dinner glass on the veranda. The view of the Seven Seas Lagoon and Cinderella Castle (in the distance) completes the experience. Reservations are recommended. The lounge here offers selections from the restaurant's menu (and does not require a reservation), as well as a full bar and an abundance of wines offered by the bottle or the glass. The dress code is business casual. **D•$$$–$$$$•**❤️**•SR**

Tea for Two (or Ten)

Teatime with all the trimmings—scones, finger sandwiches, strawberries and cream, etc.—is from 12 P.M. until 4 P.M. in the Garden View Tea Room at the Grand Floridian resort. This elegant lounge overlooks the lovingly tended gardens surrounding the resort's main swimming pool.

The menu includes custom-blended teas from around the world. Patrons may also sip coffees and spirited drinks such as port or sparkling wine. Note that guests must be at least 21 years of age (with valid photo ID) to consume alcohol.

The Grand Floridian Resort & Spa offers tea parties for kids, too. For information on these special events, turn to page 239.

For details or to make (necessary) reservations, call 407-WDW-DINE (939-3463).

1900 PARK FARE: The atmosphere is reminiscent of an old-time amusement park, but the sophisticated buffet menu and subtle decor make this one of the most elegant character restaurants in WDW. Guests may meet Mary Poppins, Alice in Wonderland, the Mad Hatter, Tigger, and Winnie the Pooh during the bountiful breakfast. Cinderella and members of her royal family visit the dining room during dinner hours. Keep in mind that the lineup of characters is subject to change.

Dinner features seafood, salads, pastas, breads, carved meats, veggie sides, and housemade desserts. Offerings change seasonally. A salad bar and dessert bar stand nearby. There's a kid-friendly buffet, too. It offers pizza, pasta, chicken bites, and corn. The restaurant's focal point is Big Bertha, a band organ built in Paris nearly a century ago. She sits in a proscenium and rises 15 feet above the floor. Reservations are recommended. Brunch is offered seasonally. **B Brunch D•$$$•♥**

VICTORIA & ALBERT'S: The dining room in the only AAA 5-Diamond restaurant in Central Florida seats just 48 guests (all of whom must have already celebrated their 10th birthday). It is indulgent without being too haute to handle (although the steep prices may curb some folks' enthusiasm) and is considered by many to be the grand dame of the Disney dining scene. As such, it's a popular destination for many a special celebration.

The 7-course "Chef's Tasting Menu" changes often, always offering a delectable selection of fish, poultry, and beef. But the beauty of this high-end experience is all the little tastes as you make your way through the $185 per-person (plus tax and gratuity) adventure. The cheese course is worth every calorie. And, even with seven courses, you *must* reserve room for the indulgent desserts. Perfect portions keep it all surprisingly manageable. The strains of a harp or violin provide a romantic backdrop. The wine list is encyclopedic. Wine pairings are available for an additional $65 per person. (Be sure to let your server know about any personal wine preferences—they aim to please.)

The main dining room and Queen Victoria room also serve a prix fixe "Chef's Degustation Menu"— a tempting selection of fish, poultry, and beef. You might start with lobster or quail, then move on to seared wild turbot or pork tenderloin. And please save room for the indulgent selection of desserts. The appetizing odyssey costs $235 per person ($385 with wine pairing), plus tax and gratuity.

For an extra-special (and extra-splurgy) experience, book the Chef's Table (for up to 8 guests; starting at $250 per person, plus tax and tip). There, you'll have a front-row seat while the Victoria & Albert's culinary team crafts your feast. Wine-pairing may be added (starting at $150 per person). With just one table, this is the restaurant's most exclusive, luxurious setting.

At the end of the meal, all guests receive a souvenir menu to commemorate the occasion. In sum, though the experience is an extremely expensive one, for many it is also quite special. Jackets are required for men. Guests must be at least 10 years old to dine at Victoria & Albert's. (There is no kids' menu.) Reservations are an absolute must. For reservations and to peruse sample menus, go to *www.victoria-alberts.com*. **D•$$$$**

POLYNESIAN VILLAGE

CAPT. COOK'S: The captain serves snacks and light fare 24 hours a day. It's a good spot for made-to-order breakfast items such as breakfast flatbreads, eggs, Mickey waffles, or the ever-popular fried, banana-stuffed Tonga toast. Lunch and dinner bring cheeseburgers, plant-based burgers, chicken wings, pulled pork nachos, hot dogs, Thai coconut meatballs, flatbreads (plain, pepperoni, seafood, and Hawaiian [marinara, pineapple, onions, ham, mozzarella, and parmesan]), salads, soup, sandwiches, and grab-and-go items such as noodle salad, yogurt, fruit, pastries, and snacks. Milk, beer, wine, and soft drinks are available. Stop there to buy and fill the Poly's refillable mug (aka Rapid Fill). **BLDS•$–$$•♥**

KONA CAFE: Warm colors and South Seas decor render the crisp, fluid design of this open dining space cozy and casual. The menu tends a tad toward the exotic side, but there's a lot to choose from. Lunch and dinner menus feature Asian-influenced entrées. Possibilities include crispy pork-vegetable pot stickers, coconut mussels, sushi, steak, market-fresh fish, and miniature seasonal desserts. The morning meal offers Tonga toast (banana-stuffed, fried sourdough bread coated with cinnamon sugar), plus traditional breakfast items. There is a solid wine list, and islands-inspired cocktails are served. The pressed-pot coffee is a fan favorite. You'll find Kona Cafe on the second floor of the Polynesian's Great Ceremonial House, just around the corner from 'Ohana. Reservations are recommended for all meals. **BLDS•$$–$$$•♥**

KONA ISLAND: A coffee bar by day, this is a super spot for a quick sip of freshly brewed Kona blend on your way to the monorail. Light breakfast items such as quiche, egg croissants, pastries, and fruit are offered, too.

Later in the day this area becomes something of a Kona Cafe annex/sushi bar. Guests may sit around the Island's counter and order from the Cafe menu. A member of the Kona Cafe waitstaff will take your order. Seating is limited, but many items may be prepared to go. Beer, wine, sake, and cocktails are served. Reservations are not accepted. Once folks discover this not-so-hidden gem, it quickly earns a spot on their list of happy places. Details may change in 2020. **BLDS•$–$$$•♥**

'OHANA: On the second floor of the resort's Great Ceremonial House, this restaurant is a meticulously themed, family-friendly eatery, complete with entertainment. An interesting twist of note: 'Ohana's family-style dinner experience—a South Pacific feast prepared in the restaurant's open-fire cooking pit—does not come with a menu, so no decisions have to be made. The oak-grilled skewers of chicken, steak, and spicy shrimp just keep coming. Honey coriander chicken wings, pot stickers, green salad, coconut bread, pan-Asian noodles tossed in teriyaki sauce, and stir-fried veggies are among the accompaniments, and dessert is bread pudding served à la mode with warm caramel sauce. Soft drinks are included. Beer, wine, and cocktails are extra.

'Ohana's setting, which features wood carvings under a vast thatched roof, is rather festive. So much so that there are periodic boisterous hula dances and coconut-rolling contests for the little ones. A singer serenades with song and ukulele rhythms.

Breakfast is also a family affair—make that extended family, as Lilo, Stitch, and their good friends Mickey and Pluto host the morning meal. Breakfast fare is basic and presented family style. Keep in mind that the character lineup does change from time to time. Reservations are strongly recommended—book early. **BD•$$$–$$$$•**🐭

OASIS GRILL: The laid-back Oasis Grill is situated next to the Polynesian's Oasis pool. It serves up items such as cheeseburgers, fish tacos, chicken avocado wraps, spinach and watermelon salad, and more. The O.G. is adjacent to the Oasis Bar. **LDS•$–$$•**🐭

PINEAPPLE LANAI: This sweet stop offers WDW's classic Dole Whip frozen pineapple dessert—served plain, twisted with vanilla soft-serve, or as a float with pineapple juice. It's possible to get a coconut rum-infused serving, too. A new menu item of note is the Te Fiti cone (lime soft-serve garnished with an orchid). The lanai is on the resort's ground level. **S•$•**🐭

TRADER SAM'S GROG GROTTO: It's impossible to be grouchy at this spot—Trader Sam will make sure of that. With a theme inspired by the Jungle Cruise and Enchanted Tiki Room attractions, Trader Sam's features drinks (tropical and otherwise) and small plates such as pan-fried dumplings, chicken lettuce wraps, and sushi rolls. Patio seating is relatively easy to snag, but securing indoor seats often requires a bit of patience. (It's worth the wait!) Doors open at 3 P.M. and close promptly at midnight. Note that folks may start lining up for the inside seats at about 2:30 P.M. **S•$–$$**

POP CENTURY

EVERYTHING POP!: The selection at this colorful food court in Classic Hall has included burgers, omelets, pizza, seared salmon, fried chicken, pot roast, rotisserie turkey, nachos, create-your-own salads, seafood, hot dogs, sandwiches (barbecue pork, turkey, and roasted vegetable), ice cream, breakfast items, and baked goods (tie-dyed cheesecake!). Feel free to join the jolly Cast Members as they dance the Twist at 8 A.M., the Hustle at 1:30 P.M., and the Mickey Mouse March at 6 P.M. **BLDS•$–$$•**🐭

PORT ORLEANS FRENCH QUARTER

SASSAGOULA FLOATWORKS & FOOD FACTORY: A food court with a Mardi Gras theme, this spot offers pizza, pasta, burgers, sandwiches, soups, salads, fried chicken, BBQ ribs, ice cream, and bakery products. The Big Easy is well represented: New Orleans–inspired menu items include classic gumbo, po' boys, chicken sandwiches, burgers, crawfish étouffée, and made-to-order Mickey-shaped beignets (with dipping sauces). **BLDS•$–$$•**🐭

HOT TIP!

Guests staying at Port Orleans French Quarter and Riverside may have pizza delivered to their rooms between 5 P.M. and 1 A.M. Call Sassagoula Pizza Express from your resort room telephone to order whole pies, drinks, and sweet snacks. There is a $15 minimum per order and the Disney Dining Plan is accepted. Guests using the Disney Dining Plan should note that pizza delivery requires two adult table-service credits per order (which includes one pizza, two beverages, and two desserts).

PORT ORLEANS RIVERSIDE

BOATWRIGHT'S DINING HALL: Southern specialties and American comfort food are the big draws in these parts: crawfish bisque, fried green tomatoes, prime rib, jambalaya, and more. Dessert can come in the form of Mississippi mud pie, red velvet cheesecake, pecan tart, gooey butter cake, or sorbet. Beer, wine, and cocktails are available, as are soft drinks. Boatwright's is the resort's only table-service spot, so reservations are recommended. Walk-up requests are typically admitted when the restaurant opens at 5 P.M. **D•$$–$$$•** 🐭

RIVERSIDE MILL: This high-ceilinged food court styled in the image of a cotton mill (complete with working waterwheel) offers a half dozen food counters. Collectively, the stands serve pizza; pasta; fried, grilled, and roast chicken; cheeseburgers; salads; Cajun chicken sandwiches; ice cream; and fresh-baked goods. They're big on "create your own" here, too. (You can customize an omelet, salad, and/or pasta dish.) There's ample seating, so it's usually possible to get a table. All items may be packaged to go. **BLDS•$–$$•** 🐭

DISNEY'S RIVIERA RESORT

BAR RIVA: Mediterranean and European-inspired beverages and bites are served at this spiffy poolside spot. **S•$–$$•** 🐭

 LE PETIT CAFÉ: Quench your thirst in an elegant manner at this chic lobby locale. A coffee bar by day and wine bar by night, Le Petit also features nibbles and sweet treats. **S•$–$$•** 🐭

PRIMO PIATTO: This quick-service trattoria serves up tasty offerings throughout the day—as well as a selection of grab-and-go items. **BLDS•$–$$•** 🐭

TOPOLINO'S TERRACE—FLAVORS OF THE RIVIERA:
 You just may feel like you're on top of the World at this new rooftop restaurant, perched on top of Disney's new Riviera resort. While eyes take in the stunning vistas of Walt Disney World, palates take a tasty tour of the Italian and French Riviera with dishes prepared in a modern expo kitchen.

Breakfast features a prix-fixe menu and appearances by favorite Disney characters. The evening meal comes with an à la carte menu brimming with possibilities—including the opportunity to enjoy a bird's-eye view of a nearby nighttime spectacular, courtesy of Epcot or Disney's Hollywood Studios.

At press time, the Terrace was expected to be open in all of 2020. To make a reservation, use the My Disney Experience app or website, visit *disneyworld.com*, or call 407-WDW-939-3463. **BD•$$$–$$$$•** 🐭 **•SR**

SARATOGA SPRINGS

THE ARTIST'S PALETTE: Set in a converted artist's loft within Walt Disney World's sprawling resort, this spot offers breakfast, lunch, and dinner. Among the selections are fresh tossed salads, made-to-order sandwiches, pizza, baked goods, and more. There are some grocery items, as well as a variety of grab-and-go selections. **BLDS•$–$$•** 🐭

THE PADDOCK GRILL: Head to this window for breakfast items such as quiche, oatmeal, grilled ham and egg croissant, bagel with cream cheese, and fruit. The lunch and dinner menu offers spicy fried chicken sandwiches, Cobb salad, bacon cheeseburgers, fish tacos, teriyaki burgers, vegetarian burgers, chili-cheese hot dogs, and housemade potato chips (which were actually invented in Saratoga Springs, New York). **BLDS•$–$$•** 🐭

THE TURF CLUB BAR & GRILL: A restaurant with an old-fashioned horse racing theme, this table-service eatery serves soup, prime rib, steak, pan-seared scallops, sustainable fish of the day, pasta, salads, New York strip steak, roasted lamb, fried chicken breast, spice-rubbed pork tenderloin, and more. **BD•$$$•** 🐭

SWAN & DOLPHIN

CABANA BAR & BEACH CLUB: An elegant poolside destination, the Dolphin's Cabana serves a sophisticated selection of starters, salads, and entrées. Appetizer options include chicken wings and fish tacos. The main bites menu offers fish and chicken sandwiches, grilled chicken BLT, buttermilk-battered chicken crisps, and burgers made from farm-raised, grass-fed, organic beef. Among the many signature cocktails are the Original Mai Tai, Solstice Margarita, and Hibiscus Cooler. Kids choose from pizza, burgers, hot dogs, grilled cheese, and chicken fingers. **LDS•$–$$**

THE FOUNTAIN: A Dolphin-based soda fountain with grown-up appeal, this is an ideal spot for a sweet snack or a satisfying meal. Homemade soft-serve ice cream is the house specialty. Be it served in a simple cone or in an elaborate sundae, the chilly treat is sure to please. Among the entrées from which to choose are cheeseburgers, hot dogs, and sandwiches. Soups and

B breakfast　**L** lunch　**D** dinner　**S** snacks　/　**$** under $15　**$$** $15–$36　**$$$** $36–$60　**$$$$** $60 and up

salads can augment the meal, as can fries, onion rings, and soft pretzels. Save room for the inventive shakes. Beer and wine are served. An adjacent walk-up window, known as Sweet Treats, has ice cream and shakes for snackers on the go. **LDS•$–$$**

FRESH MEDITERRANEAN MARKET: The Dolphin's airy eatery offers Mediterranean and American cuisine such as salads, sandwiches, and soups. The morning menu includes pastries, yogurt, fresh granola, hot cereals, eggs, pancakes, and more. It's also possible to have a light lunch here, provided that you are a salad or wrap fan. Fresh offers many wines by the glass, plus sangria, Bloody Marys, beer, and soft drinks. Reservations are recommended. **BL•$$–$$$**

FUEL: Hungry guests may fuel up at this quick-service snack bar/grab-and-go market off the Dolphin lobby. **BLDS•$–$$**

GARDEN GROVE: This Swan eatery means to transport guests to the gardens of New York's Central Park (the 25-foot oak tree is a realistic touch). It offers a full breakfast menu (with favorite Disney characters in the house on Saturday and Sunday mornings for a buffet); salads, sandwiches, and more for lunch. For dinner, different nights bring different fare. At press time, Sunday through Thursday featured a menu of salads, soups, and entrées; Friday and Saturday offered a seafood buffet. Disney characters are on hand for dinner every night. Reservations are recommended. **BLD•$$$**

IL MULINO NEW YORK TRATTORIA: A swank Swan dining destination, Il Mulino offers Italian cuisine in a vibrant trattoria-like setting. Featuring *Piatti per il Tavolo*, or family-style dining, the spot is ideal for groups. Signature items include *gamberi al Mulino* (jumbo shrimp with spicy cocktail sauce), *gnocchi bolognese* (potato dumplings with meat sauce), *pollo fra diavolo* (chicken in a spicy red sauce with sausage), and *salmone* (sautéed salmon in garlic and olive oil with wild mushrooms and broccoli rabe). *Mangia!*

Dinner begins with an antipasti tasting, on the house. Savor it while perusing the wine list's 250 or so varietals. The kids' menu offers pizza, fettuccine Alfredo, spaghetti marinara, and chicken parmigiana. Live entertainment is offered Friday and Saturday evenings from 6:30 P.M. till 10:30 P.M. To make reservations, call 407-934-1199, or visit *swandolphin.com*. **D•$$$–$$$$**

JAVA BAR: Specializing in coffee drinks, this Swan lobby bar also offers pastries, fruit, cold cereal, chips, paninis, beer, wine, and soft drinks. Hours are generally 6:30 A.M. till 6:30 P.M. Monday to Saturday and 6:30 A.M. to 11 A.M. Sunday. **BLDS•$–$$**

KIMONOS: Are you in the mood for sushi with a side of karaoke? You've come to the right place! This Swan spot is an honest-to-goodness karaoke bar (the only one within Walt Disney World's borders). Some guests come to croon, while others are drawn to the sushi, sashimi, and tempura. It's also possible to order miso soup, salad, edamame, tempura udon, gyoza, and Wagyu beef satay, among other selections. There's a full bar featuring beer, wine, and specialty cocktails. This spot is usually open from 5:30 P.M. until midnight. The singing usually gets started by 9 P.M. If you would like to get some sustenance to go, place your order with the bartender (in the back of the dining room). **DS•$–$$**

PHINS: The sleek lobby lounge serves custom-crafted cocktails, beer, wine, and soft drinks—plus a selection of small plates such as deviled eggs, wok-charred edamame, and lamb meatballs. Nibbles are offered from 3 P.M. to 10 P.M., drinks are poured until 2 A.M. **LDS•$–$$**

PICABU: This 24/7 Dolphin cafeteria/convenience store is a cut above the norm. (The folks who work there are pretty impressive, too.) Much of the food is freshly prepared—with sandwiches and salads, plus a taco and burrito station. The house coffee is Starbucks (free refills during your meal). The shop sells snacks and sundries. Picabu is a tad pricier than the average WDW quick-service eatery, but the quality is high and many portions are large enough to share. **BLDS•$–$$**

SHULA'S: This Dolphin spot specializes in generous portions of certified Angus beef, plus soups, salads, chicken and fish dishes. For dessert, there's apple crisp, vanilla cheesecake, molten chocolate lava cake, and more. The upscale eatery pays tribute to the 1972 Miami Dolphins—the year coach Don Shula led his team to a perfect NFL season. Though the interior celebrates football, this is not a casual spot. The dress code is business or resort casual. Reservations are recommended. There is a kids' menu, too. **D•$$$$**

SPLASH POOL BAR & GRILL: Just steps from the Swan lap pool and offering lake views, Splash serves contemporary lunch fare. The menu includes a Maine lobster club, fish tacos, burgers, chicken BLT, wings, Caesar salad, and Mediterranean shrimp salad. Soft drinks, beer, wine, and specialty drinks (including hibiscus coolers and frozen margaritas) are served. **LS•$$**

TODD ENGLISH'S BLUEZOO: A sophisticated member of the Disney dining scene, the menu at this Dolphin spot features coastal cuisine, incorporating an innovative selection of fresh seafood with international and New American culinary influences. The raw bar is

Resort to Resort

If you're staying in one resort and dining in another, you need to plan ahead—even if the resorts are linked by monorail or water taxi. Why? The transportation may be operating before dinner, but if you're out late enough you'll have to get yourself home another way.

The good news is you will never be stranded. Bus transportation runs until about 1 A.M.—but it's not direct. If the theme parks are closed, you'll have to take a bus to Disney Springs and transfer to a bus to your hotel. If the theme parks are open, you can take a bus to any park and transfer to one that's headed to your resort. Know that the journey can take up to 90 minutes in either direction. If that thought is unpleasant or you're running short on time, do what we sometimes do: splurge on a Minnie Van, Lyft, or Uber ride, or a trip in a taxicab. Taxis should run between $15 and $35 (before tip), depending on the destination and traffic. Minnie Vans start with a base charge of $15 charge per trip. (The final cost depends on the distance covered—each mile costs about $2.75.) Note that Uber rides are subject to surge pricing. All resort Bell Services desks can arrange for a taxi pickup.

stocked with oysters, clams, shrimp, lobster tails, and ceviche of the day. Popular starters include the clam chowder (with salt-cured bacon and oyster crackers), jumbo lump crab cakes, and zellwood corn fritters. All of the entrées are tempting: from miso-glazed mero to lobster primavera, to bluezoo's signature dancing fish (whole fish roasted on a rotating spit).

Landlubbers should consider barbecue roasted half-chicken or filet of beef. The dessert menu tempts with treats such as warm raspberry filled beignet, sorbet, and molten chocolate cake. Reservations are recommended. It's possible to order food at the bar, a plus for solo diners. Live entertainment is offered on Friday from 7 P.M. till 11 P.M. Closing time at the bar tends to vary from night to night. **DS•$$$–$$$$**

WILDERNESS LODGE

ARTIST POINT: The Enchanted Forest theme of this eatery is announced in evergreen touches and landscape murals, while tall red-framed windows look out on Bay Lake. The dining room is cavernous, but not without charm.

Part of the appeal comes courtesy of Disney characters. This new dinner experience, dubbed "Storybook Dining" invites guests to rub elbows with Snow White, Dopey, Grumpy, and—if they dare—the Queen!

The meal includes shared appetizers: mushroom bisque, shrimp cocktail, and Hunter's Terrine. Each guest selects a main course such as Cottage Beef Stew, Royal Prime Rib Roast, Magic Mirror Slow-braised Pork Shank, and Bashful's Butter-poached Sustainable Fish. For dessert, there's gooseberry pie, sponge cake with chocolate gems, and "poison" apple mousse. There are kid-friendly selections for all courses. The wine list includes more than a dozen selections from the Pacific Northwest. **D•$$$$•**

GEYSER POINT BAR & GRILL: A rustic yet modern open-air oasis, Geyser Point is nestled in the heart of the Wilderness Lodge resort near the shores of Bay Lake. A combination table-service/quick-service location, Geyser Point offers meals from a walk-up window, plus "rustic fare" in the delightful table-service lounge. The all-day menu has featured lump crab cake sandwiches, bison cheeseburgers, classic bacon cheeseburgers, smoked turkey sandwiches, salads (grilled chicken, portobello, or salmon), chocolate brownie mousse, apple-cider sorbet, coffee-infused gelato, and seasonal pies. A full bar stands at the ready. **LDS•$–$$•**

ROARING FORK: Set in a stone-walled area (a bit dungeon-like, but in a cool way), this snack bar serves three meals a day. Breakfast—which is served from 6 A.M. until 11 A.M.—features a "roaring breakfast platter" (scrambled eggs, potato hash, sausage, bacon, and a cheddar biscuit), loaded Mickey-shaped waffles, bagel sandwiches, bananas Foster French toast, plus cereal, yogurt, and oatmeal. Later in the day, feast on burgers, sandwiches, flatbreads, chicken and waffles, salads, and snacks. Beer, wine, and soft drinks are served. This is the spot to top off refillable resort mugs. **BLDS•$•**

WHISPERING CANYON CAFE: Yee-ha! A longtime family favorite, Whispering Canyon is one of the more boisterous Disney restaurants. All meals are offered à la carte and "all you can eat" style. The latter means heaping plates keep coming to the table until you say "when."

The morning air is filled with aromas of bacon and potatoes and other breakfast fare (omelets, waffles, etc.).

B breakfast **L** lunch **D** dinner **S** snacks / **$** under $15 **$$** $15–$36 **$$$** $36–$60 **$$$$** $60 and up

Lunch offers pulled pork sandwiches, bison burgers, salads, and more. For supper, expect skillets to share (BBQ, land and sea, and vegetarian), plus char-crusted New York strip steak and cedar plank salmon. Kid-friendly selections are offered. Desserts such as Granny Smith apple pie and seasonal fruit cobbler tend to garner raves. Reservations are recommended. **BLD•$$$•🐭**

YACHT & BEACH CLUB

ALE & COMPASS RESTAURANT: Capturing the breezy essence of an off-shore lighthouse, this Yacht Club spot serves New England comfort food for breakfast, lunch, and dinner. Guests can observe as chefs prepare flat-breads and other items in the onstage open-hearth oven, the focal point of the nautically themed dining area. Morning highlights include salted caramel apple French toast, red flannel hash (with chorizo, potatoes, beets, and poached eggs), and breakfast flatbreads. Later in the day, look for lobster and corn chowder, fish & chips, lobster roll, New England seafood pot pie, Coastal Clambake platters, and seared seasonal seafood—plus beef, chicken, and pasta dishes. **BLD•$$$•🐭**

BEACH CLUB MARKETPLACE: The resort's beachy setting extends to this snack bar/convenience store. There are baked goods, grocery items, made-to-order sandwiches, and packaged grab-and-go items. There is limited indoor seating. If you purchase a refillable resort mug, head here to fill 'er up. **BLDS•$–$$•🐭**

BEACHES & CREAM SODA SHOP: This recently expanded classic soda fountain is near the pool at the Beach Club. Cheeseburgers, patty melts, sandwiches, country-fried steak, fries, onion rings, soup, and chili are served for lunch and dinner. Of course, the star of the show is ice cream! Seven specialty sundaes are offered, including the ever-popular Kitchen Sink. Cups, cones, shakes, and floats round out the menu. Adult floats of note: Grasshopper, Tropical Sunrise, and Guinness Stout. Reservations are highly recommended. Select items may be ordered to go. **LDS•$–$$•🐭**

CAPE MAY CAFE: Minnie and her friends greet visitors each morning at this whimsical dining area. The breakfast buffet includes all the standards, plus a few specialties. Breakfast doesn't disappoint, but dinner is the big event here. It's an all-you-can-eat New England–style clambake buffet, and it's one of WDW's most popular meals and better values. The lineup includes crab legs, mussels, steamed clams, carved meat, salads, pastas, corn on the cob, potatoes, and desserts. Soft drinks are included, but cocktails and specialty drinks are not. Note that Disney characters are not in attendance for dinner. Reservations are recommended. **BD•$$$•🐭**

CRESCENT SOLARIUM: The afternoon tea service offers artisanal cheeses, tiny sandwiches and canapés on homemade bread, and scones served with clotted cream, lemon curd, and jam; plus pastries, cookies, and, of course, loose leaf teas. The children's option features Mickey-shaped sandwiches, a scone, cookies, and chocolate milk. Reservations are recommended. **LS•$$–$$$•🐭**

HURRICANE HANNA'S WATERSIDE BAR & GRILL: Hanna's serves cheeseburgers, barbecue pork nachos, field green salad, Caesar salad with chicken, coconut shrimp, chicken nuggets, hummus (with pita chips), french fries, and sea-salted edamame—plus cocktails and frozen concoctions. Eat at the counter or have your order delivered poolside. This is also a refillable WDW resort mug station. **LDS•$•🐭**

MARKETPLACE AT ALE & COMPASS: This upscale quick-service spot serves specialty coffees and breakfast selections such as turkey, egg, and cheese rolls; egg white wraps; and sticky buns. The rest of the day brings ham and cheese on pretzel rolls, paninis; spinach and feta pastries; and soup. There is a nice selection of grab-and-go items, too. Do you have a refillable mug? Here's a place to make it happy. **BLDS•$–$$•🐭**

YACHTSMAN STEAKHOUSE: You know you're in for a serious steak experience the moment you walk through the door. There's an actual butcher shop here. Meals begin with fresh-baked onion rolls and may continue with an appetizer such as lobster bisque. There's no skimping on the expertly prepared entrées, so good luck finding room for crème brûlée. In addition to beef (which is house-aged and prepared on an oak-fired grill), the menu includes chicken, pasta, and seafood. One could feast on side dishes alone, with sautéed mushrooms, creamed spinach, and truffle mac and cheese all vying for attention. Dessert items of note: seasonal sorbet trio, banana bread pudding, s'more sundae, and cookies & cream brownie bar. Reservations are recommended. **D•$$$–$$$$•🐭•SR**

WALT DISNEY WORLD

Name & Location	Meals	Style*	Price**	Characters	Theme
Artist Point Wilderness Lodge (page 296)	Dinner	Prix fixe menu (three course)	D: $55/33	Snow White, Dopey, Grumpy, and the Queen	Storybook fantasy
Akershus Norway Pavilion, Epcot (page 261)	Breakfast Lunch Dinner	Family-style	B: $52/31 L/D: $63/37	Belle, Jasmine, Snow White, and Aurora	Fourteenth-century Norwegian castle
Cape May Cafe Beach Club resort (page 297)	Breakfast	Buffet	B: $38/23	Goofy, Minnie, and Donald Duck	Seaside picnic
Chef Mickey's Contemporary resort (page 289)	Breakfast Brunch Dinner	Buffet	Breakfast: $46/28 Brunch: $46/28 Dinner: $55/33	Mickey, Minnie, Donald, Goofy, and Pluto	A family celebration
Cinderella's Royal Table Magic Kingdom (page 253)	Breakfast Lunch Dinner	B/L: Family-style D: À la carte	B: $73/43 L/D: $92/53	B, L, D: Princesses B, L, D: Cinderella greets guests in the Castle lobby	Medieval banquet
The Crystal Palace Magic Kingdom (page 256)	Breakfast Lunch Dinner	Buffet	B: $38/23 L/D: $52/31	Pooh, Eeyore, Tigger, and Piglet	Sunlit conservatory
Garden Grill Epcot (page 260)	Breakfast Lunch Dinner	Family-style	B: $38/23 L/D: $52/31	Mickey, Pluto, Chip, and Dale	Home-style country cooking

* Family-style and buffet meals are all-you-can-eat dining experiences. Family-style features a set menu and table service; buffet-style meals usually present more dining options and are self-serve.

** Adult prices are followed by children's prices (diners ages 3 through 9). Prices quoted represent "peak" times of year. With the exception of Cinderella's Royal Table, prices do not include tax or gratuity. All prices are subject to change.

CHARACTER DINING

Featured Items	For Dessert	Tip	Wins for . . .
Prime rib roast, roasted chicken, butter-poached sustainable fish, and seafood stew	Gooseberry pie, sponge cake, and cracked maple popcorn with a ganache heart	Meeting the Queen is optional—so if your kids aren't ready, they can easily skip an encounter with the Disney villain.	Best place to mingle with characters from the Enchanted Forest. It's also the only place to meet the evil Queen.
B: Scrambled eggs, potato casserole, dill salmon gravlax, bacon, sausage, cheese, fruit L/D: Norwegian fare and kid-friendly selections	Chocolate mousse cake, traditional rice cream topped with strawberry sauce	The eatery is about a half-mile from Epcot's front entrance—allow extra time for travel.	It's not Cinderella's Castle, but it's still pretty cool. (It's easier to score a reservation here, too.)
Eggs, breakfast pizza, Mickey waffles, sausage, cereal, grits	Doughnuts, muffins, Danish, fresh fruit	For guests staying in the Epcot area, Cape May is one of the best breakfast options.	Best Chance of Getting a Table Without Reservations (But make the arrangements, anyway—there's usually a wait to get in.)
B: Eggs, fruit, pancakes, Mickey waffles, cereal Brunch: BBQ ribs, salmon, mac and cheese, and more D: Carved meats, pasta, seafood, veggies, pizza, salads	Make-your-own sundaes, cheesecake, cookies, and other fresh, housemade desserts	A celebration happens every 45 minutes. Be sure to stick around for at least one little napkin-swinging party.	Best All-Around Character Meal (It has a fun and festive setting and a kid-pleasing menu.)
B: Frittata, lobster and crab crepes, eggs, French toast, bacon, pastries L/D: Catch of the day, pork shank, beef short ribs, and beef tenderloin	Seasonal cheesecake, flourless chocolate cake, and dessert trio	Payment in full is required at time of booking for all meals.	Best Setting (The restaurant is inside Cinderella Castle!)
B: French toast, eggs, cereal, frittatas, fruit L/D: Shrimp, carved meats, pasta, veggies, pizza, salad	B: Sticky buns L/D: Cakes, pies, make-your-own sundaes, cookies	Don't be put off by this restaurant's size—the characters make the rounds surprisingly quickly.	Best Theme Park Buffet (Crystal Palace scores points for its lovely setting, convenient location, and appetizing menu.)
B: Sticky buns, scrambled eggs, fruit, waffles L/D: Pot roast, turkey, veggies, potatoes (mac and cheese for kids)	Freshly made desserts	The room rotates very slowly throughout the meal. It's hardly noticeable to most, but may be disorienting to those highly sensitive to motion.	Best for vegetarians (Be sure to ask for the vegetarian meal—it's usually a tasty seasonal selection.)

All characters, menu items, and prices are subject to change. Prices are rounded to the nearest dollar. Call 407-WDW-DINE (939-3463) for details or to make reservations. This listing is not comprehensive. Character meals are also presented at the Hilton Lake Buena Vista (Sunday breakfast at Covington Mill) and Buena Vista Palace (Sunday breakfast at Letterpress). See pages 108 and 110 for details.

Name & Location	Meals	Style*	Price**	Characters	Theme
Garden Grove Swan resort (page 295)	Breakfast (week-ends) Dinner (daily)	Breakfast: Buffet Dinner: À la carte	B: $26/17 D: $$$ (plated)	B: Goofy & Pluto (Sat.); Goofy, Pluto, Chip, & Dale (Sun.) D: Goofy & Pluto (Sat.–Thurs.); Goofy, Pluto, Chip, & Dale (Fri.)	Picnic in the park
Hollywood & Vine Disney's Hollywood Studios (page 270)	Breakfast Lunch Dinner	Family-style	B: $38/23 L: $52/31 D: $52/31	Breakfast: Doc McStuffins, Fancy Nancy, Vampirina, and Roadster Racer Goofy Lunch and dinner: Minnie and friends	A salute to Playhouse Disney or a seasonal celebration
Trattoria al Forno Bon Voyage Breakfast at BoardWalk resort (page 287)	Breakfast	Prix-fixe menu	$38/22	Rapunzel, Flynn Rider (aka Eugene Fitzherbert), Ariel, and Prince Eric	Pre-adventure party
Topolino's Terrace Disney's Riviera Resort (page 294)	Breakfast	Prix-fixe menu	For details, call 407-939-3463	Mickey Mouse and friends such Minnie Mouse, Donald Duck, and Daisy Duck	Elegant rooftop dining
'Ohana Polynesian Village resort (page 293)	Breakfast	Family style	$36/21	Lilo, Stitch, and others, such as Pluto and Mickey	Polynesian family feast
1900 Park Fare Grand Floridian resort (page 292)	Breakfast Brunch (seasonal) Dinner	Buffet	B: $38/22 D: $52/31	B: Stars like Mary Poppins and Alice D: Cinderella and friends	Turn-of-the-twentieth-century circus
Tusker House Donald's Dining Safari at Animal Kingdom (page 274)	Breakfast Lunch Dinner	Buffet	B: $38/23 L: $52/31 D: $52/31	Donald, Daisy, Goofy, and Mickey	Safari feast

* Family-style and buffet meals are all-you-can-eat dining experiences. Family-style features a set menu and table service; buffet-style meals usually present more dining options and are self-serve.

** Adult prices are followed by children's prices (diners ages 3 through 9). Prices will be higher during select "peak" times of year. All prices may increase in 2020.

Featured Items	For Dessert	Tip	Wins for . . .
B: Omelets, grits, sausage, French toast, fresh fruit D: Prime rib, roast chicken, cedar plank salmon	Fresh pastries	Dinner, Sunday–Monday offers a choice of entrée with unlimited soup, salad, and dessert buffet; Friday and Saturday features Seafood Sensations Buffet ($36 for adults; $17 for kids).	Best-kept Secret (Garden Grove allows for a classic Disney character dining experience without major pre-planning. A true bonus at WDW!)
B: Mickey waffles, scrambled eggs, yogurt L: Salads, pasta dishes, fish, and chicken D: Offerings vary seasonally	Pineapple upside-down cake, Key lime tart, cookies	Request Play 'N Dine when you reserve breakfast and Minnie's Seasonal Dine when booking lunch or dinner.	Tot-Pleasing (Little ones love to dine along with Doc McStuffins, who appears at breakfast.)
Scrambled eggs, frittatas, pancakes, egg-white omelet with smoked salmon, oak-grilled steak, cheesy egg torte, calzone	Cherry turnovers, clam shells, vanilla and blueberry muffins, fruit	Expect lots of photo ops, but no PhotoPass photographers. Be sure to bring your camera or smartphone to capture magical moments.	Best Place to Meet Flynn Rider and Prince Eric (It's also the only place to meet these gents,)
Sour cream waffles, spiced sausage hash, wood-fired steak, eggs, fruit	Blueberry scones, cheese Danish, chocolate-avocado spread	This eatery is a Disney Dining Plan Signature Restaurant for dinner, but breakfast only requires one table-service credit per person.	Best Views Perched atop the Riviera resort, Topolino's Terrace offers majestic bird's-eye views of the World below.
Mickey-shaped waffles, eggs, biscuits, fruit, bacon	Sweet baked goods	Don't forget your autograph book and camera. The characters spend a good amount of quality time at each table.	Speediest Service (Servers keep those family-style platters coming fast and frequently.)
B: Pancakes, eggs, waffles D: Prime rib, pasta, seafood	B: Sticky buns, muffins, Danish D: Key lime pie, cheesecake, bread pudding	Breakfast here is a nice way to start a Magic Kingdom day. The park is just one monorail stop away.	Fanciest Foods (The quality is superior to many buffets, and there's plenty to please the kids.)
B: Simba and Nala waffles, eggs, frittata, fruit L/D: Spit-roasted chicken and pork, vegetarian offerings, salmon, salads, bread, fruit chutney	B: Danish, muffins L and D: Warm banana bread pudding with vanilla sauce, brownies, cookies	This spot is just steps from the Kilimanjaro Safaris attraction, making it an ideal location for a pre-safari breakfast or post-safari lunch.	Best Place to Dine with Donald Duck (The Duck and his pals greet guests at breakfast, lunch, and dinner.)

All characters, menu items, and prices are subject to change. Prices are rounded to the nearest dollar. Call 407-WDW-DINE (939-3463), or visit www.disneyworld.com/dining/ for updates or to make reservations. This listing is not comprehensive.

RESTAURANT ROUNDUP

Dining Disney style is one of the most enjoyable aspects of the vacation for many visitors. But with so many different restaurants to choose from, it can be difficult to select the spots that will best suit your family. Regulars to WDW are quick to recommend their favorites to newcomers. We, of course, are no exception to the rule. What follows is a rundown of the restaurants that we always try to include in our trips to the World and wholeheartedly recommend to those who are planning a visit. To pick these Birnbaum's Bests, we considered such factors as food quality, restaurant atmosphere, location, and overall value.

TOP WDW RESTAURANTS FOR FAMILIES WITH KIDS

TABLE SERVICE

Boma—Flavors of Africa .... Animal Kingdom Lodge resort (p. 285)

Cape May Cafe .... Beach Club resort (p. 297)

Chef Mickey's .... Contemporary resort (p. 289)

Cinderella's Royal Table .... Magic Kingdom (p. 253)

The Crystal Palace .... Magic Kingdom (p. 256)

50's Prime Time Cafe .... Disney's Hollywood Studios (p. 270)

Garden Grill .... Epcot (p. 260)

1900 Park Fare ....Grand Floridian resort (p. 292)

Rainforest Cafe .... Animal Kingdom and Disney Springs (pp. 274, 283)

Sci-Fi Dine-In Theater .... Disney's Hollywood Studios (p. 271)

T-Rex Cafe .... Disney Springs (p. 284)

Tusker House .... Animal Kingdom (p. 274)

Via Napoli .... Epcot (p. 266)

Whispering Canyon Cafe ....Wilderness Lodge resort (p. 296)

QUICK SERVICE

Columbia Harbour House .... Magic Kingdom (p. 256)

Cookes of Dublin .... Disney Springs (p. 279)

Earl of Sandwich .... Disney Springs (p. 279)

Everything Pop! .... Pop Century resort (p. 293)

Flame Tree Barbecue ....Animal Kingdom (p. 274)

Restaurantosaurus .... Animal Kingdom (p. 276)

The Mara .... Disney's Animal Kingdom Lodge (p. 286)

Pinocchio Village Haus .... Magic Kingdom (p. 254)

Sunset Ranch Market .... Disney's Hollywood Studios (p. 273)

Sunshine Seasons .... Epcot (p. 261)

BEST PLACE TO CELEBRATE A CHILD'S BIRTHDAY

Chef Mickey's .... Contemporary resort (p. 289)

RUNNER-UP
Hoop-Dee-Doo Musical Revue .... Fort Wilderness (p. 315)

BEST SPLURGE FOR GROWN-UPS

Victoria & Albert's .... Grand Floridian resort (p. 292)

RUNNERS-UP
The Boathouse .... Disney Springs (p. 278)
California Grill .... Contemporary resort (p. 288)
Cítricos .... Grand Floridian resort (p. 291)
Flying Fish .... BoardWalk resort (p. 287)
Jiko—The Cooking Place ...... Animal Kingdom Lodge resort (p. 285)
Monsieur Paul .... Epcot (p. 263)
Paddlefish.. Disney Springs (p. 282)
Yachtsman Steakhouse .... Yacht Club resort (p. 397)

BEST CHARACTER MEAL

Cinderella's Royal Table .... Magic Kingdom (p. 253)
Hollywood & Vine (dinner)...... Disney's Hollywood Studios (p. 270)

RUNNERS-UP
Akershus Royal Banquet Hall .... Epcot (p. 261)
Artist Point .... Wilderness Lodge (p. 296)
Tusker House .... Disney's Animal Kingdom (p. 274)
1900 Park Fare .... Grand Floridian resort (p. 292)

BEST DINNER SHOW

Hoop-Dee-Doo Musical Revue: This crowd-pleasing saloon hall show has been going like gangbusters since 1974. Enjoy the music and silly humor while feasting on buckets of ribs, fried chicken, mashed potatoes, corn, and strawberry shortcake. Presented at Fort Wilderness (p. 315).

BEST ROOFTOP RESTAURANT

California Grill .... Contemporary resort (p. 288)
RUNNER-UP
Topolino's Terrace—Flavors of the Riviera ......Riviera resort (p. 294)

BEST WINE LIST

Wine Bar George ....
.......................Disney Springs (p. 284)
RUNNERS-UP
California Grill ....
.... Contemporary resort (p. 285)
Cítricos ....
............Grand Floridian resort (p. 291)
Flying Fish ....
.......................Boardwalk resort (p. 287)
Shula's Steakhouse ....
..........................Swan resort (p. 295)

BEST HAPPY HOUR

Jock Lindsey's Hangar Bar ....
.......................Disney Springs (p. 320)
RUNNERS-UP
House of Blues ....
.......Disney Springs, West Side (p. 320)
Paddlefish..
.......................Disney Springs (p. 282)
STK Orlando ....
.......................Disney Springs (p. 283)

BEST BRUNCH

Raglan Road...
.......................Disney Springs (p. 283)
RUNNERS-UP
California Grill ....
...............Contemporary resort (p. 288)
Maria & Enzo's ....
.......................Disney Springs (p. 281)
Paddlefish..
.......................Disney Springs (p. 282)

BEST ROOM SERVICE

Swan and Dolphin resorts.............
................(pages 83 and 294–296)

BEST SPORTS BARS

ESPN Club....................................
...............BoardWalk resort (p. 287)
City Works Eatery & Pour House....
...................Disney Springs (p. 279)

BEST FIXIN'S BAR

Cosmic Ray's Starlight Cafe............
.................Magic Kingdom (p. 258)

BEST CRAB CAKES

Paddlefish.....................................
...................Disney Springs (p. 282)

RUNNERS-UP
The Boathouse...............................
...................Disney Springs (p. 278)
Ale & Compass Restaurant.............
................Yacht Club resort (p. 289)

BEST ITALIAN FARE

Enzo's Hideaway .... Disney Springs (p. 280)
RUNNERS-UP
Il Mulino New York Trattoria .... Swan resort (p. 294)
Tutto Italia .... Epcot (p. 266)
Trattoria al Forno................................ BoardWalk resort (p. 287)

BEST THEME

50's Prime Time Cafe .... Disney's Hollywood Studios (p. 270)
RUNNERS-UP
Sci-Fi Dine-In Theater .... Disney's Hollywood Studios (p. 271)
T-Rex Cafe .... Disney Springs (p. 284)

BEST OUTDOOR DINING

The Boathouse .... Disney Springs (p. 278)
RUNNER-UP
Raglan Road .... Disney Springs (p. 283)

BEST BUYS

Trail's End Restaurant .... Pioneer Hall, Fort Wilderness (p. 290)
Boma—Flavors of Africa .... Animal Kingdom Lodge (p. 285)

BEST SEAFOOD

The Boathouse .... Disney Springs (p. 278)
Paddlefish .... Disney Springs (p. 282)
RUNNERS-UP
Flying Fish ....BoardWalk resort (p. 287)
Narcoossee's ....Grand Floridian resort (p. 291)

BEST STEAK

Yachtsman Steakhouse .... Yacht Club resort (p. 297)
RUNNERS-UP
California Grill .... Contemporary resort (p. 288)
Le Cellier Steakhouse .... Epcot (p. 262)
Narcoossee's .... Grand Floridian resort (p. 291)
Shula's .... Dolphin resort (p. 295)

BEST SUSHI

Kimonos .... Swan resort (p. 295)

RUNNERS-UP

California Grill .... Contemporary resort (p. 288)
Kona Cafe .... Polynesian Village resort (p. 292)
Splitsville .... Disney Springs West Side (p. 283)

BEST RESORT SNACK BAR

Picabu .... Dolphin resort (p. 295)

RUNNERS-UP

Capt. Cook's .... Polynesian Village resort (p. 292)
Contempo Cafe .... Contemporary resort (p. 289)
Gasparilla Island Grill .... Grand Floridian resort (p. 291)

BEST COFFEE

Kona Cafe .... Polynesian Village resort (p. 292)

RUNNERS-UP

Boma—Flavors of Africa ...... Animal Kingdom Lodge resort (p. 285)
Starbucks .... (multiple locations; see Index)
Ghirardelli Ice Cream & Chocolate Shop ..... Disney Springs (p. 280)

BEST PIZZA FOR GROWN-UPS

Blaze Fast Fire'd Pizza .... Disney Springs (p. 278)
California Grill .... Contemporary resort (p. 288)
Via Napoli .... Epcot (p. 266)

BEST PIZZA FOR KIDS

California Grill .... Contemporary resort (p. 288)
Pinocchio Village Haus .... Magic Kingdom (p. 254)
Pizzafari .... Animal Kingdom (p. 275)
Pizza Ponte .... Disney Springs (p. 282)
Via Napoli .... Epcot (p. 266)

BEST FIREWORKS VIEWS

California Grill .... Contemporary resort (p. 288)
La Hacienda de San Angel .... Epcot (p. 263)
Narcoossee's (outdoor verandah) ..... Grand Floridian resort (p. 291)
Topolino's Terrace .... Riviera resort (p. 294)

BEST ICE CREAM

Ample Hills Creamery.......................
................BoardWalk resort (p. 286)
Beaches & Cream Soda Shop..............
................Beach Club resort (p. 297)
L'Artisan des Glaces........Epcot (p. 268)

BEST MILK SHAKE

Ample Hills Creamery.......................
................BoardWalk resort (p. 286)

RUNNERS-UP

Vivoli il Gelato..................................
................Disney Springs (p. 284)
Beaches & Cream Soda Shop.............
................Beach Club resort (p. 297)

BEST PIÑA COLADA

Tambu Lounge...................................
.... Polynesian Village resort (p. 322)

WHERE TO FIND...

From french fries to filet mignon, fried chicken to seared scallops with black truffle spaghettini, Disney dishes truly run the gamut. To help you zero in on the eateries that best fit your needs, we've created a handy index of specialized lists:

BAKERIES/PASTRY SHOPS
Beach Club Marketplace (Beach Club resort)
BoardWalk Bakery (BoardWalk resort)
Gasparilla Island Grill (Grand Floridian resort)
Goofy's Candy Co. (Disney Springs, Marketplace)
Kringla Bakeri og Kafe (Epcot, World Showcase)
Kusafiri Coffee Shop & Bakery (Animal Kingdom, Harambe)
Les Halles Boulangerie Patisserie (Epcot, World Showcase)
Main Street Bakery (Magic Kingdom, Main Street, U.S.A.)
Sunshine Seasons (Epcot, The Land)
Trolley Car Café (Disney's Hollywood Studios)

BARBECUE
Flame Tree Barbecue (Animal Kingdom, Discovery Island)
House of Blues Smokehouse (Disney Springs, West Side)
The Polite Pig (Disney Springs, Town Center)
Whispering Canyon Cafe (Wilderness Lodge resort)

BEST BANG FOR THE BUFFET BUCK
(all-you-can-eat)
Biergarten (Epcot, World Showcase)
Boma—Flavors of Africa (Animal Kingdom Lodge)
Cape May Cafe (Beach Club resort)
Chef Mickey's (Contemporary resort)
Hollywood & Vine (Disney's Hollywood Studios)
Trail's End Restaurant (Fort Wilderness resort)
Tusker House (Animal Kingdom, Harambe)

BEST WITH BABIES (table service)
Akershus Royal Banquet Hall (Epcot, World Showcase)
Biergarten (Epcot, World Showcase)
Chef Mickey's (Contemporary resort)

Crystal Palace, The (Magic Kingdom, Main Street, U.S.A.)
Garden Grill (Epcot, Future World)
Hollywood & Vine (Disney's Hollywood Studios)
'Ohana (Polynesian Village resort)
Olivia's Cafe (Disney's Old Key West resort)
Rainforest Cafe (Animal Kingdom and Disney Springs)
Tony's Town Square (Magic Kingdom, Main Street, U.S.A.)
Trail's End Restaurant (Fort Wilderness resort)
Tusker House (Animal Kingdom, Harambe)

BRUNCH
California Grill (Contemporary resort; Sunday)
Chef Art Smith's Homecomin' (Disney Springs, Town Center; Saturday and Sunday)
Chef Mickey's (Contemporary resort)
House of Blues (Disney Springs, West Side; Sunday)
Maria & Enzo's (Disney Springs; Sunday)
Paddlefish (Disney Springs, The Landing; Sunday)
Raglan Road (Disney Springs, The Landing; Saturday and Sunday)
Trail's End (Fort Wilderness; Saturday and Sunday)

BUFFET (all-you-care-to-eat)
Akershus Royal Banquet Hall (Epcot, World Showcase—*appetizers only*)
Biergarten (Epcot, World Showcase)
Boma—Flavors of Africa (Animal Kingdom Lodge)
Cape May Cafe (Beach Club resort)
Chef Mickey's (Contemporary resort)
Crystal Palace, The (Magic Kingdom, Main Street, U.S.A.)
Garden Grove (Swan resort)
Hollywood & Vine (Disney's Hollywood Studios)
1900 Park Fare (Grand Floridian resort)
Trail's End Restaurant (breakfast and dinner; Fort Wilderness)
Tusker House (Animal Kingdom, Harambe)

BURGERS

Backlot Express (Disney's Hollywood Studios)
Beaches & Cream Soda Shop (Beach Club resort)
Cabana Bar & Beach Club (Dolphin resort)
Capt. Cook's (Polynesian Village resort)
Cosmic Ray's Starlight Cafe (Magic Kingdom, Tomorrowland)
Contempo Cafe (Contemporary resort)
D-Luxe Burger (Disney Springs, Town Center)
Edison, The (Disney Springs, The Landing)
ESPN Club (BoardWalk resort)
Food Courts (All-Star resorts)
Fountain, The (Dolphin resort)
Geyser Point Bar & Grill (Wilderness Lodge resort)
Pecos Bill Tall Tale Inn & Cafe (Magic Kingdom, Frontierland)
Restaurantosaurus (Animal Kingdom, DinoLand)
Riverside Mill (Port Orleans Riverside resort)
Sassagoula Floatworks & Food Factory (Port Orleans French Quarter resort)
Sci-Fi Dine-in Theater (Disney's Hollywood Studios)
Sunset Ranch Market (Disney's Hollywood Studios)

CHEAP EATS—FAST FOOD

Backlot Express (Disney's Hollywood Studios)
Columbia Harbour House (Magic Kingdom, Liberty Square)
D-Luxe Burger (Disney Springs, Town Center)
Everything Pop! (Pop Century resort)
Flame Tree Barbecue (Animal Kingdom, Discovery Island)
Harambe Market (Animal Kingdom, Harambe)
House of Blues Smokehouse (Disney Springs, West Side)
Katsura Grill (Epcot, World Showcase)
Les Halles Boulangerie Patisserie (Epcot, World Showcase)
Landscape of Flavors (Disney's Art of Animation resort)
Main Street Bakery (Magic Kingdom, Main Street, U.S.A.)
Pinocchio Village Haus (Magic Kingdom, Fantasyland)
Pizzafari (Animal Kingdom, Discovery Island)
The Polite Pig (Disney Springs, Town Center)
Restaurantosaurus (Animal Kingdom, DinoLand)
Sommerfest (Epcot, World Showcase)

Sunset Ranch Market (Disney's Hollywood Studios)
Sunshine Seasons (Epcot, Future World)
Wolfgang Puck Express (Disney Springs, Marketplace)
Woody's Lunch Box (Disney's Hollywood Studios)
Yorkshire County Fish Shop (Epcot, World Showcase)

CHEAP EATS (relatively speaking)
Table Service

Beaches & Cream Soda Shop (Beach Club resort)
Cape May Cafe (Beach Club resort)
ESPN Club (BoardWalk resort)
Geyser Point Bar & Grill (Wilderness Lodge Resort; lounge)
Kimonos (Swan resort)
Kona Cafe (Polynesian Village resort)
Olivia's Cafe (Disney's Old Key West resort)
Planet Hollywood (Disney Springs, West Side)
Plaza Restaurant (Magic Kingdom, Main Street, U.S.A.)
Rainforest Cafe (Animal Kingdom and Disney Springs, Marketplace)
Spice Road Table (Epcot, World Showcase)
Trail's End Restaurant (Fort Wilderness resort)
T-Rex Cafe: A Prehistoric Family Adventure (Disney Springs, Marketplace)
Tusker House (Animal Kingdom, Harambe)
Via Napoli (Epcot, World Showcase)
Yak & Yeti (Animal Kingdom, Asia)

DISNEY CHARACTERS (dining with)
(see pages 298–301)

INTERNATIONAL EATERIES
African

Boma—Flavors of Africa (Animal Kingdom Lodge)
Harambe Market (Animal Kingdom, Harambe)
Jiko—The Cooking Place (Animal Kingdom Lodge)
Restaurant Marrakesh (Epcot, World Showcase)
Sanaa (Animal Kingdom Lodge, Kidani Village)
Spice Road Table (Epcot, World Showcase)
Tangierine Cafe (Epcot, World Showcase)
Tiffins Restaurant (also serves Indian cuisine; Animal Kingdom, Discovery Island)
Tusker House (Animal Kingdom, Harambe)

American

Artist Point (Wilderness Lodge)
Big River Grille & Brewing Works
  (BoardWalk resort)
Boathouse, The (Disney Springs, The Landing)
Boatwright's Dining Hall (Port Orleans
  Riverside resort)
California Grill (Contemporary resort)
Edison, The (Disney Springs, The Landing)
ESPN Club (BoardWalk resort)
Fife & Drum Tavern (Epcot, World Showcase)
50's Prime Time Cafe
  (Disney's Hollywood Studios)
Flying Fish (BoardWalk resort)
Funnel Cake (Epcot, World Showcase)
Garden Grill (Epcot, Future World)
Grand Floridian Cafe (Grand Floridian resort)
Hollywood Brown Derby (Disney's
  Hollywood Studios)
House of Blues (Disney Springs, West Side)
Liberty Tree Tavern (Magic Kingdom,
  Liberty Square)
Narcoossee's (Grand Floridian resort)
1900 Park Fare (Grand Floridian resort)
Olivia's Cafe (Old Key West resort)
Sci-Fi Dine-In Theater (Disney's Hollywood
  Studios)
Trail's End Restaurant (Fort Wilderness
  resort)
Wave . . . of American Flavors, The
  (Contemporary resort)

British

Earl of Sandwich (Disney Springs, Marketplace)
Rose & Crown Pub & Dining Room (Epcot,
  World Showcase)
Yorkshire County Fish Shop
  (Epcot, World Showcase)

Canadian

The Daily Poutine (Disney Springs, Town
  Center)
Le Cellier Steakhouse (Epcot, World Showcase)

Chinese and Southeast Asian

**Jungle Navigation Co. Ltd. Skipper
  Canteen** (Magic Kingdom, Adventureland)
Lotus Blossom Cafe (Epcot, World Showcase)
Nine Dragons (Epcot, World Showcase)
Yak & Yeti (Animal Kingdom, Asia)

French

Be Our Guest Restaurant (Magic Kingdom,
  Fantasyland)
Chefs de France (Epcot, World Showcase)
Les Halles Boulangerie Patisserie (Epcot,
  World Showcase)
Monsieur Paul (Epcot, World Showcase)

German

Biergarten (Epcot, World Showcase)
Sommerfest (Epcot, World Showcase)

Italian/Mediterranean

Blaze Fast Fire'd Pizza (Disney Springs)
Il Mulino New York Trattoria (Swan resort)
Mama Melrose's Ristorante Italiano
  (Disney's Hollywood Studios)
Spice Road Table (Epcot, World Showcase)
Tony's Town Square (Magic Kingdom, Main
  Street, U.S.A.)
Trattoria al Forno (Disney's BoardWalk)
Tutto Gusto (Epcot, World Showcase)
Tutto Italia (Epcot, World Showcase)
Via Napoli (Epcot, World Showcase)

Japanese

Kabuki Cafe (Epcot, World Showcase)
Katsura Grill (Epcot, World Showcase)
Kimonos (Swan resort)
Morimoto Asia (Disney Springs,
  The Landing)
Teppan Edo (Epcot, World Showcase)
Tokyo Dining (Epcot, World Showcase)

Mexican/Latin American

Frontera Cocina (Disney Springs, Town Center)
La Cantina de San Angel
  (Epcot, World Showcase)
La Hacienda de San Angel (Epcot,
  World Showcase)
Maya Grill (Coronado Springs resort)
Paradiso 37 (Disney Springs, The Landing)
Pecos Bill Tall Tale Inn (Magic Kingdom,
  Frontierland)
San Angel Inn (Epcot, World Showcase)

Norwegian

Akershus Royal Banquet Hall (Epcot,
  World Showcase)
Kringla Bakeri og Kafe (Epcot, World Showcase)

FAMILY-STYLE (all-you-can-eat)

Akershus Royal Banquet Hall (Epcot, World Showcase)
Cape May Cafe (Beach Club resort)
Garden Grill (Epcot, Future World)
Garden Grove (Swan resort)
Hoop-Dee-Doo Musical Revue (see page 315)
Liberty Tree Tavern (Magic Kingdom, Liberty Square)
Pizzafari (Animal Kingdom, Discovery Island)
'Ohana (Polynesian Village resort)
Spirit of Aloha (see page 315)
Tusker House (Animal Kingdom, Harambe)
Whispering Canyon Cafe (Wilderness Lodge)

FRUIT

Aloha Isle (Magic Kingdom, Adventureland)
Harambe Fruit Market (Animal Kingdom, Harambe)
Liberty Square Market (Magic Kingdom, Liberty Square)
Prince Eric's Village Market (Magic Kingdom, Fantasyland)
Sunset Ranch Market (Disney's Hollywood Studios)
Sunshine Seasons (Epcot, Future World)

GOOD FOR GROUPS

Boathouse, The (Disney Springs, The Landing)
Boma—Flavors of Africa (Animal Kingdom Lodge)
California Grill (Contemporary resort)
Cape May Cafe (Beach Club resort)
Crystal Palace, The (Magic Kingdom, Main Street, U.S.A.)
Enzo's Hideaway (Disney Springs, The Landing)
Flame Tree Barbecue (Animal Kingdom, Discovery Island)
Flying Fish (BoardWalk resort)
Hollywood & Vine (Disney's Hollywood Studios)
House of Blues (Disney Springs, West Side)
'Ohana (Polynesian Village resort)
Paddlefish (Disney Springs, The Landing)
Raglan Road (Disney Springs, The Landing)
Sunshine Seasons (Epcot, Future World)
Teppan Edo (Epcot, World Showcase)
Todd English's bluezoo (Dolphin resort)
Trail's End (Fort Wilderness)
Tusker House (Animal Kingdom, Harambe)

Via Napoli (Epcot, World Showcase)
Wave . . . of American Flavors, The (Contemporary resort)
Wolfgang Puck Bar & Grill (Disney Springs, Town Center)

HOT DOGS

Backlot Express (Disney's Hollywood Studios)
Casey's Corner (Magic Kingdom, Main Street, U.S.A.)
Dino Diner (Animal Kingdom, Dinoland)
Dockside Diner (Disney's Hollywood Studios)
Fairfax Fare (Disney's Hollywood Studios)
Lunching Pad, The (Magic Kingdom, Tomorrowland)
Sommerfest (Epcot, World Showcase)
Sunset Ranch Market (Disney's Hollywood Studios)
Wetzel's Pretzels (Disney Springs, Marketplace)

ICE CREAM AND FROZEN TREATS

Aloha Isle (Magic Kingdom, Adventureland)
Ample Hills Creamery (BoardWalk resort)
Anandapur Ice Cream Truck (Animal Kingdom, Asia)
Beaches & Cream Soda Shop (Beach Club resort)
Cheshire Cafe (Magic Kingdom, Fantasyland)
Dino-Bite Snacks (Animal Kingdom, DinoLand)
Fife & Drum Tavern (Epcot, World Showcase)
The Fountain (Dolphin resort)
Gaston's Tavern (Magic Kingdom, Fantasyland)
Ghirardelli Ice Cream & Chocolate Shop (Disney Springs, Marketplace)
Golden Oak Outpost (Magic Kingdom, Frontierland)
Hollywood Scoops (Disney's Hollywood Studios)
L'Artisan's des Glace (Epcot, World Showcase)
Pineapple Lanai (Polynesian Village resort)
Plaza Ice Cream Parlor (Magic Kingdom, Main Street, U.S.A.)
Plaza Restaurant (Magic Kingdom, Main Street, U.S.A.)
Refreshment Outpost (Epcot, World Showcase)
Storybook Treats (Magic Kingdom, Fantasyland)
Sunshine Tree Terrace (Magic Kingdom, Adventureland)

Tamu Tamu Refreshments
(Animal Kingdom, Harambe)
Vivoli il Gelato (Disney Springs, The Landing)

KIDS' FAVORITES

Akershus Royal Banquet Hall
(Epcot, World Showcase)
Cape May Cafe (breakfast; Beach Club resort)
Casey's Corner (Magic Kingdom, Main Street)
Chef Mickey's (Contemporary resort)
Cinderella's Royal Table (Magic Kingdom, Fantasyland)
Cosmic Ray's Starlight Cafe (Magic Kingdom, Tomorrowland)
Crystal Palace, The (Magic Kingdom, Main Street)
50's Prime Time Cafe
(Disney's Hollywood Studios)
Hollywood & Vine (Disney's Hollywood Studios)
Hoop-Dee-Doo Musical Revue (see page 315)
Restaurantosaurus (Animal Kingdom, Dinoland)
1900 Park Fare (Grand Floridian resort)
'Ohana (Polynesian Village resort)
Pinocchio Village Haus (Magic Kingdom, Fantasyland)
Pizzafari (Animal Kingdom, Discovery Island)
Rainforest Cafe (Animal Kingdom and Disney Springs, Marketplace)
Sunset Ranch Market
(Disney's Hollywood Studios)
Sunshine Seasons (Epcot, Future World)
T-Rex Cafe: A Prehistoric Family Adventure
(Disney Springs, Marketplace)
Tusker House (Animal Kingdom, Harambe)
Whispering Canyon Cafe (Wilderness Lodge)
Woody's Lunch Box
(Disney's Hollywood Studios)

KNOCKOUT VIEWS

Big River Grille & Brewing Works (outdoor seating; BoardWalk)
Boathouse, The (Disney Springs, The Landing)
California Grill (Contemporary resort)
Coral Reef (Epcot, Future World)
Jock Lindsey's Hangar Bar
(Disney Springs, The Landing)
La Hacienda de San Angel
(Epcot, World Showcase)
Paddlefish (Disney Springs, The Landing)
Sanaa (Animal Kingdom Lodge; select seats)

Terralina Crafted Italian (Disney Springs, The Landing)
Topolino's Terrace—Flavors of the Riviera
(Riviera resort)

KOSHER (fast-food selections)

ABC Commissary (Disney's Hollywood Studios)
Artist's Palette, The (Saratoga Springs resort)
Cosmic Ray's Starlight Cafe (Magic Kingdom, Tomorrowland)
Everything Pop! (Pop Century resort)
Food Courts (All-Star and Port Orleans Riverside resorts)
Gasparilla Island Grill (Grand Floridian resort)
Kusafiri Coffee Shop & Bakery (Animal Kingdom, Harambe)
Landscape of Flavors (Art of Animation resort)
Mara, The (Animal Kingdom Lodge)
Pizzafari (Animal Kingdom, Discovery Island)
Satu'li Canteen (Animal Kingdom, Pandora—World of AVATAR)
Roaring Fork (Wilderness Lodge)

LOUNGES AND BARS (with food)

Big River Grille & Brewing Works
(BoardWalk resort)
Boathouse, The (Disney Springs, The Landing)
Cabana Bar & Beach Club (Dolphin resort)
California Grill Lounge (Contemporary resort)
Cítricos Lounge (Grand Floridian resort)
Crew's Cup (Yacht Club resort)
Crockett's Tavern (Fort Wilderness resort)
The Edison (Disney Springs, The Landing)
ESPN Club (BoardWalk resort)
Gurgling Suitcase (Old Key West resort)
Hurricane Hanna's (Yacht & Beach Club resorts)
Il Mulino New York Trattoria Lounge
(Swan resort)
Jock Lindsey's Hangar Bar (Disney Springs, The Landing)
Kimonos (Swan resort)
Leaping Horse Libations (BoardWalk resort)
Mardi Grogs (Port Orleans French Quarter resort)
Martha's Vineyard (Beach Club resort)
Mizner's (Grand Floridian resort)
Muddy Rivers (Port Orleans Riverside resort)
Narcoossee's (Grand Floridian resort)
Nomad Lounge (Animal Kingdom, Discovery Island)

Paddlefish (Disney Springs, The Landing)
Paradiso 37 (Disney Springs, The Landing)
Phins (Dolphin resort)
Raglan Road (Disney Springs, The Landing)
Rainforest Cafe (Magic Mushroom bar; Animal Kingdom and Disney Springs, Marketplace)
River Roost (Port Orleans Riverside resort)
Rix Sports Bar & Grill (Coronado Springs resort)
Rose & Crown Pub (Epcot, World Showcase)
Sanaa Lounge (Animal Kingdom Lodge)
Shark Bar at T-Rex Cafe (Disney Springs, Marketplace)
Siestas Cantina (Coronado Springs resort)
Sommerfest (inside Germany; Epcot, World Showcase)
Splash Terrace (Swan resort)
Tambu Lounge (Polynesian Village resort)
Territory Lounge (Wilderness Lodge)
Trader Sam's Grog Grotto (Polynesian resort)
Tune-In Lounge (Disney's Hollywood Studios)
Turf Club Bar & Grill, The (Saratoga Springs Resort & Spa)
Turtle Shack (Disney's Old Key West resort)
Tutto Gusto (Epcot, World Showcase)
Uzima Springs (Animal Kingdom Lodge)
Wine Bar George (Disney Springs, The Landing)
Yak & Yeti Lounge (Animal Kingdom, Asia)

OPEN 24 HOURS

Capt. Cook's (Polynesian Village resort)
Gasparilla Island Grill (Grand Floridian resort)
Picabu (Dolphin resort)
Sundial Cafe 24-7 (Wyndham hotel)

PIZZA

Blaze Fast Fire'd Pizza (Disney Springs, Town Center)
BoardWalk Pizza Window (BoardWalk resort)
California Grill (Contemporary resort)
Capt. Cook's (Polynesian Village resort)
Everything Pop! (Pop Century resort)
Food Courts (All-Star resorts)
Gasparilla Island Grill (Grand Floridian resort)
Mama Melrose's Ristorante Italiano (Disney's Hollywood Studios)
Pinocchio Village Haus (Magic Kingdom, Fantasyland)
Pizzafari (Animal Kingdom, Discovery Island)

Pizza Ponte (Disney Springs, The Landing)
PizzeRizzo (Disney's Hollywood Studios)
Riverside Mill (Port Orleans Riverside resort)
Roaring Fork (Wilderness Lodge)
Sassagoula Floatworks & Food Factory (Port Orleans French Quarter resort)
Sunset Ranch Market (Disney's Hollywood Studios)
Trail's End Restaurant (Fort Wilderness resort)
Trattoria al Forno (Boardwalk resort)
Via Napoli (Epcot, World Showcase)
Wolfgang Puck Bar & Grill (Disney Springs, Town Center)
Wolfgang Puck Express (Disney Springs, Marketplace)

SALADS

ABC Commissary (Disney's Hollywood Studios)
Artist's Palette, The (Saratoga Springs resort)
Big River Grille & Brewing Works (BoardWalk resort)
Boathouse, The (Disney Springs, The Landing)
Boma—Flavors of Africa (Animal Kingdom Lodge)
Chef Art Smith's Homecomin' (Disney Springs, Town Center)
Columbia Harbour House (Magic Kingdom, Liberty Square)
Earl of Sandwich (Disney Springs, Marketplace)
El Mercado de Coronado (Coronado Springs resort)
Gasparilla Island Grill (Grand Floridian resort)
Hollywood Brown Derby (Disney's Hollywood Studios)
Il Mulino New York Trattoria (Swan resort)
Picabu (Dolphin resort)
Pinocchio Village Haus (Magic Kingdom, Fantasyland)
Plaza Restaurant (Magic Kingdom, Main Street, U.S.A.)
Rainforest Cafe (Animal Kingdom and Disney Springs, Marketplace)
Sunshine Seasons (Epcot, Future World)
Wave . . . of American Flavors, The (Contemporary resort)
Wolfgang Puck Bar & Grill (Disney Springs, Town Center)
Yak & Yeti (Animal Kingdom, Asia)

SEAFOOD

Ale & Compass Restaurant (Yacht Club resort)
Artist Point (Wilderness Lodge)
Boathouse, The (Disney Springs, The Landing)
California Grill (Contemporary resort)
Cape May Cafe (Beach Club resort)
Columbia Harbour House (Magic Kingdom, Liberty Square)
Coral Reef (Epcot, Future World)
Flying Fish (BoardWalk resort)
Kimonos (Swan resort)
Kona Cafe (Polynesian Village resort)
Monsieur Paul (Epcot, World Showcase)
Narcoossee's (Grand Floridian resort)
Paddlefish (Disney Springs, The Landing)
Sebastian's Bistro (Carribbean Beach resort)
Todd English's bluezoo (Dolphin resort)
Tokyo Dining (Epcot, World Showcase)
Victoria & Albert's (Grand Floridian resort)

SNACK BARS (at the resorts)

Beach Club Marketplace (Beach Club resort)
Cabana Bar & Beach Club (Dolphin resort)
Capt. Cook's (Polynesian Village resort)
Contempo Café (Contemporary resort)
Fuel (Dolphin resort)
Gasparilla Island Grill (Grand Floridian resort)
Mara, The (Animal Kingdom Lodge)
Picabu (Dolphin resort)
Roaring Fork (Wilderness Lodge)

SOLO DINERS

Boathouse, The (Disney Springs, The Landing)
California Grill Lounge (Contemporary resort)
Cítricos lounge (Grand Floridian resort)
Crew's Cup (lounge, Yacht Club resort)
Enzo's Hideaway (Disney Springs, The Landing)
ESPN Club (BoardWalk resort)
Flying Fish (BoardWalk resort)
Il Mulino New York Trattoria (Swan resort)
Jiko—The Cooking Place Lounge (Animal Kingdom Lodge)
Narcoossee's Lounge (Grand Floridian resort)
Nomad Lounge (Disney's Animal Kingdom, Discovery Island)
Paddlefish (Disney Springs, The Landing)
Raglan Road (Disney Springs, The Landing)
Tune-In Lounge (Disney's Hollywood Studios)
Wine Bar George (Disney Springs, The Landing)

STEAK

Be Our Guest Restaurant (Magic Kingdom, Fantasyland)
California Grill (Contemporary resort)
Flying Fish (BoardWalk resort)
Jiko—The Cooking Place (Animal Kingdom Lodge resort)
Kona Cafe (Polynesian Village resort)
La Hacienda de San Angel (Epcot, World Showcase)
Le Cellier Steakhouse (Epcot, World Showcase)
Monsieur Paul (Epcot, World Showcase)
Paddlefish (Disney Springs, The Landing)
Narcoossee's (Grand Floridian resort)
STK Orlando (Disney Springs, The Landing)
Teppan Edo (Epcot, World Showcase)
Shula's (Swan resort)
Yachtsman Steakhouse (Yacht Club resort)

SUPER SPLURGES (for grown-ups)

Boathouse, The (Disney Springs, The Landing)
California Grill (Contemporary resort)
Chefs de France (Epcot, World Showcase)
Cinderella's Royal Table (Magic Kingdom)
Enzo's Hideaway (Disney Springs, The Landing)
Flying Fish (BoardWalk resort)
Hollywood Brown Derby (Disney's Hollywood Studios)
Il Mulino (Swan resort)
Jiko—The Cooking Place (Animal Kingdom Lodge)
Le Cellier Steakhouse (Epcot, World Showcase)
Monsieur Paul (Epcot, World Showcase)
Morimoto Asia (Disney Springs, The Landing)
Narcoossee's (Grand Floridian resort)
Paddlefish (Disney Springs, The Landing)
Sanaa (Animal Kingdom Lodge)
Tiffins Restaurant (Animal Kingdom, Discovery Island)
Victoria & Albert's (Grand Floridian resort)
Wine Bar George (Disney Springs, The Landing)
Yachtsman Steakhouse (Yacht Club resort)

SUSHI

Benihana Steakhouse and Sushi (Hilton Lake Buena Vista hotel)
California Grill (Contemporary resort)
Kabuki Cafe (Epcot, World Showcase)
Katsura Grill (Epcot, World Showcase)
Kimonos (lounge; Swan resort)

Kona Cafe (Polynesian Village resort)
Kona Island (after 5 P.M.; Polynesian Village resort)
Morimoto Asia (Disney Springs, The Landing)
Splitsville (Disney Springs, West Side)
Tokyo Dining (Epcot, World Showcase)

TERRIFIC THEMING

Akershus Royal Banquet Hall (Epcot, World Showcase)
Be Our Guest Restaurant (Magic Kingdom, Fantasyland)
Biergarten (Epcot, World Showcase)
Boathouse, The (Disney Springs, The Landing)
Cinderella's Royal Table (Magic Kingdom, Fantasyland)
The Edison (Disney Springs, The Landing)
Enzo's Hideaway (Disney Springs, The Landing)
50's Prime Time Cafe (Disney's Hollywood Studios)
Jungle Navigation Co. Ltd. Skipper Canteen (Magic Kingdom, Adventureland)
Liberty Tree Tavern (Magic Kingdom, Liberty Square)
Maria & Enzo's Ristorante (Disney Springs, The Landing)
'Ohana (Polynesian Village resort)
Rainforest Cafe (Animal Kingdom and Disney Springs, Marketplace)
Sanaa (Animal Kingdom Lodge)
Sci-Fi Dine-In Theater (Disney's Hollywood Studios)
T-Rex Cafe: A Prehistoric Family Adventure (Disney Springs, Marketplace)
Tusker House (Animal Kingdom, Harambe)

VEGETARIAN SELECTIONS

Boma—Flavors of Africa (Animal Kingdom Lodge)
Columbia Harbour House (Magic Kingdom, Liberty Square)
Cosmic Ray's Starlight Cafe (Magic Kingdom, Tomorrowland)
Everything Pop! (Pop Century resort)
Food Courts (All-Star resorts)
Jiko—The Cooking Place (Animal Kingdom Lodge)
La Hacienda de San Angel (Epcot, World Showcase)
Les Halles Boulangerie Patisserie (Epcot, World Showcase)

Mama Melrose's Ristorante Italiano (Disney's Hollywood Studios)
Pinocchio Village Haus (Magic Kingdom, Fantasyland)
Pizzafari (Animal Kingdom, Discovery Island)
PizzeRizzo (Disney's Hollywood Studios)
Rainforest Cafe (Animal Kingdom and Disney Springs, Marketplace)
Sanaa (Animal Kingdom Lodge)
Sunset Ranch Market (Disney's Hollywood Studios)
Sunshine Seasons (Epcot, Future World)
Teppan Edo (Epcot, World Showcase)
Tony's Town Square (Magic Kingdom, Main Street, U.S.A.)
Tusker House (Animal Kingdom, Harambe)
Tutto Italia (Epcot, World Showcase)
Via Napoli (Epcot, World Showcase)
Wolfgang Puck Express (Disney Springs, Marketplace)

WINE AND DINE (great wine lists)

Artist Point (Wilderness Lodge)
Be Our Guest Restaurant ([dinner] Magic Kingdom, Fantasyland)
Boathouse, The (Disney Springs, The Landing)
Boma—Flavors of Africa (Animal Kingdom Lodge)
California Grill (Contemporary resort)
Chefs de France (Epcot, World Showcase)
Cítricos (Grand Floridian resort)
Enzo's Hideaway (Disney Springs, The Landing)
Flying Fish (BoardWalk resort)
Hollywood Brown Derby (Disney's Hollywood Studios)
Il Mulino New York Trattoria (Swan resort)
Jiko—The Cooking Place (Animal Kingdom Lodge)
Monsieur Paul (Epcot, World Showcase)
Morimoto Asia (Disney Springs, The Landing)
Narcoossee's (Grand Floridian resort)
Paddlefish (Disney Springs, The Landing)
Sanaa (Animal Kingdom Lodge)
Shula's Steak House (Dolphin resort)
Tiffins Restaurant (Animal Kingdom, Discovery Island)
Victoria & Albert's (Grand Floridian resort)
Wine Bar George (Disney Springs, The Landing)
Wolfgang Puck Bar & Grill (Disney Springs, Town Center)
Yachtsman Steakhouse (Yacht Club resort)

Reservations Explained

Disney's reservation system, formerly known as "priority seating," covers most full-service restaurants on Walt Disney World property. The name may have changed, but the procedure is the same. It was designed to provide the assurance of a reservation without delays caused by no-shows and latecomers. Here's how it works: You call ahead to request a seating time; you arrive five minutes before the assigned time and check in at the podium; you receive the next available table that can accommodate your party.

It is virtually impossible to walk into a table service eatery without a reservation—secure yours as far in advance as possible. Seating times can be reserved up to 180 days ahead (see box below) for most Walt Disney World eateries by calling 407-WDW-DINE (939-3463), by visiting *www.disneyworld.com/dine*, or via the My Disney Experience app or website. The phone hotline is open daily from 7 A.M. to 10 P.M. The number of tables available in advance varies. If you are unable to book in advance, try to make same-day arrangements. *Note that a fee of $10 per person will be charged to guests who do not show up or cancel a reservation less than one day in advance.*

Most Disney resorts have a phone in the main lobby that provides direct contact with the Dine Line. Simply touch 55—the call is free. From other locations, dial 407-WDW-DINE (939-3463). Once at the theme parks, reservations can be made at the eatery itself; at City Hall in the Magic Kingdom; in Epcot at Guest Relations by Spaceship Earth; by Hollywood Junction in Disney's Hollywood Studios; and at Guest Relations in Animal Kingdom. Bookings can also be made at Guest Relations at the Welcome Center in Town Center.

Advance Planning

While some Walt Disney World restaurants may have an occasional open table (like Marrakesh in Epcot's World Showcase), most are booked far in advance. The restaurants for which careful planning is essential include Be Our Guest and Cinderella's Royal Table in the Magic Kingdom (call 180 days ahead and keep your fingers crossed!), Le Cellier Steakhouse and Via Napoli in Epcot, Tusker House breakfast and lunch in Disney's Animal Kingdom, California Grill in the Contemporary resort, plus many others.

While the Walt Disney World reservation system is often successful, there are times when the wait for a table can be unexpectedly long. This is most likely to occur during peak mealtimes at restaurants that offer buffets or family-style meals, where patrons will often opt for seconds (or thirds). For this reason, be sure to check in at the restaurant particularly early for all character-hosted meals.

HOT TIP!

At most WDW restaurants, reservations are scheduled in five- or ten-minute intervals. If they don't have a 6 P.M. availability, check for 6:10 P.M.

Reservations are necessary for the Hoop-Dee-Doo Musical Revue and the Polynesian Village resort's Spirit of Aloha; they can be made by calling 407-WDW-DINE (939-3463). Reservations can be booked up to 180 days in advance. If you can't reserve a table for an early performance, consider a later one (they are usually less heavily booked). Another popular dinner show, Mickey's Backyard BBQ, will not be offered in 2020.

Keep in mind that, with the exception of dinner shows, a Walt Disney World seating time does vary from a traditional reservation—you may have to wait a bit when you arrive at your assigned time. Your party will be given the first table that opens up.

Note: Because the dining scene at Walt Disney World is ever-evolving, we advise calling 407-WDW-DINE (939-3463) to confirm specifics.

For Disney Resort Guests Only

Do you have a confirmed reservation at a Disney–owned-and-operated resort? If so, you are entitled to a special perk: Call 180 days prior to the first day of your hotel reservation and you can make dining reservations for up to 10 days of your stay. That's like getting a 1- to 10-day jump on everyone else! (Stays longer than 10 days will require a second call. Inquire when you make your first set of dining reservations.) Have your resort confirmation number handy when you book a table.

Dinner Shows

The fact that Disney is expert in family entertainment is nowhere more readily apparent than amid the whooping and hollering troupe of singers and dancers who race toward the stage at Fort Wilderness resort's Pioneer Hall. As guests plow through filling barbecue fare (ribs, fried chicken, strawberry shortcake, beer, wine, and soft drinks), these enthusiastic performers sing, dance, and joke up a storm.

Most of the gags are groaners, but the audience eats 'em up. It's all in the course of an evening at the **Hoop-Dee-Doo Musical Revue**, presented nightly at 4 P.M., 6:15 P.M., and 8:30 P.M. The cost is about $64 per adult and $38 for children (ages 3 through 9) for Category 3 seating; about $67 for adults, $39 for kids in Category 2; and about $72 and $43 for Category 1. (The best views are in Category 1—seating is on the main floor.)

HOT TIP!

The Hoop-Dee-Doo Musical Revue is a perennially popular show. Make your reservations as far in advance as possible.

Note that the dining room in Pioneer Hall can be chilly year-round. Bring a sweater to combat the sometimes intense air-conditioning.

Disney's luau show is called **Spirit of Aloha**. Set in the beachfront backyard of a Hawaiian house (at the Polynesian Village resort), the show invites guests to join in a musical celebration.

The luau experience combines traditional music as well as more contemporary ditties. The performers' dancing is some of the most authentic this side of Hawaii. The Spirit of Aloha is presented in an open-air dining theater in Luau Cove, near Seven Seas Lagoon.

The all-you-can-eat feast is influenced by the flavors of Polynesia and includes draft beer, wine, soft drinks, and dessert. Menu items include roasted chicken, BBQ pork ribs, fresh pineapple, Polynesian-style rice, and vegetables. The kids' menu features PB&J sandwiches, mac and cheese, chicken nuggets, and hot dogs. The cost is about $66 for adults and $39 for kids in Category 3; about $74 and $44 for Category 2; and about $78 and $46 for Category 1 (the best views are from Category 1 seats). Some of the seats in Categories 2 and 3 require guests to walk up a few stairs.

Plan to arrive at least 30 minutes before showtime, and allow extra time for transportation and parking.

(Note that all prices are subject to change.) The show may be canceled due to inclement weather (though tables are sheltered).

Reservations: Arrangements for dinner shows may be made up to 180 days in advance by calling 407-WDW-DINE (939-3463). Groups of eight or more should call 407-939-7707. Prices include tax and gratuity and may be higher during peak seasons.

A credit card number is required for all dinner show reservations. Full payment is required upon booking. It's also possible to redeem Disney Dining Plan credits for dinner shows. At press time, all Disney dinner shows were participating in the dining plan. All dinner shows are considered Signature meals and cost two table-service credits per person.

Notes: Cancellations for dinner shows must be made at least 48 hours prior to showtime to avoid paying full price. The Spirit of Aloha may be cancelled due to inclement weather.

Special occasions may be acknowledged during Disney dinner shows (no charge). Celebration cakes are available for an additional charge and should be ordered 48 hours in advance by calling 407-827-2253.

HOT TIP!

Mickey's Backyard BBQ, a Fort Wilderness favorite, is on hiatus while Disney Imagineers build the new resort: Reflections—A Lakeside Lodge. For updates on the beloved western-style dinner show, visit *disneyworld.com* or use the My Disney Experience mobile app or website.

Bars & Lounges of WDW

What distinguishes Walt Disney World pubs and lounges from many bars in the real world? Well, in addition to over-the-top theming, you can almost always get a savory nibble to accompany that cocktail. Most Disney lounges serve food, be it from their own menu or from that of a neighboring restaurant.

Hours vary, but theme park watering holes (at Epcot, Disney's Hollywood Studios, and Animal Kingdom) shut their doors at park closing time. Pool bars at the resorts keep daytime pool hours. Last call at resort lounges can be anywhere from about 10 P.M. to midnight. Disney Springs Marketplace spots stay open till the shops close, usually 11 P.M. Other lounges may keep things going until about 1 A.M.

ALL-STAR MOVIES, ALL-STAR MUSIC & ALL-STAR SPORTS

POOL BARS: There are small poolside oases in All-Star Movies, All-Star Music, and All-Star Sports: Silver Screen Spirits, Singing Spirits, and Grandstand Spirits, respectively. Each serves a selection of beer, wine, traditional cocktails, and specialty drinks.

ANIMAL KINGDOM PARK

DAWA BAR: A shady spot in a busy neighborhood, Dawa is a pleasant place to take a load off weary feet and sip Safari Amber beer and other cocktails. It's next to Tusker House, on Kivulini Terrace. There is occasional live music, too.

NOMAD LOUNGE: Adventurers can take a load off and relish in a savory snack and/or frosty beverage at this exotic Animal Kingdom destination. The lounge proffers libations from the world over. The freshly prepared cuisine at Nomad includes vegetarian pad Thai, Indian butter chicken wings, African-spiced Wagyu beef skewers, and honey-glazed, coriander-spiced pork ribs. Festive banners post questions about world travel and the thrill of discovery. Jot your answers on a decorative (and free) tag and Cast Members will post them to a chandelier for all the world to see. This escapist oasis owns a spot on our favorites list.

THIRSTY RIVER BAR & TREK SNACKS: Standing in the shadows of Expedition Everest, this casual outdoor oasis offers many spirited selections, including specialty drinks known as Himalayan Ghost, Durbar Margarita, and Khumbu Icefall. Savory snacks are available too. The menu has featured hummus with fresh vegetables, popcorn, assorted chips, and Mickey pretzels (plain or with cheese dip). Refillable souvenir popcorn buckets are available, too.

RAINFOREST CAFE: The Magic Mushroom bar serves, among other things, fruit blends and specialty drinks. Bar stools resemble animal legs (hooves and all). Guests may order from the restaurant's menu, too. The bar is inside the Rainforest Cafe. Admission to Animal Kingdom park is not necessary to enter. Note that Rainforest Cafe may keep longer hours than the park.

YAK & YETI LOUNGE: A small but escapist space inside one of the restaurant's themed dining areas, the Yak & Yeti lounge has a fully stocked bar and seating for six. (There's standing room, too.) House specialties include the Yak Attack, Rickshaw Ricky, Big Bamboo, and Pink Himalayan. Beer, wine, sake, and assorted soft drinks are also served.

ANIMAL KINGDOM LODGE

CAPE TOWN LOUNGE AND WINE BAR: Sip African wines at this intimate space adjacent to Jiko—The Cooking Place. In addition to a full menu, it has the largest selection of African wines in the United States.

MAJI: A poolside bar (*maji* means "water" in Swahili) serves beverages when the Samawati Springs pool is open (in Kidani Village).

♥ Disney Dining Plan participant at press time   **SR** Signature Restaurant

SANAA: Located in the resort's Kidani Village, this lounge is within the restaurant of the same name. South African beers and wines are served.

UZIMA SPRINGS: The bar near the main pool serves beer, wine, and specialty drinks during pool hours. The (alcohol-free) Lava smoothie is an excellent antidote to the steamy Florida heat.

VICTORIA FALLS: On the mezzanine level overlooking Boma—Flavors of Africa, this lounge offers coffee and spirits, plus the soothing sounds of the falls. (The actual Victoria Falls are located in Africa, between Zambia and Zimbabwe, and are nearly a mile wide.)

ART OF ANIMATION

DROP OFF BAR: Open from noon until midnight, this poolside location offers a variety of cocktails (with and without alcohol), soft drinks, and smoothies—plus sandwiches, fruit, and other snack items.

BOARDWALK

ABRACADABAR: A "curious cocktail lounge," adjoining Flying Fish, AbracadaBAR merges the Golden Age of Magic with the magic of the Mouse. The sophisticated social club, once frequented by famous magicians and boardwalk illusionists, is back in the spotlight and open to all. Concoctions of note: The Magic Hattan, The Conjurita, and Pepper's Ghost. Curious Cocktails include alcohol-free options. 🐭

ATLANTIC DANCE: This club has music, videos, and a deejay. The design is Art Deco, but the tunes are more current. It's open Tuesday through Saturday nights, and guests must be at least 21 (with government-issued photo ID) to enter Atlantic Dance.

BELLE VUE LOUNGE: A full bar accompanies old-time tunes from antique radios in this casual space. Continental breakfast is offered (from 6 A.M. until 11 A.M.). Board games are usually available for on-site use (free of charge). There's limited seating at the bar, but there are plenty of tables and comfy couches to relax on. The lounge starts serving cocktails at about 5 P.M. 🐭

BIG RIVER GRILLE & BREWING WORKS: Big River patrons may order appetizers at the bar and sample the brewmaster's flagship ales and specialty beers. They may even get to watch as a new batch is brewed. In addition to fresh-brewed beer, drink selections include fresh-squeezed lemonade, strawberry lemonade, pomegranate lemonade, and more. Note that Big River Grille & Brewing Works does not accept reservations and can get crowded during mealtimes (and right after Epcot closes for the evening). 🐭

ESPN CLUB: The sports bar provides live radio and TV broadcasts along with a full menu. With nearly 100 screens, chances are you'll find the game you seek. The place fills up quickly on big game days—arrive at least an hour early on such occasions. Note that on NFL Sundays, the match-ups scheduled for screening are often noted right on the TVs. If not, ask the bartender or inquire at the podium near the front entrance. 🐭

JELLYROLLS: Dueling pianos and lively sing-alongs are the draw at this club, serving beer, wine, and other drinks. There is a cover charge in the neighborhood of $15, and guests must be at least 21 years old to enter. (Government-issued photo ID is required.) Requests are encouraged. And don't forget to tip the piano players before you leave. Note that it can be exceptionally cool here: Bring a sweater.

PHOTO BY JILL SAFRO

LEAPING HORSE LIBATIONS: The pool bar—designed to resemble a carousel (hence, the leaping horses)—offers cocktails, sandwiches, soft drinks, and simple snacks during pool hours.

CARIBBEAN BEACH

BANANA CABANA: In the running for best pool bar, the open-air lounge offers a relaxing respite from the real world. It features a full bar and nummy nibbles.

CONTEMPORARY

CALIFORNIA GRILL LOUNGE: Perched atop the Contemporary resort, this revitalized space tops many a "must-visit" list. Tucked within the acclaimed restaurant, the lounge offers the full menu and shares access to California Grill's exquisite wine selection.

In addition to wine, the lounge features sake, craft beers and ciders, mixed drinks, alcohol-free signature drinks, and more. Guests of the lounge may order anything off the restaurant menu (including the spectacular sushi). Just as with the restaurant itself, all guests hoping to visit the California Grill Lounge must check in at a desk on the Contemporary's second floor. From there they are escorted to an express elevator. The lounge does not accept reservations. ♥

COVE BAR: Set beside the pool in the resort's Bay Lake Tower, Cove Bar serves sweets (apple slices with caramel dipping sauce, fruit, and frozen desserts) and lunch items (shrimp cocktail, turkey BLT wrap, nachos with cheese, veggie wrap, hot dog, and sushi). Wash it all down with one of their specialty drinks, such as the Banana Cabana or Poolside Plunge. ♥

OUTER RIM: Located on the resort's fourth floor across from Contempo Cafe, this modern lounge has about seven bar stools and an abundance of tables with cocktail service. The main draw here is not the view of the large-screen TV, but rather the sweeping views of Bay Lake and the natural wonder of Fort Wilderness (on the lake's far shore). Parts of this lounge may host guests waiting for a table at the popular Chef Mickey's restaurant, so it can be a tad congested here at mealtimes. Beer, wine, sangria, specialty drinks, and alcohol-free kiddie cocktails are served from about 11:30 A.M. till 10 P.M.

SAND BAR: A full bar is offered poolside, weather permitting. Quick-service snacks, salads, and sandwiches are served at an adjacent counter. ♥

PHOTO BY MIKE CARROLL

THE WAVE . . . OF AMERICAN FLAVORS LOUNGE: On the first floor of the resort, this spacious bar boasts a wine list that is mostly screw cap (yes, that's a good thing)—a quaffable selection of quality vintages. About 50 are available by the glass; tasting flights are a great choice for those who wish to sample several selections. Also poured: organic beers, ports, and specialty drinks. Guests may order from The Wave's menu, too.

CORONADO SPRINGS

RIX SPORTS BAR & GRILL: Located in the resort's main building, this upscale, eye- and palate-pleasing lounge serves specialty drinks, beer, wine, soft drinks, and a full menu. In addition to traditional sports bar fare, Rix offers lobster sliders, corn chowder, mahi Reubens, and New York strip steak. Sweet treats include Key lime pie, chocolate lava cake, and a sorbet trio. The 300-seat venue features about 40 TVs—ensuring that you will catch the big game—and a Mediterranean-inspired atmosphere. ♥

SIESTAS CANTINA: Swimmers can take time out for burgers, sandwiches, tacos, and cocktails at this spot near the pool in the Dig Site area. ♥

HOT TIP!

At some Walt Disney World lounges, you may order food from a neighboring or nearby restaurant's menu. Just ask.

DISNEY'S HOLLYWOOD STUDIOS

BASELINE TAP HOUSE: Sonoma Valley wines and California craft beers are specialties of this house. Pair them with cheese and charcuterie, soft pretzels with beer cheese fondue and spicy mustard, coffee-rubbed rib eye steak puff with olive salad and/or spiced almonds. Or wash them down with a sweet soft drink: black cherry soda or wild strawberry lemonade.

THE HOLLYWOOD BROWN DERBY LOUNGE: An inviting alfresco enclave, the Derby Lounge serves as an extension of the elegant eatery to which it is attached. The all-day menu touts specialty cocktails (including the Grapefruit Cake Martini) and small plates. Choose from items such as andouille-crusted shrimp, Wagyu beef sliders, and Florida tomato soup. For a sweet treat, consider the warm blueberry cobbler or banana toffee cake.

OGA'S CANTINA: Come to the cantina to quench your thirst and rub elbows (or not!) with bounty hunters, smugglers, and travelers of all ages. As guests quaff spirited beverages such as the Jedi Mind Trick, Bad Motivator IPA, or Toniray wine, they're treated to bold musical entertainment courtesy of droid DJ R-3X, a former Starspeeder 3000 pilot. (He was the original Star Tours pilot.) Non-alcoholic specialty drinks are served, too. Guests of all ages are welcome to enjoy Oga's hospitality, but valid ID is required for alcohol.

TUNE-IN LOUNGE: A sitcom living-room setting with comfy stools and couches characterizes this lounge next to the 50's Prime Time Cafe. Old TV sets play scenes from beloved sitcoms (all of which feature food). Appetizers, cocktails, beer, wine, and soft drinks are served. This joint is always jumpin'.

> # HOT TIP!
> The spirits are forever flowing at Disney Springs. In addition to the dynamic destinations detailed on these pages, the following Disney Springs venues also boast ever-so-lovely lounges: Paddlefish, The Boathouse, Chef Art Smith's Homecomin', The Polite Pig, Morimoto Asia, and STK Orlando. Cheers!

DISNEY'S OLD KEY WEST

GURGLING SUITCASE: This friendly, pocket-size lounge on the Turtle Krawl boardwalk serves an assortment of Key West specialties, along with traditional cocktails, beer, and wine—plus an unexpectedly large selection of nibbles.

TURTLE SHACK: Refreshments at this poolside counter include frozen drinks, beer, and edibles such as hot dogs, pizza, salads, and sandwiches.

DISNEY SPRINGS

DOCKSIDE MARGARITAS: Get "a taste of the Sunshine State" at this waterside bar at the Marketplace. In addition to blended margaritas, this breezy spot serves rum runners, mojitos, and locally brewed craft beers and wines. Live entertainment is provided most evenings.

THE EDISON: If not for the fact that there's another Edison in L.A., we'd say the word "unique" was invented for this place. Part eatery, part cabaret, The Edison serves food and drink with a side of eclectic entertainment. There are 3 bars within the restaurant. Guests arriving after 10 P.M. must be at least 21 years of age and dressed appropriately: Slacks, jeans, or dress shorts are fine. Jackets are optional. Ball caps, sleeveless shirts, and flip-flops are not allowed.

ENZO'S HIDEAWAY TUNNEL BAR: A sprawling, underground establishment, this speakeasy locale has a marble-topped bar and an impressively massive menu of potent potables. In addition to beer, wine, cocktails, and specialty drinks, Enzo offers a vast array of scotches and "antique" specialty rums. The bar is set within a restaurant and is accessed via tunnel. (Hence, the name.)

HOLE IN THE WALL: Blink and you miss it. This tiny establishment is bookended (and dwarfed) by Raglan Road on the left and Cookes of Dublin on the right. A full bar is available, but the Irish stout stands out. In addition to the outstanding nibbles (whipped up over at Raglan Road), this diminutive spot boasts something that is beyond rare at Walt Disney World: Happy Hour specials (from 3 to 6 or 7 P.M.).

HOUSE OF BLUES BAR: Set in the back of the eatery section of H.O.B., this bar serves drinks that are as cool as the atmosphere. It's also possible to have drinks in the enclosed Voodoo Garden (table-service only). Guests may order from the restaurant menu.

JOCK LINDSEY'S HANGAR BAR: A waterside lounge with an aviation theme, Jock Lindsey's seats about 150 adventurous guests at a time (both in- and outdoors). Visitors may savor beer, wine, cocktails, or specialty drinks and nibble on small-plate treats such as Snakebite Sliders, Fräulein's Flatbread, Mac's Pork Belly Sliders, hot wings, and Air Pirates Pretzels (with housemade mustard and beer cheese fondue). You'll find the exotic dive bar on The Landing, between The Boathouse and Paradiso 37 restaurants.

F.Y.I.: Jock Lindsey is Indiana Jones' frequent pilot and the proud owner of a pet snake named Reggie. (Reggie also happens to be the name of the boat that sits outside the lounge. And, yes, guests may sit inside Reggie. The boat, not the snake.)

MAGIC MUSHROOM BAR: When the Rainforest Cafe restaurant is mobbed, we recommend taking in the thunderstorms and waterfalls from this central bar. You can sip a cocktail and order a snack from the restaurant's menu. There is another Magic Mushroom Bar inside the Rainforest Cafe at Disney's Animal Kingdom. Details may change in 2020.

PARADISO 37: The bar at Paradiso 37 has an international wine list, an extensive selection of tequilas, frozen margaritas, and the "coldest beer in the world." This spot offers indoor and outdoor seating. It is possible to order items from the restaurant's menu, too.

PLANET HOLLYWOOD OBSERVATORY: The redesigned Planet Hollywood lounge space includes an inviting outdoor terrace—perfect for sipping cocktails under the stars.

RAGLAN ROAD: Top o' the evening to you! This jovial joint is an authentic Irish pub and simply oozes Irish charm. The polished interior is a meticulously decorated Emerald Isle oasis—complete with freshly prepared Irish cuisine and live entertainment (the latter starting at about 4 P.M. on weekdays, noon on weekends). Oh, and of course, Raglan Road serves pints of Irish stout and other spirited beverages. This place is quite popular and can get quite crowded on weekend evenings—get there early if you can.

SHARK BAR: This space, inside the T-Rex Cafe, puts the water in watering hole. Anchored under the belly of a giant Technicolor squid, the aqueous area serves all kinds of cocktails, plus items from the restaurant's menu. (One of our favorite things to order here is the tomato soup. Your tastes may differ.) Guests must be at least 21 years of age to sit at the bar.

🐭 Disney Dining Plan participant at press time   **SR** Signature Restaurant

WINE BAR GEORGE: The brainchild of Master Sommelier George Miliotes, this 200-seat establishment resembles a winemaker's estate. It's a cozy yet elegant environment in which to savor sips from acclaimed wineries and promising up-and-comers. They pair perfectly with small plate offerings and family-style entrées. F.Y.I.: George Miliotes is one of just 256 Master Sommeliers in the world.

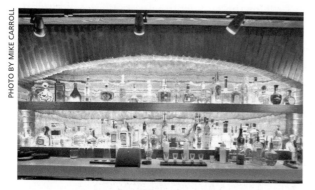

EPCOT

Most eateries, including several fast-food spots, serve alcoholic beverages. A few other Epcot locales actually specialize in liquid refreshments.

LA CAVA DEL TEQUILA: A warm glow envelopes guests in this little lounge in the big pyramid at the Mexico pavilion—and that's before they sample any of the 70-plus tequilas on the menu. In addition to blended margaritas (many made with fresh fruit and spices), guests may sip Mexican beer, wine, cocktails, and soft drinks. Snacks include fresh guacamole and chips and salsa. This 30-seat escape is open from about noon until Epcot closing time.

ROSE & CROWN PUB: This classic pub—a veritable symphony of polished woods, brass, and etched glass—adjoins the Rose & Crown Dining Room in the United Kingdom pavilion. English, Scottish, and Irish beers are available, along with a score of specialty drinks and appetizing snacks imported from the other side of the Atlantic. If you're lucky, there will be live (and lively) piano music during your visit. Feel free to sing along. (Showtimes are listed in the park's Times Guide.) Seating indoors and out is limited and available on a first-come, first-served basis. 🐭

SOMMERFEST: Just outside the Biergarten in Germany, there's a window serving soft pretzels, bratwurst, frankfurters, apple strudel, and other treats. Wash 'em down with a cold German beer. Sommerfest also dispenses German Riesling, bottled water, and fountain drinks. There are tables nearby. 🐭

> # HOT TIP!
>
> Grand Floridian visitors, take note: The resort's grand lobby is a divine setting in which to savor a fine wine or a frosty brew. While there's no in-lobby service, guests may buy a drink at a new *Beauty and the Beast*-inspired lounge and sip it while relaxing on an overstuffed lobby chair or comfy couch. If you time it right, you'll be serenaded by the lobby pianist or band.

TUTTO GUSTO: Tucked into the heart of the Italy pavilion, this rustic room offers 200 different wines (including grappa), beers imported from Italy, Italian specialty drinks, coffee drinks, and a small-plate menu. The best time to visit Tutto Gusto is in the afternoon (that's when crowds are usually lightest). Reservations are not available.

FORT WILDERNESS

CROCKETT'S TAVERN: You needn't brandish a coonskin cap to belly up to the bar in this rustic saloon, merely a government-issued photo ID to prove you're not a young'un (all guests must be at least 21 years of age to drink spirits of any kind). Tucked into a corner of the Trail's End restaurant, this spot is small but cozy, and the barkeeps are as amiable as they come. Last we visited, there were a couple of domestic beers on tap, plus a full bar. Pizza, chicken wings, and nachos are served, too. The television is usually tuned to the big game of the moment. 🐭

🐭 Disney Dining Plan participant at press time   **SR** Signature Restaurant

GRAND FLORIDIAN

CÍTRICOS LOUNGE: As inviting as any lounge on Disney property, this place has one stellar wine list. Old World, New World, red, white, sparkling . . . you name it, they got it (by the glass or the bottle). Beer, port, sherry, and creative cocktails (think along the lines of a Citropolitan or Pomegranate Splash) are available, too.

Cocktails and appetizers may be ordered until about 10 P.M. (If it's very busy, the bar may continue to serve drinks until the crowd dwindles.) Menu selections have included lamb meatballs, wild-caught halibut, slow-roasted pork belly, seasonal flatbread, artisanal cheese board, and veal Bolognese. There are a handful of seats at the bar and roughly ten tables in the lounge. If you sit at a table, be sure to place your order with the bartender before grabbing a seat.

NARCOOSSEE'S LOUNGE: This upscale bar-within-a-restaurant offers a little bit of everything: appetizers, entrées, desserts, and cocktails (including dessert drinks). There is an extensive list of international wines, 20 of which are available by the glass. How serious are they

about wine here? Our last bartender was a certified sommelier. A large selection of bottled craft beers is available, too. Note that the dress code for this lounge is "business casual." ❤

POOL BARS: Relax by the pool while sipping a specialty cocktail, beer, wine, or soft drink. The Courtyard Bar, near the big pool, also serves light snacks. Beaches Bar & Grill (by the zero-depth-entry pool) stands by with a full grill menu and a Rapid Fill Mug station.

POLYNESIAN VILLAGE

BAREFOOT BAR: Adjacent to the Lava pool (near the beach), this unassuming bar serves beer, wine, frozen tropical drinks (with and without alcohol), and soft drinks. Items of note: frozen strawberry daiquiri and piña colada. (We recommend them mixed together, aka The Lava Flow.)

OASIS BAR & GRILL: Set beside the resort's "quiet" pool, Oasis offers a full bar and a number of specialty cocktails. Spirited concoctions of note: Black Cherry Lemonade, Banana Cabana, and the oh-so-refreshing Frosty Pineapple. It's exclusively available to Polynesian Village resort guests.

TAMBU: Adjoining 'Ohana, this small tiki bar offers cocktails and specialty drinks in a tropical setting. There is seating at the bar and at tables. Note that the table section serves as the waiting area for guests dining at 'Ohana, so it tends to get very busy at mealtimes. Libation of note: the Lapu Lapu. It's a mixture of rum and fruit juices served in a fresh pineapple.

TRADER SAM'S GROG GROTTO: There's so much to see in this festive first-floor lounge that guests may not notice there is a world beyond Sam's walls. Guests may enjoy tropical drinks and small plates in the richly themed locale (Jungle Cruise meets the Enchanted Tiki Room). Drink favorites include the Krakatoa Punch, the Nautilus, and Dark and Stormy. Sam's doors may open at 3 P.M. Guests under 21 are not admitted after 8 P.M. Seats on the patio, aka Sam's Tiki Terrace, tend to be a tad easier to come by than those inside. If you simply must infiltrate the grotto, arrive at about 2:30 P.M. and wait for the doors to open.

❤ Disney Dining Plan participant at press time   **SR** Signature Restaurant

(Don't be surprised if there is already a line when you arrive.) You can also put your name on a list and be reached via pager when a spot opens up. This boisterous bar is quite the crowd-pleaser.

POP CENTURY

PETALS: This poolside watering hole serves beer, wine, and cocktails. Specialty cocktails of note: Captain's Mai Tai, Hula Hoop, and Lava Lamp. Petals is located near the resort's main pool area.

PORT ORLEANS
FRENCH QUARTER

MARDI GROGS: Beer, specialty drinks, and snacks are among the offerings at this pool spot.

SCAT CAT'S CLUB: Next to the Sassagoula Floatworks & Food Factory, this large, informal lounge pays tribute to the uniquely American music that is jazz. In fact, live jazz music is presented four nights a week (Wednesday through Saturday, from 8 P.M. till about 12 A.M.). In addition to the usual brews and blends, this happening spot specializes in Southern drinks—including Hurricanes. There is an appetizer menu, too.

PORT ORLEANS
RIVERSIDE

MUDDY RIVERS: Conveniently situated on Ol' Man Island, the poolside bar serves beer, wine, soft drinks and cocktails—including several of the frozen variety.

RIVER ROOST: Set in a room designed as a cotton exchange, this spacious lounge features specialty drinks, as well as light hors d'oeuvres. Sink into a comfy chair, beside the glow of the fireplace, and sip cocktails with a Southern flair. There are stools at the bar and tables, too. Live entertainment is presented on select evenings (usually Wednesday through Saturday, from 8 P.M. until about midnight).

RIVIERA RESORT

BAR RIVA: Meander to this poolside oasis for European- and Mediterranean-style fare, plus specialty beverages, soft drinks, and snacks.

LE PETITE CAFE: The grand lobby of the Riviera is filled with the soothing scent of coffee concoctions by day and the sounds of clinking glasses by night. A popular coffee/wine bar destination, this lobby locale also serves soft drinks, pastries, and other sweet snacks for guests on the go.

SARATOGA SPRINGS

THE TURF CLUB LOUNGE: This casual, frill-free corner of the resort serves all manner of spirits (from a walk-up window). Lounge fare is offered from 5 P.M. until 9:30 P.M. Look for items such as creamy buffalo chicken dip, fried buttermilk calamari, shrimp tacos, burgers, wedge salads, and charcuterie plates. There's a pool table, too. (No charge to play. Sweet!)

SWAN & DOLPHIN

CABANA BAR & BEACH CLUB: Come for the food, stay for drinks. This Dolphin spot's sophisticated air and edgy design is a definite draw for the grown-up set, yet the place doesn't take itself so seriously that it fails to please little ones (think pizza, fruit bars, and lemonade). Grown-up pleasers include fish tacos, crab salad, burgers made with organic, grass-fed beef, bowls featuring Mongolian vegetables, seared sesame ginger beef, and tuna poke, and the grilled chicken BLT.

Classic cocktails share the spotlight with creative, original creations (Hula Mala, Bird of Paradise, Hibiscus Cooler, etc.). Frozen libations abound, as do beer (micro- and macrobrews), rum, and tequila. Wine, scotch, cognac, cigars, and soft drinks are available, too.

IL MULINO NEW YORK TRATTORIA LOUNGE: A lovely spot (at the Swan) to sip wine, cognac, single malt scotch, cocktails, and soft drinks, and/or enjoy the bar menu, this lounge features live music on Friday and Saturday evenings. There are lots of seats at the bar, plus tables and comfy couches. It's usually open for business starting in the late afternoon.

KIMONOS: This Swan lounge, attractively decorated in Japanese style, has a full bar, as well as sushi and other culinary treats. It opens in late afternoon/early evening, and last call is usually between 10:30 P.M. and 1 A.M. The karaoke starts cranking at about 9:30 P.M.

PHINS: The edgy Dolphin lobby bar serves beer, wine, cocktails, soft drinks, and small plates such as a Bavarian hot pretzel with mustard and cheese sauce, deviled eggs, and hummus with naan bread. Phins' hours are generally 3 P.M. until about 10 P.M.

SHULA'S LOUNGE: This small, austere Dolphin saloon within Shula's Steak House features rich wood tones and plush seating—the perfect place to sip a cocktail while playing armchair quarterback.

SPLASH TERRACE: A poolside oasis near the Swan, Splash offers Maine lobster club and chicken BLT sandwiches, chicken wings, giant pretzels, Caesar salad, Mediterranean salads, soft drinks, beer, wine, cocktails, and specialty drinks. Kids choose from grilled cheese, chicken tenders, cheeseburgers, and cheese pizza. Open seasonally.

PHOTO BY MIKE CARROLL

TODD ENGLISH'S BLUEZOO BAR: The underwater mojo of Todd's bluezoo restaurant extends to the lounge area (booths and tables augment the bar seating, easily accommodating large parties). In addition to the liquid refreshments, this is a genuine raw bar—many guests order a cocktail with a side of something fishy.

Last call varies, depending on how crowded the place is at any given moment. Figure on getting the boot at any time between 9 P.M. and 11 P.M.

WILDERNESS LODGE

TERRITORY LOUNGE: Located between Artist Point and Whispering Canyon Cafe, this rustic homage to the explorers of the Great West is a nice spot for a

pre-dinner treat. Appetizers, soft drinks, beer, wine, and cocktails are served. The Pomegranate Sparkler is a no-alcohol treat.

TROUT PASS: This poolside bar serves beer, wine, cocktails, soft drinks, and frozen drinks (available with or without alcohol).

YACHT & BEACH CLUB

ALE & COMPASS LOUNGE: The boisterous, nautically themed Yacht Club lobby lounge offers a full drink menu with premium spirits and appetizers (oven-roasted oysters and clams, garlic shrimp, baked goat cheese, and more). Ale & Compass Lounge is usually open until at least midnight. 🐭

PHOTO BY MIKE CARROLL

CREW'S CUP: Styled after a traditional New England waterfront pub, this casual lounge has a seafaring feel to it. It's next door to the Yachtsman Steakhouse and has well over 25 beers. There is also a tempting menu. This is one of our favorite places to relax after a long day in the parks. Nibbles are generally served from about noon until midnight.

HURRICANE HANNA'S WATERSIDE BAR & GRILL: This poolside oasis is a sophisticated yet casual place to sip a beverage and enjoy a savory snack (until about 9 P.M.). The menu includes items such as coconut shrimp, hummus with pita chips and fresh veggies, bacon cheeseburgers, barbecue pork nachos, Caesar salad with chicken, and more. This is also a Rapid Fill mug refilling station. 🐭

MARTHA'S VINEYARD: While a full bar is available, a small but satisfying selection of wines from Martha's Vineyard (and other areas) is this Beach Club bar's specialty. Light appetizers are served, too—usually from 5 P.M. until 10 P.M. Savory snack selections may include sautéed mussels, salt and pepper calamari, pork sliders, cheese plate, and seafood poppers.

🐭 Disney Dining Plan participant at press time   **SR** Signature Restaurant

DISNEY CRUISE LINE

"Imagination has no age, dreams are forever." —Walt Disney

BIRNBAUM BONUS

326 Land & Sea Vacations

328 Sample Itineraries

330 Before You Sail

340 All Aboard!

Walt Disney World, which boasts one of the largest fleets of pleasure craft on the planet, has an inimitable nautical neighbor: Disney Cruise Line. And three of its majestic ocean liners— the award-winning *Wonder*, *Dream*, and *Fantasy*—set sail from Central Florida's Port Canaveral. That's a mere 50 miles from Walt Disney World, making the prospect of pairing a visit to WDW with a Disney Cruise a convenient temptation for many a World traveler.

A voyage with Disney Cruise Line, however, is atypical in a number of ways. First, there's the simultaneous catering to families with kids and grown-ups sans offspring. In fact, each ship has programming designed to draw young and old, and those in between, to entirely different recreational areas. Then there's the innovative "rotational dining system," a lineup of lavish musical productions, deck-shaking dance parties, and, of course, the possibility of a unique grand finale: a full day at Castaway Cay—Disney's private, tropical island.

Like swaying in a hammock in the aforementioned paradise, the process of selecting a cruise package and combining it with a stay at Walt Disney World should be as carefree as possible. Within this Birnbaum bonus chapter, you'll find detailed information meant to ensure that planning a "land and sea" holiday is smooth sailing. Bon voyage!

Land & Sea Vacations
Pairing a Disney Cruise with a Walt Disney World Vacation

It's the ultimate surf-and-turf experience for Disney fans—a Walt Disney World vacation that's paired with a Disney cruise. (What better way to chase the Pirates of the Caribbean attraction than by visiting the Caribbean?! Minus real pirates, of course.) And with three Disney ships sailing out of Port Canaveral, Florida, throughout the year, "land and sea" opportunities abound. The pages that follow describe how Land and Sea vacations work and give a brief overview of the Disney Cruise Line fleet.

If you have been to Disney's world before (or read the first 300 or so pages of this book), you know that it is not a small one. In fact, it covers 40 square miles—and with about as many attractions, restaurants, and places to stay as one might expect from an area that size. There are four theme parks, two water parks, more than two dozen hotels, a dining, shopping, and entertainment district, championship golf courses, boating, fishing, tennis, and more. Add a cruise to the mix, and even the most seasoned Disney veterans run the risk of becoming overwhelmed.

The good news is that a customized vacation package can include just about everything you would ever want. That frees you up to focus on a very important goal: having fun.

HOT TIP!

Disney Cruise Vacations offers a day-before option at a non-Disney resort with some packages. For information, contact a travel agent or call 800-951-3532.

SURF & TURF

Folks dreaming of a "land and sea" escape can customize that dream vacation with (or without) a little help from Disney Cruise Line or a travel agent. In addition to settling on a budget, there are decisions to be made:

1. Do you want to cruise before or after you visit WDW?
2. How long do you wish to play on land and on sea?
3. Where do you want to stay while you're on Land?
4. Which sailing itinerary is best for you? (See page 328

Disney Cruise Line Air Program

If you plan to fly to the port, consider allowing the Disney Cruise Vacations Air Program to help you make the arrangements. In addition to lining up round-trip airfare for your whole party, they will secure motor coach ground transportation and baggage transfers.

The service is available in more than 150 cities in the United States, United Kingdom, and Canada. At press time, this service was not included in the price of any Disney Cruise Line vacation packages. For more information and pricing, call 877-566-0967.

Combination Vacation

Walt Disney World/Disney Cruise Line combination vacations can include accommodations on land (at a WDW resort) and a stateroom on a Disney ship. In addition to accommodations, shipboard meals, snacks, soft drinks, and entertainment are included with all Disney Cruise Line packages.

What's not included in a "Land and Sea" combination vacation? Meals and beverages at Walt Disney World (unless the WDW Dining Plan is purchased in advance), transfers to Port Canaveral (these may also be purchased in advance), airfare, excursions, meals ashore in ports of call—with the exception of Castaway Cay, where food and soft drinks are included (refer to page 355)—extra gratuities, laundry or valet services, parking at the port, or any other items not specifically included.

What can be added? Just about everything. Options include tickets to Walt Disney World theme parks, water parks, dinner shows, and more. For details, visit *www.disneycruise.com*, or call 800-951-3532.

---

for a selection of popular itineraries that depart from Central Florida's Port Canaveral. Note that the *Disney Magic* sails out of Miami in 2020.)

To pair a visit to Walt Disney World with a Disney cruise, contact a travel agent or call 800-951-3532. (That's the number to call if you'd like help finding a hotel near Disney Cruise Line's other home ports, too.)

PHOTO BY JILL SAFRO

WALT DISNEY WORLD RESORT OPTIONS

The following is a comprehensive list of Walt Disney World—owned-and-operated resort hotels. Many guests choose to visit WDW before they cruise, while others enjoy a post-cruise visit with the Mouse. As an extra-special treat, there's always the option of sandwiching a cruise between two WDW resort stays—if time and budget allow, of course! For details on these resorts and other hotels at Walt Disney World, turn to our *Transportation & Accommodations* chapter.

DELUXE:
Animal Kingdom Lodge (see page 100)
BoardWalk (see page 92)
Contemporary Resort (see page 76)
Grand Floridian Resort & Spa (see page 80)
Old Key West Resort (see page 98)
Polynesian Village Resort (see page 78)
Riviera Resort (see page 86)
Saratoga Springs Resort & Spa (see page 97)
Wilderness Lodge (see page 82)
Yacht & Beach Club (see page 87)

MODERATE:
Cabins at Fort Wilderness resort (see page 82)
Caribbean Beach Resort (see page 85)
Coronado Springs Resort (see page 102)
Port Orleans French Quarter (see page 95)
Port Orleans Riverside (see page 96)

VALUE:
All-Star Movies (see page 99)
All-Star Music (see page 99)
All-Star Sports (see page 99)
Art of Animation (see page 104)
Campsites at Fort Wilderness resort (see page 83)
Pop Century (see page 103)

SAMPLE ITINERARIES

Three Disney ships—the *Wonder*, *Dream*, and *Fantasy*—are scheduled to cruise out of Port Canaveral, Florida, in 2020. The *Magic* will sail from Miami, Florida. (Though some visit other home ports, there are usually at least two ships to choose from at all times.) What follows is a sampling of the itineraries offered from Port Canaveral, the port closest to Walt Disney World—and most logically paired with a WDW vacation. Note that most include a stop at Disney's private island, Castaway Cay (see page 355). Some include two stops at the popular island paradise. For a complete list of ports and itineraries, visit *www.disneycruise.com*.

3-NIGHT BAHAMIAN CRUISE • *DISNEY DREAM*

DAY	ITINERARY
DAY 1	Check in at Port Canaveral Terminal. Aboard by 3:45 P.M.
DAY 2	Ashore at Nassau at 9:30 A.M. Aboard by 5:15 P.M.
DAY 3	Ashore at Disney Castaway Cay at 8:30 A.M. Aboard by 4:45 P.M.
DAY 4	Ship at Port Canaveral beginning at 7:30 A.M.

4-NIGHT BAHAMIAN CRUISE • *DISNEY DREAM*

DAY	ITINERARY
DAY 1	Check in at Port Canaveral Terminal. Aboard by 3:45 P.M.
DAY 2	Ashore at Nassau at 9:30 A.M. Aboard by 5:15 P.M.
DAY 3	Ashore at Disney Castaway Cay at 8:30 A.M. Aboard by 4:45 P.M.
DAY 4	Full day at sea.
DAY 5	Ship at Port Canaveral beginning at 7:30 A.M.

4-NIGHT BAHAMIAN CRUISE • *DISNEY DREAM*

(with two stops at Castaway Cay)

DAY	ITINERARY
DAY 1	Check in at Port Canaveral Terminal. Aboard by 3:45 P.M.
DAY 2	Ashore at Castaway Cay at 8:30 A.M. Aboard by 4:45 P.M.
DAY 3	Ashore at Nassau at 8:30 A.M. Aboard by 5:15 P.M.
DAY 4	Ashore at Castaway Cay at 8:30 A.M. Aboard by 4:45 P.M.
DAY 5	Ship at Port Canaveral beginning at 7:30 A.M.

7-NIGHT EASTERN CARIBBEAN CRUISE • *DISNEY FANTASY*

DAY	ITINERARY
DAY 1	Check in at Port Canaveral Terminal. Aboard by 3:45 P.M.
DAY 2	Full day at sea.
DAY 3	Full day at sea.
DAY 4	Ashore at Tortola, British Virgin Islands, at 7:30 A.M. Aboard by 5:45 P.M.
DAY 5	Ashore at St. Thomas, U.S. Virgin Islands, at 7:45 A.M. Aboard by 4 P.M.
DAY 6	Full day at sea.
DAY 7	Ashore at Disney Castaway Cay at 8:30 A.M. Aboard by 4:45 P.M.
DAY 8	Ship at Port Canaveral beginning at 7:30 A.M.

7-NIGHT WESTERN CARIBBEAN CRUISE • *DISNEY FANTASY*

DAY	ITINERARY
DAY 1	Check in at Port Canaveral Terminal. Aboard by 3:45 P.M.
DAY 2	Full day at sea.
DAY 3	Ashore at Cozumel, Mexico, at 8:30 A.M. Aboard by 4:45 P.M.
DAY 4	Ashore at Georgetown, Grand Cayman, at 10:30 A.M. Aboard by 5:30 P.M. (This port requires tendering.)
DAY 5	Ashore at Falmouth, Jamaica, at 7:30 A.M. Aboard by 4:45 P.M.
DAY 6	Full day at sea.
DAY 7	Ashore at Castaway Cay at 8:30 A.M. Aboard by 4:45 P.M.
DAY 8	Ship at Port Canaveral beginning at 7:30 A.M.

Before You Sail

What to do, what to do. There are many factors to consider when pairing a cruise package with a stay at Walt Disney World. Among the most important are destination, budget, time available, stateroom needs, and preferred itinerary.

If you want to take the most inexpensive cruise possible, then a shorter cruise in a standard inside stateroom is probably a good choice. If money is no object, consider a 7-night adventure in the super-deluxe Walter E. Disney suite. Of course, there are plenty of things in between.

CHECK YOUR CALENDAR

Determining the length of your cruise depends on several things—the first, how much time do you have in your busy schedule to devote to leisure? If your answer is only four days, don't despair: Disney has short cruises to the Bahamas (most of which include a stop at Disney's

www.disneycruise.com

We've done our best to provide accurate, current information regarding all things Disney Cruise Line. That said, rates, itineraries, excursions, and other specifics are subject to change. For additional information or to book a cruise, shore excursion, and more, visit *www.disneycruise.com*. It's one of the most user-friendly websites we have ever seen.

own private island, Castaway Cay). If you have at least a week to sail, you may choose a 7-night-or-longer cruise to the Caribbean. For details, call 800-910-3659, or visit *www.disneycruise.com*.

CHECK YOUR CHECKBOOK

The cost of your cruise is the next issue on the planning board. Budget constraints can be eased in several ways: by taking one of the shorter cruises, choosing a less-expensive stateroom class, and by limiting the number of land tours and excursions you take at the various ports of call. (We often forgo pricey excursions because the ships themselves have so much to offer.) Plan to eat aboard the ship, too—meals and snacks are included in the vacation package, as are many extras, such as stage shows, movies, tours, lectures, games, bands, deck parties with Disney characters, and more.

SELECTING A STATEROOM

Sure, you'd like the largest suite on the ship. No question, you want the biggest verandah. And, of course, you absolutely must have a great view. But if these don't fit your budget, there are other appealing options. Consider this: Every stateroom boasts nautical decor, has ample closet space, a television, and a small safe. Inside staterooms can be a bit less expensive and not much smaller than their outside counterparts; on the *Dream* and the *Fantasy* they have virtual portholes (aka "magical" portholes, these high-tech wonders have HD digital screens). On the other hand, should you decide to splurge, know that there are concierge rooms and larger suites with private verandahs where you can savor a refreshing beverage and read the newest page-turner, periodically taking a moment to gaze out at the sea.

Of course, there are other factors to think about when selecting a stateroom. How many people are in your party? Are you traveling with young children? Perhaps a Deluxe Stateroom would suit your family's needs. Most of these accommodations have queen-size beds, bunk beds for the young'uns, and a split bath (one room with a sink and a toilet and another with a sink and a shower/tub). A curtained divider provides a bit of privacy.

Of course, there's always the Walter E. Disney Suite and the Roy O. Disney Suite—so if money is no object, treat your crew to one of the thousand-plus-square-foot

WHAT'S NOT INCLUDED WITH A CRUISE?

Rest assured that all of your basic vacation needs are covered by the "all-inclusive" price of the cruise. However, there are always "extras" for which you may want to ante up a little cash. Here's a list of items and services that carry an extra charge while aboard Disney ships:

- Child care for tots ages 6 months to 3 years (see pages 336 and 353)
- Port Adventures (aka shore excursions)
- Expenses incurred while on land in ports of call (with the exception of food and most soft drinks at Castaway Cay)
- Alcoholic beverages and Royal Court Tea
- Palo and Remy (These optional, reservations-necessary, adults-only restaurants carry an extra charge: about $40 per person for dinner and brunch at Palo; about $75 per person for champagne brunch and about $125 for dinner at Remy.)
- Vanellope's Sweets & Treats (on the *Dream*)
- Refreshments at any bar

- Sweet on You (on the *Fantasy*)
- Spa and Bibbidi Bobbidi Boutique services
- Merchandise purchased onboard
- Sports simulators
- Photos snapped by the ship's photographers
- Internet usage (see page 337)
- Cell phone usage (see page 339)
- Ship-to-shore telephone calls (There is a sizable fee for all calls, incoming and outgoing. Calls within the ship are free.)

With the exception of non-Disney ports of call, all "incidental" charges will be billed to your stateroom, provided that you leave a credit card number upon check-in. It's a good idea to have some cash on hand (we bring about $300, just in case), but there are few chances to use it. Except for tips, cash isn't accepted on the ships. Same goes for Castaway Cay, with the exception of the post office—stamps must be purchased with cash. Most of the non-Disney port shops accept major credit cards, and most accept U.S. currency.

homes away from home. No matter what your requirements, chances are pretty good that Disney Cruise Line can meet them.

HOW TO BOOK A CRUISE

In addition to using *www.disneycruise.com* or calling Disney Cruise Line (800-910-3659), many guests book through travel agents.

PAYMENT METHODS: Cruise packages, as well as incidentals, gratuities, hotel bills, and deposits, may be paid by major credit card (Visa, MasterCard, JCB Card, American Express, Diners Club, etc.), Disney gift cards, Disney Rewards Redemption cards, traveler's check, cashier's check, money order, or personal check. Personal checks must bear the guest's name and address, be

drawn on a U.S. bank, and be accompanied by proper identification (a valid driver's license with photo or government-issued photo ID). The reservation number must be written on the face of the check. Checks will not be accepted within 21 days prior to vacation commencement date. The final payment for a cruise package must be made between 75 and 150 days prior to the cruise, depending on the itinerary and category. The final payment due date varies for special itineraries.

Payments sent via mail should be addressed to: Disney Cruise Line, P.O. Box 277763, Atlanta, GA 30384-7763.

Payments that are sent via courier service (e.g., FedEx or UPS) should be sent to: Disney Cruise Line, Bank of America, Lockbox Services, Lockbox 277763, 6000 Feldwood Road, College Park, GA 30349 (407-566-3500).

DEPOSIT REQUIREMENTS: When you book a Disney cruise, you will be given a "due date" for a deposit. The deposit is 20 percent of the total fare. Reservations will be canceled if a deposit is not received by the deadline. (Packages that are booked within the final payment due date or in categories IGT, OGT, and VGT come with special instructions.)

CANCELLATION POLICY: Cancellations may be made by phone or mail (we prefer the phone). To avoid

GROUND TRANSFERS

Disney Cruise Line provides reliable, friendly service aboard its motor coaches (aka: buses). Getting to the buses is easy. Upon arrival at Orlando International Airport, take a shuttle to the Main Terminal. Once there, proceed to Disney's Magical Express Welcome Center. It's on Level One, Side B. The real bonus here is the baggage handling: For flights before 10 P.M., Disney reps will pull your tagged luggage and make sure it gets delivered to your room. (Guests arriving after 10 P.M. may collect their luggage and proceed to the Magical Express Welcome Center.) From the airport, a bus will take you to Port Canaveral or a WDW hotel. (For guests with transfers included in their package, your bus departure location and information is included in your cruise documentation.) What if you're staying at a resort that's not designated as a departure location or at an off-property hotel? You'll have to get yourself to one of the WDW departure spots to catch a bus to the ship. Here's the pricing for Orlando ground transfers:

TRANSFER TRIP	PRICE*
Airport to select WDW resort (one-way)	Free**
Select WDW resort to Port Canaveral	$39
Round-trip from Orlando International Airport (MCO) to Port Canaveral	$78
Land and Sea vacation (Orlando airport to select WDW resort; WDW resort to Port Canaveral; Port Canaveral to airport)	$78

*Prices are per person, were correct at press time, and are subject to change.

**Disney's Magical Express transportation is a free service for WDW resort guests.

For pricing details about transfers to and from other locations, call 800-951-3532.

the sad fate of paying for a canceled cruise, we recommend insuring your trip.

Fees paid for canceling a cruise depend on when that call is made. For cruises of less than 10 days where embark or debark is a United States port, cancellation fees are as follows:

• For all suites and concierge rooms, the deposit is nonrefundable regardless of when the reservation is canceled.

• For each non-suite/concierge stateroom guest, canceling 74 to 45 days before sailing will cost you the whole deposit.

• For all rooms, a cancellation within 44 to 30 days costs 50 percent of the vacation price.

• For all staterooms, a cancellation within 29 to 15 days costs 75 percent per guest.

• Should a cruise be canceled less than 14 days ahead, you'll pay for the whole package.

For cruises that are 10 days or more *or* less than 10 days where embark and debark is a non-U.S. port, the fees are as follows (this does not apply to cruises out of Port Canaveral, Florida):

• For all suites and concierge rooms, the deposit is non-refundable regardless of when the reservation was canceled.

• For all non-suite/concierge staterooms, canceling within 119 to 56 days before the sailing costs the whole deposit per guest.

• Canceling within 55 to 30 days costs 50 percent of the vacation cost per guest.

• Canceling within 29 to 15 days costs 75 percent of the vacation package per guest.

• Canceling less than 14 days ahead means you will pay for the whole package.

WHAT TO PACK

"Cruise Casual" is the operative phrase with Disney. Shorts, T-shirts, sundresses, and the like are fine daytime wear. At dinnertime, casual takes on a more formal meaning: Set aside flip-flops and plan on nice slacks (jeans are okay, as long as they're in good condition) and a collared shirt for men, with real shoes, as opposed to the tennis kind. The same goes for women, while dresses are fine, too. There is an optional dress-up night, too. On 7-night-or-longer cruises, there is a semi-formal and a formal night. While some folks don black tie and

HOT TIP!

Guests who plan to arrive at Port Canaveral the night before setting sail might consider staying at one of these resorts on nearby Astronaut Boulevard:

Country Inns & Suites by Carlson. Rates range from about $89–$129, and there is a shuttle to the cruise terminal; 321-784-8500 or 888-201-1746.

Residence Inn by Marriott. Rates range from about $169–$220; 321-323-1100 or 800-331-3131.

Identification Papers

Unlike a visit to Disney's Epcot, where it only feels as if you're leaving the country, in the case of a Disney Cruise Line vacation, you usually do. Given that, you will need a passport to provide proper proof of citizenship when passing through Customs for most cruises. (There are some itineraries for which U.S. citizens may use other forms of proof of citizenship such as a state-issued birth certificate.) U.S. government regulations related to passport requirements are subject to change at any time. Therefore, all guests are advised to have a valid passport for all cruises. Visit *http://travel.state.gov*, or call 877-487-2778 for current requirements. Non-U.S. citizens are required to travel with valid government-issued passports at all times.

sequins, it's fine to sport a less formal look. The *Personal Navigator* (see page 342) will tip you off as to the appropriate attire. Many guests travel with their own pirate garb, too, in anticipation of "Pirates IN the Caribbean" party night—don't forget to pack your puffy shirt and eye patch. (The pirate party takes place on most sailings.)

Bathing suits are a must, as are beach shoes, wraps, sunscreen, sunglasses, and hats. Some sundries, such as shampoo and body lotion, are provided. Others are available for purchase, but the prices are steep, and the shops aren't always open (U.S. Customs limits the operating hours).

PACK A DAY BAG: Guests may check in at the port and board the ship as early as 1 P.M., but your checked luggage may not arrive until 6 P.M. (though usually earlier). Keep in mind that you will have access to your stateroom beginning at 1:30 P.M., along with most shipboard amenities, including all pools, so pack your swimsuit in a day bag. This should serve as, or fit in, a carry-on, as checked bags will be out of your hands once you surrender them. (Day bags can't be larger than 9 inches by 14 inches by 22 inches and do not count as part of the two-bags-per-passenger quota.) The bag should also include your passports, valuables,

HOT TIP!

You must show your "Key to the World" card (stateroom key and ID) when disembarking or boarding the ship. Adults also need a government-issued photo ID (a passport is ideal). Your Walt Disney World MagicBand or hotel key won't work on the ship.

WHAT'S IN A NAME?

A whole lot, when it comes to Disney Cruise Line accommodations. Here's a listing of the types of rooms available on each of the ships. Note that it is possible to request side-by-side staterooms, but it can't be guaranteed.

- **Standard Inside Stateroom**
- **Deluxe Inside Stateroom**
- **Deluxe Ocean-view Stateroom**
- **Deluxe Family Ocean-view Stateroom** (*Dream* and *Fantasy*)
- **Deluxe Ocean-view Stateroom with Navigator's Verandah** (*Magic* and *Wonder*)
- **Deluxe Ocean-view Stateroom with Verandah**
- **Deluxe Family Ocean-view Stateroom with Verandah**
- **Concierge Family Ocean-view Stateroom with Verandah**
- **Concierge 1-Bedroom Suite with Verandah**
- **Concierge 2-Bedroom Suite with Verandah** (*Magic* and *Wonder*)
- **Concierge Royal Suite with Verandah**

breakable items, and anything else you might need during those first hours on board. Note that most airlines require that carried-on liquids be in 3.4-ounce (or smaller containers) and fit into one quart-size, clear, plastic zip-top bag.

BOOKING SHORE EXCURSIONS

Shore Excursions, aka Port Adventures, book early. To reserve yours, visit *www.disneycruise.com*. To make last-minute arrangements, visit your ship's Port Adventures desk. Port Adventures are not operated by the Walt Disney Company—not even those on Castaway Cay (refer to page 355).

For descriptions of all of the excursions offered in more than 70 destinations around the world, including Castaway Cay, visit *www.disneycruise.com*. (We considered including all of them here, but that would have added about 600 pages to this book!)

Cancellations or changes to reservations must be made at least 3 days before a cruise starts to receive a refund. Certain restrictions apply.

HOW TO GET TO PORT CANAVERAL

BY PLANE: Fly to Orlando International Airport (MCO). We prefer to arrive the night before or take a flight that is scheduled to arrive in the early morning hours. (That helps avoid potential travel delays.) If you get there on the early side, you can make a day of it. And, if your flight is delayed, you'll still have a shot at making it to the port before the ship sails. (When you book your cruise, ask about the check-in cutoff time. Don't be late!)

FROM THE AIRPORT: As you get off the airport shuttle and enter the main terminal, proceed directly to the Disney Magical Express Welcome Center. It's on Level 1, Side B of the terminal. After your party has checked in, a Disney representative will direct you toward a motor coach. Don't worry about checked luggage. For guests with transfers, all bags bearing appropriate tags will be claimed by Disney and delivered to your stateroom. (If you plan to drive to the ship, refer to the information at the right.)

The following details apply specifically to cruises departing from Port Canaveral, Florida. For details about departure ports in other cities (such as Miami, New York, San Diego, Vancouver, or Barcelona), visit *www.disneycruise.com,* or call 800-910-3659.

DISNEY MOTOR COACH: The bus journey from Orlando International Airport or a Walt Disney World resort to Port Canaveral takes about 90 minutes (without traffic). While on board, you can fill out paperwork (though it is best to do this online in advance). There's a restroom onboard. Motor coach transportation may be purchased with a cruise package.

CAR SERVICE: Ride-sharing services Lyft and Uber may drop guests at the port. Noris Limousine and Florida Towncar also offer service between Orlando International Airport (MCO) and Port Canaveral. For rates, information, or to make a reservation with Noris Limousine, call 407-240-4533, or visit their website: *www.norislimousine.com*. For Florida Towncar, go to *www.floridatowncar.com*, or call 407-277-5466. Reservations are necessary, and cancellations must be made at least 24 to 48 hours in advance. Disney Cruise Line's reservations department can handle car service requests, as well.

AUTOMOBILE: Disney Cruise Line's Port Canaveral Terminal is located at Cruise Terminal 8 (CT8); 9155 Charles M. Rowland Drive, Port Canaveral, Florida 32920. It's approximately a 90-minute drive from Orlando International Airport (MCO) and from Walt Disney World. The parking facility, which is operated by the Canaveral Port Authority, accepts cash (U.S. currency), Visa, MasterCard, and traveler's checks only. Personal checks are not accepted. Parking costs about $17 per day. Rates are subject to change. Guests may also make a reservation for a parking space prior to arrival. To do so, have a credit card handy and visit *http://portcanaveral.com/cruising/parking.php*.

From Orlando International Airport, take State Road (S.R.) 528 East (Beachline Expressway). Continue over the Indian River and the Banana River. Turn right onto S.R. 401, which will loop and head north over the channel locks. Stay in the right-hand lane and follow signs to the "A" Cruise Terminals. S.R. 528 is a toll road.

If you are driving from Walt Disney World, take State Road 536 East to 417 (the GreeneWay). Follow 417 to S.R. 528 East (Beachline Expressway). When you come to a fork in the road, veer right to stay on S.R. 528. Continue over the Indian and Banana rivers. Turn right onto S.R. 401. Stay in the right lane and follow signs leading to the "A" Cruise Terminals. Note that 417 and 528 are toll roads.

Guests who are driving from North Florida should take I-95 South exit number 205 for S.R. 528 East (Beachline Expressway). Continue over the Indian and Banana rivers. Turn right onto S.R. 401. Stay in the right lane and follow signs to "A" Cruise Terminals.

Drivers originating in South Florida should take I-95 North. Exit at number 205 for S.R. 528 East (the Beachline). Take S.R. 528 to S.R. 401. Keep to the right and follow the signs to "A" Cruise Terminals.

GETTING TO PORT CANAVERAL FROM WALT DISNEY WORLD WITHOUT A CAR:
Disney Cruise Line has buses to take guests directly from many WDW resorts. One-way transfers cost $39 per person, while $78 will cover the round-trip. Guests with transfers will get a letter in their resort room with departure details. Bell Services will automatically pick up luggage when transfers have been prearranged. (Car services make the trip to and from Port Canaveral, too. Refer to page 334 for details.)

CUSTOMIZED TRAVEL TIPS

TRAVELING WITH BABIES:
Cribs: If you are traveling with a baby, it is possible to have a playpen-like, foldaway crib sent to your stateroom. (The cribs are 39.8 inches long, 28.25 inches wide, and 31.25 inches high.) Request one when you

make a reservation, and confirm it before leaving home. Supplies are limited. Bring your own blanket, as the cribs come with fitted sheets only.

Diaper Service: It is possible to have a disposable diaper system sent to your stateroom. You can request it when you make a reservation, or speak with your Stateroom Host or Hostess upon arrival.

Food: Staterooms on all Disney ships have small refrigerators, perfectly safe for storing formula and food. Note that homemade baby food is not permitted on board any Disney ship. At least one shop on board sells diapers, formula, and a limited selection of baby food. (The shop isn't always open, as U.S. Customs limits its hours.) If you'd like to save money, pack as many baby rations as possible.

Cold and Flu Advisory

Disney Cruise Line follows extraordinary sanitation efforts to ensure the safety and comfort of guests. Even so, humans do get sick from time to time. If you or a member of your party experiences any symptom of illness (cold, flu, stomach flu, etc.) within 72 hours of sailing, you may be assessed by the medical team during the embarkation process. (If necessary, Cruise Line representatives will direct you to someone to help your party make alternate plans if you are too ill to sail.) Fees apply at the Health Center.

Once on board, all guests are asked to wash their hands frequently and thoroughly, as this is a highly effective barrier to spreading germs. If you or someone in your party does become ill during your trip, please contact the Health Center. You'll be taken care of there, and immediate treatment will help limit the potential impact to others.

Nursery: Onboard baby care is available for tots ages 6 months to 3 years (for most cruises). The cost is $9 an hour for the first child, with a one-hour minimum stay. Each additional child (who must be the first child's sibling) is $8 per hour. The service is offered in the ship's It's a Small World nursery. Reservations for the ship's nursery can be made at *www.disneycruise.com* or on board (based on availability). In-room babysitting is not offered on any Disney vessel.

Other Supplies: Diapers, pacifiers, pool toys, and more can be purchased on board. The ships' shops aren't always open, so take inventory and plan ahead to avoid being caught short. If it's an emergency, inquire at Guest Services. They can help with just about any onboard crisis involving supplies.

Bottle sterilizers and warmers are available at the Guest Services desk.

TRAVELERS WITH DISABILITIES: Measures have been taken to make your stay as comfortable and effortless as possible. Disney Cruise Line offers special equipment and facilities for guests with disabilities. Each ship has staterooms that are equipped for guests using wheelchairs. They have ramped bathroom thresholds, open bed frames, bathroom and shower grab bars, fold-down shower seats, handheld showerheads, and lowered towel and closet bars. Captioning is available for stateroom televisions, and for some onboard video monitors and movies. Stateroom communication kits may be reserved upon request. They include door-knock and phone alerts, bed shaker notification, and a strobe light smoke detector; a text typewriter (aka TTY) may also be requested. There is no charge for the kit, but supplies are limited. Make your needs known when you make

> **HOT TIP!**
>
> If you will be using an ECV (Electronic Conveyance Vehicle) during your cruise, be sure to book an accessible stateroom (other rooms can't accommodate ECVs). No ECV parking is allowed in stateroom corridors or on elevator landings. There are ECV parking stations on Deck 6 midship on the *Magic* and *Wonder*, and on Deck 2 midship, outside Enchanted Garden, on the *Dream* and *Fantasy*.

your reservation and confirm them prior to sailing. Wheelchair-accessible restrooms are available in several common areas on board. There are pool lifts on the *Magic*, *Wonder*, *Dream*, and *Fantasy*. A small number of sand wheelchairs are available on Castaway Cay. American Sign Language (ASL) interpretation is available for a variety of onboard performances on various cruise dates. (The service is not available on every cruise, so be sure to start planning your trip as far in advance as possible.) For further information or to make special requests, ask your reservationist. For more information via TTY (text typewriter), please call 407-566-7455.

TRAVELERS WITHOUT CHILDREN: This being a Disney cruise, one could argue that you—the footloose, fancy-free folks—are on their turf. And, as such, you might expect to have youngsters underfoot at all times. This is simply not the case. The Disney ships were designed with three specific types of vacationers in mind: families, kids, and grown-ups without kids. On board, there is an adults-only deck area, complete with its own pool (not to mention music and games). There's a gourmet restaurant (two on the *Dream* and *Fantasy*) and a cozy coffee bar. It goes without saying that those spots, as well as several lounges, are strictly for the grown-up set (as in adults with legal proof of age). Plus, there are countless other ways to enjoy a

grown-up getaway in the various ports of call. With that in mind, Castaway Cay (Disney's private island) guarantees you and your ilk a piece of prime beach-front real estate where you can bask in the sun or read a novel in the shade without the fear of sand being kicked in your face. You can even have a massage in a cabana overlooking the ocean. Can you manage to spend days on end without encountering the wee ones of our species? No way. But who'd want to?

MEDICAL MATTERS: The ship's Health Center, located forward on Deck 1, is open daily to provide non-emergency medical care throughout each cruise. All Disney Cruise Line ships have a physician and nurse on call 24 hours a day (even while in port) for conditions that require immediate attention. All medical services are provided by a company independent of Disney Cruise Line, and standard prevailing fees will be charged for all medical services. Fees will be charged to your stateroom account.

In extreme cases, Disney Cruise Line will arrange to have a passenger taken to the nearest port to receive medical care. The cost of this varies with the location of the ship and the nearest port. Because all health care provided qualifies as "care outside the United States," you will be responsible for paying any charges that are

New Ships on the Horizon

Ahoy! Disney Cruise Line's family is growing—three new ships, currently being constructed, are expected to join the DCL fleet in the not-too-distant future. The new vessels will be slightly larger than the *Disney Dream* and *Disney Fantasy*, each weighing approximately 135,000 gross tons and housing about 1,250 staterooms. At press time, the ships had not been named. What do you think they'll be called? It's a lot of fun to speculate.

incurred while on board prior to debarkation. The Health Center will provide you with the paperwork you'll need to process any claim through your health insurance provider. In extreme cases, Disney Cruise Line will arrange to have a guest taken to the nearest port to receive medical care. The cost for that varies based on the location of the ship and the proximity of the nearest port.

If you get sick while on shore, your guide should direct you to your ship's tour director at the dock, who will help you get back to the ship.

Regarding younger passengers, know that any child exhibiting symptoms of illness will not be allowed to participate in the youth activities or be cared for in the ship's nursery. No exceptions.

FINGERTIP REFERENCE GUIDE

BUSINESS SERVICES: Wait a minute, aren't you here to relax? For those of you who must get a little work done while at sea, there are some business services available for an additional charge. Among them are fax transmission, copies, and AV equipment. Wireless Internet service is available throughout the ships (including staterooms) for a fee. Guests access the Web via cell phone and various personal computing devices. Computer devices are available for rental (at the ships' Connect@Sea desk). Note that the Wi-Fi service at sea can best be described as "low speed." As you sail, you may experience buffering and dropped connections. Internet connectivity can be intermittent based on satellite connectivity. All staterooms have phones (ship-to-shore rates apply), and electrical outlets are laptop friendly. Note that the ships' computers don't accept uploads and do not run any Microsoft Office applications (so any attachments from associated email accounts cannot be opened). There is, however, a handy printer at the ready. Are you planning on holding meetings during your cruise? For details on business services, visit *www.disneymeetings.com*.

Getting Around It

Travelers with disabilities already know that travel requires a lot of advance planning. Disney has equipped all of its ships with a variety of amenities geared toward those guests with special needs.

Wheelchair-accessible staterooms are equipped with ramp entrances to bathrooms, fold-down shower seats, handheld showerheads, lowered towel and closet racks, and emergency call buttons (contact Guest Services to activate).

There is a limited number of sand wheelchairs available on Disney's private island, Castaway Cay (first come, first served). **Note:** If you'll need a wheelchair throughout the cruise, you are encouraged to bring your own.

Wheelchair-accessible restrooms are located throughout every Disney Cruise Line ship. Pool lifts are also located on all DCL vessels.

Guests with hearing disabilities need not miss any of the fun on board. In-stateroom TVs are equipped with captioning, and assistive-listening devices may be rented from Guest Services and be used at most theaters and show rooms. Also available are communication kits equipped with alarm clock, door-knock, and telephone alerts with bed shaker notification. Make your needs known when you book your cruise.

CAMERA NEEDS: By all means, bring a camera. Memory cards and accessories are sold on board. There are also roving photographers capturing moments throughout the day. You'll find shots taken at "static locations" (e.g., character sets in the lobby) are available for viewing at photo kiosks at Shutters (the photo store on all Disney ships). These photos may be viewed and purchased during the cruise. (Some photo packages may be purchased in advance, with special promotions.) Pictures taken by roaming photographers (e.g., in the dining rooms, by the pool, on Castaway Cay, etc.) may be previewed, printed, and purchased at Shutters on all four Disney ships. Photographs may be purchased on a single media USB storage device—one-stop shopping. The photos are very high in quality (which is reflected in the price).

DRINKING LAWS: The drinking age on Disney's ships is 21 and is strictly enforced. Valid government-issued photo ID is required. Disney Cruise Line reserves the right to refuse alcohol sales to anyone. On cruises departing from European countries where the legal age is lower than 21, a legal guardian who is sailing with a passenger between the ages of 18 and 20 may sign a waiver allowing their charge to imbibe.

MAIL: Letters and postcards may be mailed from the post office at Disney's private tropical island, Castaway Cay. Stamps are the only things available for purchase here (cash only). It is also possible to mail items from other ports—it's just less convenient. Postcards and stamps may be purchased on the ship. If you plan to buy stamps from the Castaway Cay post office, do so early. The office is operated by Bahamian authorities and may not be open late in the day. Even if it's closed, you can still mail letters from the post office, and items will be stamped with a Castaway Cay postmark.

MONEY MATTERS: There is no need for cash on the ship. You will apply a credit card to your account during check-in. (Most major credit cards, including Master-Card, JCB, Visa, and American Express, are accepted.) From then on, all you'll need to do is sign for extras you want (including excursions booked on the ship), and these amounts will be charged to that card.

Cash or credit cards will be necessary for meals, taxis, and other purchases made in ports and during some shore excursions. Purchases made at Castaway Cay, however, are covered with a stateroom key (except for stamps, which must be bought with cash). A few hundred dollars should suffice for port purchases. Standard gratuities are automatically attached to your cruise folio. Extra gratuities may be charged to a stateroom or paid in cash. Special envelopes will be delivered to your stateroom. They may be used to present extra gratuities and/or receipts for prepaid tips.

Automated teller machines may be available in ports of call, but there are none on the ship. Be sure the machine dispenses U.S. currency before you use it. It's a good idea to alert your bank and credit card company to the fact that you'll be using cards while travelling.

HOT TIP!

If you plan to use your cell phone during your cruise, be sure to check with your wireless provider before leaving home. Ask if you will be able to get service through them while on board and how much voice, data, and text service costs—including roaming rates.

SMOKING: All Disney ships are, for the most part, smoke-free zones. Smoking (including e-cigarettes) is prohibited in all staterooms and verandahs. (Guests who violate this policy are subject to a $250 deep-cleaning fee.) There are designated smoking areas on every Disney ship.

TELEPHONE CALLS: All staterooms have telephones with ship-to-shore capability. Rates range from about $7 to $9.50 per minute (rates are subject to change). Toll-free and collect calls can't be placed from ship phones. Wireless mobile service is available on the ship (fees apply). Be sure to check with your mobile carrier (before you leave home) for talk and text rates and roaming fees. Note that text rates are usually lower than talk rates. Some ports have pay phones (you will need an international calling card to use them).

TIPPING: Some servers, such as bartenders, receive an automatic 15 percent gratuity each time you call upon their services, while spa services have an automatic 18 percent tip. That said, folks such as your dining room servers and stateroom host or hostess rely on guests to tip them appropriately. Suggested gratuity amounts will be posted to your account during the cruise (it's okay to leave more if you deem the service to be outstanding).

All Good Things

How time flies when you're having fun. You blink and it's time to go home! Here are a few tips about the debarkation process.

The day before your return to the debarkation terminal, you'll receive an information packet that includes a set of character luggage tags. The character coding designates the area of the terminal in which you can pick them up. Be sure to remove the original tags from the inbound trip before you put new tags on all bags. (Guest Services has extra tags.) You will also receive a U.S. Customs form when applicable. Hand this form in as you leave the cruise terminal (one form per household).

On the night before debarkation, you'll place luggage outside your stateroom. (Bags will be collected and delivered to a color/character-coded area in the terminal.) Keep all valuables, clothing for debarkation, medications, tickets, passports, and other key documents with you. (You have the option of "express walk off" if you're able to take your own bags off the ship in the morning.) Your waitstaff will tell you about last-morning breakfast options. After breakfast, it's time to leave the ship, taking all your happy memories and, quite possibly, the promise to return again soon. Of course, guests participating in onboard airline check-in don't have to claim bags until their plane lands at their home airport. Certain restrictions apply.

About to begin the "land" part of your vacation? Fetch your bags in the terminal and make a beeline for the bus depot. Flash your Key to the World card (to show you purchased the transfer) and climb aboard. You're going to Disney World!

If you prefer to pay in cash, inform Guest Services at the beginning of the cruise. For those guests dining at Palo and Remy, the total gratuity amount is at the discretion of the guest.

WEDDINGS: Whether you are saying your "I do's" for the first time, committing yourselves to each other, or renewing your vows, Disney Cruise Line has the means to make the occasion exceptionally memorable. Ceremonies may be performed on the ship or on the pristine sands of Disney's private Caribbean island, Castaway Cay. Some happy couples invite family members along for the trip, while others prefer to have this time to themselves.

For details, visit *https://disneycruise.disney.go.com/featured/weddings-honeymoons-vows/*, or call 800-951-3532, or contact your travel agent. Make your plans as far in advance as possible.

All Aboard!

The moment you cross the gangway, you'll realize this vessel is no ordinary home away from home. Step into the grand, multi-story atrium, and, amidst the happy hubbub, your presence is made known in dramatic fashion—with a heartfelt announcement for all to hear. And so begins your high-seas adventure.

The *Disney Magic*, *Wonder*, *Dream*, and *Fantasy* rank among the world's finest ocean-going vessels. The ships are casually elegant and designed to capture the majesty of early ocean liners. They're equipped to satisfy most cruisers, with a mix of traditional seafaring diversions and classic Disney touches. Though some theming and entertainment vary from ship to ship, the accommodations and amenities are similar. As is the service, which is expertly provided by a cast of thousands (representing dozens of countries). All staterooms aboard the quartet of ships are a cut above normal cruising quarters—with an average of 25 percent more space than the industry standard. All of the ships were designed to lure families and grown-ups without offspring to entirely different recreational areas. So, cast aside any preconceived notions you may have about cruising, and expect the unexpected.

CHECKING IN

No matter where it is they call home—be it Bangkok or Boca—all Disney Cruise Line guests begin their respective journeys by checking in at a port terminal. Most Bahamas- and Caribbean-bound guests leaving from Port Canaveral check in at Cruise Terminal 8 (CT8). Guests may choose from several different queues at check-in: Concierge, Castaway Club (for repeat guests), and general check-in. For details on other ports the ships may visit throughout 2020, call 800-910-3659, or go to *www.disneycruise.com*.

Though no one may board the ship until 1 P.M., guests are welcome to arrive earlier—but they may have to wait until their boarding number is called. Guests who check in online choose assigned boarding times in advance. (All guests must board the ship by 3:45 P.M.) The terminal has restrooms and ample seating to relax in while waiting to board. (At Port Canaveral, Florida, there's also a nifty model of the ship to give you a preview of the real thing.) And, if little ones get antsy, there's lots of room for them to roam around, plus a TV that runs a loop of Disney cartoons. Mickey Mouse and his friends occasionally greet guests in the terminal, too.

Okay, we may have gotten a little ahead of ourselves. Before you can enter the main part of the terminal, all members of your party must go through a security checkpoint. It's a lot like airport security, so save the holey socks for the second day of your trip (you may be asked to remove your shoes, along with jackets, glasses, belts, etc.). Since kids must go through the security check, too, we recommend having snacks and games to entertain them while you wait (in case the line is more than a few minutes long). Once you've cleared security, your whole party needs to go to the check-in counter so ID photos may be taken.

At the counter, you will be asked to present a valid passport for yourself and each member of your party (see page 333). This is also where you'll be asked for all of your completed cruise paperwork (which can also be completed via the Internet at *www.disneycruise.com* under the "My Online Check-in" section; be sure to select your port arrival time, print the forms, and remember to bring them with you) and a major credit card. This card will be the one to which all of your extra cruise expenses are charged. If you'd like to split expenses with another guest (or guests) staying in your room, it is possible to register multiple credit cards. Once the cruise begins, you'll use your stateroom key—aka Key to the World card—to make purchases and to open your stateroom door. The card also serves as ID for debarking and reboarding purposes (though all ports of call also require a photo ID such as a driver's license for guests over age 18). If you'd prefer that any member of your party not have charging privileges, advise a representative at check-in (or indicate your preference when you check in online).

Once the check-in process is complete, it's time to sit back, relax, and wait for the boarding process to begin. Be sure to listen for your boarding number (all parties are assigned one). The numbers may be displayed on a monitor, too. When your boarding number is called (or splashed on the screen), grab the kids and your day bags and head for the gangway. All aboard!

THE BOARDING EXPERIENCE

After you slip through the entry portal, you'll enter a subdued hallway. This is where you may have your "pre-cruise" photo taken by a Cruise Line photographer. Try to look as stressed out as possible. That'll make the post-boarding shots that much more enjoyable. (You can view/buy the photo on the ship later that day or soon after. Just stop by Shutters, the ship's photography shop.)

Beyond the photo-op area, there's a portal leading to a gangway. Cross that gangway and you'll be deposited into the ship's grand lobby—a dramatic backdrop for a dramatic entrance.

Depending on the time (staterooms are usually ready at about 1:30 P.M.) and your level of starvation, you may want to make a quick stop, change, and head out for lunch or a snack. Ships' pools are usually open all afternoon. After that, it's safety drill time! The mandatory safety drill takes place at 4 P.M. on all Disney ships for most itineraries. Once the safety drill is complete, you may head back to your room to prepare for a cruise kickoff party known as the Sailing Away Party (offered on all Disney Cruise Line ships). If you have an early dinner seating, this is the ideal time to change into your evening attire.

Finally, we simply cannot overemphasize the importance of making reservations for spa treatments and for Palo and Remy (adults-only eateries) as early as possible. (It's best to book before the trip begins, via *www.disneycruise.com*.) Make last-minute spa appointments at the spa itself. For Palo, which begins accepting reservations at about 1 P.M. on day one of the cruise,

HOT TIP!

Disney Cruise Line has called Port Canaveral home since 1998 and will do so for the foreseeable future. For details on how to sail from ports such as New York, Miami, Vancouver, Barcelona, San Diego, and more, visit *www.disneycruise.com*.

head for Fathoms (*Magic*), Azure (*Wonder*), or D Lounge (*Dream* and *Fantasy*). Reservations for Remy (upscale dining for grown-ups on the *Dream* and *Fantasy*) may be made here, too. If you haven't already registered the kids for youth activities via *disneycruise.com*, you should do so soon after boarding.

THE DISNEY SHIPS

The Disney ships are equipped to satisfy even the most savvy of cruisers, with a mix of traditional seafaring diversions and Disney touches. The ships' classic exteriors recall the majesty of early ocean liners. Guests enter a three-story atrium, where traditional definitions of elegance expand to include bronze character statues and subtle cutout character silhouettes along a grand staircase. Recreation areas are designed to draw families and kid-free adults to different parts of the ship. By day, fun in the sun alternates with touring, lunching, indoor distractions, snoozing, and perhaps even a little bingo action. Evenings give way to sunset sailaway celebrations, themed dining experiences, and theatrical extravaganzas.

STATEROOMS

The accommodations on Disney's ships range from standard inside rooms to suites with verandahs. All staterooms are a cut above the standard cruising cabin. On average, Disney's staterooms offer more space; most have a split bath (one room with a sink and toilet and another with a sink and a shower/tub), and the majority of them are outside rooms with ocean vistas—many with verandahs.

Staterooms are decorated in a nautical theme with natural woods and imported tiles. Universal amenities include a TV, Wave phones that allow you to call or text another member of your party while on board (two phones are included per stateroom—extras may be rented), telephone with voice mail (and ship-to-shore capability), USB charging outlets, a safe, a room service menu, and lots of drawer space. All staterooms also come equipped with small refrigerators. After that, different types of accommodations—which are labeled by category—offer different amenities.

THE PERSONAL NAVIGATOR

A super handy app/in-house publication called the *Personal Navigator* will help you make the most of every day. Updated daily and available via the (free) Disney Cruise Line Navigator app or at the Guest Services Desk, the *Personal Navigator* is a comprehensive listing of a day's onboard activities, events, and entertainment. Note that the app is free of charge and must be downloaded prior to the sail away.

The *Personal Navigator* is an indispensable tool. Read it thoroughly. In addition to listing the lineup of activities scheduled for the rest of the day, it provides handy bits of information such as the suggested evening attire for that day. It changes from day to day, so be sure to take note. The *Personal Navigator* also gives the time and location of character appearances, any points of interest the ship may have scheduled, and a notification of any time zone changes, as well as any special offers or promotions for merchandise, events, or services aboard the ship.

Additional features of the DCL Navigator mobile app include the ability to chat with other cruisers (that you connect with), port information, menus, and account balance (charges made to your onboard account).

DINING

A Disney cruise is not the place where you'll want to count calories—although most special dietary needs can be accommodated upon request. There's no shortage of rations on these ships. If your tastes are simple (say, a hot dog) or sublime (how does a juicy filet mignon, prepared at Palo, sound?), rest assured you'll never be hungry. Or understimulated, for that matter, as many of the restaurants are downright entertaining. And, thanks to a system called "rotational dining," you will get to experience three restaurants, all the while being made to feel like a VIP by your serving staff. That means you will eat at a different one of the three main restaurants each evening, often with the same table guests, and enjoy the services of the same waitstaff. Your serving team gets to know you, as well as your likes and dislikes, very well. The system, which is unique to Disney Cruise Line, tends to get the thumbs-up from cruise veterans and newcomers alike. The only exceptions are Palo and Remy, the adults-only, reservations-necessary restaurants.

How do you know where to go on which night? Easy. Your dining rotation is printed on your Key to the World card. Check the day's *Personal Navigator* to note the style of attire for the evening.

TABLE SERVICE

ANIMATOR'S PALATE: The pièce de résistance—as far as Disney creativity goes—is without a doubt Animator's Palate, a place where diners not only have to decide what to eat, but also what to watch! Simple surprises abound at each stage of the evening meal. There is an Animator's Palate eatery on each of the four ships, but the dining experience varies depending on which ship you are sailing. The Animator's Palate experience on the *Disney Magic* and *Disney Wonder* is a culinary journey—from black-and-white to full color: Upon entering the monochromatic room, note the soft background music and the black-and-white sketches along the wall. While you're doing so, drinks and appetizers will be served. If you ignore this distraction and keep your gaze fixed on the walls, you may notice a bit of color creeping into that sketch of Cinderella. By the time the entrées make their entrance, the room is ablaze in living color.

If you are sailing on the *Dream* or *Fantasy*, your Animator's Palate experience will be a bit different. Like its siblings on the *Magic* and *Wonder*, the decor was inspired by the magic of Disney and Pixar animation. It's teeming with everything you'd expect to find in an animator's studio: character sketches, paintbrushes, colored pencils, computer workstations, and other tools of the animation trade. Scenes and characters from Disney films adorn the walls, and that totally awesome, animated turtle called Crush actually interacts with diners on the *Dream* and *Fantasy*.

The *Magic* and *Wonder* also feature a show called Animation Magic on select itineraries. The experience encourages guests to express themselves with a drawing—and over the course of dinner, they'll witness their drawings being brought to life through the magic of Disney animation. The impressive show is a hit with artists of all ages.

Dining room details vary, but the menu is the same on all four ships. It has featured starters such as smoked salmon tartare, sliced serrano ham with Manchego cheese and olive bread, and black truffle pasta purseittes. Entrées have included grilled herb-crusted pork chop with wine sauce, lemon-thyme marinated all-natural chicken breast, black bean chipotle cakes, and ginger-teriyaki-dusted beef tenderloin. If they are available, we recommend starting with the butternut squash soup and ending with a slice of white chocolate fudge cheesecake or the crunchy walnut cake.

ENCHANTED GARDEN: This picturesque spot, which is located on the *Dream* and *Fantasy*, seems to be truly enchanted, as the immersive, outdoorsy environment transforms from day to night over the course of dinner.

Breakfast, served buffet style, is offered on select days of each cruise. Ditto for lunch. The daily dinner is a four-course affair of seasonal selections. For an additional charge (plus gratuity), guests may enjoy bar drinks,

bottled water, and specialty coffees. Soft drinks (coffee, soda, fruit juice, milk, and tea) carry no charge. Note that this eatery is only accessible via the midship stairs and elevators.

LUMIÈRE'S: Located on the *Magic* only, this elegant spot provides fine dining in a setting inspired by Disney's *Beauty and the Beast*. The sprawling dining room is elegant and softly lit, though a bit more raucous than its cosmopolitan contemporaries. Note that the later seating is usually a bit more sedate (fewer small children).

Menu selections at dinner have included crispy roasted duck breast with braised napa cabbage, and aged Angus beef tenderloin. Vegetarians can opt for the mushroom-stuffed pasta in a vegetable broth. And vegetarians won't feel at all cheated by the grilled marinated tofu. For dessert, consider crème brûlée, chocolate mousse, or traditional ice cream sundae.

TRITON'S: Passengers aboard the *Wonder* may dine in the elegant Triton's, where the specialty of the house is seafood. The ocean theme is enhanced by subtly changing lighting with every course, the room getting more

under-the-sea-like as the meal progresses. The menu has featured French onion soup; Conchiglie pasta with buttered lobster in a tomato, shrimp, and tarragon brandy sauce; oven-baked salmon royale crowned with king smoked salmon; and roasted rack of lamb. For dessert, there's chocolate mousse, Grand Marnier soufflé, sundaes, and more.

TIANA'S PLACE: A jubilant homage to New Orleans' dining and entertainment, Tiana's Place takes its

inspiration from Disney's animated feature *The Princess and the Frog*. The *Wonder* exclusive transports guests to an era of Southern charm, spirited jazz, and street party celebrations. The walls are lined with Princess Tiana's family photos and culinary awards. Chefs cook up all of her favorite recipes, drawing inspiration from the flavors of the Louisiana bayou. The cuisine is complemented with live music. Performed on the main stage, rhythmic notes of jazz, swing, and blues set the tone for a lively, Big Easy–style supper club.

RAPUNZEL'S ROYAL TABLE: It's Rapunzel's birthday *and* the anniversary of her return to the Kingdom of Corona—and *Disney Magic* guests are invited to the celebration! The festivities take place in a chamber inspired by the royal ballroom in the film *Tangled*. The regal room is adorned with Rapunzel's artwork and illuminated with floating wish lanterns. It's the perfect setting in which to mingle with characters such as Rapunzel and Flynn Rider, enjoy a little song and dance, and enjoy a feast fit for a princess.

The menu has offered items such as the Snuggly Duckling Platter (charcuterie), Maximus salad, *Tangled* pasta, a seared sea bass filet in a Champagne-truffle vinaigrette, grilled steak, and roasted prime rib. Finish the meal with a birthday cake sundae; warm, braided apple strudel; or Rapunzel's Fry Pan Sweet Bread.

ROYAL PALACE/ROYAL COURT: This regal restaurant (Royal Palace on the *Dream* and Royal Court on the *Fantasy*) got its inspiration from classic Disney animated features such as *Sleeping Beauty*, *Cinderella*, and *Beauty and the Beast*. You will find the eatery on Deck 3, midship.

French-inspired, continental cuisine is offered for breakfast, lunch, and dinner. Breakfast is offered on select mornings of each cruise, as is a full-service lunch. A four-course dinner takes place nightly. One of the favorite appetizers at dinner is the *escargots gratinés* (herb-marinated snails). Grilled beef tenderloin and shrimp is a featured entrée. Vegetarian selections such as mushroom-filled pasta are served, too. And do save room for an ice cream sundae, crème brûlée, peanut butter mousse, or other tempting treat. Yum!

RESTAURANT SEATING TIMES AND SITUATIONS: There are normally two seating sessions for dinner; however, the times vary depending on what itinerary the ship is sailing at the time. The most common times are 5:45 P.M. and 8:15 P.M. If you have a preference, tell your travel agent or reservationist the moment you book your cruise. Requests for any seating cannot be guaranteed. If you get closed out of a preferred seating time, check with Guest Services after boarding. Seating times may open up after boarding. Most seating at table-service restaurants is communal, except at Palo and Remy. If you are traveling as a family with kids, expect to be seated with similar travelers. Adults dining without children will be seated together if possible.

Parents of young children, listen up! There is a dining convenience designed especially for you. Dine and Play lets parents with late dinner seatings check their kids (ages 3 to 12) into the Youth Activities programs starting about 45 minutes after dinner seating has begun. In other words, after the youngsters have

Laundry Facilities

Laundry and dry cleaning services are available on all Disney ships for a small fee. Items will be picked up and delivered to your stateroom. If you'd rather go the self-service laundry route, you can do so in one of several Guest Laundry Rooms. There you'll find washers, dryers, and ironing equipment. (Due to safety concerns, the laundry room is the only place in which iron use is permitted.) There is no fee to use an iron. Machines run about two bucks a load. Laundry detergent may be purchased here, too. At press time, a small box costs about $1. Simply swipe your Key to the World card and charge it to your stateroom account.

downed kid-friendly fare, they can go play while you finish your meal in a leisurely manner. Neat, huh? If you wish to partake of the complimentary Dine and Play service, simply inform your servers upon arrival in the dining room. They will make sure your kids get their meals quickly, while serving the grown-ups at a much more relaxed pace.

Youth activities counselors arrive in the restaurant 45 minutes after the seating begins and assign children to groups right there in the dining room. No need for parents to escort Junior to Deck 5. (Though they will eventually have to pick the kids up!) Remember, this service is for guests with late dinner seatings only.

PALO: For adults only (age 18 and up), Palo is an ideal spot for special celebrations or just a quiet, romantic evening. Offering brunch and dinner, Palo is worth the per-person surcharge (at press time, prices were $40 for brunch and dinner) to indulge in a five-star dining experience that includes an ocean view.

HOT TIP!

To avoid being charged for canceling a Palo or Remy reservation, you must cancel at least 24 hours prior to the reservation time.

Guest Services Desk

If you have any questions or concerns while on board, head to the Guest Services Desk (Deck 3, midship). This is also the place to go to secure printed copies of the *Personal Navigator*, color-coded luggage tags (for use on the last day of the cruise), and postage stamps. Should you have any type of problem while on board, bring it to their attention. More often than not, they will resolve the issue in a matter of minutes.

True to its roots (*palo* means "pole" in Italian), the eatery has echoes of Venice, Italy—and the menu reflects some of the best continental fare you'll find on either side of the Atlantic. Dinner appetizers include *fritto di calamari e gamba* and soft potato gnocchi tossed in a piennolo tomato sauce. The entrée menu tempts with items such as roasted rack of lamb with caponata and olive potatoes, and *parpadelle con aragosta*.

A warning: Reserve room for dessert, or you will never forgive yourself. The chocolate soufflé (with hot chocolate and vanilla sauces) is beyond amazing. Of course, just about every one of Palo's homemade treats yield raves, too.

Brunch at Palo is a special event. (It's only offered on select cruises, making it even more special!) The buffet is so vast that it requires a guided tour. Expect fruit, salads, seafood, heavenly flatbreads, pastries, made-to-order omelets, fish, and chicken entrées, and more.

Palo is for diners age 18 years and older. Make reservations at *www.disneycruise.com*; at Promenade Lounge on the *Magic* and *Wonder*, and at Enchanted Garden on the *Fantasy* and *Dream* on the first day of the cruise.

REMY: For adults (guests age 18 and older) on the *Dream* and *Fantasy*, Remy is a ritzy, palate-pleasing delight. Considered the most upscale dining experience available on the ship, Remy serves fine French-inspired cuisine for dinner (on all cruises) and brunch (select cruises). The luxurious dining room has Art Nouveau touches and a rich color scheme. Tables are set with Frette linens, Riedel glassware, Christofle silverware, and custom-created Bernardaud china.

The evening meal begins with a champagne cocktail and continues with 8 to 9 small (and delectable) courses. There's nothing more thrilling than a tableside visit from the trolley of international cheeses—except, perhaps, for the wine decanting stations and after-dinner coffee service.

The private Chef's Table experience takes place in a special 8-seat dining room and features *Ratatouille*-inspired decor.

Oenophiles appreciate the lovely Wine Room, which accommodates up to 8 guests. Here, guests dine in a glass-walled room with marble flooring amid 900 bottles of wine.

Reservations are required to dine at Remy, and meals come with a $125 per-person surcharge for dinner, $60 for the decadent Dessert Experience, and $70 per person for brunch. Reservations may be made online (75 days ahead for first-time cruisers, 90 days ahead for Silver

Castaway Club members, 105 days ahead for Gold members, and 120 days in advance for concierge guests and Platinum members).

Like its neighbor, Palo, Remy also has a dress code. Dinner is much more formal here than at Palo: jackets, dress pants, and dress shoes for men (ties are optional); dresses, suits, blouses, and dress pants for women. Leave the jeans, shorts, tank tops, yoga pants, sandals, flip-flops, and sneakers in your stateroom. Jackets are optional for men at brunch.

What to Wear for Dinner: Generally speaking, "cruise casual" is the way to go in all spots except for Palo and Remy: collared shirts, blouses, cotton pants, jeans (Palo only, and they must be in good condition, without holes), and sundresses are generally acceptable for evenings in all other restaurants—swimsuits, T-shirts, hats, flip-flops, tennis shoes, and tank tops are not. On select nights, there will be a theme: pirate attire, semi-formal, etc. On such days, the desired style of dress will be noted in the *Personal Navigator*. (While parents are the best judges

Disney Cruise Line Gifts

Whether you will be celebrating a special occasion or simply consider a cruise to be a special occasion in and of itself, you may want to have a gift delivered to your stateroom. Among the items that can be pre-ordered by calling 800-601-8455 or visiting *disneycruise. com* are floral arrangements, food and beverage packages, wine packages, cakes, and Disney Cruise Line merchandise. Specialty cakes must be ordered at least 7 days in advance. Other orders must be placed at least 72 business hours before your sail date.

of what attire is appropriate for their children, most guests over the age of 13 are usually comfortable wearing attire that is similar to what is recommended for all passengers.) Note that Palo and Remy, grown-ups-only destinations, are considered more formal and guests are asked to dress accordingly: long pants and shirt are required for men (a jacket is optional at Palo, but is required for Remy), and a dress or pants and shirt combo for women. No ripped jeans, shorts, flip-flops, or sneakers, please. Likewise, the indoor area of Meridian Bar, located between Palo and Remy, has the same formal dress code as Palo. However, the outdoor patio of the Meridian Bar has a slightly more relaxed vibe (think business casual).

Wine and Dine: All table-service restaurants offer many vintages by the glass or by the bottle. If you order a bottle and fail to finish it by meal's end, ask your server to store it for you. (You'll get it with the next evening's meal.) Disney offers two wine packages (premium and classic selections).

Special Dietary Needs: Certain special dietary needs may be met aboard Disney cruise ships. All requests should be made well in advance, preferably at the time of booking the cruise package. It's always a good idea to confirm the request prior to setting sail.

SELF-SERVE, FAST FOOD, AND SNACKS

VIBE: This teens-only spot—which can be found on all ships—serves up fruit smoothies and other soft drinks. There are lots of games and activities, and the refreshments are free of charge. This area is hopping all day—and often past midnight.

BEVERAGE STATION: There is a self-serve station on every ship. On the *Magic* and *Wonder*, it's on Deck 9, aft (port side). On the *Dream* and *Fantasy*, look for the beverage station on Deck 11, midship (there is a station on each side of the Mickey pool). Help yourself to water, juice, soda, tea (iced or hot), lemonade, coffee, and hot cocoa. There is an ice machine, too. The station is open 24/7, though not all selections are available at all times. Soft drinks are free here and with meals, but not at bars or through room service.

CABANAS: Located on all four ships, this casual indoor eatery serves three meals a day. This spot recalls a breezy boardwalk along the coast, with a dash of Disney (e.g., colorful *Finding Nemo*–themed mosaics). Made-to-order breakfast and lunch selections are offered "on the boardwalk" on most days (you can refer to the day's *Personal Navigator* for times and specifics). In other words, a variety of food stations proffer freshly prepared edibles. Dinner is a table-service affair. Spirits may be ordered from the Clam Bar. Cabanas is located on Deck 11, aft on the *Dream* and *Fantasy*; Deck 9 aft on the *Magic* and *Wonder*.

COVE CAFE: A cozy, adults-only lounge, Cove Cafe can be found on all ships. It features specialty drinks, coffee, and tea all day. In the evening, guests over age 21 may also enjoy beer, wine, and cocktails. Complimentary snacks are available; fees apply for drinks. Books and magazines are on hand for on-site perusing. Board games may be borrowed, too. Guests must be at least 18 years old to visit Cove Cafe, located near the Quiet Cove pool.

DAISY'S DE-LITES: *Magic* and *Wonder*: Visit Daisy's for bagels, fresh fruit, salads, sandwiches, cookies, and more. Hours are usually 11 A.M. till 6 or 7 P.M. daily.

DUCK-IN DINER: *Magic*: Situated near the Splash Zone, this spot serves chicken tenders, burgers, veggie burgers, hot dogs, and chicken and lamb shawarma.

EYE SCREAM: Guests craving a chilly treat can find satisfaction at this self-serve, soft-serve station inspired by famous eyeball Mike Wazowski.

FLO'S CAFE: *Dream* and *Fantasy*: Flo's Cafe, located on Deck 11 near the Donald pool, is actually a trio of side-by-side walk-up windows, all themed to characters from the animated feature *Cars*. Here you'll find Luigi's Pizza, Tow Mater's Grill, and Fillmore's Favorites. Menu

options at these filling stations include pizza (often featuring a special pizza of the day), chicken tenders, salads, sandwich wraps, fruit, burgers, and more. Luigi's tends to stay open the latest of the three.

FROZONE TREATS: On the *Magic*, *Dream*, and *Fantasy*, this snack spot pays tribute to Frozone from *The Incredibles* and serves made-to-order mixed fruit smoothies and cocktails (for a fee).

PETE'S BOILER BITES: On the *Magic:* Looking for a tasty treat without the formality of a table-service eatery? Or perhaps a nibble between meals? Head here! Pete proudly serves chicken tenders, burgers, hot dogs, veggie burgers, plus chicken and lamb shawarma.

PINOCCHIO'S PIZZERIA: *Magic* and *Wonder:* This counter-service spot serves spirits and soft drinks (for a fee), and cheese and pepperoni pizzas (no charge for food). There is often a special pizza of the day. Be sure to ask before you order.

SULLEY'S SIPS: *Wonder:* Stop at this poolside spot for smoothies, cocktails, and snacks (for a fee).

SWEET ON YOU: *Fantasy:* Sundaes, shakes, and other frozen concoctions are served at this cheery ice cream parlor. Fees apply.

VANELLOPE'S SWEETS AND TREATS: *Dream:* Race to this dessert window for hand-scooped gelato, ice cream waffle cones, baked treats, and candy. Fees apply.

ROOM SERVICE

Stateroom dining service delivers 24 hours a day (except on the final night of a cruise, when service stops promptly at 1 A.M.)—handy if you're traveling with kids or if you have a snack craving in between meals. Most menu items are included with your cruise package. At press time, selections included soups, salads, sandwiches, burgers, pizza, cookies, and selections for kids. There is a charge for some beverages and snack selections (such as candy, popcorn, wine, beer, soda, and bottled water). Note that a gratuity is not always included.

SPECIAL DINING EXPERIENCES

PIRATES IN THE CARIBBEAN PARTY: If there's one thing Disney really knows how to do right, it's throw a party. On one night during most cruises, guests enjoy a buccaneering soirée. If you own any pirate attire or regalia, wear it to the big event. (You may purchase some from a ship shop, too.) It takes place on the upper decks, where pirate villains set their sights on taking over the ship. An epic battle ensues as the good guys take on the villains. The greatest spectacle of all is the show's grand finale—fireworks (offered on most itineraries). A feast fit for a pirate king is served post pyrotechnics (usually served in Cabanas).

CHARACTER BREAKFAST: An up-close-and-personal morning starring favorite characters is a very Disney way to start the day.

The character breakfast is offered on select itineraries, usually the 7-night-or-longer cruises with at least two days at sea. To attend, you will need a ticket. Reserve tickets *before* your cruise begins by visiting My Cruise Line Activities at *disneycruise.com* within your advanced booking window. (For additional information about the character breakfast, call 800-951-3532.)

Many of the character breakfast selections remain staples—eggs, bacon, cereal, fruit, yogurt, and French toast, for example.

BARS AND LOUNGES

From elegant lounges with live piano music to lively sports bars, Disney ships have a bounty of bars and lounges—many of them located in the ships' grown-up-only entertainment zones (Europa on the *Fantasy*, The District on the *Dream*, and After Hours on the *Magic* and *Wonder*).

AZURE: A celebration of the sights and sounds of the sea sets the stage for this lively dance club. A deejay often keeps the place grooving till the wee hours. All manner of drinks are available at this After Hours venue on the *Wonder*.

BON VOYAGE: A casual lounge located on Deck 3, midship (*Dream* and *Fantasy*). Beverages are available throughout the day.

CADILLAC LOUNGE: Unique to the After Hours zone aboard the *Wonder*, this sophisticated spot celebrates classic cars with soothing music, wine, martinis, and other drinks.

COVE CAFE: This cozy adults-only destination can be found aboard all Disney ships. It has specialty coffees and a full bar (charges apply). Snacks are available, too (no charge). Books and board games may be borrowed for on-site use.

CROWN & FIN PUB: Unique to the grown-ups only After Hours zone aboard the *Wonder*, this jolly spot resembles a classic British pub.

CURRENTS: A breezy spot with stellar ocean views, Currents is on Deck 13, forward (*Dream* and *Fantasy*).

DANCE CLUB: A butterfly-themed hot spot, Evolution celebrates all styles of music on the *Dream*. On the *Fantasy*, it's The Tube, a dance spot that pays tribute to the city of London. The venues feature various

---

HOT TIP!

Palo and Remy reservations will not appear on your Personal Navigator. (It's not *that* personal.) Make sure you don't miss it—there's a per-person charge for all meals. Call 800-910-3659 for specifics.

---

activities and dance parties. (Guests must be at least 18 years old to come here at night, 21 to imbibe.)

DISTRICT LOUNGE: This intimate watering hole is located in the *Dream*'s grown-ups-only entertainment zone, the District.

FATHOMS: This After Hours joint (*Magic*) fancies itself a celebration of the sea. It uses special effects, lighting, and sound to create different festive atmospheres. There's a dance floor, plus tables and bar seating. Themed parties are thrown on select evenings.

KEYS: The *Magic*'s version of an intimate piano bar, this lounge serves cocktails and wines by the glass. Keys provides a refined retreat.

LA PIAZZA: The *Fantasy*'s celebration of Italian cities features a festive carousel bar. Venetian masks and glasswork add to the fun.

MERIDIAN BAR: Found on the *Dream* and *Fantasy*, Meridian is located on Deck 12, aft, and has indoor and outdoor seating. The dress code for the interior area: Dress pants and shirt are required for men and a dress or dress pants for women. On the outside deck, the dress code is cruise casual (jeans and shorts are okay, swimsuits and tank tops are not).

OOH LA LA: A *Fantasy* champagne bar, this space was inspired by a French boudoir.

PINK: WINE AND CHAMPAGNE BAR: An elegant nightspot designed to look like the inside of a champagne

---

A TENDER SUBJECT

Some ports require a process called "tendering." This means, rather than pulling right up to a dock, the ship will pull close to port and drop anchor. Ferries take guests back and forth to shore. It's an efficient system, but it could knock you for a loop if you're not expecting it—especially if you've got an early excursion booked. In this case, you may have to leave a bit earlier than you originally anticipated. That is accounted for in the "meet time" for all excursions.

HOT TIP!

The midship elevators are the most crowded throughout the day—especially at mealtimes. Try to use the forward and aft elevators whenever possible.

bottle, this lounge is in the *Dream*'s District entertainment zone. Pink definitely gets an A+ for atmosphere.

PROMENADE LOUNGE: This busy lounge serves spirited beverages, soft drinks, and appetizers on the *Magic* and *Wonder*. At night, it offers live music.

SIGNALS: On Deck 9 of the *Magic* and *Wonder*, this poolside spot serves cocktails and soft drinks.

SKYLINE: The *Dream*'s District area and the *Fantasy*'s Europa boast Skyline, a cosmopolitan bar with majestic views of famous cities from around the world. The city scapes change over the course of the evening.

SPORTS BAR: This lounge has a big screen (often featuring a big game), plus suds, wings, hot dogs, or other munchies. It's Pub 687 on the *Dream* and O'Gills Pub on the *Fantasy* and *Magic*.

THE TUBE: Housed in the *Fantasy*'s Europa district, The Tube is a metropolitan dance club themed to the London Underground (aka the tube).

VISTA CAFÉ: *Dream* and *Fantasy* guests in need of a java jolt can head to this cheery destination on Deck 4, midship. Snacks and cocktails are served, too.

WAVES: An open-air bar on the *Fantasy* and *Dream*, this spot serves beverages all day.

HOT TIP!

Beer drinkers, take note: If you purchase a refillable mug during the cruise, you're entitled to discount suds for the duration of your stay on the ship (e.g., 20 ounces for the price of 16). You must present the beer card token to net the discount.

ENTERTAINMENT

For some, a deck chair, a good book, and a steady stream of sunshine are all the entertainment required. Others may delight in an evening of dancing or a bingo-filled afternoon. And some are satisfied with nothing short of a Broadway-style stage show. Fortunately, Disney Cruise Line has it all, plus first-run movies, game shows, variety acts, and more. Note that all shows are not presented every day or on every cruise. The lineup is tweaked from time to time, so details may differ during your cruise.

BEAUTY AND THE BEAST: Find adventure and song in a dazzling musical inspired by the live-action, feature film version of the classic tale. This version of the "tale as old as time" is presented on the *Disney Dream*. It's quite the crowd-pleaser.

THE GOLDEN MICKEYS—A TIMELESS TRIBUTE: A dynamic production, this awards show pays tribute to the musical legacy of Walt Disney Studios. It's got all the glitz and glamour of a Hollywood celebration, paying homage to the comedy, romance, and heroes (plus a few villains) of classic Disney animated films. This theatrical event is presented on the *Wonder* and *Dream*. It's a classic crowd-pleaser worthy of its own Golden Mickey.

FROZEN, A MUSICAL SPECTACULAR: The *Disney Wonder* proudly presents a heartwarming, humorous retelling of the beloved motion picture. The *Frozen*-inspired musical show transports guests to the icy, beautiful land of Arendelle and stars favorite characters from the animated feature: Anna, Elsa, Kristoff, Olaf, and Hans (okay, Hans may not be a favorite, but he *was* in the film).

DISNEY'S ALADDIN—A MUSICAL SPECTACULAR: A comic musical, this production showcases a variety of classic (and new) tunes and characters from Disney's animated feature *Aladdin* and regales guests with theatrical treats. The action often spills out into the audience, such as when a magic carpet soars overhead or the evil Jafar turns into a gigantic snake (warn timid tots). Rest assured, it all ends happily! The show is a *Fantasy* exclusive.

DISNEY'S BELIEVE: Who doesn't believe in the power of pixie dust? A little girl named Sophia certainly does. But her serious-minded father, Dr. Greenaway, is a much tougher sell. Follow his journey from skeptic to believer in this rousing musical stage show. In addition to classic Disney tunes, this crowd-pleaser features the lovely original song "What Makes a Garden Grow." It is presented on the *Dream* and *Fantasy*.

DISNEY DREAMS—AN ENCHANTED CLASSIC: This bedtime story features a galaxy of Disney stars, including Peter Pan, Aladdin, Cinderella, Tinker Bell, and Pinocchio. Together and through the power of song and dance, the characters teach a skeptical girl about the power of dreams. It takes place on the *Magic* and *Wonder*.

TWICE CHARMED—AN ORIGINAL TWIST ON THE CINDERELLA STORY: A Broadway-style extravaganza (presented on the *Magic* only), this musical production begins with the wedding of Cinderella and Prince Charming. Things take a sudden turn when the wicked Fairy Godfather makes his presence known and, after granting a wish to one evil stepmother, sends the family back in time, where—*gasp*—the glass slipper gets broken! Does this turn of events destroy Cinderella's chances of living happily ever after? You'll just have to catch the show to find out.

DISNEY'S WISHES: As high school kids face graduation day, they discover that the secret to becoming a grown-up is to stay connected to your inner child. And what's a wonderful way to do that? By making a wish and spending a fun-filled, musical—and magical—day at Disneyland. It's a *Fantasy* exclusive.

TANGLED—THE MUSICAL: A Disney Cruise Line original, this show follows the story of Rapunzel, from her escape from the tower and the clutches of the evil Gothel to her unlikely friendship with the crown-stealing bandit, Flynn Rider. With a mix of familiar and new songs (all written by Alan Menken and Glen Slater), Tangled—The Musical is fun for all ages. This one-hour show is presented on the *Magic*.

DECK PARTIES

When it comes to on-deck celebrations, the area surrounding the family pool is party central. Starting with a Sailing Away Celebration and continuing with daily dance fests with Disney characters, live bands, and fireworks (on most itineraries), it seems like there is always a reason to party. Deck parties are offered on all sailings on Disney Cruise line vessels.

FAMILY ENTERTAINMENT

D LOUNGE: This family-friendly lounge and nightclub is on all ships (Deck 4, midship). Head here for dance parties, character greetings, games, and more. Mickey Mania lets you put your knowledge of Disney trivia to the test, while Karaoke Night encourages families to take the stage and sing together. Finally, the Family Dance Party gives everyone a chance to kick up their heels (or sneakers) and enjoy a party for guests of all ages. Keep in mind that the entertainment lineup, though always dynamic, is subject to change from time to time.

CHARACTER BREAKFAST: On most cruises that are 7 nights or longer, a bountiful breakfast is hosted by familiar Disney friends. Tickets (no cost) are required.

FOR GROWN-UPS ONLY

The 18-and-over set aboard the *Magic* and *Wonder* can attend demonstrations (e.g., Disney's Art of Entertaining), tours, and special nighttime events (such as Match Your Mate, a game show in which you and your chosen one will find out how much you actually know about each other), plus theme nights, cabaret shows, and more.

On the *Dream* and *Fantasy*, adults have the chance to participate in interactive cooking demonstrations as part of the Anyone Can Cook! series; learn the secrets of Disney animation in the Illusion of Life series; and attend a presentation about the making of the ship.

JUST FOR KIDS

The wildly popular kids' programs and activities tend to elicit raves from participants and parents alike. For starters, adults who leave their kids at supervised facilities can be assured that the watchword here is safety. There are plenty of counselors on hand, and the secured programming ensures that they know where every child is at any given time. Kids are checked in with Youth Activities when entering and signed out when exiting with an authorized guardian. Upon check-in, each child is given an Oceaneer wrist band. (It assists with the check-in and checkout process and adds an additional level of security to all youth venues.)

Parents have Wave Phones (which can be found in all staterooms) and can be contacted with them (or via the Disney Cruise Line app) if their child has a problem or just wants to see them. (Though it has been our experience that most youngsters rarely, if ever, want to leave the kids' programming areas.)

Kids' programs are concentrated on Deck 5, and kids registered into secured programming always remain in either the Lab or Club. The specially tailored programming is open to kids age 3 and older who are completely potty-trained, able to interact comfortably within the counselor-to-child ratio groups and mix well with peers. There is no extra charge for youth activities. (Non-potty-trained tykes, ages 6 months to 3 years, may go to a cheery nursery. Fees apply.) Cleanliness is a priority. In fact, kids entering the Oceaneer Club and Lab are promptly asked to wash their hands.

Kids between ages 3 and 12 can choose to play in the Oceaneer Club or Oceaneer Lab based on whatever interests them. Siblings and friends between the ages of 3 and 12 can play together regardless, as kids are not segregated by age group. And don't worry about little ones ever being dominated by bigger kids—participants are closely monitored at all times.

Kids who show any symptoms of illness will not be allowed to participate without approval from the onboard medical center. If a child becomes disruptive, he or she will be asked to play with a parent or guardian during open house hours.

Except for the nursery, there is no fee for youth activities on any Disney ship. The following descriptions of activities were accurate at press time, but specifics are subject to change from time to time.

OCEANEER CLUB: A wonderfully detailed adventure zone, this club has several distinctly themed areas on every ship. In addition to computer games, costumes, and other games, there are many organized activities. It's open to all kids ages 3 to 12 (potty-trained) on all ships (provided the kids show no sign of illness).

At the Oceaneer Club, kids find a combination of free play and structured activities featuring interactive, playful experiences with Disney characters. These may include reading a story with Belle and playing games with Mickey Mouse. Lunch and dinner are served (at no extra charge) on all days except for embark day. It's usually open daily from 9 A.M. till midnight.

OCEANEER LAB: The Oceaneer Lab is open to (fully potty-trained) kids ages 3 to 12 on all Disney ships. It is located on Deck 5, midship. The entertaining space is filled with wacky inventions and opportunities for exploration. There are costumes, books, toys, tablet games, drawing materials, and more. As with the Oceaneer Club, there are also many organized activities. It is usually open daily from 9 A.M. till midnight.

HOT TIP!

If your mobile phone, laptop, or tablet is equipped for wireless Internet access, bring it along. Most areas on the Disney ships offer Wi-Fi service known as Connect@Sea. Rates may vary, but expect to pay 25 cents per megabyte (mb) of data or buy a package of 100 mb for $19, 300 mb for $39, or 1,000 mb for $89. Prices are per stateroom, and packages may be shared. For additional information, visit *www.disneycruise.com*. For the most up-to-date rates, refer to the information provided in your stateroom or contact a Connect@Sea rep, located inside Promenade Lounge on the *Magic* and *Wonder* or on Deck 4, midship aboard the *Dream* and *Fantasy*. All prices are subject to change.

Programs here allow young guests to be very hands-on while learning the skills of Disney animators or becoming a sleuth to solve mysteries with Disney characters. Refer to a *Personal Navigator* for specific dates and times for various activities while on board. Participants are served lunch and dinner each day (no extra charge) except for embark days.

Reminder: Kids ages 8 to 12 may check themselves in and out of the Oceaneer Lab and Oceaneer Club with their parents' permission.

EDGE: There are video games, arts and crafts, and movies in this tween-only hangout. Guests ages 11–14 may enjoy evening activities such as scavenger hunts and karaoke, too. Edge can be found on Deck 9 on the *Magic* and *Wonder*.

Also a tween space on the *Dream* and *Fantasy*, Edge is located on Deck 13 inside the forward funnel. Its high-tech features include an illuminated dance floor, a video wall, and game-playing.

IT'S A SMALL WORLD NURSERY: Open to kids ages 6 months through 3 years (except for trans-Atlantic cruises, during which the minimum age is 12 months), these colorful spaces are the ships' baby care centers. For an hourly fee, the nursery offers activities and a quiet area, complete with cribs.

Food is available at the nursery, but if parents provide prepared bottles or jarred food that is clearly labeled with a child's name, staffers will happily feed their hungry tyke. Space is limited and gets booked early. Reservations are accepted via *www.disneycruise.com* and throughout the cruise on a first-come, first-served basis. Due to the high demand, multiple requests might not be honored—so don't count on securing several sessions, though it can't hurt to try. The fee for the service is $9 per hour for the first child, $8 per each additional child with a one-hour minimum (only siblings net the discount). Nurseries are generally open from 9 A.M. until 11 P.M. Stateroom baby care is not offered on any Disney ship.

VIBE (TEENS ONLY)

Guests ages 14 through 17 have their own zone while aboard Disney ships. Vibe is their exclusive place to hang out. (If you are old enough to vote, KEEP OUT!—unless you're one of the specially trained Disney counselors.) It has music, games, dance parties, big-screen TVs, and more. Other programs may include karaoke, sports activities, pool parties (*Dream* and *Fantasy*), and more. Specialty soft drinks, including smoothies are free. Vibe is generally open from 11 A.M. till 2 A.M.

FUN AND GAMES

BINGO: Perhaps it's something in the ocean air, but nothing brings out the bingo fanatic in you like a few days at sea. The closest thing to gambling that you will find on a Disney Cruise Line vessel, the bingo sessions are extremely popular. You have to be at least 18 to play, but kids can watch over a grown-up's shoulder and cheer them on.

GAMES: Foosball, shuffleboard, basketball . . . they're all here. Equipment can usually be found by the tables or courts. (Don't monopolize it—it's for all to share.) Kooky competitions are sometimes held poolside. The *Dream* and *Fantasy* offer mini-golf and sports simulators (there is a charge to use the simulators). Refer to the ship's *Personal Navigator* and the associated app for further details.

MOVIES: The Buena Vista Theatre shows new film releases—some in 3-D. This is the perfect place to head when the weather is less than ideal. Get there early, as the seats fill up quickly.

If you prefer your flicks alfresco, head up to the Goofy, Donald, or Mickey pool. A jumbo movie screen (on the ship's forward funnel and dubbed Funnel Vision) broadcasts Disney features, live sporting events, and more throughout the cruise.

SHOPPING

While on board Disney's ships, you can enjoy tax-free (on all items) and duty-free (select items) shopping.

The ship's shops have limited hours due to U.S. Customs regulations and can't operate during any time when the ship is in port. Use your stateroom key (Key to the World) to buy items in the ship's shops and on Castaway Cay. Purchases will be charged to your stateroom account. Note that the Castaway Cay post office does not honor Key to the World cards—it accepts cash only. Shops in all other ports of call generally accept major credit cards, and many accept United States currency.

ONBOARD SHOPS

PRELUDES (all ships): There is a snack bar/concessions window on both sides of the Walt Disney Theatre. Among the items for sale are cookies, candies, nuts, and assorted drinks.

MICKEY'S MAINSAIL (all ships): The Mainsail stocks Disney and Disney Cruise Line merchandise, including souvenirs, clothing, beach towels, mugs, costumes, postcards, frames, books, watches, snack items, and plush toys. The shop is located on Deck 3 (*Dream* and *Fantasy*) and Deck 4, forward (*Magic* and *Wonder*).

QUACKS: This ducky spot sells swim supplies—including Disney Cruise Line bathing suits, T-shirts, towels, and the all-important sunscreen. It's on Deck 9, midship, on the *Magic* and *Wonder*.

SEA TREASURES (all ships): Located on Deck 3, forward, the treasures here may include jewelry and Disney collectibles. There may be shirts, sweatshirts, purses, fragrances, headwear, jackets, and other Disney Cruise Line logo items.

WHITE CAPS (all ships): This is the place for duty-free items such as perfume, watches, jewelry, and liquor. Note that any liquor purchased here may not be consumed while on board. It will be delivered to your room on the last evening of your cruise. It may be possible to pick up sundries, sunglasses, and snacks—plus Disney Cruise Line-themed souvenirs.

WHOZITS & WHATZITS (*Dream* and *Fantasy*): A tiny shop located on Deck 11, midship, near the Donald pool, Whozits & Whatzits sells deckwear, sunscreen, towels, and other poolside necessities.

SPORTS AND RECREATION

FITNESS CENTER: The fitness center is located within the Senses Spa & Salon on all ships. There is no fee to use the equipment, which includes treadmills, bikes, stair-climbing machines, free weights, and more. (Some of the machines sport TVs—bring headphones or borrow a pair at the Front Desk.) Fitness consultations are offered. The fitness center is generally open from about 6 A.M. to 10 P.M., while spa hours run from about 8 A.M. to 8 P.M.

WIDE WORLD OF SPORTS DECK (*Magic* and *Wonder*): Deck 10 is home to the Wide World of Sports deck. Though open to everyone, it's a huge kid and teen magnet. The basketball hoops are hopping day and night. Basketballs and other equipment are on-site (no charge). Ditto for Ping-Pong and soccer. This deck is also a wonderful place to gaze out at panoramic views of the ocean—making it popular with casual strollers. (Though jogging on the *Magic* and *Wonder* is relegated to Deck 4, where one lap is about one-third of a mile. Deck 4 is where you will find the shuffleboard court on all ships, too.)

GOOFY'S SPORTS DECK (*Dream* and *Fantasy*): Located on Deck 13, aft, the always bustling Goofy's Sports Deck is an all-ages, open-air activity center. The area has a basketball court and a sports simulator (soccer, golf, football, hockey, and basketball; fees apply for the simulator) and an honest-to-goodness (or is that Goof-ness?) mini golf course.

AQUADUCK (*Dream* and *Fantasy*): Tired of all that poolside relaxation? Head for Deck 12 and the ship's ultimate adrenaline inducer: the AquaDuck. This 765-foot-long "water coaster" propels guests through a clear tube on a journey that includes a trip over the ocean and through the forward funnel, and a 4-deck drop. Check a *Personal Navigator* for operating hours. Guests must be at least 42 inches tall to ride the Aqua-Duck and 54 inches tall to ride alone. Kids under age 7 must be accompanied by someone 14 years of age or older. It's a hoot—and not as scary as it looks.

AQUADUNK (*Magic*): Step into the 3-story, translucent tube, the trapdoor opens and . . . kerplunk! The ride is quick and splashy. Guests must be at least 48 inches tall to take the plunge. It is accessed via steps on Deck 10.

AQUALAB (*Magic, Wonder,* and *Fantasy*): Found on Deck 12, aft, on the *Fantasy* and Deck 9, aft, on the *Magic* and *Wonder*, AquaLab is a family splash zone. This interactive playground is open to guests age 3 and up. Families may frolic among pop jets, bubblers, and geysers, and slip along the "Twist 'n' Spout" waterslide. (Guests must be at least 38 inches tall to ride.)

DORY'S SPLASH ZONE (*Wonder*): Deck 9, aft, is home to the *Wonder*'s watery fun zone for the under 3 set. It's a great spot for tots to cool off. Swim diapers are a must.

NEPHEWS' SPLASH ZONE (*Magic*): Deck 9, aft, is home to the *Disney Magic*'s "splashtacular" zone. Designed for guests age 3 and under, the 500-square-foot play area features geysers and bubble jets and a soft deck surface. Non-potty-trained guests are required to wear swim diapers in this play area.

SATELLITE FALLS (*Dream* and *Fantasy*): A watery haven for grown-ups, this Deck 13, forward, spot has a circular splash pool with benches and a cascading curtain of water. The shaded Satellite Sundeck has comfy lounge chairs, available on a first-come, first-served basis.

SWIMMING (*Dream* and *Fantasy*): Deck 11 is pool central on these ships. Donald's Pool is the family pool and can be found midship. Mickey's Pool is strictly for youngsters and their guardians, and the Quiet Cove pool is a grown-ups-only splash zone. Nemo's Reef is a spray zone for the toddler set (swim diapers are required at all times). Floats, rafts and fun noodles cannot be brought onboard and are not permitted in the pools.

SWIMMING (*Magic* and *Wonder*): There are three guest swimming areas aboard the ships, all located on Deck 9: AquaLab (*Magic* and *Wonder*) is located toward the back, or aft; Goofy's Family Pool is midship; and the Quiet Cove Adult Pool is on Deck 9, forward.

Though the names are self-explanatory, we'll state the obvious: AquaLab and splash zones are for young'uns and their guardians. The Quiet Cove pool is earmarked for splashers age 18 and up. Don't let the name fool you; Quiet Cove may be for grown-ups, but it isn't always the picture of serenity. Finally, Goofy's Pool is for everyone, but kids under age 12 must be accompanied by an adult, and swimmers must be potty-trained. (Life jackets may be borrowed for free.) Goofy's Pool and Quiet Cove have two whirlpools each.

SPA & SALON (all ships): Pampering and relaxation, Disney style, can be enjoyed at the ships' ocean-view spas and salons—known as Senses on all Disney Cruise Line ships. Here, fitness-minded folk can work with a trainer, take a class, or work out solo. As for the pampering, well, that can come by way of any number of indulgent spa treatments.

Appointments may be booked ahead of time by visiting *www.disneycruise.com*, or go to the spa when you board the ship. The spa and salon are open to guests age 18 and older.

The spa is open from 8 A.M. to 8 P.M. every day, except on days when the ship is docked at its home port. Prices are posted in the spa. If you miss a reserved treatment, your stateroom will be charged 50 percent of the treatment cost. Note that Cabana Massages (located at Serenity Bay on Castaway Cay) and the Senses Spa Villas (indoor-outdoor treatment villas for one or two at Senses Spa) may be booked here, too.

Spa amenities include sandals and robes for use during treatments, steam room, sauna, locker room, showers, and more. A selection of beauty products is available for purchase.

CASTAWAY CAY

If you've ever dreamed of getting away to a private, tropical island, the folks at Disney Cruise Line have made it easy to fulfill that fantasy. Most Disney Cruises that depart from Port Canaveral or Miami, Florida, wrap up with a visit to Castaway Cay (pronounced *key*), a tiny island in the Abacos, one in the string of Bahamian isles. This patch of paradise was secured for the sole use of passengers cruising on Disney ships. It's small—only 3.1 miles long by 2.2 miles wide—and most of it was intentionally left undeveloped so that nature lovers may enjoy the still-unspoiled terrain.

Here you can take a ride in a glass-bottom boat, go back to nature on a kayak adventure, try your wings at parasailing, or go snorkeling offshore—and then return to a barbecue feast. Of course if you'd prefer to loll about in a palm-tree-shaded, beach-side hammock, refreshing beverage in hand, well, that can be arranged.

Other island amenities include biking, beach games, organized activities for kids and teens; a shaded pavilion complete with billiards, table tennis, basketball, shuffleboard, and more; Disney character greetings; plus a secluded grown-ups-only stretch of beach.

Returning guests (they always come back!) will be pleased to see that this happy place has gotten even happier—recent additions include an expansion of the family beach, two water play areas known as Pelican Plunge and Spring-a-Leak, and nearly two dozen furnished beach cabanas.

For details or to book Castaway Cay port adventures, visit *www.disneycruise.com*.

CHILL SPA (all ships): A spa within a spa, Chill is exclusively for teen guests ages 14 through 17. It offers a variety of spa services and treatments, including facials, massages, and manicures.

Reservations for Chill Spa may be made by phone or on-site any time after 1 P.M. on the first day of your cruise. Appointments book fast—book A.S.A.P.

Index

A

accommodations, 66–112
  All-Star resorts, 72
  Animal Kingdom Lodge, 70
  Art of Animation resort, 72
  Bay Lake Tower, 76
  Beach Club resort & villas, 72
  BoardWalk resort, 70
  cancellation policy, 67
  Caribbean Beach resort, 72
  check-in and checkout times, 68
  Contemporary resort, 70
  Coronado Springs resort, 72
  deposit requirements, 67
  Disney Cruise Line, 342
  Disney Vacation Club, 94
  Disney's Riviera Resort, 86
  Dolphin resort, 70
  Fort Wilderness resort and campground, 74
  Four Seasons Orlando, 111
  Grand Floridian Resort & Spa, 70
  for guests with disabilities, 53
  Hotel Plaza Boulevard resorts, 106–110
  money-saving tips, 28–29
  Old Key West resort, 72
  online check-in, 67
  payment methods, 67
  Polynesian Village resort, 70
  Polynesian Village Villas & Bungalows, 70
  Pop Century, 74
  Port Orleans French Quarter, 72
  Port Orleans Riverside, 72
  reservation guide, 24, 31, 69
  resort finder (rating system), 70–73
  Saratoga Springs Resort & Spa, 72
  Shades of Green, 110
  special room requests, 50, 67
  Swan resort, 70
  tipping, 60
  Wilderness Lodge & Villas, 70
  Yacht Club resort, 72
admission prices, 21–27
  Blizzard Beach, 231
  Disney's Animal Kingdom, 197
  Disney's Hollywood Studios, 177
  Epcot, 145
  Magic Kingdom, 117
  Magic Your Way tickets, 21–24
  Typhoon Lagoon, 227
Adventureland, 120–121
Africa, 202–204, 274, 316
African entertainment, 212
air travel, 15
shuttle service from Orlando Airport to WDW, 14, 16
Alien Swirling Saucers, 184
All-Star resorts, 72
  lounges, 99, 316
  restaurants, 99, 285
AMC Theatres, 45, 278
America Gardens Theatre, The, 165, 171
American Adventure, The, 164–165, 266, 267, 268
Amphicar, 246
archery, 249
Ariel's Grotto, 127
Art of Animation resort, 72, 104–105
Asia, 206–207, 274, 316
Astro Orbiter, 132
ATMs, 58
  Disney's Animal Kingdom, 198
  Disney's Hollywood Studios, 178
  Disney Springs, 216
  Epcot, 146
  Magic Kingdom, 117
automobile clubs, 15
Avatar Flight of Passage, 205

B

Baby Care Centers, 46
  Disney's Animal Kingdom, 198
  Disney's Hollywood Studios, 178
  Epcot, 146
  Magic Kingdom, 116
Backstage Magic, 235
banking. See ATMs; money matters
barbers, 56, 134, 220
Barnstormer, The, 129
Basin, 217
basketball, 81, 249
Bay Lake Tower, 76
Beach Club resort, 72
  lounges, 88, 323–324
  restaurants, 87, 297
beaches, 70, 76
Beauty and the Beast—Live on Stage, 180–181
beauty salons, 56, 81, 83, 91, 102, 112, 240, 355
behind-the-scenes tours, 150, 156, 183
Behind the Seeds, 156, 235
Be Our Guest restaurant, 253
Best Western Lake Buena Vista, 107
Big Thunder Mountain Railroad, 124
biking, 83, 84, 94, 95, 96, 97, 98, 102, 232, 249
B Resort & Spa, 109
Birnbaum's Walt Disney World for Kids, 17, 46

Blizzard Beach, 229–230
BoardWalk Inn & Villas resort, 70, 92–93
  entertainment district, 225
  lounges, 93, 317
  restaurants, 92–93, 286–287
boating, 75, 77, 79, 81, 88, 90, 232, 246
Boneyard, The, 208
bowling, 283
bus travel, 16
  in WDW, 65, 115, 145, 177, 197, 216
business services, 56
Buzz Lightyear's Space Ranger Spin, 130–131

C

cameras and film, 56
  Disney Cruise Line, 338
  Disney's Animal Kingdom, 198
  Disney's Hollywood Studios, 178
  Epcot, 146
  Magic Kingdom, 116
campfire program, 48, 75, 81, 83, 84, 88, 91, 104, 232
campsites at Fort Wilderness, 83
Canada, 158, 262, 268
Caribbean Beach resort, 72, 85–86
  lounges, 86, 318
  restaurants, 85, 287–288
Caring for Giants, 235
car sharing service, 65, 116
car travel, 14–15
  automobile clubs, 15
  parking, 62, 115, 145, 177, 197
  rentals, 63
  road maps, 14–15
  service and maintenance, 56
Casey Jr. Splash 'N' Soak Station, 129
cash machines. See ATMs
Castaway Cay, 355
cell phones, 60, 339
check-in and checkout times, 68
Chester & Hester's Dino-Rama!, 208–209
children, traveling with, 46–48
  Birnbaum's Walt Disney World For Kids, 17, 46
  child care, 46, 47
  Disney Cruise Line, 352–353
  lost children, 46–47, 116, 146, 178, 198
  restaurant dining suggestions, 302
  "rider switch" policy at theme parks, 46
  schedules with young children, 34, 36, 38, 40, 41
  special programs for, 239
  stroller rentals, 48, 68, 117, 134, 146, 158, 178, 198, 216

See also Baby Care Centers
China, 168–169
Christmas festivities, 8, 12, 139, 171, 234, 261
Cinderella Castle, 127
Cinderella Wishing Well, 127
Cinderella's Royal Table, 253
Cirque du Soleil, 222
climate. See weather
clothing suggestions, 17
Club Cool, (closed)
clubs. See BoardWalk; Disney Springs West Side
Colortopia, (closed)
Contemporary resort, 76–77, 93
    lounges, 77, 318
    restaurants, 76–77, 288–289
convention and meeting facilities, 89
Coronado Springs resort, 93, 102
    lounges, 102, 318–319
    restaurants, 102, 289–290
Country Bear Jamboree, 122
credit cards, 117, 146, 178, 198
crowd patterns, 8–9, 11, 119, 199, 264
cruises
    specialty cruises, 242
    See also Disney Cruise Line
Curl by Sammy Duvall (closed)

D

Daredevil Disney (theme-park alternative thrill rides), 238
dining. See restaurants
dinner shows, 315
DinoLand U.S.A., 208–210, 211, 274
Dinosaur, 209–210
disabilities, hints for travelers with, 50, 53–54, 116, 146, 178, 198, 272, 336, 338
    transportation, 53
    wheelchair rental, 53, 117, 146, 178, 198, 216
Discovery Island, 200–201
Disney & Pixar Short Film Festival, 153
Disney characters (where to find)
    at Disney's Animal Kingdom, 44, 201, 210
    at Disney's Hollywood Studios, 38, 43, 191, 300
    at Epcot, 42, 172, 298
    at Magic Kingdom, 11, 139, 298
    meals with, 110, 111, 298, 300
Disney Conservation Fund, 209
Disney Cruise Line, 325–355
    accommodations, 342
    business services on board, 337
    booking shore excursions, 333
    cancellation policy, 331–332
    cell phone usage, 338, 339
    checking in, 340–341
    children's programs, 352–353
    deposit requirements, 331

drinking laws, 338
entertainment, 350–352
    adults only, 352
    children, 352–353
    teens, 353
ground transfers, 332
Guest Services, 345
how to book a cruise, 331
identification papers, 333
Internet access, 337, 352
Key to the World, 332, 341, 342, 353
land and sea packages, 327
    WDW resort options, 327
    what's included, 327
laundry facilities, 344
lounges, 348–350
mail, 338
medical matters, 336, 337
money matters, 338
packing, 332–333
payment methods, 331
Personal Navigator, 342
pets policy, 339
planning, 326–327
restaurants, 342–348
    meals with Disney characters, 348
    reservations, 344, 345
room service, 348
sample itineraries, 328–329
shopping, 353–354
smoking policy, 339
sports, 354–355
staterooms, 330, 333, 342
swimming, 355
telephone calls, 339
tipping, 339
transportation to, 332, 334
travelers with disabilities, 336, 338
traveling with children, 335–336
weddings, 339
Disney Cruise Line Air Program, 326
Disney Dining Plan, 20, 252
Disney Dollars, 27, 58, 67, 117, 146, 178, 198, 267
Disney Dream (Disney Cruise Line ship), 325
Disney Fantasy (Disney Cruise Line ship), 325
Disney Florist, 11
Disney Information Center, 17
Disney Junior Dance Party!, 182–183
Disney Magic (Disney Cruise Line ship), 325
Disney Movie Magic, 187
Disney Skyliner, 65, 160
Disney Springs, 216–224
    resorts, 95–98
Disney Springs, The Landing, 220
    hours, 13
    lounges and restaurants, 319–320
    shopping, 220
    transportation to, 216
Disney Springs Marketplace, 217–219

hours, 13
lounges, 319–320
restaurants, 278–280, 284
shopping, 217
transportation to, 216
Disney Springs Town Center, 224
Disney Springs West Side, 221–223
    hours, 13
    kiddie rides, 219
    lounges, 319–320
    resorts, 95–98
    restaurants, 221–223, 278–283
    shopping, 221
    transportation to, 216
Disney Vacation Club, 94
Disney Wonder (Disney Cruise Line ship), 325
Disney World monorail system, 63
Disney's Animal Kingdom, 195–214
    admission prices, 197
    Africa, 202–204, 274, 316
    Asia, 206–207, 274, 316
    best times to visit, 8–9
    camera needs, 198
    crowd patterns, 199
    DinoLand U.S.A., 208–210, 211, 274
    disability information, 198
    Discovery Island, 200–201, 211
    Disney characters, where to find, 44, 201, 210
    entertainment, 204, 212
    first aid, 198
    getting oriented, 197
    Guest Relations, 198
    hours, 13, 197
    information, 198
    Kilimanjaro Safaris, 202
    lockers, 198
    Lost and Found, 198
    lounges, 316–317
    map, 196
    money matters, 198
    Oasis, The, 199
    Pandora—The World of Avatar, 205
    parking, 197
    resorts, 99–102
    restaurants, 274–275
        reservations, 314
    same-day re-entry, 198
    sample schedules, 39–40, 44
    security check, 198
    shopping, 211
    stroller and wheelchair rentals, 198
    tips, 212
    transportation to, 197
    travelers with disabilities, 198
Disney's Animal Kingdom Lodge, 70, 100–101
    lounges, 101, 316–317
    restaurants, 101, 285–286
Disney's Family Magic Tour, 235

Disney's Fastpass+. See Fastpass+
Disney's Hollywood Studios, 175–194
  admission prices, 177
  attractions, 179–188
  camera needs, 178
  disability information, 178
  Disney characters, where to find, 191
  entertainment, 187, 191
  first aid, 178
  getting oriented, 177
  Guest Relations, 178
  holiday happenings, 10–12
  Hollywood Boulevard, 187, 189
  hours, 13, 177
  lockers, 178
  Lost and Found, 178
  lounges, 271, 319
  map, 176
  money matters, 178
  parking, 177
  restaurants, 270–273
    reservations, 314
  same-day re-entry, 178
  sample schedules, 37–38, 43
  security check, 178
  shopping, 189–190
  stroller and wheelchair rentals, 178
  Sunset Boulevard, 179–181, 189
  tips, 192
  transportation to, 177
  travelers with disabilities, 178
Disney's Magical Express service, 14, 16, 64, 332
Disney's Magical Holidays, 8, 12
Disney Movie Magic, 187
Disney's Old Key West resort, 72, 98
  lounges, 98, 319
  restaurants, 98, 290
Disney's PhotoPass, 135
Disney's Riviera Resort, 86
  lounges, 322
Disney's Saratoga Springs Resort & Spa, 72, 97
  lounges, 323
  restaurants, 97, 294
  spa, 97, 241
Disney's Vero Beach Resort, 94
Disney's Winter Summerland miniature golf course, 249
DiveQuest, 156, 235
Dixie Landings. See Port Orleans Riverside
Dolphin resort, 70, 89–91
  lounges, 90, 323
  restaurants, 90, 294–295
  spa, 241
Dolphins in Depth, 156, 235–236
DoubleTree Suites by Hilton, 107–108
drinking laws, 56, 338
D23, 152
Dumbo the Flying Elephant, 128

E

Easter festivities, 10, 139
Echo Lake, 186
Electrical Water Pageant, 233
electric cart rentals, 233
Electric Conveyance Vehicles (ECVs), 53, 64, 117, 134, 146, 160, 178, 198, 211, 336
Enchanting Extras Collection, 19
Enchanted Tales with Belle, 129
Enchanted Tiki Room, The, 121
Epcot, 143–174
  admission prices, 145
  best times to visit, 8, 141
  camera needs, 146
  crowd patterns, 8–9
  disability information, 146
  Disney characters, where to find, 42, 172, 298
  entertainment, 171
  first aid, 146
  getting oriented, 145
  Guest Relations, 146
  holiday happenings, 10–12, 171
  hours, 13, 145
  information, 145
  lockers, 145
  Lost and Found, 145
  lounges, 321–322
  map, 144
  money matters, 146
  parking, 145
  resorts, 85–94
  restaurants, 260–269
    reservations, 31, 252, 314
  same-day re-entry, 146
  sample schedules, 35–36, 42
  security check, 146
  stroller and wheelchair rentals, 146, 160
  tips, 172
  transportation to, 145
  travelers with disabilities, 160
  See also Future World; World Showcase
Epcot Character Spot, 172
Epcot Forever (fireworks), 171
Epcot International Festival of the Arts, 10
Epcot International Food & Wine Festival, 11, 265
Epcot Seas Aqua Tour, 156, 236
ESPN Wide World of Sports Complex, 248
Expedition Everest, 207
Extra Magic Hours, 13, 22

F

Fairytale Garden, 127, 138
Fantasia Gardens Miniature Golf complex, 249
Fantasmic!, 181, 273
Fantasyland, 127–129, 252–255
fast food and snack spots. See restaurants
Fastpass+, 25, 27
Festival of Fantasy Parade, 138
Festival of the Lion King, 203
Finding Nemo—The Musical, 210
fireworks displays, 8, 11, 139, 171, 181, 191, 242, 259, 289, 348, 351
  IllumiNations: Reflections of Earth, 171
first aid, 50, 54, 57–58, 116, 146, 178, 198, 228, 231
fishing, 77, 79, 81, 83, 86, 95, 96, 102, 233, 247
fitness centers. See health clubs
Flag Retreat, 138
florist, 11
foreign currency exchange, 52, 59, 117, 146, 178, 198
For the First Time in Forever: A Frozen Sing-Along Celebration, 186
Fort Wilderness Resort & Campground, 70–71, 83–84, 232–234
  activities, 232–234
  archery, 84, 232
  campfire program, 84, 232
  family entertainment after dark, 84
  lounge, 84, 232
  restaurants, 84, 232, 290–291
  transportation to, 84, 234
Fossil Fun Games, 209
Four Seasons Orlando, 111–112, 241
France, 161–162, 253, 254, 257, 258
Friendship Landing, 160
Frontierland, 122–124, 255
Frontierland Shootin' Arcade, 122
Frozen attraction, 169
Frozen Ever After Sparkling Dessert Party, 266
Future World, 45, 147–156
  Caribbean Coral Reef, 150
  Imagination!, 153
  Innoventions, 149
  Land, The, 151
  map, 144
  Mission: SPACE, 155
  restaurants, 260–261
  Seas with Nemo & Friends, The, 149, 150
  Soarin' Around the World, 152
  Spaceship Earth, 148
  Test Track, 154
  Turtle Talk with Crush, 150
  Universe of Energy (closed)

G

Germany, 167–168, 262, 269
Ghirardelli Ice Cream & Chocolate Shop, 280
golf, 81, 97, 212, 244–245
  miniature, 249

Gorilla Falls Exploration Trail, 203
Gran Fiesta Tour Starring the Three
    Caballeros, 170
Grand Avenue, 185
Grand Floridian Resort & Spa, 70,
    80–81, 94
    lounges, 81, 291–292
    restaurants, 80, 291–292
    spa, 81, 240
Grand I (yacht for specialty cruises),
    242, 288
Great Movie Ride, The (closed)
Guest Relations, 116, 146, 178, 198
    tips for international travelers, 52
guided tours
    behind-the-scenes tours, 150, 156,
        183, 235–238

H

Hall of Presidents, The, 125
Halloween, 12, 139
Happily Ever After (fireworks), 137, 258,
    288, 289
Harambe Wildlife Parti, 204, 212
Haunted Mansion, The, 126
health care. See medical matters
health clubs, 75, 77, 79, 81, 83, 88, 90,
    91, 94, 95, 98, 99, 101, 102, 112
Hidden Mickeys, where to find, 141,
    173, 192, 213
Hilton Buena Vista Palace, 110
    spa, 110
Hilton Lake Buena Vista, 108–109
Holiday Inn (at the Walt Disney World
    Resort), 109
holiday happenings, 8, 10–12, 138–139,
    171, 238, 261
Hollywood Boulevard, 187, 189
honeymoons, 55
Hoop-Dee-Doo Musical Revue, 315
horseback riding, 234, 250
Hotel Plaza Boulevard, resorts on,
    106–110
hotels. See accommodations
hours, 13
    Disney's Animal Kingdom, 197
    Disney's Hollywood Studios, 177
    Epcot, 145
    Magic Kingdom, 115
House of Blues, 280, 281, 320

I

ID cards, 117
IllumiNations: Reflections of Earth,
    147, 171
ImageWorks Labs, 154
Imagination!, 153–154
Impressions de France, 161
Indiana Jones Epic Stunt Spectacular, 186
information sources, 17–18, 116, 146,
    178, 198, 216

Innoventions, 149
insurance, vacation, 18, 24, 50
International Festival of the Holidays
    celebration, 8, 12
International Gateway, 160
international travelers, tips for, 52
Internet
    access at WDW, 341
    address for WDW, 8
Islands of the Caribbean Pirate Cruise,
    239
Italy, 166, 266, 269, 321
It's a Small World, 128
It's Tough to be a Bug!, 201

J

Japan, 163–164, 265, 267, 268
Jedi Training: Trials of the Temple,
    183, 187
jogging, 77, 79, 85, 86, 104, 105, 108,
    250, 354
Journey Into Imagination With
    Figment, 154
Jungle Cruise, 120
Jungle Cruise–themed eatery, 252
Just for Kids (special programs), 239

K

Kali River Rapids, 206
Keys to the Kingdom tour
    (guided tour), 236
Kidcot Fun Stops, 171
Kilimanjaro Safaris, 202, 211
kosher meals, 264, 310

L

Lake Buena Vista golf course, 244
Land, The, 151–156
Landing, The (Disney Springs), 220
Launch Bay Cargo, 190
Leave a Legacy program, 147
Let the Magic Begin!, 138
Liberty Belle Riverboat, 126
Liberty Square, 125–126, 255–256
Lightning McQueen's Racing Academy,
    181
Living with the Land, 151
lockers, 57, 68, 116, 146, 178, 198
lost adults, 60
lost children 46, 116, 146, 178, 198
Lost and Found, 57, 116, 145, 178, 198
lounges, 316–324

M

Mad Tea Party, 129
MagicBands, 24, 52, 68, 135, 149
Magic Behind Our Steam Trains, The
    (guided tour), 236
Magic Carpets of Aladdin, The, 121

Magic Kingdom, 113–142
    admission prices, 117
    Adventureland, 120–121, 135,
        252–253
    barbershop, 56
    best times to visit, 8–9
    camera needs, 116
    Cinderella Castle, 127
    crowd patterns, 8–9, 119
    Disney characters, where to find, 139
    entertainment, 137–139
    Fantasyland, 127–129, 136, 253–254
    first aid, 116
    Frontierland, 122–124, 135, 255
    getting oriented, 115
    Guest Relations, 116
    holiday happenings, 12, 138–139
    hours, 13, 115
    information, 116
    Liberty Square, 125–126, 136, 255–256
    lockers, 116
    Lost and Found, 116
    Main Street, U.S.A., 118–119
    map, 114
    money matters, 117
    parking, 115
    resorts, 76–84
    restaurants, 136, 252–259
    reservations, 252, 314
    same-day re-entry, 117
    sample schedules, 33–34, 41
    security check, 117
    shopping, 133–136
    stroller and wheelchair rentals, 117, 134
    tips, 140
    Tomorrowland, 130–132, 136–138,
        258–259
    transportation to, 115
    travelers with disabilities, 116
Magic Strollers, 68
Magic Your Way packages (vacation
    package), 19–24
Magnolia golf course, 244
Maharajah Jungle Trek, 206–207
mail, 57, 338
Main Street, U.S.A., 118–119, 256–258
Mandara Spa at the Dolphin, 241
Many Adventures of Winnie the Pooh,
    The, 129
map(s)
    Disney's Animal Kingdom, 196
    Disney's Hollywood Studios, 176
    Epcot, 144
    Hotel Plaza Blvd. area, 106
    Magic Kingdom, 114
    road maps, 14–15
Marketplace (Disney Springs), 217–219
Marketplace rides, 219
mealtime tips, 258, 259, 269, 273
medical matters, 57–58, 337
meetings and conventions, 89
Mexico, 170, 263, 267, 321
Mickey & Minnie's Runaway Railway, 187

Mickey's Backyard BBQ, 315
Mickey's Boo-to-You Halloween Parade, 12
Mickey's Not-So-Scary Halloween Party, 11, 12
Mickey's Once Upon a Christmastime Parade, 12, 139
Mickey's PhilharMagic, 127
Mickey's Royal Friendship Faire, 138
Mickey's Very Merry Christmas Party, 8, 12, 138
miniature golf, 249
Minnie Van service, 64
Miss Adventure Falls, 227
Mission: SPACE, 155
mobile phones, 60, 339
money matters, 58–59
    coupons, 365
    Disney Cruise Line, 338
    Disney Dollars, 27, 58, 67, 117, 146, 178, 198, 267
    Disney's Animal Kingdom, 198
    Disney's Hollywood Studios, 178
    Epcot, 146
    foreign currency exchange, 52, 59, 117, 146, 178, 198
    Magic Kingdom, 117
    payment methods at WDW resorts, 67
    See also ATMs
money-saving tips, 28–29
    discounts, 29, 233
    making a budget, 30
monorail system. See Disney World monorail system
Monsieur Paul, 263
Monsters, Inc. Laugh Floor, 131
Morocco, 162–163, 264, 265, 269
motels. See accommodations
MouseGear, 149
Move It, Shake It, Dance & Play It!, 138
Muppets Present . . . Great Moments in American History, The, 125, 138
Muppet*Vision 3-D, 185
My Disney Experience, 55

N

Na'vi River Journey, 205
NBA Experience, The, 221
New Year's Eve celebration, 12, 139
nightlife
    BoardWalk, 225
    dinner shows, 315
    Disney Springs West Side, 221–223
    lounges, 319–320, 348–352
    specialty cruises, 242
Norway, 169, 261, 268

O

Oak Trail golf course, 244
Oasis, The, 199
O Canada!, 158

older travelers, hints for, 50
Once Upon a Time, 137
Orlando-area highways, 62
Orlando International Airport, 14–16

P

packages (package tours), 8, 18
    Magic Your Way package, 19–24
packing suggestions, 17, 332–333
Paddlefish, 282
Palm golf course, 244
Pandora—The World of Avatar, 205
parades, 8, 11, 12, 138
Paradiso 37, 282
parasailing, 355
parking, 62, 63, 115, 145, 177, 197
Perfectly Princess Tea Party, 239
Personal Navigator, 342
Peter Pan's Flight, 128
pets, traveling with, 59, 339
pharmacies, 58
Phineas and Ferb, 158
physicians. See medical matters
picnicking, 84, 98, 140, 231
pin trading, 35, 83, 135, 217
Pirate Adventure Cruise, 86
Pirate's Adventure—Treasure of the Seven Seas, A, 120
Pirates & Pals Fireworks Voyage, 242
Pirates of the Caribbean, 121
Planet Hollywood, 282
planning the trip, 7–60
    admission prices, 21–24
    booking a cruise, 331
    crowd patterns, 8–9
    getting there, 14–16
    holiday happenings, 10–12
    hours, 13
        Extra Magic Hours, 13, 19, 22
    international travelers, 52
    making a budget, 30
    money-saving tips, 28–29
    packages, 8, 18–20
        Magic Your Way package, 19–24
    packing, 17
    reference guide, 56–60
    reservations guide, 24
    sample schedules, 32–45
    special events calendar, 10–12
    teens, tips for, 48
    telephone calls, 52
    theme park tickets, 21–27
    travelers with disabilities, 53–54
    traveling with children, 46–48
    traveling without children, 49–51
    weather, 13, 60
    weddings and honeymoons, 55, 112, 339
    when to go, 8–12
Polite Pig, The, 282
Polynesian Village resort, 70, 78–79, 94
    lounges, 79, 322

restaurants, 78, 292–293
pontoon boats, 242, 246
pony rides, 234, 239
Pop Century, 74, 93, 103
    lounges, 103, 322
    restaurants, 103, 293
Port Orleans French Quarter, 72, 92
    lounges, 96, 322
    restaurants, 92, 293
Port Orleans Riverside, 72, 93, 96
    lounges, 96, 322
    restaurants, 96, 294
Power of the Park Side (tour), 178
prescriptions, 57
Primeval Whirl, 208–209
Prince Charming Regal Carrousel, 127
Princess Fairytale Hall, 128

R

Rafiki's Planet Watch, 203–204
rainy days, 45
rating system for WDW resorts, 70–73
refillable mugs, 285
Reflections of China (film), 168
religious services, 59
Remy's Ratatouille Adventure, 161
rental cars, 108, 252, 314
reservations, 67, 314
    for dinner shows, 315
    Disney Dining Plan, 20, 252
    for fishing excursions, 247
    for golf courses, 245
    special room requests, 50, 67
    time line, 31
restaurants, 243–283
    advance planning, 20, 252, 314
    All-Star resorts, 99, 285
    Art of Animation, 104, 286
    Beach Club resort, 87, 297
    Blizzard Beach, 231
    BoardWalk, 92–93, 286–287
    Caribbean Beach resort, 85, 287–288
    Cinderella's Royal Table, 253
    Contemporary resort, 76–77, 288–289
    Coronado Springs, 102, 289–290
    dining with children, 259
    dining with Disney characters, 110, 111, 298, 300
    dinner shows, 315
    Disney Cruise Line, 342–348
    Disney Dining Plan, 20, 252
    Disney's Animal Kingdom, 274–275
    Disney's Animal Kingdom Lodge, 101, 285–286
    Disney's Hollywood Studios, 270–273
    Disney's Old Key West resort, 98, 290
    Disney's Riviera Resort, 294
    Disney Springs, 278–284
    Dolphin resort, 83, 294–296
    Epcot, 260–269

ESPN Wide World of Sports Complex, 248
Fort Wilderness, 84, 232, 290–291
Four Seasons Orlando, 111–112
Grand Floridian resort, 80, 291–292
Magic Kingdom, 252–259
mealtime tips, 258, 259, 269, 273
Polynesian Village resort, 78, 292–293
Pop Century, 100, 293
Port Orleans French Quarter, 92, 293
Port Orleans Riverside, 96, 294
recommended restaurants, 302–305
reservations, 252, 314, 348
Saratoga Springs, 97, 294
special requests, 264
Swan resort, 83, 294–296
Typhoon Lagoon, 228
Wilderness Lodge, 83, 296–297
Yacht Club resort, 87, 297
"rider switch" policy (in the theme parks), 46
Rivers of Light, 204
Rock 'n' Roller Coaster Starring Aerosmith, 180
Royal Sommerhus—Meet Anna and Elsa, 169

S

sailing, 335
salons. See beauty salons
sample schedules, 32–45
Sanaa, 101, 286, 317
Savor the Savanna, 236
scuba diving, 150
Seas with Nemo & Friends, The, 149, 150
security check
    Disney's Animal Kingdom, 198
    Disney's Hollywood Studios, 178
    Epcot, 146
    Magic Kingdom, 117
Segway tours, 234
Senses (spa), 240, 241
service animals, 54, 59, 339
Seven Dwarfs Mine Train, 129
Shades of Green, 110
shopping
    Disney Cruise Line, 353–354
    at Disney's Animal Kingdom, 211
    at Disney's Hollywood Studios, 189–190
    at Disney Springs The Landing, 220
    at Disney Springs Marketplace, 217
    at Disney Springs West Side, 221
    at Magic Kingdom, 133–136
    for necessities, 59
    package pickup, 117, 118, 134, 146, 161, 178, 198, 211
    See also World Showcase
single travelers, hints for, 51
Slinky Dog Dash, 184
smoking policy, 60, 339
Soarin' Around the World, 152

solo travelers, hints for, 51
Sorcerers of the Magic Kingdom, 124
Space Mountain, 132
Spaceship Earth, 148
spas, 81, 88, 91, 97, 240–241, 250
special events
    calendar of, 10–12
    weddings & honeymoons, 55
    See also holiday happenings
specialty cruises, 242
speedboating, 81
Spirit of Aloha, The, 315
Splash Mountain, 123
Splitsville Luxury Lanes, 223
sports, 244–251
    basketball, 81, 249
    biking, 83, 84, 94, 96, 97, 98, 102, 232, 249
    boating, 75, 77, 79, 81, 88, 90, 232, 246
    ESPN Wide World of Sports Complex, 248
    fishing, 77, 79, 81, 83, 86, 95, 96, 102, 233, 247
    golf, 81, 97, 212, 244–245
    health clubs, 77, 79, 81, 83, 86, 88, 90, 91, 97, 101, 102, 112
    horseback riding, 234, 250
    jogging, 77, 79, 85, 86, 104, 105, 108, 250, 354
    parasailing, 355
    reservations guide, 245, 247, 250
    scuba diving, 150
    speedboating, 81
    surfing, 238
    swimming, 77, 79, 81, 83, 86, 88, 91, 94, 95, 96, 97, 98, 99, 101, 102, 103, 105, 108, 247
    tennis, 75, 77, 88, 94, 95, 98, 101, 103, 105, 234, 245
    volleyball, 77, 88, 90, 98, 102, 108, 112, 232, 233, 248, 250
stamps, 57, 134, 331, 338
Starbucks, 233, 261, 283
Starlight Safari at Disney's Animal Kingdom Lodge, 236
Star Tours—The Adventures Continue, 186
Star Wars: A Galactic Spectacular, 191
Star Wars: Galaxy's Edge, 188, 190, 272
Star Wars Guided Tour, 183
Star Wars Launch Bay, 183
stroller rental, 48, 68, 117, 134, 146, 160, 178, 189, 198, 211, 216
Sunset Boulevard, 179–181, 189
surfing, 238
Swan resort, 89–91
    lounges, 90, 323
    restaurants, 83, 294–296
swimming, 77, 79, 81, 83, 86, 88, 91, 94, 95, 96, 97, 98, 99, 100, 101, 102, 103, 105, 247
Swiss Family Treehouse, 120

T

Tables In Wonderland, 290
taxi service, 14, 65, 216
teenagers, tips for, 48
telephone calls
    cell phones, 52, 60, 339
    dos and don'ts, 52
    local, 60
temperature, year-round, 13
tennis, 75, 77, 88, 94, 95, 98, 101, 103, 105, 234, 245
Test Track, 154
tickets. See admission prices
tipping, 60, 339
Todd English's bluezoo, 295–296, 323
Tomorrowland, 130–132, 258–259
Tomorrowland Speedway, 132
Tomorrowland Transit Authority PeopleMover, 131
Tom Sawyer Island, 122–123
tours. See guided tours; packages
Town Square Theater, 119
Toy Story Land, 184–185
Toy Story Mania!, 185
trail rides, 234, 238, 250
train travel, 16
transportation, 14–16, 63–65
    from airport to WDW, 14
    to Blizzard Beach, 230
    to Disney Cruise Line, 332
    Disney's Magical Express service, 14, 16, 19, 64, 332
    to Disney's Animal Kingdom, 197
    to Disney's Hollywood Studios, 177
    to Disney Springs, 216
    to Epcot, 145
    to ESPN Wide World of Sports Complex, 248
    to Fort Wilderness, 84, 234
    to Magic Kingdom, 115
    Orlando-area highways, 62
    resort to resort, 296
    taxi service, 14, 65, 216
    travelers with disabilities, 53
    traveling arrangements, 17–18
    to Typhoon Lagoon, 228
    WDW transportation, 63–65
    See also air travel; bus travel; car travel; train travel
Transportation and Ticket Center (TTC), 27, 53, 57, 58, 63, 65, 77, 79, 81, 112, 115, 116, 145
traveler's checks, 58–59
Tree of Life, The, 200–201
Triceratop Spin, 209
Tri-Circle-D Ranch, 234, 239
TRON Lightcycle Power Run, 131
Turtle Talk with Crush, 150
Twilight Zone™ Tower of Terror, The, 179
Typhoon Lagoon, 226–228

U

Under the Sea—Journey of The Little Mermaid, 129
Undiscovered Future World, The (guided tour), 156, 237
United Kingdom, 159–160, 264, 269
UP! A Great Bird Adventure, 207
Up Close With Rhinos, 237

V

vacation insurance, 50
valet parking, 62
Village Traders, 168
VIP Tours, 20 (See also Enchanting Extras)
visual disabilities, hints for guests with, 54
volleyball, 77, 78, 90, 98, 102, 108, 112, 232, 233, 248, 250
Voyage of The Little Mermaid, 182

W

wagon rides, 234
Walt Disney: Marceline to Magic Kingdom (tour), 237
Walt Disney Presents, 183
Walt Disney's Carousel of Progress, 132
Walt Disney Travel Company, 8, 18, 19, 24, 51, 107
Walt Disney World Annual Passes, 22–23
Walt Disney World Marathon Weekend, 10
Walt Disney World Railroad, 115, 119, 236
Wanyama Safari, 237
water parks, 13, 226–231
   Blizzard Beach, 229–230
   Typhoon Lagoon, 226–228, 277
weather, 13, 60
   rainy days, 45
websites
   www.disneycruise.com, 313
   www.disneyhoneymoonregistry.com, 55
   www.disneyvacationclub.com, 91
   www.disneyweddings.com, 55
   www.disneyworld.com, 8
   www.disneyworld.com/dining/, 244
   www.gardengrocer.com, 60
   www.swandolphin.com, 87
weddings and honeymoons, 55, 112, 339
wheelchair rental, 53, 54, 117, 134, 160, 178, 189, 198, 211, 216
Wild Africa Trek, 237
Wilderness Back Trail Adventure, 238
Wilderness Cabins, 74, 82
Wilderness Explorers, 201
Wilderness Lodge, Villas, & Cabins, 82–83
   lounges, 82, 323

restaurants, 82, 296–297
Wine Bar George, 278, 284
Winged Encounters—The Kingdom Takes Flight, 201
Wolfgang Puck Bar & Grill, 271
Wonderland Tea Party, 239
World Showcase, 157–169, 261–269, 321
   American Adventure, The, 164–165, 266, 267, 268
   Canada, 158, 262, 268
   China, 168, 263, 268
   entertainment, 165, 171
   France, 161–162, 262, 263, 268
   Germany, 167–168, 262, 269
   International Gateway, 160
   Italy, 166, 266
   Japan, 163–164, 265, 267, 268
   map, 144
   Mexico, 170, 263, 265, 266
   Morocco, 162–163, 264, 265, 269
   Norway, 167, 261, 268
   performers, 165, 171
   restaurants, 261–269
   shopping, 157–170
   Showcase Plaza, 170
   stroller and wheelchair rentals, 146
   United Kingdom, 159–160, 264, 269
World Showcase: Destinations Discovered (tour), 156, 238
World Showcase Nighttime Spectacular, 171
Wyndham, 108

Y

Yacht Club resort, 72, 87–88
   lounges, 84, 234
   restaurants, 84, 296
Yak & Yeti, 274
Yuletide Fantasy (tour), 23

Where in the World?

(photo locations)

Magic Kingdom:
1. The Haunted Mansion, Frontierland
2. Peter Pan's Flight, Fantasyland
3. Mad Tea Party, Fantasyland
4. Mickey's Friendship Faire, Cinderella Castle
5. Splash Mountain, Frontierland
6. Dumbo the Flying Elephant, Fantasyland (Storybook Circus)

Epcot:
1. Frozen Ever After, Norway (World Showcase)
2. Soarin' Around the World, The Land pavilion (Future World)
3. Imagination! pavilion, Future World
4. Germany pavilion, World Showcase
5. Gran Fiesta Tour, Mexico pavilion (World Showcase)
6. View of Spaceship Earth and World Showcase Lagoon from the Italy pavilion, World Showcase

Disney's Hollywood Studios:
1. Alien Swirling Saucers, Toy Story Land
2. 50's Prime Time Cafe
3. PizzeRizzo, Grand Avenue (restaurant near Muppet*Vision 3-D)
4. Vampirina meet-and-greet, Animation Courtyard
5. Voyage of The Little Mermaid, Animation Courtyard
6. Prop near Indiana Jones Epic Stunt Spectacular (Echo Lake)

Disney's Animal Kingdom:
1. Donald's Dino-Bash, Dinoland U.S.A.
2. Expedition Everest, Asia
3. Kilimanjaro Safaris, Africa
4. It's Tough to be a Bug!, Discovery Island
5. Kali River Rapids, Asia
6. Winged Encounters—The Kingdom Takes Flight (show), Discovery Island

COUPONS

10% OFF
FOOD & BEVERAGES

(Excludes alcohol)

Subject to terms and conditions on reverse side.

10% OFF
a chocolate purchase or

$1 OFF
a specialty sundae

Subject to terms and conditions on reverse side.

B

BASIN

15% OFF Merchandise

Subject to terms and conditions on reverse side.

WOLFGANG PUCK
EXPRESS

PRESENT THIS COUPON TO
ENJOY 20% OFF
YOUR EXPERIENCE

DISNEY SPRINGS™ MARKETPLACE
1780 East Buena Vista Drive
Lake Buena Vista, FL 32830
(Behind Days of Christmas)
407-828-0107

Open Daily at 9am
Breakfast Served until 11am

THE VOID

THE MOST IMMERSIVE VIRTUAL EXPERIENCE EVER

10% OFF TICKET PURCHASE
AND FREE DIGITAL PHOTO

when you say *VOID FAN* at check-in

Subject to terms and conditions on reverse side.

FREE TRAIN OR CAROUSEL RIDE
with the purchase of one ride

Little ones and the young at heart can enjoy an old-fashioned
carousel or train ride on the Marketplace Carousel or the
Marketplace Train Express.

Subject to terms and conditions on reverse side.

TERMS AND CONDITIONS

Valid at *Disney Springs*® Marketplace location only.

Coupon cannot be combined with
any other offers or discounts.
Must present original coupon at time of purchase.
Reproductions of coupon not accepted.
No cash value in whole or in part.
Offer subject to change without notice.

For more information, call 407-934-8855.

Expires 12/31/20

TERMS AND CONDITIONS

No minimum purchase required. Not valid with any other
offers or discounts. One coupon per visit, per check.
Unauthorized distribution prohibited. No cash value.
Excludes catering, tax, alcohol, and purchase of gift cards.
Valid at Earl of Sandwich at *Disney Springs*® Marketplace
only. Offer subject to change without notice.

Earlofsandwichusa.com

407-938-1762

Expires 12/31/20

54996-8000-3030

TERMS AND CONDITIONS

Valid at *Disney Springs*® Marketplace location only.

Cannot be combined with any other offers.

Cannot be redeemed for cash in whole or in part.

Reproduction of coupon not accepted.

Must present this coupon at time of purchase.

Alcohol, tax, and gratuity not included.

Offer subject to change without notice.

For more info, call 407-828-0107.

www.wolfgangpuck.com

Expires 12/31/20

TERMS AND CONDITIONS

Offer good at *Walt Disney World*® Basin locations.

Coupon cannot be combined with any offer.

Not valid on gift cards or previous purchases.

Reproductions of coupon not accepted.

Coupon may not be redeemed for cash
in whole or in part.

Offer subject to change without notice.

Expires 12/31/20

1-888-77-BASIN | BASIN.COM

TERMS AND CONDITIONS

Located in the heart of *Disney Springs*® Marketplace.

Guests of all ages may ride.

At carousel, guests under 42 inches tall must be
accompanied by an adult (who does not have to pay)
18 years of age or older. At train, kids under 36 inches
tall must be accompanied by an adult (who does not
have to pay) 18 years of age or older.

Coupon must be surrendered at time of purchase.

Coupon cannot be combined with any other
discount or offer.

Reproductions of coupon not accepted.

No cash value.

Offer subject to change without notice.

Expires 12/31/20

Say *"VOID FAN"* at check-in to receive 10% off your ticket
purchase and a free digital photo of your experience.
1 photo per party. Valid only at the *Disney Springs*®
Marketplace location.

One photo per coupon per party with ticket purchase.

All guests must be 48" (122 cm) or taller and age 10 or older.

Guests are required to sign a liability waiver. Parent or
guardian's signature required if participant is under 18.

Advance reservations recommended.

Coupon cannot be combined with any other offers.

Reproduction of coupon not accepted.

Must surrender coupon at time of purchase.

Coupon not redeemable for cash in whole or in part.

Other restrictions may apply.
Offer subject to change without notice.

www.thevoid.com
Expires 12/31/20

COUPONS

10% OFF*

YOUR NEXT VISIT

*SEE REVERSE FOR DETAILS

The Original. World's #1.™

20% OFF

ENTIRE PURCHASE

Famous yo-yos and skill toys, Est. 1929.

Subject to terms and conditions on reverse side.

Edward Beiner™

PURVEYOR OF FINE EYEWEAR

15% OFF

PLUS FREE LENS CLEANER

with your eyewear purchase

Subject to terms and conditions on reverse side.

UNDER ARMOUR.

10% OFF

ENTIRE PURCHASE

Sports and casual apparel for men, women, and youth

Subject to terms and conditions on reverse side.

FREE

MYSTERY GIFT WHEN YOU SPEND $100

Authentic American Resort Wear
for Women and Girls

Subject to terms and conditions on reverse side.

#SmilePassItOn

20% OFF

ENTIRE PURCHASE

A brand on a fun and comfy quest
to make your feet smile

Subject to terms and conditions on reverse side.

COUPONS

10% OFF
ADMISSION
for up to 4 guests

Immerse yourself in a fascinating and educational dolphin encounter open to all guests ages 13 and up.

Call 407-WDW-PLAY (407-939-7529) for reservations.

Subject to terms and conditions on reverse side.

15% OFF
admission to the Behind the Seeds Tour at The Land for up to 10 guests

Bring the entire family backstage for a one-hour, interactive tour of the greenhouses and fish farm at The Land. For same-day reservations, present coupon at the Tour Desk next to the entrance of Soarin'. Or call ahead to 407-WDW-PLAY (407-939-7529) and mention the Birnbaum offer. Admission to Epcot® is required.

Subject to terms and conditions on reverse side.

10% OFF

Epcot® Dive Quest admission

Dive into a scuba diving adventure open to all certified scuba divers ages 10 and up.

Call 407-WDW-PLAY (407-939-7529) for reservations.

Subject to terms and conditions on reverse side.

10% OFF
ADMISSION

This amazing aqua adventure takes you on a tour of the aquarium and into the water to explore The Seas with Nemo & Friends marine environment using a Scuba-Assisted Snorkel unit.

Call 407-WDW-PLAY (407-939-7529) for reservations.

Subject to terms and conditions on reverse side.

20% OFF
Food, beverages, and merchandise

(offer good for lunch and dinner; excludes alcohol)

Subject to terms and conditions on reverse side.

10% OFF
Nine Dragons Restaurant, Lotus Blossom Café, and merchandise

(offer good for lunch and dinner; excludes alcohol)

Subject to terms and conditions on reverse side.

TERMS AND CONDITIONS

Admission to Epcot® theme park is required.

Reproductions of coupons will not be accepted.

Coupon may not be redeemed for cash
in whole or in part.

All tours and experiences are subject to availability.

Offer subject to change without notice.

© Disney

Expires 12/30/20

TERMS AND CONDITIONS

Epcot® admission is not required or included.

Reservations recommended and are subject
to availability. Ages 13 years and up.

No jewelry allowed in the aquarium; no cameras allowed
in backstage areas. Forfeit entire price of the tour if you fail
to show or cancel within 2 days of your reservation.

Reproductions of coupon not accepted.
Coupon may not be redeemed for cash in whole
or in part. Offer subject to change without notice.

All minors must be accompanied by a paying adult.

© Disney

Expires 12/31/20

TERMS AND CONDITIONS

Epcot® admission is not required or included.

Reservations recommended and are subject
to availability. Ages 8 years and up.

No jewelry allowed in the aquarium; no cameras allowed in
backstage areas. Forfeit entire price of the tour if you fail to
show or cancel within 2 days of your reservation.

Reproductions of coupon not accepted.
Coupon may not be redeemed for cash in whole or in part.
Offer subject to change without notice.

All minors must be accompanied by a paying adult.

© Disney

Expires 12/31/20

TERMS AND CONDITIONS

SCUBA certification is required for this program.

Epcot® admission is not required or included.

Reservations recommended and are subject
to availability. Ages 10 and up.

No jewelry allowed in the aquarium; no cameras allowed in
backstage areas. Forfeit entire price of the tour if you fail
to show or cancel within 2 days of your reservations.

Reproductions of coupon not accepted.
Coupon may not be redeemed for cash in whole or in part.
Offer subject to change without notice.

All minors must be accompanied by a paying adult.

© Disney

Expires 12/31/20

TERMS AND CONDITIONS

Located at Epcot®

Park admission is required.

Coupon cannot be combined with any other offers.

Coupon cannot be redeemed for cash
in whole or in part.

Reproduction of coupon not accepted.

Offer subject to change without notice.

Expires 12/31/20

TERMS AND CONDITIONS

Located at Epcot®

Park admission is required.

Coupon cannot be combined with any other offers.

Coupon cannot be redeemed for cash
in whole or in part.

Reproduction of coupon not accepted.

Offer subject to change without notice.

Expires 12/31/20

COUPONS

20% OFF

Food, beverages, and merchandise

(offer good for lunch and dinner; excludes alcohol)

Subject to terms and conditions on reverse side.

ORIGINS

FREE MINI FACIAL

FEEL GOOD FAST AND FOR FREE!

Kick back for 20 minutes and let our Guides
treat you to a perfectly pampering experience.

Subject to terms and conditions on reverse side.

Where soccer and golf come together

2 for 1
FOOTGOLF

Greens Fees

Book your tee time now by calling 407-WDW-GOLF
or go online at *www.golfwdw.com/footgolf*

Subject to terms and conditions on reverse side.

20% OFF
FOOD AND BEVERAGES
(Excludes alcohol)

Experience the magical flavors
of **Joffrey's Coffee & Tea Co.** at
Walt Disney World® Resort.

Subject to terms and conditions on reverse side.

FREE PRETZEL

**When you purchase 2 pretzels
of equal or greater value**

Subject to terms and conditions on reverse side.

TERMS AND CONDITIONS

Located at Epcot®

Park admission is required.

Coupon cannot be combined with any other offer.

Reproductions of coupon not accepted
in whole or in part.

Offer subject to change without notice.

www.moroccopavilion.com

Expires 12/31/20

TERMS AND CONDITIONS

Offer good on Disney's Oak Trail FootGolf course.
Must present coupon at check-in to receive this offer.
Photocopies or other replications will not be accepted.
Offer only valid with non-discounted Day Guest and
Resort Guest rates. This may not be combined with
any other offer and is not valid for twilight, super
twilight, or other discount offers. Offer not valid for
tournament, group, league, or any other organized
group play. May not be redeemed for cash. Offer
subject to change without notice.

For more info visit *www.golfwdw.com*

© Disney

Expires 12/31/20

TERMS AND CONDITIONS

Valid at *Disney Springs*® Town Center location only.
Not available at Sephora.

Your Origins Mini Facial includes:
Personalized skincare consultation
Nature's gentle exfoliation
Facial mask for your skincare concern

Limit one mini facial per coupon. Reproductions of coupon
not accepted. Coupon must be presented to receive offer.

See store for details. Some restrictions may apply.
Offer subject to change without notice.

Call, stop by, or go online to book your appointment.

https://www.origins.com/book-appointment

407-560-0888
Expires 12/31/20

TERMS AND CONDITIONS

Valid only at *Disney Springs*®
West Side and Marketplace locations.

Coupon not valid with any other offers or discounts.

Limit one per coupon.

Coupon must be surrendered at time of purchase.

Reproductions of coupon not accepted.

Not redeemable for cash in whole or part.

Offer subject to change without notice.

www.wetzels.com

Expires 12/31/20

TERMS AND CONDITIONS

Birnbaum 2020

Valid at **Joffrey's Coffee & Tea Co.** locations throughout
Walt Disney World® Resort.

Coupon cannot be combined with any other offers or be
redeemed for cash in whole or in part.

Must present coupon to receive offer.

Only valid for one time use.

Reproduction of coupon not accepted.

Offer subject to change without notice.

Excludes alcoholic beverages.

WWW.JOFFREYS.COM

Expires 12/31/20

COUPONS

FREE UPGRADE

Book at *www.alamo.com*,
or call 1-800-462-5266.

Reference coupon code **AU5592DJK**
at the time of reservation.

Subject to terms and conditions on reverse side.

H2O+ ™
BEAUTY

**FREE Oasis Hydrating Treatment
Deluxe Mini**

Our gift to you for your
Disney Parks vacation with any
purchase at *h2oplus.com*

Use code **DISNEYGIFT20**

Subject to terms and conditions on reverse side.

Disney's
HILTON HEAD ISLAND
RESORT
A Disney Vacation Club Resort

**Save on Accommodations
on select dates in 2020**

*For offer details and to check availability, call 407-939-7652
and ask about the Birnbaum offer.*

Subject to terms and conditions on reverse side.

Disney's
VERO BEACH
RESORT
A Disney Vacation Club Resort

**Save on Accommodations
on select dates in 2020**

*For offer details and to check availability, call 407-939-7652
and ask about the Birnbaum offer.*

Subject to terms and conditions on reverse side.

$5 OFF

One single or double stroller rental

To make a reservation, go to
www.magicstrollers.com

Subject to terms and conditions on reverse side.

$75 SAVINGS

**ONE-TIME MEMBERSHIP FEE
WAIVED FOR BIRNBAUM READERS**

To sign up for "the purple place to store your
vacation stuff," go to *www.ownerslocker.com*

Subject to terms and conditions on reverse side.

TERMS AND CONDITIONS

Free H2O+ Beauty Oasis Hydrating Treatment Deluxe Mini added to any purchase at *h2oplus.com*.

Use code DISNEYGIFT20 at checkout, no need to add to bag.

Offer expires 12/31/20 at 11:59 P.M. Pacific Time.

Limit one per person. Valid exclusively at *h2oplus.com* while supplies last, another deluxe mini may be substituted for any reason.

Offer subject to change without notice.

www.h2oplus.com

Offer valid through 12/31/20

This offer is valid on Compact through Midsize size vehicles reserved in advance for travel 10/1/2019 through 12/31/2020 at participating locations in the U.S. and Canada. Vehicle must be returned by 01/31/2021. Reservations must be made at least 24 hours in advance of scheduled pick-up time. A minimum one-day rental is required, and a 27-day maximum applies. For more information, including an estimate of your total rental cost, visit our Internet website at *www.alamo.com* or *www.alamo.ca*. This offer cannot be combined with any other discount and cannot be applied to a previous or existing reservation or rental. Alamo reserves the right to terminate the offer or change the terms at any time. Offer is subject to vehicle availability at the time of booking. Renter and additional driver(s) must meet standard age, driver and credit requirements. Please check your auto insurance policy and/or credit card agreement for rental vehicle coverage. Other restrictions, including holiday and blackout dates, may apply. Non-transferable. Void where prohibited.

TERMS AND CONDITIONS

The number of rooms allocated for this offer is very limited. Length of stay requirements may apply.

Receive 20% off the non-discounted rate most nights: 1/3–3/7/20, 3/29–5/7/20, 8/16–12/25/20

Receive 10% off the non-discounted rate most nights: 1/1–1/2/20, 3/8–3/28/20, 5/8–8/15/20, 12/26–12/31/20

Excludes 3-bedroom Beach Cottages at Disney's Vero Beach Resort.

Cannot be combined with any other discount or promotion. Advance reservations required.

Offer subject to change without notice.

For information about Disney's Vero Beach Resort, visit *https://beachresorts.disney.go.com*

Offer expires 12/31/20   © Disney

TERMS AND CONDITIONS

The number of rooms allocated for this offer is very limited. Length-of-stay requirements may apply.

Receive 20% off non-discounted rates most nights: 1/1–4/9/20, 4/19–5/21/20, 8/23–12/17/20

Receive 10% off the non-discounted rate most nights: 4/10–4/18/20, 5/22–8/22/20, 12/18–12/31/20

Excludes 3-bedroom Grand Villas at Disney's Hilton Head Island Resort.

Cannot be combined with any other discount or promotion. Advance reservations required.

Offer subject to change without notice.

For information about Disney's Hilton Head Island Resort, visit *https://beachresorts.disney.go.com*

Offer expires 12/31/20   © Disney

TERMS AND CONDITIONS

To save $75, visit *www.ownerslocker.com*. Sign-up and choose "I read about it in the Birnbaum Guide" when asked "How you heard about Owner's Locker." When selected, the $75 one-time membership Fee will be waived. Owner's Locker reserves the right to require this printed coupon be presented when the Locker is picked up for the first time. Not valid with any other promotion or discount. Offer subject to change without notice.

Expires 12/31/20

TERMS AND CONDITIONS

Limit one stroller reservation per unique coupon code. Reservation must be made online at *www.magicstrollers.com*

The coupon code below must be entered to make the reservation. The unique coupon code can only be used once. This coupon must be returned with the stroller at the end of the rental to receive the discount. Not valid with any other promotion. Offer subject to change without notice.

Coupon code:

849725820

Expires 12/31/20

COUPONS

PADDLEFISH

10% OFF

WHEN YOU SPEND $30

(Discount excludes alcohol)

Enjoy fresh seafood, waterfront dining, and 360-degree rooftop views

THE BOATHOUSE

GREAT FOOD • WATERFRONT DINING • DREAM BOATS

ORLANDO, FL

$25 OFF

YOUR VINTAGE AMPHICAR TOUR

(excluding Splash Tour)

Experience the World's only Amphicar Tour

Erwin Pearl®

ESTABLISHED 1952

10% OFF

Your purchase of $150 or more

Renowned for unique, beautiful, and exclusive fashion jewelry and accessory collections.

極度乾燥(しなさい) Superdry.

15% OFF

ENTIRE PURCHASE

Unique Apparel & Accessories
where vintage Americana, Japanese-inspired graphics, and British style come together

fresh ★ natural
rinse
bath & body co.
www.rinsesoap.com
monroe, georgia

FREE LIP BALM

WITH $10 PURCHASE

Natural bath & body products for the entire family

(Located near Paddlefish)

CRAFTED
TERRALINA
ITALIAN

20% OFF FOOD

Authentic Italian dishes and handmade pastas inspired by Italy's Lake District

TERMS AND CONDITIONS

Located at *Disney Springs*® The Landing

Offer excludes Splash Tour.

Not valid with any other discount or offer.

Reproductions of coupon not accepted.

No cash value.

Minors must be accompanied by a paying adult.

Tours are from 10 A.M. to 10 P.M. (weather permitting)

Up to 3–4 people per car, per tour.

Offer and hours subject to change without notice.

http://www.theboathouseorlando.com

407-939-2628

Expires 12/31/20

TERMS AND CONDITIONS

Located at *Disney Springs*® The Landing.

Excludes alcohol and gift cards.

Reproductions of coupon not accepted.
Coupon may not be redeemed for cash in whole or in part.
Coupon cannot be combined with any other offer or discount. All minors must be accompanied
by a paying adult.

Offer subject to change without notice.

For reservations, call 407-934-2628, or visit
www.paddlefishrestaurant.com

Expires 12/31/20

TERMS AND CONDITIONS

Offer valid at *Disney Springs*® The Landing location only. Coupon cannot be combined with any in-store or online promotions or other offers or discounts. Not valid on sale items or gift cards. No cash value. Original coupon must be surrendered at time of purchase. Reproductions not accepted. Other restrictions may apply; see store for details. Offer subject to change without notice.

www.superdry.com/us/
321-251-3351

Expires 12/31/20

TERMS AND CONDITIONS

Valid only at the *Disney Springs*® The Landing location.

Offer excludes 14Kt, BOGO, and all
sale/clearance merchandise.

Coupon cannot be combined
with any other offers or discounts.

Coupon not redeemable for cash in whole or part.

Coupon must be surrendered at time of purchase.

Reproductions of coupon not accepted.

Exchange within 14 days of purchase. No refunds.

Other exclusions may apply; see store for details.

Offer subject to change without notice.

For more information, call (407) 560-9945.

www.erwinpearl.com

Expires 12/31/20

TERMS AND CONDITIONS

Located at *Disney Springs*® The Landing

Offer valid for food only; excludes alcohol, tax, and gratuity.

Cannot be combined with other offers or discounts.

Not redeemable for cash in whole or part.

Reproduction of coupon not accepted.

Must present coupon at time of purchase.

Offer subject to change without notice.

www.terralinacrafteditalian.com
407-934-8888

Expires 12/31/20

TERMS AND CONDITIONS

Valid only at the *Disney Springs*® The Landing location.

Not valid on previously purchased items.

The purchase price is calculated after discounts
and does not include tax.

Coupon not redeemable for cash.

Reproductions of coupon not accepted.

Coupon must be surrendered at time of purchase.

Offer subject to change without notice.

www.rinsesoap.com

Expires 12/31/20

COUPONS

20% OFF LUNCH or 10% OFF DINNER

for up to 8 guests in the HOB Restaurant
(discount on food and non-alcoholic beverages only)

Enjoy distinctive Southern-inspired cuisine in an
enjoyable atmosphere filled with creative folk art.

Subject to terms and conditions on reverse side.

SAVE 15%
and get a FREE 24 oz. FOUNTAIN DRINK
when you spend $30

Located next to
the Orange Garage at
Disney Springs® Town Center

Subject to terms and conditions on reverse side.

pop gallery Orlando

10% OFF
ENTIRE PURCHASE

Experience Art that Pops!
Embellish your life with unique
art, gifts, toys, and jewelry.

Subject to terms and conditions on reverse side.

planet hollywood™

10% OFF
FOOD & BEVERAGES

(Excludes alcohol)

Subject to terms and conditions on reverse side.

planet hollywood™

10% OFF
MERCHANDISE

(Entire purchase of regular-priced merchandise)

Subject to terms and conditions on reverse side.

TERMS AND CONDITIONS

Valid at Coca-Cola Orlando Store Only. Located at *Disney Springs®* Town Center next to the Orange Garage. One coupon per customer. Cannot be combined with any other discounts. Excludes all Magic Memories photography, beverages, and food. Void if copied, scanned, altered, transferred, purchased, sold, or prohibited by law. Customer is responsible for any applicable sales tax on all purchased items. No cash value.

Offer expires December 31, 2020
and may be revoked at any time.
Offer subject to change without notice.

©2019 The Coca-Cola Company. All rights reserved.

For more information, call 407-560-0107.

TERMS AND CONDITIONS

Valid only in the House of Blues Restaurant & Bar at *Disney Springs®*

Not valid with any other offers, discounts or at The Smokehouse.

Excludes alcohol, tax, and gratuity.

One offer per check for up to 8 guests.

Must present coupon to receive offer.

Offer subject to change without notice.

Opens daily at 11:30 A.M.; Lunch hours are 11:30 A.M. to 5 P.M.

For reservations, call 407-934-2623.

www.Houseofblues.com/orlando

Expires 12/31/20

TERMS AND CONDITIONS

Valid only at the *Disney Springs®* West Side location. Coupon cannot be combined with any other offers or discounts. Discount does not apply to published art, gift cards, or sales items. Coupon not redeemable for cash in whole or part. Coupon must be surrendered at time of purchase. Reproductions of coupon not accepted. Offer subject to change without notice.

For more information, call (407) 827-8200.

www.popgalleryorlando.com

Expires 12/31/20

TERMS AND CONDITIONS

Offer valid at *Disney Springs®* location only.

Coupon cannot be combined with any other promotions or discounts.

Not valid on sale items or gift cards.

Must present coupon at time of purchase.

Offer subject to change without notice.

www.planethollywood.com
407-827-7827
Expires 12/31/20

89800-1040-8000

TERMS AND CONDITIONS

No minimum purchase required.
Not valid with any other offers or discounts.
One coupon per visit, per check.
Unauthorized distribution prohibited. No cash value.
Excludes group menus, tax, alcohol,
merchandise & purchase of gift cards.
Valid at Planet Hollywood Orlando only.
Offer subject to change without notice.

www.planethollywood.com
407-827-7827
Expires 12/31/20

71890-6000-9080

COUPONS

COUPONS

SEPHORA

Free Makeup Mini & Free Cosmetic Sample

Pop in for a **FREE** single feature Makeup Mini and receive a **FREE** cosmetic sample of your choice.

Subject to terms and conditions on reverse side.

arribas brothers

10% OFF
ENTIRE PURCHASE

Offering authentic Disney collectibles, exquisite crystal mementos, and sparkling hand-blown glass gifts.

Subject to terms and conditions on reverse side.

FREE CHEF'S APPETIZER
with the purchase of an adult entrée

Subject to terms and conditions on reverse side.

Orlando HARLEY-DAVIDSON®

RECEIVE 20% OFF
A SINGLE ITEM

Limited to Orlando Harley-Davidson® License Product

Subject to terms and conditions on reverse side.

20% OFF
FOOD & NON-ALCOHOLIC BEVERAGES

Subject to terms and conditions on reverse side.

TERMS AND CONDITIONS

Valid at the Arribas Brothers stores at the Magic Kingdom at Crystal Arts on Main Street, U.S.A., and near Pirates of Caribbean, at Epcot® in the Germany and Mexico Pavilions (park admission is required), and *Disney Springs*® Marketplace at Crystal Arts by Arribas Brothers, Royally Yours, and Silhouette Portraits.

Coupon excludes shipping charges and online purchases. Other restrictions apply. Discount cannot be combined with any other offers or discounts. No cash value. Coupon must be presented at time of purchase to receive discount. Reproductions not accepted. Offer subject to change without notice.

For more information, visit *www.arribas.com*, or call (407) 828-4840.

4 09915 01645 6

Offer valid through 12/31/20

ABFLBIRN

TERMS AND CONDITIONS

Redeemable at *Disney Springs*® Town Center location only.

Coupon must be presented to receive offer. Not valid with any other offers or discounts. Not valid on prior purchases. Limit one single feature Makeup Mini per coupon. Free sample limited to selection available at the time of the makeover. Limited to stock on hand. Photocopies will not be accepted. Non-transferable, non-negotiable. See store for details, as some restrictions may apply.

Offer subject to change without notice.

Offer valid through 12/31/20

TERMS AND CONDITIONS

Valid at *Disney Springs*® Town Center location only.
Located at the bottom of the escalators, adjacent to the Lime Garage.
Not valid on catering orders.
Appetizer selection subject to availability.
Limit one coupon and one free appetizer per transaction.
Cannot be combined with any other offers.
Coupon not redeemable for cash in whole or in part.
Reproduction of coupon not accepted.
Must present and surrender coupon at time of purchase.
Offer subject to change without notice.

politepig.com

407-938-7444

Expires 12/31/20

TERMS AND CONDITIONS

Located at *Disney Springs*®, the Landing
Valid only for food & non-alcoholic beverages.
Not valid with any other offer or discount.
Tax & gratuity are excluded.
One coupon per table.
Offer subject to change without notice.

paradiso37.com

Expires 12/31/20

TERMS AND CONDITIONS

Located at *Disney Springs*® Town Center

Valid at 5 conveniently located Orlando Harley-Davidson® stores. Visit *OrlandoHarley.com/Locations* for map, hours and directions. One use per person and must be presented prior to purchase. Cannot be combined with other coupons or offers, including dealership promotions or employee discounts. Returns and exchanges are subject to reduction in price after discount is applied. No cash value. Not to be used in conjunction with other offers, previous purchases, or purchase of gift cards. Reproductions of coupon not accepted. Offer subject to change without notice.

www.shoporlandoharley.com

Expires 12/31/20

Notes

Notes